Public Relations and Communication Management in Europe

Public Relations and Communication Management in Europe

A Nation-by-Nation Introduction
to Public Relations Theory and Practice

edited by
Betteke van Ruler
Dejan Verčič

Mouton de Gruyter
Berlin · New York

Mouton de Gruyter (formerly Mouton, The Hague)
is a Division of Walter de Gruyter GmbH & Co. KG, Berlin.

⊚ Printed on acid-free paper which falls within the guidelines
of the ANSI to ensure permanence and durability.

ISBN 3-11-017611-4 hb
ISBN 3-11-017612-2 pb

Bibliographic information published by Die Deutsche Bibliothek

Die Deutsche Bibliothek lists this publication in the Deutsche
Nationalbibliografie; detailed bibliographic data is available in the
Internet at <http://dnb.ddb.de>.

Table of contents

Acknowledgements

This book could not have been produced without the help of numerous people. First of all, the authors of the chapters. We are extremely grateful to all of them for producing – and reproducing – their insiders' view on public relations in their respective countries: there would have been no book without them. We feel certain that this book is a major contribution to the knowledge about and understanding of public relations and communication management in our respective countries as well as abroad.

Second, we like to thank our English editor, Peter Kahrel of Lancaster, UK. Language is one of the big problems to overcome in projects such as this one. He was able to understand the sometimes rather deficient use of the English language of all of us, non-native writers, discussing every word he did not understand. Some of the chapters raised lengthy discussions between him and the author, due to cultural and linguistic differences and problems. If any of us now knows about public relations and communication management in Europe, it is Peter Kahrel. The book would have been an even more endless project without him.

Third, we want to thank Anke Beck and Birgit Sievert of our publishing house, Mouton de Gruyter, in Berlin. They have had to wait quite a while for the manuscript to be fit for print – we hope it was worth their while.

Betteke van Ruler and Dejan Verčič
June 2003
Amsterdam/Ljubljana

Foreword

Larissa A. Grunig and James E. Grunig

This text reflects broad interests, not only in public relations but also in how that critical organisational function varies across countries in Europe. Taken together, the chapters expose the extraordinary pace of the development of public relations in Europe. Individual authors show how public relations is being reshaped – some would argue transformed – by such factors as education in the field, escalating management expectations, professional societies, economic privatisation and concomitant consumer demand, grassroots activism and increasingly powerful NGOs and communication technologies.

Such forces, we believe, are likely to continue to have profound, rapid, and "lumpy" effects on the study and practice of public relations. That is, we cannot trace a clear trajectory from where public relations begins in a given state to where it inevitably ends up. Instead, as these chapters illustrate, the development of the field tends to happen in fits and starts, with moments of glory and others that dismay its detractors and supporters alike.

Make no mistake, though: the profiles of public relations in the countries included in this book establish that development has changed how the function is organised, funded and appreciated by the dominant coalitions of the organisations it serves. We are convinced by the authors brought together on this momentous project that public relations will continue to evolve for the foreseeable future to the point where – if not already – it will have profound effects on organisations, their publics, and even the societies in which they co-exist.

The inevitable outcome of this development, in our view, is that public relations research, education, and practice will become increasingly central to organisational and societal life throughout Europe. Of course, the European context is changing as well. The public relations described in several chapters here suggests that communication managers not only can help their organisations anticipate that societal transformation but actually lead it. Having a significant impact on the continent, however, also seems to require a commonality of understanding of what public relations is – its contributions to organisational effectiveness, its role as social conscience, its imperative to empower even external publics, and so forth. Thus, we cannot overstate the potential impact of this first-of-its-kind text.

To begin, though, consider the book's role in explicating a European identity for public relations. Some sociologists are asking whether "identity" is a useful or desirable concept, given its unfortunate history since psychoanalyst Erik Erikson first used it in the 1950s to understand personality crises in adolescents. After that, many scholars – sociologists, psychologists, marketers, business management types, and of course communicators – have confounded it with "image". The term, once used uncritically to reflect a sense of belonging, now may reflect only central fictions of organisational life. However, the exploration of practice in this book that goes beyond individual countries to encompass a regional study is immensely valuable.

At the same time, the book does not homogenise European public relations practice across nation states. Individual contributions maintain a healthy respect for different approaches to professionalism, to research and education and to practice. The result is a deep and fascinating interpretation of how public relations is studied, taught, and implemented in geographically similar yet idiosyncratic political, economic, media, language, and cultural systems. Each chapter presents a place-specific picture and a definable national story. Authors have taken care to highlight the significant historical developments that explain that story.

Of course, we could argue that nations represent overlarge units of analysis. Like many contemporary historians, we could suggest instead that only by studying subnational regions can we truly and deeply analyze public relations. (Changes in the world arguably diminish the relevance of any single nation as the object of inquiry.) On the other hand, scholars in area-studies programs would suggest just the opposite: that given today's greater interregional economic, cultural and political ties, it makes sense to focus on the supranational – looking, for example, at the "Atlantic" region. We believe this book successfully navigates the chasm between these two concerns. Each individual chapter is written by such local experts that their resulting analyses provide the necessary depth and truth value or credibility. Thus the chapters have the additive effect of providing for larger geographical connections and comparisons across Europe – Eastern, Central and Western.

Editing a volume like this represents hard work against long odds. Who but someone with the brains, the experience, the motivation, the dedication, the depth of understanding, the persistence, the grace, and the personal networks of a Dejan Verčič or a Betteke van Ruler could have pulled this off? To that list of qualities van Ruler and Verčič might want to add a bit of luck, meticulous organisation, exhaustion, and a good stock of aspirin to deal with all the headaches that accompany a project of this magnitude. We trust their relationships with colleagues included as authors here have survived the intricacies of editing and translation. Those colleagues represent the best and the brightest among European professionals and scholars, and we would place van Ruler and Verčič at the pinnacle. Van Ruler has just accepted a prestigious full professorship at the highly respected University of Amsterdam, in the largest department of communication science in the Netherlands. Verčič almost single-handedly established public relations as a legitimate academic discipline in Slovenia while founding and managing Pristop, the country's most successful public relations firm.

Read each of the authors' entries here and you may find yourself reflecting on how public relations has shifted in its meaning and practice – generally in the direction of greater respect, more solid education, increasing support from professional societies, dawning of the ethical imperative, bigger contribution to the organisational bottom line, replacing asymmetry with symmetry, expanding roles from the technical to the managerial, a fledgling acknowledgement of the interdependence between organisation and publics, and escalating reach from media relations or publicity to relationships with a range of strategic constituencies. Are these European trends alone? Probably not, but the authors have used their individual lenses to pick up the beams of light emanating from twenty-seven European countries and – in the process – they have provided readers with enough understanding to answer the question at least to our own satisfaction.

We have no doubt that this seminal treatise will launch numerous research studies and considerable emulation. Undoubtedly some such work is in progress, but where is our compendium of public relations in Africa? In South America? When all such research and writing is complete, we will have a body of knowledge for public relations that is simultaneously broader, more reflective, and more inclusive than ever before. Even now, this book sets the stage for dialogue among university-based scholars and professionals, as well as between European practitioners and educators and their counterparts around the world. We all owe a debt to Betteke van Ruler and Dejan Verčič for bringing us together through this work. We look forward to the debate.

Chapter 1

Overview of public relations and communication management in Europe

Betteke van Ruler and Dejan Verčič

Public relations is widely practiced in Europe, although rarely under that name. Because of all kinds of societal, economic and technological reasons, CEOs become more and more aware that public acceptance of and trust in their companies is a fundamental condition for the survival of their organisations. They are also aware that this is a matter of strategic management of their public relations, though in their own national language this is often called "information management" or "communication management". They frequently hire professionals, in-house or from consultancies, to give advice and handle the organisation's communicative and relational well-being. Public relations is a flourishing industry in many countries, and all over Europe young people are interested in studying it and becoming a professional.

In Europe, public relations has a history of at least one century. Bentele and Szyska (1995), for example, refer to Krups as the first company with a department dedicated to press relations, set up in 1870. L'Etang (1999) places the beginning of public relations in England in the 1920s. Van Ruler (2003) shows that, although the first public relations departments in the Netherlands emerged at the beginning of the twentieth century, the industry is much older. Nevertheless, little is known about typical aspects of public relations in Europe and to date, there has been little exchange of knowledge. In order to gain insight in public relations in European countries, we carried out two projects, the EBOK project and the Public Relations in Europe project. This book is the outcome of the latter project. The EBOK project consisted of two phases: the Delphi research project and the development of a portal to enable on-line knowledge sharing in Europe and across the world (EBOK has a web site with the final report of the Delphi study and an electronic bibliography; see www.viewebok.org).

Project 1: The Delphi study[1]

In October 1998, the European Public Relations Education and Research Association (Euprera) initiated the European Public Relations Body of Knowledge project (EBOK). The purpose of this project is to codify the existing body of public relations literature of European origin and to enable its fuller use and recognition, which are at present restricted by linguistic, cultural and administrative barriers. The first question was what to include and exclude, and, therefore, what the parameters and content of public relations in Europe are. With Nessman's (1995) statement in mind – that although many ideas have crossed the Atlantic, public relations theory and practice in Europe have developed rather independently – it was questionable whether the parameters of the PRSA Body of Knowledge would fit the view on public relations in European countries. We therefore began to feel the need to understand what the US and Europe have in common and how they differ, and to chart the public relations idiosyncracies in European countries. In order to investigate these issues, a project team of people from the Netherlands, Slovenia, Sweden and Switzerland undertook the Delphi study, with participants from practice and science from twenty-six European countries. The study included three consultation rounds and was conducted in 1999 and early 2000 (for a full report of the research and the method used, see van Ruler et al. 2000 and van Ruler and Verčič 2002, both available at www.viewebok.org).

Discussion

In this chapter we report on five issues, all taken from the Delphi study. They were discussed at the Ninth International Public Relations Research Symposium in Lake Bled, Slovenia, 4–7 July, 2002. This discussion was the first part of the Public Relations in Europe project and eventually led to the development of this book. A comprehensive report can be found in the conference proceedings (Verčič et al. 2002).

---

1. The countries participating in the EBOK project are Austria, Belgium, Bulgaria, Croatia, Denmark, Finland, France, Germany, Hungary, Ireland, Italy, Latvia, Netherlands, Norway, Poland, Portugal, Russia, Slovakia, Slovenia, Spain, Sweden, Switzerland, Ukraine, United Kingdom and Yugoslavia (Serbia and Montenegro). After we completed the Delphi study, Greece, Malta and Turkey also joined the EBOK project.

The naming of the field in European countries
Public relations is not a very widely used name for the field in Europe, not in practice and certainly not in science. In many countries it is even "not done" to talk about public relations (especially the northern, the north-western and Central European countries). Moreover, the term "public relations" (if ever used) gets more and more replaced by such terms as "communication management" and "corporate communication". Still, in an international context many people continue to use the Anglo-American term "public relations", though there are strong reasons to believe that the term does not mean the same in Anglo-American countries and European countries, showing the different roles of what is internationally known as "public relations". The common US-oriented approach to the field focuses on public as "publics", while in some European countries at least, the roots of its science and practice seem to be much more based on public as "public sphere". An important issue in the Delphi discussion was the need to globalise the discussion on the fundamentals of public relations and start a true dialogue between the continents in order to learn from each other. Especially in the discussion at the International Public Relations Research Symposium in Bled it became obvious that we need to review terminology and theoretical approaches in order to develop a real global language.

The debate on relationships and communication
The previous point is linked with the second issue – whether public relations is about relationships or about communication. As Heath (2000: 3) mentions in the preface of his *Handbook of Public Relations*, "The new view of public relations assumes that markets are attracted to and kept by organisations that can create beneficial relationships". Hutton (1999) described the new paradigm of public relations, aimed at "building relationships with publics". In the concluding paragraphs the proposed definition of public relations ("managing strategic relationships") is said to be breaking with "some long-standing ideas" that communication is the bedrock of public relations and that "communication is a necessary but no longer sufficient foundation for public relations". From our research it is clear that – in Europe at least – even public relations researchers find it difficult to distinguish communication and relationships (see also Verčič et al. 2001). What one researcher considers "communication" may be called "relationships" by another. In the light of the European social-scientific tradition the confrontation of communication with behaviour makes no sense, communication being a form of behaviour

and at the same time being the essence of any kind of relation. A more interesting and promising point of discussion seems to be what is meant by communication and relationship, instead of having to choose between these two. Looking at the Delphi discussion, we see at least two different views of both concepts, as well as of the concept of "public". The meanings of the concepts need to be discussed thoroughly before we can start thinking about the choice for one concept rather than the other – if we can make that choice at all.

Public relations as a separate research field

The data we obtained from the research and education situation in various European nations showed that public relations is not commonly studied at a scientific level. Few European universities are actually carrying out research into public relations. In addition, scientific journals seldom contain articles by European researchers. While this will partly be due to translation problems, we believe that part of the reason is also the lack of good research. It is obvious that in European countries practice and science are not very interested in theory development in public relations. From the country reports which were made by our participants, we learned that the picture is the same when it comes to education; researchers and educators do not exactly form a critical mass. Clearly, public relations has not (yet) developed as a high-profile research or teaching area. This may be due to cultural and theoretical differences, or with the approaches to the theoretical field. Another factor, we believe, may be the lack of identity of public relations as an interesting scientific pursuit.

The parameters of the field

In the Delphi study we found many statements about the blurring of the borders between public relations and other fields such as integrated communication management, marketing or even the realms of corporate executives. Again, this could be a symptom of the different roles of what is internationally known as "public relations". Not surprisingly, there is almost complete agreement on the view that public relations is not or should not be just a tool of marketing or a merely one-way persuasive or informational activity to promote the organisation. According to the Delphi participants, it is impossible to do public relations without influencing the strategy of the organisation or without the responsibility for internal communications as well. The participants said that it was not obvious that external communication should or should not include communication with customers (marketing communication). We found that the reluctance to include marketing communication could partly be explained by the concept of "persuasion" as a fundamental concept for public relations. We also found that some of the participants who strongly reject that public relations is also aimed at commercial publics and/or that public relations has to do with persuasion, also prefer to see "public" as "public sphere". This could, therefore, indicate another approach to public relations, namely, one which we like to call "reflective" and which was articulated by one participant as follows:

> Public relations is also a question of continuously adjusting the decision processes within the organisation to society's changing norms and values, and, therefore, public relations is to discuss, in public, social norms and values relevant to the organisation in order to make the organisation reflect these norms and values in its decision processes, and finally communicate to the public that the organisation's behaviour is legitimate.

This drew our attention to the fact that it may be better to see public relations as a (societally oriented) approach or concept of organisation and not as a professional management function per se, as it is usually conceived of in the Anglo-American world. We therefore want to raise the question whether practice and education in Europe are too much focused on the professional function, at the expense of public relations as a concept of organisation, while the main thrust of a more global approach to public relations could be public relations as a societal concept of organisation.

Defining the field
All disciplines and professions that we know struggle with the multiplicity of often contradicting definitions. This multiplicity is sometimes explained away as a result of infancy and sometimes as a result of maturity of a field. In that respect, public relations is not different from any other academic social discipline or from any profession in practice. Though concentrating on "the single one definition" may not be very useful, we do feel that it is important to continue focusing on defining the field – finding the central concepts, for instance, or the main characteristics and parameters – even if it is a multi-dimensional concept. The first two consultation rounds of the Delphi generated a wide variety of views on public relations per se as well as on certain roles for public relations within (or on behalf of) an organisation and in society at large. After studying the answers and searching for a description of the characteristics of the domain, we clustered all statements and ideas into four aspects: reflective, managerial, operational, and educational (see Figure 1). Almost all participants agreed that these four aspects were typical of European public relations and had

to be included. These aspects refer first of all to public relations as a certain concept of organisation and, second, to a professional function at a managerial, tactical, as well as an educational level. We like to believe that defining the field in this way allows us to identify an interesting research field as well as a research agenda.

Reflective: to analyse changing standards and values and standpoints in society and discuss these with members of the organisation, in order to adjust the standards and values/standpoints of the organisation accordingly. This role is concerned with organisational standards, values and views and aimed at the development of mission and organisational strategies.

Managerial: to develop plans to communicate and maintain relationships with public groups, in order to gain public trust and/or mutual understanding. This role is concerned with commercial and other (internal and external) public groups and with public opinion as a whole and is aimed at the execution of the organisational mission and strategies.

Operational: to prepare means of communication for the organisation (and its members) in order to help the organisation formulate its communications. This role is concerned with services and is aimed at the execution of the communication plans developed by others.

Educational: to help all the members of the organisation become communicatively competent, in order to respond to societal demands. This role is concerned with the mentality and behavior of the members of the organisation and aimed at internal public groups.

Figure 1. The four characteristics of European public relations

Conclusion of the Delphi study

In our view, public relations is a practical field – that is, the practice should define what science is all about and science is only profitable if practice can work with it. Bridging theory and practice is, therefore, a fundamental asset of public relations science. The first question to be answered is, What distinguishes the public relations manager from other managers? Looking at our analysis of the Delphi study, his main contribution is the special concern for broader societal issues and approaches to any problem with a concern for implications of organisational behaviour towards and in the public sphere. He also shows his expertise in solving these problems in a certain way by delivering communication plans and communication media and helping others in the organisation to communicate better themselves.

From this angle, public relations is not just a phenomenon to be described and defined or a service to be delivered. The Delphi study shows that it is a much more complex phenomenon, being mainly a strategic process, taking an outsider's perspective of an organisation. In this respect it first of all bridges societal and organisational concepts.

Looking at all the statements of the participants of the Delphi research, its primary concern should be the organisation's inclusiveness and its preservation of the "license to operate". As marketing is viewing an organisation from a marketing perspective, so public relations is viewing organisation from a public perspective (in the sense of "public sphere"). The European approach, as constructed in the Delphi research, enabled us to broaden the relational and communicative approaches to public relations with or into a public or reflective approach of which the relational and communicative approaches of public relations can be seen as aspects of public relations – no less but also not more than that.

Project 2: The Public Relations in Europe project[2]

The Delphi study was a small study and necessarily explorative in nature. Of course, a better picture is needed of public relations in practice in European countries and the way in which cultural, societal and political systems influence the way public relations is practiced. This has led to the start of a more in-depth study of public relations. This book is the outcome of this study. We hope that it will refine our knowledge and understanding of European public relations and help us develop a research agenda about the development of public relations in Europe and abroad.

Europe consists of at least forty-three countries – if we count only internationally recognised countries at the time of the research – with the prospect of several new countries emerging in the next couple of years. In the majority of those countries there are no professional public rela-

---

2. The countries participating in the Public Relations in Europe project are Austria, Belgium, Bosnia and Herzegovina, Bulgaria, Croatia, Estonia, Finland, France, Germany, Greece, Hungary, Ireland, Italy, Malta, the Netherlands, Poland, Portugal, Russia, Serbia and Montenegro (former Yugoslavia), Slovakia, Slovenia, Spain, Sweden, Switzerland, Turkey and the United Kingdom.

tions associations. Europe has no pan-continental individual membership public relations association for practitioners. Individual practitioners are members of their national associations in the first place; only a few are also member of IABC Europe (http://www.iabc.com/districts/euroafrica/home.htm) and/or the PRSA. European national associations are organized into a confederation – *Confédération Européenne des Relations Publiques* (CERP; http://www.ipr.org.uk/cerp/index.htm) – which has been in crisis for years; some of the most important national associations, such as the Swedish Public Relations Association, have left recently. European academics used to form a section within CERP, but also left that confederation and formed their own association: European Public Relations Education and Research Associations (EUPRERA; http://www.euprera.org/). Students are formally still members of CERP, but it is now probable that they are transforming their organisation from CERP Students into European Association of Public Relations Students (http://www.cerpstudents. net/). In all, the situation in public relations in Europe is complex, under-researched and, above all, misunderstood by other continents, who sometimes see Europe as the underdeveloped 'United States of Europe'.

Insiders' view of public relations in European countries
The book is first of all a nation-by-nation introduction to historical public relations developments and current topics in European countries, written by noted national experts in public relations research, or – when no researchers were available – professionals who are able to oversee the situation in their own countries and who are well known as experts in their field. The contributions are written from an insider's perspective and combine researched facts and figures with qualitative observations and personal reviews. We accepted twenty-seven chapters. Contributing countries are Austria, Belgium, Bosnia and Herzegovina, Bulgaria, Croatia, Estonia, Finland, France, Germany, Greece, Hungary, Ireland, Italy, Malta, the Netherlands, Norway, Poland, Portugal, Russia, Serbia and Montenegro (still Yugoslavia at the time of research), Slovakia, Slovenia, Spain, Sweden, Switzerland, Turkey and the United Kingdom. This does not necessarily mean that there is no public relations activity in the remaining sixteen countries of Europe. In some countries we were indeed not able to find any expert, even after exploring all the contacts that had been built up within Euprera and Cerp. This was for example the case for countries such as Monaco and Iceland. The fact is, however, that in most of these sixteen countries, the experts in a position to write a

chapter, or those who committed themselves to write a chapter, were not able to finish their contribution after all. We hope that this book will win them over to participate in a second edition.

Conceptual statements

Since we were very curious what public relations thinking in Europe contains, and since we also wanted to reveal the most typical European concepts, we also included so-called intermezzi, in which well-known scholars in public relations show their approach. Not surprisingly, we included two different approaches from German scholars. From our Delphi research project we had already learned that Germany is one of the few countries in which public relations thinking has been developed. We included six of these conceptual statements. This does not mean that there are not any other original approaches to public relations in European countries. Again, we were unable to win over more scholars to write about approaches different from mainstream (mostly North-American) public relations approaches. And again, we hope that this book will persuade others to include their thoughts in a next edition.

We are very happy that we were able to include the following conceptual statements.

The systems approach by Klaus Merten of the University of Münster in Germany. From a radical constructivist point of view, he argues that, since we live in a media society, the societal communication system is the most relevant subsystem of society. Nothing is relevant or real if it cannot be found in the media. Since the media construct images instead of realities, public relations is invented to steer these images. For Merten, public relations is the strategy for using communication processes to generate desired effects by constructing desired realities.

The transitional approach by Ryszard Ławniczak of the Poznań University of Economics in Poland. The nature and range of public relations practices in developed market economies, such as those of the United States and the countries of the European Union, differ markedly from what can be labelled as "transitional public relations", such as Central and East European countries and independent states of the former Soviet Union. Is his view, public relations is there to educate society to help the transformation succeed.

The reflective approach, Suzanne Holmström, Roskilde University in Denmark. She focuses on the communication processes which constitute society as well as organisations. These processes, she argues, continuously differentiate, change and reproduce perceptions of legitimacy. Her approach emphasises the conflicts between differing and changing perceptions of legitimacy, which in her view are the basic objects of public relations practice.

The public sphere approach by Juliana Raupp of the Free University Berlin in Germany. She explains the concept of *Öffentlichkeit* ('public sphere') as a starting point and key concept of public relations and combines this concept with the US-based concept of publics into an integrated concept of societal public relations.

The civil society approach by Jószef Katus from Hungary, currently with the University of Leiden in the Netherlands, but most of the time working on projects in the former Eastern countries. Civil society is taking over the role of mass media and politics in the formation of public opinion. In fact, he writes, civil society is the arena where values and norms are precipitating, where social information and knowledge are created and diffused and is therefore of rapidly growing importance in the formation of public opinion. Therefore, public relations should not only take mass media into account but also – or perhaps most of all? – civil society's institutions and its role in society.

The dialogue approach, Roland Burkart, University of Vienna in Austria. Based on Habermas's theory of Communicative Action, Burkart developed a practical model for planning and evaluating public relations, called "consensus-oriented public relations". Understanding is the means for the coordination of actions, as the participants involved in this process aim at synchronising their goals on the basis of common definitions of the situation at hand.

The book opens with a foreword by the "godparents" of public relations research, Larissa and James Grunig of the University of Maryland in the United States. They argue that the inevitable outcome of the changing European public relations landscape is that public relations research, education and practice will become increasingly central to organisational and societal life throughout Europe.

Günter Bentele, of the University of Leipzig in Germany, wrote the final chapter in this book. He is the 2004 President of the European Public Relations Education and Research Association (Euprera) and a well-known professor in *Öffentlichkeitsarbeit* at the University of Leipzig. Mr Bentele gives us food for thought in his closing remarks on New Ways for Public Relations in Europe.

References

Bentele, Günter and Peter Szyska (eds.) (1995). *PR-Ausbildung in Deutschland. Entwicklung, Bestandsaufnahme und Perspektiven* [Public relations education in Germany. Development, Status quo and perspectives]. Opladen: Westdeutscher Verlag.

l'Etang, Jacquie (1999). Public relations education in Britain: A historical review in the context of professionalisation. *Public Relations Review* 3: 261–289.

Heath, Robert L. (ed.) (2000). *Handbook of Public Relations.* London: Sage.

Holmström, Suzanne (2000). The reflective paradigm turning into ceremony? Three phases for public relations – strategic, normative and cognitive – in the institutionalisation of new business paradigm leading to three scenarios. In: Dejan Verčič, Jon White and Danny Moss (eds.), *Public Relations, Public Affairs and Corporate Communications in the New Millennium: The Future. Proceedings of the 7ᵗʰ International Public Relations Research Symposium, 7–8 July 2000, Lake Bled, Slovenia*, 41–63. Ljubljana: Pristop Communications.

Hutton, James G. (1999). The definition, dimensions, and domain of public relations. *Public Relations Review* 25: 199–214.

Nessman, Karl (1995). Public relations in Europe: a comparison with the United States. *Public Relations Review* 21: 151–160.

Ruler, Betteke van (2000). *Carrière in Communicatie* [A Career in Communication]. Amsterdam: Boom.

Ruler, Betteke van and Dejan Verčič (2002). *The Bled Manifesto on European Public Relations.* Ljubljana: Pristop Communications.

Ruler, Betteke van, Dejan Verčič, Gerhard Bütschi and Bertil Flodin (2000). *European Body of Knowledge on Public Relations/Communication Management. Report of the Delphi Research Project 2000.* Ghent/Ljubljana: European Association for Public Relations Education and Research.

Verčič, Dejan, Betteke van Ruler, Gerhard Bütschi and Bertil Flodin (2001). On the definition of public relations: a European view. *Public Relations Review* 27: 373–387.

Chapter 2

Austria

Karl Nessmann

1. National profile

The democratic republic of Austria is a federal state comprising nine federal provinces lying in the heart of Europe. Historically speaking, the concept of Austria dates back to 996, when the name "Ostarrichi" was first mentioned in documents. With a population of eight million, Austria has been a member of the European Union since 1995 and is one of the wealthiest industrial nations in the world.

Of the estimated 10,000 people involved in public relations in Austria at present, around one third is employed in public relations agencies or as freelance public relations consultants, while two thirds work for institutions, authorities, associations and companies. The average age of public relations experts in Austria has remained constant at 39 years over the last few years (Haas 1987; Zowack 2000).[1]

The level of education of public relations people is exceptionally high: while 57.3 per cent had been to university in 1987, by 2000 over 89 per cent had a degree. Most of them had studied journalism and communication science, followed by business administration and economics. In addition, public relations experts in Austria set great store by advanced vocational training with 94.3 per cent regularly attending public relations courses. In 1987, 85.4 per cent of public relations experts had previously worked in another field (most frequently in journalism) while by 2000 most people at the start of their careers had a specialist professional background in public relations thanks to the wide range of courses on offer.

---

1. The data presented in this chapter are based on interviews with prominent public relations experts and on representative questionnaires on the everyday realities of the profession in Austria (Haas 1987 and Zowack 2000). Haas's survey was carried out as early as in 1984 (sample of 256 people, returns of 51.5 per cent). Zowack's survey also covered a representative sample of Austrian public relations experts and took place in 1999 (sample of 470 people, returns of 41 per cent).

Women dominate the branch: the proportion of women has been increasing constantly for years. In the mid-1980s, 80 per cent of public relations experts were men; twenty years later the opposite is true with women making up 70–80 per cent of the workforce. The studies mentioned above quite clearly show the increasing feminisation of the public relations branch in Austria, largely reflecting international trends. The negative consequences of feminisation mooted in the USA (low status, lower prestige, falling income, etc.) are not an issue for most people working in the Austrian public relations business whereby men tend to rule out such consequences more than women.

In international terms the structure of the public relations branch is small and easy to grasp. The average Austrian public relations agency has four to eight employees, while the largest agency in Austria (ECC PUB-LICO) has around sixty. That is not a great deal in comparison with the large international agencies (some of which have hundreds of employees). In fact many agencies are so-called "one-man/woman" companies: 70 per cent of public relations companies have one to five employees, 12 per cent have six to ten, and around 5 per cent have sixteen or more (Brunner 2001: 5). As far as quality is concerned, however, they certainly stand up to international comparison, as proved, for example, by the many international awards they have received. In order to increase their sphere of influence and to exchange know-how, increasing numbers of agencies are becoming involved in international co-operations (by joining large public relations networks, for instance).

2.   History and developments of public relations

2.1. Roots of public relations

To date it has not been possible to define when public relations first "developed". For as long as there is no clear definition of what public relations is, it is not possible to write a definitive history. Most experts do, however, agree that *Öffentlichkeitsarbeit* (the German term for public relations) took place in the German-speaking world long before the English term was introduced. Thus, numerous public figures in Austrian history made use of early forms of public relations, including famous emperors and statesmen from the Babenburg (tenth to thirteenth centuries) and Hapsburg dynasties (thirteenth to twentieth centuries), who employed a whole range of propaganda, from coins bearing their portraits, paintings, written and oral announcements to rallies, etc. All these efforts – which would nowadays be called the "instruments of public relations" – served the purpose of helping them to retain power, push through their interests, or increase their fame.

Another early form of "modern-style" public relations was pursued by Maria Theresa (1717–1780). In her reign, pamphlets were distributed to inform the population about forthcoming reforms, such as the introduction of a public school system. Another example of embryonic public relations in Austria is the newspaper first issued by the trade unions in 1867, which was directed at union members and opinion leaders and can be seen as an instrument of internal and external communication in today's terms.

It was also around this time that the state, business world and interest groups started to make use of public relations activities, particularly in the form of lobbying (although the term was certainly not used at the time) and press releases, reflecting contemporary socio-political developments. This is illustrated by a passage from the Austrian constitution introduced in 1867, which stated that *all citizens are equal before the law, have access to all offices, free choice of profession and enjoy freedom of worship and conscience, etc.* Citizens had a right to information, while authorities and companies were obliged to provide it. The introduction of universal suffrage in 1907 is another example of early public relations when the first large-scale political parties used posters, meetings and media reports to attract the attention of potential voters.

It was not until after the First World War, however, that the first press offices were set up, whether by the state or private enterprise, although the business sector was particularly keen on creating understanding and inspiring confidence with a wide range of communicative activities. The Austrian Chamber of Commerce, for example, employed a journalist as a press spokesman for the first time in 1927. He was responsible not only for presswork but also edited an internal paper for its members. The Austrian businessman Julius Meindl was also very progressive in the way he dealt with journalists, always inviting the economic editors of the major daily newspapers to discussions in his office, thus guaranteeing journalistic sympathies. In the First Republic (1918–1938) the Austrian government also issued press reports in periodical publications and held press conferences. Not much research has been carried out for the period of the *Anschluss* and Second World War – in contrast with Germany – but it is obvious that censorship, the banning of critical newspapers, and dismissal of journalists who did not toe the party line were the order of the day – in other words, a step backwards towards propaganda.

Modern public relations really only became established after the Second World War, when it started to become increasingly professional. From 1945 onwards, press offices in politics, business and administration were set up. In the state and public sectors, public relations developed more swiftly than in the business world, in particular within pressure groups, the Chamber of Commerce, political parties and public offices. This specifically Austrian approach to public relations work is largely due to socio-political circumstances: Austria has a virtually closed system of associations and political parties supported by a system of *Sozialpartnerschaft* ('social partnership'), which is unique in the western industrial world. In other words, conflicts of interests are largely solved by (de facto) binding arrangements between political parties and associations.

2.2. Development of public relations practice

Agencies and professional associations took their time getting off the ground. In 1963 Ernst Haupt-Stummer founded the first public relations agency in Austria (Pubrel Public Relations) while 1964 saw the launch of Publico by Prof. Mittag (Wachta 2000). In 1968 the Association of Press Officers was set up, originally with the goal of coordinating the dates of press conferences. A job outline for press officers was drawn up for the first time and the Association cultivated contacts with public relations societies abroad. In 1969 the Austrian PR Society was founded but this first attempt to set up a professional representation failed and it was not until 1975 and the PR Club Austria (PRCA) that the profession managed to assert itself. In 1980 it was renamed Public Relations Verband Austria (PRVA). Comprising 394 members in 2002, the Austrian Public Relations Association (PRVA) considers itself to be "the voluntary professional representation of professional, freelance and employed public relations professionals in companies, agencies, organisations, institutions, regional administrative bodies and politics" (cf. http://www.prva.at). Thanks to a wide range of activities, the PRVA has an important contribution to make to the professionalisation of public relations.

However, not all Austrian public relations people are PRVA members, as the PRVA pursues a clear policy of selecting its members – one reason for this being to delimit public relations as unambiguously as possible from other professions with differing aims. This arrangement inevitably means that the association demands very high standards of its members. Many communications specialists are members of other associations.[2] The most important platform and the mouthpiece of the communications branch is, however, the PRVA.

There is a wide range of associations and their sheer numbers document the increasing importance of the communications branch (cf. Frühbauer 2002). The fact that there are so many "smallish" associations is an Austrian speciality – Austria has the largest number of associations and societies of any country in Europe and most Austrians are active members of several associations.

Increasingly, public relations advice is being seen as communications management in a comprehensive and holistic sense of the word. Put so succinctly by Milan Frühbauer (2000: 140), former PRVA president and authority on the Austrian public relations scene, in the commemorative publication of the branch's *Bestseller* magazine, it is developing from "media work to integrated communication". Sketching the development of public relations in Austria, Frühbauer also discerns a widening spectrum of tools, namely, "a transformation from an emphasis on media work to an instrumental pluralism in which media activities still play an outstanding role but are no longer the "be all and end all" (Frühbauer 2000: 140). Franz Bogner, another former president of the PRVA, author and major forerunner of modern public relations work in Austria, argues along the same lines when he says that "increasing numbers of public relations practitioners are realising that the old school of public relations is outdated and that comprehensive networked communication management, or public relations strategies, is what is required. Increasing numbers of agencies and public relations people in companies and institutions are devoting their energies to networked public relations concepts; public relations departments and agencies are turning into communication units" (ÖGK 1998: 41–42).

2.3. The development of education and research traditions

Public relations (or actually *Öffentlichkeitsarbeit*) was first taught as a subject at university level at the beginning of the 1950s, with the first doc-

---

2. For example, the PR CLUB CARINTHIA, Austria's only association based in the provinces, in Carinthia. It was founded in 1985 and has circa 100 members today. It sees its task as making "the complex tasks of public relations practitioners more transparent and pointing out the essence and necessity of modern communication work" (cf. www.prclub-kaernten.at). Many communications and public relations specialists are member of other associations, for example: CERCLE INVESTOR RELATIONS AUSTRIA, EMBA (the umbrella organisation for Austrian events agencies), VIKOM (Association of Integrated Communication), etc.

torates submitted to the Faculty of Law and Political Science at the University of Innsbruck (Gröpel 1953; Schweighardt 1954). Hellmut Gröpel looked into the phenomenon of public relations from an economic perspective, identifying public relations as a new function for companies, in line with German and American authors. Kurt Schweighardt, in contrast, approached the phenomenon from a sociological viewpoint and defined public relations (also in line with German and American authors) as the "cultivation of relations and opinions" (*Beziehungs- und Meinungspflege*), classifying public relations as "human relations". For both authors, mutual understanding, trust and reputation are central goals of public relations.

The first lectures on public relations were held in 1960 at the Institute of Journalism and Communication Science at the University of Vienna. Hans Kronhuber published the first book in 1972. Entitled *Public Relations*, it is a classical introduction to public relations work. Kronhuber is a proponent of action-oriented public relations, principally defining public relations as "trustworthy behaviour" and "mutual cultivation of relations". In his words, 90 per cent of public relations is about acting properly and 10 per cent speaking about it.

The first surveys on the topic of public relations in Austria appeared in the 1980s: published under the same name, Signitzer's anthology (1984) covered practical public relations in Austria and included contributions from public relations practitioners. Alongside articles on the general principles of public relations there were numerous case studies. This work illustrates the relatively high standards that were prevalent even then. A few years later Haas (1987) analysed the first empirical study on the professional realities of public relations in Austria.[3]

Since then, hundreds of practical publications, academic papers, diploma theses and doctorates have been written in Austria. To date, these works have not been systematically recorded in the sense of a bibliography of Austrian public relations. Indeed the sheer number of publications would go beyond the scope of this chapter (for more information, see www.prtc.at).

In terms of theoretical approaches to public relations, the first works published by Signitzer (1988, 1992) and Dorer and Lojka (1991) are exemplary. They had a significant contribution to make to a sound, theoretical systemisation of public relations in Austria. Burkart (1993; 1994) at-

---

3. The most important results of this study are discussed below in connection with an up-to-date survey of how things stand in the profession.

tracted international attention with his *consensus-oriented public relations approach*, proved by the conferences that were specifically organised to discuss his approach (Bentele and Liebert 1995). Other new approaches from Austria include *personal public relations* as developed by Nessmann (2002), where people (as opposed to the enterprise) are at the centre of attention. Only at an early stage of development in comparison with Burkart, this approach views public relations as a central communicative function of people and not only of organisations.

In the mid-1980s public relations was introduced as a special subject within journalism at the three Institutes of Communication Science in Vienna, Salzburg and Klagenfurt. This meant that increasing numbers of courses were offered in this field and that more and more diploma theses and doctorates were written on this topic (cf. www.prct.at). The first extramural course at university level to concentrate solely on practical public relations was launched at the University of Vienna in 1987, a relatively early date as things stood in Europe. At that time, no comparable academic training courses for public relations practitioners existed (in the German-speaking world at least). To a certain extent, Austria was ahead of the field. In a speech on the occasion of his eightieth birthday, Albert Oeckl, one of the great pioneers of public relations in Germany, said "If you want to study public relations, you really should go to Austria" (ÖGK 1998: 42). Since then, many training courses have been set up at higher education institutions and other establishments of adult education. Private training centres also hold public relations seminars, but all these are centred around the capital city, Vienna. With the exception of Carinthia, the southernmost province in Austria, there are no adequate opportunities for university-level training in public relations outside the capital. The extramural course on public relations at the University of Klagenfurt, which was set up in 1996, provides on-the-job training directed at communications experts working in the field.

All in all, the public relations programmes in Austria are a mixture of initial and in-depth training: "initial" in the sense of basic qualifications for those starting to work in the field and "in-depth" in the sense of additional "on-the-job" qualifications for working professionals. In terms of their objectives, the Austrian public relations programmes combine the *public relations technician* and *public relations manager* models (Nessmann 1998: 40). The large number of courses does, however, have an important contribution to make to the professionalisation of the branch. This is also reflected in job adverts and applications: without having attended an appropriate course, it is almost impossible for people at the start of their careers to find a suitable job. An up-to-date overview of all training courses in Austria can be found at www.prva.at. As anybody can in fact call themselves a public relations practitioner in Austria without having to pass any exams or fulfil certain legal requirements, public relations courses are of paramount importance.

2.4. How language shapes the development of public relations

In the German-speaking world, the English term *public relations* is generally translated with 'Öffentlichkeitsarbeit', which literally means 'public work', namely, working *in, with* and *for* the public (sphere), although both the English and German terms tend to be used synonymously in Austria. In fact, the terms "public relations" and "Öffentlichkeitsarbeit" are in decline nowadays – in theory and practice – and are gradually being superseded by "communications management". This trend can be observed at all levels, whether in connection with the names given to public relations agencies or the names of courses or titles of books on the subject.

The majority of public relations experts in Austria consider themselves to be *communications managers*. The common division between *communications managers* and *communications technicians*, which is prevalent in the US, is not thought to be useful by around two thirds of Austrian public relations experts (Zowack 2000). This is probably due to the structure of the public relations branch in Austria, which has considerably smaller organisational units and not such a clear division of managerial and technical roles as in the US. In other words, Austrian public relations managers simply consider technical activities to be part of their job. As an interesting detail, it is perhaps worth mentioning that many public relations experts in Austria (mostly PRVA members) see themselves as *architects of communication*, thereby laying claim to leadership within the various disciplines of communication.

This development is also reflected in the names of agencies. An informal (and unpublished) analysis of agencies' names carried out by the author of this chapter revealed that only one third of Austria's public relations agencies still includes the classical terms of *public relations* (or *Öffentlichkeitsarbeit*) in their name; another third makes use of the term *communication* (for example, "communications planning/management/ advice" or "consultancy"), while the last third makes use of the owner's surname (mostly in tandem with one of the following additions: "public relations", "communication", "public affairs" or "lobbying", as in *Ness-mann PR & Lobbying* or *Nessmann Communications*).

At present, in conformity with public relations in practice, training programmes tend towards total integrated communication. This focus comes to the fore in all public relations courses and is even partially reflected in new titles, such as "public relations and communications management", "organisational communication/public relations" or "communications business". In fact the organisers cannot do full justice to these claims as important training modules, such as special management tools, are still missing, as Zerfaß (1998) points out.

3.   Typification of current public relations

3.1. Status of public relations in business, administration and society

Despite the worldwide recession of 2001, the public relations branch in Austria is expanding enormously, with annual growth rates of up to 30 per cent on average (Zowack 2000). This trend was also confirmed by the current president of the PRVA, Christian Kollmann, at their annual general meeting on 14 March 2002: "despite unfavourable economic developments which have intensified in the wake of September 11, the public relations branch has held its ground. In comparison with other communication disciplines, public relations has proved to be relatively immune to the economic downturn". Increasing expenditure on public relations goes hand in hand with a continual increase in the number of people working in the branch.

3.2. Major roles of public relations and typical tasks

The European view of public relations presented in the "Delphi Study" (cf. Verčič et al. 2001; Ruler and Verčič 2002) is also reflected in Austria. Thus, the four dimensions of European Public Relations (reflective, managerial, operational, educational) identified in that study are also central components for Austrian public relations practitioners and theoreticians. The results of Austrian studies of the profession largely coincide with the Delphi Study: the key concepts of a public relations definition are communication, relationships and publics. The essence of public relations is either management of communications or management of relations. The aims of public relations are building mutually beneficial relationships, mutual understanding and public trust.

Last but not least, public relations is also seen as two-way communication, as dialogue-oriented relations, in Austria, as reflected in the awards presented by the PRVA for many years now. Virtually all public relations campaigns and academic papers that have received awards make use of dialogue-oriented strategies (www.prva.at).

Technical tasks have largely stayed the same over the last 20 years: (1) writing and editing various public relations texts; (2) planning public relations measures and public relations events; and (3) setting up and maintaining contacts with the media, still count as the three most frequently performed public relations activities today (Haas 1987; Zowack 2000). Classical media work is still an important aspect of the jobs of public relations experts but it is declining. Instead managerial activities (such as strategic planning, drawing up public relations concepts, cultivating contacts and consultancy work) are becoming increasingly important in the job profiles of public relations people – whether they are working for agencies or directly for companies. As shown in two representative studies, these activities were not so pronounced twenty years ago. Agencies in particular have a higher consultative status today according to Menedetter (agency boss, member of the PRVA and an expert on the public relations scene) in an interview with Frühbauer. She continues by explaining that today it is a question of strategies and solving problems: "We are strategic consultants" (Frühbauer 2000: 142). A recent study by Roland Burkart, which has only appeared on the internet to date (cf. www.prtc.at), confirms this trend: the status of strategic public relations planning and public relations concepts is assessed very highly in this survey of Austrian communications experts.

3.3. Position of public relations in organisations

The position of public relations in the hierarchy of Austrian businesses is very high: as early as 1984, 67.4 per cent of public relations employees were found at the highest levels within their organisations – that is, directly assigned to the executive board or management (Haas 1987). This tendency has not been reversed: professional public relations work has since turned into an indispensable component of management tasks. This is just as true for politics and business as for the culture industry and non-profit organisations (Frühbauer 2000: 140). This undiminished trend is also confirmed by another expert and permanent observer of the Austrian public relations scene: "In the meantime it is almost impossible to imagine the branch without the services of strategic communication consultants, lobbyists, spin doctors or press officers" (Wachta 2000: 138).

3.4. Major textbooks and best selling practical books

Since Kronhuber (1972) published the first public relations textbook in Austria, only one further practical textbook has been published which systematically deals with the topic, namely, Bogner's (1990) *Das neue PR-Denken* ('New Thoughts on Public Relations'). Bogner's book is the most successful and most frequently quoted practical public relations textbook in Austria (with the third, expanded and updated edition published in 1999). The author has an organisation and person-related interpretation of public relations, defining it against the background of established theory as the management of communication between an organisation or a person and its public (sphere), or more specifically as an important communication function of management. For Bogner (1999: 27), public relations is principally about having the right attitude, comprising 70 per cent *wanting* and 30 per cent *doing*.

Of course, as indicated above, hundreds of books on public relations have been published in Austria, but most are concerned with very specific areas such as lobbying, issues management, media relations, crisis management, online PR) or with special fields of application (public relations for non-profit organisations or schools, for instance).[4]

3.5. Growing fields and hot issues

A brief look at the leading Austrian journal for the branch reveals that the following fields are either new or have increased particularly strongly over the last few years: lobbying, investor relations, issues management, crisis management, event management, online management, and personal public relations.

---

4. Hopfgartner and Nessmann (2000) was the first textbook published in the German-speaking word to cover public relations work systematically and comprehensively for schools. Within two years it became a bestseller and was reprinted in 2002.

Lobbying in particular is a growing field. In the German journal *PR Report* (5/2002) Austria is called the "land of lobbying". Thanks to Austria's geographical location, particularly business with south-eastern Europe is expanding fast. According to the journal, more than 1,000 internationally operating companies manage their public relations activities for eastern European countries using Vienna as a base.

Personal public relations is also growing. Here, people (as opposed to the enterprise) are at the centre of attention or the recipients of advice. The number of individuals who wish to create a position for themselves in the public sphere is proliferating: CEOs, politicians and the leading lights in society increasingly make use of the services of public relations coaches. More and more agencies and consultants offer personal coaching alongside their classical tasks, such as training for interviews and presentations, preparation for public appearances, image and personal branding, and advice on appearance. All in all, personal public relations is clearly booming and has become an important economic factor in the public relations industry (Nessmann 2002).

The new facets of public relations mentioned above are, however, creating problems in the branch as these growing fields are starting to become independent, resulting in the setting up of specialist associations and courses. What were originally seen as subsections, applications or instruments of public relations, are now developing into independent specialities. This is weakening the public relations branch as a whole. A second negative effect is that proponents of these "disciplines" (as they are self-confidently called) reduce and degrade public relations to media work or media relations. This phenomenon is particularly prevalent in lobbying, investor relations and event communications; the problem has been recognised by the PRVA and is the topic of internal discussions at present.

4. Conclusions: state of the art and future of public relations in Austria

While Austrian agencies are small on an international scale in terms of the numbers of employees, the quality of their work certainly speaks for itself. The larger agencies are members of international networks and the educational standards of people working in public relations are above average. There is a wide range of associations, contributing to professionalism within the branch with their numerous activities. There are many opportunities for initial and further training at university and adult education level, especially considering the size of the branch. The three

Institutes of Media Communications at the Universities of Vienna, Salzburg and Klagenfurt have well-established Departments of Public Relations, which are quite popular among students. The number of diploma and doctoral theses and academic publications is increasing continuously – unfortunately, without a corresponding increase in the number of staff, so that both teaching and research are suffering from the glut of students. Little support can be expected from the universities and even colleagues in the same institute do not have a particularly positive attitude towards public relations research. Indeed, public relations is the only subject which has not been recognised as an independent academic discipline. In spite of all this, awareness of the necessity and importance of professional public relations is on the increase; theory and practice are continuing to develop. The public relations branch in Austria has grown up and is becoming increasingly professional.

As far as the future of public relations in Austria is concerned, there are reasons for optimism. In comparison with advertising, for example, public relations is more resistant to recession. However, although the market is growing, it is expected that it will become saturated in the medium term, both for agencies and within companies. Fairly equal slices of the public relations cake will give way to cut-throat competition. At agency level this means that the large "full-service agencies" and the "specialist agencies" (for example, online, events, environmental, health) will probably survive and within organisations (businesses, associations, etc.) only those employees with solid, practical training who are interested in life-long education will keep their jobs. Finally, only those agencies or employees who keep an eye on international developments will maintain their hold on the market.

The question posed by the organisers as to the influence of the United States can be answered as follows: a brief glance at the history of public relations in Austria shows that it certainly has its own tradition of public relations. The first stage (eighteenth and nineteenth centuries) proceeded relatively independent of, and parallel to, the history of public relations in the US. One basic difference between Austrian and American developments is that early public relations in the US was much more defensive in nature (the "public-be-damned" phase), acting as a legitimation for "big business" versus criticism in the investigative journalism of muckrakers. In contrast, the early days of Austrian public relations were characterised by active information work – for example, the information policies of Maria Theresa (1717–1780). The second phase of development (mid-twentieth century) is characterised by mutual influences. While Europeans – Germans and Austrians in particular – have taken note of theories and approaches developed in America, they have not taken them over wholesale. Instead they reflect on them critically and develop them in their own right against the background of a European context. Right from the start it was clear to German-speaking authors that the American situation could not be transposed to Germany or Austria and that the prevailing conditions, prerequisites and forms of the media and communication society in Europe and Austria had to be taken into account (cf. Nessmann 1995, 2000). Finally, it is important to mention that Austrian communications experts have shown time and again that they have the potential to go their own way (both in terms of training and public relations as an academic discipline). The innovative public relations courses at universities and the theoretical approaches to public relations developed by Austrian authors mentioned in this chapter can be considered proof of this.

References

Bentele, Günter and Tobias Liebert (eds.) (1995). *Verständigungsorientierte Öffentlichkeitsarbeit. Darstellung und Diskussion des Ansatzes von Roland Burkart* [Consensus oriented public relations. A description and discussion of Roland Burkart's approach]. (Leipziger Skripten für Public Relations und Kommunikationsmanagement 1.) University of Leipzig: Institute of Communication and Media Science.

Bogner, Franz (1990). *Das neue PR-Denken. Strategien, Konzepte, Maßnahmen, Fallbeispiele effizienter Öffentlichkeitsarbeit* [New thoughts on public relations. Strategies, concepts, measures, case studies on efficient public relations]. Vienna: Ueberreuter Verlag.

Bogner, Franz (1999). *Das neue PR-Denken. Strategien, Konzepte, Aktivitäten* [New thoughts on PR. Strategies, concepts, activities]. Vienna: Ueberreuter Verlag. 3rd edn.

Brunner, Doris (2001). PR-Berater fit für Euroland [PR consultants fit for Europe]. *MEDIANET* 50: 5.

Burkart, Roland (1993). *Public Relations als Konfliktmanagement. Ein Konzept für verständigungsorientierte Öffentlichkeitsarbeit* [Public relations as conflict management. A concept for consensus oriented public relations.]. (Studienreihe Konfliktforschung 7.) Vienna: Braumüller Verlag.

Burkart, Roland (1994). Consensus oriented Public Relations as a solution to the landfill conflict. *Waste Management & Research* 12: 223–232.

Dorer, Johanna and Klaus Lojka (eds.) (1991). *Öffentlichkeitsarbeit. Theoretische Ansätze, empirische Befunde und Berufspraxis der Public Relations* [Public relations. Theoretical approaches, empirical findings and professional practice]. (Studienbücher zur Publizistik- und Kommunikationswissenschaft 7.) Vienna: Braumüller Verlag.

Frühbauer, Milan (2000). PR heißt jetzt Professionalität. Von der Medienarbeit zur integrierten Kommunikation. [The professionalisation of public relations. From media relations to integrated communication]. *Bestseller* (20 Jahre Festschrift), 140–144.

Frühbauer, Milan (ed.) (2002). PR-ALMANACH 2002 [PR almanac 2002]. Vienna: Manstein Verlag.

Gröpel, Hellmut (1953). Public Relations: Eine betriebswirtschaftliche Studie [Public relations; a study from the point of view of business management.], Ph.D. dissertation, University of Innsbruck.

Haas, Meta (1987). *Public Relations. Berufsrealität in Österreich* [Public relations. The realities of the profession in Austria]. Vienna: Orac Verlag.

Hopfgartner, Gerhard and Karl Nessmann (2000). *PR-Public Relations für Schulen. So gelingt erfolgreiche Öffentlichkeitsarbeit* [PR for schools – how to do successful public relations]. Vienna: Öbv&hpt Verlag. See also http://www-sci.uni-klu.ac.at/pr/PR_Schule/home.htm

Kronhuber, Hans (1972). *Public Relations: Einführung in die Öffentlichkeitsarbeit* [An introduction to public relations]. Vienna: Böhlaus Verlag.

ÖGK (1998). *Medien Journal* 22–3 [Media journal] (thematic issue *Public Relations. Qualifications and competences*).

Nessmann, Karl (1995). Public relations in Europe: A comparison with the United States. *Public Relations Review* 21–2: 151–160.

Nessmann, Karl (1998). Vermittlung von Basisqualifikationen. Berufsbegleitende PR-Bildungsprogramme [How to teach basic qualifications. On-the-job training for public relations]. *ÖGK Medien Journal* 35–40.

Nessmann, Karl (2000). The origins and development of public relations in Germany and Austria. In: Danny Moss, Dejan Verčič, and Gary Warnaby (eds.), *Perspectives on Public Relations Research*, 211–225. London/New York: Routledge.

Nessmann, Karl (2002). Personal Relations: Eine neue Herausforderung für PR-Theorie und -Praxis [Personal public relations: a new challenge for theoretical and practical public relations]. *PRMAGAZIN* 1. 47–54.

Ruler, Betteke van and Dejan Verčič (2002). *The Bled Manifesto on Public Relations.* Ljubljana: Pristop.

Schweighardt, Kurt (1954). Theorie und Praxis der öffentlichen Beziehungspflege einer Unternehmung unter besonderer Berücksichtigung der soziologischen Elemente [The theory and practice of corporate public relations with special reference to sociological elements]. Ph.D. dissertation, University of Innsbruck

Signitzer, Benno (ed.) (1984). *Public Relations: Praxis in Österreich* [Public relations and how it is practised in Austria]. Vienna: Orac Verlag.

Signitzer, Benno (1988). Public Relations-Forschung im Überblick: Systematisierungsversuche auf der Basis neuer amerikanischer Studien [An overview of public relations research: an attempted systemisation based on new American studies]. *Publizistik* 1: 92–116.

Signitzer, Benno (1992). Theorien der Public Relations [Theories of public relations]. In: Roland Burkart and Walter Hömberg (eds.), *Kommunikationstheorie: Ein Textbuch zur Einführung* [Communication theory: an introductory textbook], 134–152. (Studienbücher zur Publizistik- und Kommunikationswissenschaft 8.) Vienna: Braumüller Verlag.

Verčič, Dejan, Betteke van Ruler, Gerhard Buetschi, and Bertil Flodin (2001). On the definition of public relations: A European view. *Public Relations Review* 27–4: 373–387.

Wachta, Hansjörg (2000). Die Geschichte der Public Relations: Vom Orakel zum Onlineberater [The history of public relations: from oracles to online consultants]. *Bestseller* (20 Jahre Festschrift), 138–139.

Zerfaß, Ansgar (1998). Techniken, Tools, Theorien. Management-Know how für Public Relations [Techniques, tools, theories. Management know-how for public relations]. *ÖGK Medien Journal* 3–15.

Zowack, Martina (2000). Frauen in den österreichischen Public Relations. Berufssituation und die Feminisierung von PR [Women in Austrian public relations. Their professional situation and the feminisation of public relations]. Ph.D. dissertation, University of Vienna.

Chapter 3

Belgium

Luc Pauwels and Baldwin Van Gorp

1. National profile: facts and figures

1.1. Overview of national characteristics

Belgium became an independent state in 1830. It is a constitutional monarchy that has gradually evolved towards a federal structure through a series of institutional reforms. Today, the constitution stipulates that Belgium is a federal state consisting of communities and regions. There are three communities: the Dutch-speaking Flemish community, the French community and the German-speaking community. In addition, economic concerns gave rise to the creation of three regions with a considerable degree of autonomy: the Flemish Region, the Brussels Capital Region and the Walloon Region. Belgium's regions are, to an extent, similar to the states in the United States of America or Germany's *Länder*. The country is further divided into ten provinces and 589 communes. Reconciling regional and cultural identities in a federal structure proves to be difficult, but it is nevertheless regarded as an essential step towards bringing the decision-making process closer to the people. However, linguistic and cultural differences have had (and to an extent continue to have) disrupting effects on many aspects of Belgian society, including the institutionalisation of public relations.

Freedom of organisation in the Belgian educational system has been guaranteed under the Constitution since 1831. As Belgium is a highly industrialized society, education and training are crucially important. This explains why post-war education policy was geared explicitly towards raising the overall level of training and realizing a more democratic educational system. The financial barriers that used to restrict people's participation in education have been lowered dramatically: primary and secondary education was made free and an extensive system of social allowances and grants was introduced to encourage young people to move on to university or other forms of higher education. Today, the level of education in Belgium ranks among the highest in Europe.

1.2. Facts and figures about public relations in Belgium

Public relations consultancy by independent advisors or public relations firms developed rather slowly in Belgium. In the early 1970s, there were perhaps as few as twenty individuals or firms providing such services (Pleunes 1982: 16). In the 1980s, however, advertising agencies became more closely involved in the public relations business, most likely for economic reasons. The onset of recession, the saturation of the market and the inherently unpredictable impact of advertising campaigns prompted advertising agencies to diversify. By the year 2001, there were 1,118 VAT-registered public relations firms in Belgium according to figures from the National Institute of Statistics. Of these, 542 were located in Flanders, 225 in Wallonia and 351 in the Brussels Capital Region. This relatively high number of public relations firms for a small market such as Belgium may be due to the fact that "Public Relations Consultant or Advisor" is not a legally protected title or profession. Furthermore, many of these registered public relations firms are, in fact, one-person businesses. Others are events agencies whose articles happen to mention public relations as an area of activity. As the expertise of the Belgian branches of international consultancy firms such as Hill & Knowlton and Burson-Marsteller tends to focus on Brussels-based EU institutions and multinational corporations, there is still ample room for smaller public relations firms in other niche markets. While many public relations firms present themselves as full-service agencies, others prefer to concentrate on specialized areas, such as media relations, crisis communications, financial communication or public affairs.

2. History and development of public relations

The discipline of public relations has, quite literally, acquired a place in many organisations in Belgium and it has, moreover, developed into a recognised and popular field of study. Today, public relations activities are regarded as part and parcel of the successful management of private and public enterprises. Yet, many misconceptions persist and there is still much room for improvement in terms of the professionalism and institutionalisation of the field.

We provide an overview of the gradual development of public relations in Belgium, identifying its main characteristics and highlighting some of the principal issues and trends. In the absence of comprehensive and large-scale research into the various aspects of public relations as an academic and professional field, we draw on a wide variety of sources and materials. Indeed, the input for this chapter is provided by references in the literature and by academic work on public relations (particularly in relation to the Belgian context), interviews with public relations managers and consultants, various research reports and documents from the Belgian Public Relations Centre (BPRC) archives[1] (including newsletters, annual reports, minutes of meetings and special task force reports), and a recent online survey. In addition, the views expressed in this chapter are grounded in our own professional practice and experience, both at the organisational side of communication management and at the media side.

Some of the issues discussed here relate specifically to the Belgian context, though presumably developments in this field are similar in other European countries.

2.1. Roots of public relations

While the concept of public relations only truly arrived on the Belgian scene after World War II, some corporations, including the national electricity company, already had departments dedicated to the systematic dissemination of information long before such methods were introduced more widely from the US (Bol 1978). The first proper public relations departments were, however, only established after the war at such companies as the Belgian branch of ESSO (1946), the insurance firm *Algemene Verzekeringen* (1949) and the *Generale Bankmaatschappij*, a bank (1950).

Erik Cyprès, a Belgian correspondent with the *New York Herald Tribune*, is believed to have been the first to set up an independent public relations agency in Belgium in 1952. He also brought together a number of individuals in charge of public relations at large organisations to discuss the creation of a first professional association, but this pioneering effort failed because the participants held such divergent views.

Eventually, though, on 31 March 1953, the bilingual Belgian Public Relations Centre (BPRC) was established. Over the years, the BPRC has experienced its fair share of problems in dealing with controversies

---

1. We wish to thank D. De Marto, Director of the BPRC, charged with the daily operations, for his kind co-operation, particularly in providing unrestricted access to the well-kept archives of his organisation.

between the Dutch-speaking and the French-speaking membership, but it always managed to survive (Meiden and Fauconnier 1982). The organisation used to play and still plays an important role in the professionalisation and institutionalisation of the field. It is the oldest and largest organisation of its kind in Belgium, consisting of internal public relations professionals from private or public institutions as well as external public relations consultants and, albeit fewer, teachers and students. Yet, the organisation comprises only about 250 members, which is only a fraction of the total number of public relations practitioners in Belgium. The BPRC offers its members ample opportunity to meet and exchange information and experiences, in formal and more informal ways (through workshops, conferences, seminars, lectures, electronic newsletters, annual reports, research reports, special task forces, etc.). The BPRC has set itself the task of serving the professional interests of its members at national and international level. The organisation is, however, primarily geared towards practitioners, while public relations scholars are, on the whole, not well represented. Nonetheless, by organizing workgroups, research projects and special events, the BPRC does make an effort to establish and foster closer links between researchers and teachers on the one hand, and professionals on the other.

In 1954, the Belgian government established a public relations department, probably with a view to brush up its image that had been somewhat tarnished by the country's controversial colonial past. Not much later, Belgium became the third European country to join the International Public Relations Association (IPRA). Over the next four decades, the IPRA would develop from being a bunch of enthusiastic pioneers to its present status of representative international network of public relations professionals.

Most of the early Belgian members of the IPRA represented foreign, particularly American, companies. On the occasion of the 1958 World Exhibition, the BPRC organized the first ever world conference on public relations, an example that would soon be followed by the IPRA. In addition, the many international contacts that existed in the field gave rise to the idea of a European association of national public relations organisations. This led to the creation in May 1959 of the 'Centre Européen des Relations Publiques' (CERP, now called 'Confédération Européenne des Relations Publiques') by practitioners from Belgium (represented through the BPRC), France, Germany, Italy and the Netherlands. Headquartered in Brussels, the CERP is the umbrella organisation of national and professional public relations associations from across Europe.

In 1991, another nationwide professional association was founded, namely, the Association of Belgian Communications Directors (ABCD). This organisation was much smaller and, as the name already suggests, much more exclusive than the BPRC. It sought to create an informal forum where communication directors could exchange experiences and insights. Apart from these national organisations, a number of regional or local institutions were also established, partly as a result of the linguistic and cultural differences that continued to characterise Belgian society. These institutions included the *Association Carolorégienne de l'Information et des Relations Publiques* (ACIRP); the *Cercle Liégeois de l'Information et des Relations Publiques* (CLIRP), the *Centre Namurois d'Information et de Relations Publiques* (CNIRP), *Public Relations Antwerpen* (PRA), *Werkgroep voor Public Relations in het bedrijfsleven van de Mechelse regio* (PRIM) and *PR Limburg*.

2.2. Development of education and research traditions

In 1958, the then bilingual Catholic University of Leuven offered the very first course in public relations. In the following years, similar courses were introduced at other universities and institutions of higher education. However, until today, no university in Belgium offers separate graduate degrees in public relations or communication management. These areas of study are usually incorporated in undergraduate and graduate programmes in communication sciences. Yet, many universities recognize the growing importance of public relations, both as an academic field and as a profession, and provide students with the option of specialized programmes in "Strategic Communication" (University of Antwerp, for instance) or "Internal and External Communication" (at the University of Leuven). On the other hand, the more profession-oriented non-university institutions of higher education offer separate degrees (usually three-year programmes) in public relations, business communications, press and information, advertising, and marketing communications. Choosing one of these options within communications management training does not seem to determine or restrict the field in which graduates are subsequently employed. In any case, there is much overlap between the options within each of the available programmes. Furthermore, corporations generally do not set very specific requirements for new recruits in the fields of communications or human resources. Indeed, communication graduates must often compete with sociologists, law graduates and economists in the job market. Job advertisements tend to combine or even confuse marketing communications skills with public relations-related competencies (for example, they may require that a marketing assistant be able to write a staff newsletter or that an internal communications assistant must be able to produce marketing collateral).

While higher non-university education traditionally claims to be more practical and thus, in a sense, more professional, it is not at all clear what this actually means. For example, what practice does one refer to: execution-related tasks or strategic planning? Clearly, more time is devoted to learning communications techniques (writing press communiqués, organizing events), but, on the other hand, university graduates generally acquire a more strategic and integrated view on communications in a broader organisational context. Moreover, they may be expected to be better versed in communication theory, organisation theory and research methodologies. So while university graduates may initially find it hard to prove themselves within an organisation in a junior position (many will after all never have written a press communiqué or handled a video camera), they should – in theory – be better prepared to eventually acquire a management position.

Particularly in higher education, mandatory internship is being considered as an integral part of public relations or communication management training. However, it is not easy to find interesting positions for trainees in organisations year after year. Students inevitably lack the necessary skills and experience to contribute meaningfully to the activities of an organisation. From the organisations' perspective, a balance needs to be found between them providing relevant on-the-job training for students and the students offering something in return. This may imply that trainees should get some real work done or that the company should be allowed to thoroughly assess them as potential employees. In rare occasions, trainees are abused as a source of free labour, performing tasks that contribute little to their development. But in other instances, the trainee period can be a most rewarding experience for both parties and it may occasionally result in the hiring of the trainee after graduation.

The professional public relations organisations generally make a genuine effort to establish a closer link between theory and practice. The CERP, for instance, set up two task forces, which it called *de la théorie à la pratique* ('from theory to practice') and *synergies enseignement – profession* ('synergies between public relations training and profession'). The BPRC likewise organises a yearly event called the "Day of the Student" with the purpose of informing and enthusing students about public relations as a profession. However, as these organisations are still rather small, so too is the impact of their efforts.

2.3. How language shapes the development of public relations

Dutch speaking Belgians will routinely use the term "Public Relations" in English while the French speaking part of Belgium prefers to use its French equivalent *Relations Publiques*. But as in other countries, the very term "public relations" whether in its English or French version, is a recurring topic for debate. Some say the expression is confusing and that it is not sufficiently expansive, and they therefore put forward the more general term "communication" as an alternative. Others argue that "public relations" is far too broad a term to be useful. In other words, there is much disagreement over its exact meaning, and this is apparent in the wording of job advertisements, job titles, job descriptions and different organisational arrangements. They reflect the lack of agreement and persisting confusion regarding the precise boundaries of the field or profession. Some still tend to exclude internal communications from public relations, but this view is losing ground. The more dominant view is that commercial types of communication – that is, "marketing communications" – should be clearly differentiated (though not necessary separated) from public relations activities. Calls for integrating marketing communications and corporate communications, rather than lead towards a more integrated planning and tuning of all internal and external communications of organisations, often result in utter confusion of goals and means, even though the idea of such integration as such makes much sense.

3. Typification of current public relations

3.1. Status of public relations in business, administration and society

Public relations in Belgium has progressively extended its scope and it has, moreover, also gained some depth. The notion of communication management has gradually moved beyond merely catering for the media, producing collateral or organising events.

Over the years, many authors have repeatedly emphasised the importance of managing "internal communications". In the case of some companies, a broader understanding of the term "public" in public relations has resulted in a sharper focus on the vastly important internal publics besides numerous specialised external publics. Unfortunately, this often goes little further than looking after the internal media (personnel newsletters, web sites).

The increasing complexity of managing a business (due to growing competition, globalisation and technological innovation) has also resulted in calls for other types of specialised communications. Today, it is not uncommon for companies in Belgium to advertise in newspapers for specialists in financial communications, investor relations, health communications or indeed many other fields. Public relations, both as a professional activity and as an academic interest, has witnessed short-lived hypes as well as more enduring trends, triggered by external events, slick communication gurus or slowly maturing insights.

The increased interest for environmental and crisis communications in the 1980s may have been occasioned by such events as the explosion at a Union Carbide plant in Bhopal (1984), the nuclear accident at Chernobyl (1986) and the shipwreck off the Belgian coast of a vessel carrying radio-active waste (1984). Another sub field of public relations that has mushroomed in recent years is "public affairs", also referred to as "political public relations" or "government relations". Known primarily for one of its key techniques – namely, lobbying – this field has evolved from what was regarded a questionable practice to a widely accepted activity by powerful industries and pressure groups alike. Today, Brussels is populated by thousands of lobbyists.

Not only have we seen an increase in strategic communication with governmental bodies and institutions (public affairs), but public sector bodies in Belgium, be it local, regional, national or international, have also been taking communication much more seriously. Cities, provinces, ministries, etc., are now hiring personnel to set up specialised information offices, to produce communications plans and to introduce new communication technologies in an effort to provide better information and establish a dialogue with the citizens. This 'external' aspect of public sector communications is rather country-specific or, in the case of Belgium, community-bound and regulated. It is definitely an important area of growth. Unfortunately, because of its inevitably specific context (cultural, political, professional), there is little literature on the topic, despite the fact that expertise in this particular domain is of crucial importance. The communication responsibilities of local, regional and national government bodies are varied and complex. Their purpose and goals, and indeed the products and services they deliver to their audiences, differ significantly from those of many private, predominantly profit-oriented, organisations. Some educational institutions are trying to provide specialised courses in governmental communications, but thus far they have largely failed to tap into the specifics of this field.

In the 1980s and 1990s, much attention was paid to the application of new communication technologies (such as desktop publishing, AV production, multimedia, Internet and Intranet) and, indeed, this continues to be a major point of interest and concern for communicators. One of the more recent trends would appear to be increased attention for communications during mergers or acquisitions and the varied role communications can play in preparing people for change, guiding them through it and helping them build a new corporate culture and brand. It is also noticeable that general business principles and mindsets ("no cure, no pay", for instance) are now being applied to service providers in the communication sector.

The recent crisis in the information and communication technology sector and the allegedly fraudulent business practices of certain large corporations in the US and Belgium have again demonstrated the vulnerability of a corporate reputation. They also illustrate the crucially important role that managing both internal and external communications can play in assuring that the image of an organisation is both favourable and realistic – that is, that it reflects the corporate identity.

Research into aspects of communication within organisations is very limited and often takes a narrow approach. Sometimes the organisation itself takes the initiative for a kind of study (usually a questionnaire) or it may commission a firm to look into a particular set of problems. Small-scale research projects are also typically conducted by graduate students in communication science, usually as part of their thesis requirement.

Over the years, the BPRC has issued several interesting surveys to its members. Despite the limited number of potential respondents (compared to the estimated number of public relations practitioners in Belgium) and the overrepresentation of the Brussels Capital Region, these surveys have yielded interesting and rare data on public relations in Belgium. Some of these studies are reflexive in nature, focusing on the characteristics of the members of the BPRC and their views on how the organisation performs. Others deal with the big issues of public relations and communication management in general.

In 1996, the BPRC sent out a survey to its members asking them about their views on the strengthening of ties between the public relations profession and academia, especially by conducting more applied communication research. Most of the thirty respondents supported the idea and identified the following areas and issues as meriting further research: media relations for the non-profit sector; top managers' perception of communications management; financial communication; evaluating media relations; crisis communications; reputation management; sponsoring; content and definition of public relations and communication; and proper application of the new media. It is noteworthy, though not unexpected, that the responses indicate that public relations professionals continue to focus primarily on external communication. None suggested that large-scale research should be conducted into issues relating to internal communications. This might indicate that one prefers to keep such internal matters within the organisation or that the fundamental adage of working "inside out" in communications is still not fully understood or taken to heart.

Also in 1996, Keystone Network performed some diagnostic research on behalf of the BPRC, consisting of a series of interviews with twelve public relations leaders in organisations and ten consultants from public relations firms. These interviews confirmed some of the previous findings with regard to the status of public relations in Belgium (and abroad):

- There is no common understanding of what public relations is or should be.
- Public relations professionals have widely divergent educational backgrounds and work experience. Some are communication-science graduates, but many others have different backgrounds, have moved from other jobs within the company, or have previously worked in the mass media.
- There is a clear divide between the strategic and the purely operational levels.
- Public relations is sometimes considered to be merely a part-time task for a secretary or director.
- Public relations has a fairly negative image within organisations: it is seen as a cost factor rather than a critical-success factor. Problems encountered in measuring its impact (due to its nature and its long-term focus) tend to reinforce this view.
- Public relations has become a more stressful and more encompassing profession (more specialised, performance-oriented, more technological), in which practitioners are constantly required to prove themselves.
- The term "public relations" no longer describes the field adequately. Some propose replacing it with the term "communications" or with combined terms that include the word "communication".

The study also uncovered some of the typical tensions that exist between public relations firms and organisations commissioning their services. The latter often feel they have to pay too much for consultancy services that prove to be less specialised than the public relations firm claims. External public relations consultants, in turn, lament that organisations mainly call upon their services in times of severe crisis, or they accuse them of "brain picking" and subsequently proceeding on their own.

Two years later, in 1998, the BPRC issued a new survey to its members (fifty-five respondents) concerning their reasons for having joined the association. It emerged that the prime reasons for becoming a member of the BPRC are the opportunities it offers for informal and professional contacts, its nation-wide character and the quality of its events and initiatives. Most members are eager to learn from case studies and want to share their experiences with others. On the other hand, members feel that the BPRC is still inadequately organised and not very widely known, and that, consequently, it has a very limited impact on the professional world at large. Some also disapprove of the strong focus on Brussels or even Belgium. Almost half of the respondents state that there is a need for more specialised courses for professionals who want to keep in touch with developments in the field and for people entering into the profession from other fields (which appears to be a common occurrence).

Our own recent online survey (Pauwels and Van Gorp 2002), which yielded responses from communication managers in thirty-one large companies (with 500 or more employees) from many different sectors of industry, largely echoes the results of previous studies – but it also provides some more up-to-date information. Here are some of the findings:

- Most of the large organisations that responded (twenty-six out of thirty-one) have a separate public relations or communications department, but these rarely consist of more than three to five persons (in a few cases more than twenty and in several instances just one or two).
- Most communication managers report that they have produced a communications plan, though it is unclear for the moment what these plans encompass or how they were developed (for instance, on the basis of research?). One-third of respondents indicate that they conduct no research on internal or external communications. Of all the typical communications activities, research is most likely to be outsourced.
- A wide variety of titles and terms are used to name the field: Marketing and Communications, Corporate Communications, Press and Pub-

lic Relations, Internal and External Relations. Many of these include the word "communication" rather than "public relations". Furthermore, these titles and terms are often Dutch, French or German (Belgium's three official languages), though English is also well established in the business world.

– Apparently, public relations has acquired a relatively comfortable position in the hierarchies of the organisations. The head of the communications department often occupies a position at the middle-management level (thirteen out of thirty-one) or even at the higher management level (twelve out of thirty-one), though this does not necessarily mean that they are involved in strategic decision-making.

– Most public relations or communications heads have a college degree in humanities (communication sciences, sociology, law, economics) and the majority entered their present job from another communications function or from a marketing, sales or human resources related position.

– With respect to key competencies and skills, the respondents emphasise the importance of adequate verbal communication skills (speaking, writing and presenting) as well as social competencies and organisational ability. On the other hand, the more specific communication management skills (knowledge of communication theory, research and evaluation techniques, and media) are rated rather lowly.

– As to the image of the profession, a large proportion of the respondents lacked a pronounced opinion, while the rest held quite divergent views (ranging from very favourable to very unfavourable).

– The responses to various questions regarding specific tasks and issues confirm that most public relations personnel are primarily focused on external relations (such as reputation management, media relations).

– An open question regarding the respondents' main concerns in relation to their profession revealed that the following issues are considered to be important: establishing an appropriate mix of electronic and paper communication; differentiating between "pull" and "push" approaches; ensuring consistency and co-ordination in and between different types of communication; increasing the limited strategic impact of public relations; incorporating social responsibility into public relations activities; ensuring that top-level management takes its exemplary role to heart; effective communications coaching for diverse publics; making the organisation as a whole subscribe to the idea that good public relations is vitally important; integrating corporate communications into marketing communications.

– As regards training, the respondents to this survey – rather surprisingly – did not express an overwhelming preference for more specific or elaborate educational offerings.

3.2. Position of public relations in organisations

On a less positive note, it should be pointed out that there is still a certain degree of mistrust and prejudice between the outside world (notably journalists) and public relations people, which is only in part attributable to current practices. But even within organisations, public relations often suffers from a rather negative or distorted image. Public relations practitioners are commonly seen as big spenders who like to party but contribute very little to the realisation of corporate success. Often, public relations activities are considered "nice to have" rather than essential for the success or survival of an organisation. In times of crisis or economic recession, budgets for so-called "non-productive" or "supporting" activities tend to be slashed, whereas in relation to communication exactly the opposite is required. The Golden Sixties are over, and, perhaps fortunately to some extent, so are the times of purely "cosmetic" types of public relations, characterised by expensive image campaigns and mainly outer-directed activities that were often completely divorced from the actual identity of the organisations concerned (Buntinx 1966). But while expensive-looking brochures and posh events are no longer a prime focus of the more professional public relations departments, it is still hard to obtain a decent budget for serious research and planning of activities. Product- and event-oriented activities, and quick-hit approaches in general, still seem to dominate. In addition, means (such as personnel newsletters and press events) are easily confused with goals (such as fostering better mutual understanding with the different publics). Furthermore, some practitioners (and their leaders) are not at all convinced of the need to further professionalise the field, nor of the fact that, in order to improve overall performance, a specific body of theoretical knowledge and specialised skills and experience are needed that go beyond general organisational know-how.

The absence of a truly strategic and broad approach that is solidly founded in theory often goes hand in hand with the narrow, yet widespread view of the position, role and practice of communication management. While communication is commonly regarded to be a strategic management instrument, communication managers are, in reality, often seriously constrained when it comes to giving shape to this idea. External communications activities are typically dominated by press relations, while internal activities are often confined to supervising the internal media (personnel newsletter, website) and 'passing on' information from the top (Pauwels 2001). The purely instrumental top-down approach is still characteristic of many communication systems within organisations. The need for more-encompassing and valid types of evaluation is mostly voiced by academics.

4. Conclusion: state of the art and future of public relations in Belgium

By way of conclusion, we may say that public relations in Belgium is definitely in the process of becoming more institutionalised, both as a profession and as an academic field. Communication departments at universities and non-university institutions offering higher education in communications are proving very successful and are attracting a growing number of students. Demand from private and public organisations in Belgium for communication science graduates and experts, is also growing. However, this booming interest in communications from organisations and in academic life does not automatically translate into an overall increase in the quality of communications management within organisations. Nor does it guarantee a closer linkage of academic and professional practice. The latter issues are related to such aspects as the recognition and development of specific competencies, role definitions, expectations and perceptions held by the different players in the field (public relations practitioners, general management, educators, media people, general public, etc.), and to the means and levels of autonomy within the complex structure of an organisation. Unlike other organisational fields and functions (such as financial management), public relations or communication management is still not fully recognised as a specialised area of expertise that has a significant impact on the well-being of an organisation. The notion persists that communications-management skills within an organisation are acquired mainly "on the job". Many see an unbridgeable gap between an approach that is based purely on experience or on simplistic and outdated models (strictly linear, mechanistic, one-way) and approaches that are grounded more firmly in contemporary theory and research. Quality improvement with regard to communications management is not just a matter for managers and professionals within organisations, but also for academics specialising in this field (especially if they have acquired some real-life experience in communication management within a large and complex organisation). Whether this gap will ever be closed depends primarily on the combined efforts of these academics and the more enlightened communication professionals. Further research is needed to attain better insight into the current theory and practice within organisations in the field of strategic communication management. This insight could then help bridge the chasm between the rapidly expanding academic knowledge base with respect to organisational communication and workable approaches and applications of theory in real-life settings. In other words, research findings may further stimulate the process of professionalisation of communication-related activities within organisations and result in a more meaningful contribution from communication science education to society as a whole.

References

Bol, Jean-Marie Van, (1978). *Historische Bakens van de Public Relations in België* [*Historical Beacons of Public Relations in Belgium*] (2nd edn.). Brussels: INBEL/BPRC.
Buntinx, Hubert (1966). *Public Relations: Proeve van Analyse en Synthese* [Public Relations: Essay in Analysis and Synthesis]. Hasselt: Heideland.
Meiden, Anne van der and Guido Fauconnier (1982). *Profiel en Professie: Inleiding in de Theorie en de Theorievorming van Public Relations* [Profile and Profession: Introduction into the Theory and Theorizing of Public Relations]. Leiden/Antwerpen: H. E. Stenfert Kroese.
Pauwels, Luc (2001). Het ontwikkelen van een strategisch communicatiebeleid voor organisaties: een tien-fasen communicatie-planningsmodel [The development of a strategic communications policy for organisations: a communications planning model in ten parts]. In C. van Tilborgh en R. Duyck (eds.), *Management Jaarboek 2001* [Management Year book 2001], 177–185. Wetteren: PIMMS N. V. & Vlaamse Management Associatie.
Pleunes, Jean-Luc (1982). [No title]. *PR Contact*, October: 16.

Intermezzo

A constructivistic approach to public relations

Klaus Merten

1. Preliminary remarks

Since systems theory applies to the micro-, meso- and macro-levels of social processes and to their interrelations, it can be used fruitfully for the analysis of communication processes as well as for the management of communication and the development of the communication system.

Public relations is a strategy for using communication processes to generate desired effects by constructing desired realities. Systems theory, which is the only theory to deal adequately with communication processes, may therefore be a good base for describing and analysing public relations.

It can be shown that the communication system, probably the latest of the great societal subsystems, develops in the era of media society into the most relevant subsystem. According to the development of three realities in media society, the relation between fact and fiction changes thoroughly: fictional and "real" reality now can substitute each other and "real" action or "real" persons get some substitute in the media, which develop their own relevance – the image, for example.

It is these features which provide the basis for a profession to create, stabilise or modify images: public relations. Furthermore, the potential to create fictional realities, which can act effectively on the actual realities will give public relations, little by little, the competence of creating the daily sample of relevance which used to be the area of the journalists. The consequences of this development in media society are huge: the radius of relevant events reported by the media widens infinitely, but the possibility to rely on truth will vanish completely.

Systems theory can operate on several levels. The basic level, the simplest societal process, is the communication process. The second level is the organisational and/or group level, and the third level is the societal level. But systems theory not only operates on these levels, it can also interrelate them. Furthermore, since the development of public relations relies heavily on a continuous process of constructing suitable realities, a constructivist perspective has some advantages in comparison with other types of theory (Schmidt 1987). In other words, systems theory is the only theory that can describe communication processes and their effects, initiated by organisations to influence people in different societal subsystems, and to watch their interrelations. Consequently, systems theory may be a promising basis to look at public relations.

Public Relations, however, is a strategy to use communications in a well-defined manner. Public Relations function as a means to persuade, influence, convince the public and establish consensus (Bernays) with respect to the relevant problems at hand. Or, as Grunig (1992: 6) put it, public relations is the "management of communication between an organisation and its public".

2. Evolution of the media

From a theoretical point, the evolution of the media is an inevitable consequence of societal differentiation (Merten 1999: 207). It establishes the necessary integrative forces between the societal subsystems by means of communication. As Figure 1 shows, the evolution of the media accelerates continuously through the centuries and provides society with a growing flood of information.

The continually rising flood of information leads to an evolutionary pressure that can be imagined if one bears in mind that the evolution of media has taken place simultaneously at different places. For example, the development of literature took place about 3,500 years BC in China and at the same time in Uruk (Iraq). In 1609, the printing press was invented in Strasbourg as well as in Wolfenbüttel (Germany). In 1665, the first two journals – the *Journal de Scavants* (Paris) and the *Philosophical Transactions* (London) – were launched simultaneously. Moreover, in 1895, the brothers Skladanowsky showed the first film at Berlin, only weeks before the brothers Lumière showed their film in Paris (Merten 1999: 421).

The amount of information distributed by media grows at the same time. In 1990, for instance, media (print, radio and television) provided forty times (i.e. 4,000 per cent) more information than in 1960. The growing flow of supply and demand of social information in the post-industrial society (Bell 1976) led to the new term "information society".

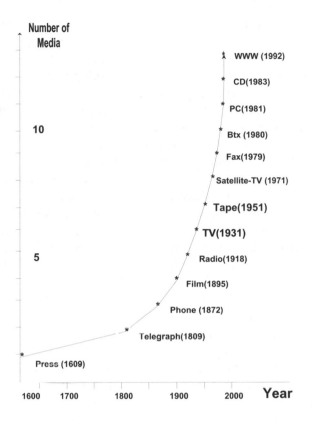

Figure 1. Evolution of the Media

3. Media society

Compared with the term "information society", the term "media society" is far more than the crossing of some level of information flow. In particular, we can distinguish at least three evolutionary developments: (1) the installation of reflexive relations, (2) differentiation of reality and (3) representation or substitution of "real" action by medial action.

3.1. Installation of reflexive relations

The increasing information-overload in modern societies demands a powerful solution of the problem which Niklas Luhmann's sociological systems theory (1970) outlines: the implementation of reflexive mechanisms. According to Luhmann, societies and societal subsystems try to make use of reflexive mechanisms whenever the demand for dealing with higher complexities are exceeded. The development of great societies, for example, made it necessary to substitute the ancient structures of natural economic exchange. The solution was the invention of money – that is, the invention of the exchange of exchange possibilities. And later we have a further implementation of a reflexive mechanism, namely, buying money with money by the invention of interest.

The same holds true for the media society. The problem at hand – the information overload – is solved by the implementation of a reflexive mechanism, that is, meta-media. Meta-media contain information about the content of other media. For example, meta-media tell us what television program we can expect at a specific time. Another type of meta-media are the search engines on the internet. Connected with these developments, the media have installed a thorough mechanism of self-observation: media report on media – for example by printing concurrent press voices, or by reporting the features of how candidates organise their public behaviour during election campaigns, or by installing media-pages and media-topics in the media themselves.

The trilogy of ancient society, industrial society and post-industrial society coined by Bell (1976) always offers the application of the same principle, namely, the networking of mass, energy and information. But networking is a communicative principle and the networking of information is the employment of networking on networking – that is, the installation of a strong reflexive relation. This leads inevitably to the fact that the developments in post-industrial society, that is, media society, will generate new and powerful structures we never came to think of before. An example for this development may be the communicative potentials offered by the World Wide Web.

3.2. Differentiation of reality

A further specific function of media society is derived from the fact that the media have gained increasingly the function of reality construction and relevance definition. The media provide us with a daily sample of relevance and a daily outline of reality. Accordingly, the media system necessarily grows more quickly than other societal subsystems such as economy or politics, and becomes the most relevant subsystem with its own binary code, which is "topical" vs. "non-topical" (Merten 2004). In this respect, topicality is the outcome of two variables: information (unexpectedness, surprise) and relevance (Merten 1973). That is to say, no sales without advertising, no election victory without public opinion, no culture without television, and no public trust without public relations. In other words, nothing is relevant and nothing is real if it cannot be found in the media.

Oh dad, if a tree has fallen in the forest and the media are not there to cover it, has the tree then really fallen?

Figure 2. What is not in the media cannot be real nor relevant

3.3. The substitution of "real" by the fictional

Behind this development is another one. Since the media substitute all real and relevant action, and the substitution of persons itself becomes a type of fictional person which we usually call image (it is no coincidence that the term "image" was first coined in the mid-twentieth century; Boorstin 1961). And since an image can be changed far more easily, quickly and cheaply than the original (person, event, organisation, etc.), media society stipulates a new profession to construct, to maintain or to change, and that is public relations.

As a consequence, fictional reality has the power to rule out the "real" reality. In the transcendence of "real" and fictional reality we get a new third type of actual reality, as a combination of the increasing fictional and the "real" reality which can substitute themselves viably (see Figure 3). Relevant societal, political or economic action can be duplicated in this way – the cost is that the term "truth" begins to vanish and has to be replaced, little by little, by processes of building real or fictional consensus or majorities (this development is supported by new technological possibilities, in particular by the word wide web and digital photography). Probably we have to face the beginning of a new era of valid virtuality, of soft lies, of clandestine realities, of pseudo-events and of false proofs and prophets.[1] But if this era has any effects, the strongest will be seen in the increase of the degrees of freedom that public relations can handle.

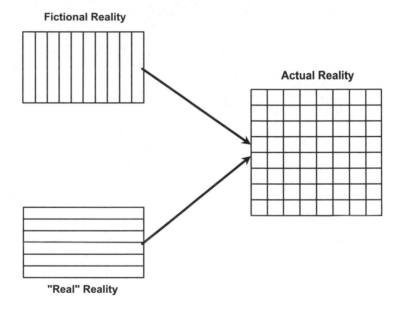

Figure 3. The three realities of the media-society

---

1. For example, in 1983 the German journal *Der Stern* began to publish the diaries of Adolf Hitler. But it took months for the diaries to be unmasked as fake. In 1992 CNN News showed a young girl cry because of the cruelties of Iraqi soldiers towards newborn babies in Kuwait. But this turned out to be a carefully orchestrated public relations stunt from an international public relations agency, ordered by the CIA. And to give a final example, in May 2000 the *Süddeutsche Zeitung*, one of the four German quality papers, was forced to admit that it had been printing fake interviews with celebrities and stars for years.

Taking this development into account, we can, in a first step, define public relations as the construction of desirable realities by means of suitable communication. In other words, public relations is the possibility of keeping the semantics of something in contingent distance to the something itself.

4. Consequences

The rise of public relations in correspondence to media evolution has far-reaching consequences for the communication system. Again, a constructivist perspective is helpful to detect the ongoing process of differentiation. The most relevant development of the communication system lies in the installation of a further reflexive relation – that is, the selection of selection – and will be demonstrated here in three steps: until the invention of the newspaper in 1609, the observation of the world, of all types of events E was limited to the authentic observation every recipient R could do by himself (Figure 4).

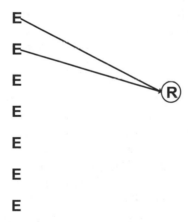

Figure 4. Authentic observation of events E

Later on, the media began to widen the radius of relevance by observing the world. The recipient, R, now had to "pay" for what first was an advantage of a broader view on the world and on its ongoing daily change, by losing the authenticity of observation that is guaranteed to an increasing part, by special observatives, J, which we call "journalists" (Figure 5).

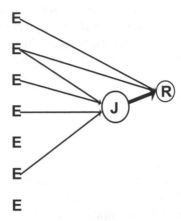

Figure 5. Primary and Second-order observation of the world

Only in the close environment of the recipient R, authentic observation is yet possible, but even there we find media witness, for instance, developments such as the intranet. In a third step, the observation of the world will be done by public relations, because public relations provides day-by-day information about organisations. Maybe this information is only of particular and not of public relevance and published with a specific intention. But if it finds its way into the media, the specific intention vanishes and the public interest is given by the pure fact that the information is in the paper, on television, etc.

As we know public relations provides about 80 per cent of all journalistic information in the media. In the long run, however, we have a decisive differentiation of the journalistic role: the journalists leave the field of primary selection of new information to public relations and strengthen their work on the secondary selection out of the primary one done by public relations. They retire from direct reality in order to improve the selective power of the information to be published (see Figure 6). This is the era of media society and typically this means a further installation of a powerful reflexive relation.

Even in the era of media society, the recipient claims a small part of world observation by himself as authentic observation. The same holds true for the journalists J: for any event E they can claim their personal competence in reporting authentically. But this is an exception.

Public relations is closest to the daily reality, coined by the events E. And public relations defines reality and relevance by the selection of events not being the most relevant events but being declared to be the

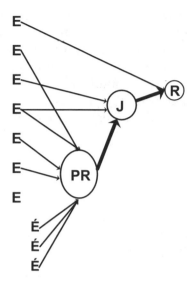

Figure 6. Improvement of information selection by selection out of selection

most relevant events. Furthermore, the development of three realities, as outlined earlier, enables public relations to create viable pseudo-events É, which have no authentically reference to the "real" reality, but neither are they able to act on the reality provided by the media and observed by the recipient R. These pseudo-events É cannot be reported by journalists: they could only report that they are not to be detected in reality.

We are to suppose, then, that the power and the competence to select the daily draft for reality will pass more and more from the journalists to the public relations consultants, and this is an increase of real power itself. Or, as a prominent public relations consultant coins it, "We don't become President, we make Presidents".

5. Conclusion

Public relations is a strategy for using communication processes to generate desired effects by constructing desired realities. Therefore, a systems theory, the only theory to deal adequately with communication processes, may be a good basis for describing and analysing public relations.

We showed that the communication system, the latest of the great societal subsystems, developed in the era of media society into the most relevant subsystem. According to the development of three realities in media society, the relation between fact and fiction changes profoundly: fictional and "real" reality now can substitute each other and "real" action or "real" persons get some substitute in the media which develop their own relevance, such as the image. These features provide the basis for a profession to create, stabilise or modify images, which is what public relations is all about. Furthermore, the potential to create fictional realities that can act effectively on the actual realities, gives public relations its specific power.

References

Bell, Daniel (1976). Welcome to the post-industrial society. *Physics Today* 29: 46–49.
Boorstin, Daniel (1961). *The Image.* New York: Vintage.
Grunig, James E. (ed.) (1992). *Excellence in Public Relations and Communication Management.* Hillsdale: Erlbaum.
Grunig, James E. and Todd Hunt (eds.) (1984). *Managing Public Relations.* New York: Holt, Rinehart & Winston.
Luhmann, Niklas (1970). Reflexive Mechanismen [Reflexive mechanisms]. In: Niklas Luhmann (ed.), *Soziologische Aufklärung* [*Sociological Explanation*], 31–53. Opladen: Westdeutscher Verlag.
Merten, Klaus (1973). Aktualität und Publizität, *Publizistik* 18: 216–235.
Klaus Merten (1999): Einführung in die Kommunkationswissenschaft. Münster/London: Lit.
Merten, Klaus (2002). Politik in der Mediengesellschaft. Zur Interpenetration von Politik- und Kommunikationssystem [Politics in media society. On the interpenetration of political and communication systems]. In: Klaus Merten, Rainer Zimmermann and Helmut Andreas (eds.), *Handbuch der Unternehmenskommunikation 2002/2003* [Handbook of corporate communication 2002/2003], 81–98. Munich/Neuwied/Cologne: Kluwer.
Merten, Klaus (2004). *Einführung in die Kommunikationswissenschaft* [Introduction to communication science]. Münster/London: Lit.
Schmidt, Siegfried (ed.) (1987). *Der Diskurs des radikalen Konstruktivismus.* Frankfurt: Suhrkamp.

Chapter 4

Bosnia-Herzegovina

Nenad Brkic and Melika Husic

1. National profile

1.1. Overview of national characteristics

Bosnia-Herzegovina's declaration of sovereignty in October 1991 was followed by a referendum on independence from the former Yugoslavia in February 1992. Neighbouring Serbia responded with armed resistance. On 21 November 1995, in Dayton, Ohio, the warring parties finally signed a peace agreement that brought to a halt the three years of inter-ethnic civil strife (CIA 2000). The Dayton Agreement divides Bosnia-Herzegovina roughly equally between the Federation of Bosnia-Herzegovina and the Republic of Srpska.

Bosnia-Herzegovina is a south-east European country. Its land mass is 51,129 sq km. It borders on Croatia, Serbia and Montenegro, and has 20 km of coastline. Because of the mostly mountain terrain and beautiful ski resorts, Bosnia-Herzegovina hosted the Olympic Winter Games in 1984. It has large quantities of natural resources (coal, iron, bauxite, manganese, forests, copper, chromium, lead, zinc, hydropower), which resulted in placing the most of the heavy industry of former Yugoslavia in Bosnia-Herzegovina.

Because of the dislocations caused by military action and ethnic cleansing, population data are unreliable, but it is estimated that approximately 3.6 million people currently live in Bosnia-Herzegovina. Sex distribution is 1.03 male for every female; the population growth rate is 3.1 per cent (CIA 2000). The population is ageing, and the youngest and brightest are emigrating. The population of Bosnia-Herzegovina includes a variety of ethnic groups – namely, Bosniak (44 per cent), Serb (31 per cent), Croat (17 per cent), Yugoslav (5.5 per cent) and some other (2.5 per cent) (1991 figures). Religiously, the country is diverse, too: there are muslims (40 per cent), orthodox catholics (31 per cent), Roman catholics (15 per cent) and protestants (4 per cent), and some other

(10 per cent). The official languages are Bosnian, Croatian and Serbian (CIA 2000).

Gross domestic product in Bosnia-Herzegovina is estimated at US$ 1,130 per capita, while the unemployment rate is approximately 40 per cent (Central Bank 2001). The official currency is KM (Convertible Mark) which is connected to the Euro through the currency board – this is why there is no inflation in Bosnia-Herzegovina.

The privatisation process has started, though its implementation is slow (International Crisis Group 2001). No one pretends that privatisation in Bosnia-Herzegovina will be easy, or free from scandal. Experiences elsewhere in Eastern Europe indicate that the process is likely to concentrate wealth in the hands of people with political influence and former directors of the state-owned firms. Yet these same experiences also suggest that new owners who are incompetent or incapable of managing the newly privatised companies quickly sell them on to owners that are more capable. In any event, it is important that the state-owned assets be transferred to the private sector, which can utilise them in a far more productive manner than the state. Over time, these assets will end up in the hands of those most capable of maximising their economic potential.

2. History and development of public relations

Information about public relations in Bosnia-Herzegovina is extremely difficult to find. No research has been done before the war. We must keep in mind that the socialist system in Bosnia-Herzegovina did not allow competition or promotion of corporation, brand or product. Two main drawbacks in this way of communication were the media, their ignorant management and journalists, and the lack of public awareness and interest in the companies' activities. The government controlled the media and the news broadcast was restricted; the public was not used to receive information. During this time, every organisation had the so-called "Sector for Informing", with public relations as their main duty. The pioneers in public relations practice were Energoinvest, Unis, Famos, Sipad, Natron-Maglaj, Soda So-Tuzla, Aluminij-Mostar, Rudi Cajavec-Banja Luka.

In small organisations, only one person was assigned to this field, but in larger ones, it could be up to fifteen or twenty people. Employees were mostly journalists, because public relations until now was considered a journalist's communication tool. These departments were in the Ministry of Information and available to journalists at any time. Their primary task was to provide press releases and interviews to the journalists, because in order to have just an interview with a manager, journalists would have to go through the press department in that organisation. As to press conferences, they were organised only for the extremely relevant events. In addition to what we mentioned earlier, large companies (with a hundred employees or more) published their own internal publications, and that was the only way of communicating with their public – that is, employees.

Events, as one of the most often used public relations tools, were organised in order to promote new projects, production facilities, increased capacity, etc., and were aimed at journalists. On extremely important occasions (anniversaries, for instance), monographs were published – these would then be followed every year by revised editions.

Media monitoring and press clipping were regular activities for every secretary, and each morning they would pass their reports to the general manager. *Tanjug* (the only press agency in the territory of the former Yugoslavia) published the so-called Red Bulletin, which included informal sayings (word of mouth, gossip and what is known in smaller circles) about specific companies. That information was not published in the regular media, and was for the benefit of just a handful of companies in the republics of ex-Yugoslavia.

Research on experience with crisis and crisis management led to anecdotes showing the way in which the information flow was controlled. The military complex Unis-Pretis in Vogosca, near Sarajevo, had an enormous explosion in early 1980s, and fires could be seen for weeks after that. At the press conference (which was chaired by a general), one journalist had the courage to ask, "I heard, you know, Sarajevo is saying, someone saw some kind of fire in Vogosca, somewhere around Unis-Pretis. Would you, by any chance, happen to know anything about that?" The only response he could get from the general was: "Sarajevo is saying, but Sarajevo should shut up." So much for being open to the press during the crises.

We find it important to reiterate that the legacy of socialism cannot be easily overcome in Bosnia-Herzegovina, the country that used to have a small and closed market with a planned supply system, and almost no competition.

Until recently, there was no education in public relations at any level, but courses are now provided both at the Faculty of Economics and the Faculty of Journalism.

The term for "public relations" in Bosnian is *Odnosi s javnoscu*. It is the same in Croatia, Serbia and Montenegro. People associate the term with press conferences, relations established only with journalists, and with one-way communication.

The main turning point, not only in public relations but also in corporate and marketing communications, were the XIVth Olympic Winter Games held in Sarajevo in 1984. The transformation in public relations practice occurred unconsciously but even then, only journalists conveyed it. Earlier, the few open-minded journalists were directed to the areas that were rather unimportant, such as show business. When the Olympics were assigned to Bosnia-Herzegovina in 1979 in Athens, Pavle Lukac was appointed as a PR director. Experts – mostly from the US and Canada – came to Sarajevo in order to establish a proper press service. Ivica Misic was appointed as director of the press centres, and Mehmed Husic as editor in chief. The international community was determined to establish public relations according to its standards. It was necessary to educate domestic staff, public opinion and the media, and to establish sections in the media dedicated to the Olympic Games and to press releases.

Two years before the grand event, weekly press conferences were held, and provided bulletins for journalists. A monthly magazine containing interesting articles was also published. Every third month, an exclusive brochure, called *Sarajevo '84* was published, and all together, ten issues can be found in libraries today. Press centres were organised as a model, so that the main media in ex-Yugoslavia were assigned to only one press centre. For example, *Vijesnik* was placed in the Olympic Hall Zetra, *Oslobodjenje* on Bjelasnica, *Delo* at Malo Polje, *Politika* was stationed in Jahorina, while the news agency *Tanjug* had the main press centre.

As to crisis management, different committees were responsible for this, even though it was all based on intuition, with no plan whatsoever. Branko Mikulic headed the main organising committee; Ante Sucic chaired the executive committee. As to sponsorship, they realised that the main income would be from television rights. The invitations for tenders appeared in 1980. The most generous offer, worth US$ 91.5 million, was made by ABC Network.

After the Olympics, the situation in public relations practice in Bosnia-Herzegovina completely changed, so we can say that this event was a precedent in corporate and marketing communications. New concepts and ideas came from developed countries, and that was the period of massive economic and social changes in this part of the world. The privatisation started with the reforms initiated by Ante Markovic. Competition was encouraged, and companies finally had to fight for their consumers, which made in public relations one of the communication tools more aggressive than before. Unfortunately, at this stage the war started in Bosnia-Herzegovina, and in 2003 we are still struggling to overcome its consequences. The current instability is caused not just by the recent war but also by the inability to overcome the ghosts of the past and the habits inherited from the socialist system. Promotional activities were very low on the priority list, so it can be said that the organised public relations practice in Bosnia–Herzegovina started after the war, when this market finally opened.

3. Typification of current public relations

3.1. Status of public relations in business, administration and society

The PR practice, as known from developed market economies, did not exist in Bosnia-Herzegovina (B-H) until about ten years ago. Only with the economic and political reforms in Bosnia-Herzegovina, public relations as social and corporate function is appearing on the surface of business and economic life. The original initiator was the government,[1] but later on other organisations and subjects followed its lead.

As never before, the public relations function is becoming very important to Bosnia-Herzegovina organisations. The changes – in both macro- and micro-environments – require appropriate reactions of organisations to emphasise the role of public relations. Unfortunately, public relations is not yet widely recognised in contemporary business. In addition, most companies still do not have public relations as a management function; and there has been some confusion about what the real role of marketing and public relations in Bosnia and Herzegovina should be. Public relations is often classified as marketing activities and equated with marketing communications.

The role of public relations in the state administration is mainly reduced to media relations, established through the information offices in

---

1. In 1993, a public relations agency was hired by the government of Bosnia-Herzegovina to rally US support for its cause. The firm sent fax updates about the war in former Yugoslavia to press contacts and managed to place op-ed pieces sympathetic to the Bosnian cause in several important US newspapers. The agency also arranged for media stakeouts in which policy makers were forced to make public comments on the issue. Perhaps as a result, Bosnia, which was virtually unknown in the United States, became an important topic in news coverage (see Dominick 1996: 391).

the administration. The function of public relations is not yet clearly defined – nor, for that matter, are the roles of spokesperson, protocol activities, receptions, sponsorship and publicity.

3.2.   Position of public relations in organisations

3.2.1. Public relations in the non-profit sector

At the end of the war, in 1995, the non-profit sector in Bosnia-Herzegovina began to develop. Now, in 2003, about 1,300 NGOs are officially registered. This expansion was strongly supported by the activities of the international community, directed towards the development of civic society, gender equality, human rights, freedom of the media, legal assistance, educational programmes, overcoming of conflicts, micro-crediting, etc. (Cicic, Brkic and Selak 2003). Some of the above organisations, especially the international organisations active in Bosnia-Herzegovina, organise their public relations activities well.

Numerous non-governmental and governmental organisations today follow the practice of the organisation and functioning of public relations in international organisations. However, the conducted research (Èièiæ, Brkiæ and Kaèmarèik 2002) did not take into account the practice of numerous non-governmental or humanitarian organisations but was focused on the organisation and functioning of the public relations departments in the international organisations acting in Bosnia-Herzegovina. These organisations are OHR (Office of the High Representative), OSCE, Mission to BiH, Delegation of the European Commission to Bosnia-Herzegovina, UNMIBH (United Nations Mission to Bosnia-Herzegovina), IOM (International Organisation for Migration), the Commission for Real Property Claims of Displaced Persons and Refugees (CRPC), UNDP (United Nation Development Programme), the World Bank Mission in Bosnia-Herzegovina and NATO/Stabilisation Forces.

The analysis of the public relations sector in the international organisations active in Bosnia-Herzegovina enabled the identification of common characteristics of all non-profit organisations, as well as access to specific practices. First, research has shown that the number of employees in the public relations departments varies from organisation to organisation. For instance, the largest public relations department based in UNMIBH employs twenty-nine full-time employees, and the European Commission Delegation in Bosnia-Herzegovina employs only two persons in the public relations department, including a counselor who is both head to the above department and assistant of the head of the public relations department in the EU office, performing administrative duties. Among the terms used for the public relations office are "Public Affairs", "Press and Public Information" and "Public Relations". After analysing the terms used, we reached the conclusion that the most important task of the offices mentioned earlier is the communication with the press. Nevertheless, our research showed that the press office has a more significant influence on organisations and more important tasks than the "sponsorship" or transmission of messages to journalists. As a rule, the heads of the public relations offices play an important role in their organisation. In principle they are the link between the organisation and the world, in particular with journalists. The majority of well-educated heads of office acquired their professional experience in journalism. Heads of the public relations offices are usually directly subordinate to the chief of mission/organisation and are members of the top management team. Somewhat less frequently they are directly subordinate to the second important person in the organisation (UN Mission, UNDP, for example). Professional staff engaged in public relations has only limited access to the deliberative process at the strategic level of the organisation.

The nationality of the head of the public relations office is an important issue for a better understanding of the public relations scene: international professionals are employed in the majority of the above jobs – domestic practitioners only very rarely. Of the other employees working in public relations offices, approximately 25 per cent belongs to the international staff, the rest to the national staff from Bosnia-Herzegovina.

In determining their target groups, the international organisations have defined the basic target groups using specific communication channels for each of them. The messages, sent by international organisations to their target groups, are based on the mandate of the organisation, its mission, fundamental principles and the ideas the organisation is promoting.

The following are the most important target groups.
– The domestic public in Bosnia-Herzegovina is important for the smooth realisation of ideas and the implementation of the organisation's mission. The domestic public is reached generally through the media/journalists – who report on the activities of the organisation or achieved results – or directly, through various forms of direct mail (brochures, leaflets, posters, letters and e-mails). Carefully prepared with the task to promote a particular idea or to provide some specific information, the infor-

mation campaign represents a specific type of communication with the target groups.

– The international community represents an important target group because they are taxpayers from countries that finance the work of the organisations mentioned earlier. Although it is not possible to establish a direct connection between the reputation of these organisations and their financial resources (they depend on political decisions, including many other factors), public relations offices based in the international organisations acting in Bosnia-Herzegovina do not want to neglect the above connection.

– Relations with the journalists. Based on the data we collected, we can conclude that the public relations offices in the international organisations accept the journalists and the media as the most important targeted public, due to the fact that they communicate with both the domestic public in Bosnia–Herzegovina and with the international community. The organisations employing a large number of people engaged in public relations, prepare press releases almost every day. The spokespersons of OHR, OSCE, UN Mission, SFOR, for instance, organise joint press conferences twice a week. Apart from these events, the organisations also prepare special press conferences in case there is a great interest in certain subjects. In addition, the press office mediates between journalists and higher ranking officials when it is necessary to organise a special interview or to participate in a particular programme. In such cases, the public relations office plays an advisory role analysing items for discussion, type of information that is to be presented, prepare for possible questions and answers, etc.

– Communications with partner organisations and diplomatic representations are mainly at the managerial level of the organisation. In this case, the role of the public relations office is reduced only to the transfer of information and reports to the media or domestic public.

– Communications with domestic political and governmental organisations is mainly at the management level and part of the daily activities. This target group is communicated indirectly and through messages sent to the media/press. The press offices/public relations offices involved play an advisory role, helping with the selection of the media and the timing of making things public. As per this target group, an important task is organising events and ceremonies where public relations practitioners sometimes perform their duties, thinking about details such as sending invitations, preparing venues, media announcements, etc. It is important to point out that communication with this target group mostly includes advocacy – where the public relations or press office has again an advisory role – and interpreting the way in which the public treats certain ideas or what would be the reaction to a particular activity.

When talking about the functioning of public relations offices in crisis situations, it is – generally speaking – easy to conclude that offices are not provided with an accurate list of potential crises. Naturally, each organisation has its own safety plan for crises in the domain of physical security but the public relations experts think that this is negative publicity.

A characteristic of public relations in the non-profit sector is the absence of the consistent measuring of the efficiency of communication activities combined with the impossibility to provide financial resources for conducting particular detailed research. The organisations involved in this research have not conducted a detailed public opinion survey of the organisation's image, how much their messages are understandable or to what extent they are accepted within their target groups. Yet, some international organisations acting in Bosnia-Herzegovina, such as NDI (National Democracy Institute), conduct surveys of measuring public opinion in Bosnia-Herzegovina on a regular basis. They forward their reports to the heads of missions of all the most important international organisations.

Media monitoring is another method of evaluating communicating activities. Some NGOs have full-time professional staff (OHR employs a team composed of seven full-time employees), whose task it is to conduct regular monitoring and analysing of articles from the international and domestic press. Such reports are prepared once or twice a day, and they contain not only quantitative but also qualitative analyses of articles (objectivity, point of view, background, etc.).

Public relations departments in the international organisations operating in Bosnia-Herzegovina have complex duties. Some of them only bridge "gaps" related to public relations activities of the PR departments of international organisations are normally undertaken by domestic governments in other countries. "It still happens that Bosnia–Herzegovina journalists address to the above organisations to get comments or responses to questions that are within the competence of domestic institutions. We have been making all necessary efforts to refer the journalists not to the international organisations but to responsible local institutions competent to provide the above answers.", as said by a PR officer of one of the international organisations in one of the interviews we had. Some of the ideas promoted by the international organisations mentioned earlier in other countries are the exclusive competence of domestic ministries (European integration, for instance). In Bosnia-Herzegovina, domestic institutions have more and more limited budgets, are understaffed and have few skilled people capable of performing such types of activity, so that the advocacy or education of the public remains the exclusive domain of the international organisations.

Reinforcement of local capacities is one of the objectives the majority of international organisations want to achieve. This means that they intend to transfer some of their activities (advocacy, mass information, education of the public in particular issues) to domestic governmental (or non-governmental) organisations after the termination of their mandate.

A basic difference between the above mentioned organisations and other non-governmental organisations acting in Bosnia-Herzegovina (NGOs or associations of citizens) is in the fact that the collection of donor or other financial resources is not directly connected with their reputation. Naturally, it does not mean that the above organisations may exist without paying attention to public opinion – the implementation of their policy – that is, the mandate of the above organisations directly depend on the attitudes of the public and of the acceptance of their ideas.

3.2.2. Public relations in the profit sector

Fast changes in business environment in Bosnia-Herzegovina are expected to produce alternate composition of marketing and communication mixes in companies that are present at the market. Therefore, the research has been undertaken to measure how specific conditions in business environments determine the character of public relations practice for domestic firms (Cicic, Brkic and Kamenica 2001).

The findings of research appear to be interesting and expected. The target groups of public relations are consumers, suppliers, banks, the government, local communities and the media. Public relations is considered mostly as a selling tool, not as a communicative tool. Accordingly, its objective is to increase sales and market share, whereas public's perception of a company is not considered as a very important objective.

In the corporate practice in Bosnia-Herzegovina, advertising in electronic and print media is a major tool of communication. Very few companies use press releases and press conferences. In addition, in organisational terms there are no units specialised in public relations, or whose work domain is restricted to it. The practice of the executive staff used in public relations is very well represented. Research findings indicate that the interest in public relations in the corporate environment of Bosnia-

Herzegovina is increasing, but the public relations practice is still lagging behind the practice in the developed countries.

In many businesses in Bosnia-Herzegovina, public relations activities were undertaken only when a particular organisation faced a crisis of confidence in its public. However, in the last decade, the public relations industry has grown in size and importance due to the fact that more organisations have recognised the need to maintain consistent and continuous communications with their public and target audiences – and not only in times of crisis.

3.3. The current state of education and character of major textbooks

Public relations in Bosnia-Herzegovina suffer from inadequate education in public relations. Pre-graduate studies in public relations do not exist. There are seven universities in Bosnia-Herzegovina, but public relations is studied only on an introductory level and only in a few courses or even a few lectures, as part of other subjects, such as marketing or journalism. But more and more students of business and journalism show interest in public relations, often exploring the possibilities of studying it or pursuing a career in it. The situation is similar in the postgraduate studies. Two master's theses on public relations will be finished in 2003 at the Sarajevo Faculty of Economics and at the Tuzla Faculty of Journalism.

In addition, the academic community in Bosnia-Herzegovina shows more and more interest in public relations. In the mid of 1990s, a doctoral dissertation dealing with public relations in the political organisations and institutions was defended. At least two assistants in universities in Bosnia-Herzegovina are developing their career in public relations and at least two theses deal with public relations. We expect further research to be conducted in the field of public relations soon. Currently, the PR internet research on the one hundred largest Bosnia-Herzegovina companies is in progress (Brkic and Selimovic 2003).

It is reasonable to expect educational programmes on public relations, mainly thanks to the increased demand for public relations professionals in business and governmental and non-governmental organisations. One project worth mentioning here was initiated in the autumn of 2001, when the London School of Public Relations (LSPR), supported by SPEM Communication Group of Maribor, Slovenia, started work in Sarajevo, Bosnia-Herzegovina. In this scheme, lecturers from Slovenia and Bosnia-Herzegovina equally participate in teaching. So far, three groups of fifty students graduated from the LSPR. The fourth generation of students started their studies in the autumn of 2003. It is interesting to mention that the attendants of the first three generations of the LSPR were employees in the numerous international organisations active in Bosnia-Herzegovina, such as UNDP, OSCE, the World Bank, NATO-SFOR, OHR (Office of the High Representative in Bosnia-Herzegovina), etc. Only a handful of attendants were from such business as international banks and companies operating in Bosnia-Herzegovina (Raiffeisen Bank, HVB Bank, Nestlé), including several domestic companies (Public Enterprise Elektroprivreda Bosnia-Herzegovina, Lijanovici Food Industry).

By the end of 2002, two other private schools for public relations had started work, one in Banja Luka, the other in Mostar. In May 2002, the Public Relations Agency (PRA) Serbia and Montenegro opened its representative body for Bosnia-Herzegovina in Banja Luka. The Banja Luka PRA branch is the first such agency in Srpska. The representative body in Banja Luka has organised several seminars attended by the representatives of the most successful companies from Serbia (Telekom, Mobis, Nova Banjaluèka banka, Vodovod, World Media, Europlakat, Elektrokrajina, Kosig Dunav osiguranje, Ministarstvo finansija) as well as specific seminars (*Biro za odnose sa javnoscu Vlade Republike Srpske, Toplana BL*). By mid-October 2002, the first generation of students from the Republic of Serbs in B-H started their studies at the Public Relations Business School in Banja Luka. The classes were attended by thirty-five individuals as well as by the representatives of successful companies wishing to improve their knowledge in this sector (Toplana, Teol, Telekom, Privredna komora RS, GTZ, Krka, Pliva, World Bank, British American Tobacco, European Commission, IMC Consulting, ALF-OM, Danish Red Cross, World media). Zoran Tomic, the former spokesman and deputy of the HDZ political party in the Federation of the B-H Parliament, together with the National University from Zagreb, initiated the School for Public Relations in Mostar.

3.4. Major textbooks and selling practical books

One problem is that the university libraries are not sufficiently provided with necessary literature in English – often they do not have any literature at all. Local university textbooks such as *Basics of Marketing* and *Marketing Communication* are the books where it is possible to read something about PR. Two leading textbooks from this field originated in the Faculty of Economics in Sarajevo: Tihi (2002) and Cicic and Brkic (2002).

It is extremely difficult to find literature on public relations in the Bosnia-Herzegovinian market; there are no books on public relations written by Bosnia-Herzegovinian authors. It is sometimes possible to find translations of foreign books; these are usually from Serbia, translated within the British Council programme there. In addition, some Croat books on marketing have some chapters on public relations (since Bosnian, Croatian and Serbian are very similar, books in Serbian and Croatian are usable in Bosnia-Herzegovina). It is very hard to find literature on public relations in any bookshop.

3.5. The local scene of public relations

Most public relations agencies in Bosnia-Herzegovina are from Slovenia – Pristop, SPEM and Imelda, and PRA (Public Relations Agency) – and from Serbia. Login Public in Sarajevo is the only local public relations agency. But recently, many advertising agencies have been opening separate public relations departments to meet the needs of their clients for integral communications. Fabrika Sarajevo, McCann-Erickson Sarajevo, Mita Group-Publicis Sarajevo, Studio Marketing-JWT Sarajevo – these are the advertising agencies that started offering their services to their clients.

As to professional organisations, Bosnia-Herzegovina does not have a national association and is not a member of any international organisation or association. The International Advertising Association (IAA) – B-H Chapter, composed of several public relations agencies, is the only communication association in Bosnia–Herzegovina.

Although professional conferences have not been held in Bosnia-Herzegovina, some individuals took part at several other international conferences with their research; an example is the Enterprise in Transition Conference in Split (Cicic, Brkic and Kamenica 2001).

3.6. Growing field and hot issues

Crisis communication and relations with the media represent the two most important public relations activities in Bosnia-Herzegovina. This is reasonable in view of the fact that currently – at the beginning of the twenty-first century – Bosnia-Herzegovina is undergoing enormous changes in economy, politics and society as a whole.

4. Conclusions on the state of the art and future of public relations in Bosnia-Herzegovina

Public relations are getting a somewhat different role in the organisations in the Bosnia-Herzegovinian environment. Environmental forces cause rapid development and changes in character of public relations. Recent research showed the growing importance of public relations as a management function.

In general, many firms use the public relations function in their business activities, though it is often not well understood or applied. The reasons are numerous, but for the most part, they are caused by the lack of knowledge, low awareness of the importance of the function and the public in general, and lack of awareness of the importance of particular stakeholders for the company.

The environment is important for companies and represents a stimulating factor for the development of public relations activities. The most important elements of the environment are the market and its participants. Even though appropriate, such an approach, only aimed at consumers, is not sufficient since it neglects the importance and influence of other stakeholders. In particular, citizens and the media are not respected. A possible explanation is that in the former political regime, they did not have any particular importance or influence, and that this has been transferred to the present situation – despite substantial changes in their role and influence in the new everyday reality.

The major objectives of public relations identified here are increased sales and market share. This indicates that there is more emphasis on the immediate and short-term objectives, rather than on building a relationship with stakeholders. Attempts to influence public opinion or to engage in crisis management are negligible, which may mean that the core concepts of the public relations function are not yet well understood. At the same time, most respondents to the survey stress the importance of public relations vis-à-vis other elements of business strategy. This may indicate a positive trend and an increase in interest in this activity at the managerial level.

Bosnia-Herzegovinian companies do not use the services of specialised public relations agencies a lot. Currently, there is only one local specialised agency in Bosnia-Herzegovina, and a few advertising agencies offer a limited range of public relations services. In addition, there are no professional associations in this sector. Several international agencies, mostly Slovenian, are currently entering the Bosnian market.

Very few companies have a separate organisational unit for public relations, whereas others organise and implement public relations activities through their marketing department. In general, a small number of people is employed and engaged in public relations activities.

It is apparent that general managers are to some extent involved and active in public relations, which indicates the transformation of public relations from a functional to a managerial activity. This could provide the consistent and familiar image for the whole range of business activities and elements for companies.

Generally speaking, it is realistic to expect a rapid development of public relations activities in Bosnia-Herzegovina. Strengthening of the country's economy, in particular, and further development of the service sector will certainly contribute to this process. Financial institutions, hotels and big privatised corporations such as telecommunication corporations are particularly interested in the development of public relations activities. The growth of the media industry, changes in the higher-education system that have recently been implemented, as well as the change in attitude towards public relations, understanding and accepting it as a strategic instrument, will also contribute to its development.

References

Brkic, Nenad and Dino Selimovic (2003). Corporate communication in the new media environment: a survey of 100 corporate communication web sites of the biggest companies in Bosnia-Herzegovina. Internal research paper, Faculty of Economics, University of Sarajevo.

Central Bank of Bosnia-Herzegovina (2001). *Annual Report*. www.cbbh.gov.ba

Cicic, Muris and Nenad Brkic (2002). *Marketing Communication*. Sarajevo: University of Sarajevo Press

Cicic, Muris, Nenad Brkic and Damir Selak (2003). Market orientation in non-profit organisations in Bosnia-Herzegovina. Collection of Papers of the Faculty of Economics, 23. University of Sarajevo.

Cicic, Muris, Nenad Brkic and Nela Kacmarcik (2002). Public relations in non-profit organisations: the case of international organisations in Bosnia-Herzegovina. Internal research paper, Faculty of Economics, University of Sarajevo.

Cicic, Mrusi, Brkic, Nenad and Kamenica, Amil (2001). Public relations practice in corporate environment of Bosnia-Herzegovina. Proceedings of the Fourth International Conference "Enterprise in Transition", 91–93. Split.

Dominick, Joseph R. (1996). *The Dynamics of Mass Communication* (5th edn.). New York: McGraw-Hill.

International Crisis Group (2001). Report for B-H. http://www.intl-crisis-group.org/projects/

CIA – The World Factbook (2000). www.cia.gov/cia/publications/factbook/

Tihi, Boris (ed.) (2002). *Basic Marketing*. Sarajevo: University of Sarajevo Press.

Chapter 5

Bulgaria

Minka Zlateva

1. National profile

Situated in the south-eastern part of Europe, at the crossroads between the East and West, Bulgaria has been the centre of cultural exchange for millennia. It is the cradle of Thracian civilisation – one of the
oldest on the European continent – and of the Cyrillic alphabet. It is to
Bulgaria that the Cyril and Methodius brothers, the creators of the Slavonic–Bulgarian alphabet, owe the preservation, dissemination and recognition of their work. Today, along with the Thracian gold treasures and
rich literature, Bulgarian culture is known for its rich folklore.

The Bulgarian state was created in 681 AD. Its 1300-year history has
been quite turbulent. The ninth century is considered the golden century
of the Bulgarian culture, while during the Ottoman rule (1396–1878) its
public and cultural developments were controlled for almost 500 years.
Not until the end of the Russo–Turkish war (1877–1878) did Bulgaria regain its independence, but it was incorporated in the Soviet bloc at the
close of World War II. The socio-political changes of 1989 heralded a new
era of liberty and democracy, culminating in the drive for European Union membership.

Its territory covers 110,993 sq. km and, according to the latest 2001 census, its population stands at 7,974,000, 69 per cent of which is urban (Statisticheski godishnik 2002: 7). The population comprises the following
ethnic groups: 6,660,682 Bulgarians, 757,781 Turks, 365,797 Rom and
121,773 other nationalities (see www.nsi.bg/statistica/Statistics.htm/). Bulgaria's population is not very mobile, with 86 per cent having inhabited
their dwelling place at least twenty years (Kacarski 1998: 161).

2.   History and development of public relations

2.1. Roots of public relations

The term "public relations" was first mentioned in Bulgaria in 1972 in an article by Svetozar Krastev as a component of marketing (Krastev 1972), though until 1989 it was difficult to talk about any development of public relations in the country's practice and educational system. The changes of 1989 initiated the development of public relations. The depolitisation of the army and the police forces, the restructuring of government authorities and institutions made it necessary constantly to inform the public about the government's activities. Numerous new but short-lived political and civil organisations appeared, all wishing to be at the centre of public opinion and expressing their attitude in the progress of the democratic process.

In the transition to the market economy, many foreign companies (the car, cosmetic, computer industries, for instance) entered the Bulgarian market with their quality products and their effective instruments of public relations and advertising to gain a large market share competing with local companies.

Whereas in the Western democracies the origin of public relations was based on the requirements of corporations and their target public, in the new democracies in Central and Eastern Europe, the function of public relations emerged in crisis conditions as a necessary means of reorganisation and stabilisation of public relations. The ensuing confidence crisis, combined with weakening conventional mechanisms for social organisation, and with the uncontrolled break-up of social relations, caused waves of changes that affected the deepest roots of social identity (Petev 1996b: 401–403). In this complicated situation of overall reorganisation of the social structures, the press was liberated through the abolition of the state monopoly on the media, and private papers and radio stations appeared. The specific character of the transition in each country of the former Eastern bloc – from vast Russia to small Bulgaria – has set American and Western-European public-communication experts tasks that were much more complex than they were used to. The presidential elections in Russia and Bulgaria showed this clearly.

2.2. Development of public relations practice

In countries in transition, it is necessary to lead a constant, serious and effective dialogue with the public, in order to reach consensus decisions in the target public. Since journalists – both in Bulgaria and other Eastern-European countries – have so far been the most experienced group in establishing contacts in their relation with the public, many of them were among the first to act as spokesperson of the new political formations, and master the techniques of public relations in various companies and non-government organisations and the press centres of various state institutions. For example, in the elections for National Assembly (Parliament) and the local authorities, of which the country has seen quite a lot since 1989, the image of the leading political parties and leaders needed to be built up. But journalists are not the only professional group naturally drawn to public relations; political scientists, advertising experts, sociologists, psychologists and directors – all experts in public speech and non-verbal behaviour – found their way into public relations.

2.3. Development of education and research traditions

Naturally, a huge interest among students in the professional education of work in the field of public communication has originated. Initial attempts to teach public relations as an academic subject were made by the first private university in Bulgaria (the New Bulgarian University in Sofia), which started to train "specialists in public relations" in 1991. Following the tradition of interdisciplinary education in humanities and engineering, the Technical University in Sofia, in its Open Faculty, initiated public relations as an optional course of future engineers in 1993. A number of newly established private companies started short-term public relations courses for their employees.

Based on a project by UNESCO and the International Public Relations Association (IPRA), a comprehensive syllabus for the preparation of bachelors and masters in public relations and advertising was produced by the Faculty of Journalism and Mass Communication at Sofia University St. Kliment Ohridski. The first degree course for the professional qualification of "experts in public relations" was launched in the academic year 1994/ 1995. The UNESCO Chair "Communication and Public Relations" was established as part of ORBICOM – the worldwide network of UNESCO chairs of Communications (www.orbicom.uqam.ca) – with T. Petev elected in ORBICOM's board of directors as its first chair (Zlateva 2002a: 34–36). The development of public relations in Bulgaria can thus be divided into two stages: an initial stage, from 1989 to 1995, and a consolidation stage, from 1995 on.

2.4. How language shapes the development of public relations

The English term "public relations" has gradually entered the vocabulary of both practitioners and theoreticians. It is popularly rendered in Bulgarian as *vrazki s obshtestvenostta* (literally, 'relations with the public'), but as this does not really cover the English term, the *Media & Reklama* magazine conducted a survey among theoreticians and practitioners in September 1999 to determine its appropriateness.

According to Raykov (1999a: 22), public relation is only one aspect of public communication, which involves the employment of specific techniques by means of which an organisation establishes contact with its public. Public relations experts organise the technological process through which effective communication of the organisation with its public is guaranteed for a given period and specific aims are achieved. He goes on to say that from 2000 on, the concept of public relations does not fully meet society's expectations of that profession and that it is important to establish mutually advantageous relations between one organisation and its public, but that it is still more important to motivate organisation and public when communicating, to promote the humanisation and prosperity of society as a whole. According to him, the philosophy of this new approach to that new technology is defined by the concept "public communication".

But certainly the term "public communication" comprises much more than "public relations". And indeed, Nikolova (1999: 22) claims that the translation 'relations with the public' gives just one aspect – namely, one-way communication – from the organisation to the public. Nikolova (in personal communication) now suggests that the translation *vrazki s obshtestvenostta* is not correct and that nobody in the field accepts it. She thinks that since such English terms as "marketing" and "management" have been adopted in Bulgarian, we might as well borrow *public relations*, without any translation, in the process borrowing its hundred years of history and connotations. Nikolova stresses that, because its meaning is different, she disagrees with those who say that using the Bulgarian translation is unproblematic. The Bulgarian word *vrazki*, which replaces "relations", means 'personal connection to help persons to do the work more quickly or to skip over the regulations and the law'. The word *obshtestvenost*, which stands for "public", means 'society', not 'public'. She goes on to say that the main problem is not the translation itself, but that the incorrect translation leads to misunderstandings about the nature of what public relations really is – and the first years of public relations in Eastern Europe demonstrate this. But on a more positive note, she concludes that, fortunately, experience shows that such old customs and habits as personal connections with journalists and paying for admission to schools are not effective any longer. And any honourable practitioners or educators call themselves "public relations practitioners", so the Bulgarian translation will fade away to become a thing of the past.

All this may be true, but the reality is that non-professionals generally continue to use "relations with the public". I would think that the German translation, *Öffentlichkeitsarbeit* (literally, 'public work'), is better than the Bulgarian 'relation with the public', but it is not optimal either. After all, public relations in practice includes activities not only for establishing, but also for maintaining, improving and consolidating these relations.

Unfortunately, instead of seeking ways for achieving consensus desperately needed by the public, in order to resolve the large-scale and complex problems of transition to a civil society, anti-consensus attitudes prevail in the Bulgarian socio-political practice. The reasons for such developments certainly are complex. One possible explanation of the emergence and existence of negative forms of public communications as forms of concealed publicity can be found in the Habermas's Consensus Theory of Truthfulness. He views the consensus as a two-step construct where only the formal, not the essential level is subject to consensus" (Reese-Schäfer 1994: 18). Formally, if the media, organisations and public actors stand for democracy, transparency and pluralism, essentially they invest these concepts with quite different meanings, dictated by their situational interests (Zlateva 2002b: 45).

In spite of all this, the two terms, "public relations" and "relations with the public", are routinely used as synonyms.

3. Typification of current public relations

3.1. Status of public relations and major roles

Bulgaria's National Institute of Statistics still does not process information about public relations, so we have no statistical data available on either the number of public relations experts in business, administration and society as a whole, or of the public relations agencies and their profiles. However, if we analyse the field and proceed from the four approaches to public relations – informative, persuasive, relational and discursive (Verčič 2002) – we can point out the following, based on our impressions:

– In companies and corporations (particularly in the foreign companies operating in the Bulgarian market) public relations is most often entwined with marketing and is practiced mainly as a function of the management.
– In politics, public relations is seen as a persuasive communication activity.
– In the relations with the public in the administrative sphere, as well as in crisis situations, the information model of the relations with the public is the most applicable as there is a need for accurate, unambiguous and timely information about the activities of each organisation.
– In academe, the leading developments are the relational and discursive models of public relations (e.g. Grunig and Hunt 1984; Burkart 1993).

Multiple departments of public relations have been established in organisations. The experts there maintain contacts with the media, act as heads of information offices or spokespersons (as in the government and the speakers' office of the Ministry of the Interior) or work in public relations and advertising departments in foreign and Bulgarian large- and medium-sized companies.

3.2. Current state of education and character of major textbooks

In the comparatively short period of four to five years, until the end of 2000, training in public relations as a separate academic subject outside Sofia was introduced in many universities in the country – Varna, Russe, Plovdiv, Bourgas, Blagoevgrad, in the G. S. Rakovski military academy and in the Academy of the Ministry of the Interior.

The syllabus of the Faculty of Journalism and Mass Communication of Sofia University St. Kliment Ohridski for the preparation of experts of public relations is constantly revised, reflecting the actual state of the practice. The scope of the lectures and practical exercises in communication skills is growing all the time: covering such topics as writing about public relations, radio and television, public speech, empirical sociological research, marketing and management, to mention just a few. Special attention is paid to integrated marketing communication, the theory and practice of the interrelations between the media and public relations, and the new information technologies.

Students have the opportunity to attend lectures of leading European scholars in the field of public communication, such as Roland Burkart

(University of Vienna), Günter Bentele (University of Leipzig), Barbara Baerns (Free University in Berlin), Jaakko Lehtonen (University of Jyväskylä, Finland), Benno Signitzer (University of Salzburg) and Tony Meehan (University of Glasgow).

The most widely used foreign authors were originally Jefkins (1993), Oxly (1993), Kunczik and Zipfel (1998) and, more recently, Cutlip, Center and Broom (1999) and Burkart (1999, 2000). More than twenty books for communication written by Bulgarian authors have appeared. Among the most popular are Petev (2001), Raykov (1999b, 2001a, 2001b), Marinov (2001), as well as the collections of the UNESCO Chair *Communication and Public Relations* of the Faculty of Journalism and Mass Communication at the Sofia University (Petev 1996a; Zlateva and Petev 1999; Petev and Zlateva 2000; Zlateva and Petev 2002; Petev and Zlateva 2002a; Petev and Zlateva 2003).

3.3. The local scene of public relations

The Bulgarian Public Relations Society, the first professional organisation of experts in public relations in the country, was established in 1996. At present it has over 300 members in Sofia, Varna, Russe, Pleven, Bourgas, Stara Zagora, Targovishte, Dobrich, Shumen, Plovdiv and Haskovo. It has been a member of IPRA since 1999, elected its ombudsman in 2000 and adopted its own code of professional standards.

The annual scientific conferences held by the UNESCO Chair *Communication and Public Relations* of the Faculty of Journalism and Mass Communication of Sofia University St. Kliment Ohridski, together with the Austrian Science and Research Liaison Office Sofia, and with the Bulgarian Public Relations Society, have proved to be particularly useful for the development of the theory and practice of public relations. Their topics focus on the "hot spots" as public communication and public organisation (1997), public relations and European integration (1998), public relations and conflicts in the democratic society (2000), public relations and the new media (2001) and media and public relations: issues of education and practice (2002). The participants at these conferences have been scholars and public relations practitioners from Bulgaria, nine other European countries and the US.

The papers of the participants in the conferences are published in collections and eventually become part of the teaching material. The conferences are important forums for young scholars in the field of public relations to meet and exchange views with established practitioners. The first doctoral students in the UNESCO Chair, among others Roussi Marinov, Galin Borodinov, Sonya Alexieva, Rumyana Abadzhimarinova, Lyudmil Gerogiev, Diana Petkova, have successfully defended their dissertations, and now teach in universities. Other material that has found its way into the educational system is the coursework developed for the summer schools in public relations at the New Bulgarian University, which have been organised since 1999. This material is routinely published.

4. Conclusion: state of the art and future of public relations in Bulgaria

So far there have been several attempts at creating professional journals in the field of public relations. Examples are *Public communication / public relations, advertising and mass media*, which was first published in 1995 and *Public Relations*, published from 1995 to 1998. Topical issues of public relations with the public are currently being commented on in two specialised journals, *Media World* and *Marketing Media*, as well as in a number of printed media, such as the *Kapital* and *Pari* newspapers. The yearbooks of the Faculty of Journalism and Mass Communication of Sofia University St. Kliment Ohridski and the Department of Mass Communication at the New Bulgarian University are partly devoted to these problems. However, a specialised periodical publication that comprises the entire thematic variety of public relations in their theoretically and practically applicable aspects is still missing.

As to practitioners, these form a heterogeneous collection. The majority are former journalists. Most of the agencies in this line of business combine public relations and advertising, thus recruiting designers, advertising experts and managers. Philologists prevail in the public relations departments of foreign companies on account of their language skills. In the process of integration with the European Union, serious work is being done on the reorganisation of the Bulgarian administration. Many government departments already have departments of public relations, but some of these departments combine the activities of public relations and the protocol performed by specialists of various qualifications.

Those involved in public relations activities in non-government organisations are mainly young people lacking special training in public communication. This lack of specific knowledge about the nature of public relations among those practicing the profession was evident from the results of only one survey carried out in 1999. The findings show that these are mainly young people aged 20 to 30, most of them being in this business up to three years, 65.5 per cent have a degree in journalism and 32 per cent have a degree in philology. As to their interests, 58 per cent stated image building as a priority in their job, whereas 33.3 per cent emphasised professional consultations and developing communication strategies in private companies (Bondikov and Galev 1999). That narrow interpretation of the nature of the professional responsibilities of public relations experts is typical both of themselves and of journalists. For 29.4 per cent of the journalists, the main activity of a private public relations agency involves "collecting accurate and authentic information and presenting it to the media" (ibid.).

Far more serious is the problem of misunderstanding the nature of public relations activities on the part of the managers of companies. That lack of corporate culture leads to, on the one hand, irrational and ineffective use of the capabilities of public relations experts in corporate activities and, on the other hand, causes problems in the communication between organisations and their public. The public relations experts take on the part of a "fire brigade" as a young practitioner aptly expressed it recently.

A recent trend is the increasing need for public relations experts. Most of them work in crisis situations, which requires detailed knowledge of the situation and available skills abroad in order to apply these creatively, adapting them, where necessary to local conditions.

The pressing need for exchange of opinions and experience in the field of public communication in Eastern-European countries is stimulating and has already established annual scientific and scientific and practical forums such as the international public relations research symposia at Lake Bled, Slovenia (from 1992), the international PR Conferences at Sofia University, Bulgaria (from 1997), the international conferences in the Poznań University of Economics in Poland (from 2001), and the Baltic PR Weekend in St Petersburg, Russia (from 2001).

In order to make the exchange of opinions among theoreticians and practitioners at an all-European scale current and mutually beneficial, I would suggest work in the following directions:

– The successful completion of the project *European Public relations Body of Knowledge*, as this would considerably assist the elaboration of a unified conceptual instrument in the field of public relations.

– Elaboration of a European calendar of the international initiatives in the field of public relations, aimed at coordinating the efforts of organisers of various forums and spread their materials to all European countries showing interest in the topics discussed there.

– As an extension of the project *Public relations in Europe* by scholars and public relations practitioners, the elaboration of a project on publishing a collection of case studies from eastern and western Europe, focusing on crisis situations in different spheres. Its preparation would stimulate the pan-European cooperation in this field and the collection could be used in the training of public relations practitioners.

– Pooling our efforts in specific joint research in public relations problems in the conditions of new information technologies, whose steady development and updating brings about various problems and highlights new and still higher requirements of the quality of the public relations products.

Bulgaria celebrated on 4th of October 2003 the centenary of the birth of John Vincent Atanasoff (1903–1995) of Iowa State University, son of Ivan Atanasoff, who originated from the village of Boyadjik in Yambol region. The computer invented by him and his graduate student, Clifford Edward Berry, in 1936–1939 and named *ABC* (Atansoff–Berry Computer) sets the beginning of the information technology age. The computer has turned the world into a global village and public relations experts are honoured with the task to work and create in it an atmosphere of public trust and understanding.

References

Bondikov, Venceslav and Todor Galev (1999). Zaklyuchitelen doklad ot provedeno empirichno sociologichesko izsledvane na tema "Sastoyanie i tendencii na PR-deynostta v Balgariya" [Final report of the empirical sociological survey carried out on the topic "state and tendencies of PR-activity in Bulgaria"]. Unpublished paper, Sofia.

Burkart, Roland (1993). *Public Relations als Konfliktmanagement. Ein Konzept für verständigungsorientierte Öffentlichkeitsarbeit* [Public relations as conflict management: a proposal for communications-oriented public relations]. Studienreihe Konfliktforschung, 7. Vienna: Braumüller.

Burkart, Roland (1999). Pablik rileyshans v konfliktni situacii: edin obshtovaliden opit za otgovor na edno orientirano kam praktikata postavyane na vaprosa [Public relations in conflict situations: a general proposal to a practical problem]. In: Minka Zlateva and Todor Petev (eds.), *Publichna komunikaciya i Evropeyska integraciya* [Public Communication and European Integration], 19–37. Plovdiv: Zenica.

Burkart, Roland (2000). *Nauka za komunikaciyata: osnovi i problemni poleta.* [Communications studies: basics and problem areas]. Veliko Tarnovo: PIK.

Cutlip, Scott M., Allen H.Center and Glen M. Broom (1999). *Efektiven pablik rileyshans* [Effective Public Relations]. Sofia: Roi Communications.

Grunig, James E. and Todd Hunt (1984). *Managing Public Relations*. New York: Holt, Rinehart & Winston.

Jefkins, Frank (1993). *Vavedenie v marketinga, reklamata i pablik rileyshans* [Introduction to Marketing, Advertising and Public Relations]. Varna: Grand Varna Management and Consulting Ltd.

Kacarski, Ivan (1998). Balgarskoto obshtestvo: kam specifichnata formula na racionalnostta [Bulgarian society: towards a specific formula of rationality]. In: V. Prodanov (ed.), *Kriza na Racionalnostta v Savremmenniya Balgarski Obshtestven Zhivot. Teoreticheski Problemi i Prakticheski Resheniya* [Rationality Crisis in Modern Bulgarian Social Life: Theoretical Problems and Practical Solutions], 155–164. Sofia: Humanity Foundation.

Krastev, Svetozar (1972). Sistemata pablik rileyshans kato komponent na komplexnata pazarna politika [Public Relations as a Marketing Component], 229–253. Sofia, Proceedings of Scientific Research Institute of Foreign Trade,6/1972.

Kunczik, Michael and Astrid Zipfel (1998). *Vavedenie v Naukata za Publicistika i komunikacii* [Introduction to the Science of Publicism and Communications]. Sofia: Friedrich Ebert Foundation.

Marinov, Roussi (2001). *Pablik Rileyshans* [Public Relations]. Sofia: Vanyo Nedkov.

Nikolova, Dessislava (1999). "Pablik rileyshans" ili "vrazki s obshtestvenostta"? [Public Relations or Relations with the Public?]. *Media & Reklama* p. 22.

Oxley, Harold (1993). *Principi na Pablik Rileyshans* [Principles of Public Relations]. Bourgass: Delfin Press.

Petev, Todor (ed.) (1996a). *Vrazki s obshtestvenostta i izgrazhdane na doverie* [Public Relations and Building Confidence]. Sofia: UNESCO.

Petev, Todor (1996b). Vrazki s obshtestvenostta: predizvikatelstvo pred vissheto obrazovanie v kraya na veka [Public Relations: Provoke to Higher Education at the End of the Century]. *Balgarsko mediaznanie* [Bulgarian media science] 1: 401–407.

Petev, Todor (2001). *Komunikaciya i socialna promyana* [Communication and Social Change]. Sofia: Sofia University.

Petev, Todor and Minka Zlateva (eds.) (2000). *Pablik rileyshans i konflikti v demokratichnoto obshtestvo* [Public Relations and Conflicts in the Democratic Society]. Sofia: Sofia University.

Petev, Todor and Minka Zlateva (eds.) (2002a). Komunikaciya v krizisni situacii [Crisis Communication]. Sofia: Friedrich Ebert Foundation.

Petev, Todor and Minka Zlateva.(eds.) (2002b). Media and Public Relations: Issues of Education and Practice.Sofia: Sofia University (This edition was printed in English in Sofia, following of Petev and Zlateva 2003).

Petev, Todor and Minka Zlateva (eds.) (2003). Medii i pablik rileyshans: problemi na obrazovanieto i praktikata. [Media and Public Relations: Issues of Education and Research]. Sofia: Sofia University.

Raykov, Zdravko (1999a). "Pablik rileyshans" ili "vrazki s obshtestvenostta"? [Public Relations or Relations with the Public?]. *Media & Reklama*, p. 22.

Raykov, Zdravko (1999b). *Publichna komunikaciya* [Public Communication]. Sofia: Darmon.

Raykov, Zdravko (2001a). *Tehnologiya i tehniki na publichnata komunikaciya* [Technology and Techniques of Public Communication]. Sofia: Darmon.

Raykov, Zdravko (2001b). *Korporativen imidzh* [Corporate Image]. Sofia: Darmon.

Reese- Schäfer, W. (1994). *Jürgen Habermas*. Frankfurt and New York: Campus Verlag.

Statisticheski godishnik 2002 [Statistical reference book 2002] (2002). Sofia: National Institute of Statistics and printing house.

Verčič, Dejan (2002). Four Approaches to Public Relations: Informative, Persuasive, Relational and Reflective. In: Todov Petev and Minka Zlateva (eds.)2002b Media and Public Relations: Issues of Education and Practice, 40–46,Sofia: Sofia University.

Zlateva, Minka (2002a). The development of public relations in Bulgaria. In: S. Averbeck and S. Wehmeier (eds.), *Kommunikationswissenschaft und Public Relations in Osteuropa* [Communication studies and public relations in Eastern Europe], 30–55. Leipzig: Leipziger Universitätsverlag.

Zlateva, Minka (2002b). Media and public relations: bridging the space to public consensus? In: Todov Petev and Minka Zlateva (eds.) 2002b, Media and Public Relations: Issues of Education and Practice, 47–54, Sofia: Sofia University.

Zlateva, Minka and Todor Petev (eds.) (1999). *Publichna komunikaciya i Evropeyska integraciya* [Public Communication and European Integration]. Plovdiv: Zenica.

Zlateva, Minka and Todor Petev (eds.) (2002). *Pablik rileyshans i novite medii* [Public Relations and New Media]. Sofia: Sofia University.

Chapter 6

Croatia

Boris Hajoš[1] and Ana Tkalac

1. National profile

1.1. Overview of national characteristics

Croatia is a Central European and Mediterranean country, situated on the crossroads between Central Europe and the Adriatic Sea, which is the northernmost gulf of the Mediterranean. Croatia stretches from the river Drava in the north, river Danube in the north-east to the Istrian peninsula in the west, Bosnia and Herzegovina and Serbia and Montenegro in the east and south-east. Its area is 56,538 sq. km and it has 4.4 million inhabitants. The majority of the population are Croats (89,63%). National minorities include Serbs, Moslems, Slovenes, Hungarians, Czechs, Slovaks, and Italians. The majority of the population is Roman Catholic (87,83%); additionally, there are Christians of other denominations and Muslims. The official language is Croatian. The capital, Zagreb, with 770,058 inhabitants, is the administrative, academic and communications centre of the country.

The main economic activities in Croatia include agriculture, the foodstuff, textile, wood, metalworking, chemical and petroleum industries, the electrical manufacturing industry, shipbuilding and tourism. Gross domestic product per capita in 2001 was $ 4.625,2, industrial output growth rate was 6%, inflation is at 2.6%. The unemployment rate is very high at 22.3%.

During the past ten years, since it became an independent country, Croatia has been going through some major changes in different parts of its society. The transition of the political and economic systems, from a semi socialist system to a market economy – followed by a transformation of the regime from an authoritative to a young democracy – has not been easy.

---

1. With special thanks to Ms Wendy Zečić, Head of Protocol Office, Government of Croatia, former PR manager of VIPNet GSM provider, and Ms Hana Klain, SPEM Communication Group Zagreb, Croatia.

The necessity of building a modern market economy and all the attributes that characterise it emphasises the role that public relations should have in Croatia.

The parliamentary elections held in January 2000 brought a new coalition between the Social Democratic Party (SDP), Croatian Social Liberal Party (HSLS), Croatian Peasant Party (HSS), Istrian Democratic Party (IDS), Liberal Party (LS) and Croatian people's Party (HNS). Two parties have left the coalition (IDS in 2001 and HSLS in 2002). In spite of the undeniable problems within the ruling coalition, the government has managed to remain relatively stable.

When in 2000 the new Croatian Government started its term in office, the Croatian economy was in recession; it was impoverished by the war and burdened by the high cost of public expenditure. Compared with other countries in transition, Croatia is lagging behind. There are numerous causes of this situation, the most important of them being:
- The situation inherited from the former Yugoslavia – a declining economy at the beginning of the 1980s, followed by structural problems and inflation.
- The war caused much damage, led to a high number of refugees and displaced persons, and was responsible for the collapse and the dissolution of the former Yugoslav market.
- The lack of a stimulating development policy.
- A wide range of social rights that could not be afforded with the available economic resourses.
- The privatisation model proved to be inadequate.
- The slow acceptance of Croatia into international associations, such as the EU.
- An ineffective legal and judiciary system.

The new Croatian government started to gradually deal with the accumulated problems and implement structural reforms, which are aimed at economic recovery and progress. The political and democratic changes are followed by various economic reforms, implemented in order to create an open economy that can be integrated as an equal partner in modern European society.

Croatia is still not an EU candidate country, although it is fully committed towards the European integration process. The government has established closer ties with the European Union and its member states over the past two years, which culminated in the signing of the Stabilization and Association Agreement in October 2001.

1.2. Facts and figures about public relations in Croatia

There is almost no research to indicate the current status of the profession. There are some undergraduate papers dealing with the development and positioning of public relations in Croatia (Almer 2001; Besedeš 2002), but they can serve only as a starting point for broader research projects that are necessary for further development of the profession.

According to estimates of professionals in the field (K. Laco, in personal communication, November 2002), in 2002 the size of the public relations market in Croatia was about € 6 million. This is a significant growth compared with the € 5 million of 2001 (this estimate includes all public relations activities such as consulting services, media relations, publications and events, but excludes any media-buying budget). The growth of the market has been exponential since 1999, but has slowed down significantly in 2002.

When both the private and the public sector are taken into consideration, there are between 1,000 and 1,500 professionals involved in different types of work in the Croatian PR industry. The background of these people differs greatly. A large proportion of public relations professionals have a journalistic background or an academic background in economics (in Croatian universities, schools of economics and business schools are not distinguished).

There are about fifty companies that offer public relations services, and these can be divided into three categories: public relations agencies, advertising agencies with public relations departments or employees, and consulting companies with public relations employees. Of these, some fifteen companies focus primarily on public relations, and they greatly differ in size, expertise and experience. The largest ones are Premisa, Hauska & Partner, Dialog, and Madison Consulting.

2. History and development of public relations

2.1. Roots of public relations

The history of public relations in Croatia can be traced to the period in which the country was still part of former Yugoslavia. Croatia's focus on tourism greatly influenced its entire economy as well as the development of the public relations profession. Following the international trends in the tourism sector, Zagreb's Hotel Inter-Continental introduced the position of a public relations manager in 1964. The job description of the hotel's PR expert included developing relations and relationships between the hotel and its – mostly economic – environment (Tomašević 2002).

The promotional activities in Croatian companies of that period were relatively well developed, but an awareness of public relations as a separate activity did not exist at the time. An important date in the history of Croatian public relations was the opening, in 1968, of a public relations position in Podravka, the biggest food-processing company in Croatia. The creation of other public relations positions in numerous hotels during the next fifteen years followed the development of the tourism industry in Croatia (Hotel Croatia in 1973; Hotel Inter-Continental in 1974; Hotel Solaris in 1980; Hotel Belvedere in 1984). On the other hand, until the 1990s there seemed to be no need for public relations professionals in the business sector or the public administration (Tomašević 2002).

The development of the profession in the rest of the former Yugoslavia was very uneven. Neighbouring Slovenia, which maintained its status of the most developed former republic, went through a period of speedy growth. In many ways it influenced the shape of public relations in Croatia. In 1989, Dejan Verčič and Franci Zavrl founded the first Slovenian public relations agency, Pristop Communications. Slovenes also formed their public relations society in 1990, which soon became the member of different international professional associations. At the same time, in Belgrade, the Institute for Journalism started organising the first Business School for public relations in cooperation with the Faculty of Public Relations in Utrecht, the Netherlands. The school started in 1991, but due to the collapse of Yugoslavia, it never managed to complete its courses. A Yugoslav public relations association was founded in Belgrade in 1993. Bosnia and Herzegovina, Macedonia and Montenegro still do not have national public relations associations.

After Croatia gained its independence, in the early 1990, the Croatian advertising market was dominated with only a few international agencies and smaller domestic ones. That was also the period in which the first spokesperson position in the Office of the President of the Republic was established. The trend of identifying public relations with spokespersons has its roots in that period and is still quite strong in Croatia. In 1990, the Office for Information at the Government of Croatia was formed and it was the forerunner of today's Offices for Information of Spokespersons in Croatian ministries, Governmental agencies and other public administrations bodies.

The foundation of the national public relations association in Croatia was delayed by the war that took place between 1991 and 1995. In April 1994, Eduard Osredečki – an expert in communication and author of a book on public relations *Odnosi s javnošću* ('Public relations') – initiated the foundation of the first Croatian public relations society under the name *Hrvatska udruga za odnose s javnošću* ('Croatian public relations association') – HUOJ. Due to various difficulties, including the lack of funds and an unclear definition of its mission, the association did not start with its regular activities until May 1998. Eduard Osredečki was the first president of HUOJ, followed by Mihovil Bogoslav Matković, the public relations officer of Croatian Electrical Power Supply, and later by Sandro Baričević, the public relations manager of Coca Cola Zagreb. In 2000, another association grew out of the first one and *Strukovna udruga za odnose s javnošću* – ('Professional Association for Public Relations') – SUOJ was formed.

The current situation in Croatia shows a lack of transparent professional standards that would define who can practice public relations and how it should be done. Nor are binding guidelines or requirements available for working in the field. Virtually anyone can take up public relations without any previous special training. However, the situation is developing rapidly. HUOJ is currently working on setting a professional code of conduct for public relations experts as well as means of accreditation and certification.

2.2. The development of public relations practice

During the 1970s (while Croatia was still a part of Yugoslavia), the adoption of certain market mechanisms was already under way, caused by the total ineffectiveness of the planned-economy system (Renko, Pavičić and Tkalac 1998). However, the major problem was the non-existence of owner responsibilities as well as the absence of any system that dealt with responsibilities for business risks that led to unreasonable and irresponsible business actions. Investments, especially capital ones, were mainly determined by the political criteria, which led to foreign debts. All this had a great impact on the economic state in the country.

In spite of the fact that the environment was not conducive, some authors wrote about marketing and advertising (Rocco and Obraz 1964; Rocco 1994), but there were still no books on public relations. The 1980s brought a more liberal affirmation of the area of communications. Academics and practitioners tried to find possibilities for efficient communication (in the area of marketing communications more than anything else) and in the involvement of international trends in spite of the fact that until 1990, Croatia had only about a dozen agencies specialised in marketing communications (Renko, Pavičić and Tkalac 1998).

However, in 1990, the situation changed substantially after radical political transformations. The marketing and advertising industries that had been present in the economy and the educational system went through a period of rapid growth, while at the same time, public relations started to distinguish itself as a profession. International advertising agencies entered the Croatian market and the area of marketing communications became very dynamic. The opening of the first specialised public relations agency and an establishment of the public relations market soon followed.

3.   Typification of current public relations

3.1. Status of public relations in business, administration and society

The development of corporate culture in Croatia is in its initial phase, which greatly affects the status of public relations. The dominant view in most companies defines public relations as an additional cost instead of an investment. Still, today, in every area of business, industry and government, there is a growing belief in the right to be informed on what is going on and why. All parts of business are expected to be accountable for their policies and actions. This is where public relations becomes important and has a definite contribution. "Public relations" means different things to different people, but professionally it means creating an understanding and, better still, a mutual understanding. Among the small (but growing) public relations community the profession is seen as a process of affecting change.

Public relations is often confused with marketing and advertising elements. For example, many people think that "publicity" is simply another way of saying "public relations" (Tkalac 2001). As a function, public relations is still not clearly differentiated from spokesman-ship, protocol activities, sponsorship activities or marketing communication activities (in which public relations is equated with publicity). Therefore the issue of defining public relations, its scope and activities, is a big problem for the profession and professionals in Croatia.

There is quite some confusion as to the roles of marketing and public relations in Croatian organisations. In general, public relations was neglected and deprived because of marketing, and still has an unclear role in the set-up of Croatian companies. The term "public relations" is often misunderstood, especially among journalists who perceive public relations as media relations and occasionally as event management. Unfortunately, "public relations" is not accepted as an essential part of management or any systematic activity of an organisation. In general, as there is no clear definition of the term, the English abbreviation is commonly used, although vaguely understood.

3.3. Position of public relations in organisations

The trend of departmentalising public relations is quite new – even though public relations specialists have been working in different organisational departments for years. Some of these units are clearly identified with the label "public relations"; others, however, operate under a variety of different names, ranging from "public affairs" to "corporate communications" (Tkalac 2001).

Only a few market leaders, be it multinational companies or big Croatian companies, have in-house public relations or corporate-communications departments with personnel in charge of internal communications, internal company bulletins, Internet sites, etc., while the external communications are mainly covered by the outsourced public relations agencies. According to Grunig and Repper (1992), when public relations is restricted to the functional level, it usually implements the strategies of other departments, such as marketing or human resources, and is restricted to the application of technique rather than the formulation of policy. This is quite true in Croatian practice, where public relations is sometimes under the auspices of the marketing or human relations departments, and there are even some cases where it falls under the jurisdiction of the financial department.

The positioning of the public relations function often presents a big problem. The organisational relation between public relations departments and marketing departments – which have a longer tradition and a wider job description – is not yet clearly defined. The lack of infrastructure almost assures competition and is seen as problematic in many Croatian organisations. The consequence of this is a fragmented image of the organisation among its various target groups and a breakdown in relationships, especially with employees (Tkalac 2001).

Public relations practitioners have to work on defining their role in the hierarchy of the company and in relations to top management, which in most cases does not support the idea of departmentalising public relations. Management usually does not recognise the essential and strategic role of public relations. Altogether, the position of public relations depends mostly upon the individual management style of each CEO, since the style of management in Croatia is very authoritative.

In the area of public administration the biggest incentive for development was the elections held in 2000. Changes that the society went through induced a need for the opening of public administration to its constituents and a better and more structured communication with various publics. This resulted in development of information offices and the appointment of public relations professionals in various branches of public administration, from local to national government level.

Today, public-administration specialists typically manage media relations and maintain Internet sites and bulletins of their respective institutions, which facilitate dialogue with the citizens. The diversity of their titles reflects the diversity of the tasks and activities they cover. Sometimes their job description defines them as spokespeople, chiefs of protocol, designers and event managers, all in one person. Background and education of professionals in public administration differ a lot (as in the business sector), but most of them have a history in journalism.

Because of the tense political situation in Croatia, public-administration professionals work under constant media pressure. There is a lot of mistrust between the media and public relations personnel – low levels of funding do nothing to improve this. Most of the additional problems in public administration are similar to the problems in other areas of public relations. These include unclear positions in the decision-making process, and unrealistic expectations of managements who often do not understand the value of continuous and strategic communication.

As the government matures and becomes more professional, it can be made more responsive to citizens' needs and concerns, give incentive to essential programs, and provide services to those who need them (Cutlip, Center and Broom 1999). The growing recognition of the importance of public relations in the government will ultimately lead to its status being comparable with other parts of the world.

3.4. Current state of public relations education and major textbooks

Many of the problems that public relations professionals face are the result of insufficient education. As Grunig and Hunt (1984) state, public relations cannot become a "full-fledged" profession until its practitioners approach their tasks with a significant level of intellectualism. However, their approach depends almost entirely on the intellectual tradition they learn as students. Education should be the primary means of providing the necessary knowledge and skills to perform well as a public relations worker.

Even though the body of knowledge in the area of public relations is almost non-existent to date, Croatian academia offers substantial academic research in related areas that could serve as a starting point in developing public relations further. The biggest problem in education lies in the insufficient number of good teachers and academic researchers specialised in this area. Since higher education (both at undergraduate and graduate level) follows the changes in employment opportunities, it can be expected that the situation in academia will improve rapidly.

Today, undergraduate education in public relations is still not offered to Croatian students. At all four Faculties of Economics and Business in Croatia, public relations is taught only as part of marketing courses. However, the interest of business students in public relations is considerable and separate public relations courses are now being offered. At graduate level – administratively more flexible in its program changes – public relations is being offered as a part of various courses. It will eventually take over entire courses and maybe even modules, in response to the request of business school graduates.

In the autumn of 2001, the Department of Culture and Tourism at the Faculty of Philosophy in Zadar (Croatia), in cooperation with University of Maribor in Slovenia and experts from the SPEM Communication Group in October 2001 started Masters (four terms) and PhD (six terms) courses in Information and Communication Sciences, journalism, and public relations. As Cutlip, Center and Broom (1999) state, because public relations have an influence that is significantly wider than the boundaries of the organisation that particular practitioners works for, these public relations experts have to take into consideration both intended and unintended consequences of the function. Collectively, through professional associations, they must take responsibility for defining standards of competence, through defining the standards of conduct and educational and accreditation requirements. Practitioners of public relations must also encourage research in order to widen the body of knowledge that guides the practice.

The research tradition in public relations is young and has leant on the US model up to now. The number of scientific articles and research studies focusing on the topic of public relations is low, but some of the young academics connected to the University of Maryland are starting to build a line of research in this area. Again, areas related to public relations show a much brighter picture, and there are numerous research projects connected with the image of the country, public opinion, etc.

Fast changes in the market and in new technologies require permanent learning, for which the only sources are special professional conferences for PR experts. In September and October 2000, two international public relations conferences were held in Croatia (the first one in Zagreb, organised by SUOJ; the second one organised in Opatija by HUOJ). The second HUOJ conference, held in Pula in October 2001, attracted more than 200 Croatian public relations experts, who shared their experience with such speakers as James Grunig and Laurie Grunig (University of Maryland), Steven Ross (Boston University) and Dejan Verčič (University of Ljubljana).

Croatia has ten IPRA members, who are united in working on the development of professional standards. They collaborated with HUOJ on the preparation of the third Croatian national public relations conference in 2002 and the IPRA Mediterranean public relations conference in 2003.

4. Conclusion: state of the art and future of public relations in Croatia

The field of public relations in Croatia is characterised by inspiration, ambition and a growing demand for professionalism, but at the same time, the necessary infrastructure still is not complete. Public relations needs to be (re)defined and (re)positioned in the education system, in the organisational structure and through ethical codes and codes of conduct. In spite of all this, the future of public relations in Croatia looks bright and the profession is evolving all the time. From the initial phase in the 1990s and the introduction of a market economy in Croatia, public relations developed under the umbrella of marketing into a profession that is becoming an important academic and business field.

The path of development of public relations in Croatia tends to follow the trends and issues that are taking place in neighbouring countries and in the rest of Europe. Increased competition is positioning public relations as an unavoidable management function and necessitates its inclusion in various organisations. The trend has already led to the opening of a relatively large number of public relations agencies, and will probably lead to a degree of specialisation.

The definition of public relations and the positioning of the profession is still a big problem for Croatian public relations practitioners. As yet, nobody has a complete and clear understanding of the field, which affects the development of the profession by reducing it to media relations and publicity.

The importance of public relations professionals and agencies in the continuing process of privatisation will have a big effect on the profession as a whole. In the privatisation of the remaining state-owned companies in Croatia, public relations experts will play an important role by defining the communication strategies. Privatisation already affected both the public relations and advertising industries through a "media war" between the two biggest mobile telephone operators – HT Cronet (a privatised state-owned company) and a new player, VIP Net.

Today, there is a growing demand for public relations in the finance sector, which is largely due to the privatisation of banks, the growth of the insurance industry and the introduction of the reformed pension system and pension funds. The trends mentioned earlier, combined with the unavoidable process of globalisation that has already brought numerous foreign public relations agencies (and with that a higher level of competition and know how), will prove to be beneficial to the development of public relations as a discipline.

The tendency towards the professionalisation of the public relations practice and the acceptance of the dignity of serving the public interest will continue to strengthen educational programs, build the body of knowledge and raise the standards of ethical professional behaviour. These improvements ensure that public relations continues to develop as a profession and guarantee a professional status for those with the necessary skills and knowledge.

References

Almer, Alice (2001). Odnosi s javnošću [Public Relations]. Diplomski rad. Ekonomski fakultet Sveučilišta u Zagrebu. [BSc. Thesis. Graduate school of Economics – University of Zagreb].

Besedeš, Iva (2002). Istraûivanje rada agencija za odnose s javnošću u Republici Hrvatskoj. Diplomski rad. Ekonomski fakultet Sveučilišta u Zagrebu [Analysis of public relations agencies in the Republic of Croatia. BSc. Thesis. Graduate school of Economics – University of Zagreb].

Cutlip, Scott M., Alan H. Center and Glen M. Broom (1999). *Effective public relations*, 8th edition. New Jersey: Prentice Hall.

Grunig, James E. and Todd Hunt (1984). *Managing public relations*. New York: Holt, Rinehart and Winston.

Grunig, James E. and Fred C. Repper (1992). Strategic management, publics, and issues. In: James Grunig (Ed.) *Excellence in Public Relations and Communication Management.* Hillsdale, NJ: Lawrence Erlbaum.

Renko, Nataša, Jurica Pavičić and Ana Tkalac (1998). The Development of Advertising in Croatia: Challenges for the Future, Advertising, paper presented at Transition, 8TH IAA World Education Conference, 1–4 October.

Rocco, Fedor (1994). *Marketing management.* äkolska Knijga, Zagreb.

Rocco, Fedor and R. Obraz (1964). *Market research – marketing.* Zagreb: Informator.

Tkalac, Ana (2001). Public relations, marketing and marketing communications – the relationship of three business functions in a transitional economy, paper presented at the Fourth International Conference on Enterprise in Transition; Split – Hvar, 24–26 May.

Tomašević, Amelia (2002). Uvod u odnose s javnošću [Introduction to public relations]. London School of Public Relations, Croatia, unpublished working paper.

Chapter 7

Estonia

Kaja Tampere

1. National profile

Estonia is a small but innovative country, with a population of
1,487,000 (1995 figure). In 2000, GDP was $ 5.8 billion, the change in
GDP was 6.9 per cent. Industrial sales increased 12.9 per cent (yearly
change). The total volume of exports was $ 3.2 billion, imports $ 4.3
bil. Estonia's current account balance is − 6.4 per cent of GDP; the
consumer-price index is 4 per cent. Estonians earn $ 339 per month on
average; unemployment stands at 13.7 of the population (Statistical
office of Estonia, Business Central Europe, EBRD; Economist Intelligence Service). Like all other post-communist countries, Estonia has
paid a high social price for its reforms. According to a nation-wide survey in 1996, 44 per cent of the Estonian population had great difficulties adapting to the market economy (Pettai 1998). The main ethnic
groups are Estonians (62 per cent of the population) and Russians
(30 per cent).

2. History and developments of public relations

2.1. Roots of public relations

Communication in communist and post-communist societies is a bit
peculiar. At the beginning of the transition period, communist influences
dominated communication in organisations. In that respect, public relations and communication management in post-communist Estonia in the
beginning of the 1990s was often similar to the public relations practice in
the US in the nineteenth century. Propaganda was used and truth was regarded unimportant, and information was manipulated. Leaders liked to
present themselves in positive and propagandistic ways (the so-called
"shirt stuffing" style was popular).

Public communication in Soviet society was ideological, managed by the Communist Party. Communism based on Lenin's doctrine looked upon journalism as a major part of the political system. To quote a well-known saying by Lenin, journalism had to be and in fact was 'not only a collective propagandist and a collective agitator, but also a collective organiser'. Lenin drew a parallel between journalism and scaffolding (journalists make all levels of the Party accessible; scaffolding makes all levels of a building accessible); both served as a means of communication between the Party and the people, thus fostering the joint construction of the edifice of Communism. The Russian Bolshevik Party, under Lenin's guidance, and dozens of other communist parties, viewed culture and communication pragmatically, discerning in them Machiavellian means of gaining power. In its treatment of journalism, Leninist-communist doctrine rested upon the following logic (Høyer, Lauk, Vihalemm 1993: 177):

– history is the struggle between classes;
– every person must inevitably take sides with one of the classes in society;
– spontaneous movement and the natural evolution of events can only lead to the domination of bourgeois ideology. In order to defeat bourgeois ideology, it is necessary to arouse the workers' class-consciousness, to organise and discipline them.

The party-principle governing journalism was absolute, and it was also acknowledged as the underlying principle of activity of all cultural and social institutions (Høyer, Lauk, Vihalemm 1993: 177). Media and communication analyses (Vihalemm and Lauristin 2001) in communist Soviet Union show that journalism realised public relations and the communication-management function itself in the Soviet Union: there was no free press in communist society and public relations as a term did not exist in this society. Communication was one-way and propagandistic – ideological, political and a struggle for a "better communist future".

Communication is a cultural tool: it is about what people actually do. According to Bourdieu, every communication practice constitutes an additional part of cultural maps. Communication can be understood as the practice of producing meanings and the way in which the system of meanings is negotiated by participants in a culture. Culture can be understood as the totality of communication practices and systems of meaning (Bourdieu 1990). Communication and culture are not separate entities or areas; they are produced through a dynamic relationship.

The definition of "communication" in a communist society can be derived from its cultural context. Communist ideology created its own communication style, referred to as "deep language" (sometimes also called "double speech") (Radzinski 2000). This refers to a style of utterances, both in speech and in writing; it was initiated by Lenin during the revolution. The whole process had to be highly secret and people were called to violent resistance with sentences such as: "We hope that it will be a peaceful demonstration" really meaning a very bloody demonstration. "Deep language" was further developed by Stalin. For example, his statement about a promotion of a comrade meant in reality his or her death sentence. "Deep language" was preserved in the language use of subsequent leaders in different forms, depending on the activity of the party and the individuality of the leader. Over time, it was ingrained in the whole society because people understood that it was safer and more beneficial to use the same style as the leaders did. This style was characterised by a "lie syndrome" (Tampere 2003), which meant that in order to understand the actual content of information one had to read between the lines and have a critical attitude towards texts. This style was born at the same time as the practice of communist ideology and it was typical of the whole period in many aspects. It was one of the instruments of the Communist Party for controlling and influencing people. Organisations in communist society used the "deep language" style mixed with the specific technocratic language typical of specialists in different areas (medicine, engineering, lawyers, etc.), that obstructed their communication with the public and gave birth to a lot of communication problems. In Western societies propaganda and communication management was totally different. In totalitarian societies technical and specialist communication was the only way to say things because all other aspects were guided by the Communist Party. In communist society personal opinion did not exist; it counted only the collective opinion of the Communist Party. No truth, no freedom, no personality, etc. Organisations were worried, because they must show victories in the working place to communist leaders very often. But reality was horrible: the planned-economy mechanism did not work and real economic results were catastrophic. On the other hand, organisations and their leaders' comfort depended on the Communist Party leaders' decisions after work results inspections; that means that organisations must lie to the Party functionaries to keep their personal privileges and comfort (in a total goods-deficit situation this was important) and organisations who were loyal and had good results got some privileges. Relationships in a communist society were based on lies and leaders' manipulations of messages, information, decisions, and privileges.

2.2. Development of public relations practice

Public relations and communication management, both in practice and at an academic level, developed rapidly after the changes of 1989. Though public relations also existed in earlier times, for example, in the First Estonian Republic (1918–1941), this period has not yet been studied sufficiently. Public relations and communication management in the modern sense of these terms have been practiced in Estonia only since 1990, and only these years of experience enable analysis and generalizations.

The government of the Soviet republic of Estonia communicated with the media and, through the media also with the public, with the help of assistants of the leaders. Important change in communication with the public took place in 1990, when Edgar Savisaar became prime minister and created the first post of Press Secretary. The first task of the press secretary was to make reports of the topics covered during government sessions, of the activities of government members and their official meetings; these reviews were presented to the press. The main channel of information flow was the state-owned Estonian Telegraph Agency (ETA, today the Stock Company News agency). According to some comments, ETA was considered the mouthpiece of the government, or its official voice, as most of the news was given to this news agency only, while the rest of the Estonian media received only the headlines and main topics. There was discussion about giving ETA official status as the government mouthpiece (comparable with the Voice of America, for instance), but that discussion died and nothing happened. In the mid-1990s the prime minister came up with the idea of weekly press conferences, after the government session (Ohlau 1999).

Other responsibilities of the press secretary were to prepare articles on political events and the viewpoints of government leaders, and the preparation of texts for leaders for their weekly radio presentations. The press secretary was also responsible for organising public-relations events, sometimes still mixed with Soviet time propaganda elements: meetings with journalists, outings to counties and even naming the prime minister as a godfather to twins in a remote village – old habits never die (Ohlau 1999). The year 1993 can be considered the birth year for public relations in Estonian business organisations, when big enterprises started to hire press representatives and to produce press releases and in-house newsletters.

One of the first Estonian enterprises to implement public relations functions was the phone company, which was established in co-operation

with the Swedes and the Finns. An information and marketing department was established with three employees: the editor of the in-house
newsletter, a press representative and a referent for everyday media clipping. This was to become a familiar pattern: public relations and communication management in Estonian companies were usually initiated by
foreign consultants and partners.

In the first years of Estonia's new independence there were problems
with defining the public relations function – public relations specialists
were not involved in structures of organisations and there were difficulties
with their job titles and job descriptions. The result was that public relations specialists worked mainly in marketing departments, communicating with the press and performing marketing tasks, as advertising was often connected with journalism. Major changes took place in 1994, when
the first public relation companies were established in Estonia. For example, Hill & Knowlton and some consultancy companies are based in the
Estonian capital. Other companies soon followed: KPMS & Partners, Ots
& Partners, Arcturus, Past and Partners, Tampere Public Relations, Rull
& Rumm, etc.

In 1995 the round table of public relations companies was established,
which was the first organisation to unite public relations practitioners in
Estonia. It was transformed into the Association of Public Relations
Companies in 1997; today its activities are rather modest. A bigger professional organisation is the Union of Estonian Public Relations Specialists (EPRA). It was established in 1996, and involves both, practitioners
and researchers; in 2002 it had forty-two members. Today Estonia is represented in IPRA by four persons, and in EUPRERA by two institutional members. The student organisation, CERP, is represented in Estonia, too.

2.3. Development of education and research traditions

The first degree course relevant to public relations dates back to 1954,
when communication and journalism degree schemes were organised at
Tartu University. More pertinently, public relations degree courses were
not organised until 1996, also at Tartu University. Public relations is taught
in the context of organisational and marketing communication, political
communication and knowledge management. This new specialisation has
broadened the scope of academic research in the field of communications beyond traditional media research. In the summer of 2000, masters

and doctoral studies in media and communication were established. Since 2000, the department has a new name: Department of Journalism and Communication. In the academic year starting in 2003, there were about 100 students at bachelor level and thirteen at masters level. Between 1996 to 2003 eight public relations students graduated at master's level, while forty eight students gained their bachelor's degree.

Until 1995, the Department of Journalism at the University of Tartu was the only educational institution in Estonia where journalism, media and communication studies were carried out. From 1995 to 1998, advertising and media, film and video production and broadcasting studies were started at the Tallinn Pedagogical University, and media and public relations studies at Concordia International University Estonia. All these courses are provided only on bachelor's level, so that the University of Tartu remains the only university in Estonia to offer media, communication and journalism at post graduate level (accredited curriculum). In 1999 the field of communication research was expanded to organisational communication, political communication, marketing communication and strategic communication. Since 2000, research concerning new media in Estonia has established itself as a new area of research.

Apart from the media and communication research, the Department of Journalism and Communication is also involved in the sociology of social and cultural transformations in the post-communist society. The main focus here is on changing values and identities, minority–majority relationships, political culture and the role of media in the democratisation process; interpretation of social changes; spatial effects of transition and factors of international competitiveness.

The Department of Journalism and Communication is the only research centre in Estonia in the field of communication, public relations and journalism, and two of its key activities are integrated communication research and raising a new generation of researchers. "Integrated research" means (a) the convergence of historical and sociological approaches; (b) focus on the media and attention to the complementary roles of the different communication forms and channels; (c) convergence of the macro- and micro-analysis and quantitative and qualitative methodologies; and (d) using media research as a tool for the analysis of society and culture.

2.4. How language shapes the development of public relations

In Estonian, the term "public relation" is translated as *avalikkussuhted ja teabekorraldus* in academia (literally, 'public relation and communication organising'), though a more common term, widely used outside academia, is *suhtekorraldus* (literally, 'organising relations'). The academic approach involves both aspects of public relations: relations and communication between the public and companies. The problem, however, is that an adequate translation is not easy to find.

3. Classification of current public relations

3.1. Status of public relations in business, administration and society

Research on the development of public relations and its usage in Estonian organisations was conducted in May 2001 (Tampere 2003). Information from the Estonian credit database shows that 35,000 active enterprises/organisations were listed in Estonia. The present researcher studied 262 of these companies, and found that only one had a public relations department. In the second round of the research these companies were questioned about the ways they had advertised their services in telephone directories. 1,980 organisations were questioned – business enterprises, government agencies, NGOs, educational and cultural institutions, etc. Only 31, or 1.6 per cent, of those questioned had an active public relations function – either the service was bought from some outside consultancy company or the organisation itself had hired a press representative, public relations specialist or an adviser. Sixty out of 1,980, or about 3 per cent, mainly used marketing communication services and advertising.

More attention was paid to the self-presentation of big enterprises and state enterprises, which made up 95 per cent of all who had implemented a public relations function. Public relations was used more in those organisations that had some foreign partnership, or that were Estonian branches of some foreign company – 87 per cent of public relations users had a foreign partnership or were branches of foreign companies.

The majority of the companies that had a public relations and marketing communication function thought that one, or at most two, persons were enough for the implementation of public relations work and 90 per cent of the companies with a public relations function did not consider it necessary to establish a public relations team. Only 10 per cent of the organisations using public relations used it strategically, developing various sub-departments (media relations, marketing communication, etc.) and teamwork.

In Estonia, "public relations" is often just a title for public relations persons, without much elaboration of their tasks, and, typically, the functions of press officers, and public relations specialist are undifferentiated. Still, there are many opportunities for the development of Estonian public relations as such. Research shows that so far there is not much planned communication management aimed at symmetry in public relations and communication, focused on different target segments. But further steps in this direction can be expected together with a higher professional level of public relations specialists.

In the first years of the development of public relations, the most sought-after services were media relations, followed by organising events and marketing services. Media relations continue to hold primary importance, but the share of marketing communications and corporate public relations, including the strategic planning and auditing of communication, has grown. According to different estimates, the total annual turnover of Estonian public relations companies is 35–40 million EEK. Services are charged at approximately 300–2,000 EEK per hour.

A new development is publicity campaigns by the public sector or NGOs, for example, integration of Russian-speaking people and Estonians in post-communist Estonia, child rights, traffic safety. Another continuing trend is higher specialisation in the market and services. The demand for media relations is diminishing, a growing demand can be expected in the field of marketing communications, lobbying, social-political public relations, corporate public relations, financial and investor relations, to be followed by services based on new media. It is important to realise that Estonia was an 'empty place' with respect to public relations in 1990. For example, public sector campaigns are totally new things in post-communist countries. In the communist period promotion included only communist propaganda, and all public sector messages expressed communist ideology. This is a change of paradigm, a change of ideologies in all possible levels in society.

3.2. Major roles of public relations and typical tasks

The roles of public relations and communication management in a transition society are specific in nature. There are several reasons for this. First, the relation between propaganda and communication is sensitive. Secondly, the countries of Central and Eastern Europe and the former Soviet republics are in a crucial phase of transforming their economies from centrally planned to market economies. Due to such a period of fundamental social and economic changes it was inappropriate to add a democratic PR aspect directly to new post-communist environment.

According to Ryszard Ławniczak, the first task of public relations during the first stage of the transition is to build up an image of "capitalism with a human face", in order to secure public acceptance of ongoing economic reforms. The second task is to create public awareness of the wide range of possible alternative market-economy models by promoting value systems and lifestyles with products and services, keeping in mind that in the former socialist countries a struggle is currently under way to determine the final shape of the market economy. And finally, the third task is to facilitate effective functioning of the market economy (Ławniczak 2001: 15). Ławniczak's main idea is that public relations in a society in transition is an instrument for systemic transformation in Central and Eastern Europe.

Based on the results of the EBOK project, *The Bled Manifesto on Public Relations*, van Ruler & Verčič (2002) stress the educational aspect that is to help members of organisations to become communicatively competent in order to respond to societal demands. This function has to do with the behaviour of the members of the organisation. In transition countries another pedagogical aspect needs to be considered, for example educating the public and different target groups of the organisation in order to help people change with society and adapt to new cultural, philosophical and economic conditions (Tampere 2003). In turn, a system of knowledge would emerge as a basis for better mutual understanding, trust and relations in the society as a whole and between the organisation and its target groups.

4. Conclusion: state of the art and future of public relations in Estonia

The PR function has historically developed through various cultures and societies. Public relations itself has been considered a phenomenon of a democratic society for years (Cutlip et al. 1985; Harrison 1995). Totalitarian regimes in Europe at the beginning of the twentieth century (from revolutionary changes in Russia in 1917 to World War II, totalitarian regimes in Russia, Germany, Italy, etc.) strongly influenced the development of communication management in Europe. According to Harrison (1995: 7), Goebbels provided a definition for propaganda in the 1930s that changed the meaning of propaganda to a great extent – mainly devaluing its meaning, and relationships between public relations and propaganda started to be problematic.

Looking at the social developments at the end of the twentieth century, it seems that the time has come to re-examine the pillars of public relations and communication management as organisational activities of crucial importance, and also to accept the development of public relations in the environment of a post-communist society. Public relations history in the democratic world, in the author's opinion, took on a new dimension in 1989, and we can call this period the opening period (Tampere 2003), which would become the cradle for the systematic public relations function in post-communist states and the beginning of new developments in European public relations. This was the beginning of the process of opening up of totalitarian states and the time when a large part of Europe changed its social order, and worldview. This is the period when transition societies were formed and developed, and the period when public relations and communication management were established in post-communist transition societies. The length of the period of opening was about ten years. Since 2000, communication management and public relations processes have taken place in the global networking and net communication period (public relations on the net) (Tampere 2003), because both in post-communist and in old democracies, as well as in Asian cultures, there has been a very rapid development of internet and information technology. This communication trend has very clearly followed the net society trend and McLuhan's ideas of the Global Village. This period can also be characterised as one of strong integration of different cultures, worldviews and philosophies, and of different functions and activities.

I would suggest one additional role of public relations, the integrative role. In the European society context it is important to discover opportunities for cooperation (Tampere 2003). The past ten years have been revolutionary in Europe – more than half the European territory changed its basic values at a very fundamental level. As a result, more than half of Europe is still experiencing the stress of change. In Europe we have met problems arising from encountering different national cultures and religious worldviews. In addition, there have been problems with economic, political, ideological, ethical and cultural differences, which are much more complicated aspects than mere differences in nationality. In my opinion, it is possible to find opportunities to integrate the experiences of different economic systems and different societies. To do this it is necessary to have special skills and tolerance, along with good and ethical pedagogical practice. Together with public relations' integrative role, it is possible to find new dimensions in the actions of PR practitioners: they will be in a much more diplomatic position, like translators between different approaches to existence.

References

Bourdieu, Pierre (1990). *The Logic of Practice*. Cambridge: Polity Press.

Cutlip, Scott M, Allen H. Center and Glen M. Broom (1985). *Effective Public Relations*. Englewood Cliffs, NJ: Prentice Hall.

Harrison, Shirley (1995). *Public Relations An Introduction*. UK: Routledge

Høyer, Svennik, Epp Lauk and Peeter Vihalemm (1993) *Towards a Civic Society*. Tartu: Baltic Association for Media Research/Nota Baltica.

Ławniczak, Ryszard (2001). Transition public relations: an instrument for systemic transformation in Central and Eastern Europe. In: Ryszard Ławniczak (ed.), *Public Relations Contribution to Transition in Central and Eastern Europe*. Poznań: Printer

Ohlau, Aili (1999). Eesti avaliku sektori asutuste avalike suhete praktika, probleemid ja perspektiivid [The practices, problems and perspectives of public affairs in Estonian state offices]. MA thesis, Tallinn Technical University.

Pettai, Iris (1998). Adaption as an indicator of integration. In: *Estonian Human Development Report 1998*, 31–37. Tallinn: UNDP. (See also www.undp.ee).

Radzhinski, Edvard (2000). *Stalin*. Tallinn: Varrak.

Tampere, Kaja (2003). Public relations in a transition society 1989–2002: using a stakeholder approach in organisational communications and relations analyses. Doctoral Thesis, Finland: University of Jyväskylä.

Van Ruler, Betteke and Dejan Verčič (2002). *The Bled Manifesto on Public Relations*. Ljubljana: Pristop.

Vihalemm, Peeter and Marju Lauristin (2001). Journalism and public relations in different normative contexts. In: Eskelinen Sari, Saranen Terhi and Tuhkio Tetti (eds.), Spanning the Boundaries of Communication. International Colloquim, Jyväskylä, 14 Feb. 2001.

Chapter 8

Finland

Jaakko Lehtonen

1. National profile

1.1. Overview of national characteristics

Finland – the home country of Nokia, manufacturer of the world's biggest-selling mobile phone, a company which started out as a manufacturer of rubber boots – has experienced a dramatic change in the communication culture during the second half of the last century. This formerly agriculture- and forestry-driven country was recently considered a laboratory for technological innovations, in which not only the latest mobile phone models, but also other innovations in the field of communication technology are tested before worldwide marketing.

Finland as a country is geographically fairly big. If it could be moved to the centre of Europe, with its southern tip placed on Rome, its northern tip would extend to Brussels. In a country in which the population is small in number, approximately five million, and distances long, communication is a prerequisite for its functioning. A country with large distances and sparse settlements has presented a fertile ground for the acquisition of new communication technologies.

The country's journey through the twentieth century has been turbulent: from being the western province of the Russian Empire at the beginning of the twentieth century, through its existence as a slowly industrialising agrarian community during the 1920s and 1930s, through two major wars, through the era of the pipeline industry, pushed on by the war-indemnity obligations, towards the post-modern, post-industrial, IT-driven information society it represents today.

On a popular post card, each member country of the European Union is represented by a caricature of a stereotypical quality, such as German humour, British cooking, and the sober Irishman. When Austria, Finland and Sweden were admitted to the Union in 1995, the artist had to add three more figures to the card. The virtue that Finland added to the stereotype of the perfect European was talkativeness: the characteristics that are most often connected with the Finns is reticence and shyness (Sajavaara and Lehtonen 1997). It is a paradox that the silent Finns today belong to the most frequent users of the mobile phone in the world, and that the country is largely regarded as a forerunner and laboratory of innovations in communication technology.

Communication technology has changed not only the life of big business. Within a few years, each of the more than 400 Finnish municipalities, all governmental offices and most non-profit organisations inform their public and offer their services over the Internet. In 2002, more than 50 per cent of homes were connected to the Internet and the percentage is growing every day. As a consequence of the conquest of new territory by IT-based public-information services, the traditional role of the communication specialist is changing. On the one hand, some of the traditional practical tasks of the public relations professional, such as writing and distributing bulletins and handouts, have been added to the responsibilities of the line foremen and the IT-officials; new strategic issues, on the other hand, such as managing the corporate reputation and customer relations, have been growing in importance in the work of the communicators.

The Internet is also changing the media relation's strategies of organisations. Today, some public and private organisations prefer to arrange virtual media conferences using the Internet instead of face-to-face meetings. On the other hand, all the media use the Internet for data collection – according to a recent estimate, up to 80 per cent of the material published in a newspaper comes from the Internet. Newspapers themselves were digitalised in the 1990s. Among the earliest were the small local newspapers; the first medium-sized newspaper to be produced digitally was *Keskisuomalainen* in 1993 (Huovila 1998).

1.2. Facts and figures about public relations in Finland

Since the 1970s, the Finnish Council of State has published recommendations concerning public information, which are to be applied in all government offices. The Finnish Prime Minister, Paavo Lipponen, signed the most recent recommendations, of May 2002. The 63 pages of the recommendations can be reduced to six principles: (1) openness in administration and trust in public decision-making are the main pillars of democracy; (2) the participation of citizens is possible only through interactive communication; (3) reliability, impartiality, coverage, and speed are es-

sential qualities in communication; (4) communication in public administration must serve the goals of administration; (5) all official bodies are
obliged to inform the citizens about how they are administered and (6)
the role of communication in the conduct of public affairs, like all state
administration, is to serve the citizens. The recommendations do not
have the status of a statute, but all offices are obliged to work out a communication plan and report on it to the Council of State (see: Informing
2001; Recommendation 2002).

Besides state's civil service departments, the municipalities are an important employer of communication specialists. Bigger cities have communication departments in each branch of administration (education, social services, health care, construction work, electricity and water mainte-
nance). Municipalities are not only a big employer of communication
specialists; they are also the most important platform for social participation and the development of civil society. The rights of the citizens to information were laid down in the law on municipal administration (*Kunta-
laki*) in 1995. A law that defines the communication obligations of all civil
servants is being prepared and should come into force in 2004.

2. History and developments of public relations

2.1. Roots of public relations

In the first two decades of the twentieth century the concept of public
relations was unknown. Its function was fulfilled by the new field of advertising (*reklaami*), which was so new that it did not have a domestic
word in Finnish until 1928, when the word *mainos* won in a competition
to find the best word with which to describe advertising. Several agencies
were established as early as in the 1920s. In 1923, the import industry set
up an Advertising Centre (*Teollisuuden Ilmoituskeskus*), and in 1924 the
very first public relations office – *Liiketaloudellinen neuvontatoimisto*
('counseling office for business administration') – was established. But
the idea of consulting companies was too new and very soon it was con-
verted into a regular advertising agency. The 1920s and 1930s were the
golden age for the advertising industry: companies established advertising departments, seminars on advertising were arranged, books on advertising theory were published, several agencies were established, and
in 1928 the first association of people in the advertising business, *Re-
klaamimiesten kerho* ('club of advertising men'), was established (Hei-

nonen and Konttinen 2001). An interesting public relations product of the 1920s, which might be considered the beginning of Finnish public relations campaigning, was the first propaganda film on Finland in 1922, which was shown all over the world with great success.

Even before World War II, several ministries had press offices of their own. With the international situation growing tense towards the end of the 1930s, the Finnish government started to develop its ability at wartime communication. In 1937, the armed forces invited a group of journalists, novelists and advertising experts to a 'second term of training' in war propaganda. In the spring of 1937 these activists founded the first Finnish public relations association, called *Propagandaliitto* ('propaganda league'). After the war many of these people, 68 in number, were hired by the central administration boards of ministries to apply their skills in peacetime public relations work.

In the late 1930s, the central goal of the *Propagandaliitto* was to make Finland known in other countries and to market the 1940 Olympic Games, which were to be held in Helsinki. Part of the *Propagandaliitto* was a private news office, *Finlandia*. The propaganda league was the first public relations organisation in Finland – but at the end of 1939, the war put an end to its activities.

When in December 1939 the Soviet Union attacked Finland – which in the secret Molotov–Ribbentrop pact was assigned to the Soviet sphere – and started the 100-days' Finnish Winter War, all public communications were brought under military control. Later, during the world war, the State Information Office, established in 1941, directed public propaganda and monitored the nation's mood. The State Information Office was reduced in size after the war in 1945, and finally closed in 1948 (Perko 1988).

After the war the public-information service was faced with several public relations challenges: the resettling of evacuees from areas occupied by the Soviet Union, feeding the people and other measures needed in the return to a peacetime society. Many of the army Public Relations officers were hired as "propagandists" in various ministries and public offices. In aftermath of the war, the propaganda officers "had to re-educate themselves on their domestic ground and acquire the ethical norms which are common to modern public relations" (Virkkunen 1958).

After 1945 some of the "public-propaganda specialists" met on a regular basis and discussed the social questions of the day. This informal club was called *virallisten elinten propagandistien neuvottelukeskus* ('the Negotiations Centre of the Propagandists of the Civil Service Departments'). They proposed the settling up of a ministry of information; however, this did not come to anything, nor did their private member's bill in parliament to create a "Finland Institute" to spread information about Finland.

In 1947 a number of these people, hired to work in various state offices, got together and founded a society, *Tiedotusmiehet*, which translates literally as 'Information Men'. They rendered the name of their association into English as 'Public Relations Society of Finland', although people from business organisations were not represented. The focus of activity was on conducting public opinion in the difficult post-war days. Initially, only journalists and government public relations officers were accepted as members. Public relations officers of the newly established public relations office of the biggest Finnish department store, Stockman, or those from the international companies – Esso, Shell and Ford – did not have access to the association until the 1950s (Virkkunen 1978). In 1983 the organisation was renamed *Suomen Tiedottajien Liitto*, and today it is called *PROCOM*. The number of members increased from 643 in 1980 to 1,371 in 1990 and to around 1,700 in 2002 – partly reflecting the increase of PR-related occupations in business and public organisations, and partly due to active recruiting. Over the years, the focus of the association shifted to business communication and since 1993, the approximately 400 communication professionals of municipalities and state offices have an organisation of their own.

In the Finnish "Big Encyclopaedia" (1980), the entry for "public relations" reads as follows: "As in all Nordic countries, the concept of public relations in Finland is associated with negative meanings". Several new concepts have been suggested as replacements to public relations, among others *yhteystoiminta* ('affiliation work'), and, recently, *viestintä*. After the war, the professionals slowly phased out the word *propaganda,* which was loaded with negative connotations, and replaced it with the new word *suhdetoiminta*, which means something like 'relationship activity'. *Suhdetoiminta* was the Finnish equivalent of "public relations" until, in the 1980s, the word *viestintä* (derived from *viesti*, based on the Russian word *vjest*) conquered the field of communication. The stem *viesti* corresponds with the English word *relay,* but for present-day Finns the word *viestintä* is opaque. The problem is that *viestintä* has become overloaded with meanings both in everyday use and in scientific writing. For many people the word has such connotations as "modern" and "interactive" – which was not the case with the older word *tiedottaminen* ('informing'). But *viestintä* is also used to cover communication technology and the administration of public communication channels (radio, television, mobile networks, etc.), and the title of the minister in the cabinet responsible for these issues is *viestintäministeri*.

2.2. Development of public relations practice

Pietilä (1987) divides the early development of public relations in Finland into five stages. The first stage ran from the beginning of the twentieth century and ended with the outbreak of the Finnish Winter War and World War II. During this stage – which was interrupted by the Finnish Civil war (1917–1918) – the Lutheran Church founded its Information Centre (1917), the Finnish Journalists' Association was established (1921), the Public Broadcasting Company started the first radio transmissions (1926) and the first advertising agencies were set up in the 1920s.

The second, and pioneering, stage began after the Second World War and ended with the General Strike of 1956. During this stage, the public relations profession started to take shape, the public relations doctrine was spread among the professionals, the first Finnish municipality, the City of Tampere, hired a public relations specialist, telex was adopted by newspapers and companies, and, in 1955, TV transmissions began. At the beginning, the focus of public relations work was on media relations and monitoring public opinion. Concord and unanimity were among the goals of post-war government communications. During this period, business organisations, too, started to direct attention to internal communication. The first personnel magazine was published as early as 1913, and was soon followed by others. In 1955 the professionals of internal communication founded a society of their own, called *Suomen Henkilöstölehtiyhdistys*, the 'Personnel Magazine Association of Finland'. The public relations association had been established by demobilised army officers; the Personnel Magazine Association, in contrast, was a women's club.

The third stage, up to the mid-1960s, was characterised by the emergence of public relations activity in industry. Organisations created public relations vacancies, books on public relations were published and professionals discussed with enthusiasm "the philosophy of public relations". The General Strike of 1956 in particular, gave business organisations an impetus to develop their relations with the trade unions. The enthusiasm was based on a belief that in the future, public relations would have the power to prevent unrest in the labour market.

The fourth phase, which lasted until the end of the 1970s, Pietilä calls the public relations boom. Typical of this period is the substantial devel-

opment of public information. A new law regulating municipal administration, defines the responsibilities of municipal communication; the government lays down regulations to be followed by the state authorities in
the organisation of internal and public communication.

The fifth phase, in the 1980s, has been called the "settling down" phase.
It includes the first signs of the emerging information society and the first
university chair of public communication with special emphasis on organisational communication. In 1970 the Finnish public relations agencies set
up an organisation of their own called The Finnish Association of public
relations Agencies. In 2002, more than forty public relations agencies
(*viestintätoimisto*, in Finnish) offer their services on the Internet. Since
1983 the public organisations that carry out public advertising campaigns
have been organised in the Association of Social Advertising in Finland.

2.3. In the new Millennium

In the summer of 2002, the Finnish Public Relations Association, together with the Finnish Association of public relations consultancies, interviewed 253 managers and public relations specialists from various
Finnish organisations. The interviewees were asked, among other things,
about the role of communication and the role of the communicator in
corporate decision-making, and the significance of communication as a
value-adding factor. They named as their essential responsibilities: external communication (69 per cent of the interviewees), media relations
(67 per cent) and internal communication (63 per cent). By contrast,
stakeholder relations and participation in strategic decision-making were
mentioned by only 11 per cent of respondents; less than 10 per cent considered lobbying and sponsoring as their responsibility. The fact that lobbying was not seen to belong to their responsibilities may be explained by
the negative connotations of the word "lobbying" in Finland. When, for
instance, the Finnish forestry industry hired a lobbyist to work in Brussels, he was not introduced to the Finnish media as a lobbyist but as a
"particular forest-industry specialist" (*Helsingin Sanomat* 22 Nov. 2002).

In their comments on the results, the Finnish PR-people expressed
their concern about the managers' mistrust in communication specialists.
The biggest discrepancy between the opinions of the CEO and those of
the communication and marketing management – more than 30 per cent
– was in the rating of external communication, the role of communication officers in running the organisation's media relations, and in the de-

velopment of corporate culture and identity. The communication specialists rated the role of communication in these areas much higher than the
general managers did. The communication people also saw communication as playing a more central role in informing and educating the public,
in discussion on the corporate vision, in consultations with the top management, and in developing and auditing the corporate image than the
CEOs did.

2.4. The development of education and research traditions

The theoretical knowledge of the early Finnish public relations professionals was imbibed from the literature, though some had also studied
public relations in the UK and the United States. The first public seminar
on public relations in Finland was arranged by the Finnish public relations Society as late as November 1956. The topics of the lectures were
personnel relations, public-opinion formation, the role of workers and
foremen in quality improvement, personal relations in customer service,
and the printed media, radio, and television as the working tools of public relations.

Since 1930 a correspondence school called *Markkinointi-instituutti*
('The Institute of Marketing') offers business people courses in various
communication skills, such as advertising and the language of business.
The first PR-related concept in the institute's program was the training of
salespeople and "advertising men", but in 1978 the school started a separate program in public relations and communication (*tiedottajakoulutus*),
combining distance teaching with face-to-face teaching. The program
consists of courses in organisational communication, business writing,
mass communication, practical journalism, new media, speech, regulation of communication, communication planning, and marketing communication. The course takes a year and a half and is concluded with a
dissertation.

Academic teaching and research in public relations was given a boost
in 1978 when the University of Helsinki offered Osmo A. Wiio a chair in
communication. As the first and only professor in Finland in the field, a
prolific writer of textbooks, and an internationally appreciated scholar,
Wiio has had an enduring effect on Finnish public relations theory. One
of the prevailing theories of the 1970s was the General Systems Theory,
which Wiio, together with G. M. Goldhaber, among others, applied to organisational communication. For Wiio, communication is a matter that

joins the organisation with its environment. However, the way in which an organisation communicates is contingent on its environment. Therefore, an organisation must accommodate its approach to communication to changes in the environment. Wiio calls this application of the contingency theories *soviteteoria* in Finnish (literally, 'accommodation theory'). His student, Leif Åberg, and other members of the "contingency school" – for example, Elisa Juholin and Miia Jaatinen, both supervised by Åberg – have applied Wiio's theory. In turn, they all passed the research tradition on to the next generation of researchers.

At present, two Finnish universities offer major studies in organisational communication and public relations. At the University of Helsinki organisational communication is a line of study within the subject "communication", and at the University of Jyväskylä, organisational communication and public relations is an autonomous subject. In both universities a student can major in organisational communication (and public relations) for MA and Ph.D. degrees. At the University of Helsinki, there is one professor specialising in organisational communication; at the University of Jyväskylä, two of the seven professors at the department of communication specialise in organisational communication and public relations. In addition to university departments, the minor courses in public relations of the two universities are also offered by the Open University system in various locations. The Open University also offers a specially tailored program in public communication for officials in municipalities who specialise in public communication.

Since 1992, the new category of educational institutions – polytechnics – formed by linking together earlier intermediary vocational schools, have radically changed the situation in public relations and communication education. Most of the twenty-nine polytechnics offer some variety of communication education, including courses in organisational communication and related topics. These programs are very flexible, which makes it impossible to describe any PR programs in detail; students are free to combine courses from the existing eighty-five programs with the core content of their own program – for instance, a student of communication can take courses in entrepreneurship, marketing, mass media, graphic design, or information technology. Combined with an internship in a business or public organisation the student acquires good practical skills for working life. For example, the communication program of the Helsinki Business Polytechnic offers courses in business reporting, assessing and planning organisational communication, mass media analysis, journalistic writing, visual communication, customer journals, etc. Because of the versatility of the courses on offer the polytechnics can recommend their communication students, who are awarded the degree of *medianom,* to a variety of professions. According to the Kymenlaakso Polytechnic study guide, for instance, medianoms are professionals in visual communication who know the areas of graphic design, new media production, network communication and public relations, depending on the direction of their studies.

Along with the public educational institutes a number of private training enterprises offer a variety of courses in PR-related issues. One of the training companies, *Inforviestintä,* specialises in courses and consultations of organisational communication.

3.   Typification of current public relations

3.1. Major roles of public relations and typical tasks

Many aspects of communication in a working community could be mentioned here that are arguably the responsibility of public relations professionals. All these improve the competitive advantage of organisations and are also the objectives of communication research, education and consultation. In recent years, these have included participatory management, facilitator leadership, team philosophy and empowerment, integrated marketing communication, total quality management, and, more recently, reputation management. But there has been one thing that has affected not only communication but organisational thinking and organisations as a whole – the new communication technology. One can hardly imagine an organisation – be a business, government, or non-profit organisation – without a web site, or without internal c-mail or some Extranet application for stakeholder communications. And at this very moment probably hundreds of software specialists are developing some portal application for customer communication or for the internal use of various organisations.

It is not only companies that have adapted the new technology to their stakeholder communications. Most cities and municipalities are developing versatile Internet services that enable interaction between citizens and public servant. Parliament and civil service look to Internet applications to improve their communications. But remote rural villages are also building up networks for cooperation using the Internet technology. These initiatives are often sponsored by various funds from the European Union, and are expected to gain even more strength with the advent of the new generation of the mobile phones that combines the mobile phone with the Internet and other functions of the traditional personal computer. In 1997, only 41 per cent of the 448 Finnish municipalities had organised Internet services for their inhabitants but five years later, in May 2002, this figure was 89 per cent. In a study by *Kuntaliitto*, carried out 2001, informing the local inhabitants was considered among the most important goals of their Internet services. After that came "creating familiarity with the municipality" and "offering a channel for dialogue and participation".

3.2. Growing fields and hot issues

As in many countries, the public relations and communication profession in Finland has feminised. At the beginning all information officers were men; the move towards a feminine majority began with the rise of organisation-internal communication in the 1950s. Although there is no detailed information about the gender distribution among communication professionals, a survey conducted in 2000 may give an idea. In this survey, carried out among their members by the two professional organisations, STiL and JAT, 80 per cent of the respondents were women. By contrast, in a similar survey organised in 1997, 74 per cent were women.

The 2000 survey also showed clear correlations between gender, on the one hand, and earnings and hierarchical position, on the other. Men typically occupy the leading positions in communication departments. This difference is, however, levelling out: in 1989 only about half of the heads of communications departments (Finnish *viestintäpäällikkö*) who are heads of their departments but not board members, were women, whereas eleven years later the share of women in this position was already 80 per cent. The higher on the ladder of power you climb, the bigger is the proportion of men: females account for 86 per cent of those communication specialists (*tiedottaja*) who either work alone or are employees in a communication department. At the other end of the ladder, only 55 per cent of communication managers (usually members of the board of managers) were females.

4. Conclusions: state of the art and future of public relations in Finland

People used to joke in Finland about a ten-year delay in the acquisition of new trends from abroad. Due to globalisation and the European integration, the inertia in acquiring new trends – if it ever really existed – is gone. The same trends that can be perceived in company life in Silicon Valley or in big European corporations can be recognised in Finnish businesses. One of the hot topics of the 1990s was environmental communication. Almost every organisation developed an environmental program, invested in internal and external environmental communication and published a statement of its environmental principles. Very often the statements consisted of the same litany about sustainable values and natural diversity. At the end of the 1990s, the enthusiasm shown for the natural environment faded away and was replaced by another emotional motive: organisational values, business ethics, and social responsibility. And again, organisations are publishing statements about business ethics, or organisational values, or corporate social responsibility, like everywhere else. It is possible that the acquisition of new trends is easier in a country with a shorter history of manufacturing and in which the layers of organisational culture are thinner, and in which traditions do not hinder development to the same extent as in some of the older European cultures. But in today's world, culture and tradition may play a minor role: either one has to adapt to the global competitive environment and do what has to be done, or surrender. In a globalising world no organisation can afford national idiosyncrasies anymore – not in business or in public relations.

References

Heinonen, Visa and Hannu Konttinen (2001). *Nyt Uutta Suomessa: Suomalaisen Mainonnan Historia* [History of Finnish Advertising]. Helsinki: Mainostajien Liitto.

Huovila, Tapani (1998). Digitaalisuus yhdistää välineominaisuuksia uutisessa [Digital technique makes the news media characteristics uniform]. In: T. Perko and R. Salokangas (eds.), *Kymmenen Kysymystä Journalismista*, 225–249. Jyväskylä: Atena Kustannus.

Kunnan viestintä (2001). Suomen Kuntaliitto [Association of Finnish Local and Regional Authorities]

Perko, Touko (1988). Sanomalehdistö sodan ja säännöstelyn puristuksessa 1939–1949. *Suomen Lehdistön Historia* [History of the Finnish Newspapers] 3: 9–137.

Pietilä, Jyrki (1987). Neljä etappia, viisi epookkia: eli suomalaisen tiedotuksen vuosikymmenet. [Four etapes, five epoches. The decennia of Finnish PR]. *Tiedottaja* 5–6.

Sajavaara, Kari and Jaakko Lehtonen (1997). The silent Finn revisited. In: A. Jaworski (ed.), *Silence: Interdisciplinary Perspectives*, 263–283. Berlin/New York: Mouton de Gruyter.

StiL jäsenkysely (2000). [unpublished opinion poll] The Finnish PR Association.

StiL jäsenkysely (2001). [unpublished opinion poll] The Finnish PR Association.

Toivonen, Pirjo (1989). Suomalainen tiedotus alusta saakka eturivissä [Finnish PR in the front rank from the very beginning]. In: Leppänen et al. (eds.), *Yhteisö viestii*, 11–22. Helsinki: WSOY.

Recommendations 2002: Valtionhallinnon viestintäsuositus (2002). [Recommendation on Public Information by the council of state] Valtioneuvoston kanslia, Valtioneuvoston tiedotusyksikkö.

Informing 2001: Informoi, neuvoo, keskustelee ja osallistuu [Informing, consulting, discussing, participating. Publication of the council of state]. Valtionhallinnon viestintä 2000-luvulla. Valtioneuvoston kanslian julkaisusarja 2001/5

Virkkunen, Veli (1958). Thirteen years of Finnish public relations. Tiedotusmiehet r.y. Yearbook 1958.

Virkkunen, Veli (1978). *Miten se alkoi...* [How did everything begin...]. Tiedotusmiehet r.y. Yearboook 1978.

Wiio, Osmo A. (1982). Viestinnästä ja muista käsitteistä [About communication and other concepts]. *Tiedottaja* 2.

Intermezzo

The reflective paradigm of public relations

Susanne Holmström

1. Preliminary remarks

The reflective paradigm[1] is a theoretical model developed to understand the evolution and character of society's legitimating processes, and in this context the function of public relations practice. It defines phenomena such as multi-stakeholder dialogue, symmetrical communication and reporting on the triple bottom line (People, Planet, Profit). Theoretically, it is based on late modern sociology.[2] Empirically, it is based on observations dating back to the 1960s on the changing role, responsibility and practice of business in Western Europe (see Holmström, forthcoming). It expresses characteristic traits of European public relations, in research and practice, respectively.

In Europe, public relations is increasingly identified and analysed as a specific social relation and activity within the larger societal context (e.g. Ronneberger and Rühl 1992; Antonsen and Jensen 1992; Bentele 1994; Holmström 1997; Falkheimer 2002). It is assumed that to understand organisational legitimacy, the overall analytical framework must be the constitution of society. Here, the analytical focus is the social communication processes, which constitute society as well as organisations (Luhmann 1995, 1998, 2000a; Leydesdorff 2001). These processes continuously differentiate, change and reproduce perceptions of legitimacy. This

---

1. The reflective paradigm was originally developed as a late modern distinction to a modern paradigm based on the theories of Niklas Luhmann and Jürgen Habermas (Holmström 1998). The concept of the poly-contextual perspective of reflection differs markedly from the mono-contextual perspective of *reflexivity*. Therefore, reflective is emphasised – as opposed to reflexive. A reflective practise is also identified as one of four characteristics of European public relations by van Ruler (2000).
2. Predominantly in one of the most important sociologists of our time, Niklas Luhmann (1927–1998). Some main works are Luhmann (1995, 1997). Luhmann never analysed public relations, and the development of the reflective paradigm is based on my research and theoretical developments.

focus emphasises the conflicts between the differing and changing perceptions of legitimacy, which are seen as the basic object of public relations practice. The reflective paradigm is based on an analysis of the diffusion of *reflection* as a specific social capability evolving in the late twentieth century to transform destructive conflicts into productive dynamics. We can define reflection as the core demand on organisational legitimacy today, and public relations as a specific reflective structure. Accordingly, the reflective paradigm is seen as part of the new forms of society's coordination, implying self-regulation of organisations within a poly-contextual reference.

2. The theoretical base

The basic characteristic of reflective learning processes is the rise from a narrow, mono-contextual perspective in the organisation to a poly-contextual perspective. This enables the organisation to see itself as part of the larger societal context. The organisation finds its specific identity, acting independently, and learns how to develop restrictions and coordinating mechanisms in its decision-making processes in recognition of the interdependence between society's differentiated rationalities – such as politics, economics, law, science, religion and mass media.[3]

In the mono-contextual perspective, society's differentiated perspectives see each other from the prejudiced position of their enclosed worldviews. This leads to conflicts, hostility and counter-action, exemplified, for example, in a practice identified with concepts such as manipulation, propaganda and asymmetrical communication. Social conflicts are transformed into a war between good and evil, between rich and poor, and between big business and individual human rights.

The rise to a reflective perspective, however, facilitates a more nuanced position. The organisation inquires about the worldview of opponents in order to understand how other social rationalities produce other perceptions of reality (Luhmann 1993: 226). It increases its sensitivity

---

3. This basic paradox of interdependence as a precondition for independence and vice versa is often seen in public relations literature. Examples are "Building relationships – managing interdependence – is the substance of public relations. Good relationships, in turn, make organizations more effective because they allow organizations more freedom – more autonomy – to achieve their missions than they would with bad relationships. By giving up autonomy by building relationships, ironically, organizations maximize that autonomy" (Grunig 1992: 69).

and respect for the socio-diversity. Reflection becomes the production of self-understanding in relation to the environment. This does not change the fundamental worldview, which integrates the organisation. However, taking business as an illustration, from a mono-contextual corporate practice with a narrow economic focus on "profit", the poly-contextual practice evolves with considerations of "planet and people" as a precondition for "profit", as illustrated in the concept of *the triple bottom line*, originally formulated by Sustainability, UK in 1994, and later adopted by, for instance, Shell (2000).

3. A trend towards reflection

Reflection, however, is not a natural social ability of organisations. On the contrary: reflection is socially resource-demanding and risky (Luhmann 1995:144; Holmström 1998: 66–68). It is resource-demanding because the poly-contextual considerations double the social communication processes and make decisions and decision processes far more ambiguous than the mono-contextual perspective. And it is risky because it may raise doubt in an organisation about its own rationality, raison d'être and social boundaries, and because it means exposure and sacrifice in the short term in return for existence in the longer term. (Researchers familiar with late modern social-systems theory will recognise the closure–openness paradox of the thesis of autopoiesis. To secure its closure, a system opens up to the environment.)

Why then did we see reflection evolve as a general social pattern towards the end of the twentieth century? The dynamics behind this social learning are the basic condition of society as being differentiated in conflicting rationalities. Today's society is poly-centered. Society has no top, no centre, not just one reality or truth. Through the latter half of the twentieth century, society's communication processes gradually clustered around various specialised functional rationalities (Luhmann 1995) – social communication systems oriented towards different functions in society. Among the most widespread are politics (Luhmann 2000a), law (Luhmann 1993), science (Luhmann 1990a), economics (Luhmann 1999), religion and the mass media (Luhmann 2000). They are basically indifferent to each other and incompatible. Each functional rationality is based on its own specific criteria of relevance, each has its specific perception of society, and of its legitimacy, role and responsiblity in society. Even if all organisations refer to several rationalities (and almost all in some way to economy), they predominantly identify themselves with one of society's different rationalities.[4] A business enterprise[5] is fundamentally integrated by the economic rationality – although, of course, the organisational decision processes refer to several other functional logics (always law, often science) (Luhmann 2000b).

Throughout the twentieth century we could observe how these social patterns stabilised, resulting in a strong specialisation and fragmentation in society. This gradually activated a conflict between, on the one hand, the increasing mutual strain of society's functional dynamics on each other, and of the strain of social processes on human beings and nature (e.g. stress, pollution), and, on the other hand, an increasing mutual interdependence between the functional areas. We see a growing focus on authorities and conventions as social constructions: risk is traced back to contingent organisational decisions (Luhmann 1993), the legitimacy of which is increasingly questioned.

In 1960s and 1970s democratic Europe these social trends led to what was then characterised as "a rebellion against the authorities that dominate society".[6] The mono-contextual perspectives were increasingly challenged (by protest movements, the mass media, and the social sciences). Several decades of conflicts and confrontations gradually provoked social learning processes towards new forms of interaction. We saw the breaking up of conventional social patterns. It is in this maelstrom of fights over the setting of social boundaries and new formations of social expectations that we may understand the emergence and growth of late modern public relations. Although the mainspring of transformations are the basic functional conflicts of society and their balancing between au-

---

4. The idea of a generalised type of rationality is to establish and maintain an identity, a structure of expectation in a boundless and unpredictable world through reduction of complexity. Consequently, if you connect to communication, then the horizon of meaning is limited: We more or less know what to expect. Communicative connection is more probable when uncertainty can be reduced because you know whether you deal with, for instance, a family, a church, a university, a government, an NGO or a business enterprise, and which expectations and meanings that are related to the social system in question, at the time in question, and in the situation in question.

5. The reflective paradigm evolves in organisations – private, non-profit, public, semi-public, etc. Here, however, business is taken as the specific field of analysis and, accordingly, the economic rationality.

6. I have previously described the evolution of society since the 1960s as a particular process taking place in specific stages, with each its corporate approach and public relations practice. The process goes from a conventional over a counter-active to a reflective practice, which is gradually being routinised into good practice and finally stabilised in a neo-conventional business paradigm (cf. Holmström 2000).

tonomy and cooperation, independence and interdependence, society's turbulences increasingly strike in organisations. They become visible as organisational legitimacy conflicts and as new demands on corporate social responsibility. Passive confidence is gradually substituted by reflective trust (Luhmann 1982), which leads to high communicative complexity of society.

Initially, these conflicts provoke counter-action, defence and closure. However, when one crisis, confrontation, boycott after the other has influenced and restricted the legitimate space for business in a conventional understanding, evolutionary learning processes towards reflection are activated in the exposed parts of the business community. The Brent Spar case of 1995 has become a symbol of this change.

4. Poly-contextual corporate legitimacy

Reflection opens up the possibility of transforming conflicts into productive dynamics, which balance the differing societal worldviews in a hyper-complex interaction (Holmström 2002). In this way, we see an evolution within business from a narrow economic rationality towards a broader perspective, which takes into consideration more values than the economic. The basic activity of business, to produce and function as the economic foundation of society, does not change. The societal conditions do, however, thus leading to transformations in the sociology of the economic rationality based on increasing corporate self-restriction. Gradually, we see a shift from a narrow shareholder focus to a broader stakeholder engagement. This is where we can identify a reflective practice as *poly-context-referential self-regulation* – a precise designation of "multi-stakeholder dialogue", "ethical programmes", "triple bottom line" and "symmetrical communication".

So, reflection is an evolutionary developed social capability of foreseeing potential conflicts between social systems, of evaluating their consequences, and of transforming the reflective observations into organisational learning processes – self-control. This does not mean that relations between an organisation and its environment now grow free of conflicts. On the contrary – conflict is the basic dynamic of contemporary society. However, reflection implies a larger sensibility to differences and diversity: conflict and respect are no longer opposites. This is expressed also in the many negotiative partnership forums that have evolved in particular since the late 1990s. They include those who earlier were struggling against each other, and are formed between conflicting logics and worldviews: in particular between business enterprises and NGOs, as well as politics and social sciences. Not to dissolve and integrate perspectives, but to reach agreements on mutually acceptable social expectations based on the socio-diversity.

In the poly-centered society it becomes obvious that we cannot claim a centre of society – as for instance politics or a public sphere – which constitutes the social expectations, which coordinate society. Corporate legitimacy is generated in a poly-contextual interplay involving a large (and increasing) number of stakeholders. In addition, the classic regulating environment of business – market and state – follows the development towards poly-contextual legitimating processes. The political system establishes 'voluntary' forms of regulation to increase social co-responsibility in business as well as on the markets and with other stakeholders. Governance structures and soft law supplement conventional law. The political mantra becomes "support and dialogue is growing more important than control" (Jespersen 1997). And indeed we see part of the markets for consumption, investment and employment change gradually, with appeals to buy and invest "ethically", which is tantamount to taking a reflective perspective.

5. The reflective paradigm of public relations

In today's poly-contextual legitimating processes we can identify reflection as the core demand on organisations. In order to improve the organisational ability to relate reflectively to the environment, reflective structures evolve to connect the differentiated social logics in a complex social order. Such mechanisms have the character of transformers, which can translate and mediate between different rationalities. It is in this context that we identify late modern public relations practice. This practice is characterised by four main organisational features.

First, the poly-contextual understanding of the environment. The trend towards poly-contextual legitimation increases and transforms the complexity between the organisation and the environment. The environment will always remain a construction of the organisational perspective. With the reflective perspective the organisation sees itself as part of the larger society. A legitimating environment appears with notions such as "public" and "stakeholders". A European frontrunner in stakeholder relations, the Danish healthcare company Novo Nordisk, thus experiments with poly-contextual stakeholder models. The company is no longer the centre; it is one of several poly-centered interacting socialities (see Figure 1). Reflection means a reference to the idea of a larger context. In practice, the poly-contextual legitimating relations are designated stakeholder relations. However, the idea of a public horizon as a mediating rationality dealing with matters of common interest is present, as a reflective perspective which continuously raises doubts, questions and opens the debate without making decisions.[7]

Figure 1. The stakeholder web sees the company as part of the poly-centered societal context. (Novo Nordisk 2002: 17)

Second, a specific approach and practice of reflective interrelations. Reflective self-observation implies that a societal functional system (such as economy) as well as the individual organisation sees itself as part of a larger societal context. So, as opposed to the asymmetric, counter-active practice's mono-contextual perspectives on an environment to be managed, the poly-contextual perspective sees an environment to be respected. This reflective relation we recognise in concepts such as dia-

7. My reconstruction of the public perspective is based in particular on Dirk Baecker (Baecker 1996) and Luhmann (1990: ch. 7, 1996, 1997, 2000a, 2000b).

logue and symmetrical communication,[8] and in semantics such as "shared responsibility", "partnerships", "negotiations" (instead of persuasion), and "to build or engage in (instead of manage) relationships".

Third, a clarification of own identity, role and function in society. Reflection means that organisations thematise their identity, role and responsibility in society. The reflective paradigm therefore activates top management and influences the overall corporate policies. Moreover, public expectations are changing dynamically, and the different particular stakeholder expectations are competing. This increases the demand for internal clarification of the organisation's identity, role and responsibility in society.

Fourth, communication of this identity. Poly-contextual legitimation is anchored not only in legality and functional sustainability, but also in complex and dynamic patterns of expectation involving a long and growing series of stakeholders. The perception of corporate legitimacy is the precondition of their trust in an organisation (Holmström 1998: 87, 94). This is where we find a growing focus on internally and externally communicating organisational values, on various new types of reporting (social, ethical or sustainability accounts, reporting on the triple bottom line) and even some forms of branding, to generate the perception of legitimacy necessary to ensure corporate resources (interdependence), and a certain autonomy and field of action (independence).

6. Sense, integrate, communicate

As a response to and an expression of the new poly-context-referential legitimating processes, the reflective paradigm implies a tripartite synthesis of three organisational functions: sensor, leadership, and communication.[9] The sensor function reflects the organisation in the larger societal context and increases its poly-contextual sensitivity (see Figure

---

8. Not identical with the symmetric ideals as they are defined in, for example, the Habermasian discourse ethics (Habermas 1981). Neither do dialogue and symmetrical communication precisely identify the reflective paradigm; however they may be seen as indications of a reflective ideal.

9. We meet this tripartition in public relations research programmes: the sociological, organisational/business economic and communicative orientation. A cross-combination of these orientations seems necessary to gain insight. Public relations education at Roskilde University in Denmark combines sociology, organisational theory, business economics as well as language theory and communication science.

2). This is where we can identify the main function for reflective public relations practice. It requires essential qualifications of the practitioner, but above all, insight into the social and societal conditions, structures and processes in which organisations are embedded. However, the reflective practice implies a synthesis of the three functions. The sensor function must be seen in close interplay with the leadership function and the communicative function (irrespective of whether they are placed in one or in more organisational departments, in one or several persons). In the reflective leadership function the focus is on values and identity policies – that is, on the integration of reflection in the organisational decision processes. In its specific communicative function, public relations practice communicates the reflective corporate self-understanding. This grows an increasingly important function as organisational legitimacy rests in perceptions, which continuously change in poly-contextual dynamics.

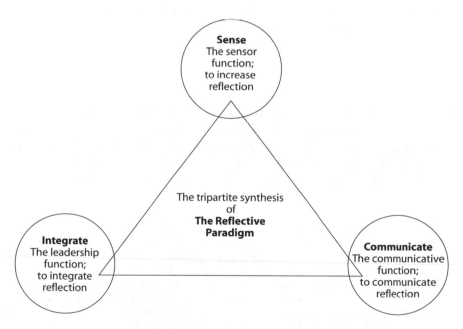

Figure 2. The tripartite SIC synthesis of the reflective paradigm: Sense, Integrate, Communicate

7. Consequences: clarification of societal identity

Organisations with a high degree of reflection are capable of being open in another way than organisations with a mono-contextual world-view. They have sufficient self-complexity to co-reflect other rationalities, and at the same time to maintain or even strengthen their own identity. Reflective organisations can endure the challenge of taking an open and understanding position towards other perspectives than their own. They tend to develop a clarified, strengthened relation to their societal identity. Conversely, organisations with a low level of complexity hardly endure reflection and tend to avoid exposure to reflection.

As the reflective paradigm catches on, we see how it gradually grows legitimate again for business to be socially responsible, based on economic criteria, though in a broader perspective than in the earlier conventional understanding. Reflection implies a change in the understanding of business of its corporate social responsibility as fulfilled by the narrow economic focus to a social responsibility based on "enlightened self-interest" (Kofi Annan in his introduction to UN Global Compact, 1999). Themes that were conventionally understood as "extra-economic" – such as nature, humans rights, animal welfare – are now seen as core issues on the corporate agenda.[10]

8. Conclusions

The reflective paradigm analytically uncovers the new forms of poly-contextual legitimating processes which challenge, increase and transform the complexity between organisation and environment, and in this context the function for late modern public relations. This does not mean that this analysis identifies all public relations practice. On the other

---

10. See for instance the statement of the World Economic Forum 2002. We may also see it as an expression of the reflective paradigm that business now increasingly takes the initiative. One example is the Nordic Partnership Forum, established by sixteen major Nordic business enterprises in collaboration with the NGO WWF World Wildlife Fund for Nature. The goal is to develop a new sustainable business model, a recipe for organisations to take on social and environmental global responsibility combined with considerations for the sales curves and shareholders. The argumentation illustrates the reflective recognition: that what is conventionally known as self-interest preconditions broader considerations, and that responsibility is ultimately rooted in the dynamics of economy.

hand, the paradigm embraces activities analytically captured as exactly relations to the public, even if they are not called "public relations".

The reflective paradigm is empirically expressed in a movement towards poly-contextual perspectives, towards mutual considerations – not to dissolve and integrate the differentiated societal rationalities, but to maintain their specialisation. Interdependence is acknowledged as a precondition of independence, autonomy and interaction, and vice versa. We see the cooperation between the different specialised dynamics of society ensured – but at the same time the autonomy and specific dynamics strengthened. We see a broader value orientation, though from the perspective of the basic rationalities.

This makes it evident that analytically uncovering the reflective paradigm is neither an attempt of legitimating, nor an idealisation of the social processes identified by the notion of public relations. It is strict analysis. The reflective paradigm bases organisational practice in "enlightened self-interest". It opposes ideas of harmony and consensus, and analytically uncovers how society learns to cope with its constitutive conflicts. Even if the reflective paradigm in the immediate perspective opens up for changes, then in the large evolutionary perspective it is seen as part of society's self-maintaining processes.

References

Antonsen, Marianne and Inger Jensen (1992). Forms of legitimacy essential to public relations. In: Mogens Kühn Pedersen (ed.), *Management and Competition*, 149–171. Roskilde, Department of Economics and Planning, University of Roskilde.

Baecker, Dirk (1996). Oszillierende Öffentlichkeit [Oscillating public relations]. In: Rudolf Maresch (ed.), *Medien und Öffentlichkeit* [Media and Public Relations], 89–107. Munich: Boer Verlag.

Bentele, Günter (1994). Öffentliches Vertrauen: Normative und soziale Grundlage für Public Relations [Public trust: normative and social basis for public relations]. In: Wolfgang Armbrecht and Ulf Zabel (eds.), *Normative Aspekte der Public Relation: Grundlagen und Perspektiven. Eine Einführung* [Normative aspects of public relations: Basics and perspectives. An Introduction], 131–158. Opladen: Westdeutscher Verlag.

Falkheimer, Jesper (2002). Framväxten av public relations i det senmoderna samhället [The emergence of public relations in the late modern society]. In: L. Larsson (ed.), *PR på svenska* [*PR in Swedish*], 19–34. Lund: Studentlitteratur.

Grunig, James E. (ed.) (1992). *Excellence in Public Relations and Communication Management*. Hillsdale, NJ: Lawrence Erlbaum Associates.

Habermas, Jürgen (1981). *The Theory of Communicative Action*. London: Heinemann.

Holmström, Susanne (1997). An Intersubjective and A social Systemic Public Relations Paradigm. *Journal of Communication Management* 2–1: 24–39.

Holmström, Susanne (1998). *An Intersubjective and a Social Systemic Public Relations Paradigm*. Roskilde: Roskilde University Publishers. (See also www.susanne-holmstrom.dk/SH1996UK.pdf). (First published in Danish in 1996.)

Holmström, Susanne (2000). The reflective paradigm turning into ceremony? In: Dejan Verčič, John White and Daniel Moss (eds.), *Proceedings of the 7ᵗʰ International Public Relations Research Symposium, Public Relations, Public Affairs and Corporate Communications in the New Millennium: The Future*, 41–63. Ljubljana, Pristop Communications.

Holmström, Susanne (2002). Public relations reconstructed as part of society's evolutionary learning processes. In: Dejan Verčič, Betteke van Ruler, Inger Jensen, Danny Moss, Jon White (eds.), *Proceedings of BledCom 2002, The Status of Public Relations Knowledge in Europe and Around the World*, 76–91. Ljubljana: Pristop Communications.

Holmström, Susanne Forthcoming: Den refleksive virksomhed (The Reflective Organisation). Ph.D. dissertation, Roskilde University.

Jespersen, Karen (1997). Ending speech. First International Conference on New Partnerships for Social Cohesion. Copenhagen: Ministry of Social Affairs.

Leydesdorff, Loet (2001). *A Sociological Theory of Communication: The Self-Organisation of the Knowledge Based Society*. USA: Universal Publishers.

Luhmann, Niklas (1982). *Trust and Power*. Chichester: John Wiley & Sons. [Transl. of *Vertrauen*, Stuttgart: Enke, 1979].

Luhmann, Niklas (1990a). *Die Wissenschaft der Gesellschaft* [The Science of Society] Frankfurt am Main: Suhrkamp.

Luhmann, Niklas (1990b). *Soziologische Aufklärung 5: Konstruktivistische Perspektiven* [Sociological Clarification 5: Constructivist Perspectives]. Opladen: Westdeutscher Verlag.

Luhmann, Niklas (1993). *Risk: A Sociological Theory*. Berlin/New York: Mouton de Gruyter. (First publ. as Soziologie des Risikos, Berlin and New York: Walter de Gruyter, 1991).

Luhmann, Niklas (1993). [1969] *Legitimation durch Verfahren* [Legitimation through Process]. Frankfurt am Main: Suhrkamp.

Luhmann, Niklas (1995). *Social Systems: Outline of a General Theory*. Stanford, Calif.: Stanford University Press. (Transl. of Soziale Systeme. Grundriß einer allgemeinen Theorie, Frankfurt am Main: Suhrkamp, 1984).

Luhmann, Niklas (1997). *Die Gesellschaft der Gesellschaft* [The Society of the Society]. Frankfurt am Main: Suhrkamp.

Luhmann, Niklas (1998). Modernity in contemporary society. *Observations on Modernity*, 1–21. Stanford, Calif.: Stanford University Press.

Luhmann, Niklas (1999). *Die Wirtschaft der Gesellschaft* [The Economics of Society]. Frankfurt am Main: Suhrkamp.

Luhmann, Niklas (2000). *The Reality of the Mass Media*. Campbridge: Polity Press (first published as Die Realität der Massenmedien. Opladen: Westdeutscher Verlag, 1996].

Luhmann, Niklas (2000a). *Die Politik der Gesellschaft* [The Politics of Society]. Frankfurt am Main: Suhrkamp.

Luhmann, Niklas (2000b). *Organisation und Entscheidung* [Organisation and Decision]. Opladen/Wiesbaden: Westdeutscher Verlag.

Novo Nordisk (2002). *Reporting on the triple bottom line 2001: dealing with dilemmas*. Copenhagen: Novo Nordisk.

Ronneberger, Franz and Manfred Rühl (1992). *Theorie der Public Relations* [Theory of Public Relations]. Opladen, Westdeutscher Verlag.

Ruler, Betteke van (2000). Future research and practice of public relations, a European approach. In Dejan Verčič, John White and Danny Moss (eds.), *Proceedings of the 7ᵗʰ International Public Relations Research Symposium, Public Relations, Public Affairs and Cor-*

porate Communications in the New Millennium: The Future, 157–163. Ljubljana: Pristop Communications.

Shell (2000). *The Shell Report 2000. The Sustainable Development Group*. London: Shell International.

UN-Global-Compact (1999). www.unglobalcompact.org

Chapter 9

France

Valérie Carayol

1. National profile[1]

1.1. Overview of national characteristics

France's territory is approximately 550,000 sq. km (c. 213,000 sq. miles –
about the size of Texas). It is the largest country in western Europe, and covers almost one fifth of the area of the European Union. It has a vast maritime zone; its exclusive economic zone extends over 11 million sq. km.

The most recent census dates back to March 1999. On 1 January 2000,
Metropolitan and Overseas France had 60.4 million inhabitants, including 4 million foreign residents, of whom 1.5 million are European Union
nationals. France accounts for 16 per cent of the European Union's population. It has 52 urban areas with over 150,000 inhabitants with a total
population of 30 million. As to household economy net average annual
earnings is € 19,938; gross average household savings are € 1,829, or
15.6 per cent of disposable income.

France's economy is the world's fourth largest in terms of GDP. The
country's assets are varied and include transport and telecommunications, agriculture and food and pharmaceutical industries, along with
banking, insurance, tourism and the traditional luxury products (leather
goods, ready-to-wear fashion, perfumes, jewels, fine wines and spirits,
etc.). In 1999 France had a trade surplus of € 18.9 billion; it is the world's
fourth largest exporter of goods (mainly durables) and ranks second in
services and agriculture (cereals and food in particular). It is the leading
producer and exporter of farm products in Europe. Sixty-three per cent
of its trade is with its European Union partners (50 per cent within the
euro area). Gross domestic product (GDP) was € 1,346.58 billion and
GDP growth was 2.9 per cent, both in 1999.

Turning to the media, 36 per cent of the French read a daily newspaper
every day. There are seven national newspapers and 160 regional papers

---

1. Source: http://www.diplomatie.gouv.fr.

(dailies and weeklies). Total annual circulation is 9 billion. As to periodicals, among the top 100, six have a circulation of over one million copies, eight over 500,000 copies. With 1,354 copies sold for every 1,000 residents, the French are the most rapacious magazine readers. But watching television remains the favourite leisure activity of the French, with an average of 3 hours 15 minutes per person per day. There are more than 130 television channels. These include four national public channels: France 2, France 3, Arte (Franco–German cultural channel) and La Cinquième (educational channel); three national private channels: TF1, M6 and Canal Plus (pay channel with 6.6 million subscribers in France and 6.9 million abroad); over 20 national and local cable channels (35 per cent of households are connected to a cable network). Finally, 7.1 per cent of households subscribe to specific cable channels.

While computers are considered primarily as tools for work and are used as such by 46 per cent of the French, an increasing proportion, currently 23 per cent of households, now own one. The French have rapidly taken to the internet, with four million users at school, work and home. Internet use in France has grown swiftly in a few years: virtually every institution, daily newspaper, government department and business now has its own website.

1.2. Facts and figures about public relations in France

Over the past twenty years, communications occupations in France have undergone considerable change, which has been explained variously by sociological, microeconomic or macroeconomic, and political considerations (Floris 1996; Mattelart 1990; Miege 1989; Le Mocnne 1994). Since the late 1980s, most professionals in public relations, corporate press and institutional communications have adopted such titles as "communications manager" and "communications director". The term "public relations" has gradually been abandoned in organisations, though it is still quite popular in consultancy firms. The structure of the professional identity of communications directors has been studied since the mid 1990s (Tixier-Guichard and Chaize 1993; Walter 1995). At the same time, a debate was organised in some universities[2] on the development in the availability of training courses (Brillet 1992).

---

2. For example, *La communication enquête de métier. Présent et devenir du métier de chargé de communication* [Professional communication survey: present and future of the profession], GREC/O Symposium, University of Bordeaux, 1992.

Today, the organisational communications professions appear to have matured – whether they are organised in consultancy agencies or in organisations. A specialised professional press exists, as do academic journals, which have contributed to the legitimisation of this sector (Bernard 1998; Deveze 1998). Professional associations and syndicates have developed. In addition, according to the various studies available, between 40 and 50 per cent of companies say that they have had a "communication position" for more than ten years.

In this chapter we describe public relations in France today from the point of view of the collective project that drives us. Because of the constraints imposed by the format of this book, we cannot deal with all aspects of French public relations, for which longer and more comprehensive studies are required. Rather, this chapter may serve as a springboard for future work. The following study is based on literature study and a field study performed recently by a team of Bordeaux students under our direction.

2. History and development of public relations

2.1. Roots of public relations

The few existing historical surveys are the fruit of the work of professionals who have worked on the legitimisation and the emergence of public relations as a profession. They often take the form of "narratives" that relate the structuring and construction of the field. A recent symposium of organisational communication researchers was interested in the corpus of studies used in research. It demonstrated the virtual absence of historical studies of a scientific character. Some researchers (Delcambre 2000, for instance) advocate working on archives and monographs to piece together the birth and development of communication services. For the time being, if we want to reconstruct a chronology for the emergence of public relations, it is necessary to go back to existing chronologics (Lougovoy and Huisman 1981, for example) and the few analyses of the professional debates and practices of some researchers (Cavallier 1992; Walter 1995).

Various sources (see, for example, Calin and Iacobescu 2002) show that the first signs of corporate communications appeared at the end of the World War I, were developed during the second World War II and really became established at the end of the last war, in the wake of the Marshall plan, especially on the initiative of the oil companies. A dozen pioneers, trained in US methods, came together in 1949 at the "La Maison de Verre" club ('The Glass House') and presented their work with reference to an American model. At that time, public relations in France was heavily influenced by North-American practices.

In the mid 1950s, the professional associations became very active. On 7 January 1955 the *Association professionnelle des relations publiques* (APROREB, 'Professional association for public relations'), founded in 1952, merged with La Maison de Verre. The new association then renamed itself *Association française des relations publiques* (AFREP, 'French association for public relations'). On 1 May 1955 the International Public Relations Association (IPRA) was founded, grouping together professionals from several European countries. The year 1957 saw the foundation of the *Union nationale des attachées de presse* (UNAP, 'National Union of Press Officers') by André Hurtrel and of the *Syndicat national des conseils en relations publiques* (SNCRP, 'National Public Relations Consultancy Syndicate') by Georges Serrel. It required a precursor, Lucien Matrat, to develop what has been described by Jacques Walter (Walter 1995) as a genuine European sociological public relations doctrine. According to Boiry (1989) "it brings an ethical dimension to the profession born in the United States". In 1959, Lucien Matrat founded the European Public Relations Centre.

In an order issued on 23 October 1964, Alain Peyrefitte, then Minister of Information, defined the professions of public relations consultant and press officer. In 1965 Lucien Matrat gave public relations genuine status and rules by creating the Code of Athens, a kind of deontological bible. This document is still used as a reference, even though the professional rules that it promulgates are not officially recognised by the public authorities or legal bodies.

In 1969 the first Ministry of Public Relations (post of Secretary of State to the Prime Minister) was created and entrusted to Jacques Baumel, who held it until 1972.

In March 1973 the *Syndicat national des professionnels de l'information et de la communication* (SNPIC, 'National Syndicate of Information and Communication Professionals') was created and France obtained a French Public Relations Federation, grouping together SNPIC, AFREP and UNAPC.

2.2. The development of public relations practice

Starting in the 1980s, the communicational paradigm supplanted that of public relations, ending in the "Communication Director model"

(Walter 1995). This transition took place under the influence of several factors: the emergence of the concept of corporate image, the development of management requirements and institutional advertising, and that of consultancy agencies in "overall communications". From then on, communications officers who relied on good knowledge of new information and communication technology to legitimise their work, managed all aspects of the company's image and its commercial communications as well as its information policy.

2.3. Development of education in public relations

Training courses for public relations professionals or press officers were first proposed by private, highly practice-orientated establishments (Walter 1995). Among the first were Francis Dumont's *Institut des relations publiques* ('Public Relations Institute'), the *Collège des sciences sociales et économiques* ('College of social and economic science') and the *École Française des Attachés de Presse* (French School for Press Officers"), created in Paris and Lyon in 1961.

The number of professional university training courses on offer is extremely high today. There are short two-year courses at the IUT (*Institut Universitaire de technologie* 'University Institute of Technology'), longer four-year courses at the IUP (*Institut Universitaire Professionnalisé* 'Professional University Institute') and postgraduate courses (DESS, Masters). For example, the universities of Paris and Bordeaux offer courses in all areas of information and communications science at all training levels.

Teaching in the area of "organisational communication" was developed primarily in the mid 1980s. The first courses were often called "corporate communication", and are nowadays taught by information- and communications-science teachers. On the other hand, subjects related to public communication are usually taught by political-science teachers and by professionals.

At the same time, high-quality general university courses were developed, with students attaining a doctorate in information and communication science. Because of the high volume of university training courses on offer, the private sector played a relatively small role in education – though commercial schools (HEC, Sup de Co) offer subject combinations or options that relate to communication and are more geared towards management and marketing sciences.

2.4. Development in research traditions

The existence, since the mid 1970s, of an academic field called "information and communication science", enabled the development of numerous research projects and the emergence of a community of researchers of more than 350 people (see, for example, www.sfsic-congres-2002.com). The contributions of researchers are published in social science journals, management journals, political science journals or specialised communication journals.

An academic journal, started by CELSA – *Humanisme et entreprise* (Sorbonne, Paris) – disseminated the first articles sprouting from research projects in the field known at the time as "corporate communications". This journal is no longer published, but it made a major contribution to the emergence of the area (Bernard 1998: 95).

Another academic journal, *Communication and Organisation*, was launched in 1992. It was published by a research group called GREC/O (*Groupe de recherche en communication des organisations* at the Michel de Montaigne University in Bordeaux (see www.montaigne.u-bordeaux.fr/GRECO/). At the same time, the name of the field of study was changed to "Organisational Communication" (Communication des Organisations), expressing the enlargement of the field of investigation.

The term "public relations" is virtually absent from the vocabulary of researchers (Carayol, Laugt and Versel 2002). If some of the initial research projects towards the end of the 1980s sometimes appeared to be a function of consultancy or expertise, this tendency is nowadays poorly represented. The legitimacy of the field is based on a distancing in respect of the professional practices and critical paradigms are developing, marginalising the research known as "applied". Nowadays this theoretical field of research is dynamic, with several research groups publishing in this area, and with symposia on a regular basis. A network of researchers at *La Société Française des Sciences de l'Information et de la Communication* (SFSIC, 'The French Society of Information and Communication Science') has been set up, which works on the development of this field (see www.up.univ-mrs.fr/actualite/indexupresse.html).

3. Typification of current public relations

3.1. The communications market in France

In 2001, more than € 29 billion was invested in communications in France (www.irep.asso.fr). This is just over 2 per cent of GDP, which illustrates the importance of this sector. Media investments represent 35.8 per cent of this total, with non-media making up 64.2 per cent. The distribution of non-media investments is as follows:

Direct marketing	49.6%
Promotion	24.8%
Events	11.4%
Public relations	8.9%
Directories	4.7%
Internet space purchases	0.6%

Taking only the investments in events and public relations, some € 1,365 million were invested in these sectors in 2001; € 904 million by national advertisers and € 461 million by local and regional advertisers (www.irep.asso.fr).

The difficulties of the "net economy" in the late 1990s and early 2000s and the current international situation have had a negative effect on investments, and, consequently, on the share prices of the companies in the sector. The advertising sector seems to be the one in which investments have been most badly hit by the recent economic and stock-market downturn. Between 2000 and 2001, investments in media declined by 5 per cent, while non-media investments continued to progress – investments in public relations were 5.5 per cent higher than 2000 and those in events were up by 2.7 per cent.

The communication sector in France is an important economic sector in terms of the number of media of all types, the number of advertising departments and consultancy agencies and the number of professionals employed in organisations (private, public and non profit sector). According to UDA (the advertisers union),[3] almost 30,000 enterprises (consultancies, departments, media and service providers) are active in advertising, employing 300,000.

3.2. Communication or public relations consultancy

In the 1990s, the communication consultancy sector was faced with a moribund economic climate and with problems arising from new laws

3. The UDA (Advertisers Union) represents the main French groups that buy advertisement space. The figures cited here are from INSEE EAE (1999 figures) and *La Poste* (2001 figures), from a document entitled *Les chiffres-clés des annonceurs* [Key figures from the advertisers].

restricting its activity. Two examples of these new laws are the Evin act, which bans alcohol advertisements, and the Sapin act, which sets new rules in the advertising market to prohibit non-ethical practices. The consequences of this difficult period were restructuring, concentration and internationalisation. It is not easy to gain a clear picture of the situation in this sector, from the jobs point of view, since the figures presented in different studies contradict each other. If we confine ourselves to the most recent figures from the *Association des agences conseils en communication* (AACC, 'Association of communications consultancy agencies') the overall number of jobs at the 200 member communications agencies rose from 9,300 in 1996 to 9,700 in 1999 (see www.aacc.fr and www.kompass.fr). According to the UDA, communication consultancy agencies in all sectors employ some 20,000 people, to which 7,650 people should be added who are employed by providers – organisers of trade fairs and exhibitions.

An economic study, carried out in 2000, of activities in the communications-consultancy sector, distinguished the following categories: advertising consultancy, marketing services consultancy, public relations consultancy, financial communications consultancy, recruitment and human resources communications consultancy, design agencies, and interactive agencies (see www.strategie-online.com). Many agencies provide overall advice and this categorisation may appear artificial. However, according to figures published by *Stratégies* (see www.groupe-strategies.fr) the top-ten public relations consultancy groups are these:

1. i&e Group
2. Burston Marsteller (parent company Yong & Rubicam, WPP Group)
3. Euro-RSCG PR&Corporate (parent company Euro-RSCG Corporate)
4. GCI Moreau & associates (parent company GCI group)
5. Porter Noveli France Group (parent company DAS, Omnicom)
6. Brodeur SRRP (parent company Brodeur Worldwide)
7. DDB&Co PR centre (parent company DDB & Co)
8. TBWA/corporate PR centre (parent company TBWA France)
9. Edelman (parent company Edelman Public Relations worldwide)
10. Rumeur Publique

Overall turnover in the sector is estimated at € 1,650 million (see www.irep.asso.fr).

Syntec-rp (see www.syntec-rp.com) is a professional organisation that groups together some of the largest agencies specialising in French public relations. It regularly carries out surveys of activities in the sector. One of these surveys, carried out among twenty-eight agencies representing 45 per cent of the estimated consultancy market and dating from 1999, established these sectors of activity of the agencies in 1999, together with their distribution:

Products and brands communication	27%
"External" institutional communication	25%
Specialist communication (health, etc.)	19%
Internal communication	7%
Crisis communication	8%
Financial communication	8%
Communication with the public authorities	6%

Though the field of public relations is viewed in a fairly broad manner here, some consultancy agencies specialise. For example, the events communication sector has its own association – *Association nationale des agences d'évènements* (ANAé Evénements, 'National association of events agencies', www), and a specialist journal, *L'événementiel* (see www.cvenementiel.fr). The most recent survey on this sector (Chapuis 2001), covering 2000, indicates that there were about 58 specialist agencies, employing about 2,325 people. Of these, 20 per cent are very large, accounting for 73 per cent of overall turnover, 24 per cent are medium-sized with 16 per cent of overall turnover and, finally, 55 per cent are small, representing 10 per cent of overall turnover. Since 1999, turnover has increased by an average of 35 per cent, and has tripled in five years. The number of event-agencies has doubled in the past two years.

On the basis of an initial analysis of the various data we can say that the clear distinction made between activities of a commercial nature and those directed more towards "corporate civics", which defined the field of traditional public relations, appears to be giving way to a refocusing on operational and technical capacities that can be mobilised in different sectors. This initial observation, if it were to be confirmed, would go against the sector's traditional legitimisation discourse (Walter 1995).

3.3. Communication in companies and institutions

Several recent national and regional studies made it possible to draw up a list of the positions of the corporate communication function. A recent analysis of job vacancies in the sector (Arzeno-Martin 2001) showed that there were about forty-five different titles describing occupations in organisational communication. In 66 per cent of the advertisements, the terms "communication manager" and "communication director" are used, while the term "public relations" is encountered in only 9 per cent of the vacancies.

Data on big firms are provided by a survey among the top 1,500 French companies, conducted by UDA, to which 264 companies responded (Union des Annonceur 2000). Following two disappointing years, there is optimism in the sector. The survey shows that more than one company in two has had a communication department for over ten years. The numbers have remained relatively stable for two years, but the budgets are on the increase. Among the more recent changes in their jobs, officers quote the very rapid development of multimedia, which is at the top of the tools used by companies. The use of outside subcontractors is on the increase, as is the creation of crisis centres, which exist in more than one in two companies. The male–female distribution in 2000 was 53 per cent males vs. 47 per cent females; the age of officers has been rising for several years: the number of employees aged over 45 has gone from 27 per cent in 1992 to 46 per cent in 2000.

Another survey was conducted in 2001 in the Aquitaine area on the initiative of the *Association des Professionnels Aquitains de la COMmunication* (APACOM, 'Association of Aquitaine Communications Professionals') among 300 companies and local authorities. The results give a good idea of communication practices in region: 49 per cent of companies and 78 per cent of public authorities have a communication department; 40.6 per cent of the departments have existed more than ten years, 50 per cent of the public authorities departments have existed less than six years.

More than one department in two is made up of only one or two people, which explains why the use of service providers is common: 74 per cent of public authorities and 58.8 per cent of companies make use of them.

In departments made up of several people, the percentage of professionals trained in communications is 46.2 per cent for companies and 75 per cent for public authorities. Other differences are also notable between companies and public authorities, since 37 per cent of the former say they have an Internet site, compared with 64 per cent of the latter. The differences between the two types of companies are big, with service companies much better equipped than distribution companies.

A study carried out by Occurrence – see www.syntec-rp.com – on behalf of UDA and Syntec-RP, in 1999, provides us with some of the characteristics of French public relations practices. The term "public relations" as referred to in the survey encompasses all forms of organisational communication, whether of a commercial character or otherwise. The study reveals that the communication practices deemed to be the most important are:
– Trade communication (commercial, brand, etc.) (70%).
– Institutional communication (60%)
– Press relations (53%)
– Internal communication (33%)

Crisis communications gets only 7 per cent, "public affairs" 4 per cent. The most commonly used practices are:
– Press relations (97%)
– Institutional communication (91%)
– Internal communication (89%)
– Trade communication (commercial, brand, etc.) (88%)
– Strategic consultancy (71%)
– Patronage-sponsoring (64%)
– Public affairs (64%)
– Studies and audits (60%)
– Financial communication (57%)
– Crisis communication (52%)

Of those surveyed, 97 per cent said that they evaluate their communications operations, even though 40 per cent do not allocate any specific budget to this.

A comparison made in this study, using figures for Europe and the US,[4] showed that France still largely manages its communications operations internally (35 per cent of all communications operations), compared with 16 per cent for the whole of Europe and 9 per cent for the United States. Apart from this, the survey also shows that internal communication has been practised much more in France than in other parts of the world: it is at third place, compared with thirteenth and fourteenth places for the US and the whole of Europe, respectively. Brand and product communication are also practised much more in France than any-

4. Source: International Association of Public Relations Professionals.

where else. On the other hand, crisis communication, which is very popular in the US (third place) and in Europe (fifth place), is only at eleventh place in France.

3.4. The professional press and professional associations

The professional press in the field of communications occupations is fairly dynamic. Not counting purely marketing-orientated media, it includes:
– Weeklies. For instance, *CB News* and *Stratégies*, orientated towards the communication economy, advertising communication and agency consultancy; see www.toutsurlacom.com.
– Monthlies, some of which are more or less general: *Faits de Sociétés*, *L'expression d'entreprise*; and others are specialized: *L'évènementiel*, *Culture Pub.*
– Quarterly specialist literature such as *L'actualité du Mécénat* and other on-line literature, sometimes daily; see www.admical.asso.fr.

We should also mention here a weekly television programme on the M6 channel, entitled *Culture Pub* (see www.m6.fr), which this year celebrates its fifteenth anniversary. It concerns advertising and presents thematic documentaries and news.

The corporate/economic press also frequently carry articles about communication.

There are many professional associations, both national and regional ones, some promoting an activity or occupation, others dealing with public communication or communication in the private or non-profit sector.

3.5. The perception of the occupation of organisational communicator by professionals

In May 2002, a qualitative-type perception study of communications occupations was conducted (Cornand et al. 2002), using semi-directive interviews, among thirty-six Aquitaine communicators from the public, private and non-profit sectors.

On the basis of several observations (Carayol 1992), the variety of structures, titles and positions of the departments in the organisations could be charted. Even today, many interviewees deplore the lack of recognition of their occupation in their hierarchy and their weak involvement in the organisation's strategic orientations. The majority of interviewees think that there are several roles to be played in communication, such as: "I'm a conductor" or "I'm a director". The most interesting results relate to the variations in the conception of the role of communicators as a function of the sector in which they work.

Communicators who work in the private sector define themselves more as operational technicians, in the sense that they often implement instructions and use practices to obtain concrete results for the company. The technicians are confined to results based on a target that is predefined by management. Typical comments are "I'm a technician – I implement the boss's instructions" and "You have to be familiar with technology so as not to make mistakes".

Despite the technical dimension of the role, it is preferable, according to the technicians, not to be in total opposition to the organisation's values. Support is justified by ethical and efficiency considerations: you have to believe in the message or the product in order to be convincing.

Communicators working for the social and non-profit economy consider that they mainly have a mediator role. They are liaison agents between the various actors and can be classified as informer or teacher. Typical comments here are "I'm the interface between the members of the association, but also the membrane allowing passage from the inside to the outside and vice versa" and "You have to listen to the people you work with internally so as to improve communications between them". The implication for the project and the organisation's values is very marked and is regarded as indispensable. As two interviewees put it, "I'm 200 per cent in favour", and "It must be love at first sight".

In the public sector there appears to be a mosaic of roles, ranging from mediator to technician via strategic expert. The technical nature here relates to abilities in terms of tools. In his role of mediator, the communicator sees him- or herself as a link and a disseminator of information. The strategic experts, who remain the prominent figure, describe themselves as a communication consultant who casts a critical look at the work done and makes suggestions on future operations. Some sample comments are "We bring some competence and some value added to the institution" and "My role as strategist is primarily one of assistance and advice".

An implication is claimed for the values of "public service" and the "collective good", which are considered politically neutral. Elements can be found here that were already revealed in another study (Carayol,

Mignot and Versel 1998); that is, a certain denial of influence and power, a willingness to stand back in relation to the communication messages, and the claim to be serving a mission rather than an organisation. On the other hand, an absence of training missions in the technical sense of the term is noted, something which applies to the three sectors. Concern for society does not appear to be a major preoccupation of the people surveyed, except in the private sector, where it is seen in a consumerist perspective; a response to the needs of future consumers. Concern for technology, on the other hand, is common to all sectors.

Outside the sector of activity, the conception of the occupation also seems to vary according to seniority and level of qualification. People with less than ten years' experience and with a university education in communications expressed their willingness to widen their sphere of action. They wish to be a force of proposition and to become strategists in their organisation; they more often claim a status that could be compared with that of an engineer. Typical comments are "We are perceived too often as mediators, but that's not really my job – communication is a true strategic position" and "I'm a coherence producer".

If this image of the communicator is more dominant in the public sector, it is also because people have more often had an education in communication. Conversely, people who have been employed for a long time do not express this claim for a strategic role.

The results of this qualitative study obviously indicate only some tendencies, discernible among a sample of average structures, and should be confirmed in a more extensive study, possibly of a quantitative type. The same study among large companies would probably have given different results, since the debate about the strategic role of communication is quite dominant in the professional press and among professionals in large structures.

4. Conclusion: state of the art and future of public relations in France

The image of communication professionals in France seems to follow a pendulum motion. It was fairly poor at the start of the development of public relations, since the abbreviation "PR" were soon translated "public rubbish". The development of public relations to the "Communication Director" model seems to have marked a positive change initially. The 1980s saw flamboyant communication officers flourish, holding enthusiastic debates about the company's image and attempting to reconcile trade and civic logic, particularly through ambitious politics of patronage. Communication thus helps the company to shine and to increase its fame and visibility. Some professionals have almost achieved guru status to certain company managers.

In the 1990s, laws and regulations introduced to "moralise" the advertising professions, raised doubts about the virtues of the communications environment. Subjected to criticism and hit by the repercussions of the economic crisis, the professionals developed deontological charts and a debate about corporate citizenship. This has manifested itself in policies that closely combine internal and external communication and in renewed attention to questions of social and environmental responsibility. The practices and debates have become more modest, and the consumers have been subjected to greater attention with the emergence of consumer clubs, whose aim is to make them more loyal, and customer relations departments to deal with their suggestions. The listening, contact and interactivity debate has become dominant.

The image of the communication occupations varies. Suspicion seems to be recurrent. Communications practices are the object of frequent debates, particularly between communicators and journalists, who maintain passionate relations. During the major electoral ballots, communications practices are the object of virulent criticism and are embellished with every possible evil. The present prime minister of France, Jean Pierre Raffarin, used to work in communication. He is now targeted by many cartoonists and humorists – a sign of the ambiguous status of these professions.

References

APACOM (Association des Professionnels Aquitains de la communication) (2001). Allo la com'?. *La lettre de l'APACOM*, Special issue [Survey of 300 enterprises and associations].

Arzeno-Martin, Hélène (2001). Qualités et compétences: des offres d'emploi pour expliquer un métier [Qualities and competences: Employment offers to explain a trade]. *La lettre de l'APACOM*. Special edition, p. 8.

Bernard, Françoise (1998). La communication organisationnelle, parcours vers une légitimité scientifique [Organisational communication: Towards a scientific légitimity]. Dissertation, University of Aix Marseille.

Boiry, A. Philippe (1989). *Les relations publiques ou la stratégie de la confiance* [Public Relations or the Strategy of Confidence]. Paris: Eyrolles.

Brillet, Frederic (1992). École de communication: le trop plein [School of communication: an abundance]. *Stratégies* 791.

Calin, Anna Maria and Iacobescu Aurore (2002). *Historique des relations publiques en France* [History of public relations in France]. MS, University Michel de Montaigne.

Carayol, Valérie (1992). Les structures de communication [Communication structures]. *Communication & Organisation* 2: 122–141.

Carayol, Valérie, Olivier Laügt and Martine Versel (2002). Une analyse de discours des chercheurs francophones en communication organisationnelle [A speech analysis of the french-speaking researchers in organisational communication]. In: F. Bernard (ed.), *Les recherches en communications organisationnelles. Quels concepts? Quelles théories?* [Research in organisational communication. Which concepts? Which theories?]. Rennes: Presses Universitaires de Rennes.

Carayol, Valérie, Marie Pascale Mignot and Martine Versel (1998). *Voyage au cœur de la communication locale: dix ans de programme de Cap'Com soumis à une analyse de discours* [Travel to the heart of local communication: Ten years of Cap'Com programs through a speech analysis]. MS, Cap'Com.

Cavallier, Marcel Paul (1992). *Vingt ans de communication d'entreprise* [Twenty Years of Business Communication]. Nancy: Presses Universitaires Nancy

CECCOPOP (Centre d'études Comparées en Communication Politique et Publique) (1997). Communicateurs publics, quels statuts, quelles carrières? [Public relationists: Which statutes? Which careers]. *Communication Publique* 45.

Chapuis, Muriel (2001). Communication évènementielle: la belle reprise de 2000. *L'évènementiel* 100.

Cornand Stella, Charlotte Guitton, E. Leroy, J. Maillard, M. Riboullet and D. Vanderperre (2002). Perception des métiers de la communication par les communicants [Perception of communication occupations by professionals]. Dissertation, Université Michel de Montaigne.

d'Almeida, Nicole (2001). *Les promesses de la communication* [The Communication Promises]. Paris: PUF.

Deveze, Jean (1998). La communication d'entreprises face au choc des réalités; légitimité et légitimation par les discours des professionnels [Business communication facing the shock of reality; légitimacy and légitimation through the speeches of the professionals]. In: C. le Moenne (ed.), *Communications d'entreprises et d'organisation* [Communication of Businesses and Organisations]. Rennes: Presse Universitaires de Rennes.

Floris, Bernard (1996). *La communication managériale: la modernisation symbolique* [Management Communication: The Symbolic Modernisation]. Grenoble: Presse Universitaires de Grenoble.

Moenne, Christian le (1994). Étudier les communications d'entreprises: problèmes et problématiques. [Studying business communications: Problems and problematics]. Dissertation, University of Grenoble.

Moenne, Christian le (ed.) (1998). *Communications d'entreprises et d'organisations* [Communication of businesses and organisations]. Rennes: Presse Universitaires de Rennes.

Linon, Jean P. (1967). Les relations publiques [Public relations]. *Humanisme et Entreprise* 41.

Lougovoy, Constantin and Huisman Denis (1981). *Traité des relations publiques* [A Course in Public Relations]. Paris: PUF.

Mattelart, Armand (1990). *La publicité* [Advertising]. Paris: La Découverte.

Miege, Bernard (1989). *La société conquise par la communication* [Society conquered by communication]. Grenoble: PUG.

Tixier-Guichard Robert and Chaize Daniel (1993). *Les dircom* [The communication managers]. Paris: Seuil.

TMO Consultants (1989). Les responsables de la communication locale parlent de leur métier [local communication professionals talk about their trade]. *Le Monde*, 26 Sept. 1989.

Union des Annonceur 2000 Baromètre UDA sur la communication d'entreprise: enquête 2000. See www.uda.fr.

Walter, Jacques (1995). *Directeur de la communication* [Communication director]. Paris: L'harmattan.

Chapter 10

Germany[1]

Günter Bentele and Ivonne Junghänel

1. National profile

1.1. Overview of national characteristics

The Federal Republic of Germany, with an area of 356,790 sq. km and nearly 82 million inhabitants, is the country with the largest population in Central Europe. The national territory is bordered to the north by the North Sea, the Baltic Sea and Denmark, to the East by Poland and the Czech Republic, to the South by Austria and Switzerland, and to the West by France, Belgium, Luxembourg and the Netherlands. Germany is a federal nation with sixteen "Länder" (individual states). About 7.3 million foreigners live in Germany, which is 9 per cent of the total population. There is freedom of religion. In 2000, the protestant and catholic churches each counted about 27 million members; the next largest religious community is the Muslims with approximately 2.8 million members.

The media system in Germany divides into the privately owned print market and the broadcasting market – essentially, the latter is nowadays a "dual" market, consisting of private and public sectors. The basic types of print medium are daily newspapers, weekly newspapers, magazines and free newspapers (Noelle-Neumann, Schulz and Wilke 2000: 382, 398–412). Due to the technical development of cable and satellite, the point of a technically limited distribution of television and radio programs, i.e. a limited number of channels, became obsolete in the 1970s. Private broadcasting was introduced in the 1980s (Stuiber 1998). Public and private broadcasting are subject to different legal regulations. Public broadcasting has to serve public welfare and guarantee the basic programmes (information, sports, entertainment, culture). It has a central integrating function since it articulates the interests of minor-

---

1. This chapter is partly based on a chapter by Stefan Wehmeier in Bentele and Wehmeier (2003).

ities and encourages interaction between different interest spheres
(Hesse 1999: 115 ff.). For that reason, public broadcasting carries out a
strict internal pluralistic concept: every program has to reflect the actual diversity of the society. Private broadcasting, on the other hand,
since it depends on income from advertising, faces less high constitutional demands. As an indirect consequence of economic competition,
the concession of private broadcasting activities is expected to result in
an increasing diversity of offerings and thus in more choices for the radio and television user. This demand for a minimum variety of TV
channels is met when at least three channels that cover all general interests are distributed all over Germany by at least three different provid-
ers/owners. Besides the dual broadcasting system, and as compensation
for the concession of large private providers, some provisions for "citizens' broadcasting" have been made. Citizens are allowed to produce
their own radio and television programs for these "open channels", and
they can also publish printed products. They are responsible for their
activities, but they can ask the *Land* media institutions for technical
support. However, due to the low quality of these programs, they are
not very popular.

An exact monitoring system enables the measurement of how people
use the media. On average, people use the media for up to 8.5 hours a
day. Of this use, radio accounts for 41 per cent (3.4 hours), television for
37 per cent (circa 3 hours). Public stations mainly meet the need for information, whereas private television is preferred for entertainment. In East
Germany, people watch 30 minutes more than in West Germany – the
former also watch more entertainment programs. About 40 per cent of the
total population use the internet for at least 13 minutes a day. Every
week day, 80 per cent of the Germans spend 30 minutes reading the
newspaper (*Media Perspektiven* 3/2001: 102; 4/2001: 162). In 2001, there
were 136 "media units" in Germany – a media unit is an independent
complete editorial office, with a politics department and all the other editorial departments. This amounts to 386 daily newspapers with 28.4 million copies sold. Adding local and regional editions the number rises up
to nearly 1,600 newspapers. On top of that, there are 23 weeklies (circulation 1.9 million), 845 popular magazines (circulation 129.7), and 1,094
professional journals (circulation 18 million) (*Media Perspektiven* 2001:
45). Most daily newspapers are sold through subscriptions; seven street-
selling newspapers (a total of 43 editions) account for a total circulation
of 5.7 million copies. Among these, *Bild* is the biggest street-selling newspaper with 4.2 million copies.

1.2. Facts and figures about public relations in Germany

Though the present state of the profession in Germany has been discussed in a number of empirical studies (Becher 1996; Böckelmann 1988, 1991a, 1991b, 1991c; Merten 1997b; Röttger 2000; Wienand 2002; Zühlsdorf 2002), a *representative* study that covers the entire field in Germany does not yet exist.

The total number of full-time public relations practitioners in Germany is estimated to be at least 20,000. Around 40 per cent work with a company, 20 per cent in organisations such as associations, unions, churches, etc., and another 20–30 per cent in different social and political institutions (such as political and municipal administration and courts). Approximately 20 per cent of the public relations practitioners work in public relations agencies (Fuhrberg 1998). The number of public relations practitioners is increasing more quickly than the number of journalists.

As to the level of organisation, only an estimated 10 per cent of all public relations professionals (around 1,800) are members of the DPRG (German PR Association), which was founded in Bonn in 1958. The number of organised public relations practitioners in the German Journalists Association – most of who work in press departments – is estimated to be 4,000.

In 1973, the leading public relations agencies founded their own association (*Gesellschaft PR-Agenturen*, GPRA; 'Association of PR Agencies'). At present it counts as members about thirty public relations agencies, representing nearly 1,500 employees. It is difficult to give a detailed overview of the entire public relations counseling market in Germany. This applies both to the produced turnover and to the actual number of consultancy firms and employed public relations consultants. Many agencies and individual consultants offer public relations services, yet they act under the name of other professions (such as advertising agencies, management consultants, free-lance journalist). In addition, the open access to the profession and the high fluctuation rate make an exact count of public relations consultants and agencies even more difficult. Though the GPRA, DPRG and the Stamm publishing house evaluate data on the state of the German agency field every year, the information varies because of different criteria and indicators (Fuhrberg 1998). The prognosis of *PR Report* (2001: 5) says that in 2001, the top 100 German public relations consultant agencies employed about 3,460 permanent employees and had a turnover of fees of approximately € 351 million. The biggest German PR agency (ECC KothesKlewes) had a staff of 364 employees in 2001 and returned a profit of more than € 37 million (*PR-Report* 2001: 5).

After adding the data of the employees of smaller agencies and the data of all registered individual consultants, we estimate that there are nearly 5,000 public relations practitioners in public relations agencies.

The degree of professionalisation of this branch, which is strongly interconnected with the training facilities, has been increasing since the beginning of the 1990s. In general, the public relations profession is academically institutionalised: 70 – 80 per cent of the public relations practitioners have a degree (from a university or a polytechnic) or even a Ph.D. (Becher 1996; Merten 1997a, b). Though these data show an increasing general education level of public relations practitioners, they do not say anything about the actual degree of professionalisation – that is, the existence of a PR-related academic education. Only about 15 per cent of public relations practitioners have a PR-related education and training (such as public relations courses or majors) (Röttger 2000: 317).

Where do public relations practitioners come from? Public relations is still very much an "open" field, a profession for practitioners with backgrounds in such diverse professions as journalism, law, and engineering. This is shown by a 1989 survey of DPRG members as well as by a more recent study by Becher (1996). Both studies showed that a third of all interviewed persons originally came from journalism, another third came from business or administration, and about 15 per cent had previously worked in advertising and market research. Interestingly, about 20 per cent had had no other occupation before entering public relations (Becher 1996: 194; DPRG: 1990).

Finally, "feminisation" is a feature that developed into a distinct characteristic of the German public relations field. Whereas in the late 1980s less than 15 per cent of the people working in PR in businesses, administration, and associations were female (Böckelmann 1988, 1991a, 1991b), Merten (1997a, b) showed that by 1996, women accounted for 42 per cent of the work force. This is confirmed not only by the present proportion of females among the members of the professional association DPRG (43 per cent in 2001), but also the proportion of female students of public relations reached more than 60 per cent.

2.   History and development of public relations

2.1. Roots and developments of public relations practice

The development of public relations in Germany has always been shaped by political, economic and social conditions. In this context, the changing types of state had a decisive impact on the history of German PR: the German Alliance (1815–1866) as an alliance of states of German princes and free cities was succeeded by the German Reich (1871–1918) and the Weimar Republic (1918–1933), followed by the national-socialist dictatorship of the Third Reich, and eventually the establishment of two German states, which reunited in 1990. These turning points in the history of Germany are reflected in the attempts to structure the history of German public relations into periods.

A scientific German PR historiography is just emerging. However, there are already some models of dividing history in some periods (Avenarius 2000; Bentele 1997), some case studies (Binder 1983; Döring 1997; Wolbring 2000; Zipfel 1997), an effort of an overview of German PR history until 1933 (Kunczik 1997) and a volume reflecting on PR-historiography (Szyszka 1997).

Bentele distinguishes six periods of German public relations history (Bentele 1997). The first period is called "development of the profession". It starts in the middle of the nineteenth century and ends at the close of the first World War in 1918. The development of the first press offices in politics and economy as well as in communities (Magdeburg's first municipal press office was established in 1906, for example), associations and organisations, originated in this period. The first political press department was established in 1841 in Prussia; it was called *Ministerial-Zeitungsbüro* ('governmental bureau of newspapers'). Alfred Krupp, founder of the steel company Krupp, established the first press department in a private company in 1870 – Krupp had been aware of the necessity to hire a "literate" since 1866. The duty of this "literate" was to read all newspapers that were considered important to the firm and at the same time to write articles, brochures and "correspondences" in order to advertise products and the firm as a whole (Wolbring 2000). It was probably in this period that the first standard tools of press relations emerged, such as media relations, arranged interviews, press conferences and press reviews. A characteristic feature of this first period is that public relations was used both to inform and to manipulate.

The second period, which covers Weimar Republic (1918–1933), can be described as a phase of consolidation and growth. It is characterised by new social conditions: the parliamentary-democratic of state and an economically independent and active press, no longer directed or controlled by the state. This new freedom led public relations to experience an immense growth in different social realms; for example, many communal press departments were established. Due to the economic boom of the "Golden Twenties", more and more firms recognised the necessity and the use of public relations (Kunczik 1997: 166, 290).

After the national-socialists came to power, the conditions of public relations changed abruptly. In sharp contrast with the Weimar period, the media were now controlled and manipulated by the party. This period lasted about twelve years, from the end of the Weimar Republic to the end of the second Word War (1933–1945).

The fourth period in the history of German public relations can be called "revival", and starts with the end of the Second World War. Not only did public relations had to redefine itself under the new conditions of a parliamentary democracy, it also had to dissociate itself from (Nazi) propaganda. The US influence on West German society was widely felt in the development of post-war public relations: besides new German advertising and public relations agencies, branches of US agencies started to settle in Germany. From today's point of view it is interesting that the twelve years of Nazi dictatorship had not only cut off all staff-related connections to press relations activities of the Weimar Republic but also all relations to the pre-nazi public relations literature, i.e. to the literature of reflecting public relations practitioners: all the literature of the Weimar republic remained unknown until the beginning of the nineties.

The year 1958, when the German Public Relations Association (DPRG) was founded, can be seen as the beginning of the fifth period, which can be described as "consolidation of the field". Conferences, discussion groups and the foundation of the DPRG further encouraged the discourse about the self-understanding of the occupational field and enabled a systematic dialogue about relevant questions of PR as well as about training activities.

At the same time, a "socialist public relations" developed in (then) East Germany from the mid-1960s. There was an occupational field of public relations, which according to practitioners involved about 3,000 people. As in (then) West Germany, public relations was conducted in all social fields, but socialist public relations in East Germany was constrained by strong political-propagandistic regulations. However, it was a professional field clearly distinct from journalism, advertising and pure political propaganda.

In the mid-1980s, the boom in public relations and the beginning of its professionalisation mark the sixth period in the development of German public relations (1985 until today). Public relations agencies developed very fast and gained more and more relevance, especially when compared with advertising agencies. The public relations departments in private companies and other organisations grew in size and relevance, and research in public relations established itself in several universities.

Pre-history: Official press politics, "functional" public relations, development of instruments

Period 1 (mid-19th century–1918) Development of the occupational field	Development of the first press offices in politics and firms; war press release under condition of censorship
Period 2 (1918–1933) Consolidation and growth	Fast and wide spread of press offices in different social fields: economy, politics, municipal administration
Period 3 (1933–1945) Media relations and political propaganda under the Nazi Regime	Media relations and journalism controlled by the nationalist-socialist party
Period 4 (1945–1958) New beginning and upturn	Post-war development; upturn and orientation to the American model starting in the early 1950s; development of a new professional identity under the conditions of democratic structures (PR defined as distinct from propaganda and advertisement); rapid development of the professional field, predominantly in the economic sphere
Period 5 (1958–1985) Consolidation of the professional field in West Germany and establishment of "socialist public relations" in East Germany	West Germany: development of a professional identity; foundation of the professional association DPRG (*Deutsche Public Relations Gesellschaft* 'German Public Relations Association'); this association initiated private training programs. East Germany: "socialist public relations", dominated by the SED, developed in the mid-1960s
Period 6 (1985 until today) Boom of the professional field, professionalisation	Strong development of PR agencies, professionalisation of the field, beginning and development of academic PR-education; improvements in the training system; scientific application and enhancement of PR-instruments; development of PR as a science

Figure 1. Periods in German public relations upturn (*Source*: Bentele 1997: 161)

2.2. Development of education and research traditions

While public relations can draw on a gradually evolved history, good education in public relations and research in public relations are in their infancy. Though young, research can be divided into two main areas: basic research and applied research (Bentele 1999). Basic research is mostly pure or purpose-free research conducted in university settings. Examples are theory-building, historiography and meta-research – that is, the generation, testing, and perfection of general basic findings about a specific field. There are two different types of theory within the field of theory-generation: middle-range PR theories and general theories. Most theoretical approaches to PR belong to the group of middle-range theories. For example, Baerns (1985) conceived the Determination Hypothesis, and Bentele, Liebert and Seeling (1997) developed their intereffication approach. Both mark the beginning of a theoretical research tradition with many empirical studies (Bentele 2002). To this group of theories can be added Burkart's (1992) consensus-oriented public relations approach and Bentele's (1994) theory of public trust and his Discrepancy Hypothesis. On the other hand, so far there is only one systematic and comprehensive German general public relations theory – it goes back to Ronneberger and Rühl (1992). Basic research can also be taken to include the research that deals with the systematic description of the public relations of individual organisations, branches, and social realms, as well as with aspects of public relations education and training, professionalisation processes and ethical problems.

In contrast, applied research – which on the whole is privately financed – docs not aim to extend general knowledge about public relations, but to solve concrete practical questions and problems. Applied research in public relations uses general social-science methods such as polls, content and media resonance analyses, communicator and audience research; it is typically performed by universities, but also by specialised service providers such as market-research firms and public relations agencies; and it is sometimes also carried out by businesses themselves.

For a long time, public relations training in Germany was "training on the job". In the 1960s and 1970s, the DPRG and some private institutions (such as the *Akademie der Führungskräfte* in Bad Homburg ['Academy of management staff']) offered the only training and advanced courses. These course took one or several weeks. Only since the early 1980s was public relations institutionalised at universities and polytechnics (*Fachhochschulen*) as a marginal field of communication studies programs. For example, the universities of Erlangen-Nürnberg, Hohenheim, Bamberg, Berlin, Bochum and Munich offered seminars on PR-related topics. A decade later, in the early 1990s, a development boom started to improve significantly the situation of public relations and public relations training. By now several German universities established public relations courses within their communication-studies programs (Berlin and Leipzig, for instance). Furthermore, there have been some PR degree schemes (B. A. programs and schemes which can be finished with a German "diploma degree") at polytechnics and universities since 1999 (Hannover, Osnabrück, Leipzig, for example). Several universities plan to establish public relations courses, too. Equally important, the professional associations established a training and examination academy (*Deutsche Akademie für Public Relations* ['German Academy of Public Relations'], DAPR) in 1991, and there are some forty other private academies and institutes which offer PR training courses as well as further education courses of different character (evening schools, distance-learning courses, etc.). However, in the near future, public relations training will shift more and more to the traditional education institutions (polytechnics and universities) (Bentele and Szyszka 1997; Brauer 1996; von Schlippe, Martini and Schulze-Fürstenow 1998).

The content of academic training programs and of many general courses offered by private institutions is very diverse. They cover the entire spectrum of the profession: the basics of communications and public relations, history of public relations, public relations theories, methods and tools of practical public relations, and several aspects of communication management (such as media relations, investor relations, event management, internal communication, crisis public relations, methods of evaluation, methods of empirical communication research and social research). Economic, legal and ethical topics are included in most courses at universities and sometimes also at private academies. As to literature, many titles exist in practitioner's literature (how-to-do-literature). Practitioners wrote it for practitioners. Besides this type of literature, the body of scientific literature has been growing since the beginning of the 1990s (Bentele 1999); it often deals with problems of the occupational field, to public relations techniques, public relations tools and problems of organisational communication. Both types of research are brought together in the journal *PR-Forum* and on the internet at www.pr-guide.de/.

2.3. How language shaped the development of public relations

Towards the end of nineteenth century, public relations practitioners were usually called 'literates' (*Literaten*), press departments were called "literary bureaus" or "press bureaus", the work itself was called *Pressearbeit* ('work for the press'). Albert Oeckl proclaimed to have come up with the translation of the term into *Öffentlichkeitsarbeit* (work for the public sphere) in 1950 or 1951. However, some research, conducted in Leipzig (Döring 1997; Liebert 1997) showed that this term had been used as early as in 1917 by August Hinderer, an important protestant journalist, who tried to refer to some broader type of communicative practice which had more than just the press as its main public.

In 1937 or 1938, during the Nazi period, Carl Hundhausen, the grand old man of German public relations, introduced the American term "public relations" in Germany (Hundhausen 1951: 24; Nessmann 1995: 9). Today, both terms are used. Taking into account that for some years now the German language has been strongly anglicised, the term "public relations" (or PR as the short form) is considered to be more modern and progressive, particularly by the younger generation. Economists and PR-consultants also prefer the English term, whereas political organisations, municipal administrations, and associations more often apply the term *Öffentlichkeitsarbeit*. Terms such as "information" or "communication" (as in "corporate communication") are also frequently mixed with public relations. For some years now, "communication management" has been used more and more to refer to a special type of PR – namely, PR with high professional standards – or to refer to public relations in general. The reasons for this development could be that the term "PR" is often connected with slightly negative connotations.

3. Typification of current public relations

3.1. Status and position of public relations in businesses, administration and society

Public relations associations and academics claim for themselves the highest possible hierarchical ranking of public relations practitioners within the organisation they work for. Becher (1996: 175) found that 41 per cent of her interviewees worked in independent departments, which were rated as below the management department. Another 22 per cent worked in departments that were part of the organisation's management (for example, the head of public relations is a member of the board). In Merten's (1997a, b) survey, 68 per cent of the interviewees said they held a "leading position". In his representative survey among businesses from 1993, Haedrich found that 26 per cent of all companies ranked PR as a line position, 71 per cent as a staff position. Of these companies, 33 per cent graded public relations as top level in the corporate hierarchy, 54 per cent into the second highest level – that is, directly under the executive level – 12 per cent into the third level, and 1 per cent graded public relations even lower (Haedrich, et al. 1994: 4). The same study also found that the bigger a business was the more independent the PR departments were, in some cases they were even higher in the hierarchy than the marketing department. At the same time it is evident that the subordination of public relations under marketing or at least the mixing of these two is more apparent in small and medium-sized firms. A follow-up survey in 1997 carried out by the wbpr agency interviewed 3,000 businesses and showed that the rating of PR within businesses has improved since the first study of 1990. Public relations had a "very high" rank for 16 per cent of the interviewees and a "high" rank for 56 per cent (wbpr 1997: 9). A recent representative survey among companies (Zühlsdorf 2002) indicated that 80 per cent of the heads of communication departments work on the top hierarchical level. These results show that public relations departments in German businesses are rated relatively highly.

The differentiation of public relations roles – investigated in American studies and in the Delphi study (Ruler et al. 2000: 20) does not play a big role in Germany. Wienand (2002: 361) argues that the managerial and technician public relations roles do not easily carry over to the German situation. Based on our own knowledge of the field, we assume that in larger organisations both the managerial and the technician roles exist. The heads of public relations departments and the senior consultants in the public relations agencies have managerial roles whereas the employees of the public relations departments have technician roles. Getting ahead in an organisation is normally combined with a change of role. The "reflective" and "educational" dimensions (Ruler et al. 2000) should be understood as dimensions of the managerial role.

But there are other concepts, which refer to the different ways public relations practitioners, see themselves. An empirical study conducted by Bökkelmann differentiates the following three professional roles: representative (of the organisation), journalist (oriented to the public sphere) and mediator (between organisation and publics) (Böckelmann 1988: 54, 1991a: 66, 1991b: 80).

The image of the public relations field varies considerably. The wider public has a rather diffuse image – if at all – of public relations and can hardly perceive it directly. Media representatives and journalists often have an ambivalent image of public relations: they recognize that public relations is indispensable as a source of information, but at the same time they often use such characterizations as "PR gags", "PR pretence", "typical PR". These expressions refer to events which are considered overstated and lacking content. In contrast, communication experts are treated by journalists as partners, colleagues "on the other side of the desk". Especially in company boardrooms, the image of the communication expert has significantly improved over the last two decades. While in the 1960s heads of public relations departments were still called *Frühstücksdirektor* (someone who has a directors' position but only dines with guests) in order to disparage the public relations profession, today the necessity of professional communication management is mainly unquestioned and public relations has established itself as an independent organisational function.

4. Conclusions: state of the art and future of public relations in Germany

As with social, technical and media-related developments, the requirements for the occupational field of public relations change continuously. New trends and practices of public relations emerge all the time, of which we name only these: about five years ago, numerous businesses (amongst those were young start-up firms, but also slowly developed corporations) entered the stock market, which led to a boom. As a result, investor relations especially, as part of financial relations, experienced an immense upturn (Hansen 2000; Kirchhoff and Piwinger 2001; Rolke and Wolff 2000). Additionally, issues management (Röttger 2001), crisis communication, employee relations and event public relations gained more and more relevance for practical PR activities (and PR research). New trends at bigger public relations agencies are, for example, "change communication", "sustainability communication", "brand PR", "corporate citizenship", and "impression management" (Bentele, Piwinger and Schönborn 2001). Another hot issue is corporate communication (and public relations as its part), understood as an element of the process of corporate value creation.

Some characteristics of public relations are typical for Germany. Among these we can mention the process of professionalisation – including scientifically based PR education and an emerging PR science – and the on-going feminisation. Ethical problems are discussed in the scientific community – much more seldom in the practical field. But there was a case during the summer of 2002 (the "Hunzinger case" through which the ministry of defense, Rudolf Scharping had been dismissed by chancellor Gerhard Schröder because Scharping was suspected to have taken some advantages for his own interest from the lobbyist Moritz Hunzinger) through which ethical questions of public relations ("What is Lobbying?"; "To what extent is 'contact management', aimed at bringing politicians and business together, unethical?") were widely discussed in all media.

As a last trend, we return to the different situations in the eastern and western parts of the country. Public relations in the eastern part of Germany – thirteen years after the opening of its borders – is not as developed as in the western part, which is largely due to economic reasons. In addition, there are only small public relations agencies in the eastern part that, in order to survive, have to offer additional services – typically, advertising services. In that sense the situation has not changed much since the mid 1990s (Bentele and Peter 1996).

References

Avenarius, Horst (2000). *Public Relations: Die Grundform der gesellschaftlichen Kommunikation* [Public Relations: The basic form of social communication]. Darmstadt: Wissenschaftliche Buchgesellschaft. (2nd edn.)

Baerns, Barbara (1985). *Öffentlichkeitsarbeit oder Journalismus: Zum Einfluß im Mediensystem* [Public relations or journalism: On the influence in the media system]. Köln: Wissenschaft und Politik.

Becher, Martina (1996). *Moral in der PR? Eine empirische Studie zu ethischen Problemen im Berufsfeld Öffentlichkeitsarbeit* [Moral in public relations? An empirical study on ethical problems in the field of PR]. Berlin: Vistas.

Bentele, Günter (1994). Öffentliches Vertrauen: Normative und soziale Grundlage für Public Relations [Public trust: normative and social basis for public relations]. In: Armbrecht, Wolfgang and Ulf Zabel (eds.), *Normative Aspekte der Public Relation: Grundlagen und Perspektiven. Eine Einführung,* 131–158. [Normative aspects of public relations: Basics and perspectives. An Introduction]. Opladen: Westdeutscher Verlag.

Bentele, Günter (1997). PR-Historiographie und funktional–integrative Schichtung: Ein neuer Ansatz zur PR-Geschichtsschreibung [PR historiography and functional–integral stratification: A new approach to PR historiography]. In: Peter Szyszka (ed.), *Auf der Suche nach Identität: PR-Geschichte als Theoriebaustein,* 137–169. [The quest for identity: PR history as theoretical constituent]. Berlin: Vistas.

Bentele, Günter (1999). Public relations research and public relations science in Germany: An overview. In: Hans-Bernd Brosius and Christina Holtz-Bacha (eds.), *The German Communication Yearbook*. 181–210. New York: Hampton.

Bentele, Günter (2002). Parasitism or Symbiosis? The inter-effication model under discussion. In: Sari Eskelinen, Terhi Saranen and Tetti Tuhkio (eds.), *Spanning the boundaries of Communication*. 13–29. Dept. of Communication, University of Jyväskylä.

Bentele, Günter and Grazyna-Maria Peter (1996). Public relations in the German Democratic Republic and the New Federal German states. In: Hugh M. Culbertson and Ni Chen (eds.), *International Public Relations: A Comparative Analyses*. 349–350. Mahwah, New Jersey: Lawrence Erlbaum Associates.

Bentele, Günter, Tobias Liebert and Stefan Seeling (1997). Von der Determination zur Intereffikation: Ein integriertes Modell zum Verhältnis von Public Relations und Journalismus. [From determination to inter-effication: An integrated model of the relationship between public relations and journalism.] In: Günter Bentele and Michael Haller (eds.), *Aktuelle Entstehung von Öffentlichkeit: Akteure, Strukturen, Veränderungen*, 225–250. [Current development of public. Actors, structures, changes.] Konstanz: UVK Medien.

Bentele, Günter and Peter Szyszka (eds.) (1997). *PR-Ausbildung in Deutschland*. [PR education in Germany.] Opladen: Westdeutscher Verlag.

Bentele, Günter, Manfred Piwinger and Gregor Schönborn (eds.) (2001). *Handbuch Kommunikationsmanagement: Strategien, Wissen, Lösungen*. [Handbook of communication management: Strategies, Knowledge, Solutions]. Neuwied: Luchterhand.

Bentele, Günter and Stefan Wehmeier (2003). From "literary bureaus" to a modern profession: The Development and Current Structure of Public Relations in Germany. In: in Sriramesh, Krishnamurthy and Dejan Vercic (eds.) (2003). The Global Public Relations Handbook: Theory, Research, and Practice 199–221. Inc. Mahwah, N.J.: Lawrence Erlbaum Associates.

Binder, Elisabeth (1983). *Die Entstehung unternehmerischer Public Relations in der Bundesrepublik Deutschland* [The development of businesslike public relations in the Federal Republic of Germany]. Münster: Lit.

Böckelmann, Frank E. (1988). *Pressestellen in der Wirtschaft*. (Pressestellen I) [Press offices in the economy. Press offices I]. Berlin: Spiess.

Böckelmann, Frank E. (1991a). *Die Pressearbeit der Organisationen* (Pressestellen II) [Press offices in organisations. Press offices II]. München: Ölschläger.

Böckelmann, Frank E. (1991b). *Pressestellen der Öffentlichen Hand*. (Pressestellen III) [Press offices in public organisations. Press offices III]. Berlin: Ölschläger.

Böckelmann, Frank E. (1991c). Pressestellen als journalistisches Tätigkcitsfeld [PR offices as a field of activity for journalists]. In: Johanna Dorer and Klaus Lojka (eds.), *Öffentlichkeitsarbeit: Theoretische Ansätze, empirische Befunde und Berufspraxis der Public Relations*, 170–184. [Public Relations. Theoretical Approaches, Empirical Findings and Practice of Public Relations]. Wien: Braumüller.

Brauer, Gernot (1996). *Wege in die Öffentlichkeitsarbeit. Einstieg, Einordnung, Einkommen in PR-Berufen*. [Roads into Public Relations: Entrance, Fitting in, Income]. Konstanz: UVK Medien.

Burkart, Roland (1992). *Public Relations als Konfliktmanagement: Ein Konzept für verständigungsorientierte Öffentlichkeitsarbeit. Untersucht am Beispiel der Planung von Sonderabfalldeponien in Niederösterreich* [Public Relations as Conflict Management: A Concept of Consensus-Oriented Public Relations. A case study about the planning of a special waste ground in Lower Austria]. Wien: Braumüller.

Döring, Ulrike (1997). Öffentlichkeitsarbeit der evangelischen Kirche in Deutschland: Eine Bestandsaufnahme. Historische Entwicklung, theologische und kommunikationspolitische Determinanten sowie kritische Analyse berufsfeldbezogener Verständnisse und Tätigkeitsmuster [The Public Relations of the protestant church in Germany: An account of the present situation. Historical development, theological and communication-political determination and a critical analysis of professional understandings and activity patterns]. Ph.D. dissertation. Leipzig: Institut für Kommunikations- und Medienwissenschaft.

DPRG (1990). *Auswertung der DPRG-Mitgliederumfrage 1989* [Analysis of the 1989 DPRG member survey]. Bonn: DPRG.

Fuhrberg, Reinhold (1998). PR-Dienstleistungsmarkt in Deutschland [The PR service market in Germany]. In: Günter Bentele (ed.), *Berufsfeld Public Relations*. Studienband 1, 241–268. [The occupational field of Public Relations. Study guide 1]. Berlin: Kommunikation & Management.

Haedrich, Günther, Thomas Jenner, Marco Olavarria and Stephan Possekel (1994). *Aktueller Stand und Entwicklungen der Öffentlichkeitsarbeit in deutschen Unternehmen: Ergebnisse einer empirischen Untersuchung* [Current Situation and Developments of Public Relations in German Businesses: Results of an Empirical Study]. Berlin: Institut für Marketing, Lehrstuhl für Konsumgüter- und Dienstleistungs-Marketing.

Hansen, Jürgen Rolf (2000). *Professionelles Investor-Relations-Management* [Professional Investor Relations management]. Landsberg a. Lech: Verlag moderne Industrie.

Hesse, Albrecht (1999). *Rundfunkrecht* [Broadcasting law]. (2nd edn.) München: Vahlen.

Hundhausen, Carl (1951). *Werbung um öffentliches Vertrauen* [Advertising for public trust]. Essen: Girardet.

Kirchhoff, Rainer and Manfred Piwinger (eds.) (2001). *Die Praxis der Investor Relations: effiziente Kommunikation zwischen Unternehmen und Kapitalmarkt* [Practical Investor Relations: Efficient Communication Between Businesses and Capital Market]. (2nd edn.) Kriftel: Luchterhand.

Kunczik, Michael (1997). *Geschichte der Öffentlichkeitsarbeit in Deutschland* [History of Public Relations in Germany]. Köln: Böhlau.

Liebert, Tobias (1997). Über einige inhaltliche und methodische Probleme einer PR-Geschichtsschreibung [On some content-related and methodical problems of PR historiography]. In Peter Szyszka (ed.), *Auf der Suche nach Identität: PR-Geschichte als Theoriebaustein*, 79–99. [The quest for identity: PR history as theoretical constituent]. Berlin: Vistas.

Media Perspektiven (2001). *Basisdaten: Daten zur Mediensituation in Deutschland 2001* [Basic data: Data on the media situation in Germany in 2001]. Frankfurt/Main.

Media Perspektiven (3/2001), Frankfurt/Main.

Media Perspektiven (4/2001), Frankfurt/Main.

Merten, Klaus (1997a). Das Berufsbild von PR: Anforderungsprofile und Trends. Ergebnisse einer Studie [The image of PR: Requirements and trends. Results of a survey]. In: Günther Schulze-Fürstenow and Bernd-Jürgen Martini (eds.), *Handbuch PR: Öffentlichkeitsarbeit in Wirtschaft, Verbänden, Behörden*, 1–23. [Handbook of PR: Public Relations in Business, Associations, Administration]. Neuwied: Luchterhand.

Merten, Klaus (1997b). PR als Beruf: Anforderungsprofile und Trends für die PR-Ausbildung. [PR as a profession: Demands and trends in PR education]. *PR-magazin* 1: 43–50.

Nessmann, Karl (1995): *The Origins and Development of Public Relations in Germany and Austria. Second International Public Relations Research Symposium*. Beld, Slovenia, 6–9 July.

Noelle-Neumann, Elisabeth, Winfried Schulz and Jürgen Wilke (2000). *Fischer Lexikon. Publizistik, Massenkommunikation* [Fischer Encyclopedia. Publicity and mass communication]. (6th edn.) Frankfurt/Main: Fischer.

PR-Report (2001). *Ende des Booms, Anfang der Zukunft.* [End of the boom, start of the future]. *PR Report* 1808: 4–7.

Rolke, Lothar and Volker Wolff (eds.) (2000). *Finanzkommunikation: Kurspflege durch Meinungspflege. Die neuen Spielregeln am Aktienmarkt* [Financial Communication: The Care for Quotations as Care for Opinions. New rules for the stock market]. Frankfurt/ Main: FAZ-Institut für Management-, Markt- und Medieninformation.

Ronneberger, Franz and Manfred Rühl (1992*). Theorie der Public Relations: Ein Entwurf.* [A theory of Public Relations. A draft.] Opladen: Westdeutscher Verlag.

Röttger, Ulrike (2000). *Public Relations: Organisation und Profession. Öffentlichkeitsarbeit als Organisationfunktion. Eine Berufsfeldstudie* [Public Relations: Organisation and Profession. Public Relations as Organisational Function. A Field Study]. Wiesbaden: Westdeutscher Verlag.

Röttger, Ulrike (ed.) (2001). *Issue Mangagement: Theoretische Konzepte und praktische Umsetzung. Eine Bestandsaufnahme* [Issue Management: Theoretical Concepts and their Translation into Practice. An account of the Present Situation]. Opladen: Westdeutscher Verlag.

van Ruler, Betteke, Dejan Verčič, Gerhard Buetschi and Bertil Flodin (2000). European body of knowledge on public relations: communication management. Report of the Delphi Research Project 2000. European Association for Public Relations Education and Research. Ljubliana.

von Schlippe, Bettina, Bernhard-Jürgen Martini and Günther Schulze-Fürstenow (eds.) (1998). *Arbeitsplatz PR. Einstieg, Berufsbilder, Perspektiven*, 187–216. [Public Relations: Start, Career, Perspectives]. Neuwied: Kriftel.

Stuiber, Heinz-Werner (1998). *Medien in Deutschland*, Vol. 2: *Rundfunk.* [The media in Germany, Vol. 2: Broadcasting]. Konstanz: UKV Medien.

Szyszka Peter (ed.) (1997). *Auf der Suche nach Identität: PR-Geschichte als Theoriebaustein* [The Quest for Identity: PR History as Theoretical Constituent]. Berlin: Vistas.

wbpr (1997). *Wo ist der Schlüssel? Zweite Untersuchung zur unternehmensspezifischen Bedeutung von Public Relations. Eine Untersuchung der wbpr Gesellschaft für Public Relations und Marketing GmbH in Zusammenarbeit mit dem LUMIS-Institut der Universität-GH Siegen und dem Wirtschaftsmagazin Capital* [Where is the Key? Second Survey on the Specific Meaning of Public Relations in Business. A survey by the PR company wbpr in co-operation with the LUMIS institute at the University Siegen and the *Capital* business magazine]. München and Potsdam: wbpr.

Wienand, Edith (2002). Public Relations als Beruf: kritische Analyse eines aufstrebenden Kommunikationsberufs. [Public relations as a profession: a critical analysis of a rising area]. Unpublished Ph.D. unpublished dissertation, Münster.

Wolbring, Bettina (2000). *Krupp und die Öffentlichkeit im 19. Jahrhundert* [Krupp and the public in the 19th century]. München: C. H. Beck.

Zipfel, Astrid (1997). *Public Relations in der Elektroindustrie: Die Firmen Siemens und AEG 1847 bis 1939* [Public Relations in the Electronics Industry: Siemens and AEG between 1847 and 1939]. Köln: Böhlau.

Zühlsdorf, Anke (2002). *Gesellschaftsorientierte Public Relations: Eine strukturationstheoretische Analyse der Interaktion von Unternehmen und kritischer Öffentlichkeit* [Society-oriented Public Relations: A structural-theoretical analysis of the interaction between business and the public]. Wiesbaden: Westdeutscher Verlag.

Chapter 11

Greece

Prodromos Yannas[1]

1. National profile

1.1. Profile of the country

Public relations emerged in Greece in the early 1950s. At that time, Greece was recovering from the ravages of World War II and of the civil war that ensued and was ready to embark on a capitalist/liberal-democratic form of development. From its inception, public relations practice in Greece was constrained by the relative small size of the national market, approximately 10 million inhabitants, and the structural characteristic of the economy which was made up mainly by family-owned and -operated small- and medium-size enterprises. In the 1950s and 1960s, small enterprises concentrated on production and did not pay too much attention to promotion, marketing or public relations techniques. The first practitioners of public relations in Greece worked either as independent consultants or as employees of large private or state enterprises. Beginning in the 1970s, there has been a marked increase in the share, both in absolute and relative terms, of the tertiary-service sector to the national economy. An indication of the rise of the service sector is the fast growth of the advertising industry, which was given a boost with the entry of affiliates of foreign companies in the 1980s and 1990s.

1.2. Facts and figures about public relations in Greece

Global trends in the marketing of product and services, the consolidation of democratic rule in Greece since 1974, the integration of the

---

1. The author would like to thank public relations professionals Rita Malikouti and Christiana Pirasmaki, as well as Professor George Panigyrakis, for their helpful comments and suggestions on earlier versions of this chapter. Needless to say, the responsibility for omissions and shortcomings is his own.

Greek economy with the rest of Europe through the country's membership of the European Union (EU) since 1981 and the affiliation of Greek-based firms with multinational companies – all these have had a profound impact on the practice of public relations. The most significant development has been the emergence of firms, independently operated or affiliated with advertising agencies, which exclusively focus on public relations. The "home base" for public relations is no longer the advertising agency but the public relations agency. Currently, more than thirteen public relations agencies have grouped together to form the Hellenic Public Relations Consultancies Association. It is estimated that approximately 1,500 professionals make up the human capital of the public relations industry. Most of the industry is concentrated in the capital city, Athens, and to a much lesser extent in the second largest city, Thessaloniki, in the Macedonian region of northern Greece. Of a total 146 public relations agencies and public relations consultants operating in Greece, 120 (82 per cent) are located in Athens, 20 (14 per cent) in Thessaloniki and six (4 per cent) in the major cities of Patras, Larissa and Heraclio of Crete (Guide of Public Relations 2001–2: 111–120). In addition, there are public relations practitioners employed by firms, non-governmental organisations (NGOs) and the public sector. There are no reliable figures on the number of people employed by NGOs and the public sector. In the business world, large firms under Greek or foreign ownership with more than 150 employees each, maintain an in-house public relations department (Panigyrakis and Ventoura 2001: 65–66).

The people employed by the industry differ in terms of their professional experience and educational background. A good number of them possess prior experience in the advertising industry or in the media. A significant number of people have worked for the marketing, sales or publicity departments of companies or organisations and have gradually developed an expertise in public relations. In terms of their educational background, the picture is much more blurred. In the last ten years, a number of young professionals have acquired postgraduate degrees in public relations, corporate communication management or marketing management from abroad and have returned to Greece to staff public relations consultancies. According to Rita Malikouti, a PR professional with many years of experience, "the new generation of public relations people has an excellent educational background. What is missing in the industry are well-qualified middle- and senior-level staff". Most of the professionals have a university degree in the social sciences, the humanities or in business administration and supplement their skills with training-seminars provided either in-house or by various institutes – such as the Institute of Public Relations – and organisations. There is also a segment of the PR community with no formal higher education that has managed to acquire skills through on-the-job training, seminars, etc.

The research that Panigyrakis and his associates conducted in 1998–1999 on the Greek public relations scene brings to light for the first time important information depicting the personal, educational and professional profile of the Greek PR practitioners (Panigyrakis and Veloutsou 1998; Panigyrakis and Ventoura 2001). Looking at the personal characteristics among a sample of 180 public relations officers working for industry, the researchers found that in terms of gender, females (66.7 per cent) outnumber males (33.3 per cent) by 2 to 1 in PR positions in firms operating in Greece. As far as age is concerned, most of the practitioners fall within the 41–45 age group (27.8 per cent) followed by the 31–35 age group (22.2 per cent). The most appropriate age for entry into the profession seems to be between 26 and 30, signaling that a prospective applicant for a public relations position must neither be too young nor without some business experience. As to educational background, an equal number of public relations officers hold university (41.2 per cent) and postgraduate degrees (41.2 per cent) with only a minority (17.6 per cent) holding post-secondary degrees. In terms of previous professional experience, the overwhelming majority (66.7 per cent) has six or more years of experience in the field, with the remaining ranging from four to five years (20 per cent) to two and three years (13.3 per cent).

2. History and developments of public relations

2.1. Roots of public relations

The issue of the origins of public relations in Greece is a question of debate among long-time practitioners. According to some accounts (Papamichalakis 1996: 105; Magliveras 1997: 41) the planning for the first public relations activity in Greece was conceived in 1947 and implemented in 1951. The activity revolved around festivities and events celebrating the 1900th anniversary of the coming of St Paul, the Apostle, to Greece. The principal organisers were the Greek Orthodox Church, the Greek state and the theological seminaries of the Universities of Athens and Thessaloniki, respectively. According to other accounts (Koutoupis 1992: 23–24; Mantas and Koutroumanos 1992: 25) public relations activity in Greece originated in 1951 with the public call for a Public relations program funded by the American Mission for Aid to Greece for the benefit of the Hellenic Tourist Organisation. In 1952, Eric Williams of the Foote Cone & Belding agency of the United Kingdom came to Greece to implement the first public relations campaign for the Hellenic Tourist Organisation. Whether public relations was home grown, so to speak, or was implanted from abroad is of no particular importance. What *is* important is the fact that the public relations concept was quickly adopted in the Greek context with transfer of know-how from abroad. The first company to implement public relations programs was Izola, an electrical manufacturing company, in 1952. Izola's example was taken up by a number of large private Greek firms (Piraeki Patraiki, Titan Cement) and foreign-owned firms, as well as by government agencies and state enterprises in the 1950s. The implementation of public relations programs by foreign giants – such as Shell, Mobil and BP in petroleum products, Philips in electrical appliances, American Express in banking and by Greek companies such as Commercial Bank, Public Power Corporation, Olympic Airways and the Hellenic Telecommunications Organisation – was crucial in providing strong foundations and building up support for public relations activities.

2.2. Development of public relations practice

The days when public relations was a one-shop operation run as a family-owned business are long gone. Public relations in Greece has been on an upward slope in the past twenty years and this positive trend is not likely to be reversed in the near future. Currently, public relations practice has reached the stage of adulthood, characterised by increased professionalism. On the supply side, specialised public relations consultancies and public relations experts offer public relations services. With professionalism, the range of public relations services has been widened to incorporate new developments in technology, such as the use of the internet in internal, external and crisis communications and new areas of expertise, as for instance sponsoring and public affairs/political marketing. On the demand side, increasingly, companies and organisations have begun to realise the value of public relations and have made it an integral part of their communication strategy (Panigyrakis 2001).

2.3. Development of education and research tradition

Formal education has lagged behind practice in the field of public relations but in the last few years great strides have been made in the direction of course offerings and in developing public relations as a distinct area of study and research. In 1999, the first academic department that exclusively focused on public relations was established in Greece at the Technological Educational Institution (TEI) of Western Macedonia. Before 1999, public universities and TEIs, comprising the higher education sector in Greece, were offering introductory courses or more specialised courses in public relations, without however granting degrees. In the business-oriented universities, the Athens University of Economics and Business and the University of Macedonia, and in the business schools of the TEIs courses in public relations were introduced in mid 1980s. The establishment of Communication and Media Departments in the early 1990s in Panteion University, Athens University and the University of Thessaloniki increased course offerings in public relations. As of now, there does not exist a postgraduate degree in public relations in the Greek higher education system, but there are good prospects that a program leading to a Master's degree will be established in the near future at the Athens University of Economics and Business by George Panigyrakis and his research team.

It is evident that public relations education in Greece has evolved both from a business and a communication perspective. It yet remains unclear what effects, if any, this two-headed evolution will have on the future direction of the field. In terms of research, it will be interesting to see whether key research questions will be addressed from a business perspective or whether a more sociological route is taken. It is still too early to pass a judgement since the scientific field is in its infancy and is struggling at the moment to form a distinct identity. What is certain, though, is that institutional considerations do and will play a role in the creation of the public relations body of knowledge that will be produced.

2.4. How language shapes the development of public relations

Practitioners and academics think of the term "public relations" in similar ways. Both groups emphasise the management function in public relations for the purpose of establishing and maintaining mutual understanding between an organisation and its public. The adoption of the

British Institute's definition of public relations fits very well with the professional role that Greek public relations practitioners want to craft for themselves as managers developing and implementing strategies rather than as technicians performing various tasks. Although the majority of professionals in the field identify themselves as public relations officers, some prefer to be called communication or corporate communication officers. On the part of Greek academics, this Anglo-American understanding of public relations has gone unchallenged. Partly this is due to the foreign import of ideas and partly it reflects the lack of a serious research tradition in Greece up until very recently.

It is worth, however, pondering on the meaning of the term in Greek. If public relations is taken to mean 'relations with the public(s)', then one is struck to realise that the term used for 'public(s)' in Greek (*koino, koina*) is different from the term 'public' (*demosies*) used to characterise relations. The 'public' in "public relations" shares the same Greek base (*demos*) with such terms as "publicity", "public international law", "public interest", "public administration", "public affairs" and "public sector". The term "public" as in 'target group(s)" or "audience" shares the Greek base (*koino*), which means what is common among people, with words such as "public opinion", "society" and "social worker". One way to make sense of the two different roots is to think that they correspond to the two attributes that Arendt (1958: 50–58) ascribes to the term "public" in an effort to distinguish the public from the private realm. The base *demos* comes closer to the public performance in the Ancient Greek city-state and to the modern conception that everything that is seen and heard warrants publicity. The word base *koino*, on the other hand, denotes Arendt's second attribute of "public", namely, the gathering of everybody, in relation and in separation to one another. This second dimension is related to the emergence of the social realm in modernity. It may be no accident that all modern Greek words that begin with the base *koino* acquire in English translation the Latin base *soci*, meaning 'associate'. This dual meaning of the term "public" in Greek may be the starting point of shifting away from an organisation-based perspective of public relations and opening up the space of contested issues, relations and identities among entities that constitute today's civil society. In this sense, the Greek word bases provide additional support to the claim of the initiators of the EBOK (European Body of Knowledge) Project, who underline that "what distinguishes the public relations manager when he sits down at a table with other managers is that he brings to the table a special concern for broader societal issues and approaches to any problem with a concern for implications of organisational behavior towards and in the public sphere" (Verčič et al. 2001: 382).

3. Typification of current public relations

3.1. Status of public relations in business, administration and society

In the past twenty years, public relations has grown professionally in Greece, both in quantitative and qualitative terms. Professional associations have been formed, a good number of qualified public relations professionals with advanced degrees have returned to Greece to take up key positions in many sectors of the economy and new degree programs have been created at the higher education level. Notwithstanding these considerable gains, public relations is still considered the poor cousin of advertising. In monetary terms, the advertising budgets of firms are in many cases ten times bigger than the budgets allocated to public relations programs. In terms of creating value for the firm a number of large firms appreciate the role of public relations. The same is the case with the community of communication professionals, who have begun to acknowledge the valuable role of public relations in promotional activities. A lot of groundwork will have to be done in education, where professors need to instil upon students the view that public relations is not a subdivision of marketing.

3.2. Major roles in public relations and typical tasks

An empirical study conducted early in 1999 by Centrum Research – on behalf of the Hellenic Public Relations Consultancies Association – may provide clues regarding the four dimensions the EBOK project has identified for European PR: managerial, operational, reflective and educational (Ruler and Verčič 2002: 14). The findings of the study (*To Vima* 1999: D16), drawn from a sample of 203 firms, clearly support the prevalence of the operational dimension among firms of up to twenty employees and of the managerial dimension among firms which employ more than forty persons. Small-size firms, which adopt the operational dimension, employ public relations technicians who see their role as building personal contacts with customers (37 per cent of the sample). Larger-size firms with over forty employees ascribe to a more managerial view of public relations, placing emphasis on the promotion of the company's name, products and services (24 per cent of the sample). Large firms also share the managerial dimension and multinationals that assign to their public relations departments the task of formulating the company's image and identity (24 per cent of the sample). The educational dimension is practiced by a limited number of large firms that offer training seminars to their employees. The reflective dimension is, in my view, quite underdeveloped and the questioning of dominant values and practices is only very recently beginning to emerge as firms confront issues of social responsibility.

Public relations consultancies in Greece distinguish job titles in public relations in the following rank order:
- Managing Director or General Manager
- Group Account Director
- Account Director
- Senior Account Manager
- Account Manager
- Senior Account Executive
- Account Executive
- Junior Account Executive
- Trainee

On-the-job experience seems to be the decisive factor that public relations staff working for public relations consultancies must have in order to climb the professional ladder.

3.3. Position of public relations in non-profit and profit organisations

The non-profit sector in Greece includes approximately 1,040 organisations, excluding government departments and agencies (Elefterotypia 2001). This figure represents the entire spectrum of philanthropic and non-governmental organisations, foundations, trade unions, chambers of industry and commerce, church-related organisations, civil not-for-profit institutions and local chapters of international NGOs. Although the figure of over 1,000 organisations may look impressive, one should bear in mind that only an estimated 300–400 organisations remain truly active. The Hellenic Ministry of Foreign Affairs has enlisted approximately 200 NGOs, focusing in the area of international cooperation and development. Other major areas of concern for NGOs in Greece relate to the environment, human rights, rights of women and children and health-related issues.

The lack of the profit motive, the provision of a public service and the dependence on fundraising are some characteristics that differentiate NGOs and the non-profit sector from for-profit businesses. In soliciting funds and in bringing their message across to various audiences, NGOs engage in various public relations activities such as lobbying, planning and executing information campaigns and event management.

Unlike in businesses, public relations tasks in the NGO sector of Greece are not carried by in-house public relations professionals, but by volunteers. Reliance on volunteer work may form an integral part of the philosophy of the organisation and it may even spare the organisation from spending much-needed funds. However, volunteer work cannot be a substitute for the work undertaken by public relations professionals. Officials in NGOs must realise the critical role of public relations in promoting the mission of the organisation and in fundraising. NGOs which are recipients of EU funds have in the past ten years began to appreciate the added value of seeking professional public relations counsel and have on a number of occasions engaged the services of independent public relations professionals and consultancies.

3.4. Current state of education and character of major textbooks

Public relations education in Greece varies in quality and duration and is offered by a number of providers. At the level of higher education, academic education in public relations is provided by public universities, technological education institutions and by private colleges. A number of private colleges operating in Athens and Thessaloniki offer academic programs in collaboration with foreign – mostly English – universities. However, their degrees are not recognised by the Greek government due to an article of the Greek Constitution, which stipulates the public and free-of-charge character of higher education. Be that as it may, it should be acknowledged that a private college named "Eurocentre" was the first institution to offer a program of studies in public relations in 1988 (Koutoupis 1992: 26).

In the public sector, the only academic program at undergraduate level that focuses exclusively on public relations is offered by the Department of Public Relations and Communication of the Technological Educational

Institution (TEI) of Western Macedonia in the city of Kastoria, in northern Greece. The above-mentioned department started operating in September 1999 and since then, more than 1,000 students have enrolled and are attending studies in public relations. Public relations education is also provided by other public universities and TEIs in the broader context of either communication or business administration studies. PR has been offered as an academic concentration in the Communication and Media Departments of Panteion University in Athens, of Athens University and of the University of Thessaloniki. Public relations has also been featured as a concentration of the business-administration programs of the Athens University of Economics and Business, the University of Macedonia in Thessaloniki and of the TEIs of Athens and Thessaloniki, respectively. At graduate level, a public relations concentration has been included and is available to students enrolled at the Masters of Business Administration (MBAs) programmes of the University of Macedonia and the Athens University of Economics and Business respectively.

At the level of training, public relations education is provided in the form of courses, seminars and lectures by a number of institutes, associations and companies. The Hellenic Society of Public Relations ran a two-year program in public relations for a number of years (from the late 1980s to the mid 1990s). The Institute of Public Relations, which was founded in January 1999 in Athens, offers seminars, organises conferences and produces educational material in the field of public relations for its members, the public relations community at large. Centres of professional training, firms or organisations such as the American–Hellenic Union offer introductory courses in public relations intended for people seeking entry-level positions.

Turning to textbooks, the Greek market is replete with introductory books that have been written with a lay audience in mind. Most textbooks cover the same terrain, with topics dealing with the public relations concept, public relations publics, ethics and public relations, development and execution of public relations programs, market research and media relations. Moreover, depending on training and expertise of the author, introductory books may include a number of chapters on special areas of practice (sponsorship, crisis management, internal relations, investor relations, government relations and lobbying, etc.). Greek authors write the majority of introductory textbooks but a good number of American and English textbooks have been translated in Greek (Magnissalis 2002; Jefkins 1994). In university and TEI courses, instructors are more inclined to use books written by Greek academics, who may hold advanced degrees in marketing, sociology or international relations but have professed a keen interest in public relations (Arnaoutoglou and Douroudakis 1999; Piperopoulos 1999; Panigyrakis and Ventoura 2001). Even though these books are addressed to an academic audience, they tend to dwell upon practical issues to the detriment of theoretical concerns. For example, none of the books mentioned discusses the four public relations models (press agentry/publicity, public information, two-way asymmetric and two-way symmetric models) and their relevance to the Greek setting.

3.5. Best selling practical books

Magliveras (1997) has been among the first public relations consultants who collected, classified and analysed material pertaining to public relations. His book, which addresses theoretical as well as practical questions, was first published in 1971 and is currently in its tenth edition. Also going through the tenth edition is an introductory book written by public relations educator and researcher, Magnissalis (2002). Another widely used popular book, with a plethora of tips on "how to" practical questions, was written by a well-respected public relations consultant (Koutoupis 1992). In this book one encounters an insider's view of the profession, its evolution, problems and prospects, as well as a discussion, followed by interesting tips on how to organise events, deal with the media and conduct public relations activities for various economic sectors (such as industry, tourism, government relations).

3.6. The local scene of public relations

Public relations practitioners can become members of a number of professional associations. The Hellenic Society of Public Relations was founded in 1960 and numbers over 250 members (Koutoupis 1992: 27). Over the years, the Society has organised a number of lectures and conferences on special and current issues. According to the definition of the Hellenic Society, public relations is "a social calling of two-way communication, which – following research and investigation of the objective elements of the given environment and the accurate information of the interlocutors – attempts, through free dialogue, to present the true image of one another in order to accomplish in a climate of mutual understanding the development of their relations on the basis of mutual interest" (Baskin, Aronoff and Lattimore 2001: 22).

Public relations practitioners who operate out of Thessaloniki are likely to be members of the Society of Public Relations of Northern Greece. The Society was founded in 1972 and in the past five years has been particularly active organising an equivalent number of annual symposia, bringing together practitioners, academics and students. In March 2000, a third professional association was founded by 42 members in Athens, under the name "Association of Communication and Public Relations Officers".

A number of well-qualified public relations professionals have managed to become members of the International Public Relations Association (IPRA). Currently, eighteen members comprise the National Chapter that is chaired by Christiana Pirasmaki, the Greek National Coordinator since 1999. Manos Pavlidis, the doyen of Greek public relations, has served as President and Honorary Secretary of IPRA for the periods 1973–1976 and 1964–1970, respectively. Another Greek professional who has served as an officer of IPRA is Marcel Yoel, in the position of Honorary Treasurer for the period 1964–1970.

In 1996, the leading seven Greek public relations consultancies decided to establish the Hellenic Public Relations Consultancies Association. In a very short period of time, six more consultancies joined the seven founding members. The Association functioned as an independent entity up until June 2001, when its member-consultancies transferred their allegiance to the newly formed Association of Advertising and Communication Agencies. During its short-lived history, the Hellenic Public Relations Consultancies Association managed to draft a code of professional practice, laid the foundations for the establishment of the Institute of Public Relations, participated in the International Committee of the Public Relations Consultancies Association and organised two international conferences in Athens. The first conference, held in April 1999, assessed the state of public relations in various areas of practice while the second conference, held in May 2001, focused on sponsorship and sponsoring.

Since June 2001, the Greek public relations agencies comprise the Public Relations section of the Association of Advertising and Communication Agencies. This new Association is an outgrowth of the Association of Advertising Agencies, which had been in existence for more than fifty years. Throughout the year 2000 the Association of Advertising Agencies amended its by-laws, in order to enlarge its membership and expand its scope to encompass all aspects of communication. The transformation was completed in June 2001. Twelve out of the thirteen consultancies of the Hellenic Public Relations Consultancies Association joined as a whole the new association. Nine out of the twelve public relations consultancies that make up the public relations section of the new association collaborate closely or are affiliated with advertising agencies. Besides the public relations section, the Association of Advertising and Communication Agencies maintains an advertising section with forty-six agencies, a media units section with nine member agencies and a sales promotion and direct marketing section with nine members. Affiliated with the Association of Advertising and Communication Agencies is the Institute of Communication, a not for profit institution, which was set up in November 2002 in order to engage in training, develop a resource-information centre and promote research on communication issues including public relations.

According to figures made available by the public relations section of the Association of Advertising and Communication Agencies (*Marketing Week* 2002), the twelve PR agencies employed 137 staff and offered their services to 242 clients in 2000. The comparable figures for 2001 raise the number of staff to 160 and the number of clients to 291. This quanti tative increase is underestimated, considering that one agency did not submit figures for 2001. Based on the 2001 figures, a Greek public relations agency has on average about 14.5 employees and 26.5 clients. It should however be pointed out that the market for public relations services is much larger than these figures seem to suggest. To get a comprehensive picture of the Greek public relations scene, one should take into account the additional forty agencies that provide public relations services which are not members of the newly formed Association, as well as the work of approximately thirty independent public relations consultants and many public relations officers who staff in-house departments of firms and/or organisations (Chaimanda 2002: 26).

3.7. Hot issues in Greek public relations

Technological, economic, political and cultural developments do play a role in defining what issues are important at a given point in time. Internet public relations is certainly an area that a lot of public relations agencies, firms and organisations monitor. Many agencies are exploring the applications of Internet public relations in internal communication, in crisis communication, in publicity and two-way communication between a company and its clients. Another area which seems to be getting the attention of companies is crisis management or – to be more to the point – crisis prevention. Large companies increasingly realise that a well-functioning public relations department is a prerequisite to crisis prevention and to the effective handling of the crisis once it erupts (Gortzis 2002: 10). Financial and investor public relations is a specialty sector that a number of public relations agencies developed in the mid to late 1990s – a period marked by mergers and acquisitions and a considerable boom in the Greek stock exchange. Entering the twenty-first century, financial and investor relations have suffered from three consecutive years of downturn of the Greek stock exchange. Sponsoring-sponsorship is a speciality that has been given a boost by the hosting of the 2004 Olympic Games in Athens. A number of large Greek firms either have been named "grand sponsors" – for example, the Hellenic Telecommunications Organisation (OTE) and Alpha Bank – or have become sponsors as formal supporters and formal suppliers along designated product and service categories – that is, milk and dairy products, the beer, car, and energy sectors, airlines, insurance, maritime shipping, etc. Of course, the Olympic Games and the many artistic events scheduled to take place in the context of the Cultural Olympiad, spanning a period of at least two years, offer public relations agencies and public relations consultants ample opportunities in the areas of sponsoring planning and implementation and event management. Finally, large firms, Greek as well as multinational, pay more and more attention to issues of corporate social responsibility and corporate reputation. In the year 2000, sixteen large firms and industry associations formed the Hellenic Business Network for Social Cohesion. Within the public relations community, agencies, departments and consultants have also begun to pursue this area of specialty. Moreover, beginning in 2001, Tradelink Reputation Management, a private company, in collaboration with the Reputation Management Institute of Greece have developed and began estimating the reputation quotient of a number of large Greek-based firms.

4. Conclusions: state of the art and future of public relations in Greece

Public relations in Greece has undergone considerable changes in the last twenty years. There has been a marked trend towards professionalism and an appreciation of the value of public relations both in the private and in the non-profit sectors of the economy. The increased professionalism is evidenced in the emergence of public relations consultancies, the increased share of public relations activities in the communication mix of businesses and organisations and the entrance of qualified new public relations experts in the field. The trend towards professionalism is aided significantly by the development of degree programs focusing partly or exclusively on public relations at the level of Greek higher education. Large businesses in the consumer goods industry and the services sector consider public relations activities absolutely essential to their reputation and future growth and integrate them within their overall strategy. Small- and medium-size enterprises are slower in understanding the added value of public relations. In this regard, there is reason for optimism as managers become more familiar with the work of public relations experts and more convinced of the effectiveness of public relations activities. NGOs have also engaged in partnership with public relations consultancies and independent public relations experts in order to carry out fundraising tasks and meet communication objectives specified by their governing bodies or their funding agencies and organisations.

Last, but not least, interviews with public relations professionals reveal two areas of development for public relations: the public sector and the potential provided by the expansion of business activities in the Balkan region. The EU funds allocated to Greece – as part of the three successive community support-frameworks – have had a beneficial impact on the perception and value of public relations held by officials in the public sector. Government agencies administering EU funded projects have turned to public relations consultancies for carrying out publicity and other communication tasks. Indicative of this trend is the involvement of public relations consultancies in project work for various Greek Ministries and in all phases of the Euro-awareness campaign. In the foreseeable future, Greece will continue to be a recipient of EU funds and the public sector will be in constant need of professional public relations services. The second growth area concerns the expansion of Greek-originated business activities in the Balkan region. In the post-communist period, Greek businesses have seized the opportunity to trade and/or invest in the Balkan countries by taking advantage of the availability of cheap labour and low transportation costs. Along with the expansion of business activity, Greek managers have felt comfortable contracting out public relations consultancies and professionals with whom they have collaborated in Greece, in order to help them support the communication function of their new business ventures in the new environment of the Balkan countries.

References

Arendt, Hannah (1958). *The Human Condition*. Chicago/London: University of Chicago Press.

Arnaoutoglou, Elefteria and Manolis Douroudakis (1999). *Dimosies Sxesis* [Public Relations]. Athens: Interbooks Publishing Co.

Baskin Otis, Craig Aronoff and Dan Lattimore (2001). *Dimosies Sxesis: To Epagelma ke I Askisi tou* [Public Relations: The Profession and the Practice]. Athens: Papazissis Publishers.

Chaimanda, Sonia (2002). Dynamismos ke kerdoforia [Dynamism and profit-making]. *Odigos Dimosion Sxeseon 2001–2002* [Guide to Public Relations 2001–2002]. Athens: Imerissia.

Elefterotypia newspaper (2001). Anthropismos, I parigoria tou 21ou aiona [Humanism, the consolation of the 21st century]. Special issue, 17 July.

Gortzis, Antonis (2002). Se trochia anaptyxis o klados [On the path of development the field]. *Odigos Dimosion Sxeseon 2001–2002* [Guide to Public Relations 2001–2002].Athens: Imerissia.

Jefkins, Frank (1994). *Dimosies Sxesis* [Public Relations]. Athens: Klidarithmos.

Koutoupis, Thalis (1992). *Practicos Odigos Dimosion Sxeseon* [Practical Guide to Public Relations]. [3rd edition]. Athens: Galeos.

Magliveras, Denis (1997). *Public Relations* [10th edition]. Athens: Papazissis Publishers.

Magnissalis, Kostas (2002). *Dimosies Sxesis: Theoria ke Techniki ton Sxeseon me to Koino* [Public Relations: Theory and Technique of Relations with the Public]. [10th edition]. Athens: Interbooks Publications.

Mantas N. and K. Koutromanos (1992). *Isagogi stis Dimosies Sxesis* [Introduction to Public Relations]. Athens: Contemporary Publications.

Marketing Week (2002). I Katataxi ton eterion dimosion sxeseon 2001 [Classification of public relations agencies 2001]. 8 April. 2002, p. 16.

Panigyrakis George and Cleopatra Veloutsou (1998). Sex-related differences of public relations managers in consumer-goods companies in Greece and Italy. *Women in Management Review* 13–2: 72–82.

Panigyrakis, George (2001). Public relations management in the services sector in Greece. In: *Volume of Essays in Honour of Late Professor D. Kodosakis*, 811–828. Piraeus: University of Piraeus.

Panigyrakis, George and Zoi Ventoura (2001). *Sychroni Diikitiki Dimosion Sxeseon* [Contemporary Management of Public Relations]. Athens: Benou Publications.

Papamichalakis, Ioannis (1996). Ellinikes Dimosies Sxesis [Greek public relations].Deltion Ellinikis Enoseos Symvoulon Dimosion Sxeseon [*Bulletin of the Greek Association of Public Relations Consultants*] 2.

Piperopoulos, George (1999). *Epikoinono, ara Yparcho* [I Communicate, Therefore I am]. [6th edition]. Thessaloniki: Zygos Publishers.

To Vima (newspaper) (1999). Epichirisi "Dimosies Sxesis" [Operation "public relations"]. 13 June, p. D16.

Ruler Betteke van and Dejan Verčič (2002). *The Bled Manifesto on Public Relations*. Ljubljana: Pristop Communications.

Verčič, Dejan, Betteke van Ruler, Gerhard Butschi and Bertil Flodin (2001). On the definition of public relations: a European view. *Public Relations Review* 27: 373–387.

Chapter 12

Hungary

György Szondi

1. National profile

1.1. Overview of national characteristics

Hungary is located in the centre of Europe. It has a population of 10 million people and about five million Hungarians live beyond the borders. Hungarians are of Finno-Ugric origin and as a people have lived in their present-day homeland, the Danube Basin, for more than 1,000 years.

Hungary has become one of the most successful countries in its transition to a market-oriented economy following the collapse of the Berlin wall and one of forerunners for EU membership. Since 1997, economic growth has been impressive, with the Hungarian economy recording growth rates of around 4 per cent per year. GDP growth at 5.2 per cent in 2000 was the highest since the transition, mainly pushed by export growth rates of over 20 per cent. Despite the world-wide economic slowdown, Hungary's economy grew at 3.8 per cent in 2001, and at 2.9 per cent in the first quarter of 2002.

Precise information about the number of public relations practitioners in Hungary is not available. An estimated 5,000–6,000 people are working in the field but this number is based on a broad interpretation of public relations activities. The situation is further complicated by the fact that anybody can start working in public relations and anybody can claim to be a public relations expert without any prerequisites or consequences – the market is not regulated. One measure could be the membership of the Hungarian Public Relations Association (HPRA). The Association had 200 members in 1994, 435 members in 1999 and currently has 212 members. From 2002 only those who have paid their membership fee are considered members. Very little information is available about the background of the members. The only available data is that most members have a degree in higher education and 20 per cent of them live in the countryside. Public relations is concentrated in Budapest, the capital, where 90 per cent of the agencies are located.

The number of graduates majoring in public relations might be another index, but it cannot be considered reliable because not all graduates end up in the profession. Two independent pieces of research (www.btl.hu and Szondi 1999) found that the average Hungarian practitioner has been working in public relations for four years. In-house public relations departments are staffed by one or two people on average. Consultancies have an average of eight practitioners.

Because public relations departments tend to be small, there are hardly any opportunities for internal promotions. Both in-house departments and consultancies are characterised by a high turnover of practitioners.

1.2. Facts and figures of public relations in Hungary

When talking about the development and current state of the art of public relations in Eastern Europe, it must be kept in mind that each country has its unique evolution and customs, even though some countries may share some common characteristics. Reviewing studies on public relations for the region published in American and Western-European journals and periodicals (e.g. Hiebert 1992a, b; Gruban 1995; Culberston and Chen 1996; Tampere 2002), one could easily get the impression that public relations shows a homogeneous picture across Central and Eastern Europe. In contrast, studies that originated in Central or Eastern Europe – often based on a limited number of interviews, observations and opinions – cannot be generalised to the whole region. The different country reports in this book will cast light on the similarities and differences of public relations in the region and will probably also prove that these countries can boast some serious results and achievements. The dramatic changes in the political and economic systems saw public relations emerging within a few years in the region and its evolution is rather rapid comparison with Western European or American practices. After comparing the results one might ask whether Eastern European countries have their own flavour of public relations – maybe they are just followers of fashion?

2. History and developments of public relations

2.1. Traces of public relations during the communist era

If we do not accept propaganda as a form of public relations (Verčič, Grunig and Grunig 1996: 42), the roots of Hungarian public relations can be dated to the late 1960s and early 1970s, when economic reforms resulted in more openness towards Western countries. József Lipót published the first book on public relations in Hungarian in 1968, with the title *Public Relations a Gyakorlatban* ('Public Relations in Practice'). The book was soon banned, however, and no books with the words "public relations" were allowed to be published for a long time. But this did not prevent some enthusiasts from organising seminars, clubs and lectures on public relations using a Hungarian term (*közönségkapcsolatok*), which does not cover the meaning of "public relations" very well. Further political détente in the 1980s enabled the English term to re-emerge, but more as a chapter in marketing and advertising textbooks, following the marketing view of public relations. The other line of development was related to libraries as several discussions and seminars were devoted to the theoretical concepts of developing relations with the public. Even some limited campaigns were organised to make libraries more popular, which included inviting the public to the libraries to get to know each other and the functions of the libraries. It is difficult to judge to which extent these traces could be considered as a form of public relations.

2.2. Public relations emerges

The political and economic changes in 1989 enabled public relations to gain grounding in Hungary. Turning a centrally planned economy into a free-market economy in a very short period of time presented great challenges, not only for companies, but for the whole society as well. The customer entitled to freedom of choice and rights was in the centre of the evolving consumer society. Rapid privatisation was carried out, often ignoring cultural and ethical dimensions. The political process was dramatically changed by the emergence of inexperienced political parties and free elections. Civil society needed to be created.

It was this turbulent but democratic political, economic and societal environment which enabled public relations to set foot in Hungary. The first ten years of the Hungarian public relations industry were characterised by a variety of initiatives and achievements. The Hungarian Public Relations Association (HPRA) was established in December 1990 with 40 members. In 1992 public relations became a recognised profession by the Office of Central Statistics under the chapter of "Business Counselling". In the same year the HPRA developed and accepted a standardised public relations terminology. The first public relations courses at undergraduate level were launched in 1992 when the number of public relations agencies had been mushrooming.

The Foundation for Public Relations Development was established in 1995 at the initiative of HPRA. The Foundation strives for higher standards in and wider recognition for public relations by constantly modernising and developing the methods and techniques used in public relations. It has a crucial role in coordinating research in the public relations industry and in further developing public relations education. The first public relations magazine, *PRHerald* was launched in the same year.

Within the framework of IPRA's annual conference, which was held in Budapest in 1996, the first International public relations Film and Video Festival Prince Award was launched. The purpose of the festival, endorsed by IPRA and CERP, is "to maintain the dynamic development of the art and knowledge of public relations as well as providing opportunity for presenting professional PR films, videos and different types of multimedia". In 1999 the first public relations "ball" was organised by the Hungarian Public Relations Association.

Budapest hosted the first regional IPRA conference for Central and Eastern Europe in May 2002. The conference was concluded with the "Budapest Statement" on the establishment of IPRA's Central and Eastern European Regional Chapter.

HPRA issued four fundamental documents. The "Gárdony Declaration", adopted in 1993, defines the terminology of public relations, the basic principles and areas of the field. In the "Székesfehérvár Declaration", HPRA clearly defined the role and function of public relations in organisations and the different levels and the relevant responsibilities of the PR practitioners. The "Veszprém Declaration", adopted in 1995, is concerned with the relationship between marketing and public relations. The "Codes of Ethics", adopted in 2000, was based on the professional standards and ethical guidelines of IPRA and CERP. HPRA members have always regarded international relations as of high importance for the development of the practice. Several Hungarian practitioners belong to international professional organisations, sometimes fulfilling a high position.

2.3. Public relations agencies

The first public relations agency, Publicpress, was established in October 1989 and today there are some 50 agencies nationwide. The big multinational companies arriving in Hungary often brought along public relations as part of their practice. Besides the international public relations agencies – such as Burson Marsteller, Hill and Knowlton, Noguchi and Peters Communication, Sawyer Miller Group and M&H Communications – several domestic consultancies offer full public relations services to a variety of local and international clients.

The number of public relations agencies has resulted in tough competition and the last ten years have seen many consultancies flourishing and disappearing. The local branches of the international agencies were often set up and headed by professionals who had been living and working abroad. Many of them had been working as diplomats in the USA or Western Europe or had worked as commercial representatives of Hungarian companies abroad. These professionals brought along certain knowledge, as well as expertise and attitude towards public relations. At the same time, this meant that in the beginning there were only very few practitioners in agencies who could fulfil the senior-advisor role while educating a new cohort of practitioners. The public relations agencies played a significant role in educating the clients about the function and role of public relations. Much effort and time were devoted to making CEOs and in-house liaison officers realise the relevance and importance of public relations activities, as well as justifying the actions of the agency.

In 2001, ten leading consultancies founded the College of Public Relations Agencies, with the aim of safeguarding the profession and professional values. The College seeks more respect and recognition for public relations. It develops recommendations and advises the Association of Hungarian Communications Agencies, which unites advertising, marketing and public relations agencies. One of the latest issues is the copyright of creative work, ideas and proposals developed by public relations consultancies and presented to potential clients. The College has worked out guidelines on how to handle situations when a company implements proposals itself, after turning down public relations agencies.

Specialisation and integration co-exist in the Hungarian public relations industry. Although some agencies have focused on special areas – such as on-line communication, financial PR, public affairs or health communication – most agencies cannot afford to narrow down their market. A more common practice is integrated communication, initiated when marketing and advertising agencies began to set up public relations divisions or merge with public relations consultancies to satisfy clients' expectations of integrated communication. Other reasons for integration are the decreasing number of open tenders for public relations activities and the rationalisation of the public relations market and business, which is booming less than in the 1990s. The economic recession in late 2001 and early 2002 meant a turning point for most public relations agencies as the demand for public relations activities decreased.

The hard work and creativity of PR practitioners is recognised by many international awards. IPRA Golden World Award for Excellence has been awarded to Hungarian public relations programmes several times.

2.4. The development of education and research traditions

Education in public relations is characterised by numerous vocational courses at secondary and post-secondary levels and by academic undergraduate programmes. Vocational courses range from some weeks to a complete academic year; their qualities differ considerably. The first school to offer courses at this level was SKULL, School of Communication, founded in 1992. The course is designed to serve the needs of the public relations consultancies and in-house PR departments. Its focus is very much on practical aspects of public relations. The programme is endorsed and accredited by the Hungarian Public Relations Association and the content was set according to the recommendations of the Public Relations Education Trust Matrix. Public relations practitioners deliver the course in 226 lessons. Applicants must have a higher education degree or two years experience in the field of public relations. After completing the two semesters, students receive a diploma issued by the SKULL school and the Hungarian Public Relations Association. Some 600 students have so far graduated from the institution.

At academic level, the first – and so far the only – PR department was established at the College of Business and Management Studies in 1994; this department is the forerunner of public relations education in Hungary. Students at this institution graduate with a Bachelor degree in international communication, majoring in PR, and are proficient in two foreign languages. Today there are eight universities or colleges that offer undergraduate public relations courses and/or degrees schemes full-time, part-time or as a distance-learning scheme. Departments of communication or media studies host most public relations courses. Interdisciplinary studies and approaches do not have a long tradition in Hungary and still need further grounding and development. Geographically, despite the strong concentration of public relations jobs in the capital, public relations education is evenly distributed across the country.

Master-level education in public relations does not exist yet. Several MBA courses are offered both in English and Hungarian but none of them include or touch the field of public relations. There are only two people in Hungary with a Masters degree in PR (one graduated in the USA, the other in the UK) and the only Ph.D. dissertation in public relations was written by the founder of the only public relations department, Márta Németh, in 1993.

The institutions that provide public relations courses are teaching-oriented, rather than research-oriented organisations. Instructors teaching public relations courses have degrees in marketing, sociology, linguistics, law or education. Due to the lack of instructors with the relevant background and lack of time, scholars do very little systematic research. Undergraduate dissertations make up the main body of research, and the majority of these are qualitative studies using interviews, observations, and focus groups as research methods. In most cases they are case studies or develop communication plans for profit or non-profit organisations. Quantitative research methods (statistics) are hardly used in these works despite the fact that they are taught at the College for Management and Business Studies – though in fairness, this college is the only place to teach them.

Each year some 300 students graduate with a public relations degree in Hungary but the demand for public relations graduates is much lower. We could probably conclude that in Hungary there is mass education in public relations at the undergraduate level, which is not necessarily a bad thing. Although it is very difficult to find jobs in public relations as a fresh graduate, the number of people with basic understanding of the principles of public relations with positive attitudes towards the discipline is increasing in this way.

Unfortunately, there is a serious gap between practitioners' attitudes and behaviour towards education. They all acknowledge the importance of education as a way of improving the status and quality of public relations, but they seem to be critical towards the current level of education and do not participate in any further training. Several national and international training programmes have been organised but most of the courses had to be cancelled due to the lack of interest among public relations and communication practitioners. The most significant forum of further training and professional developments are probably the in-house courses and seminars of the public relations agencies, such as the Hill and Knowlton Colleges. These courses are short in duration but very focused and practice-oriented, and often take place abroad. Another popular and well-attended forum of development is the *PR Club*, organised by HPRA; however, this takes places irregularly.

2.5. Major textbooks on public relations

The number of Hungarian textbooks and other publications on public relations is extremely limited. The first textbooks were written in the early 1990s on the basis of Austrian and German publications – the reason why German books were adapted, not American or British titles, was that the authors were more likely to speak German than English and had contacts with German-speaking universities. Thus the interesting thing is that the basic theory of (American) public relations entered Hungary through the work of Austrian and German scholars, who adapted and further developed these theories. It was this "Germanised" version that appeared in Hungary and was tuned to the Hungarian market. (Hungary has always been, on the other hand, under the influence of German traditions and culture. Several research findings underpin the similarities between the German or Austrian and the Hungarian corporate cultures.)

Six books and several articles were published by Péter Szeles, who is probably the only recognised author in public relations in Hungary. Mr Szeles was elected three successive times as the president of HPRA; he is one of the founders of Hungarian public relations. His books are concerned with image and corporate identity, and concentrate on public relations techniques. These publications heavily rely on British titles, research findings as well as the IPRA Gold Papers. Theoretically and practically oriented textbooks that are comparable to the American or British basic textbooks are still to be written. The latest initiative is the so-called *Big PR Book*, which attempts to incorporate the theoretical foundations as well as the practical know-how of the Hungarian public relations practice. It is being published chapter by chapter – it will take some time to complete.

The College of Business and Management Studies is the only institution where textbooks are published; other colleges use these textbooks as they are the only ones available. The ORBICOM network supports curriculum and textbook developments. Under the leadership of Rosa Nyárády, the current Chair of Public Relations, the department participates in several projects supported by UNESCO, such as the ethical aspects of communication, media and new information technologies, and public relations in the focus of communication.

A very practical and easy-to-use English–Hungarian, Hungarian–English Public Relations Dictionary was published in 1996 by PeppeR Communication Agency, enabling better and easier translation and usage of English terminology. A few books were published on crisis communication, an area that is probably the best developed in terms of both theory and practice. Quality issues in public relations are still to be developed but the Hungarian translation of the booklet *Quality Standards in Public Relations* by Kirsten Berth and Göran Sjöberg could contribute to better results.

The publishers of the monthly public relations journal issued three booklets on public relations. The first one was concerned with the principles of crisis communication; the second provided national and international case studies. The third publication was a manual on *Who is Who in the Hungarian Public Relations?* and provides the short résumé of 340 practitioners. This initiative was well reveived by the profession despite the fact that it also includes marketing experts.

The major source of information was a monthly journal, *PRHerald*, first published in 1995 but it went bankrupt in April 2001. This publication was a popular forum for public relations practitioners, providing up-to-date information, case studies, theoretical articles about the Hungarian and foreign trends and developments. A professional publication is very much needed to fill the void. The author of this chapter has been working on the launch of a new professional journal, *Kommunikáció Menedzsment* ('Communication Management'), within the framework of a series called *Business Class*. The first issue was published in March 2003. Every fourth issue will be in English, which will enable practitioners and scholars in other countries to learn about current issues and achievements of the Hungarian public relations industry.

3. Typification of current public relations

3.1. How language shapes the development of public relations

Hungarian, together with Finnish and Estonian, belongs to the Finno-Ugric language family and thus the statement that "German and Slavonic languages cover the whole Northern, Central and Eastern Europe" (van Ruler and Verčič 2002: 4) is incorrect. Instead the variety and colourfulness of peoples and languages throughout the region is more clearly demonstrated. Hungarian public relations practitioners did not make much effort to find an adequate translation for the term "public relations", which would have been an unsuccessful and unnatural attempt. Instead they had heated debates on whether these two words should be pronounced as in English (pi: a:(r)) or as in Hungarian (pé er), and whether it should be written in lower or upper case. In the end, the Hungarian Public Relations Association ruled in favour of the Hungarian pronunciation, written in lower case. One can hardly find any publications about the Hungarian PR industry in English.

3.2. Position of public relations in organisations

The most extensive research about the public relations activities of Hungarian companies was developed by Annax International Communication Agency (http://www.btl.hu). The research was carried out in 2002 and surveyed the top-200 companies. Fifty-six per cent of these companies have a separate public relations department and the marketing or Human Resources departments manage public relations activities in the rest of the cases.

Foreign investors own nearly half of the companies surveyed. Forty-one per cent of the respondents referred to the initiatives of these investors as the main reason for engaging in public relations activities, which are often developed and controlled by the foreign headquarters of these multinational companies.

The most frequently quoted purpose of public relations was the need to enhance the reputation of the company. In the light of these attitudes it is not surprising that most companies engage in public relations to develop a better image and to generate trust towards products or services among employees and the external. In half of the companies, public relations does not contribute to developing business strategies or to the decision-making process. Public relations is brought into play when the decisions have already been made and need only to be communicated to the public (82 per cent). In most cases, public relations comes down to establishing and maintaining effective media relations (93 per cent) and to organising and managing events (86 per cent). Other areas, such as internal communication, investor relations and sponsorship, are managed under the auspices of other departments, such as the marketing department.

Seventy-seven per cent of the firms surveyed have already employed a public relations agency and 50 per cent are currently working with at least one agency. Twenty-six per cent of the respondents reported negative experiences with the services of agencies; only 17 per cent were completely satisfied. The rest of the answers included mixed experiences. More development and effort are needed in the fields of strategic communication, issues management, public relations evaluation and more effective media relations.

The surveyed companies rarely employ communication or public relations experts when they engage in lobbying – one of the most popular public relations activities in Hungary – where personal contacts and influence are being employed instead of professional strategies and techniques of public affairs.

Another extensive and empirically based research project aimed to identify the behaviour and attitudes towards evaluation of Hungarian practitioners (Szondi 1999). The study involved 68 practitioners, both in-house employees and consultants. Seventy-eight per cent of the practitioners valued the role of evaluation in public relations as important or very important, in contrast to 12 per cent who did not attribute any importance to it at all. The view that it is possible to measure effectiveness was shared by 47 per cent of respondents and a third thought it was impossible. Hungarian practitioners identified effectiveness in public relations with effectiveness at the programme level, and only one practitioner mentioned that it should be assessed in relation to organisational goals. A fifth of the respondents considered evaluation as an opportunity to justify their own work to clients or the management, a phenomenon typical of a relatively young profession. Press clippings are the most widely used method to measure output, followed by media content analysis to evaluate public relations efforts in terms of outcome. The former method was mentioned by half of the respondents, which suggests that measuring output is more important to practitioners than outcome assessment. A third of the Hungarian practitioners rated the intangible and unquantifiable aspect of evaluations as most serious, closely followed by the lack of time and that of budget.

Consultants expressed the fear that evaluation exposes them to criticism, an element that is related to accountability and requires the agency to prove the return on the client's investment. In an ex-communist country, where trust is still often absent, accountability is of great importance. It is no coincidence that one of the definitions accepted by HPRA at the beginning of the 1990s was "Public relations is the art of trust building". This is an important point, as the transition process left many people disappointed with and distrustful of politics and economic processes.

Eighty-six per cent of respondents wanted more information on how to measure and evaluate their activities systematically, and almost nine out of ten showed willingness to participate in a workshop devoted to evaluation. In a young profession where most practitioners do not have formal education in public relations, continuing professional education can be of great importance – especially if practitioners themselves show commitment.

3.3. Accreditation's vicious circle

Accreditation of public relations practitioners has always been on the agenda in Hungary, but with little success. It is considered an important step towards professionalism, which is why a proposal for an accreditation system was developed as early as 1998. The criteria for enrolment were a degree in higher education and at least five years' experience. To become an accredited practitioner, candidates were to pass written and oral examinations – overseen by an examination board – and achieve a minimum 70 per cent result. Accredited practitioners would be entitled to call themselves "accredited PR experts"; accreditation would be renewable after five years. The accreditation programme was developed but died, mainly because of the jealousy among public relations practitioners and lack of interest. But apart from that, several dilemmas contributed to the failure of the initiative. First, who should be the first delegates in the examination board and who should be in the position of judging others? Second, what should be measured during the examination; the basics of the profession or very specific knowledge, incorporating professional and theoretical concepts and knowledge. Third, should an existing accreditation system be adopted, based on, for example, the US system or the Universal Accreditation Programme, or should a system be implemented tailored to the Hungarian environment and conditions? Though the preparations for the system were well under way – the accreditation committee even started to compile a manual on public relations, which would have the basis for the examination materials – there have not been any concrete results yet.

3.4. Major roles of public relations practitioners

To date, role models in public relations have not been investigated in Hungary. Of the four characteristics of European public relations identified by the Delphy study (van Ruler and Verčič 2002), the reflective, operational and educational dimensions are the dominant ones. Two-way communication and dialogue-oriented practice is paid lip service, though public relations consultants show more commitment here than government or in-house practitioners. Two-way symmetrical communication is still a rare phenomenon among Hungarian firms and the craft public relations model (Grunig and Grunig 1992: 312) seems to better suited to the practice than the professional model.

The Hungarian Public Relations Association identified different public relations job titles and clearly defined the responsibilities of each position. The job titles used in the Hungarian practice do not reflect any hierarchy at all and are used interchangeably, despite the efforts of the Association. These job titles are:
− Public relations executive/manager
− Spokesperson
− Public relations specialist
− Press officer
− Public relations assistant

In public relations agencies, three levels can be distinguished: junior account executive, account executive and senior account executive; in agencies more attention is paid to the job titles and hierarchy. Corporate communication, Public Affairs departments, or the relevant comparable positions − all these are nearly non-existent in Hungary.

3.5. Growing fields and hot issues

Several issues have contributed to the general mixed perceptions of public relations. As a recent phenomenon, public relations as an activity has politicised to a great extent in Hungary. Favouritism still occurs, but, fortunately, is not widespread.

Political communication has undergone a serious development since the first years of democracy, when political parties and politicians did not know much about communication and campaigning (Odeschalchi 1999). Political public relations (the term "political marketing" is more common) has started to gain ground in the last few years. The term "public relations" became widely known between 1998 and 2002, under the then conservative government, lead by FIDESZ (Federation of Young Democrats). It was the first government to consciously use public relations. Public relations was introduced to the public by FIDESZ and the term appeared in the newspapers much more frequently than before. Szondi (2003) showed that the newspapers close to the government were using the term "public relations" in a positive context, while the journalists not in favour of the government had very negative attitudes towards public relations, associating it with manipulation, propaganda and fake activities. All this came to a head during the elections in April 2002, when the two main political parties, FIDESZ and MSZP (Hungarian Socialist Party), engaged in a PR war, in which neither party shunned unethical methods. The communication strategies and methods used in this period by the different parties have been investigated, but mainly by sociologists, marketing experts or politicians, who interpret public relations in a broad way.

In order to communicate a positive image about Hungary abroad, the conservative government set up the Country Image Centre (*Országimázs Központ*) in 1998. The centre was staffed by marketing specialists, rather than by communication and public relations experts. It lacked clear visions and strategies, and its activities met with so much resistance that the centre was closed.

Another issue is the well-known antagonistic relationship between public relations practitioners and journalists. In order to improve understanding and relations between these two groups, a dialogue has been started. The media have changed and developed a lot during the last twelve years and the field's professionalisation is taking place parallel with that of the public relations practice. The independence of public broadcasting is always on the agenda, with one political party accuse the other of influencing the media when the latter is in power. Journalists in Hungary have strong political stances, which are seldom hidden, and as a result the press is also politicised to a certain extent.

In 2003 the hottest issue is the public relations aspects of the enlargement of the European Union. There are two issues here. First, public communications campaigns have been launched to improve public knowledge and understanding of the European Union as well as to explain the implications of accession. The short term goal was to further increase the support for integration which culminated in the referendum on 12 April 2003 when Hungarians voted for joining the European Union. These campaigns engage the citizens in a dialogue, in which public relations agencies and government information practitioners play a leading role. Second, a public relations offensive has been launched to create a positive image of Hungary, especially in the EU, but also in the rest of the world. Hungary, together with other Central and Eastern European candidate members, makes a big effort to develop a "Euro conform"' identity and to invest in

communicating it to the EU. All these countries seem to distance themselves from the old image of "Eastern Europe" by rebranding themselves.

4. Conclusions: state of the art and future of public relations in Hungary

One of the challenges for the future is to improve the quality of education and the status of public relations. Launching Master programmes
would significantly contribute to improving the situation. Much more
systematic research in the field is needed, and more textbooks and professional publications.

The Hungarian Public Relations Association must take a more active
and leading role. Currently, it is not an opinion maker or guide in the field
of communication. The organisation's opinions are seldom sought when
decisions are being made – marketing and journalists associations are more
active and visible in their own areas. The Association itself needs better
public relations, both among its members and to the outside world. It
should play a more active role and contribute more to the professionalisation of the field. At the same time, Hungarian practitioners should be more
united and should have the profession's interest more at heart than they do
now – too often, personal interests are pursued. It is not too late to start; the
profession is still young and dynamic enough to readily absorb changes.

Public relations in Hungary is practised as an activity at a tactical level.
But deeper understanding of the discipline both by managements and
the public, as well as launching Master and Ph.D. education, will lift the
profession to a more strategic level. It is still too early to speak about
professionalism of the practice, but it is clear that Hungary has made the
first steps on the long road to professionalisation. Learning from the long
tradition and experiences of western colleagues might help to shorten
this challenging but rewarding process.

References

Culbertson, Hugh and Ni Chen (eds.) (1996). *International Public Relations*. Hillsdale, NJ:
    Lawrence Erlbaum.
Gruban, Brane (1995). Performing public relations in Central and Eastern Europe. *Public
    Relations Quarterly* 40: 20–24.
Grunig, James E. and Larissa Grunig (1992). Models of public relations and communica-
    tion. In: J. E. Grunig (eds.), *Excellence in Public Relations and Communication Manage-
    ment*, 285–325. Hillsdale, NJ: Lawrence Erlbaum Associates.

Hiebert, R. E. (1992a). Global public relations in a post-communist world: A new model. *Public Relations Review* 18–2: 117–126.

Hiebert, Ray (1992b). Public relations and mass communication in Eastern Europe. *Public Relations Review* 18–2: 177–187.

Lipót, József (1968). *Public Relations a gyakorlatban* [Public Relations in Practice]. Budapest: Közgazdasági és Jogi Kiadó.

Odescalchi, Daniel (1999). Democracy and elections in the new East-Central Europe. In: Bruce Newman (ed.), *Handbook of Political Marketing*, 587–603. Thousand Oaks, CA: Sage Publications

Ruler, Betteke van and Dejan Verčič (2002). *The Bled Manifesto on Public Relations*. Ljubljana: Pristop Communications.

Szondi, György (1999). Evaluation in the Hungarian public relations industry. Unpublished M.Sc. dissertation, University of Stirling.

Szondi, György (2003). The image of public relations in the print media. *Kommunikáció Menedzsment,* 1: 9–14

Tampere, Kaja (2002). Post-communist societies experience as a new development in European relations: Estonian case study. *The Status of Public Relations Knowledge in Europe and Around the World*. Proceedings of BledCom 2002 in conjunction with 2002 Euprera Annual Congress, Pristop Communications.

Verčič, Dejan, Larissa Grunig and James E. Grunig (1996). Global and specific principles of public relations: evidence from Slovenia. In: Hugh Culbertson and Ni Chen (eds.), *International Public Relations*: a comparative analysis, 31–65. Hillsdale NJ: Lawrence Erlbaum.

Chapter 13

Ireland

Francis Xavier Carty

1. National profile

This chapter covers public relations in the Republic of Ireland – it does not include Northern Ireland. The Public Relations Institute of Ireland (PRII) was formed in 1953 and the Public Relations Consultants Association of Ireland (PRCAI) in 1989. Northern-Ireland practitioners join the UK Institute of Public Relations (IPR). Friendly links between practitioners in the Republic and in the North go back to 1964. Two northern consultancies are members of the PRCAI and northern entries feature prominently in the annual PRII/PRCAI awards for Excellence in Public Relations.

The 2002 Irish Census (see www.cso.ie) recorded just over 3.9 million people, the highest since 1871 and an increase of 290,000 since 1996. This is a young, highly-educated population with the highest EU birth rate (14.3 per 1000) and lowest death rate (8.2 per 1000). In 2000, at the peak of the Celtic Tiger years – as the recent economic boom was termed – Ireland had the third highest gross domestic product per head of population in the EU at 118 per cent of the average, behind only Denmark (120 per cent) and Luxemburg (192 per cent) (IPA 2002). There has, however, been a downturn in 2001 and 2002. Ireland has always looked to Europe and sought to join the EU from the very start, but its entry was delayed until 1973 because of the French veto on British entry. Ireland has gained greatly from the EU to the extent that from being one of the poorest members in 1973, in recent years it has become, relatively, one of the most prosperous.

The economic success has been reflected in the growth of public relations and an increase in PRII membership. Full membership went up from 165 in 1995 to more than 300 in 2003. Adding student membership of more than 500, with affiliate and associate members, gives a total of about 1,100 (PRII 2001). The PRCAI, with thirty-eight members, includes most of the consultancy sector. It is difficult to gauge the real size of the industry, but it is likely that PRII caters for about 60 per cent of practitioners. Carty (1998) found the mean size of an Irish consultancy was 9.7 people, and 5.2 for in-house departments.

Fees at the top level, for the most sought-after consultants, can be up to € 300 an hour. Hardiman (2000) wrote, "Ireland's PR firms have never had it so good. Fee income is soaring in a buoyant economy that has created the perfect conditions for the service industry to thrive".

PRII is represented by John P. Gallagher, a founding member, at the Global Alliance for Public Relations and Communication Management. In October 2000, Gallagher joined representatives from twenty-two other public relations associations to clarify the goals and objectives of the Alliance. Members benefit by access to regional and international conferences, case studies, awards programmes and benchmarking research. The Alliance also enhances networking opportunities, and acts as a framework through which ethical standards, universal accreditation options and other initiatives can be examined (PRII 2001).

Media relations feature strongly in Irish practice but closeness to the UK and the sharing of a common language, English, means that British media have made a deep penetration into the Irish market, with several national UK papers publishing separate Irish editions and printing them in Ireland. There are four Irish-based national daily newspapers with a combined circulation of 450,000; two evening papers, 132,000, and five Sunday papers, 800,000. There are some forty regional weekly newspapers covering the entire country with a combined circulation of nearly 700,000. The magazine press amounts to about 200 titles and there is a proliferation of on-line titles.

Radio Telefis Eireann (RTE) is the state-owned broadcasting authority with three television channels and four radio stations. It has a public-service remit and is financed by a licence fee and advertising. There is one independent national radio station, one television station, and about thirty local radio stations.

Independent News & Media plc, headed by Sir Anthony O'Reilly, is the dominant player in the Irish media. Grown from one morning, evening and Sunday newspaper thirty years ago, it is now a leading international group, operating in Australia, Ireland, New Zealand, South Africa and the UK. It owns the *Independent* titles in the UK and the leading metropolitan group of newspapers in Northern Ireland. It publishes more than 200 newspaper and magazine titles with a weekly circulation of more than 15 million copies. The group employs 12,900 people (IPA 2002).

2.   History and developments of public relations

2.1. Roots of public relations

In the dark ages of Europe from the fifth century, when civilisation was nearly totally destroyed, Irish monks painstakingly copied the ancient books and then emigrated to found monasteries throughout Europe. The Irish monks were among the first public relations practitioners and experts in communication and negotiating relationships with key stakeholders.

2.2. Development of public relations practice

Modern public relations, like so many other features of Irish life, can be traced back romantically to 1916 when, in the words of the poet William Butler Yeats, "a terrible beauty was born". The Irish Volunteers, led by an unlikely group of writers, teachers and socialists, rebelled against British rule and, on Easter Monday, occupied the principal public buildings in Dublin. They declared Ireland an independent republic, thus starting the War of Independence, which led to the creation of the modern state in 1922. These revolutionaries, from the occupied General Post Office in the centre of Dublin city, made what was possibly the world's first ever radio news broadcast. Using morse code on the shipping wavelength, they tapped out the news that the republic had been declared (Gorham 1966: 2). It is not certain whether any ships picked up the news but these rebels, under siege, ten years before the Irish radio station 2RN was set up, sent their messages to the world. But apart from this, public relations in the 1920s was dominated by the political situation and was, for the most part, propaganda. There were a small number of commercial publicists, but never in the sense that they existed in the US or even in Britain. They were usually hawkers of advertising for the newspapers and a growing number of commercial and trade publications.

Formal public relations practice in Ireland started with the state bodies. The Electricity Supply Board (ESB) appointed Ned Lawler as public relations officer in 1927 and he played a major role in awareness campaigns, particularly the rural electrification scheme which continued to the 1950s. He had been political correspondent with the *Irish Independent*. Leslie Luke founded the PRII when he suggested to Lawler a "meeting of public relations officials". It was held in Dublin on 28 October

1953 and Lawler was elected chairman and convenor. Six of the ten founding members were from the state sector. The first Irish consultants emerged in the 1950s. Bill Kelly, later a sports journalist, said that he set up the first consultancy in the early 1950s (Kelly 1983: 117), but others attribute this distinction to Leslie Luke.

The Irish television service opened on 31 December 1961, creating new opportunities and a major culture change. Since 1926, broadcasting had been run directly by the civil service and there had been no political debate, nor interviews with politicians or church leaders in a state where 95 per cent of the people were Roman Catholics. But this soon changed with television. Public relations grew in the commercial sector through the 1960s, as did the consultancy business, but most of it was controlled by advertising agencies.

War in Northern Ireland

The Civil Rights campaign in Northern Ireland in 1968 was followed by sectarian and political violence. There was fear that war might break out all over the island. The Irish Government, keen that its policy against partition and against British rule in Northern Ireland be heard, despatched the public relations heads of the state bodies and government departments to Irish embassies in London, Canberra, Washington, Madrid and Stockholm. They remained at their posts for some months, until that phase, of what was to be a thirty-year crisis, eased.

Niall O'Flynn, in his PRII Presidential address in 1969, pointed to the "entire unhappy situation in Northern Ireland" and said it was a "glaring example of the complete neglect of the practice of public relations". He had no doubt that the "timely use of professional public relations would have averted much of the hardship and bitterness which afflicted that part of the island" (PRII archives).

A maturing industry

Tim Dennehy, from the National Transport Authority (CIE) and Michael Colley, from the Electricity Supply Board (ESB), were two senior practitioners in state bodies who articulated the maturing of public relations. For instance, Dennehy (1967) told an Army training course that public relations has been "concisely described as 'getting the reputation one deserves'. It is not, in the common jargon, concerned with image-building but with the creation of mutual understanding [...] it is not so much an activity as an attitude of mind [...] By the very nature of the State and the size of its population there has been little opportunity for the development of the gimmicky fringe activities of public relations practice in this country".

Looking ahead to the new decade, Michael Colley wrote (1970: 22):

> The new demands are likely to place the accent on the development of the corporate rather than the product image, the implementation of more frank and aggressive PR information programmes and the creation of effective machinery to provide an accurate inflow of information which can contribute to the formulation of policy, in the light of probable public reaction. It is pretty certain that management will demand the same sort of planning in public relations activity, as they already achieve in production, marketing, development and construction [...] The concept of long term PR planning is not a new one in theory. Its practice has not been so obvious in this country. Too often the practice has been on an ad hoc basis and 'fire brigade' action has been as common as the long term plan.

Some consultancies, which had been part of advertising agencies, became independent. Others were formed without advertising connections – an example was Murray Consultants. Joe Murray, managing director, said his company intended to specialise in corporate relations, "selling companies instead of products" (in *Business & Finance* 1974). Murray told *The Irish Times* (1978), "Public relations and advertising are two different worlds. Advertising agencies have done a lot of damage to the reputation of public relations by using the service too much as a back-up or after-sales service to their advertising accounts". By 1979 only eight of the twenty-two listed consultancies were associated with or owned by advertising agencies (IPA 1979).

The Papal visit
One of the most significant events in the history of the PRII was the visit of Pope John Paul II to Ireland in 1979. The Institute volunteered the services of its members and more than 100 took part in what was probably the biggest ever media event in the country, with more than 3,000 journalists attending. Lyons (1995) reported that public enthusiasm was overwhelming. The entire country came to a halt.

Further development
As other areas of corporate public relations developed through the 1970s, Myles Tierney, an elected county councillor, was the first lobbyist and, through lectures and papers, developed his 'theory of repose' to explain the purpose and dynamics of lobbying (Tierney 1982).

The 1980s saw greater awareness of public relations management. John McMahon, President of PRII wrote in 1980: "Public relations may well be the career path to the chief executive's chair in the last two decades of the twentieth century [...] Public relations has a new, more exacting role, far beyond organising press conferences and gathering press cuttings for management or clients. The role is in the area of communications".

2.3. Development of education and research traditions

The first course in public relations was held in 1951 at the Rathmines High School of Commerce in Dublin, now part of Dublin Institute of Technology. The lecturers were predominantly from the state sector. Rathmines held a longer course in 1954–1955, in conjunction with the PRII, which awarded its (first) diploma to successful students, thus making them eligible for membership. This seems to be the earliest link between educational qualifications and Institute membership. Standards were stringent. A total of 114 students enrolled but only seventy-six survived to take the examination and only fifty passed (PRII 1956).

In this first generation of Irish nation-building, the emphasis seems to have been on Grunig's public information model. This reversed the trend in, say, the US, where the press agentry era came first. It was in the 1960s, however, that several of the advertising agencies opened public relations departments. The press agentry model gained a foothold from this time, as the commercial publicity and promotions side of public relations was emphasised, advertising clients often getting the public relations services added on for free.

While the PRII ran successful part-time courses, maintaining its interest in education, the first full-time course started in 1978 at Dublin Institute of Technology, with the support of PRII. Originally a certificate course for school-leavers, it became a postgraduate diploma in 1990 and a Master's degree in 1997. PRII introduced mandatory educational qualifications for membership in 1985 and launched its own two-year night course in 1986. From the start, this course attracted more than a hundred students each year.

The popularity of the DIT and PRII courses led to other colleges setting up courses. This risked confusion as to the relative merits and standards of each course, leading the PRII, in 1997, to introduce its own National Syllabus Diploma to set the syllabus and examine all the other institutions apart from DIT. Three colleges run the PRII National Diploma one year full-time and four run it two years part-time, with a total enrolment of more than 500 students.

Public-relations research in Ireland is still in its infancy, but there has been steady development through the MA degree scheme at DIT, with some 160 graduates to date, and it has produced many exploratory studies in public relations practice.

2.4. How language shapes the development of public relations

The PRII archives show several indications of a mature view of public relations from as early as the 1950s. For instance, Eamon de Valera, survivor of 1916 and then nearing the end of his long career as Taoiseach (Prime Minister) was asked in the Dail (Parliament) in November 1957 what qualifications, if any, were necessary for the post of Director of the Government Information Bureau, and whether press experience was required. He said:

> The qualifications are those generally required of a public relations officer, and, in particular, a knowledge and appreciation of the Government's social and economic policy and of the working and activities of the various Departments of State and branches of public administration, and a sense of news values. A knowledge of the Irish language should, I think, also be regarded as essential. Journalistic experience, while desirable, would not be essential in the case of a person otherwise adequately qualified. (PRII 1958)

Erskine Childers, a Government Minister and President of Ireland (1973–1974), called for more public relations at an advertising conference in 1954, saying that:

> The whole panoply of public relations is insufficient in this country. There are no continuous publications covering the productive aspects of national life, and no highly skilled public relations officers in a number of important Government Departments with the exception of the Department of Health. The taxpayer should be told how his money is distributed. The vehicle taxpayer is not given any information on the number of roads repaired or reconstructed for his money. There is no publicity campaign to treat agricultural production in peace time as an ideal of the nation. (PRII 1954)

Jeremiah Dempsey, for many years head of the national airline, Aer Lingus, told PRII (1974) that the true test of public relations is "its capacity for contingency action in unpredictable circumstances – and the acceptance by the public of the organisation's actions in these circumstances". He added that "a company thrives in good public relations which is the medium through which it establishes its reputation which is in turn its very life-blood".

The name of the academic discipline in Ireland is "public relations". The profession describes itself as "public relations" and nobody has suggested any change in the name of the PRII or PRCAI. Numerous consultancies, however, have changed their names from "XXX Public Relations" to "XXX Communications" because of the negative perceptions that the term "public relations" often creates in the media and popular imagination.

Michael Colley (1971) noted that in one European country "PR men are turning over to the term 'relationists'. In the US you find that there has been a move to create 'public affairs' divisions." "Relationists" did not catch on but the term anticipated the current research emphasis on relationship management.

Despite some superficial impressions, there is growing realisation among Irish practitioners of the importance of building dialogic relationships with the entire network of their clients' stakeholders. Impressionistic evidence suggests that the quality of the practice is very professional, skilled and ethical. This is reflected in the confidence of international companies that are paying relatively large sums to buy Irish consultancies. Furthermore, organisations perceive the good value from their public-relations expenditure as witnessed in the number of new consultancies being formed and the growth in PRII membership.

3.   Typification of current public relations

3.1. Status of public relations in business, administration and society

PRII Chairman, Lesley Luke, said (PRII 1959): "Public relations does not enjoy here the status it should. As a study and a specialised practice of communications and relationships it is essential to the welfare of every Irish firm and organisation".

Public relations is still, somewhat grudgingly, criticised. Leaders in politics, business, and the voluntary sector recognise its importance and are increasingly using its services. This respect is most evident in the financial and political areas, inspired by the large number of corporate financial developments of recent years and the fact that no Irish Government was re-elected from 1969 to 2002.

Niall O'Flynn told PRII students in 1991 that "the reality is that every major decision has public-relations implications. The bigger the decision, the larger the company, and the greater the number of people that are affected, the more significant the PR component becomes". Niall Delaney, consultant, said in a *Sunday Tribune* supplement in 1992: "The good PR person now works in a barrister-like fashion, developing cases and arguments and presenting them in a way that is meaningful".

3.2. Major roles of public relations and typical tasks

There is plenty of evidence to show that media relations play an important role. Murray Consultants were the envy of their peers in 1995 and
got a PRCA Award for Excellence by persuading President Bill Clinton
to be photographed drinking a pint of Murphy's Irish Stout in Cassidy's
pub in Camden Street, Dublin. Media exposure gained for the brand
(Murray's client) at national and international level was "exceptional",
much to the chagrin of Guinness, who claimed that Clinton also tasted
their rival product on the same occasion (IMJ 1996).

Carty (1998) found that "media publicity" outscored all other forms of
public relations for "level of involvement of your organisation", with 290
out of a possible 315. "Business-to-Business" came second with 238. When
respondents were asked to rank roles in order of importance from 1 to 5,
"media relations" totalled 210 out of a possible 215, with "counselling/ad-
visor to management" third at 142.

There has always been a reluctance to admit to this emphasis on media
relations. As early as 1960, the PRII told members: "To restrict public relations to mere press relations is to place, wrongly, public relations on the
same level as advertising and this confused situation may only be the
source of misunderstanding with newspapers and advertising agencies"
(PRII 1960). Richard O'Farrell (PRII 1965) said: "There are still unfortunately far too many people who think that public relations is nothing more
than the sending out of numerous press releases, irrespective of the extent
to which they are published". One wonders, however, was it wishful thinking when Dennehy (1977) wrote, "I would say that press relations is only
about one-tenth of the totality of public relations today".

When asked what their primary role was as a public relations practitioner, 43 per cent emphasised the manager role and 27 per cent, the technician role (Carty 1998). Murphy (2000) found support among consultants for the hypothesis that they see themselves as strategic managers
while they believe others see them as spin doctors. Murphy (2000: 39) cites
the Chambers 21st Century Dictionary, as also cited by Richards (1998: 7)
that a spin doctor is "someone, especially in politics, who tries to influence
public opinion by putting a favourable bias on information presented to
the public or to the media" and Richards' comment (1998: 8) that "the
modern spin doctor is more than just a propagandist or publicist. The role
of the truly powerful spin doctor can be as an advisor, counsellor and
trusted friend to leaders". Murphy (2000: 73) concluded that "public relations is becoming more strategic" in Ireland. This claim was backed up by

the increasing presence of consultants' at the boardroom table and also the "senior status that they are afforded by the organisations that commission them". Murphy found a clear consensus to indicate "that public relations is about the management of an organisation's reputation and communication".

Some have grown to like the term "spin-doctor" and see it nearly as a term of endearment, realising that they could be and have been called many worse things. One former government press secretary, who has since resumed his career in broadcasting, titled his memoirs, *One Spin on the Merry-go-round* (Duignan n.d.).

While there is undoubtedly a lot of what some call "joke" public relations (often associated with marketing support, promotions and pseudo-events – the latter being an event that is not news in itself, but is created by an organisation solely to attract publicity) the level of advice at the corporate level has grown immensely since the early 1990s.

3.3. Position of public relations in organisations

While most of the best consultants deal directly with chief executives in client companies, the past twenty years has seen a growing influence of marketing. Consultancies are taking on a greater amount of marketing work, often answering to the marketing directors. This has led to a perception that public relations is essentially marketing support with an emphasis on product publicity and promotion. It can be argued that public relations, in this respect, has lost some of the independence that it seemed to be gaining from the 1970s.

Many practitioners see a large proportion of their public relations activity as practised in a marketing context (Carty 1998). Twenty-two per cent saw it between 20 and 30 per cent; 18 per cent at 31– 40 per cent; and 19 % at 41–50 per cent. The remaining 41 per cent saw it as more than 50 per cent. More half of the respondents, 54 per cent, saw public relations in the future becoming more allied with marketing.

3.4. Current state of education in public relations and major textbooks

Carty (1998) found strong support for education with 45 per cent of all respondents saying courses were very valuable, and another 45 per cent, some value. Among those respondents (one third of total) who had taken courses, 48 per cent said very valuable and 44 per cent, some value.

Following its successful investment in pre-entry education, PRII turned its attention to continuing professional development and launched a comprehensive program in 2002, describing it as "a flexible framework within which companies and individuals can plan and recognise professional development and learning". It has been expanded in subsequent years.

The MA programme at DIT does not prescribe a core textbook in public relations, but holds the best ones in its library. Grunig and Hunt (1984), White (1991), Grunig (1992), Dozier et al. (1995), White and Mazur (1995), Cutlip, Center and Broom (2000), Heath (2001), Theaker (2001) and Grunig, Grunig and Dozier (2002) are the most frequently recommended, and recourse to the professional journals is also mandatory for students. The National Syllabus Diploma of the PRII prescribes, as its core text, a new Irish title written by Ellen Gunning (2003): *Public Relations – A Practical Approach*.

3.5. The local scene of public relations

Most of the consultancies are still Irish-owned and headed by their founder-owner, but Edelman, Lopex, Ogilvy and Hill & Knowlton came in the 1980s and recent years have seen an expansion of the international presence. Shandwick bought Financial & Corporate Communications for a reported sum of nearly € 5.08 million in 2000. In the same year, Drury Communications was sold to BBDO Worldwide for € 8.25 million. Fleishman-Hillard bought out the remaining 41 per cent of the Irish company, Fleishman-Hillard Saunders in 2001 for € 7.62 million and soon after a young consultancy, Gallagher & Kelly, formed only in 1999, was bought by the US Conduit Communications for a total reported package of € 15.24 million. It now trades as Financial Dynamics Ireland.

Text 100 have been in Ireland since the early 1990s, Manning, Selvage & Lee have a link with Pembroke Communications, as do Burson Marsteller with Park Communications. Several other companies have differing forms of association with internationals.

3.6. Hot issues in public relations

The respondents in the Carty (1998) survey were generally optimistic about the future, but often viewed it through the perspective of the dominant media relations role. An example of an optimist: "[Public relations] will become a more respected discipline and gain credibility due to increased professionalism and better educated practitioners". While one of the few pessimists said: "Media relations will become more difficult in terms of obtaining coverage for 'softer' PR stories – sponsorships, launches – consumer PR in general". Linking theory with practice, replies were more positive than might often be the impression in informal conversation and media quotes. Fifty-four per cent believed "a knowledge of theoretical models of public relations is relevant to the daily practice of public relations", while this rose to 65 per cent among those with educational qualifications.

Another issue is the attitude of the media towards public relations. This attitude is similar to that in other countries, but at an individual level there is respect on both sides. Criticism of public relations is seldom malicious. Shaw (1999: 97–98) concluded that Irish and American practitioners and journalists share similar views on their relationship with one another. "Indeed, despite differences in perceptions and understanding of each other's role, Irish public relations practitioners and *The Irish Times* journalists find themselves mutually dependent and view their relationship as conditionally co-operative". To Shaw, however, it appeared that journalists in Ireland and America "intuitively" perceive involvement with practitioners as collusion and somehow a threat to the principles of an independent press.

4.   Conclusions: state of the art and future of public relations in Ireland

4.1. Trends

In 1997, the PRII President, Roddy Guiney, asked senior members to indicate trends in the profession. Barbara Wallace, a former president, focused on the new technological developments and asked whether they improve the quality of communication. Pat Barry, of Guinness Ireland, asked "are we sufficiently focused on giving, or more importantly, showing that we give value for money?" With increasing specialisation, he hoped there would still be room for the generalist at the end of the next decade. Eileen Gleeson, managing director of Financial & Corporate Communications, saw people, technology, media operations, client management and evaluation as the main issues facing the industry (PRII 1997).

Another trend is the emphasis on media relations, and this is borne out through MA research. Public-relations practitioners are often seen only as people to handle the media, despite their own common perception that they are strategic managers. This view is perpetuated by their tendency to sell themselves to clients on the strength of their contacts with the media. Indications are that their own research is frequently confined to media relations, but more still has to be done on the subject. Further observation and conversation indicates that there is a strong tendency, even in more sophisticated companies, to see media coverage as an end in itself, without reference to overall corporate culture and business objectives.

Evaluation is also an issue. Much lip service is paid to it, but there still seem to be obstacles to its implementation, especially in the consultancy area where clients are reluctant to pay for it. Evaluation is often strong in the sponsorship area, where organisations such as the Electricity Supply Board (ESB) have built in sophisticated measures to show the extent of attitude shifts through each element in their extensive programme. A 1997 survey by marketing students from University College, Dublin, found that 65 per cent of respondents, from 1,000 organisations across a wide variety of industries, stated that they had no means of evaluating public relations (*Sunday Business Post* 1997)

Here we should also mention an over-emphasis on techniques. The development of the new technologies and new media is not necessarily creating better public relations and attention to the community, described by Wilson (2001) as the ultimate stakeholder, the most important public. Information flows so rapidly that there is frenetic activity and a fear that this will lead to an even greater emphasis on short-term tactics and techniques rather than strategies.

A final trend to mention here is the gender shift. Public relations is becoming a more female profession, with applicants for the courses about 80 per cent women. This is reflected in the number of women who now hold senior positions: 14 of the 38 PRCA members and 26 of the 74 consultancies now listed in the IPA Yearbook (IPA 2002) are owned and/or headed by women. Almost 60 per cent (178) of the 300 full members of PRII are women. Carty (1998) did not detect any barrier to the promotion of women in Irish public relations.

4.2. Other special features of interest

The tendency to see public relations as a technical rather than a management function still persists and there is still a strong tendency to recruit journalists because of their media experience and contacts. Confusion is strengthened by the fact that the British-based National Union of Journalists covers Ireland and still has a branch to cater for public relations, of which this author has been a member for more than thirty years.

Lobbying ethics

In 1999 the opposition Labour party introduced a Registration of Lobbyists Bill. The PRII/PRCAI opposed it and met the politicians to make their case (PRII 1999). It was defeated, mainly because of difficulty in putting it into a form that would work.

The debate about the role of lobbyists has been intensified since an allegation was made to a Government Tribunal of Inquiry in 2000 by former government press secretary and lobbyist, Frank Dunlop, that he gave money to Dublin county councillors to buy votes for the rezoning of land, that is to allow a change of use from, for instance, agricultural use to industrial, residential, educational or so on. Dunlop immediately resigned his membership of PRII and his firm's membership of PRCAI. The Tribunal, set up in 1997, submitted a preliminary report in October 2002 and it is expected to continue its investigations and to sit for some more years.

The future

How do Irish practitioners see the future? When asked by PRII (*Communique* 2001), they were optimistic, despite fears of world-wide economic downturn and recession. Robin O'Sullivan, a consultant, said, "Today, Ireland's PR industry operates from a good strong base. We're working in a different climate, thankfully, than we had earlier. There is at long, long last a greater appreciation of the fact that PR has an important training service to offer. A company that manages its internal and external communications well will always, I believe, do better in times of adversity". Martina Byrne, of Statoil, said that the public relations industry, in previous time of economic difficulty, was generally one of the first to be hit. "It was often seen as an easy way to cut costs within a company. People then didn't value the services PR offered". She holds that now the public relations industry has developed into "an integral part of a good company's brand and marketing communications strategy" and that if this is the case "clients will not desert their PR advisors now".

Grunig and Hunt (1984: 536–540) predicted that the future was bright for the field of public relations but not so bright for practitioners; there was plenty of opportunity but practitioners were not necessarily equipped to avail of it. They saw the key to the future in education, not just of practitioners, but of the public. Cutlip et al. (2000: 496) cited Ed Block, vice-president for public relations at AT&T: "If the essence of good public relations has long ago been so adequately described [...] why is it that so many corporations continue to commit so many fundamental blunders?"

There is still a job to be done in convincing clients that public relations is an essential part of their strategic management, inextricably linked to the business plan and corporate objectives, and that while its skills can be used with advantage in media relations and marketing communications, it is a lot more than that.

References

Business & Finance (1974). *Report on formation of Murray Consultants*, 27 Apr. 1974
Carty, Francis Xavier (1998). Perception and practice of public relations in Ireland, Dublin. Private circulation email fxcarty@indigo.ie.
Colley, Michael (1970). A PR swing in the seventies. *Business & Finance* 6: 22.
Colley, Michael (1971). Role of PR men expanding rapidly. *Cork Examiner*, 12 June 1971.
Communique (2001). Face to the future. *1–1*. Dublin: PRII
Cutlip, Scott M., Allen H. Center and Glen M. Broom (2000). *Effective Public Relations* (8th edn.). Upper Saddle River, N.J.: Prentice-Hall International.
Dempsey, Jeremiah F. (1974). *Public relations in the public company*. Lecture, PRII, 17 Apr. 1974
Dennehy, Tim (1967). *Public relations*. Lecture, Curragh Camp, 28 Nov. 1967
Dennehy, Tim (1977). Looking to the future for PR. *Irish Marketing Journal* 3–8: 11.
Dozier, David M., James E. Grunig and Larissa L. Grunig (1995). *Manager's Guide to Excellence in Public Relations and Communication Management*. Mahwah, NJ: Lawrence Erlbaum Associates.
Duignan, Sean (n. d.) *One Spin on the Merry-go-round*. Dublin: Blackwater Press. (c.1996).
Gorham, Maurice (1966). *Forty years of Irish Broadcasting*. Dublin: Talbot Press
Grunig, James E. (ed.) (1992). *Excellence in Public Relations and Communication Management*, Hillsdale, NJ: Lawrence Erlbaum.
Grunig, James E. and Todd Hunt (1984). *Managing Public Relations*. Fort Worth: Holt, Rinehart & Winston.
Grunig, Larissa, James E. Grunig and David M. Dozier (2002). *Excellent Public Relations and Effective Organizations*. Hillsdale, NJ: Lawrence Erlbaum.
Gunning, Ellen 2003 *Public Relations – A Practical Approach*. Dublin: Gill & Macmillan.
Hardiman, Cyril (2000), in *Irish Independent*, 19 Oct. 2000, p. 7.
Heath, Robert L. (ed.) (2001). *Handbook of Public Relations*. London: Sage.
IPA (1979). *Administration Yearbook and Diary*. Dublin: Institute of Public Administration.

IPA (2002). *Administration Yearbook and Diary.* Dublin: Institute of Public Administration.

IMJ (Irish Marketing Journal) (1996). *The best of public relations* (Special report), June–July 1996. Vol 22 – 6/7.

Irish Times (1978). *Planned communications in two different worlds* (Special report on advertising agencies), 15 March 1978.

Kelly, Bill (1983). *Me Darlin' Dublin's Dead and Gone.* Dublin, Poolbeg Press.

McMahon, John (1980). PR as career path for the 80s Chief Executive. *Irish Marketing Journal.* Vol 6, No. 8, August 1980, p. 11

Murphy, Sharon (2000). Public relations: the insider's perspective. MA dissertation, Dublin Institute of Technology.

O'Flynn, Niall (1969). PRII archives.

O'Flynn, Niall (1991). Managing the in-house PR department. Lecture, Dublin, April, 1991.

PRII (1954). Newsletter, October 1954.

PRII (1956). Newsletter, April 1956.

PRII (1958). News Bulletin, January 1958.

PRII (1959). Newsletter, May 1959.

PRII (1960). Newsletter, October 1960.

PRII (1965). Newsletter, May 1965.

PRII (1997). PRII News, May/June 1997.

PRII (1999). Annual Report.

PRII (2001). Annual Report.

Richards, Paul. (1998) *Be Your Own Spin Doctor.* Harrogate, UK: Take That.

Shaw, Thomasena F. (1999). Friend or foe: an exploratory study of how Irish public relations practitioners and journalists view their relationship with one another. MA dissertation, Dublin Institute of Technology.

Sunday Business Post (1997). PR survey. *Sunday Business Post,* 14 Sept. 1997.

Sunday Tribune (1992). *Public relations enters a golden age.* Special report, Jan. 1992.

Theaker, Alison (2001). *The Public Relations Handbook.* London: Routledge.

Tierney, Myles (1982). *The Parish Pump: A Study of Democratic Efficiency and Local Government in Ireland.* Dublin: Able Press

White, Jon (1991). *How to Understand and Manage Public Relations.* London: Business Books.

White, Jon and Laura Mazur (1995). *Strategic Communications Management: Making Public Relations Work.* Wokingham: Addison-Wesley.

Wilson, Laurie J. (2001). Relationships within communities. In: Robert L. Heath (ed.), *Handbook of Public Relations,* 521–526. London: Sage.

Intermezzo

The transitional approach to public relations

Ryszard Ławniczak

1. Preliminary remarks

Since the early 1990s, the countries of Central and Eastern Europe (CEE) and those of the former Soviet Union have witnessed a unique historical process in which a group of former "socialist", centrally planned economies (or, as some would call them, communist countries and societies), are undergoing a process of transition from planned to market economies, from party dictatorship to democracy, and from socialism to capitalism (Mygind 1994). There have been no precedents in the last two centuries of such a comprehensive transition from one political and economic system to another.

This process is difficult and, for some social groups, has proven to be long and painful. A key factor in its success will be the degree to which social awareness can be changed. This would include the immediate elimination of negative habits related to "socialist" thinking and attitudes towards work, along with the removal of remaining fears and prejudices towards capitalism. Public relations strategies and instruments have proved to be a useful tool in helping to achieve such desirable transformations in social consciousness in the shortest time possible, and ensuring a smooth transition from one socio-political and economic system to another.

2. Transitional public relations: the new stage in the development of international public relations

Together with the historically unprecedented experience of transition, also the new stage in the development of international public relations began (Tampere 2002: 115). For the first time in the history of public relations, its strategies, policies and instruments could be applied to assist in the peaceful transition from one system to the other. This happened not only in one country and society, but also in a group of countries in a region with the common heritage of socialist command economy.

However, the nature and range of public relations practices in developed market economies, such as those of the United States and the countries of the European Union, differ markedly from what can be labelled as "transitional public relations" – that is, public relations performed in the transition economies of Central and East European countries and independent states of the former Soviet Union. There are two main features that distinguish those types of public relations. One is the burden represented by the legacy of the former system retained in the minds of the people and in the basic economic conditions in which transition economies operate. The other type is made up of the additional "transitional" role (function or dimension, besides such as: managerial, technical, reflective and educational) (Ruler 2000), which public relations assumes in transition economies, that are not observed in developed market economies (Ławniczak 2001).

Such an approach is based on the assumption that by using the contribution of analysts of comparative economic systems, one should give greater consideration to differences between economic systems defined as a "set of mechanisms and institutions for decision-making and the implementation of decisions concerning production, income, and consumption within a given geographic area" (Gregory and Stuart 1989). Differences between those elements in market-economy countries and transition economies, have – in my opinion – a strong effect on public relations strategies and practices in all C&EE countries.

However, Verčič, Grunig and Grunig (1996) concluded that "there are generic principles of public relations that can be applied in every political and economic system subject to change", but they also note that "political and economic systems provide strong constraints on the application of generic principles of public relations".[1] Although I agree with these postulates, it could also be argued that public relations practitioners in C&EE countries need to account for the influence of the political–economic system (which is one of the five specific variables) to a much larger

---

1. These are the nine generic principles: (1) involvement of public relations in strategic management; (2) empowerment of public relations in the dominant coalition or direct reporting to senior management; (3) integrated public relations function; (4) public relation as a management function separate from other functions; (5) the role of public relations practitioners; (6) two way symmetrical model of public relations; (7) a symmetrical system of internal communication; (8) knowledge potential for managerial role and symmetrical public relations; (9) diversity embodied in all roles.

extent. This is because the legacy of the former socialist system, as reflected in ways of thinking, the structure of the economy, and the mechanism for resource allocation, creates a unique combination of constraints on the application of the universal principles of public relations. For this reason, we may speak of transitional public relations.

For present purposes, I adopt the specific approach of a comparative economic system to explain in a more detailed way two things: (1) the sources of the above mentioned constraints, brought upon former centrally planned economies in C&EE countries and the way in which specific political and economic features of centrally planned economies influence public relations practices in such countries;[2] and (2) the additional roles played by public relations in C&EE countries that are not performed by public relations functions in developed western European countries and the reasons why such roles have been assumed.

3. The legacy of the socialist-economic system and its impact on public relations strategies and practices

The conditions under which transformations began in C&EE were fashioned by both external and internal factors. The external factors that have had the strongest impact on the initial conditions of the economic and political transformations include (a) the structure of economic and political ties with foreign partners (economic and political dependency from Soviet Union); and (b) the role of international financial institutions (World Bank, IMF), particularly for the strongly indebted countries. The key internal factors affecting transition economies include the level of economic development; the historical cultural environment; and the legacy of the centrally-planned economy.

The legacies that, in my view, have had the strongest impact on public relations practices in C&EE countries include (a) ways of thinking, fash-

---

2. A good illustration of how the constraints mentioned earlier of the socialist system influenced public relations practices in the 1990s, can be provided by examining the rise and fall of Burson-Marsteller in Poland. In 1991, the company was the first major Western public relations agency to set up operations in Poland. The news in March 2001 that Burson-Martseller would close its Polish and Moscow offices on 30 April shocked professional circles in Warsaw. In my opinion, this leading American agency failed to account for the above mentioned "legacies" of the former system that have persisted in the Polish market. When the office was closed, the annual volume of business in the Polish public relations market was estimated at about US$ 100 million.

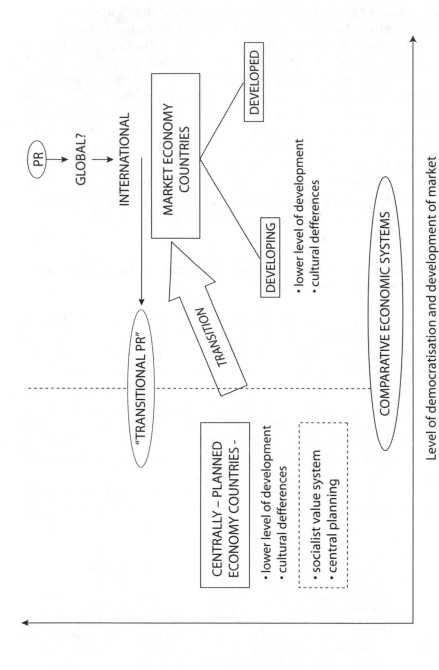

Figure 1. The sources of the concept of transitional public relations

ioned by socialist systems of values, social security and education; (b) the structure of the economy and, in particular the role of the public sector, and primarily, that of state-owned industrial enterprises, the prevalence of monopolies, the structure of the labour market and the role of trade unions, and the weakness of the financial sector; and (c) the use of central planning in allocating resources, which ultimately leads to shortages (Kornai 1980).

To this day, after more than ten years of transition process, the legacy of "socialist democracy" and central planning is manifested in many areas of social life – including the practice of public relations – in almost all the transition countries of C&EE and former Soviet Union. It still can be seen, among other things, in the following areas:
– the common perception of public relations as suspicious propaganda; this view stems from the historic role that censorship used to play in the mass media, the subjugation of all such media to a single doctrine, and the resulting stereotypical conviction that "the press lies";
– the failure to understand the point of marketing and promoting products and businesses, and building the images of companies and their executives; this problem originates from the fact that, at a time of severe shortages, all goods manufactured in the socialist economy were readily sold;
– the belief that companies, their owners and/or their successes are better left unprompted as high profiles may bring on additional tax sanctions; this view stems from the fact that, for ideological reasons, all privately owned operations were considered suspicious and subject to ad hoc taxation.

These characteristics have had a significant impact on the development and current status of public relations in Poland, but also in the other transition countries of the region. As a result, the evolution of public relations in the former communist countries followed two tracks. On the one hand, the systemic transformation created opportunities for establishing broader foreign contacts, allowing for foreign investment and privatisation to enter the country. In effect, numerous Western enterprises that recognised their need for public relations services, moved into the local market. Some of their demand was satisfied by foreign agencies that established branch offices in Poland, such as Burson Marsteller, which opened its Warsaw office in 1991. On the other hand, before establishing certain market instruments, mechanisms and institutions (such as the stock exchange, or VAT) absent in the command economy, the C&EE governments (such as Poland and Slovenia) engaged public relations agencies to carry out public information campaigns. Financing for such campaigns came from foreign sources (e.g. the PHARE fund from European Union). Since the public relations market was virtually non-existent in these countries, their governments hired Western companies, which relied on the help of local consultants. In this way, although external funds went to external contractors, the transformation gave an impulse for the emergence of the public relations industry in transition economies.

One might argue that political, social and economic transformations are responsible for creating a demand for public relations services and for the arrival of public relations experts and agencies, mainly from the West. But it can also be claimed that public relations has played the role of an important and useful instrument that facilitates and accelerates the political and economic transition of all the former communist countries (in the case of Slovenia, public relations professionals who employed their generic principles "have been successful in changing the political-economic system in Slovenia to a more democratic one" (Verčič, Gruning and Grunig 1996: 46).

4. The specific role and tasks of transitional public relations

Public relations in well-developed economies can be defined as "the management function which evaluates public attitudes, identifies the policies and procedures of an individual or an organisation with the public interest, and plans and executes a program of action to earn public understanding and acceptance" (Cutlip, Center and Broom 1994: 3). Because public relations practices, teaching and research are largely US-oriented, the European Public Relations Body of Knowledge project (EBOK) has formulated a "European Approach" (which in the author's opinion represents the Western European approach only) that recognises the following four aspects, roles or dimensions of "European" public relations (Ruler 2000):

1. Managerial: maintaining relationships and managing communication with publics in order to gain public trust and/or mutual understanding. This function has to do with organisational strategies.

2. Reflective: discussions regarding organisation conducted with the society that is to assume responsibility. This function has to do with organisational values and norms and can be seen as a developing function of public relations and as a contribution to the discussion on socially responsible behaviour in organisations.

3. Educational: helping members of organisations become communicatively competent in order to respond to societal demands. This function has to do with the behaviour of the members of the organisation.

4. Operational: to execute communication plans. This function has to do merely with execution. It is not supported as a view on public relations, but mentioned as a common aspect.

To accommodate the C&EE transition economies, a fifth aspect to the roles, dimensions or functions of public relations is necessary. This additional role should be labelled "transitional", and is defined as "helping to introduce and adopt the mechanisms and institutions of the market economy and democracy in former command economies". More specifically, in my opinion, the transitional role, which may also be treated as a new systemic transformation instrument, involves these points:
– Evaluations of public attitudes towards the manner and pace of transition to a market economy and the conditions behind such a transition.
– The formulation of tasks and the creation of instruments to be used by economic entities (such as private entrepreneurs and foreign businesses) or by non-profit organisations (such as charities and non-governmental organisations) in their relations with the public at large.
– The planning and execution of actions aimed at earning public approval and support for the principles and mechanisms of the market economy with a view to facilitating their effective implementation.
The need to adjust Western-style public relations to the unique conditions of the burgeoning market economy has its roots in the legacies of the former system, as described above.

5. The main tasks of public relations during the first stage of systemic transformation

Public relations, during the initial stage of the transition process, has several important tasks. First, to reverse the fears of and prejudices against "ruthless capitalism", instilled during the socialist era. One generation in Central and Eastern Europe and two in the former Soviet Union were raised under this system. The average Polish citizen, and especially older Poles, associate capitalism with unemployment, the lack of a welfare safety net, the negative consequences of substantial social inequalities, the negative social consequences of monopolistic practices and a fear of foreign capital; the latter is believed to be part of a plan to "take over the country". Simply put, the task of public relations during the first stage of the transition is to build an image of "capitalism with a human face", in order to secure public acceptance for ongoing economic reforms.

The second task is to create public awareness of the wide range of possible alternative market-economy models and of the fact that both in Poland and in other formerly socialist countries, a struggle is under way to determine the final shape of the market economy by promoting value systems and lifestyles along with products and services. Such promotion is to be aimed at gaining market share and securing the best possible terms from investors willing to put their money in particular industries and businesses (Albert 1992; Fleck and Ławniczak 1993).

Third, to facilitate effective functioning of the market economy by:
- Promoting entrepreneurship;
- Promoting and assisting in the implementation of the privatisation process as a tool for more effective management (a case in point: NFI (the National Investment Fund);
- Attracting foreign capital which can potentially boost the effectiveness of management;
- Enabling local (domestic) businesses to participate in the process of creating a market economy.

These three tasks of public relations activities are in practice realised by practitioners applying public relations, strategies, policies and instruments in following areas (with different intensity in different countries):
- Public relations in state-run enterprises. The goal is to secure the acceptance among workers and society at large for necessary restructuring and possible privatisation.
- Public relations in privately owned business. The goal: to secure public acceptance for the concept of private property.
- Public relations of government institutions (the chancelleries of the Prime Minister and the President, ministries, government funds, etc.). The goal is to gain acceptance of the public for governmental policy, for example stricter taxation policy.
- Public relations for "new" market economy institutions (stock exchange, banks, National Investment Funds). The goal is to educate and encourage the public to use their services.
- Public relations in foreign companies. The goal is to gain public acceptance for foreign investments.
- Promotion of cities and regions. The goal is to attract potential investors, among other things.
- Promotion of the country. Here, the goal is to secure the support of international financial institutions, attract foreign capital, and achieve acceptance for attempts to integrate with the European Union or by joining NATO.

6. Conclusions

By analysing the strategies and policies of public relations applied in the C&EE and former Soviet Union countries, we can draw several conclusions. First, together with the historically unprecedented experience of transition from a centrally planned to a market economy in C&EE and the former Soviet Union began the new stage in the development of international public relations. For the first time in the history of public relations, its strategies and instruments could be to applied to assist in the peaceful transition from one political–economic system to the other. This happened not only in one country and society, but in a group of countries in a region with the common heritage of socialist command economy. Second, it will take some time until Western public relations theory and practice will be able to accommodate the unique realities of countries in transition. Third, although I agree with Verčič, Grunig and Grunig (1996), who postulated that certain "generic principles of public relations" exist that may apply in every economic system, I argue that public relations practitioners in Central and Eastern Europe need to account for the influence of the former communist political and economic system to a much larger extent, because of the constraints such a system imposes on the efficient deployment of public relations strategies and policies. Fourth, the legacy of the former system, as reflected in ways of thinking, the structure of the economy, and the mechanism of resource allocation, has created a unique combination of constraints on the application of the universal principles of public relations. For this reason, we may speak of transitional public relations, as a specific brand and stage in the development of international public relations. And, finally, the sources of this concept are based on a methodological contribution of the theory of comparative economic systems, as presented in the Figure 1.

References

Albert, Michel (1994). *Kapitalizm kontra kapitalizm [Capitalism Contra Capitalism]*. Kraków: Znak

Cutlip, Scott M., Allen H. Centre and Glen M. Broom (1994). *Effective Public Relations* (7th edn.). Prentice-Hall.

EBRD (2001). *Transition report 2001*. London: European Bank for Reconstruction and Development.

Fleck, Hans-George and Ryszard Ławniczak (eds.) (1993). *Alternative Models of Market Economy for Transition Economies*. Warsaw: Sorus Press.

Gregory, Paul R. and Robert C. Stuart, Robert C. (1989). *Comparative Economic Systems.* Boston: Houghton Mifflin, 3rd edition.

Gruban, Brane (1995). Performing public relations in Central and Eastern Europe. *Public Relations Quarterly* 40: 20–24.

Hiebert, Ray E. (1992a). Global public relations in a post-communist world: a new model, *Public Relations Review* 18–2: 117–126.

Hiebert, Ray E. (1992b). Public relations and mass communication in Eastern Europe. *Public Relations Review* 18–2: 177–187.

Kornai, Janos (1980). *Economies of Shortage.* Amsterdam: North-Holland.

Ławniczak, Ryszard (2001). Transition public relations: an instrument for systemic transformation in Central and Eastern Europe. In: Ryszard Ławniczak (ed.), *Public Relations Contribution to Transition in Central and Eastern Europe.* Poznań: Printer.

Mygind, Niels (1994). *Societies in Transition.* Copenhagen: Copenhagen Business School.

Ruler, Betteke van (2000). Future research and practice of public relations: a European approach. In Dejan Verčič, John White and Daniel Moss (eds.), *Proceedings of the 7th International Public Relations Research Symposium, Public Relations, Public Affairs and Corporate Communications in the New Millennium: The Future,* 157–163. Ljubljana: Pristop Communications.

Tampere, Kaja (2002). Post-communist societies experience as a new development in European relations: Estonian case study, in: Dejan Verčič, John White and Daniel Moss (eds.), *Proceedings of the 7th International Public Relations Research Symposium, The Status of Public Relations Knowledge in Europe and Around the World.* Ljubljana: Pristop Communications.

Verčič, Dejan, Larissa A. Grunig and James E. Grunig (1996). Global and specific principles of public relations: evidence from Slovenia. In: Hugh M. Culbertson and Ni Chen (eds.), *International public relations: A comparative analysis,* 31–65. Mahwah, NJ: Lawrence Erlbaum Associates.

World Bank (2002). *Transition. The first ten years: analysis and lessons for Eastern Europe and the former Soviet Union.* Washington: World Bank.

Chapter 14

Italy

Toni Muzi Falconi & Renata Kodilja

1. National profile

1.1. Profile of the country

Despite the stereotype of being a very ancient nation, Italy is a young democracy: a united country since 1861 and a parliamentary democracy since 1946. Until 1992, for almost fifty years Italy lived in what political scholars define as a "blocked democratic system": with the largest communist party in the western world, but unable to participate in the government because of Italy being a member of Nato. This irremovable obstacle forced other Italian political parties into various forms of coalitions around the central, pro-Vatican Christian Democratic Party (DC). For some fifty years the Italian democratic system – despite stereotypes of constant instability based on recurring cabinet reshuffles – enjoyed a surprising, albeit somewhat arteriosclerotic, stability as cabinet ministers were more or less always the same, even if in different positions.

In 1992 the Italian communist party dissolved and a semi-majoritarian electoral reform introduced the option of alternative government coalitions. In 1994 a conservative majority won the elections and television tycoon Silvio Berlusconi was elected premier. However, this unstable government soon collapsed, which led to new elections in 1996. These, in turn, were won by a centre-left majority, led by Romano Prodi, who subsequently was replaced by Massimo D'Alema (the first ex-communist to become prime minister) and this, again, led to Berlusconi sweeping the following 2001 elections, thus returning to power.

With 60 million inhabitants, Italy is today home of the oldest population in the world in terms of average age. Italians are also known as prime supporters of the European Union and last to adopt its directives. Recognised for having the world's largest cultural heritage, Italy also has the lowest number of university graduates as well as book and newspaper readers per inhabitant in Europe.

1.2. Facts and figures about public relations

Public relations in Italy in 2003 is characterised by two features: multi-faceted and developing strongly. The relationship between the academic community and professional practice, traditionally distant, begins to move to a harmonious integration and mutual completion. The organisation of public relations professionals, rooted and consolidated in Italy since the mid 1950s (FERPI, *Federazione Relazione Pubbliche Italiana*, as a federation of pre-existing associations since 1970, Assorel since 1983 and *Associazione Comunicazione Pubblica* since 1991) are now supplying resources, know-how and contribution to the definition of formative goals for the four recently developed (the first, IULM University of Milan, one decade ago) undergraduate courses in public relations. The university environment, on its own side, is consolidating the practice of internship asking public relations professionals to directly contribute to the improvement of students' education.

The development of the discipline has qualitative and quantitative aspects. The quantitative growth is reflected in clear numbers: 70,000 practitioners in all sectors of the market place, and some 40,000 students enrolled in undergraduate courses in public relations, and, more commonly, in communication sciences. The qualitative aspects are related to a truly new awareness of the pervasiveness of the profession in every walk of Italian society. Public relations is progressively less confused with propaganda, persuasion and manipulation. Italy shows a trend towards the development of quality in relationship management. Although the term "public relations" still has negative connotations, in recent years public relations theories and techniques have been associated with innovative cultural statements.

1.2. Status of public relations in business, administration and society

The actual "legal status" of public relations in Italy, a status limited only to the public sector, is a consequence of cultural and political changes in the 1990s. Stefano Rolando, director of the communication department of the government's Council of Ministers in the 1980s and early 1990s, who in 1991 founded – as an offshoot of FERPI – the Italian Association of Public Sector Communicators (with some 1,500 members today), in 1994 succeeded in convincing the newly elected Prime Minister Berlusconi (the great communicator!) to sign a decree instituting in every single branch of the national, regional and local public sector an office of relations with the public (the first of these offices dates back to 1954 in the Province of Bologna).

In 2000, the Italian parliament also approved a law (law no. 150), which was the result of a joint lobbying effort of the Association of Public Sector Communicators and the legally chartered Guild of Italian Journalists – with FERPI leadership then conspicuously absent. This law formally recognises communication as a strategic task for the public sector and public sector communicators as relevant protagonists of the public sector's much-needed reform. Though extremely valuable, the law also has a few flaws, one of which is 'preposterous': after stating that all segments of the public sector are to create three different communication departments – the spokesperson (of the political leadership), the media relations office and the office for relations with the public – Article 9 of the law stipulates that only members of the journalistic guild (an organisation which by law holds an exclusive of the journalistic profession) may access and work for the media relations departments in the whole Italian public sector!

2. History and development of public relations

2.1. Roots of public relations

As distinct from advertising or propaganda, public relations arrived in Italy in the summer of 1943 in the wake of the allied troops landing in Sicily. As Italy was the first enemy country to be invaded in Europe, its scene was considered particularly relevant by the US-dominated alliance as an interesting territory in which to identify and experiment with viable ways of building amicable relationships with existing local communities.

Antecedents
However, as with Cutlip's well-known interpretation of public relations antecedents in the US, some are also to be found in Italy. An interesting book by contemporary historian Simona Colarizi (Colarizi 1991) explains details of the highly sophisticated interactive public opinion monitoring systems adopted by the fascist regime, which in their structure and processes we would today consider very advanced. A second and more specific antecedent dates back to 1936, when Mussolini decided to invade Ethiopia, bypassing strong opposition by the British government. Recent documents found in the archives of Italy's foreign minis-

try recount that the Italian dictator was worried that British lobbying efforts in Washington might succeed in moving the then US position on the planned invasion from neutral to negative. He subsequently sent Bernardo Bergamaschi, a senior officer in the Propaganda Ministry, to the United States to select a public relations agency capable of counter-lobbying in Washington through a grass root campaign, which mobilised major US based Italo-American communities into explaining to the Congress and the White House the reasons for the proposed annexing of Abyssinia. Unfortunately, the documents do not tell us which agency was selected – though they do tell us that the campaign was a success and also that it bore no cost to the Italian state budget.

Again in the 1930s, Linoleum, then a company of the Pirelli group, under the leadership of Giuseppe Luraghi, opened a public relations department assigning its responsibility to two relevant intellectuals: Leonardo Sinisgalli (after the war he became editor in chief of IRI's sophisticated corporate magazine, *Civiltà delle Macchine*) and the poet Alfonso Gatto. In 1934, publicist Dino Villani convinced the Motta company to launch the *Premio Notte di Natale*, a classic public relations event based on best individual philanthropic practices. Villani is also known for having invented the 'five thousand lire for a smile' prize (tied to a toothpaste manufacturer) as well as for having formed and edited the periodical *Ufficio Moderno*, which after the war became a centre of attraction for many young intellectuals seduced by modern industry and mass communication practices.

The late 1940s and 1950s
In early post-war Italy, Vanni Montana, Italo-American and public relations officer of the US based trade union AFL CIO, is the most active inspirer and a direct protagonist of the 1947 break-up of the Italian socialist party. This would change the course of Italian post-war politics. When the socialist–communist coalition eventually lost the elections in 1948, an American led organisation – USIS (United States Information Service) – which had been operating undercover in Italy since 1943, outed and sparked off an articulated and highly successful public relations program throughout the country aimed at permeating Italian society with western (i.e. US) values. This campaign continued well into the 1960s and became the foremost training ground for many Italian public relations operators, mostly concentrated at the time in Milan (private sector) and Rome (public sector).

In 1952 in Milan a group of operators, led by Roberto Tremelloni, a respected social democrat who would later become Finance Minister, founded the *Istituto per le Relazioni Pubbliche* (IPR, 'Institute for Public Relations'), whose aim was to disseminate the public relations approach to management both in the private and the public sector. In 1954 IPR launched the *Oscar del Bilancio* ('Oscar for Annual Report') and the first prize was won by Motta "because it was the first company to publish its annual turnover figures"! The *Oscar del Bilancio* still exists and is now run by FERPI and reputed to be the most authoritative and desirable recognition of transparency and best communication practices by the private, the public and the non-profit sectors of society.

But it was the Olivetti typewriter company, under the charismatic leadership of intellectual Adriano Olivetti, that marked the foremost maturation of visionary and local as well as global public relations practices in those years. Many young architects, poets and philosophers are attracted by Adriano to become public relations operators in its broadest interpretation, including, of course, internal, corporate, marketing and visual communications. The Olivetti experience, even after Adriano's death in 1960, runs as Italy's best practice well into the 1970s.

The first professional public relations associations were formed in the 1950s: *Associazione italiana per le Relazioni Pubbliche* (AIRP, 'Italian Association for Public Relations') and the *Sindacato Nazionale Professionisti Relazioni Pubbliche* ('National Union of Public Relations Professionals). The former was based in Milan and catered mostly for corporate practitioners; the latter was based in Rome and attracted consultants and public sector practitioners. In October 1956, in Stresa, the two collaborated to organise the first-ever international conference on public relations in Italy (Aa.Vv. 1956; Aa. Vv. 1957; Quaglione & Spantigati 1989).

The 1960s

In 1963, the Christian Democrat Party decided to call on the services of the then famous US consultant Ernst Dichter. Dichter is called late in the campaign and, not unexpectedly, suggests that the party should present a "younger face" and therefore renew its leadership. The party implements this reasonable advice by designing a poster with a healthy and smiling young country girl with a strong bosom and a bouquet of flowers in her hand under the headline "DC is twenty years old!". As soon as Palmiro Togliatti, charismatic leader of the communist party, sees the poster he orders his militants to write by hand on every poster – as an add-on pay off – the sentence: "and it's time to screw her!" It will take some thirty years for another famous American political consultant to play an active role in an Italian general election: Francesco

Rutelli used Jack Greenberg in his losing 2001 campaign against Silvio Berlusconi.

Private sector companies active in public relations activities in the 1960s, besides Olivetti, were mostly Pirelli – with an admirable program of spreading principles of modern management practices in the rest of the private sector through publications, workshops and seminars – and Ferrania, the film company that had been acquired in 1964 by 3M, which ran until the early 1970s a very intense public relations campaign to support young Italian photographers and researchers developing the major publicly available archive on historic and contemporary photography.

The 1970s

On 17 March 1970, the two professional associations, IRP and AIRP, reunited to form the *Federazione Italiana Relazioni Pubbliche* (FERPI, 'Federation of Italian Public Relations'). Since its inception in 1970, FERPI claims to pursue legal recognition of the profession and an intimate relationship with the media; it recognises the IPRA ethics code. These are intense years for the association: from 1972 to 1978, four national, "provocative", conferences were organised. In these years, the association also embarked on a full program of professional development for its members, including seminars and workshops on marketing, research, programming as well as evaluation and measurement of public relations effectiveness.

The year 1976 marks the birth of SCR Associati, soon to become Italy's largest and most influential public relations agency. In 1990 it was sold to the then UK Shandwick Group. And again in 1976, thanks to the efforts of professional Giuseppe Roggero (then chairman of SCR) and sociologist Francesco Alberoni, Milan opened the first public relations undergraduate course in the IULM Institute, followed a year later by a second evening course organised by Isforp, founded by Aldo Chiappe. IULM became a full-fledged university in the 1980s and the State therefore recognises the first ever public relations undergraduate course in Italy.

Since the early 1970s, the Italian political system becomes paralysed, social unrest moves from students to trade unions, entrepreneurs leave core internal information and communication activities into the hands of trade unions after fierce negotiations in 1974. The situation explodes in the mid 1970s with major corruption scandals in the private and public sectors and in the political leadership. Terrorism strikes hard and public relations activities are virtually suspended. It will take more than ten years for major corporations to recoup internal and external public relations as a relevant management task.

Many companies begin to indulge in cultural sponsorships, image campaigns, logo restyling and other so-called "worst practices" in media and editorial relations. As a result – particularly in the 1980s – they create a smokescreen that succeeds in covering their increasingly illegal practices with the State.

The 1980s

An integrated and powerful coalition between media tycoon Silvio Berlusconi and socialist-party secretary Bettino Craxi forces regulatory boundaries in favour of private television and opens full broadcast activities to advertising and corporate values into a lazy pauper communist–catholic oriented civil society. Mass consumption explodes. Intellectuals call this period the reign of the "culture of image" and "the culture of visibility". In 1985, Luca di Montezemolo – after resigning as head of public relations of the Fiat group – soothes Italians to dream along with the adventure of Azzurra in the America's cup: Azzurra is the first ever public relations consortium formed by major Italian corporations.

In 1986, for the first time, corporations spend more on market research into the effects of their communication, rather than into what consumers think of their products. In the second half of the decade, SCR, the agency which was by then one hundred people strong, collectively elaborates and successfully experiments the public relations methodology GOREL (government of relationships) which, many times updated since, is today often adopted as a scrapbook reference to public relations governance, evaluation and measurement of effectiveness.

The 1990s

In 1992 the *Mani pulite* ('clean hands') scandal erupts, involving a considerable number of public relations professionals involved in mediating illegal operations between businesses, political and media communities. A Rome-based association of educators and professionals named *Correnti* (still active today, and inspiring) theorises that only an organisation which communicates factual behaviour is credible and that, after so many years of consociate public policy making between majority and opposition as wells between both the above and the private sector, the identity of an organisation is the result of its success in distinguishing itself from other organisations: i.e. positioning comes of age.

A much-touted campaign for the privatisation of state-owned companies is launched in 1993 by a new transition government headed by Carlo Azeglio Ciampi; today President of the Republic. His public relations assistant Paolo Peluffo proposes as a blueprint for the Italian model the UK privatisation model, where public relations consultants lead all communication efforts. This unexpected move relaunches Italy's public relations practice, which had received a severe blow from the *Mani pulite* scandal (Spantigati 1995; Trupia 1992; Trupia 1989).

2.2. Public relations in practice: present scenario

A recent estimate by FERPI, based on a census by the government's Ministry of Public Function, indicates that some 70,000 individuals operate professionally in public relations in the public, private and non profit sectors of Italian society. More than 50 per cent operate in the public sector. To these one should add some 10,000 in the private sector, about 5,000 in civil society and some 15,000 who work as consultants and service providers to all sectors. Of the latter, about 1,000 operate in large agencies, mainly based in Milan and Rome, while the rest work in smaller or solo consultancies in the two large cities, but also in many other areas of the country.

FERPI has some 1,200 members, to whom one should add circa 1,500 members of the association of public sector communicators. Therefore, about 3,000 professionals, less than 5 per cent of the total, are members of professional associations.

Overall, the estimated annual investment in public relations activities in Italy in 2002 was is in excess of € 10 billion euro. This figure derives from the (moderate) assumption that average annual gross cost to the organisation of a pr professional is 50 thousand euro, that this figure, if the person is productive, needs to be tripled in terms of inducted expenses and that therefore $50,000 \times 3 \times 70,000$ equals more than € 10 billion euro.

2.3. Development of education and research traditions

Despite the fact that, beginning in the early 1960s, two different institutes, IPR (*Istituto per le Relazioni Pubbliche*, 'Institute for Public Relations') and IPSOA (*Istituto Post-Universitario per lo Studio dell'Organizzazione Aziendale*, 'Postgraduate Institute for the Study of Corporate Public Relations') ran courses in public relations mainly for practitioners, Italy has no consolidated tradition in public relations education.

IULM University in Milan was the first university in Italy (in 1993) to have a formally recognised undergraduate course in public relations; it was organised in the Faculty of Communication Sciences. Since then, three more undergraduate courses have been opened in other areas of the country: the University of Udine (by the Faculty of Foreign Languages, in 1998); the University of Catania (by the Faculty of Political Sciences) and again in IULM University, but now in the ITC branch at Feltre, near Padova.

In recent years the Italian university system has also opened forty-four undergraduate courses in communication sciences (one in almost every university) which, at least in theory, include the teaching of public relations. Communication sciences, however, suffer from the lack of teachers, who are usually not academics but professionals hired in temporary contracts. As to students, there are about 40,000 of them who take public relations as either their main studies, or as a subsidiary course.

Fearing an overspill of thousands of new entries in the profession with no true specific knowledge background, FERPI and Assorel (the association of agencies), also on the basis of an opinion poll which indicated that some 80 per cent of public relations and 38 per cent of the communication sciences students wished to enter the profession, in January 2002 embarked on a complex and ambitious project, named *Consulta Educa-tion*. In cooperation with Euprera, educators and student representatives from some thirty universities participated in a forum, during which FERPI and Assorel presented an offer to sign with each university an agreement by which
– the associations contribute to the formation and adaptation of the curricula;
– the associations will supply lists of expert educators from the profession willing to fill in teaching vacancies before purpose-trained teachers are available (see the next point);
– the associations will co-finance three-year research doctorates in public relations with the objective of creating full-time public relations educators;
– the associations will organise research and workshop projects with universities;
– the associations will press their members to take on young students for brief work experiences in their organisations.

This proposal was met with interest by the invited universities and, in the next few months, twenty-two expressed their willingness to sign the agreement. This obliged the associations to search for funds in order to co-finance the doctorates. Some funds have so far been found and agreements have been signed with the Universities of Milan (IULM), Udine (Gorizia) and Rome (Sapienza).

As to research in public relations, there are very few – if any – activities. Some individuals are active in research; institutionally, research is carried out only at Correnti in Rome, as mentioned earlier. However, the general feeling in the community is that the new doctorate programs will soon fill the huge gap in this area.

2.3. How language shapes the development of public relations

Considering the naming issue, Italy is plagued by a unique misnomer. Most Italians, and what is even worse, most professionals translate the term "public relations" in *pubbliche relazioni* instead of *relazioni pubbliche*, as it should be. It is as if the French used the term *publiques relations* rather than *relations publiques*, as they in fact do. The mistake in the translation was probably made in analogy with the equally wrong but established terms *pubblica amministrazione* ("public administration"), and *pubblica sicurezza* ("public security", i.e. the police). One could speculate that all three mistakes have to do with organisations which are viewed by public opinion as "weak" and "unrespected". As a result, that both terms (*relazioni pubbliche* and *pubbliche relazioni*) are sidestepped by many organisations, many serious professionals preferring to use the terms *relazioni esterne* ('external relations'), *immagine* ('image'), *comunicazione* ('communication') or *immagine e comunicazione* ('image and communication'). "PR" or even *Pi-erre* are often used to abbreviate the more denigrating concepts of public relations. In every-day language there are many confusions, for example, some newspapers once published classified ads for prostitutes and special massages under the title "PR". Recently, FERPI succeeded in getting publishers to stop this practice. Despite this "naming game", FERPI has decided, after many discussions, to maintain the name *relazioni pubbliche* and to use it provocatively and proactively as a matter of principle.

If one considers as public relations the sum of all these different names given to the profession at large, one can say that today the function is duly recognised as having a proper "licence to operate" by Italian business, media, public sector and non-profit communities.

In general we can say that responsible Italian leadership recognises the role of public relations in its broadest sense, which includes specifically media relations (except in the public sector as anticipated), opinion leader relations, support of marketing and advertising, corporate and financial relations, relations with the public policy process.

3. Typification of current public relations

3.1. Major roles of public relations and position in organisations

Referring to the description of the four roles of public relations set out in the *Bled Manifesto* (Ruler and Verčič 2002), we can sum up the Italian reality as follows:
- technical/operative professional role is by far dominant in the present scenario;
- the managerial role is sometimes present in larger organisations;
- the strategic or reflective roles as well as the educational ones are very rare.

In marketing-oriented companies the public relations function usually reports, in the best of circumstances, to marketing or, in the worst, to the advertising function. In corporate or institutionally oriented organisations, the function reports to the CEO, to the general secretary, to the COO or, sometimes, to the CFO. In the public sector, and keeping in mind the tri-partition of roles dictated by the new law mentioned earlier, the spokesperson reports directly to the politically elected leadership, while the media relations and relations with the public functions usually report to the highest bureaucratic role in the administration. In the non-profit sector, public relations and fundraising operators report to the leadership.

3.3. Current state in education

Currently, the Italian undergraduate system includes different public relation practices. Unable to refer to a consolidated academic discipline or to an established research tradition, universities are outlining formative routes on the basis of the possible professional applications. In contrast with Italian university tradition in other disciplines, undergraduate courses in public relation are now much closer to professional requirements.

We identify four trends in curricula. First, the classic corporate curriculum, often linked to the organisation of big events: it aims to train operators in marketing and corporate public relations in all its aspects of mass media, publishing, tourism. The adopted approach is communication management science: the education is intended as teaching the tools in order to realise an effective communication with public opinion, consumers and opinion leaders. Probably because it is perceived as the classic profession for public relation practitioners, this curriculum is actually the more popular with Italian students; besides, it represents the clear identity of some undergraduate courses.

Second, the small- and medium-size business curriculum, economic–communicational oriented. This aims to produce experts in integrated communication, marketing, negotiation and management of human resources and of corporate image and identity. It represents the curriculum oriented to the needs of small and medium Italian firms, which seem to discover the value of internal and external communication, of attention for human resources management and of quality in services and products. This curriculum is a kind of "bridge" between disparate educational traditions – namely, economics and communication/social science. They are combined thanks to a sense of business logic; so much so that in some universities this has been placed in the economics faculty).

Third, the institutional/public sector curriculum. This is directly related to the consequences of the new law (law 150, mentioned earlier), which aims to train experts in internal and external institutional communication and in public administration. There are three professional roles, each clearly defined by ministerial decrees: the spokesperson – who has an important political–institutional role – the media-relations office and the office of relations with the public. To allow public relations to enter state administration is in a way a revolution in the Italian culture of public services: it takes into consideration the citizen's point of view and focuses on quality and the increase of the public sector's effectiveness. This is the sector valued as the easiest for job opportunities by public relations graduates, but at the same time it is the least popular.

Fourth, the European–international curriculum. This trains experts in cultural, political–institutional, and language mediation. It is the new figure of the public–international mediator with relationship abilities on different levels (political–institutional, normative and socio-cultural management) and capacities in mediation between different European national realities. It is a curriculum born of the needs of the multiform

EU reality, as a bridge between the tradition of European political studies and the needs of communication and cultural–linguistic mediation.

Despite these articulations, many in Italian universities question the true essence of public relations and its basic disciplines. The base-education, on which is engaged the specific education, finds its roots in sociological, psychological, historic–geographic, legal and economic disciplines.

3.4. Major textbooks in public relations

Traditionally, the textbook used in most public relations undergraduate courses was the Italian translation of the Cutlip and Center book containing a long introduction by Giuseppe Roggero (Cutlip and Center 1997). More recently, Emanuele Invernizzi, the only full-time academic teaching public relations today (in IULM) has published with McGraw Hill two huge manuals (Invernizzi 2001, Invernizzi 2002), which are now widely used in various courses.

Recently published by Toni Muzi Falconi, *Governare le relazioni* ('Governing relationships'), represents for practitioners, scholars and students a critical as well as practical guide to the application of public relations tools in social, economic and political sectors (Muzi Falconi 2002).

Other books published in Italy reflect the growing interest in public relations practice, but most of them are concerned with specific areas, such as corporate image and corporate identity (Baldassi 2002), institutional communication for public administration (Grandi 2001), advertising (Lombardi 2001, 2002), marketing, etc. Moreover, in undergraduate courses, public relations is often taught using textbooks written by social and organisational psychologists, communicational sociologists and corporate economists.

3.5. Growing fields and hot issues

Ethics
Recently, the Global Alliance for Public Relations and Communication Management was formed, and this organisation is determined to define a new global protocol of ethic codes for all its member associations. This has sparked an intense discussion on ethics in public relations, which involves educators, professionals, researchers, ethicists, philosophers and

management consultants. In addition, the association of public sector communicators has embarked, in cooperation with FERPI, on the development of an ad hoc code for public sector professionals. This issue – which covers most of all the various aspects of the profession's responsibility to societal demands rather than only considering expectations of colleagues, employers, clients and specific stakeholder groups – is likely to last for some time as the Global Alliance protocol demands that each national association needs to review its own code of ethics in order to make sure that it is consistent with the global protocol. This issue also covers the enforcement issue. It appears that Italian professionals, although agreeing on the relevance of continued education through case histories, do not agree that, as in the US, enforcement of the ethics code should be abandoned.

Regulation

Though only a small minority of FERPI's members advocate regulation of the profession, this is undoubtedly a hot issue as more and more individuals enter the profession. The approach which seems to be gaining ground in order to foster some sort of "protection" from the declining reputation for public relations includes: (a) putting the protection of stakeholders and of the general interest before the protection of professionals, and (b) making sure that members of professional associations are constrained by a constant education process, by an updated code of ethics, by more viable internal enforcement obtained through legal recognition of the associations, thus obliging the latter to entrust to third party organisations the formal certification of member practitioners.

Alongside this, associations would also proactively advocate soft and, where necessary, hard regulations *erga omnes* by regulatory bodies and the state in those specific public relations practices which more than others are felt to have more impact on the public discourse, the public policy process and investor/consumer decisions (i.e. lobbying, political consultancy, media relations, financial and investor relations, life science and pharmaceutic public relations, consumer and marketing public relations).

Social responsibility

The discussion which is presently taking place is about how to avoid a public perception of the social responsibility issue as a "smokescreen exercise" and how to position professionals in an educational role in the organisations for which they operate. The discussion involves, besides professionals, a number of other communities including entrepreneurs, private, public and non-profit sector management, as well as academics and researchers.

Media relations

The whole area of the growing interdependence of public relations and the media community is a hot topic with Italians on both sides of the fence, and will continue to be a hot issue at least until the anomaly of article 9 of law 150, mentioned earlier, is resolved.

Measurement

Accountability and qualitative–quantitative measurement methods, both for relationship-oriented public relations and messaging media relations and events-based public relations, are constantly being requested by organisations who invest in public relations. In both areas there is a constant search for sophisticated and convincing methodologies.

4. Conclusions: state of the art and the future of public relations in Italy

4.1. State of the art

Seen as a whole, the Italian scenario of public relations appears composite and in marked evolution. The panorama includes several distinctive elements.

– *Practice*. One observes an increase in operators in the various domains and positioned frequently in the middle-lower level. At the same time, the associations of practitioners (FERPI, ASSOREL and others) have grown, consolidated professionalism through continuous and mandatory training and through the growing awareness of their members, as well as a growing influence on public opinion and opinion leaders.
– *Universities*. Universities and the specialised educational community have assisted in the recent development and growing success of courses which are practical rather than academic. This evolution was launched from inspirational principles of the recent reform of the Italian university system, even if this change is not always reflected in the organisation of specific courses. The new reality of public relations has set new requirements to start and consolidate specific research activities. Nowadays the intellectual community formed by psychologists, sociologists, communications specialists and business economists is united by the need and in-

tent to highlight common denominators in the interpretation, education, practice and research of public relations.

– *Social and cultural aspects*. These include the effects of the general explosion of interest in communication and the effects of the refined needs of the business community, or the requirements of public administration, public relations has taken new roads. The directions are marked by the need for fuller awareness and higher standards, by the need of quality in interpersonal and institutional relationship management and in the tools leading to effective governance, management and services.

– *Small- and medium-sized businesses*. This sector has discovered the value of public relations. The use of this profession in businesses has multiplied and diversified; it is not only the traditional use of advertising and marketing, but new application of public relaters in many traditional business functions and in new specialist sectors. The pervasiveness of public relations did not bring an immediate reflection on the distribution of roles. Many of these, when they are strategic, reflective and educational, are largely undervalued; and even if managerial roles progressively emerge, those which are used in technological sectors are prevalent.

4.2. Trends

If carefully observed, the evolution of public relations in Italy in these recent years clearly shows three trends that guide researchers and practitioners. First, relationships reflect the need to study and apply the perspective of symmetric relations of quality. The traditional approach of social psychology and of other human sciences and the use, more or less consciously, of persuasive and manipulative tools are slowly beginning to be replaced by different paradigms. Relationship management is becoming a profession in itself characterised by trust, credibility, symmetric and transparent relationships, and lack of ambiguity. This feature upsets traditional research paradigms of social psychology, of persuasion and of the classical communication theories. Today research begins to focus on issues related to relationship quality: exchange, trust, satisfaction and commitment. On an applied level, the corporation – but the public administration, too – appears impatient to transform this speculative knowledge in operative instruments that may enhance the value of relationships with stakeholders, opinion leaders, influent publics and public opinion.

Second, communication–public relations, in its social representation but also in everyday practice, is strongly correlated to communication theories and practices in advertising, business, institutional and interpersonal communication. These "blood-ties" partly explain the settlement of undergraduate courses in public relations in the legal cluster of communication sciences. In this sense, traditional research on communication, in the different fields – from sociology to psychology – shows the need for convergence towards innovative ad hoc paradigms applied to public relations.

And, finally, third, we can identify a trend in the growth of organisational knowledge and know-how. This trend reflects the need to rationalise organisational systems, to manage resulting excess capacities and to improve service and products by applying European norms of quality certification. Any public relations action – image-enhancement campaigns, significant events, the rationalisation of organisation charts and communications flows – when strategically and successfully created necessary implies the *forma mentis* of a rigorous organisation. In this sense, the art of good organisation becomes a new challenge, pushing ahead to create new territories for research and professional applications.

References

Aa.Vv (1956). *Atti della prima Conferenza Internazionale Relazioni Pubbliche* [Proceedings of the Second International conference on Public Relations]. Milan: Franco Angeli.

Aa.Vv (1957). *Atti della seconda Conferenza Internazionale Relazioni pubbliche* [Proceedings of the Second International conference on Public Relations]. Milan: Franco Angeli.

Baldassi, Carlo (2003). *Piccole e Medie Imprese Che Crescono* [Small and Medium Sized Enterprises That Grow]. Udine: arti grafiche fulvio 2003

Colarizi, Simona (1991). *The Opinion of Italians Under The Regime 1929–1943*. Bari: Laterza.

Cutlip, Scott M., Allen Center and Glen M. Broom (1997). *Nuovo manuale di relazioni pubbliche*. Milan: Franco Angeli [Transl. of Effective Public Relations, Englewood Cliffs, NJ: Prentice Hall, 1994].

Grandi, Roberto (2001). *La comunicazione pubblica. Teorie, casi profili normativi* [Public Communication: Theory and Case Studies]. Rome: Carocci.

Invernizzi, Emanuele (ed.) (2001). *Relazioni Pubbliche. Le competenze, le tecniche e i servizi di base* [Public relations: Competence, technique and core service]. Milan: McGraw-Hill.

Invernizzi, Emanuele (ed.) (2002). *Relazioni Pubbliche. Le competenze e i servizi specializzati* [Public relations: Specialist competences and services]. Milan: McGraw-Hill.

Lombardi, Marco (ed.). (2001). *Il dolce tuono* [The soft thunder]. Franco Angeli.

Lombardi, Marco (2002). *Il nuovo manuale di tecniche pubblicitarie. Il senso e il valore della pubblicità* [The new manual of technical advertisement: The meaning and value of publicity]. Milan: Franco Angeli.

Muzi Falconi, Toni (2002). *Governare le Relazioni* [Governing Relationships]. Milan: FERPI e Il Sole 24 ore.

Quaglione, Valeria and Federico Spantigati (1989). *La comunicazione in Italia: 1945–1960* [Communication in Italy: 1946–1960]. Rome: Bulzoni.

Ruler, Betteke van and Dejan Verčič (2002). *The Bled Manifesto on Public Relations.* Ljubljana: Pristop.

Spantigati, Federico (1995). *La comunicazione nella Seconda Repubblica* [Communication in the Second Repuclic]. Rome: Bulzoni.

Trupia, Piero (1989). *La democrazia degli interessi* [The democracy of interests]. Milan: Il Sole 24 Ore.

Trupia, Piero (1992). *La scuola italiana della comunicazione* [The Italian School of Communication]. Rome: Bulzoni.

Chapter 15

Malta

Carmel Bonello

1. National profile

1.1. Overview of national characteristics

Any account of the current state of public relations in Malta has to take
into account a number of considerations peculiar to this small sovereign
state in the centre of the Mediterranean Sea. These include its geographical position and size, its past and present neo-colonial history, the historic stronghold of the Catholic Church on the people (Sultana 1994: 34),
the economic situation, the gender issue as well as mass media. Malta has
two official languages: Maltese (a Semitic language that has undergone
much influence from Italian) and English.

Situated 96 kilometres from the southern tip of Italy and 290 km from
North Africa, Malta's geographical position reflects its culture and value
systems. It has a population of 380,000 in a surface area of 316 sq. km,
making it the fifth most densely populated country in the world. The
Knights of St John (1530–1798) and the British (1800–1964) left their
mark not only through massive defensive architectural projects that
today serve as valuable tourist attractions, but also on the commercial
and social life.

The British colonial legacy is amply evident. English is widely spoken
and, together with the Maltese language, Malta's official language.
Today's educational, financial, commercial structures, general institutions
and business culture are all modelled on British bureaucratic culture and
make ample use of the English language. This neo-colonial legacy is sustained through the continuous flow of British consultants, conference
speakers, examiners and trainers, who are constantly supplying business
ideas and educational contacts.

Values in Malta are shifting towards greater individualisation. This
shift does not have any special connection with the fact that Maltese are
islanders (Tonna 1996: 161), but, as Collins (1992: 54) suggested, it is a

permanent mixture of the cultural sky of modern societies. A values survey conducted by the Maltese sociologist Anthony Abela in 1995 found that the priorities for what Maltese consider to be important in life are family, work, religion, leisure, friends and politics (Abela 1996: 52–54).

Notwithstanding its limited resources and the inherent difficulties generated by its small geographical size, Malta has a thriving economy. After the closure of the British military base in 1979, on which Malta has been largely economically dependent for nearly 180 years, successive Maltese governments pursued a policy of restructuring and diversification. This was based on tourism with 1.18 million total arrivals in 2001, and on manufacturing for export with over 880 million Maltese lira (€ 2,128 million) in 2001, mainly to European Union countries (Central Bank of Malta 2002).

Indicators reveal a significant economic development. GDP per capita places Malta 45th in the world, which is considerably higher than other EU candidate countries such as the Czech Republic (54th), Hungary (56th), Poland (63rd) and Estonia (67th) (The Economist 2002: 26). From the 1990s onwards, Malta's international finance and maritime facilities were developed and marketed internationally.

Other important developments in the last two decades include the digitalisation of the telecommunication system, the establishment of a major 'offshore' business centre, the Malta Stock Exchange and the Malta Freeport, which is one of the most active in the Mediterranean. Legislation enacted in 1988, and further refined in 1997, resulted in the expansion of foreign investment in manufacturing industry (particularly in non-traditional fields such as electronics, information technology and pharmaceuticals). In 1997, the Institute for the Promotion of Small Enterprise (IPSE) was established to cater for the setting up and development of small enterprises. (In the fourth quarter of 2002 a plan was launched to amalgamate MDC, IPSE and the Malta External Trade Corporation into one organisation – the Malta Enterprise Board.)

1.2. Facts and figures about public Relations in Malta

Notwithstanding the significant developments mentioned earlier, public relations in Malta has not developed in terms of quantity and, even more importantly, in terms of quality. The main reasons are the nature of organisations, the nature of the public relations agencies, and the background of in-house practitioners. As to the nature of organisations, very few can afford to employ public relations practitioners or retain public relations consultants; these are government ministries, para-statal companies (enterprises in which the Maltese government is the biggest shareholder), government funded agencies and authorities and a small number of the major commercial companies. But the vast majority of organisations in Malta are small or micro-enterprises that either do not understand the need for public relations activities or cannot afford it. As a result, only a few marketing communication agencies have (small) public relations units. Other agencies deal with public relations activities through their advertising account-handling teams. The lack of any substantial public relations budgets also explains why international public relations companies have not yet set up shop in Malta – although some Maltese agencies work with these companies in the Maltese context where international campaigns are concerned.

There are no properly structured courses on public relations available in Malta that go beyond an introductory level. One cannot equip oneself with the necessary practical and analytical skills for a professional career specifically in public relations, unless one has the necessary financial support to follow either a distance-learning programme or a full-time course with a university overseas. The overall general level of public relations education is low and generally does not go beyond Grunig and Hunt's (1984) textbook level. But things are gradually changing: an increasing number of practitioners are university graduates, or have obtained a marketing communication certification, generally from British institutes. A good number of these practitioners are bringing with them a more solid approach based on theoretical underpinnings. They regularly deal with their foreign counterparts, gaining valuable experience and insights in the process.

Practitioners move out of the public relations field after a relatively short number of years (four to five years maximum). For the professionalisation process this presents both a brain-drain and a continuation problem, both of which need to be addressed.

Maltese public relations practitioners do not have their own national body. It is therefore difficult to come up with an exact number of those practising public relations and with descriptions of their qualifications and their respective jobs or, more importantly, to embark on a structured professionalisation process. One thing that is evident, though, is the increasing visibility of women employed in public relations as opportunities in the field expand. This positive note is generated through an increase over the last years in the number of female university graduates, who – it is hoped – would go on to consolidate their careers and gain promotion to higher status. From an insignificant percentage in the late 1970s, we estimate that over 30 per cent of all public relations positions in 2002 are occupied by women. In a country where there is still some resistance to the changing roles of men and women as currently taking place in the advanced industrial societies (Abela 1994) it may be surprising that about one third of Maltese practitioners in such a recently introduced occupation are females.

2. History and developments of public relations

2.1. Roots of public relations

The first organised efforts in public relations on a national scale in Malta were carried out by the Central Office of Information (COI), set up in 1955. The COI's aims were to ascertain that the Maltese people were kept informed about the government's plans, policies and achievements and that, through publicity campaigns, the government's plans are introduced and achieved (COI 1956). The COI was responsible for the Government's Printing Press, the official *Government Gazette*, the Educational Broadcasting Office which was set up in 1949, as well as for other government print and broadcast material. While in other colonies a department of information or propaganda was set up by the colonisers, who used it to boost the colonial government's credibility, Malta was probably the only British colony where this happened the other way round (Beng 1994).

In the 1960s, the economy in Malta started moving out of the confines of the immediate post-World War II period. With the advent of the Maltese government, following the 1964 independence, together with an increase in tourism and a booming construction industry, the Maltese market was ready for a significant increase in the range of imported products. The people employed by importing and manufacturing companies not only gained job experience in public relations from their British counterparts, but went on, in the 1970s and 1980s, to obtain marketing certificates and diplomas with a public relations content that were recognised in the UK.

2.2. Development of public relations practice

Up till the late 1980s, the public relations efforts of private industry were still mostly unstructured and unscientific. It was only in the late

1980s that private industry in Malta began to discover the power of public relations and was prepared to pay for public relations consultancy services. Though they had large media advertising budgets, the majority of major private companies had previously expected advertising agencies to write one-off press releases free of charge – that is, as an extra service for the fees agencies were earning from advertising revenue (this information was corroborated by various senior practitioners in the advertising field in Malta). By the early 1990s, the producers of local alcohol beverages and soft drinks followed the largest tobacco company in contracting public relations services, while the two major Maltese banks and the new mobile telephony followed suit by signing public relations consultancy retainer agreements. Hierarchically, the public relations departments in these organisations were usually located in the marketing departments.

The development of professional public relations in Malta is still in its initial stages. Companies manufacturing for export – both the local and the foreign-owned companies – rarely engaged in visible and planned public relations activities, either in Malta or abroad. They base all their efforts on the one-to-one contacts that are generally established during international specialised fairs, or during trade visits abroad organised by the Malta Export Trade Corporation (METCO).

Companies manufacturing for the local market focus their marketing communications strategy on advertising and participation in local specialised fairs. Thus, through a tradition of good quality products in a small market, they have built a loyal clientele for their products and services. The culture in which the managers of these companies have been bred does not consider spending hard-earned money on marketing communications as an investment to build and maintain a hospitable environment for their organisation.

So far, international public relations campaigns have only been carried out by Air Malta and the Malta Tourism Authority, mainly in Western Europe. Other Maltese organisations, such as the Malta Maritime Authority, the Malta Development Corporation, and the Maltese government itself, have arrived at a point where they are embarking on international public relations exercises to explain their respective functions and attract investment to Malta.

On the political front, in the 1970s a group of public relations officers (PROs) attached to Labour cabinet ministers or employed by para-statal organisations (such as Air Malta, Sea Malta, the former Telemalta now known as Maltacom, and two large commercial banks), emerged on the Maltese scene. Although some of these PROs had journalistic experience, most of them had no academic qualifications, though they did have experience of political militancy and co-ordination at grass-root, district and national party levels. They were appointed to sensitive and powerful posts, and eventually gained further access to greater power, to the point that their power at times went far beyond the limits normally associated with such posts.

At one point in the mid-1980s, in a clear attempt to curb the power of the Ministers' PROs, the Labour administration instructed all ministries that all press releases and media appointments had to be issued only through the government's Department of Information (DOI). This can be seen as an attempt by the Prime Minister of the day to contain the perceived advantage of extensive political exposure generated by these PROs for their respective Ministers.

The accumulated power and success in communicating messages of the Labour government were not to be repeated by the PROs of the Nationalist (Christian Democrat) administration when the latter was in power between 1987 and 1996 and from 1998 till today. Examples abounded where the benefits of developments carried out by the government, some of them accomplished even before other more developed countries (such as digital telecommunication and advanced health care services) were not adequately communicated to the people. As a result, the public remained unaware of the extent of the transformations. This lack of communication led many Nationalist Party (PN) members to believe that it was one of the main factors that contributed towards their loss of government in the October 1996 elections.

Aided by marketing techniques, the style of political performance in the last four general elections (February 1992, October 1996, September 1998 and April 2003) was packaged in a way to make it more acceptable to the public. Gone were the series of village-corner meetings with the participation of district candidates; instead, home visits and walk-abouts were the order of the day. The electoral campaigns of both major parties were increasingly transformed into road shows, that were planned, managed and manipulated with increasingly propagandistic skills. The Malta Labour Party is credited to have won the 1996 election by targeting with particular precision the floating voters, while in 1998, the PN succeeded in swinging back the electorate in its favour by using the same technique. (In Malta, a few thousand votes can sway a general election, yet the major difficulty lies in the ability of targeting these particular voters without alienating others.) Repeat positive performances were executed by the pro-European Union PN during Malta's EU Membership Referendum held in March 2003 and in April 2003, General Elections that actually gave the green light for the Maltese Prime Minister to sign the EU accession treaty.

There is no doubt that the constant use that the political parties make of the news media has increasingly politicised the Maltese society. Another contributing factor is the introduction of broadcasting pluralism, which provides more opportunities for political, commercial and non-profit making organisations to voice their opinions – all this in a small and fragmented market. Aided by political public relations, politicians still dictate and manipulate the country's news agenda. Following Malta's EU membership, one may envisage, however, that politicians may soon have to contend with a culture shift towards more individualisation, which may – in the medium to long term – reverse the present trend.

2.2. Development of public relations education and research traditions

The University of Malta, founded in 1694 and the oldest in the British Commonwealth outside the United Kingdom, provides education in the fields of accountancy, agriculture, architecture, communications, dental surgery, economics, education, engineering, law, management and medicine. It does not offer programmes in public relations beyond the introductory level.

But though various BAs communication students have completed dissertations in the area of public relations, research on public relations in Malta is limited and in itself does not constitute a comprehensive scientific discipline.

2.3. How language shapes the development of public relations

As stated above, due to the British neo-colonial heritage and an Anglo-American business marketing education, the Maltese term *relazzjonijiet pubblici* is rarely used in everyday practice. Instead its English version or the abbreviation "PR" is commonly used – even in Maltese conversation. The same happens in the case of key words, such as "publics" and "designations" – with the exception of *Segretarju Informazzjoni,* which is generally used in political party structures and by some NGOs.

In commercial organisations, public relations documents, as other written communications, are usually authored in English. In recent years, however, there has been an increase in the use of the Maltese language, especially when communicating with external publics of organ-isations and in particular present and potential customers and share-holders. Two reasons may be behind this move: a re-found respect for an important aspect of the Maltese national identity, both by Maltese com-panies desiring to highlight their Maltese-ness as a differentiating factor and by international foreign companies seeking acceptance in the Mal-tese market.

3.   Typification of current public relations

3.1. Status of public relations in business, administration and society

Public relations is slowly emerging as a field of its own. With the expan-sion of the news media through broadcast pluralism, more opportuni-ties are open for business, not least through sponsored events. In politics, the techniques of public relations – together with propaganda techniques – played a major role in the process of forming an opinion in favour of EU membership prior to the 2003 General Elections that sealed the country's decision to join the EU.

The functions of public relations manager and public relations officer ("technician", in Dozier and Broom's 1995 terms) have been the two most frequent role models (Bonello 1999). However, other titles, such as "communication manager" and "officer/executive" are used increasingly, which may lead the blurring of boundaries between public relations and other marketing communication tools.

3.2. Position of public relations in organisations

Research in Malta demonstrates that official designations do not reflect the work done by the respective practitioners. Hence, the respective designation may not be the best key to understanding what practitioners actually do, and designation status is only a label to describe individual cases. The profile of Maltese practitioners was surveyed through five ref-erence frames (Bonello 1999):

1. Professionalisation: including a code of ethics, the need for system-atic knowledge, training and qualifications, and a professional association.

2. Respectability: the practitioners' belief that public relations is con-sidered a prestigious occupation.

3. Monopoly of knowledge: the belief of the practitioners that public relations can be practiced only by qualified people.

4. Dissemination of information: their perception of disseminating information about public relations to their respective managements.

5. Negative regard: the practitioners' perception that management does not consider public relations to be a prestigious occupation.

Significant differences were found among practitioners concerning years in same public relations position, gender, location of public relations department and salaries.

Years in the same public relations position: the most significant difference registered by this variable was the contrast between those with more than ten years in the position who had a very low mean (more than 1 standard deviation below the factor mean) for negative regard (−1.18), and who were significantly different ($p < 0.077$) from practitioners with one to three years in position who had a just above the mean score (0.08) for negative regard.

Gender: there was one significant gender difference. This was only for the "negative regard" reference frame. Female practitioners were perceived with higher negative regard by managements (0.51 above the mean) compared to the male practitioners whose negative regard was −0.39 below the mean.

Location of public relations department: among those in-house practitioners who form part of their respective chairman/CEOs office, there is a higher attitude toward professionalisation and a perception of more positive regard for public relations from their respective employers.

Salaries: there is a significant difference ($p < 0.033$) between the lowest paid practitioners (less than € 12,550 in 1998) and the highest paid practitioners (more than € 18,875 in 1998) in terms of their perception of negative regard by their employer. The lowest paid group perceives a high negative regard (mean 1.14) whilst the highest paid group perceives a low negative regard (mean −0.88).

No significant differences were registered for such variables as years employed in public relations, age group, area of tertiary study and number of staff in public relations department. The issue of encroachment is sometimes at play in the relationship with other in-house professional areas. It is often the case that public relations practitioners are striving to regain the initially lost public relations' ground from other professionals, mainly accountants and lawyers and to a lesser extent from engineers and architects, rather than the other way round.

One could say that other professions feel that they do not like losing total control over the organisation's public relations, as the price would be the loss of the high visibility that public relations used to offer them. At the same time, public relations practitioners are generally aware of the possible negative repercussions that such a shift may create and, through a negotiated process, tend to avoid such a conflict. They usually achieve this by integrating, where possible, ideas of these professionals and by exposing, where and when appropriate, these other professionals in their respective professional role.

There are no marked differences between practitioners in profit organisations and public administration, while in the non-profit sector public relations is carried out on a totally voluntary basis, sometimes by practitioners who work in public relations in their full-time job.

3.3. Current state of education and character of major textbooks

Courses in public relations are limited to an introductory course in the BA Communications degree at the University of Malta, an evening course at the Malta College for Science and Technology and a series of short courses run by a private education company.

There are no specific Maltese textbooks; the books used in teaching public relations are British or American publications. This author is presently writing the first textbook about public relations in the Maltese language.

3.5. The local scene of public relations

There are forty-five agencies offering marketing communications, or mainly advertising and graphic design services in Malta. However, there are no public relations agencies as such. High-profile marketing communications agencies provide all the public relations services required by their clients through dedicated public relations units within the respective agency.

Maltese practitioners have a good standard of primary skills (such as high computer literacy and competency, writing press releases, translating public relations texts in a bi-lingual society and internal communication). Specialisation, which serves to increase both the value of public relations on the market and enhances their social standing, is lacking. At the same time, in most cases where the need for such a function has been recognised by management, practitioners have to perform single-handedly a broad range of public relations functions, which in other much larger organisations (in other countries) are dealt with by specialists for each respective function. This lack of specialisation is also reflected in the salaries earned by the average Maltese public relations practitioners. These salaries (€ 16,250 in 1998) are generally in the mid-range of the Maltese government's schedule of assimilated grades. The steady influx of graduates into public relations, while proving a cause of concern to existing practitioners without tertiary education, could certainly serve to inject a more professional approach to public relations.

Perhaps one of the most striking features in Malta is that public relations as a function within an organisation is often under the direct responsibility of top management. This could be due to senior management's desire to control, and at the same time profit from the subsequent benefits of public relations.

A higher degree of professionalisation and perceived recognition toward public relations is evident when this function is located at the chairman/ chief executive office, and not made subservient to some other department. This indirectly supports earlier research on the ideal location of public relations departments within organisations, namely, that by Acharya (1985), Benn (1982), Broom and Smith (1979), Cutlip, Center and Broom (1994), Dozier (1992), Grunig and Hunt (1984) and Schneider (1985). When placed within the chairman/chief executive office, as is frequently the case in Malta, there would be scope for Maltese public relations to become a valuable mechanism for managing its interdependence with its strategic publics (Ehling, White and Grunig 1992). On the other hand, Maltese practitioners have high expectations of their managements to help them financially to further their studies in public relations. Practitioners are aware that public relations cannot be pursued by anyone indiscriminately and that they therefore need to acquire a systematic body of public relations knowledge. This would help them to secure a monopoly of knowledge and improve their economic position. At the same time, monopoly of knowledge would avoid encroachment by "non-public relations professionals to manage the public relations function" (Dozier 1988: 6–13).

Maltese practitioners value respectability, and perceive themselves to possess it as well. Public relations is perceived by Maltese practitioners as a prestigious occupation. Journalists are ranked the lowest in terms of respectability by practitioners, who regard journalists as ambivalent in their respect of practitioners. This low regard of journalists was replicated as only 10.4 per cent of Maltese adults admit to trusting journalists (MISCO 1998). One interpretation of these results could be that management of organisations that employ practitioners either consider public relations to be related to overall effectiveness of the organisation in fulfilling its mission (McElreath 1977) and/or that practitioners have passed the acid test of contributing to the bottom line (Hon 1997: 5).

The importance of brand and corporate public relations – in that order – followed by internal communications, continue to be the main current issues in public relations in Malta. On the other hand, as competitive forces play a more significant role due to increased prospects of privatisation and imminent trade liberalisation, practitioners seem to be slowly expanding their activities to other functions. These include advising management and lobbying, issues management, financial public relations, corporate social responsibility, and investor relations. These are activities that increasingly portray the practitioner as an analyst of the social, political and economic contexts in which their clients operate. Culberston and Jeffers (1992: 54) argue that this type of activity – "widely viewed as central to the PR practitioner as a manager" – distinguishes the true public relations professional from the publicist or hack.

4. Conclusion: state of the art and future of public relations in Malta

It is evident that, collectively, Maltese practitioners have not, to date, consciously embarked on a "professionalisation project". The overall picture, however, seems to indicate that they are at a stage where they could be sufficiently prepared to start making a serious attempt to turn their occupation into a professional practice and themselves into professionals (Hughes 1963). In Malta, the main focus of the practice is still on press agentry/publicity and public information models of public relations (Grunig and Hunt 1984). It is no surprise, therefore, that the most characteristic services offered by Maltese practitioners are media relations and internal communications – both generally performed at present as a one-way, source to receiver, message production in which practitioners "seek to gain awareness of a client, perhaps to keep … turnstiles clicking" (Culberston and Jeffers 1992: 54). A further and, possibly, more relevant reason for this state of affairs is the nature of the para-statal sector. This includes the "'arterial' economic enterprises supplying other sectors of the economy and still operates within a protected market system considered by some as [consisting of] 'pure monopolies'" (Scicluna 1993: 17).

This sector appears to need the public relations function either to justify its present monopolistic position due to Malta's small size (economies of scale) and to serve national developmental needs or, in other instances, to raise the overall corporate profile prior to partial or full privatisation.

Although the importance of public relations is recognised, Maltese practitioners are still far removed from the point where they can demand legally accredited recognition. To begin with, they do not have a public relations association that could co-ordinate such an effort. At the same time, there exists an awareness of the need for practitioners, and hence a future public relations association, to embark on the initial phase of an information campaign about the role of public relations. This campaign should target practitioner–members' respective managements, managements of other organisations, and particular publics such as other professional associations.

Defining the field of public relations should be considered among the most pressing objectives for a public relations association for the advancement of public relations in Malta, as it would set the course toward social closure. This could be achieved by establishing and maintaining the independence of public relations from other disciplines and by emphasising the importance of education in contributing to the professionalisation of the field, as well as by an interactive approach towards professionalisation (l'Etang and Pieczka 1996: 3).

Education should be one of the logical objectives of a future national professional association as the organisation of education in public relations is another concern among practitioners. One of the hallmarks of a profession is establishing and maintaining a specialised body of knowledge (McElreath and Blamphin 1994). Empowerment of practitioners through "a formal education in which specialised skills are learned" (Lauzen 1992: 68) combined with expertise gained in the field, both of which significantly lessen individuals' feelings of powerlessness, may present a solution to this problem. It is therefore imperative that Maltese practitioners drastically improve both their academic level and their public relations knowledge through specialised courses devised for immediate and relevant application to the local scenario. Such courses may be organised both in conjunction with the University of Malta as well as by the proposed national association, in order to attain individual accreditation, following the development of an education and training matrix. This matrix will serve to establish the range of knowledge and skills necessary for public relations professionals. If certified by the University of Malta, the courses would more likely encourage the majority of practitioners to pursue them.

Finally, there seems to be a growing need for the establishment of a code of ethics among Maltese practitioners. This would provide a framework for practitioners as part of a more general effort to avoid encroachment by others, and members would be able to claim jurisdiction and be perceived as professionals.

References

Abela, Anthony M. (1994). Values for Malta's future. In: Ronald G. Sultana and Godfrey Baldacchino (eds.), *Maltese Society: A Sociological Enquiry*, 253–270. Malta: Mireva.

Abela, Anthony M. (1996). Shifting values: in Malta and Western Europe', *The Sunday Times (of Malta)*, 13 Oct.

Acharya, Lalit (1985). Public relations environments. *Journalism Quarterly* 62–3: 577–584.

Beng, Yeap Soon (1994). The state of public relations in Singapore. *Public Relations Review* 20–4: 373–394.

Benn, Alec (1982). *The 23 Most Common Mistakes in Public Relations*. New York: AMA-COM.

Bonello, Carmel (1999). The state of public relations in Malta. Unpublished M.Sc. thesis, University of Stirling.

Broom, Glen M. and George D. Smith (1979). Testing the practitioners' impact on clients. *Public Relations Review* 5–4: 47–59.

Central Bank of Malta (2002). *Quarterly Review*

COI (1956). Annual report. Central Office of Information Malta.

Collins, Randall (1992). Sociological Insight. New York, Oxford, p. 54

Culbertson, Hugh M. and Dennis W. Jeffers (19929). The social, political and economic contexts: keys in educating the true public relations professional. *Public Relations Review* 18–1: 53–65.

Cutlip, Scott M., Allen H. Centre and Glen M. Broom (1994). *Effective Public Relations* (7th edn.). Prentice-Hall.

Dozier, David M. (1988). Breaking public relations' glass ceiling. *Public Relations Review* 14(1): 6–13.

Dozier, David M. (1992). The organizational roles of communications and public relations practitioners. In James E. Grunig (ed.), *Excellence in Public Relations and Communication Management,* 327–355. Hillsdale, NJ: Lawrence Erlbaum Associates.

Dozier, David M. and Glen M. Broom (1995). Evolution of the manager role in public relations practice. *Journal of Public Relations Research* 7–1: 3–26.

Ehling, William P., Jon White and James E. Grunig (1992). Public relations and marketing. In James E. Grunig (ed.), *Excellence in Public Relations and Communication Management*, 357–393. Hillside, NJ: Lawrence Erlbaum Associates.

l'Etang, Jacquie and Magda Pieczka (eds.) (1996). Public relations education. *Critical Perspective in Public Relations*. London: International Thomson Business Press.

Grunig James E. and Todd T. Hunt (1984). *Managing Public Relations*. New York: Holt, Reinhart and Winston.

Hon, Linda Childers (1997). What have you done for me lately? Exploring effectiveness in Public Relations. *Journal of Public Relations Research* 9–1: 1–30.

Hughes, Everett C. (1963). Professions. *Deadalus* 92–4: 655–668.

Lauzen, Martha M. (1992). Public relations roles, introrganizational power, and encroachment. *Journal of Public Research* 4 – 2: 61–80.

McElreath, Mark. P. (1977). Public relations evaluative research: summary statement. *Public Relations Review* 3 – 4: 129–136.

McElreath, Mark, P. and John M. Blamphin (1994). Partial answers to priority research questions and gaps – found in the Public Relations Society of America's *Body of Knowledge. Journal of Public Relations Research* 6 –2: 69 –104.

MISCO International Survey Report (1998). Commissioned by the Media Centre, Blata l-Bajda, Malta.

Schneider, Larissa A. (1985). The role of public relations in four organizational types. *Journalism Quarterly* 62 – 3: 567–577.

Scicluna, Edward (1993). The restructuring of the Maltese economy. Malta, FOI publications.

Sultana, Ronald G. (1994). Perspectives on class in Malta. In: Ronald G. Sultana and Godfrey Baldacchino (eds.), *Maltese Society: A Sociological Inquiry*, 29 –53. Malta: Mireva.

The Economist (2002). *Pocket World in Figures.*

Chapter 16

The Netherlands

Betteke van Ruler

1. National Profile

1.1. Overview of national characteristics

With nearly 16 million inhabitants, the Netherlands is one of the smaller countries of Europe. Population per square kilometre is a little over 450, which is exceeded only by Bangladesh, Taiwan and South Korea. The Dutch economy has risen to an all-time high during the 1990s, thanks to an explosive services sector, which contributes almost 70 per cent to the gross domestic product (GDP). Compared with the US, Dutch GDP is 110:145 (i.e. Netherlands: US = 110:145) – compared with Poland, for example, which has a GDP of 110:38 (Netherlands : Poland = 110:38; 1998 figures). Employment is high, with less than 5 per cent unemployed in 2001 and just 13 per cent employed by the government. Nevertheless, one million of the potential labour force of seven million people are not able to work because of long-standing physical or mental illnesses, and are maintained by a government support system. In 2001, 13.5 per cent of the population was older than 65 and therefore without a labour agreement. In a few decades, this will be about 20 per cent or even higher. Of course this will challenge the rather generous state assistance and pension system.

The Netherlands is a country of reasonable diversity. One third of the population state that they are (passive or active) Catholic; almost one third call themselves Protestant of any kind; and the remainder are of miscellaneous denominations (almost 1 million are Islamic) or without religion. This does not mean that religion is institutionalised; one can easily state to be a Catholic without going to church or even without giving any attention to the pope. Most people have been Dutch for generations; 1.7 million are first- or second-generation immigrants. Although Dutch women are not as emancipated as in the Scandinavian countries, the gender development index is almost 0.7, which is rather high.[1]

Ever since the seventeenth century, the Netherlands have been known for its high level of wealth, both economically and culturally. The country is famous for painters like Rembrandt and van Gogh. Many people in other continents had contact with the Dutch because of their entrepreneurial nature, business sense and because of their questionable history of colonisation. It is said that the Dutch were as successful as they were because they had to overcome the poor level of Holland's natural resources, and therefore developed an earthy nature, strict working ethics and a very strong propensity to negotiation and consensus. At the same time the Dutch have built the questionable reputation of pretending to know how people in other societies in the world should behave. The Oxford Dictionary defines talking to people as a "Dutch uncle" as "lecturing them paternalistically" (Hofstede 1987: 5). The expression "Dutch party" stands for ungenerous behaviour with money. And the country is famous (or notorious) because of its liberal behaviour with respect to drugs, which – at least by the Dutch themselves – is seen as the best way to cope with this problem: drug trafficking is illegal but the use of it is allowed.

The Dutch have always had a strong outside orientation, but at the same time a very tight societal concept. This concept is often characterised by "pillarisation" (civil society was in all its institutions and partly still is built on four pillars: Catholic, Protestant, socialist and liberal), "corporatism", and "consensus" (see Ruler 2003). Freedom of speech, religion and assembly, and respect for people's spiritual freedom are the basis of the constitution. Moreover, civic literacy is seen as the primary basis of democracy, and institutionalised in the law on public information. Transparency of and involvement in politics is therefore a basic requirement of the functioning of the democratic political system.

According to Vossestein (2001), basic values of the Dutch were always egalitarianism and a high working moral. He claims that the Dutch have difficulty in dealing with hierarchy, always trying to maintain a balance between being aware of the hierarchical aspects of a relationship and not wanting to make that awareness too obvious. Common people are the norm, the elite can be mocked – that has been a motto in the Netherlands for decades. Although the labour market in the Netherlands is highly com-

---

1. See Gallagher, Laver and Mair 2001. This index measures the degree of women's representation in key areas of political and economic life, taking into account the number of women in national parliaments, women's share of earned income, and their levels of occupancy in a range of professions.

petitive, competition has not been appreciated that much. One certainly never may compete at the expense of weaker players or colleagues. "Act normal, that is strange enough" and "Never put your head above the parapet" are widely known expressions. Moreover, those with talent should deploy it for the benefit of all, not just for themselves, according to Vossestein.

Another characteristic of the Netherlands is the fragmentation of its politics. Many parties compete for electoral and parliamentary support and none of these is in a position to win a working majority on its own. That is why every government is a system of coalitions and alliances. The major parties still represent the ideological pillars of the last century: socialist, liberal, religious (Catholics and Protestants now work together in one party), but apart from them, all kinds of interest groups can form their own party and contest for control of the parliament.

1.2. Facts and figures of public relations in the Netherlands

Public relations is an established industry in the Netherlands. Nine out of ten organisations with more than fifty staff employ personnel with "communication duties". Six out of ten of these organisations also have special departments aimed at the "coordination of their communications". We can therefore conclude that public relations – or "management of communication", as it is called in the Netherlands – is a normal fact of division of labour. In a general labour market of about six million, some 30,000 people are employed in public relations within organisations (of which, however, 50 per cent have other tasks as well, in personnel or marketing departments, office management, etc.) and about 25,000 in consultancies (Ruler and Lange 2000). About 20 per cent of the communication employees work in the public sector (government and semi-governmental organisations), at national, provincial and local levels. The average communication-unit employs six people. Marketing communication is included in these figures as in the Netherlands it is impossible to distinguish marketing communication/advertising and public relations/corporate communication. What some call "public relations" is better seen as (part of) marketing communication; others speak of communication management – but in fact mean advertising – or use "marketing communication" in such a broad sense that others would label it "corporate communication" or "communication management".

Until the beginning of 2002, consultancy was a booming sector with some 11,500 consultancy firms. At least three thirds of these firms are one-person operations; 90 per cent have fewer than ten employees – so it is a branch with many small businesses. In an analysis of its service supply, van Ruler and de Lange (2000) found that the consultants typify their work most often as "communication advice", followed by "advertising", "creative work" and "public relations" (in the sense of publicity-seeking). The consultancy sector is clearly a young sector: almost half of the firms have existed five years or less. The age of the consultancies correlates directly proportionally with their size: the longer they have existed, the larger they are. There is also an almost linear relationship between size and profitability; according to the rules of the VPRA – a Dutch association of some 60 consultancies – consultancies with less than seven employees have a very low profitability. That means that the long-term viability of most of the consultancies is very much at risk.

2.   History and development of public relations

2.1. Roots of public relations

The period of Enlightenment, as developed in the eighteenth century in France and Germany, strongly influenced the evolution and practice of public relations in the Netherlands. In the eighteenth century, science and knowledge were no longer seen as being relevant only for the elite, but had to be diffused. The means for this diffusion was *voorlichting*, which is a literal Dutch translation of 'enlightenment'. The idea of *voorlichting* is based on an expression of Kant: *sapere aude* (literally, 'dare to know') and which was meant as "all people must have the intention to be informed on what is going on and must be enlightened, so that they can take part in the ongoing debate about and development of society". This is equivalent to what Habermas (1962) means by the "open bourgeois debate". Besides 'education', *voorlichting* was seen as the main instrument to help people get informed. In the nineteenth century the concept of *voorlichting* developed into "giving full information to all people to mature and emancipate". The administration as well as civil society organisations started to introduce *voorlichters*, specialists who travelled around to give information about health, good farming, housekeeping, education, politics, etc.

At the same time, the elite remained sceptic about this full enlightening of ordinary people. That is why most of the time *voorlichting* was also used to show people how to conduct themselves as good citizens and to control them. The history of public relations in the Netherlands can therefore be seen as a history of the battle between information and emancipation on the one hand, and education and persuasion on the other hand – but always under the ("Dutch uncle") dogma of "knowing what is best". In all theories of *voorlichting* the rather pedantic premise is, that it is given for the benefit of the person or group to be enlightened, even when the "victims" did not want to be enlightened at all – or at least not in that way.

The characteristics of the practice of this *voorlichting* can still be seen in the daily practice of public relations departments and consultancies. The evolution of public relations in the Netherlands cannot therefore be captured in terms of "publicity" or "press agentry" but all the more in terms of "public information" and well-meant (but patronizing) soft-selling "persuasion".

Due to changing management styles, this is, nowadays, blurring with publicity and imagery. At the same time, dialogue, negotiation and consensus-building are natural exponents of Dutch culture, which for centuries has relied on the practice of consultation and the involvement of as many people as possible in decision-making (Hofstede 1987). Every issue bearing even the remotest risk of disagreement has a forum of its own in which all interested parties are represented, whether it be traffic issues, defence matters, or education affairs. Kranenburg (2001: 38) showed that this culture has many repercussions in politics. "The more the relevant bodies agree, the less freedom of movement remains for the politicians. It was under these conditions that the now well-known "polder model" emerged in the early 1980s.("Polder" is a Dutch word for reclaimed land, made out of water or swampland.) At that time, politicians planned to intervene in the country's wage levels and to tackle the high rate of unemployment in the 1980s by sharply reducing labour costs. Facing the loss of their freedom of negotiation, trade unions and employers agreed to a voluntary wage restraint in return for a reduction in working hours. The political establishment had no choice but to bow to this "voluntary" agreement between employers and unions. The symmetrical model is, so to speak, "the" model by which the Dutch have done business for ages. What the public relations sector has added to this are the idiosyncrasies of *voorlichting*.

2.2. Development of public relations practice

Many state that public relations was invented in the United States and crossed the ocean together with Marshall Aid after World War II. This is certainly true for the term, but not for the practice. The origins of Dutch communication management can be found as early as in the seventeenth century. At the time, consular civil servants had to report regularly on

events in the country where they were stationed, which might be important for shipping, trade and industry. Later, civil associations hired specialised *voorlichters* to give information on better housekeeping, farming,
and on sexuality, for instance (Katus 2001). When industrialisation became
a fact, industries started to provide information on their well-being to the
press as well as to the general public. The first press departments originate
in the beginning of the twentieth century. The government followed soon
and founded departments to inform journalists. Dutch journalists, however, preferred to keep direct access to administrators and politicians.
Thanks to the strong pillarisation of society, with each pillar using its own
media and therefore its own political contacts, their lobby was successful
for a long time and the governmental public relations departments were
forced to aim their press releases to foreign journalists only.

Moreover, according to Kickert (1996) the Netherlands can be seen as
an almost perfect example of the modern non-static concept of what he
calls "neo-corporatism". This (European) model emphasises the interests
represented by a small, fixed, number of internally coherent and well-
organised interest groups that are recognised by the state and have privileged or even monopolised access to the state. Usually, the most important groups in a corporatist society are employers, employees and the
state. However, in the Netherlands, all kinds of single-issue pressure
groups are also involved in the system.

These characteristics have influenced the practice of public relations.
Civil society is seen as the basis of society-building in the Netherlands and
pressure groups are a natural part of life. Many authors state that this is due
to the consensus-building nature of the Dutch, and that pillarisation and
corporatism therefore never resulted in a strongly polarised society, even in
the turbulent 1960s. Moreover, pressure groups have been allowed great involvement in decision-making, in politics and nowadays also in the corporate arena, as long as they are not too violent in their approach. That is why
cooperation is an important strategy of Dutch pressure groups. Van Luijk, a
professor in business ethics in the Netherlands, calls it "democratisation of
moral authority" and sees it as a trend (Luijk and Schilder 1997). As a result, aggressive persuasion is not an acceptable public relations strategy.

2.3. Development of education and research traditions

The first courses in public relations were offered as optional courses at a
university level as early as in the late 1940s, always under the umbrella of

"mass communication" and "journalism". Public relations was most of all seen as "working for the public, with the public, and in public", and was therefore seen as a function in the larger societal communication system (Ruler and Verčič 2003). In such a societal approach, public relations serves the same kind of (democratic) function as journalism does, as they both contribute to the free flow of information and its interpretations, and to the development of the public sphere in volume ("How many people are involved in public life?"), in level ("What is the level at which we discuss public matters?"), and in quality ("What are the frames used in the debates?"). Education and research in public relations was for a long time closely related to education and research in journalism, not because the practitioners have to deal with journalists, but because of these overlapping functions in society (see Meiden 1978). This is changing. Both education and research are nowadays approached from a management perspective and as a result, research changed direction, too: more and more it addresses the effects of certain public relations approaches to publics, and hardly the (unintended) consequences in society.

2.4. How language shapes the development of public relations

In the early days, the discipline was called *voorlichting*, "in- and external relations", "press contacts", or "public relations". *Voorlichting* was the common name in the public sector, the other names could be found in the non-profit and profit sectors. Courses and books often used the combination "public relations and *voorlichting*" when describing the discipline. *Voorlichting* covered public information and emancipation on the one hand, and, on the other hand, education and persuasion. Public relations has been reduced mainly to all activities that can be covered by "in-house journalism", "publicity seeking" and "pampering those that the organisation wants a relation with".

As in many European countries, public relations in the Netherlands is not called "public relations" anymore (if it ever had been). This is because of the negative connotations of the term, but also because of the one-way and non-scientific orientation of the practice. Nowadays, the term is only used in a negative way, to define what can be seen as bad for one's image ("This is bad PR for you"), and by some consultancies which work for US enterprises and are oriented at publicity seeking. Currently, the most common names for the field are "corporate communication", "communication management", or just "communication". Van Riel (1995) provided the theoretical foundations of existing ideas, and showed the need for co-ordinated and integrated communications. This broadening goes hand in hand with the growing discussion in the profession on what management of communication entails.

Pre-period: enlightenment	First monitoring system by civil servants for industry and trade in the seventeenth century; first *voorlichters*, who provided information on farming, housekeeping, sexuality, etc. in the eighteenth century.
First period: public information (1920–1940)	First press departments in industry and government.
Second period: institutionalisation (1945–1965)	1946 First association of professionals; institutionalisation of the profession, named public relations and *voorlichting*.
Third period: professionalisation (1965–1985)	1964 First chair in *voorlichting*; 1976 First public relations chair; 1978 first BA program; start of many courses at different levels; 1980 Law on Public Information.
Fourth period: corporate persuasion (1985–1995)	Rapidly growing influence of the corporate communication concept; change of name into 'communication'.
Fifth period: back to the roots? (1995–	Governmental campaigning shows hardly any effect; image building is under pressure: its effects are now seen as dubious; main topics become responsiveness, transparency, identity and dialogue.

Figure 1. Development of public relations practice in the Netherlands

3. Typification of current public relations

3.1. Status of public relations and major roles

The field of what is now called "communication management" or "corporate communication" is widely accepted. Almost all organisations have "communication employees" or at least structural contacts with communication consultancies. Managers see communication as an important or even as a critical factor for success. Recently, an official commission advised the prime minister on how to cope with communication in the new information age and was very positive about the necessity of good communication management in the public sector (Commissie Toekomst Overheidscommunicatie 2001).

The European study on the parameters of public relations showed four characteristics of public relations in Europe: the reflective, the managerial, the operational and the educational elements (Ruler and Verčič 2002a). Accordingly, four professional roles can be found.

(1) Counseling the organisation on their answers to changing values in society (issues management).
(2) Planning communication programs in order to secure the trust of publics and public opinion.
(3) Service-providing in order to facilitate the communications of the (members of the) organisation;
(4) Coaching the members of the organisation to communicate competently (Ruler and Verčič 2002b).

According to a trend-watch of the Association of Communication service providing is a dominant characteristic of public relations in the Netherlands (Lebbing 2002). The educational sector strives for more planning of communication activities. Governmental communication professionals have introduced the "Silver Standard" several years ago, which stipulates that all campaigns must be evaluated; there is growing attention in the profession for evaluation methods. The debate in the professional journals and at congresses however concentrates on counseling and coaching roles. These are seen as the new challenges of the profession. This goes hand in hand with a discussion on the identity of the profession.

3.2. Position of public relations in organisations

A large representative survey (Ruler and Lange 2000) on the structural representation of communication in organisations with more than fifty staff showed that almost all these organisations have communication employees and that the responsibility for communication activities is placed at a high level. However, the internal visibility of the profession is still rather low. Of those responsible for communication activities, less than half (42 per cent) reported to have a job title that relates to communication in one way or another (including external communication, *voorlichting*, public relations and advertising). Unsurprisingly, communication-related job titles correspond with the presence of single departments coordinating different communication activities (though this correspondence is not complete). Many respondents indicated that there is one special department in which communication activities are coordinated, but that these departments are not always headed by a "real" communication manager – that is, a departmental head who is named as such. In such cases, the management of communication activities is obviously "encroached" by another department. Remarkably, if a job title has the word "communication" in it, its hierarchical position is different compared with titles that refer to, say, "marketing". Staff functions and positions at middle management or operational level coincide more often with the use of "communication" in the title, whereas among members of the management team, marketing-related titles prevail. This indicates that communication under the marketing denomination often has a management position. Single communication departments, however, participate less in the board of directors. It is clear that communication management is seen as important within organisations, but not via a visible and specialised department at the managerial level.

Another indication of internal visibility is budget. Almost half the respondents in the study indicated that there was no structural budget for communication activities (40 per cent) or that they did not know what this budget was (9 per cent). Communication management is apparently given a position at a higher staff or management level of responsibility, but this is far from being translated yet into a structural communication budget. All in all, communication management is a normal part of job differentiation, but it definitely cannot yet be regarded as being fully established in the hierarchy of organisations – at least not at managerial and strategic levels, as normative theory presumes.

Recently, the Association of Communication has developed levels of practice: assistant, communication employee, senior communication consultant, communication manager, and has built a lists of competencies (www. communicatie.com). Next step will be to develop profiles within the levels.

3.3. Current state of education and character of major textbooks

At first sight, the Dutch communication industry is professionalised. The educational system in public relations is very well developed, although still focused on the vocational level. There is a well-developed system of education in craft communication activities, both at undergraduate and at graduate levels. Almost all (about thirty) polytechnics offer full BA programs in organisational communication or communication management (240 European credits), and almost all the thirteen research universities offer BA streams in this area, of about 20, 60 or 120 European credits. Education at Masters level has not yet been fully developed. There is one university-based Masters program in applied communication science (aimed at organisational communication problems and rated as one of the best Master programs ever), one in Corporate Communication (post-initial education), one in Policy, Communication and Organisation, and two in what used to be called *voorlichting*. Most universities are currently working on new Masters programs and communication management will be one of the programs most universities will be offering. The Netherlands School of Communications Research, (NESCoR), offers a Ph.D. program in communication science. However, communication management is hardly researched yet. In 2003, two chairs in organisational communication will be founded. This will be helpful in developing organisational communication and its management as new themes in this research school, and it elevate the production of a body of knowledge.

Still, knowledge reproduction is not a professional norm either. Of those responsible for communication, 90 per cent have no educational background that has anything to do with communication. This could, of course, be partly caused by the fact that most educational programs have been developed only since 1980s. One could say that long experience could be equalised with higher education. But also 90 per cent of those responsible for communication have been in the field less than three years. It is obvious, then, that it is not a sector for which a special background is needed in order to get a job. The figures indicate that this will change: the Monitor mentioned earlier showed that the younger the communication managers, the more often educated they are. Clearly, the profession does not yet meet the classic criteria of professionalism. Indicators of professionalism are: a well-functioning knowledge-production and knowledge-reproduction system.

Turning now to textbooks, judging by the number of new titles in corporate/organisational communication and communication management, the Dutch communication management book-publishing industry must be flourishing. A bibliography of the Association for Communication, developed in 1999, showed more than 350 Dutch titles. Best-selling practical books are those written by professionals, aimed at such topics as organisational change, organisational culture, internal communication, crisis communication, reputation and corporate identity. The more checklist based and standardised it is, the better it sells. But most books are relatively shallow and unscientific. For example, most authors feel no necessity to define what they mean by communication, and they hardly use any communication models to explain what they mean. If anything, Shannon's mathematical communication model is used, blurred with the ingredients of the Berlo's SMCR model, and fused down to a linear flow model of communication, sometimes referred to as "the classic communication model" (Ruler 1996).

Some scientific books have been produced by researchers for use in education. However, at the vocational level it is no longer common practice to use books: most teachers produce readers for their students with all kinds of written materials and Internet links. At the scientific level, the best-selling books are the Anglo-American textbooks published by the international publishers. Earlier the German scientific literature on communication science was used as well. However, since German has become an optional course in secondary schools, this is no longer the case.

3.4. The local scene of public relations

After the Second World War, Dutch society had to be rebuilt and it became important to promote business and social goods (Katus 2001). Because of the Nazi propaganda during the war, people had a strong aversion against any form of promotion of ideas from above – stronger than ever. There was therefore a strong debate in society about the ethics of any kind of promotional activity. According to Lagerwey, Hemels and van Ruler (1997), the Dutch tend to solve these problems by creating associations. The first professional association was established in 1945, initiated by a journalist but open to public relations professionals as well as journalists. The goal of this association was to facilitate the exchange of knowledge between journalists and public relations officers (representing government, corporations and agencies) and to remove the fear of political and official information, which was strongly associated with Nazi propaganda. This first professional association was followed, in 1946, by the first specialist public relations association, called *Vereniging voor Openbaar Contact* ('Association for Public Contact'). As a forum for press officers of corporations and the government, it was later renamed as the Association for Public Relations in the Netherlands (now called the Dutch Association for Communication). The primary aims of this association were to promote knowledge development among practitioners, to provide networking opportunities and to help develop an identity for the profession. In 1967 those members who worked in consultancies decided to form their own association, and in 1978 they finally established the Association of Public Relations Consultancies (VPRA). Nowadays, this association comprises about sixty consultancies, mostly small ones. Some of the larger consultancies are associated in the former Association of Advertising Bureaus (the VEA), nowadays aimed at the association of communication consultancies. Until five years ago, almost all consultancies were Dutch. Today, at the beginning of the twenty-first century, most of the larger consultancies are associated with or owned by international firms, most of which are American. They form their networks within their own consultancies and seem no longer interested in the development of the profession in the Netherlands.

In 1968, the communication professionals of the public sector started their own association, as did the in-house journalists, who started the Association of In-House Journalists (which merged with the Dutch Association for Communication in the late 1990s). This was followed by the establishment of the Contact Centre of Public Relations for professionals in public relations, advertising, journalism and marketing (in 1973) and the establishment of a section *Voorlichting* of the Association of Journalists in 1977 (originating from an independent Association of "Honest Enlighteners") and the National Association of Communication (in 1988; now merged with the Dutch Association for Communication). Besides these national associations, there are numerous local, regional and sector-focused associations and informal networks.

3.5. Growing fields and hot issues

There are no real "hot issues" in the public relations scene. In the 1960s and 1970s the public relations community had long and hot debates on its core issues and its relation to other managerial areas. These debates are over. However, it could well be that a new debate is forthcoming, due to two factors. The first factor is the decline of the economy and, consequently, of communication budgets. The second factor is the vague identity of the profession. As long as it was just *voorlichting* it was obvious what the profession stood for. Now that it is tagged with such labels as "communication management" and "communication advice", its goals do not spring to mind automatically – the profession has not yet been able to define what in essence it has to offer or what the big issues could be.

4. Conclusion: state of the art and future of public relations in the Netherlands

There are several indications that public relations will change enormously in the next few years. The government commission on the future of governmental communication management stated in 2001 that "communication belongs to the heart of decision-making and communication specialists have to support this communication" (Commissie Toekomst Overheidscommunicatie, 2001).This favours the counseling and coaching roles that were identified in the European Delphi study as upcoming roles for communication management (Ruler and Verčič 2002a). It is striking that there is a structural decline in campaigning and image building in favour of identity building, with a strong emphasis on internal communication. Internal communication is said to become *the* or at least an important service supply of the consultancy sector and communication departments. A recent search for the most compelling themes in the profession showed top priority for "the increasing demands on the profession to give advice on the role of communication in organisational change" (Lebbing 2002). Moreover, trend watchers point out the trend of increased accountability of general management. This will give room to planning and evaluation and well-defined communication programs. Last but not least, there is an upcoming orientation in the public sphere on norms and values in society and social responsibility of corporations. Public moral is becoming rather strong in this matter nowadays and law becomes more restrictive in this respect.

These issues urge for a renewed discussion on the identity of public relations. Image building is never been seen as the normal way of doing business, but rather as "the American way". The Dutch don't mind that as long as they can use it, but the norm is swerving back to "Never make yourself bigger than you are". Normative theory on public relations as image building gets much attention, but it is increasingly seen as untrustworthy. That is why working on identities is increasingly seen as a better investment than working on images, as a leading professional, Ron van der Jagt, stated in a series of articles in the journal of the public relations practice *Communicatie*. In this debate, the cultural roots of *voorlichting* and the idiosyncrasies of Dutch nature cannot be neglected.

References

Commissie Toekomst Overheidscommunicatie (2001). *In dienst van de democratie. Het rapport van de Commissie Toekomst Overheidscommunicatie* [In democracy's service: report by the commission The Future of Government Communication]. The Hague: SDU.

Hofstede, Geert (1987). *Gevolgen van het Nederlanderschap: gezondheid, recht en economie* [The results of Dutch citizinship: health, justice and economy]. Inaugural lecture, University of Maastricht.

Katus, Joszef (2001). Government communication: development, functions and principles. In: Joszef Katus and and Fred Volmer (eds.), *Government Communication in the Netherlands*. The Hague: SDU.

Kickert, Walter J. M. (1996). Expansion and diversification of public administration in the postwar welfare state: the case of the Netherlands. *Public Administration Review* 1.

Kranenburg, Mark (2001). The political wing of the "Polder Model". In: *The Netherlands: A Practical Guide for the Foreigner and a Mirror for the Dutch*. Amsterdam and Rotterdam: Prometheus and NRC Handelsblad.

Lagerwey, Eric, Joan Hemels and Betteke van Ruler (1997). *Op Zoek Naar Faamwaarde: Vijftig Jaar Public Relations in Nederland* [Searching Fame's Value: Fifty Years Of Public Relations In the Netherlands]. Houten: Bohn Stafleu Van Loghum.

Lebbing, Teus (2002). Onzekerder dan ooit? Communicatiemens: nog meer manusje van alles. [More uncertin than ever before? Communication person: even more jack-of-all-trades]. (7) *Dialoog*, Nov./Dec.: 4–6.

Luijk, Henk van and Arnold Schilder (1997). *Patronen van verantwoordelijkheid: ethiek en corporate governance* [Patterns of responsibility: ethics and corporate governance]. Schoonhoven: Academic Service.

Meiden, Anne van der (1978). *Wat zullen de mensen ervan zeggen? Enkele visies op het publiek in de ontwikkelingsgang van de public relations* [What will people say? Some views of the public in the development of public relations]. Inaugural lecture. The Hague: NGPR.

Riel, Cees B. M. van (1995). *Principles of Corporate Communication*. London: Prentice Hall.

Ruler, Betteke van (1996). *Communicatiemanagement in Nederland* [Communication management in the Netherlands]. Houten: Bohn Stafleu Van Loghum.

Ruler, Betteke van (2003). Public relations in the polder: the case of the Netherlands. In: Krisnamurthy Sriramesh, Krisnamurthy and Dejan Verčič (eds.), *Handbook of International Public Relations*. Hillsdale, NJ: Lawrence Erlbaum Associates.

Ruler, Betteke van and Rob de Lange (2000). Monitor communicatiemanagement en -advies 1999: de stand van zaken in de Nederlandse beroepspraktijk [Monitoring communication management and advice 1999: the state of affairs in the Dutch professional practice], *Tijdschrift voor Communicatiewetenschap* 28–2: 103–124.

Ruler, Betteke van and Dejan Verčič (2002a). *The Bled Manifesto on Public Relations*. Ljubljana: Pristop Communications.

Ruler, Betteke van and Dejan Verčič (2002b). Twenty-first century communication management: the people, the organization. In: Peggy Simcic Brønn and Roberta Wiig (eds.), *Corporate Communication: A Strategic Approach to Building Reputation*, 277–294. Oslo: Gyldendal Akademisk.

Ruber, Betteke van and Dejan Verčič (2003). Reflective Communication Management, a Public View on Public Relations, Paper presented at the 53rd Annual Conference of the International Communication Association, May, San Diego, USA.

Vossestein, Jaap (2001). *Dealing with the Dutch. The cultural context of business and work in the Netherlands in the early 21st century*. Amsterdam: KIT Publishers.

Chapter 17

Norway

Pål Horsle

1. National profile

Norway can be characterised as a homogeneous pluralistic society in transition, a mixed economy of private and public economies and relatively
well-developed social services. Coastal livelihood and natural resource
management have gradually changed into oil activities, which today is a
major factor in Norwegian economy. Norway has a population of 4,554 000
(January 2003) and a surface area of 385,155 sq. km (*Statistics Norway*).

Though Norway is a small country, it has officially two written languages, *Bokmål* (Dano-Norwegian) and *Nynorsk* (New Norwegian).
They have equal status, which means that they are both used in public administration, schools, churches, and on radio and television. Books, magazines and newspapers are published in both languages. Everyone who
speaks Norwegian – whether it is a local dialect or one of the two standard
official languages – can be understood by other Norwegians. On the other
hand, Sami, an ethnic minority language, is not related to Norwegian, and
is incomprehensible to Norwegian speakers who have not learned it.

The EU debate and multi-ethnic Norway are among tendencies that
have contributed to self-examination and a critical debate about the concept of "Norwegianess". The dominating theme in the 1994 EU membership debate (when Norwegians voted against membership for the second
time) related to the preservation of Norwegian identity and cultural
character. Those in favour of EU membership claimed that closer ties
with Europe would enrich Norwegian culture, and at times it was claimed
that the alternative to a common European identity would be cultural
dominance by the United States. EU-sceptics emphasised unique aspects
of Norwegian society and culture – such as regional support policies, the
social security system, an egalitarian society, the second official language
Nynorsk and subsidies to Norwegian-language literature – which they
feared would be jeopardised by EU membership.

The differences in life style between, say, Oslo and Milan, are not as accentuated as one would guess, especially if one were to take popular national symbols seriously. According to Norwegians' self image, Norwegians are mainly a nation of fishermen and farmers who live close to nature, they're simple and bucolic, and they tend to act awkwardly and clumsily when traveling abroad. This national-romantic image has little to do with reality – in many ways the majority of Norwegians share the same lifestyle as other Europeans. The national symbols give Norwegians a strong feeling of national identity, but provide a poor description of the nation's actual culture (*About Norway*, Ministry of Foreign Affairs).

Many countries have special press or media legislation covering the rights and obligations of the press and other media in their country. There is no such law in Norway. The Norwegian constitution contains some basic principles governing the press, while other stipulations regarding the media are contained in ordinary legislation – but a great deal is entrusted to watchdog organs established by the media themselves. A lot of the media are subsidised by the state. There is a wide variety of local, regional and national newspapers attracting a high numbers of readers.

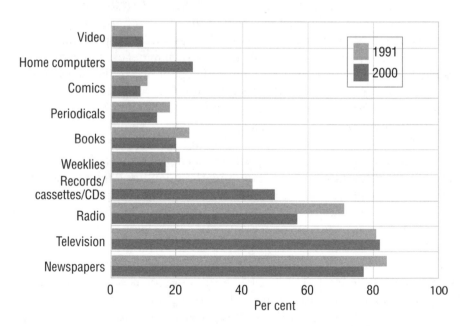

Figure 1. Percentage of people who has used various types of mass media on an average day (Source: Statistics Norway)

2.   History and developments of public relations

2.1. Roots of public relations

During World War II the Norwegian Government, which was in exile in London, established an Office of Information (Strand 1995). The Norwegian Public Relations Club was established in 1949. The policy for the exclusive club of selected people from central government administration and other public institutions was to be ethical and honest. Public relations were defined delimited and quite simple. "If, when a boy meets a girl, he tells her how lovely she looks, that is sales promotion. If he impresses her how wonderful he is, that is marketing. But if the girl seeks him out because she has heard from others what a splendid person he is, that is public relations" (Mørk 1994: 16).

Eight years later the Public Relations Club opened for membership from the private sector. Ten years after the foundation, it had forty-three members; nine of whom came from the private sector, twelve were managers of media relations or public relations in public institutions and sixteen were editors, managers of media relations or public relations in non-profit organisations. Four members were based abroad and within ten years the PR Club had already two honorary members. Of the forty-three members, just one was female. By 1957, the number of women doubled (to two) and the number of members had passed 100. In the 1960s, Norway experienced considerable economic growth, including public relations functions in all types of organisations, especially media relations.

Due to a growing public sector influenced by social democratic politics executed at the time and with great emphasis on public education and information, the Norwegian Central Government Information Service was established in 1965. Ten years later similar public bodies were established in Sweden and Denmark. There was an overall understanding of professionally exercised information as a key factor or tool for development of democracy and transparency in the Scandinavian societies (Jäger 2001).

The Norwegian public relations associations were eager to learn and soon became involved in international public relations organisations. In 1950, 180 Norwegians joined the Annual General Meeting of the British Institute of Public Relations in London. They joined and chaired The International Public Relations Association (IPRA) very soon. The Norwegian Odd Medbø became the first president of IPRA in 1955 (Mørk 1994). Later and during the 1970s the international involvement changed into a similar Nordic cooperation.

In the late 1960s and during the 1970s the expressions "public relation" and "PR" disappeared in job titles because of the public's association with propaganda. The terms "information" and "communication" have since been the proper expressions in Norway instead of the Anglo-American expression "public relations". Differing opinions emerged between the public and private sectors on how to practice the growing trade. An association of public relations staff members in the public sector – *Foreningen for Offentlig Informasjon* (FOI) – was established in 1975. In 1982 the Norwegian Information Association was established as the result of a merger between the old association and a corporate editor's association (*Norske bedriftsavisers redaktørforening*). They emphasised mainly the private sector. The two organisations merged into the Norwegian Communication Association in 2000 for practical reasons. The argument was, "Why have two separate organisations with 1,000 members each when they are in the same line of business".

2.2. Development of public relations in practice

The history of public relations in Norway also describes the development of the practice. But still there is no scientific research on the impact of public relations. From the outset the public sector has played a major role in the development. A strong public sector would be the main explanation for this development, but a book written by Haug about the status in the early 1990s emphasised that most of the written analysis was carried out as public research or public reports though not scientific research. The growth and impact of public relations were strong in the public sector but also in the corporate and private sectors. A growing understanding that CEOs need to be assisted in order to manage the media relations, or the marketing function, or even the internal relations, contributed to a growth in corporate departments of information and communication. There has been endless discussion about the nature of public relations, and a concomitant demand for standards, ethical codes of conduct and quality norms in order to create a professional framework for the industry (Mørk 1994; Haug 1992).

Several detailed public reports on the state's need of a special responsibility in the field of information stated that information is a management responsibility and determined a need for thorough research and analysis (NOU 1978: 37, 1992: 21). A strong public sector which emphasised consumer-oriented public education and information (Abrahamson 1972) changed into a two-way symmetrical communication model (Grunig 1992).

The introduction of the Norwegian Information Policy in the early 1990s advanced information and communication in a strategic direction. The principal objectives of this information policy are (a) to ensure that each citizen and organisation has real access to information on activities in the public domain, to provide all citizens with information on their rights, obligations and opportunities, and (c) to secure general and equal access to achieve participation in the democratic process. The five principles are comprehensiveness (holistic principle); line management responsibility; information as a management responsibility; active information; and the main principle of communication (Ministry of Labour and Government Administration 1994).

By the principle of active information (planning) and communication the government aimed to improve the participatory democracy. On the basis of Grunig and Cutlip, the principle of communication was given a normative scientific and professional element. In addition, the information policy was given public legitimacy. The Norwegian Central Information Service was the administrative body of the information policy and had resources to implement strategies and methods based on scientific research and models. In the case of Norway, the strong societal corporate philosophy of the welfare state seems to have provided the right circumstances for the implementation of a two-way symmetrical communication model (Grunig 1998: 28). Unlike the private sector, the public sector had resources to implement research and analysis. The focus was still on democratic participation in all levels and groups, even when the latter were in weak positions (Simonsen 1998).

The various public relations practitioners have always advocated a great variety of events, arrangements, seminars and conferences. All this activity can be explained by the large number of interested corporations and due to the corporative tradition in Norway. In addition, the commitment, special interest and eagerness to learn about public relations are highly developed. For example, at the *Kommunikade* conference in 2000, more than 500 people participated, which is approximately a quarter of all members of the Norwegian Communication Association, gathered in one single event.

2.3. The development of education in public relations

Despite the early recognition of the importance of formal education, actually very little happened until the end of 1980. The National Public Relation Association established an education board in 1964, consisting of three persons (Mørk 1994: 24). Different types of practical daily or weekly courses have since been supported by the different national information associations. The state district-colleges of Hedmark and Volda were the first to offer formal and scientific public relations education. In 1989, the university college of Hedmark established an annual course under the title 'Information and Community Relations' (*Informasjon og samfunnskontakt*). In 1991 a two-year programme was established at the university college of Volda. Today their undergraduate 2–3 years public information study programmes aim to qualify students for information work in the public sector in particular, but also in non-governmental organisations and private enterprises. Students work on analytical tools, enabling them to interpret and understand problems in the field of information studies and to combine theoretical understanding with practical work. A student who has passed every course and has completed the programme has earned the degree "College graduate in Communication Management" – the Norwegian equivalent of a Bachelor's degree.

Apart from universities, business schools offer a varied combination of smaller courses that combine a three-year diploma (sixty credits) or a four-year degree in business. Still, journalism and media studies dominate the scene of education for practice of public relations in Norway.

In the beginning of the 1990s the University of Oslo established an equivalent bachelor's degree and later a postgraduate programme in media and communications. This programme focuses on the media as institutions, the content of media and its audience, history and the context in society, the legitimacy of power, ethical questions, expressions and linguistics. The studies are multidisciplinary in the sense that they are founded on both social sciences and humanities. The University of Bergen also offers undergraduate and postgraduate programmes in Media Studies, equivalent to the programme in Oslo but more focused on film, video and digital medias.

There are not any specific Ph.D. programmes in the field of public relations offered. Though grants are available, they are awarded only when the work is related to other scientific disciplines.

Currently, a new degree structure is being introduced, replacing the present system which encompasses the old degrees and vocational qualifications. The model for the new degree structure, adopted from the Bologna Process, will be Bachelor's Degree (three years) plus Master's Degree (two years) plus Ph.D. (three years). In a few subject areas, students will enroll for a five-year integrated Master's degree course.

2.4. The development of research traditions in public relations

Despite an increasing number of educated professionals both quantitatively and qualitatively, there is no scientific research about the industry itself, such as the number of PR educated people working in the field or its influence. Although research work on media, media channels and messages dominate, there has been little progress in research in the past decade in the field of public relations or communication. An increase in the demand of an institutionalised body to maintain this kind of research, especially from the public sector, has yet to give results.

This lack of scientific research may also be an answer to the question why there is no independent scientific discipline of public relations. But for a long time – even among the practitioners – there has been a demand for scientific research. A search for identity, the absence of legitimacy and the overall lack of a profession may in my opinion be an answer. Still, some bright spots exist despite the underfunding and lack of initiatives, especially in the public sector.

A study of successful elements of public information about citizen rights and obligations given at alterations of law, regulations and principles were initiated and sponsored by the Norwegian Government Central Information Service by 1.4 m. NOK (appr. € 179,000; Asplan Viak 2000). A research grant of 700.000 NOK (appr. € 90,000) was awarded to the Ph.D. study *Persuasion theory and formative research in a mediated anti-smoking campaign directed at adolescents* (Haug 2002). Similarly, 250,000 NOK (appr. € 32,000) was granted to the Ph.D. study *Mapping the strategic orientation of public relations managers* (Brønn 2000).

The multidisciplinary background in education and research in Norway is well demonstrated by scholarships at postgraduate level. The submitted proposals came from different disciplines such as sociology, political science, journalism, media, marketing, languages, mass communication and public relations. Papers were even submitted from foreign universities. The scholarship is granted by *Statskonsult* (the former Norwegian Government Central Information Service) and the purpose is to initiate research and within the public sector. For example, an analysis of the National Council on Nutrition and Physical Activity in their strategic communication maintaining a general awareness of food safety (Jensen 2001), and reactions on a modernisation initiative of a one-stop shop model of public information called Public Offices of Service (Melhus 2003).

Overall there is very little scientific research in Norway. Compared to other Nordic countries, Norway is the "bad guy". While the Swedes in 2001 spent 10,300 NOK per capita on research, Norway spent just 5,400

NOK (Research Council of Norway). Lack of money is one explanation for the state of scientific research in the field of public relations in Norway – but the lack of a profession is even more striking.

Despite the lack of empirical research and resources I will like to add that there is a growing amount of research done in monitoring and semi-academic research work carried aut by practitioners.

2.5. How language shapes the development of public relations

In this chapter I use the term "public relations" as a synonym of "information and communication", as these are the most commonly internationally used terms. By 1975 less than 10 per cent of the members in the national public relations association used the term "PR" in their job titles (Mørk 1994: 36). The association in the public mind with propaganda was the formal excuse, but we may add different opinions between the public and private sector on how to practice the "profession" as much as it also is a political and ideological explanation. In the same context the difference in use of "publics" in a public sphere and organisations "stakeholders" have to be understood (Verčič et al. 2001).

The most common titles given today in Norwegian and the English translation are the following.

Informasjonsdirektør 'Director of Public Relations and Communication'
Informasjonssjef 'Head of PR & Communication'
Informasjonsrådgiver 'Press Officer, Account Executive, Information Consultant'
Informasjonsansvarlig 'PR Manager'
Informasjonsmedarbeider 'PR Assistant'

The title *informassjonssjef* ('Information Director') is most often used as the advanced or highest job title in the public sector. The job titles are given in descending order of importance.

3. Typification of current public relations

3.1. Status of public relations in business, administration and society

The Norwegian Public Relations Agencies Association (*Norske informasjonsrådgivere*, NIR) consists of thirty-two mainly small agencies and had an estimated income in 2001 of total 560 m. NOK (approx. € 71,700).

The average income employee was estimated at 980,000 NOK (approx. € 125,500 (ResearchLab 2002). By the end of 2001 the number of employees passed 500, but due to the state of the market may have decreased during the last few years.

The Norwegian Communication Association (*Norsk Kommunikasjonsforening*, similar to the Institute of Public Relations in the UK) had 2,500 members by the end of 2002 (annual report). Some could have double membership and the figures are not directly related to the number involved in public relation in the diversified business. Norway follows international trend of female share in the business, with approximately 60 per cent of the members women (Communication 2002: 3). Does this mean that public relations is moving towards a discipline of feminism? Is it right that gender should have an impact on communication excellence? Do we have to consider that female top communicators may have to work harder to develop strategic expertise while they must engage in technical activities that are not expected of men?

An increasing number of the professionals today have a university degree from the social sciences, humanities or in business administration and further their skills with training seminars provided in-house either by various institutes or by the Norwegian Communication Association. There are also segments of public relations practitioners with no formal higher education who have acquired skills through on-the-job training, seminars, etc.

Fifty per cent (about 500) of the staff in private agencies have an undergraduate degree. The dominating field of study is information or public relations studies from abroad; economical studies and journalism form the second-most common educational background. Approximately one out of ten working for the private agencies have recently just passed their exams, but most (29 per cent) come from other agencies (ResearchLab 2002).

Findings from a Ph.D. study about managers indicates that, in general, public relations managers in Norway are characterised by a lack of education in their field. The most common degree held was the four-year Norwegian undergraduate degree *cand. mag.* (similar to a BA degree) in related studies (Brønn 2000).

3.2. Major roles of public relations and typical tasks

According to the Delphi study and the Bled Manifesto, the four characteristics of European relations are reflective, managerial, operational

and educational (Ruler and Verčič 2002). I'll summarise these characteristics briefly.

- Reflective: to analyse changing standards and values and standpoints
  in society and discuss these with members of the organisation, in order
  to adjust the standards and values/standpoints of the organisation accordingly. This role is concerned with organisational standards, values
  and views and aimed at the development of the mission and organisational strategies.
- Managerial: to develop plans to communicate and maintain relationships with public groups, in order to gain public trust and/or mutual understanding. This role is concerned with commercial and other (internal
  and external) public groups and with public opinion as a whole and is
  aimed at the execution of the organisational mission and strategies.
- Operational: to prepare means of communication for the organisation
  (and its members) in order to help the organisation formulate its communication. This role is concerned with services and is aimed at the execution of the communication plans developed by others.
- Educational: to help all members of the organisation become communicatively competent, in order to respond to social demands. This role
  is concerned with the behaviour of the members of the organisation
  and aimed at internal public groups.

The three roles (reflective, educational and technical) should be understood in the sense of the superiority of the managerial function and strategic role. In regarding the reflective role, organisational issues are important for understanding the role of public and government information
as political issues. This may be the part of private sector, too – in the understanding of strategic goals – but in a market oriented meaning. Every
organisation has a different framework of existence. As to the educational role, this should be understood as a comprehensive image of an organisation. The role of education or the advisory role aim at making public relations understandable as a strategic function in every subgroup and
functions as an organisational goal. The overall picture of the different
roles is in Norway partly supported in practice but not in research.

As to the type of work done, in private agencies, 27 per cent of the employees define their work as dealing with strategic issues, 14 per cent work in
design, 10 per cent in journalism, 8 per cent in media relations and 6 per cent
are active in lobbying and financial communication (ResearchLab 2002).

Findings from a Ph.D. study about managers indicate that, in general,
public relations managers in Norway are characterised by a lack of edu-

cation, a lack of previous experience in their field, and a mixture of reporting lines (to the chief executive officers). Only 17 per cent could be
said to believe they execute a strategic orientation, while around 26 per
cent espoused a strategic orientation. The positive aspect is that those es-
pousing a strategic orientation is greater than those who believe they are
enacting one (Brønn 2000).

If these results can be generalised, it means that chief executive officers
in the field of public relations are not acting or supporting strategically, despite their strategic title and positions. In order to act as a manager it is not
enough to access, or be a member of, the top management team. Even public relations education does not support acting with strategic orientation.

An explanation held by the senior executives themselves of the unclear boundaries between an operational and managerial role, indicates
that size docs matter. In the many small- and medium-sized organisations in Norway, their managers fulfil both the managerial and the operational roles.

3.3. Characteristics of major text books and best selling practical books

Obligatory literature in under- and postgraduate studies differs, but US
inspired textbooks dominate. There are exceptions of course, such as *Internal Communication* – a practical guideline for planning and organising
(Erlien 1997). There is also a growing number of Norwegian authors in
compendiums – a collection of Norwegian articles or a particular subject
published in English.

Unsurprisingly, introductory books on public relations are among the
best selling and popular, even though these books seem to lack references to scientific knowledge and models. This type of book is very often
based on practical experience, but without references to research. For a
practitioner, referencing sources is not common. From an academic point
of view, these books tend to be extremely normative. But we have to remember that books of guidelines and practical examples are written by
practitioners for practitioners.

3.4. Growing fields and hot issues

Ethics is an ongoing consideration. Now and then it is provoked by what
is observed as the unethical conduct of a practitioner or consultancy

(Communication 2002: 4). For all practitioners this is an important issue and it is which is discussed in the profession, especially when business ethics becomes a more and more important issue concerning the credibility of top management and as an element of corporate social responsibility.

Opposite, ethics is also the topic of an interesting Ph.D. study. *When the news sources ask for a dance: the edited or directed reality* by Sigurd Allern, which is a critical study on the power and influence of public relations agencies. Between source, media and the public opinion, there is an ongoing trade of change. The public relations agencies attempt to subsidise information in order to lower the journalistic production price and to comfort the media. In fact the study strongly blames the journalists and the media how they exercise their ideal of being critical and independent (Allern 1997).

Besides a bad image of public relations, lack of strategic influence is also confusing the PR directors. The arguments given are the preponderance of bad practice and because others do not understand the importance of public relations.

Brand and image building as part of an international trend is an issue to unite marketing and public relations. It has also been an issue for the Norwegian Government, mainly due to reduced public legitimacy.

'Issues management', 'environment monitoring', or 'competitor intelligence' are different ways to translate the Norwegian term *omverdensanalyse* which is meant to be excellence in public relation in practice (Communication 2003: 3). This is a system of managing information based on systematically collected data; it may be a part of the reflective role and gives the public relations adviser a role as boundary spanner (Choo 1998).

Other hot issues are crisis management, financial public relations, integrated communication, lobbying, mergers, and new technology in information and communication.

4. Conclusions: state of the art and the future of public relations in Norway

The main characteristics of public relations in Norway need to be separated into three parts. Norwegians have a tradition of high commitment and eagerness to learn public relations. The highly developed Scandinavian corporative system has given opportunities to develop two-way symmetrical communication. Norway and Canada are the only countries which have adopted a governmental information policy. Despite this, the image of highly developed practice, education and research in Norway, is beginning to crack. Empirical data from research indicate a lack of education in our field and a lack of strategic orientation.

There is a need to bridge the gap between academics and practitioners. In order to play a managerial, strategic, symmetrical and ethical role in an organisation, there is a need to establish a professional basis of knowledge. Public relations contribute to organisational effectiveness when it helps to reconcile the organisation's goal with expectations of its strategic clients. This contribution has also monetary value to the organisation. Public relations are able to establish effectiveness by building high-quality long-term relationships with strategic clients.

We depend on excellent education and research in order to use the expression "profession of public relations". In Norway there is a lack of both excellent education and research. The Swedish university education programmes are not adequate for students who wish to study the important field of strategic communication (Flodin 2002: 2), but the situation in Norway is even worse. Therefore Norway needs to establish communication programmes and offer special programmes for Ph.D. studies. If we manage to bridge the gap between academics and practitioners we will soon be able to use the expression Profession of Communication and Information (or "public relations" to use the Anglo-American term). Despite the high quality of the Norwegian 'trade', Information and Communication needs to produce research data on which to base future training and activities – extensive practical experience is not enough.

References

Abrahamson, Kenneth (1972). Samhällskommunikation. Samhälle i utvcekling, studentlitteratur [Public communication. Development in society]. Lund: University of Lund.

Allern, Sigurd (1997). Når kildene byr opp til dans [When the news sources invite to dance: the edited or directed reality]. Ph.D. dissertation, University of Oslo.

Asplan Viak (2000). Informasjon ved lov- og regelendringer: en analytisk tilnærming [Information given at alterations of law, regulations and principles]. Oslo: Asplan Analyse.

Brønn, Peggy S. (2000). Mapping the strategic orientation of Public Relations managers. Ph.D. dissertations, Henley Management College, England.

Choo, Chun Wei (1998). *Information management for the intelligent organisation*. (Asis Monograph series). Toronto: Information today.

Erlien, Bente (1997). Intern kommunikasjon: planlegging og tilrettelegging [Internal communication: planning and organising]. Oslo: Tano/Aschehoug.

Grunig, James E. (ed.) (1992). *Excellence in Public Relations and Communication Management*. Hillsdale, NJ: Lawrence Erlbaum Associates.

Grunig, James E. (1998). Strategic, symmetrical public relations in government: from pluralism to societal corporatism. Paper presented at the fifth Annual International Public Relations Research Symposium in Bled, Slovenia.

Haug, Magne (1992). Informasjon eller påvirkning? [Information or persuasion?] Oslo: Bedriftsøkonomenes Forlag.

Haug, Magne (2002). The use of persuasion theory and formative research in a mediated anti-smoking campaign directed at adolescents. Ph.D. dissertation, University of Oslo.

Jäger, Charlotte (2001). Historien om Kommunikade og utviklingen av informasjonsfaget i offentlig sektor. Statens informasjonstjeneste [The history of Kommunikade and the development of the profession of information in public sector]. Oslo: Statens informasjonstjeneste.

Jensen, Ina Porsholt (2001). Trygg mat og strategisk krisekommunikasjon [Through safety and strategic crisis communication]. MA thesis, University of Oslo.

Melhus, Ole Christian (2003). Offentlige servicekontor: hvordan reagerer statlige etater på et moderniseringsprosjekt initiert av sentrale myndigheter? [Public offices of servie: how do public services respond to a modernisation project initiated by Central Government]. MA thesis, University of Oslo.

Mørk, Egil (1994). Et slag med halen. Informasjonsforeningens historie 1949–1994 [A stroke by the tail. The Norwegian Public Relations history 1949–1994]. Oslo: Informasjonsforeningen.

NOU (1978). Norwegian Public Report. Offentlig informasjon [Public information].

NOU (1992). Norwegian Public Report. Ikke bare ord ... Statlig informasjon mot ar 2000 [Not merely words... Governmental information towards the year 2000].

ResearchLab (2002). Benchmarkundersokelse. [Benchmark research]. Oslo: Norwegian Public Relations Agencies.

van Ruler, Betteke and Dejan Verčič (2002). The Bled Manifesto on public relations. Ljublana: Pristop Communication.

Simonsen, Arne (1998). Deltaker i samfunnet [Participant in society]. Oslo: Kommuneforlaget. (2nd edition).

Statens informasjonstjeneste (1990). God informasjon er gull verdt [Good information is worth its weight in gold]. Oslo: Statens informasjonstjeneste.

Strand, Odd (1995). Informasjon på terskelen til år 2000 [Information on the threshold to year 2000]. Oslo: Tano.

The Ministry of Labour and Government Administration (1994). The Norwegian Government Information Policy. Oslo.

Verčič, Dejan, Betteke van Ruler, Gerhard Butschi and Bertil Flodin (2001). On the definition of public relations: a European view. Public Relations Review 27: 373–387.

Chapter 18

Poland

Ryszard Ławniczak

1. National profile

1.1. Overview of national characteristics

Since 1989, Poland has been undergoing a political shift toward democracy and an economic transition from a command to a market economy. Some of the features that distinguish Poland from among the region's other transition economies are the size of its population and area, outstripped only by those of Russia and the Ukraine; its long democratic traditions compared with the rest of Eastern Europe (the process of building democracy in Poland began as early as 1956 with the opposition to the government, backed by Poland's strong Catholic Church); Poland's relatively strong private sector in agriculture, operating since the Second World War (the country's private farmers held approximately 85 per cent of farmland); a significant private business ownership in the trade, crafts and service sectors since 1956; and Poland's historic role as a pioneer of transformation and its success in applying the so-called shock therapy that brought about phenomenal economic growth – GDP grew by 7.0 per cent in 1995, 6.0 per cent in 1996 and 6.8 per cent in 1997 – a drop in inflation, and eliminated consumer goods shortages, but later contributed to a rise in unemployment to about 18 per cent, social disparities and a slowdown in GDP growth to 1 per cent in 2001. In effect, Poland should be assessed in the context of all of the region's transition economies, which form an environment substantially more volatile than that of Europe's other market economies. Not considering former Yugoslavia, Poland was among the countries that blazed trails toward a more liberal economy, democracy, and opening up to the West. Its efforts have led to the introduction of the fastest and most radical market reforms.

1.2. Facts and figures about public relations in Poland

A key factor affecting the current status and the ongoing evolution of public relations in Poland (and other former command economies) is the legacy of the old centrally planned economy that still exists in the minds of its citizens and in the structure of today's economic institutions.

The legacy can still be seen in a number of different ways:

- The common perception of public relations as suspicious propaganda. This view stems from the historic role that censorship used to play in the mass media, the subjugation of all such media to a single doctrine and the resulting stereotypical conviction that the press lies.
- The failure to understand the point of advertising and promoting products and businesses, and building the images of companies and their executives. This problem stems from the fact that, at a time of severe shortages, all goods manufactured in the socialist economy were readily sold.
- The belief that companies, their owners and their success are better left un-promoted, as high profiles may bring on additional tax sanctions. This view stems from the fact that, for ideological reasons, all privately owned operations were considered suspicious and subject to ad hoc taxation.

These characteristics continued to have an influence on the development and current status of public relations in Poland. One might argue that political, social and economic transformations are responsible for having created the demand for public relations services and for the arrival of public relations experts and agencies, mainly from the West. On the other hand, public relations has played the role of an important and useful instrument that facilitated and accelerated political and economic transitions. One may therefore postulate that in Poland, as well as in other transition economies, public relations have a fifth transitional dimension added to the four dimensions characteristic of developed economies of Europe – namely, managerial, technical, reflective and educational (Ruler and Verčič 2002).

With little more than a decade of history, Poland's public relations market is relatively young. Its emergence and evolution were a response to transformations occurring in the transitional economy. Today, the approximate annual value of the public relations market is estimated at US$ 100 million, with public relations services offered by some 500 specialised agencies. Only about fifty of these are fully professional (Łaszyn

2001), offer a wide range of services, operate on a long-term basis and seek to establish lasting relationships with their clients. Other agencies, typically run by one or two owners, have been set up by journalists and public relations experts who have chosen to leave their jobs in corporate public relations departments or large public relations agencies.

2. History and development of public relations

2.1. Roots of public relations

Even in the 1970s, information on the nature of public relations trickled into Poland from Western Europe and the US, carried by Polish researchers who maintained scientific links with the West. The year 1973 marked the publication of the article *Public relations in the socialist economies* (Żelisławski 1973), which most likely was the first published article on public relations. Yet, principally, Polish public relations is the direct product of the country's systemic transformation and the need to communicate with the environment, brought about by the transition to a market economy.

2.2. Development of public relations practice

The evolution of public relations in Poland followed two routes. The first route was the systemic transformation. This created opportunities for establishing broader foreign contacts, allowing for foreign investment and privatisation to enter the country. In effect, numerous Western enterprises that recognised their need for public relations services moved into the local market. Some of their demands were satisfied by foreign agencies that established offices in Poland; these included Burson Marsteller, which opened its Warsaw office in 1991. It was a year earlier, however, that the first two other public relations agencies – First Public Relations and Alcat Communications – were formed.

As to the second route, before establishing certain market instruments, mechanisms and institutions (such as the stock exchange) that were absent in the command economy, the Polish government engaged public relations agencies to carry out public information campaigns (Barlik 2001). An example is the use of such agencies during the levying of direct and indirect taxes on the introduction of the national privatisation program in the

1990s. Financing for such campaigns came from foreign sources, mainly from the PHARE – EU fund for Poland and Hungary. Since the Polish public relations market was virtually non-existent, the government hired western companies that relied on the help of Polish consultants. In this way, although external funds went to external contractors, the transformation gave an impulse for the emergence of the Polish public relations industry.

From 1990 to 1994, only eleven newly established companies claimed to have made public relations their core business. Still, their actual focus was on advertising. Nevertheless, thanks mainly to big governmental contracts (the above mentioned public information campaigns, for instance), the first five years of public relations evolution in Poland witnessed a rapid development of the market with annual growth proceeding at the rate of 12 per cent (Czarnowski 1999). In 1995, the annual sales of the largest agency – SIGMA International (Poland) – reached US$ 8.3 million (*Rzeczpospolita*, 26 June 1996). By comparison, the market's annual growth between 2000 and 2002 was below 5 per cent (Łaszyn 2001).

The years between 1995 and 2000 saw further dramatic growth of public relations in Poland. During most of the period, the growth was mainly quantitative. It was not until the late 1990s that actual quality improvements were made, as the need for crisis communication (in the wake of the Russian crisis of 1998), internal public relations and investor relations were recognised and actions in these areas were undertaken.

From 2000, a growing number of agencies recognised the need for specialisation. This formerly fragmented market was consolidated through mergers and acquisitions. Many agencies were pushed out of business, partly because the first stage of transformations had been completed by then, and the government no longer offered large contracts to big Western agencies. In addition, many smaller agencies were hit hard by the worsening economic recession. On the other hand, this is also a stage in the development of public relations when professionalisation and internationalisation began in Poland. In October 2001 in Berlin, Warsaw-based "Business Communications Associates" (BCA) won three Golden World Awards from IPRA. One of their prize-winning programs was also nominated to receive a United Nations award.

2.3. Development of education and research traditions in public relations

The origins of public relations education date back to the early 1970s, which is when the first public relations course was offered at the former

Table 1. Public relations evolution in Poland

1990–1993 **Infancy**	1994–1999 **PR flourishes and slowly matures**	2000 – **PR becomes professional, specialised and international**
First PR agencies established, first large governmental information and educational campaigns	*Dominance of media relations; PR combined and confused with marketing*	*Economic stagnation, diminishing PR and marketing budgets, tight competition, specialisation and first international achievements*
1990 Establishment of first two Polish PR agencies: First PR (March) and Alcat Communications (September). **1991** Burson Marsteller opens branch office in Warsaw. **1992** Publication of first two Polish textbooks in PR **1992** NGO's campaign "Myths in the economy". **1992–1993** Two large governmental tax information campaigns (budget of US$ 2.5 million).	**1994** Establishment of Polish Public Relations Society (PPRS) (August). **1995** First two doctoral dissertations in PR. **1995** First issue of Information Bulletin of the Polish Public Relations Society. **1995** International conference on "Public Relations as the new tool of systemic transformation" held in Poznań (co-organised by Deutsche PR Gesellschaft). **1995** Establishment of the first regional office of the Polish Public Relations Society in Poznań (October). **1996** Code of Ethics of PPRS. **1997** The first Polish internet PR page. "www.piar.pl"	**2000** Doctoral studies at the Poznań University of Economics. **2001** Establishment of the Association of Public Relations Firms. **2001** Customer Relations Code of the Association of Public Relations Firms. **2001** First issue of a new version of the bulletin of the Polish Public elations Society *Na linii* ('On the line'). **2001** Burson Marsteller withdraws from Poland (April). **2001** Biggest achievement of Polish PR: BCA wins three Golden Awards of IPRA and is nominated for a special UN award. **2001** 2nd edition of the Public Relations Project Contest. regular, yearly conferences organised for theoretitians and practitions of PR in Rzeszów the new professional internet service for PR practitioners – "internetPR.pl" (May) **2003** the new internet service of PPRS – "prsp.org.pl".

Main School of Planning and Statistics. At that time, the course was a lecture given on an elective basis by Krystyna Wójcik, the author-to-be of what today is a primary public relations textbook. Since 1989, the course has been a core requirement in the Economic Journalism specialisation program offered by the Poznań University of Economics. Two first textbooks on public relations came out in 1992 (Wójcik 1992; Zemler 1992). Starting in the mid 1990s, the teaching of public relations has gained popularity, both in state universities and in private business colleges. Today, nearly all major state and private institutions of higher education offer public relations programs. The "secrets" of public relations can be explored mainly in universities of economics but also, to a smaller extent, in humanities-oriented institutions and, even more sporadically, in institutes of technology.

Turning to research in Poland, public relations is a relatively recent research area. Some of the first public relations studies were conducted in the early 1990s. Their authors focused on general rather than specific issues. The approach is understandable as the discipline was new in the Polish business practice. Poland's first two dissertations in public relations were defended in 1995. By 2002, thirty-eight dissertations in public relations were submitted, fourteen of which were in the final stages of approval. The first higher-level dissertation was defended in 2002. Paradoxically, as of mid 2002, public relations has not been given the status of a scientific discipline (according to the classification of the Scientific Research Committee). As public relations evolves and as the body of research in the field grows, the focus of studies is gradually shifting from general public relations issues to more detailed areas. The year 2001 marked the first time an original Polish theoretical concept appeared in an English-language publication. The concept is "transitional public relations", that is, a form of international public relations specific for former post-socialist countries (Ławniczak 2001).

Since 2001 one could also observe pronounced increases in the volume of research in the field. This is reflected in the growing number of dissertations on topics related to public relations. There are however relatively few large research projects in public relations bringing together large teams of scientists. The research scene is greatly fragmented and diversified. The majority of PR research is conducted by the Warsaw School of Economics, the Poznan University of Economics, the Kraków University of Economics, the Wrocław University of Economics, the Warsaw University, the Jagielonian University of Kraków, and the private University of Information Technology and Management in Rzeszów, the organiser (since 2001) of yearly conferences for public relations theoreticians and practitioners. In summary, the significance of public relations as a field of research and teaching continues to rise. Yet, experts claim that the real growth of public relations as a discipline of science is still to come.

2.4. How language shapes the developments of public relations

There is no Polish equivalent for the term "public relations". Although a great number of attempts have been made at translating it, no proposal accurately expressed the idea. In effect, the English term is commonly used. While the most common abbreviation of the term is PR, there is a recent trend of using the Polish phonetic transcription, spelled "piar". Similarly, some specific public relations concepts, such as internal and media relations, are left untranslated.

Another concept gaining popularity in the Polish language is *komunikacja społeczna* (social communication) derived from the English term "communication". Part of the reason why the Polish equivalent was provided is to comply with the law of 2001 on the purity of the Polish language. On the other hand, faced with an oversupply of marketing specialists under pressure to move to other areas of business, many such experts transfer to public relations simply by adopting the term "communication", as in "marketing communication".

3. Typification of current public relations

3.1. Status of public relations in business, administration and society

Systemic transformations have forced the business community to revisit its standing in the new and unknown reality of the market economy. State-owned enterprises were forced to reform their communications policies to get their foreign shareholders to support privatisation and retrenching. Public relations became an important instrument for supporting the transition of large enterprises from the command to market economy (Ławacz 2001).

Nevertheless, the main client for public relations services in Poland was not state-owned companies, but, rather, international corporations and companies whose majority shareholders were foreign enterprises. The second largest group of public relations customers was a new generation of large Polish private businesses; privatised State Treasury companies ranked in the top ten of Poland's largest business organisations. The group least aware of the need for public relations are small and medium-sized entrepreneurs and large state-held enterprises that have not yet undergone privatisation.

3.2. Major roles of public relations and typical tasks

For the reasons mentioned earlier, the key roles played by public relations in Poland differ somewhat from those adopted in Western Europe and the US. A critical responsibility of public relations in today's Poland is to communicate with external publics. Thus, the dominant roles are managerial and technical, while the adoption of reflective and educational roles (defined as internal or influencing members of organisations) will require considerably more time. However, in the context of today's transition economy in Poland, there is a need for adding a fifth role of public relations, appropriate also for all other transition economies. This additional role should be labelled "transitional" and be defined as support for the introduction and adoption of market and democratic mechanisms and institutions into former command economies (Ławniczak 2001).

3.3. Position of public relations in organisations

A study carried out in 2000 by euroPR Agency has helped define the place of public relations in Polish enterprises. Forty-four per cent of the companies have placed the public relations function in their marketing departments, 22 per cent in their sales departments, 15 per cent in their management board offices and 10 per cent in their advertising departments. Only 5 per cent maintain a separate public relations unit reporting directly to the management board. The choices made by companies in this respect are summarised in Figure 1. The study also shows that public relations offices/departments can be found in a large number of companies. It also demonstrates differences in approach to public relations between companies established before and after 1989. Thirt-six (84 per cent) of companies with long-standing traditions deliberately use public relations in their day-to-day business. This is in contrast to a mere 22 (36 per cent) of companies established after 1989. Only 28 per cent of the surveyed companies indicated that they maintain long-term relations with the media, while 18 per cent rely on external publications to promote themselves and their products. Only 46 per cent of organisations make use of image-building campaigns whereas 31 per cent have a crisis-prevention policy in place.

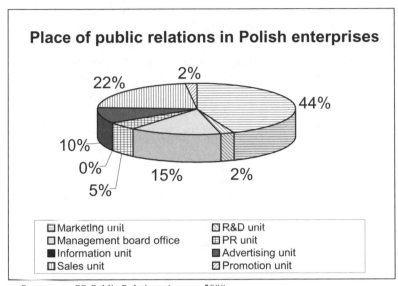

Place of public relations in Polish enterprises

Source: euroPR Public Relations Agency, 2000

Figure 1. Place of public relations in Polish enterprises

Interesting insights are provided by an analysis of the goals that enterprises have formulated for their public relations function. The priority goal for 22 per cent of the companies is to create and maintain a good company image. Nineteen per cent of the companies focus on informing the external public, while 17 per cent aim at maintaining good relations with customers and at increasing sales. Shaping public opinion is a priority goal for a mere 9 per cent of the companies, while 4 per cent of the surveyed seek to concentrate on the need to liaison with the media and organise campaigns. The smallest proportion (1%) indicated a focus on lobbying and internal communications. As to the work force, the study shows that 40 per cent of employees are not familiar with the concept of public relations and that only 12 per cent of the surveyed understand the difference between public relations and advertising.

The level of education of those in charge of public relations leaves much room for improvement. Only 45 per cent have a degree in public relations. The largest proportion of public relations practitioners are economists (53 per cent), holders of degrees in engineering (23 per cent), human sciences (12 per cent), and law (approximately 4 per cent).

From July to September 2001, GFMP Management Consultants surveyed Polish enterprises for information on communications and related issues (see Figure 2). The study was carried out in response to a growing role of communications in ensuring the proper performance of companies. One of the most notable findings of the study was the determination of challenges and barriers to internal and external communication. The surveyed individuals tended to be most aware of such external challenges as increasing employee dedication and eliminating employees' reluctance to change. Next in the order of priority was the strengthening of company image and reaching customers more effectively – both these are external communications goals.

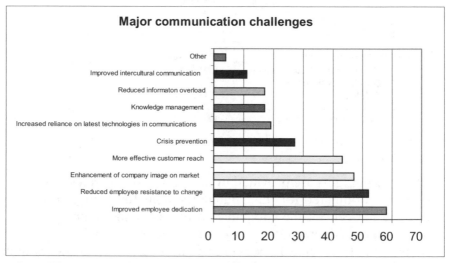

Source: GFMP Management Consultants, July–September 2001

Figure 2. Major communication challenges

The perceptions of challenges faced by businesses vary widely across the sectors and industries in which they operate. Some of the priority challenges indicated by trading companies are to enhance external communications (in order to be more effective in reaching customers and to improve the company's image). Manufacturing companies, on their part, stress the need for personnel dedication and overcoming employee resistance to change.

The primary need of state-owned enterprises is to improve the market perception of their organisations. Companies with foreign participation were the most likely to point to the need for increased employee dedication. Transformations have also had an effect on public administration. Some market institutions absent in centrally planned economies, such as the stock exchange and the Securities and Exchange Commission, were created. Public administration was placed in charge of educating the public in previously unknown instruments and institutions of the market economy and, most of all, of alleviating fears of the negative consequences of capitalism. Their underlying goal was to drum up public support for the ongoing systemic reform.

The responsible ministries have pursued all these goals since the early 1990s. Educational tasks were outsourced to foreign companies (such as Ogilvy Adams & Rinehart) and financed with foreign funds. In July 2002, in its new strategy for administrative reform – drawn up to the European Commission's recommendations for Polish tax administration – the Exchequer resolved to establish sixteen public relations units at local and regional tax offices by 1 January 2004. Today, full-time in-house professionals employed in newly formed public relations departments perform most public relations actions carried out by the central administration. The scope of responsibilities of such departments is defined by changing the responsibilities of the spokesperson, which was known even in the socialist era. Some of its work is outsourced to specialised public relations agencies.

The majority of public relations tasks handled by Polish institutions of public administration involve some sort of media relations. For this reason, public relations officers at all levels of Polish administration are employed in Press Relations, Promotion and Information or Public Relations Offices. In addition to media relations, their key responsibilities include promotion of organisation activities and creating and writing publications and web site postings. At lower levels of administration, public relations responsibilities are commonly placed in the hands of spokespersons.

The year 1989 brought about a rapid growth of the non-profit sector. The sector was highly vulnerable in its beginnings as it found it difficult to secure public approval due to the unfavourable associations with the previous system, in which the communist party closely controlled similar organisations. It was soon discovered, however, that the main way to establish public support is by building an image through emphasis on reliability and credibility. In effect, many public relations departments were formed – most of them, however, were established in national organisations. Local non-profit organisations did not have sufficient budgets to finance such actions. In the case of other grass roots initiatives and non-governmental organisations engaged in providing social assistance and protecting the environment, public relations efforts are rarely carried out in-house. Rather, volunteers, who are not trained professionals, usually perform the tasks.

In an overwhelming majority of cases, public relations campaigns carried out by public administration bodies or the non-governmental sector involve some form of media relations. All other aspects of public relations are given substantially less attention.

3.4. Current state of education and major textbooks

Although public relations education in Poland goes back to the early 1990s, it was not until the late 1990s that a dramatic rise in the number of educational offerings in the field was observed. The growth of the public relations education market was the direct result of the development of the public relations industry.

Today, Polish institutions offer public relations programs at undergraduate, graduate, and postgraduate levels. Undergraduate and graduate programs in public relations usually focus on an area, such as public relations, spokesman, media relations and communication). The specialisations are offered within major programs in economics, sociology, journalism, political science, management and marketing. The programs are three years at the undergraduate level and four and a half or five years at graduate level (with two years reserved for the public relations specialisation). Most commonly, however, public relations education in Poland is offered in two-year postgraduate courses.

The emergence of public relations programs coincided with the rise in the number of public relations textbooks and other books on public relations related topics. A total of about fifty titles have been written on the subject, mostly by Polish specialists, some (seven) are translations of English-language books. Most of the Polish textbooks provide general information and Western case studies. Titles providing in-depth discussions of specific issues or tools and case studies set in the Polish context are still in short supply. The authors of these publications are both theoreticians (Wójcik and Goban-Klas being the most popular) and practitioners, contributing descriptions of their experience (such as Drzycimski, who was responsible for public relations support for then-President Lech Wałęsa). The first original Polish publication on public relations theory and research translated into English came out in Poznań in 2001. It was first presented at the world congress of IPRA in Berlin (Ławniczak 2001). At the time of writing, the bestselling titles in the Polish public relations market are two textbooks written by Polish authors: Wójcik (2001), an expanded and modified version of the author's first 1992 book, and Goban-Klas (1995) and Kadragic and Czarnowski (1996).

3.5. The local scene of public relations

In 2002 the public relations services market in Poland comprised about 500 agencies, the majority of which are small, often one-person, companies commonly ran by former journalists. Probably only a limited number of these companies are true public relations agencies. Most of them (85 %) are native agencies.

Even today, Poland is home to only a few branches of foreign public relations chains. These include The Rowland Company and Prisma International. Burson Marsteller, which has operated in Poland since 1991, closed its Warsaw office in April 2001. The company probably failed because of its inability to adapt to the specific requirements of transition public relations. Nearly all the company's Polish employees who gained experience in its Polish operations have become heads of Poland's top public relations agencies.

Poland's biggest and best agencies are linked with reputable Western international companies. These include BCA (the winner of three Golden Awards in Berlin), affiliated with Edelman PR World Wide, Sigma – with Weber Shandwick World Wide, ComPress – with Fleishmann Hilard, United Public Relations – with Manning, Selvege & Lee, Feedback – with Hill and Knowlton. In a ranking of Poland's best public relations agencies published by IMPACT in July/August 2002, the main player in terms of sales is Sigma, which posted revenues of approximately € 4.5 million, employing fifty-seven staff (Rzeczpospolita 7 Aug. 2002).

A classification of Polish public relations agencies by year of establishment shows that most were formed between 1996 and 1999. A classification by geographic location indicates that more than 70 per cent of all agencies operate outside Warsaw.

The rapid growth of the public relations market seen in the 1990s has given rise to the demand for the establishment of an organisation associating public relations practitioners and theoreticians. The first such institution, the Polish Public Relations Association (PPRS), was set up in 1994. As of early 2002, 184 owners or employees of public relations agencies have applied for membership, as well as university professors and staff of public relations departments in business organisations and bodies of local and state administration.

The goal of the PPRS is to define and promote the concept of public relations, demonstrate differences between public relations and advertising establish and implement a code of professional ethics in public relations, popularise public relations, offer education in the field and create a proper image of companies and individuals involved in public relations. This goal will be carried out mainly by creating a platform for the exchange of information among its members, establishing relations with and joining similar associations abroad, initiating and carrying out various types of training, courses and seminars designed to improve the qualifications of association members and by cooperation with state institutions and social organisations as well as institutions and individuals working towards goals included in the Association's mission. One example of such co-operation was the formation of the Association's first Western branch, in collaboration with the Deutsche Gesellschaft für Public Relations. This took place in Poznań in 1995. In 2002, again for formal and legal reasons, the work of local branches of the Association was left unregulated. Since 1995, the Polish Public Relations Association has been publishing its own information bulletin, first entitled *PR News*, and later *Na linii – Public Relations* ['On the line – Public Relations']. The Association contributed to organising the international congress EUPRERA, entitled *Public Relations Education in Europe: In Search of New Inspirations* and held in Warsaw in 2001.

The other public relations association operating in Poland is the Association of Public Relations Firms (APRF), established in 2001 to represent the business of professional public relations services. Its members include sixteen leading agencies. Five other agencies applied to join in 2002. The APRF's aim is to protect the rights of its members, represent members in dealings with the authorities as well as legal and natural persons, and strengthen the position of and disseminate knowledge on public relations professions. The APRF achieved a number of important things, such as the organisation of the MEDIUM Public Relations Contest (in collaboration with ESKADRA), which is the largest contest in the industry. It should also be noted that at an IPRA conference in 2001, one of the agencies associated within the Association of Public Relations

won as many as three Golden World Awards, known as highly prestigious
distinctions. As the Association became more professional, it joined international public relations industry organisations. In August 2001, the
Association was admitted to the International Communications Consultancy Organisation (ICCO). In the same year it also signed a cooperation
agreement with the International Public Relations Association (IPRA)
and joined the Polish Confederation of Private Employers.

At the moment of writing, these two are the only public relations associations operating in Poland. In view of the size of Poland's public relations market and its evolution, described earlier, it is unlikely that any
other associations will be established in the near future.

3.7. Growing fields and hot issues

The following is a list of hot issues in Polish public relations as of the
early twenty-first century:
– The use of public relations as a tool for the illegal transfer of resources
  from state owned and/or state controlled corporations.
– The habit of politicians and corporate executives of relying on the
  services of real and false image creation experts.
– The stagnation of the public relations services market resulting from
  the economic recession originated in 2001.
– Tighter competition, leading ultimately to price wars between public
  relations agencies and independent consultants.
– New areas of public relations activities such as "social responsibility"
  and public relations ethics.
– Efforts to protect the profession of the public relations expert – as of
  early, such experts were not included in the list of professions pursued
  in Poland.
– Relationships between journalists and public relations practitioners
  and cases of journalist corruption (Wielowicjska, 2000).

The relations between public relations agencies and mass media in Poland are fairly poor, as confirmed by studies by SMG/KRC Poland Media
conducted in June 2001. The studies showed that more than one half of
the journalists use materials provided by public relations agencies and/or
press spokesmen as often as several times a week (see Figure 3). Yet, as
much as 47 per cent of the surveyed journalists believe the materials are
neither useful nor useless. Close to 57 per cent of journalists believe that

the information supplied to them is "unattractive", probably because – as is believed by 60 per cent of journalists – public relations experts are rarely aware of the needs of journalists and make few attempts to respond to them. To make things worse, as much as 46 per cent of journalists claim to have been approached at least once by public relations specialists attempting to dissuade them from publishing specific material.

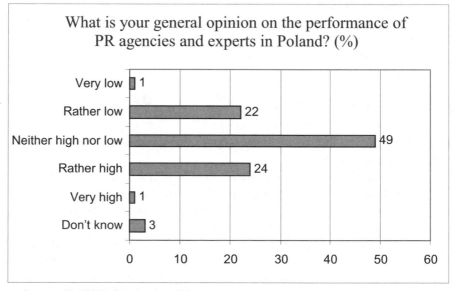

What is your general opinion on the performance of PR agencies and experts in Poland? (%)

Source: SMG/KRC Poland, poll by CATI, June 2001

Figure 3. Journalists on public relations

4. Conclusions: state of the art and future of public relations in Poland

The most recent characteristics of public relations in Poland are strong competitive pressures, including cases of price wars, resulting from an economic downturn that begun in 2000 and from constraints on marketing and public relations budgets. Related trends are the increase in the level of specialisation, the growing level of professionalism among public relations practitioners, and the integration with Western European markets, especially after Poland's accession to the European Union.

The legacy of the socialist (communist) system, as preserved in the minds of the citizens of Poland and other formerly centrally planned economies ("communist economies") and in the structure of their economies and political institutions, provides a context sufficiently distinct to postulate the demand for a whole new brand of international public relations, namely – transitional public relations.

References

Barlik, Jacek (2001). Public awareness campaigns in Poland and Slovenia: lessons learned by government agencies and PR practitioners. In: R. Ławniczak (ed.), *Public Relations Contribution to Transition in Central and Eastern Europe. Research and Practice.* Poznań: Printer.

Czarnowski, Piotr (1999). Polskie public relations: jakie jest, każdy widzi [Polish Public Relations: a Showcase]. Paper presented for Polish Association of Public Relations, July 1999.

Goban-Klas, Tomasz (1995). *Public relations czyli promocja reputacji. Pojęcia, definicje, uwarunkowania* [Public Relations or the Promotion of Reputation. Concepts, Definitions, Conditions]. Warsaw: Rzeczpospolita, Business Book.

Kadragic, Alma and Czarnowski, Piotr (1996). *Public relations czyli promocja reputacji. Praktyka działania* [Public Relations or the Promotion of Reputation. Work Practice]. Warsaw: Rzeczpospolita Business Book.

Łaszyn, Adam (2001). Poland's PR slowdown. *IPRA Frontline,* Oct. 2001.

Ławacz, Piotr (2001). Public relations for state enterprises during the restructuring process. In: Ławniczak, Ryszard (ed.), *Public Relations Contribution to Transition in Central and Eastern Europe. Research and Practice.* Poznań: Printer.

Ławniczak, Ryszard (ed.) (2001). *Public Relations Contribution to Transition in Central and Eastern Europe. Research and Practice.* Poznań: Printer.

Ruler, Betteke van and Dejan Verčič (2002). *The Bled Manifesto on Public Relations.* Ljubljana: Pristop Communications.

Wielowiejska, Dominika (2000). Korupcja mediów [Corrupt Media]. *Gazeta Wyborcza,* 31 March 2000.

Wójcik, Krystyna (1992). *Public Relations, Czyli Jak Zjednać Otoczenie i Tworzyć Dobra Opinię* [Public Relations, or How to Unite People and Create a Good Image]. Międzyborów: Centrum Kreowania Liderów.

Wójcik, Krystyna (2001). *Public Relations od A do Z [Public Relations from A to Z].* Warsaw: Agencja Wydawnicza Placet.

Zemler, Zbigniew. (1992). *Public Relations, Kreowanie Reputacji Firmy* [Public Relations: Creating Corporate Reputation]. Warsaw: Poltext.

Żelisławski, Jerzy (1973). Public relations w gospodarce socjalistycznej [Public Relations in Socialist Economies]. *Reklama* 6.

Intermezzo

The public sphere as central concept of public relations

Juliana Raupp

1. Preliminary remarks

The concern with the "public sphere" as one of the central concepts of public relations is assumed to be a specifically European approach; as such it is related to a "reflective dimension of public relations" (van Ruler and Verčič 2001: 5). German public relations theoreticians, too, lay claim to the public sphere as a key category of public relations and organisation communications (cf. Szyszka 1999). Nonetheless, the concept of the public sphere has not yet been consistently used as a starting point for a public relations theory. The systematic development of the concept of the public sphere is rendered more difficult, moreover, by the ambiguity of the terms 'public' and 'public sphere'.[1] At least three different meanings of the terms are immediately discernible when used with reference to public relations.

- "Public" is used, firstly, to denote such affairs that affect everyone or that are generally accessible. With the rise of nation states, the adjective *public* became a synonym of *state-run* or *state-owned*. This meaning of *public* is evoked when, for example, authorities are legally obliged to inform the population in general and the media in particular about policy decisions.
- The term "public sphere", by contrast, is used in the opposite sense – that is, to denote a domain appropriated by citizens and thus one which is not state-run or state-owned. Habermas (1990) used this aspect of

---

1. In German literature on communication and media studies, the terms "public relations" and the German term *Öffentlichkeitsarbeit* (literally, 'public sphere work') are used synonymously. In professional practice, however, *Öffentlichkeitsarbeit* is mainly used to describe the activities of public authorities and institutions in publishing information, whereas public relations is used, above all, in business and industry. Nevertheless, in practice one can observe a certain overlap of the two terms. Moreover, further terms are catching on, such as "corporate communications" and "communication management".

the meaning in an attempt to formulate a social analysis which is based on an ideal concept of the public sphere. "Public sphere" points in a normative way to the mode of communication developed by the emancipating bourgeoisie – rational discourse.
– Third, "publics", in the plural, are conceived of as groups of persons in the environment of an organisation. This standpoint is to be found in organisation-related public relations research. From the organisation's point of view, public relations is the "management of communication between an organisation and its publics" (Grunig and Hunt 1984: 6).

These different notions of publics and the public (sphere) correspond to different approaches towards public relations theory. While PR theories at a societal level tend to have recourse to the concept of the public sphere, organisation-related approaches have adopted the term 'publics'.[2] In this respect approaches at a societal level are traditionally rooted in German-speaking public relations research whereas organisation-related approaches to public relations have been developed largely in the US (cf. Röttger 2000: 26).

Considered in isolation, however, each standpoint is incomplete since public relations is related both to the public sphere and to publics, albeit in different ways. What is necessary is an integrative perspective. My aim is to develop such a perspective by correlating the two concepts of publics and the public sphere. In its societal function, public relations is related to the public sphere while in its organisation-related function, it is related to publics. How do the public sphere and publics relate to one another and how is the position of public relations to be located within this relationship? In order to answer these questions, in Section 1 I develop theoretically the concept of the public sphere as a structured and differentiated space for communication. This theoretical framework enables publics to be conceived of as groups within the public sphere, which is set out in Section 2. Finally, Section 3 argues a dual linkage of public relations to the public sphere.

2. The public sphere

The public sphere is regarded here as a space for communication, which in principle is available to all. Certain rules apply in this communication

2. On the categorisation of the main perspectives of public relations theory, see, for example, Signitzer (1992: 135 ff).

space, and it is characterised by certain structures. Formal structures develop as a result of legal norms relating to the public sphere: laws governing the freedom of speech, the freedom of opinion and the freedom of the press. Pertinent structures are formed through the functional logic of the public sphere which are aimed at attracting attention for certain messages and issues. Here, the rules of the economy of attention apply (Franck 1998). "Attention" is a commodity in short supply; succes in attracting attention depend on the resources which the actors who communicate in the public sphere are able to invest. One important resource in attracting attention is celebrity, which is not only given to individuals, but also to organisations or ideas. Celebrity also has an accumulative effect: the more famous a person or cause, the more probable it is that the person or cause attracts attention, which in turn leads to a greater degree of celebrity. This circumstance points at the same time to the difficulty which non-celebrities or unknown causes have in attracting attention.

A further structural feature of the public sphere as a space for communication derives from the number of people potentially involved in the communication and the area covered by the information. The public sphere is a differentiated one and, accordingly, is divided into different levels. With their so-called "arena model", the sociologists Gerhards and Neidhardt have developed a system for dividing up the public sphere (cf. Gerhards and Neidhardt 1991: 49 ff). According to this model, three levels – or arenas of the public sphere – can be distinguished (for an alternative gradation of the public sphere, see e.g. Faulstich 1999).

1. The smallest form of the public sphere is made up of public encounters, in which individuals come into direct contact with each other.
2. The level of public meetings includes such forms as the traditional speech given in the market place or at modern political rallies.
3. The largest public arena is that of the mass media.

Taking the "arena model" as a point of departure, one can identify rules governing attention which are relevant to public relations.

What distinguishes encounters is the fact that they take place under conditions of direct interaction, which includes the opportunity of immediate response and feedback. As a rule, encounters involve individuals meeting face to face, but this can be simulated in certain media, for example in the form of "live chats". Encounters provide those involved with a comparatively large scope of action and interpretation with, at the same time, a limited differentiation of roles. In encounters the participants receive an immediate response to their communication activities (which may also manifest itself in silence or other forms of non-verbal communication), that is, each individual taking part in the communication has the opportunity of testing the effect of his or her own words and of reacting accordingly.

Like individual encounters, public meetings or rallies give participants the opportunity to interact. However, in this larger arena there is a distribution of roles, which offers the participants a variety of repertoires of behaviour and expression. One must distinguish between the role of speaker and that of listener. The latter is rather limited: it is true that the listeners may try to influence the course of the communication process, for example by heckling. As a rule, however, the audience's options are restricted to expressive forms of communication such as clapping, booing, getting up and leaving – or falling asleep. Differentiated contents cannot be conveyed in this way. For the speakers this distribution of roles has certain consequences: contents must be prepared in such a way that they are understandable to many people at the same time, whereby attention is easily lost. Reducing the complexity of issues, repetition and visual underpinning are essential preconditions for achieving the desired communication effect in the arena of meetings or rallies.

The public sphere embraced by the mass media is the largest arena of communication. In this arena all the issues are discussed which are important to our information society as well as those that are less important. Individual messages can become issues only when they have been taken up by the mass media. However, in the process they undergo change. In the arena of the mass media issues develop a momentum of their own which is no longer controllable by the individual actors involved. The processes of mass communication are shaped by entirely different structures from those of direct communication, with the activities of sending and receiving messages taking place at different times and in different places. Direct feedback only occurs in exceptional cases. The communication process conveyed by the mass media is characterised by a greater reduction of complexity, and at the same time by greater complexity: greater reduction of complexity inasmuch as many different activities of sending messages are condensed to standardised complexes of symbols and the activities of receiving messages are limited to giving one's attention. The communication processes are of greater complexity inasmuch as the number of actors and roles are significantly increased. In the arena of communication conveyed by the mass media it is mainly corporative actors (organisations) that appear as primary communicators;

journalists act as professional intermediaries (for a specification of communicators in this arena see Bentele, Liebert and Seeling 1997: 227).
With the emergence of communication routines on the part of the communicators, the roles of the (corporate) communicators, as well as those
of the intermediaries, became permanently fixed; there is virtually no
change of roles. The activities of all communicators – public relations actors and journalists alike – are directed towards the mass media. Nonetheless, public relations communicators and journalistic communicators
have different functions in relationship to the mass media: public relations may be described as self-perception and presentation of one's own
particular interests, while journalism can be considered as a function of
the general interest (cf. Baerns 1987: 90).

PR as a professional role developed out of the requirements resulting
from the rules governing attention in the arena of public communication
constituted by the mass media. For only by preparing messages in such a
way that they can be further processed by professional intermediaries –
journalists – does an actor have the chance of attracting attention in the
arena of the public sphere constituted by the mass media. However, since
the different levels of the public sphere overlap, public relations covers
all three levels of public communication.

3. Publics

The term "audience" clearly denotes persons. Historically, it signified a
group of people present, for example, in a theatre or concert hall. The
rise of the modern mass media has led to members of the audience being
separated from each other in time and space.

The audience of mass media tends to be composed of individuals who
do not share common experiences. In relation to the communicator, the
audience of mass media tends to be relatively anonymous. On account of
the great increase in the opportunities provided by mass communication
the "dispersed audience" has now split up into many fragmented audiences (cf. Holtz-Bacha 1997). These fragmented audiences show similarities with publics as it is a common issue that brings them into existence.

In their *Situational Theory to Identify Publics*, Grunig and Hunt seek
to define PR-specific publics more accurately (Grunig and Hunt 1984:
147 ff). Publics develop around certain problems or issues. Grunig divides publics into different types according to problem recognition, subjective constraint recognition and the level of involvement. It is assumed

that the greater the degree of involvement, the more prepared the pertinent groups are to act. Accordingly, Grunig distinguishes different kinds of publics: active publics – involved in all issues – aware publics, latent publics and nonpublics.

Hallahan has developed this concept of identification of pertinent groups further. He goes beyond Grunig's concept in that he introduces a further criterion of distinguishing between groups, namely that of "informedness", that is, the extent to which a group is informed (Hallahan 2001: 33 ff).

By focusing on communication processes, situational theories to identify publics go beyond simple marketing models, which tend to neglect the complexity of communication. However, since publics are considered first and foremost at the level of social groups, the process of opinion-forming in mass media societies fades into the background. Further, no strict linkage is constructed between communication processes and the scope for action and the effects that result from them. In order to construct this linkage, the two analytical dimensions, the public sphere and publics, must be related to each other and then related to public relations.

4. The dual linkage between public relations and the public sphere

Where can public relations be positioned on the basis of the distinction developed earlier between the public sphere and publics? First of all, one must inquire into the function of public relations with reference to the public sphere. Functional approaches to public relations, whose arguments are based on a conception of the public sphere, either regard it as a constituent factor of democracy – in which case its function is creating a minimum consensus in society (cf. Ronneberger 1977) – or its task (from a constructivist, systems theoretical, point of view) is understood to be the construction of desirable realities (cf. Merten and Westerbarkey 1994). In contrast to these approaches, the function of public relations is seen here – based on the proposed definition of the public sphere as a space for communication – as the attempt to attract attention for issues and messages in the different arenas of public communication and/or to influence the processes of public discussion. In doing so, public relations is subject to legal and professional norms as well as to the pertinent laws of the economy of attention.

In contrast to the public sphere as a space for communication, the definition of publics developed above points to social actors within the public sphere who are grouped around specific issues (see Raupp 2001 on the concept of the public sphere divided up into specific issues with the art publics as an example). It is the task of organisation-related public relations to create and cultivate relationships of communication with previously identified publics relevant to the organisation by monitoring and providing issues.[3] In order to maintain these relationships – under the conditions of public communication – communication processes are planned and controlled. With regard to publics, public relations thus denotes a form of strategic action.

The concepts of the public sphere and the concept of publics which I have developed here are interdependent. They represent two dimensions of public communication: one being a structural dimension, the other pertaining to the theory of action. Both dimensions are linked with each other through the issues of public communication. Consequently, public sphere and publics are prerequisites and, at the same time, the product of public communication processes, which public relations also helps to shape by operating in the public sphere under the structural conditions of the public sphere. By providing issues for public communication, public relations as a societal function is related to the public sphere. The organisation-related function of public relations consists in strategically shaping relationships of communication with publics which are grouped around these issues.

References

Baerns, Barbara (1987). Journalism versus public relations in the Federal Republic of Germany. In David A. Paletz (ed.), *Political Communication Research: Approaches, Studies, Assessments*, 88–107. Norwood, NJ: Ablex.

Bentele, Günter, Tobias Liebert and Stefan Seeling (1997). Von der Determination zur Intereffikation. Ein integriertes Modell zum Verhältnis von Public Relations und Journalismus. [From determination to intereffication. An integrated model on the relationship between public relations and journalism] In: Günter Bentele and Michael Haller (eds.), *Aktuelle Entstehung von Öffentlichkeit. Akteure – Strukturen – Veränderungen* [Present formation of the public sphere: actors – structures – changes], 225–250. Constance: UVK Medien.

Faulstich, Werner (1999). Der Öffentlichkeitsbegriff. Historisierung – Systematisierung – Empirisierung [The term public sphere. Historization – systematization – empirization]. In: Peter Szyszka (ed.), *Öffentlichkeit: Diskurs zu einem Schlüsselbegriff der Organisationskommunikation* [Public sphere. Discourse on a key term of organizational communication], 67–76. Opladen/Wiesbaden: Westdeutscher Verlag.

3. By means of "issue monitoring", issues are prepared for discussion within the company (cf. Imhof and Eisenegger 2001: 263).

Franck, Georg (1998). *Ökonomie der Aufmerksamkeit: Ein Entwurf* [The economy of attendance. An outline]. Munich: Carl Hanser.

Gerhards, Jürgen and Friedhelm Neidhardt (1991). Strukturen und Funktionen moderner Öffentlichkeit: Fragestellungen und Ansätze [Structures and functions of the modern public sphere. Questions and approaches]. In: Stephan Müller-Doohm and Klaus Neumann-Braun (eds.), *Öffentlichkeit, Kultur, Massenkommunikation. Beiträge zur Medienund Kommunikationssoziologie* [Public sphere, culture, mass communication. Contributions to the sociology of media and communication], 31–89. Oldenburg: University of Oldenburg.

Grunig, James E. and Todd Hunt (1984). *Managing Public Relations.* New York: Holt, Rinehart & Winston.

Habermas, Jürgen (1990). *Strukturwandel der Öffentlichkeit* [The transformation of the public sphere] Frankfurt/Main: Suhrkamp (first publ. 1962).

Hallahan, Kirk (2001). The dynamics of issues activation and response: an issues processes model. *Journal of Public Relations Research* 13–1: 27–59.

Holtz-Bacha, Christina (1997). Das fragmentierte Medien-Publikum. Folgen für das politische System [The fragmented media-audience. Consequences for the political system] In: *Aus Politik und Zeitgeschichte. Beilage zur Wochenzeitung Das Parlament* [Politics and contemporary history. Supplement of the weekly magazine The Parliament]. B 42/97, 13–21.

Imhof, Kurt and Mark Eisenegger (2001). Die Basis des Issue Managements [The foundation of issues management]. In: Ulrike Röttger (ed.), *Issues Management. Theoretische Konzepte und praktische Umsetzung: eine Bestandsaufnahme* [Issues management: Theoretical concepts and practical application: An inventory], 257–278. Wiesbaden: Westdeutscher Verlag.

Merten, Klaus and Joachim Westerbarkey (1994). Public opinion und public relations [Public opinion and public relations]. In: Klaus Merten, Siegfried J. Schmidt and Siegfried Weischenberg (eds.), *Die Wirklichkeit der Medien* [The reality of the mass media], 188–211. Opladen: Westdeutscher Verlag.

Raupp, Juliana (2001). *Kunstöffentlichkeit im Systemvergleich. Selbstdarstellung und Publikum der Nationalgalerien im geteilten* [The public sphere of art. The public presentation and the publics of the National Gallery in Berlin]. Münster: LIT.

Röttger, Ulrike (2000). *Public Relations: Organisation und Profession. Öffentlichkeitsarbeit als Organisationsfunktion. Eine Berufsfeldstudie* [Public relations: Organization and profession. Public relations as an organizational function]. Wiesbaden: Westdeutscher Verlag.

Ronneberger, Franz (1977). *Legitimation durch Information. Ein kommunikationstheoretischer Ansatz zur Theorie der Public Relations* [Legitimation by information. A communication theoretical approach to the theory of public relaions]. Düsseldorf and Vienna: Econ.

Signitzer, Benno (1992). Theorie der Public Relations (Theory of public relations]. In: Roland Burkart and Walter Hömberg (eds.), *Kommunikationstheorien. Ein Textbuch zur Einführung* [Communication theories. An introductory textbook], 134–152. Vienna: Braumüller.

Szyszka, Peter (ed.) (1999). *Öffentlichkeit. Diskurs zu einem Schlüsselbegriff der Organisationskommunikation* [Public sphere. Discourse on a key term of organizational communication]. Opladen/Wiesbaden: Westdeutscher Verlag.

van Ruler, Betteke and Dejan Verčič (2001). *The Bled Manifesto on Public Relations.* Ljubljana: Pristop Communications.

Chapter 19

Portugal

José Viegas Soares and António Marques Mendes

1. National profile

1.1. Overview of national characteristics

As a sovereign European state, Portugal (see www.portugal.gov.pt and www.portugalinbusiness.com) has been an independent nation since the first half of the twelfth century. The country's borders have remained unchanged since the thirteenth century, a significant reflection of internal cohesion and stable international relations. Apart from its continental landmass, the Portuguese republic also comprises two autonomous and mid-Atlantic regions: the Azores and Madeira. There are 10.3 million Portuguese, of whom nearly 51 per cent are economically active. The greatest population density is found in Lisbon, the capital city, and Oporto, and in other larger cities near the coast (average population density 113 per sq. km). Portugal extends over 91,100 sq. km; the official language is Portuguese. The rich and centuries-old historic and cultural links that Portugal enjoys with the world are reflected in its language, spoken by more than 200 million people on continents as far flung as Asia, Africa and Latin America.

Since 1974 (the Carnation Revolution) Portugal has been a parliamentary democracy. For forty-eight years the country was under a dictatorial regime led by António Salazar and Marcelo Caetano. Until 1974 political and civil liberties were severely restricted, and general censorship was in place. In societal terms there was no freedom of speech or opinion and the media, although privately owned, were strongly restricted in their capacity to intervene and inform. The bloodless revolution of 1974 was followed by a difficult two-year post-revolutionary period, which was characterised by strong political conflicts that almost paralysed the economy and society. In 1976 a new constitutional architecture was set in place and a new democratic and pluralist constitution was published on 2 April 1976 and became law on 25 April 1976. Political stability definitely emerged in 1986 when Portugal joined the EU (then EEC) after twelve years of negotiated and legalistic political evolution. In political economic terms Portugal was a "corporatist state" before 1974, with all the implications that such a regime had over the Portuguese economic situation. Particularly important were the economic concessions that Portugal had to make to North American multinational corporations (oil, chemical industry, pharmaceuticals, motor industry) in order to benefit from the support provided by the Marshall Plan after the Second World War.

EU membership and the challenge of a wider single European market, along with traditional openness in the Portuguese economy, contributed significantly to domestic growth over the past decade. After Portugal joined the EU, the period up to 1990 saw GDP rise at an annual average of 5 per cent, stimulated by investment, consumption and exports. In 1999 the economy entered its sixth consecutive year of growth with GDP at 3 per cent, slightly below that of the previous year but above the EU average. The economy was strong in 2000, growing at slightly more than 3 per cent within the EU average. The pace slowed in 2001 and GDP is thought to have expanded by just 2 per cent. In 2003, Portugal was facing a new economic recession.

The shape of the domestic economy, driven by EU structural funds and much effort at promoting quality, design and diversification, has followed the trend seen in most other European countries, moving sharply towards the service sector. Restructuring involved various sectors – industry, tourism, distribution and financial services. Services today employ 52 per cent of the workforce, producing 66 per cent of gross added value. Almost all the media in Portugal are privately owned, with the state maintaining only two television channels (RTP1 and RTP2), three radio stations (RDP) and the LUSA press agency. There are four direct broadcast television channels (2 public and 2 privately owned) and a cable network with a large number of international channels and other channels devoted to themes of specific interest. There are three radio groups covering the whole country and hundreds of local and regional radio stations.

The expansion of public relations and its present standing can be fully appreciated only with reference to key Portuguese demographic, political and economic characteristics and their evolution, to which we turn in the next sections. Similarly, economic and political evolution explains why the profession, after a shy start – mainly in multi-national companies in the

1960s – blossomed during the 1990s in professional, educational and research areas.

1.2. Facts and figures about public relations in Portugal

There are no detailed studies on the number of practitioners active in public relations departments in companies, but our estimate is between 2,500 and 3,000. As we shall see, Viegas Soares and Costa Pereira (1999b) came to the conclusion that of the 500 largest Portuguese companies, about 90 per cent had a public relations/communication practitioner. In smaller companies, however, job prospects are not nearly as good, which is significant as about 80 per cent of the Portuguese GDP is generated by SMEs. The same study showed that the background of in-house heads of public relations departments is very diverse, which may explain the difficulties that the subject still has today in institutional terms.

Turning to public relations companies, a recent survey (Dossier Temático 2002b) reported the existence of eighty-five consultancies operating in Portugal. The PR consultancy market is worth about € 35 million. The market leader is Imago – an associated company of Incepta-Dewe Rogerson Group – which reported a turnover of almost € 3.8 million. The volume of the Portuguese market is put in perspective by figures reported by the British market leader – Weber Shandwick – which reported a turnover of € 26.3 million in 2000 (*PR Week* 2001).

We estimate that between 450 and 500 practitioners work in public relations consultancies. The market is dominated by companies with formal connections with international groups or relevant consultancies, but there is no clear market leader.

As for the Portuguese PR Consultancies, a recent study on its reputation with clients and journalists concluded that there are still some steps to be taken in the improvement and approach to the most developed European markets (Dossier Temático 2002a). Although journalists and clients point out the positive development of the professionalism of Portuguese public relations firms, they also mentioned the need to increase the scientific and "relational capacity" of those working in public relations consultancies. This conclusion strongly correlates with the available data on the academic background of those working in public relations consultancies (see Table 1). According to a survey developed especially for this study, the average gross annual salaries are € 40.300 for an account manager and € 20,000–25,000 for account executives (these are indications: salaries are performance-based).

Table 1. Background of PR consultancies staff

Background consultancies:	
Former Journalists	40–45
PR/Communication Studies	25–30
Law Studies	15–20
Other (Marketing, Advertising, Business Management)	10–20

2. History and developments of public relations

2.1. Roots of public relations

Public relations was introduced in Portugal in 1959/1960 by US multinational companies such as Mobil, and, locally, by the *Laboratório Nacional de Engenharia Civil* ('National Laboratory of Civil Engineering', LNEC), which initiated public relations activities modelled on those in foreign companies. At about the same time, in 1964, the first school was founded that offered public relations courses – the *Instituto de Novas Profissoes* ('Institute of New Professions', INP).

The development of public relations in Portugal is linked to three professional interest groups. Apart from the LNEC and INP, mentioned earlier, the COPRAI ('Training Department of the Portuguese Industrial Association') was instrumental in establishing the first public relations association, *Sociedade Portuguesa de Relacoes Publicas* ('Portuguese Society of Public Relations', SOPREP).

2.2. The development of public relations practice

The development of public relations in Portugal divides into three periods, 1959–1960, 1974–1990 and 1990 up to the present. During the first period, the political and economic context strongly influenced the evolution of public relations. The media were completely controlled by the government (censorship was widespread); the concern with propaganda ("press agentry", following Grunig's terminology); the corporatist system with its own views of job development. As a result, public relations practitioners found themselves strongly constrained in their possibilities and range of activities.

In the second period, between 1974 and 1990, the profession made substantial progress. The 1974 revolution and the following years brought about important political and economic changes, which accelerated development. Key factors in this period were the expansion of the media system; economic freedom and increased competition; change of the state intervention paradigm, which turns from positive intervention to regulation with the consequent change of the citizenship model, where the state should be responsible for the citizens. These factors had as a consequence that the public institutions and the private sector felt the need to relate actively to those on whom their success depended, the public, hence the connection we see today between public relations and marketing. On the other hand, private and public institutions felt the need to adapt to the new reality, building public information services in their structures. This was especially visible in local government – nowadays all Portuguese municipalities have a public relations department – but to some extent also at the national level. The expansion of the media system contributed to the necessity of professional relations with the media from both private and public institutions. Working first as in-house practitioners and then initiating the first public relations consultancies (mainly specialised in media relations), journalists were the biggest source of recruitment in this period. In 1979, SOPREP had 188 active associates, figures that in 1980 decreased to 93, to raise again to 124 in 1981 (the decrease was due to the reorganisation going on at the time). In 1982 SOPREP became *Associaçao Portuguesa de Relaçoes Públicas* (APREP, 'Portuguese Public Relations Association'), with a more professional character.

The third period, from 1990 on, is characterised by consolidation and expansion. There were new challenges, both in business and in the domain of public institutions; higher education improved and so did professional standards; a new breed of public relations practitioners appeared on the scene who had received specific public relations training; and, finally, international public relations companies entered the Portuguese market. All these factors contributed to public relations moving away from the confines of media relations and expand into the wider area of corporate communication and integrated marketing communication. It is with this shift in focus that public relations develops strategically.

2.3. The development of education and research traditions

The development of education in public relations divides into four periods. The first period begins with the INP mentioned earlier, in the first half of the 1960s. For a long time the INP was the only institution to offer public relations education. In the second period two moments can be distinguished; the early 1970s, with the foundation of the High School on Communication Means which, like the INP, provided training in public relations subjects, and the late 1970s, with the introduction of undergraduate degree schemes in social communication at the New University Lisbon in 1979 and at Lisbon Technical University in 1980. Essentially, these two schools introduced a degree of professionalism in public relations; they also define the beginning of the third period. This third period is a one of overwhelming acceleration and rapid growth of the communication and the public relations schools. The last available figures showed that about thirty schools were offering undergraduate degrees in public relations and related studies. Finally, the fourth period, from 2000, marks the beginning of adulthood of public relations education in Portugal, with graduate studies offered and the first Ph.D. programme in public relations (ESCS-IPL in coordination with Universidad Complutense de Madrid).

For about twenty years there was only one public relations school in Portugal. It never had more than a dozen students. This situation had practical consequences for some time, such as the lack of professional training of those working in this area (as we have seen, practitioners have a very diverse background). Of the thirty schools that exist today, fifteen are public and the other fifteen are private. Only six of the thirty schools (20 per cent) have the designation "public relations" in their name, while the others use in their names such terms as "communication sciences", "social communication", "business communication", "marketing and communication", "institutional communication" and "communication and culture".

Turning to the curriculum, three teaching areas can be distinguished; communication sciences, business studies (including economy) and social sciences. Generally, the orientation of the curriculum is practical: not a lot of academic skills are taught. As a result, quite a few (less than 20) dissertations have been written, but these degrees have not resulted in any publications. At the final meeting of the Congress of the Portuguese Communications Association (SOPCOM) in 2001, Paquete de Oliveira said that the teaching strategy has been a determinant to the investigation strategy, meaning that the immediate always supplanted the important. This may be true, but at the same time, the work done in the last five or six years has contributed to more knowledge and better understanding of the subject (Viegas Soares and Costa Pereira 1995, 1996, 1999a, 2002; Espirito Santo 1996; Viegas Soares 1997).

2.4. How language shapes the development of public relations

In Portugal the term "public relations" has acquired negative connotations. Apart from that, the term has lost most of its original content, now that most people – security guards, receptionists, sales people – say that they are active in or deal with public relations. To give the profession some new prestige several terms have come into fashion, following to a large extent trends discernable in the rest of Europe – the most popular terms are "communication management", "corporate communication" and "organisational culture", the latter linking with public relations through internal communication, a quite strong area of practice in Portugal.

3. Typification of current public relations

3.1. Status of public relations in business, administration and society

Two studies carried out in Portugal, in 1994 and 1999, on the presence of public relations in the business sector show that the importance of public relations is increasing, both in public and in private organisations (Viegas Soares and Costa Pereira 1996, 1999a, 199b). In 1994, 70 per cent of the organisations in the public sector had a public relations department, which increased to 93 per cent in 1999. For the private sector the figures are 87 per cent in 1994 and 100 per cent in 1999. These figures, summarised in the matrix below, also show that in public organisations, public relations is always bigger than in the private sector.

	1994 (%)	1999 (%)
Public sector	70	93
Private sector	87	100

The increased importance of public relations is also shown by the presence of "someone in charge of public relations activities". In 1994, 72 per cent of respondents reported to have such a person, while in 1999 this had increased to 89 per cent. Apart from this, public relations departments (or public relations sections in other departments) grew as well in this period. We should point out, though, that this involves few real public relations experts: about 90 per cent of the surveyed organisations have between one and three experts – the rest have a different background.

The 1999 study also showed that the main activities of public relations practitioners are the following.

Corporate advertising	79 %
Sponsoring	64 %
Media relations	84 %
Internal communication	75 %
Financial PR	20 %
Marketing communication	54 %
Fairs and exhibitions	61 %
Research and evaluation	41 %
Publications production	71 %
Multimedia production	45 %
Events management	82 %

3.2. Major roles in public relations and typical tasks

Our experience with and knowledge of the Portuguese public relations market lead us to conclude that the profession is mainly exercised under the category "operational" as defined in the Bled Manifesto (Ruler and Verčič 2002). Additionally, and from a different perspective, Viegas Soares and Costa Pereira (2002) concluded that Portuguese private and public institutions mainly performed under Grunig's "Public Information" model of public relations.

Taking into consideration the particularities of the corporate culture in traditional Portuguese organisations, as well as the specific characteristics of the Portuguese business sector, we think that the "reflective" and "managerial" roles are difficult to perform for regular staff. Top managers, who have decisive power, better do such performance modes.

3.3. Position of public relations in organisations

Viegas Soares and Costa Pereira's (1999) research showed some interesting data on the structural and functional position of the people in charge of PR/Corporate Communication. About 75 per cent of the PR/corporate communication managers depend hierarchically on the board of directors, while 22 per cent depend on another manager (see Figure 1), which is generally the marketing manager (about 46 per cent; see Figure 2).

Figure 1. Organisational structure dependency of the PR manager

Figure 2. Functional dependency of the PR manager

The structural position of the public relations department in Portuguese institutions seems to be the right positioning, meaning that about 30 per cent are called "Communication and Public Relation Department", while 21 per cent others are called "Image and Communication Department", answering directly to the board of directors. There are, however, some cases in which the public relations department depends on a member of the board of directors who at the same time is in charge of the marketing or the human resources department (Viegas Soares and Costa Pereira 2002).

PR/Corporate communications managers have the following educational background:

Secondary education	17%
Undergraduate degree	66%
Graduate degree	6%
Other	11%

Turning now to the position of public relations departments vis-à-vis other departments, a functional conflict can be distinguished. With respect to company-internal communication, public relations departments often seem to clash with the human resources department – the latter is seen as standing closer to the company's own employees. As these two departments have the same goal, an internal climate is created that is conducive for human development and the organisation's productivity.

3.4. Current state of education and character of major textbooks

We mentioned earlier that education in public relations has been expanding in recent years. There were 8,676 applications for public relations and related courses (out of a total of about 45,000 students in higher education). Only 1,440 candidates were accepted (Portugal has a *numerus clausus* system that restricts the number of students per field). The trend recently has been for the number of applicants to decrease, while the number of accepted candidates increases (2002 data; source: Ministry of Education). This is illustrated in the following matrix.

	Candidates	New entrants
2000	11,743	1,265
2001	10,749	1,315
2002	8,676	1,440

Higher education in public relations in Portugal awards *Licenciado* degrees, which correspond to a four-year undergraduate university degree. The higher-education system is formed by four types of institution, organised along two dimensions: public–private and university–polytechnic.

Apart from higher education institutions, professional training institutions also offer public relations courses. However, these do not award certificates or credentials. The textbooks used are mainly British and American, as there are hardly any books in Portuguese. There are some titles in Brazilian Portuguese, but due to the cultural differences between Portugal and Brazil these books are not very suitable. As to other publications, there are some technical magazines (*Marketeer* and *Portuguese Management Magazine*, for instance) which the scientific community uses as an outlet, and which are also sometimes used in teaching. Finally, there are some popular practice books, covering a small market dealing with "communication techniques" in a very general way. Most of these books are of the "How to be a successful businessman" type.

3.5. The local scene of public relations

There are two types of associations – professional and scientific. Currently, with APREP not functioning (as discussed earlier), there are no professional public relations associations in Portugal. However, some other but related professional associations make up for that. The *Associação de Comunicação Empresarial* ('Business Communication Association'), established in 1990, is a company publications association that since its beginnings has been a forum for dialogue between corporate communicators, researchers and academics. It publishes a four-monthly magazine (*Business Communication*), which publishes much research carried out in public relations. Another organisation is *Associação Portuguesa das Empresas de Conselho em Comunicação e Relações Públicas* (APECOM, 'Portuguese Association of Communication and Public Relations Consultancies'), which was founded in 1989 and is mainly for consultancies. It has twenty-three associates. Finally, there is the *Associação Portuguesa de Directores e Técnicos de Comunicaçaõ e Imagem* (DIRCOM, the 'Portuguese Association of Managers and Technicians of Communication and Image'), established in 2001, with about 150 members. DIRCOM aims to be a forum for corporate communicators, but it is not doing well and may not survive.

Turning to scientific associations, we note that there is just one: *Associação Portuguesa de Ciências da Comunicação* (SOPCOM, 'Portuguese Association of Communication Sciences'). SOPCOM was established in 1998 and unites researchers and academics from all higher education institutions in Portugal related to specific fields. It has 240 associates. In May 1999 it organised its first congress; the topic was the communication sciences at the turn of the century. The second congress, organised in 2001, was entitled "Directions of the Communication Society". Between these two congresses SOPCOM organised the First Iberian Congress of Communication in Malaga. In summary, Portugal does not have much to offer by way of associations: there is just one scientific association and no specific public relations associations at all. This may be due to the individualistic nature of the Portuguese: they simply do not have an associative spirit.

3.6. Growing fields and hot issues

The thematic surveys in professional publications that we used for this chapter (Dossier Temático 2002), show that the public relations agenda is dominated by four items: (1) fair competition among agencies (charges of price dumping are being made); (2) quality improvement in the subject area (in services and in academia); (3) the definition of professional standards; and (4) the social status of the profession.

4. Conclusions: state of the art and future of public relations in Portugal

The Portuguese public relations market continues to grow, thanks to the budget movement from other sources (direct marketing, sales promotion, etc.). There is an optimistic feeling in the market regarding the future development of this sector. Expectations of the standard of practitioners are gradually rising, in terms of both training and professionalism. As work in the field progresses, the separation into corporate and marketing communications will be consolidated. This is already showing in the specialisation of certain areas, such as crisis management, public affairs and community relations. We should also note that in societal terms, the level of activism in Portugal has been rising (environmental and consumer issues, for instance), which causes institutions to increase their image of corporate social responsibility, to respond adequately to the challenges imposed by this trend.

References

Dossier Temático (2002a). Agências de Comunicação [Communication Consultancies]. Briefing, nr. 344.
Dossier Temático (2002b). Agências de Comunicação [Communication Consultancies]. Meios & Publicidade.
Espirito Santo, Paula (1996). Comunicação Interna nas maiores empresas portuguesas [Internal Communication in the bigger portuguese companies]. *Comunicação Empresarial* 3.
Michael Page International Portugal (2000). Salary survey. *Marketeer* 64–4.

Ruler, Betteke van and Dejan Verčič (2002). *The Bled Manifesto on Public Relations.* Ljubljana: Pristop Communications.

Viegas Soares, Jose. (1997). RP: ensinar/desempenhar [PR: teaching and acting]. *Ensinus* 11.

Viegas Soares, Jose and Francisco Costa Pereira (1995). RP: perfil de uma profissão [PR: the profile of the profession]. *Ensinus* 4.

Viegas Soares, Jose and Francisco Costa Pereira (1996). A imagem das RP [PR image]. *Comunicação Empresarial* 4.

Viegas Soares, Jose and Francisco Costa Pereira (1999a). A comunicação nas grandes empresas portuguesas I [PR in Portuguese companies, part I]. *Comunicação Empresarial* 12.

Viegas Soares, Jose and Francisco Costa Pereira (1999b). A comunicação nas grandes empresas portuguesas II [PR in Portuguese companies, part II]. *Comunicação Empresarial* 13.

Viegas Soares, Jose and Francisco Costa Pereira (2002). Radiografia dos Modelos Comunicacionais nas Grandes Empresas Portuguesas [X-raying Portuguese companies: communication models and practices]. In: Jose Bragança de Miranda and Joel Silveira (eds.), *As Ciências da Comunicação na Viragem do Século* [*Communication Sciences at the turn of the century*]. Vega.

Chapter 20

Russia

Katerina Tsetsura

1. National profile

1.1. Overview of national characteristics

The Russian Federation (or Russia) is the largest country in the world, with 17 million sq. km of land. Located in the northern part of the Eurasian landmass, Russia spreads from west to east, bordering the Arctic Ocean, between Europe and the North Pacific Ocean, and includes eleven time zones. Russia unites nine *oblasts*, twenty-one republics, ten autonomous *okrugs*, six *krays*, two federal cities and one autonomous *oblast* – Chechnya. Since the collapse of the Soviet Union, Russia has struggled to establish a modern market economy and is still struggling to improve the situation for the 40 per cent of its people who live below the poverty line (as of 1999). In 2002, the GDP real growth rate was 4 per cent. Economic conditions improved in the past three years, with annual output growing by an average 6 per cent and with progress in structural reforms. Yet, serious economic and political problems persist in Russia.

Russia is one of the richest countries in natural resources, although severe climate and distance hinder their exploration. According to the CIA *World Fact Book 2002*, today the country "remains heavily dependent on exports of commodities, particularly oil, natural gas, metals, and timber, which account for over 80 % of exports, leaving the country vulnerable to swings in world prices". With a total population of about 145 million people (as of July 2002), the death rate is currently higher than the birth rate in Russia.

1.2. Facts and figures about public relations in Russia

When the first international conference on public relations was held in Moscow in May 1997, everybody – representatives of federal and local governments, leaders of the most prestigious and successful Western and

Russian public relations agencies, journalists and editors of national and regional mass media, and educators and researchers from Russian and Western institutions of higher education – agreed that public relations is a necessary field for the successful development of modern business and the free market in Russia (Pashentsev 2002). This was not the first time when Russian public relations was granted such an important role in the development of the newly emerged democracy and market economy. Yet, the field, which started to develop in Russia a little less than twenty years ago, still struggles to earn its place among the leading areas of study, research, and practice. Studying and practicing public relations in Russia nowadays face several obstacles: lack of adequate research and analyses of the field's practices, inability to properly produce and present a theoretical foundation for the field, and ethical concerns about existent Russian public relations practices.

In this chapter I address these obstacles from the perspective of a researcher who has been studying public relations theories and practices in Russia and the US to highlight major characteristics of Russian public relations and discuss historical, cultural, educational and geopolitical factors that have influenced the development of the field in the country. I first look at the emergence of theoretical approaches in the field and the first practice of public relations in Russia. Then I offer a thorough analysis of education in the field, concentrating on the history and the current state of the Russian education. Finally, I present an overview of current trends in public relations theory and practice and describe the challenges that Russian educators and practitioners are facing today.

2.   History and development of public relations

2.1. Roots of public relations

Twenty years ago, Russians were not familiar with the concept of public relations. Only one definition was found and only in reference to "marketing" in *Marketing: Collected Essays*, by Kostukhin (1974: 86), a book about "modern problems of capitalistic markets":

> Public relations – 1. Establishment of relations with publics. 2. Department for establishing such relations (its goal is to develop positive attitudes toward a company among needed publics, including a number of actions and sometimes advertising).

For many years, public relations in soviet Russia was considered to be a marketing function that was used in capitalist countries. With political and economic changes in Russia, public relations came to life, and the old literature, as well as the old understanding of public relations, was first brought into use. Scholars who had a business background began talking about public relations as an effective tool of marketing. At the same time, publishing houses began translating and releasing US literature on popular economic subjects, which also included some discussions of the concept of public relations from a business perspective. Russian professional translators, who never had any "real-life" experience with public relations, when translating public relations terms into Russian, created several controversial definitions. Some of these are: "Indirect advertising (from English 'public relations') – any contacts with public and media" "propaganda (from English 'publicity') – method of indirect advertising, which includes the usage of editorial, non-paid space in the media" (Ozhegov 1984: 156). Today, these translations seem inappropriate; at the time, however, no one had yet comprehensively studied public relations, its history and its ultimate goals, and so the translations were accepted. Later, these translations were the cause of some misunderstanding and misinterpretation of public relations activities and even created some debate on the nature and essence of public relations. The most popular polemics was a question on whether public relations is propaganda and manipulation. The debates around this issue are quite popular even today (see, for instance, Pocheptsov 2001; Tsetsura 2000a).

Some researchers switched from studying economics to studying public relations and had broadly supported already existing misunderstanding of public relations as simply a part of marketing activities. Such scholars advocated the practice of public relations only as a means of marketing support. Golubkov (1994), for instance, emphasised public relations as an effective and inexpensive way of communicating with publics. Publicity as a major component of public relations was being defined as a business tool used in Western countries. Often, publicity *was* public relations (Tsetsura 2000a).

Another approach to public relations was developing too. Scholars who examined US and European perspectives on public relations presented a competing approach. Utkin and Zaitsev (1993), in one of the first Russian works on the subject, argued that public relations was an ideology of creating reputation, responsibility, and trust, rather than just a method of gaining immediate profits. They also translated works in public relations from other countries, such as Black's *Essentials of public relations* (1993), accentuated these ideas and provided well-supported explanations of the nature of public relations.

Some of the scholars who were especially interested in public relations began an in-depth investigation of its practice. They developed theories that created a unique theory of modern Russian public relations (Pocheptsov 2001). Others, Tsetsura (2000a: 5) pointed out, were persistent in their attempts to prove that public relations was unnecessary and that attention to public relations was undeserved:

> The latter scholars argued that public relations methods were unfair and manipulative and that the only goal of this "pseudo-study" was to create a positive image without spending much money, i.e., by using any direct or indirect means, including free advertising in the media. Some journalism educators and editors actively supported this idea. They felt cheated by the new public relations practitioners who were trying to get publicity. Such opinions were very popular, and it was easy to find an explanation for these contentions: anyone who wanted to learn more about public relations and publicity used definitions from earlier published works and dictionaries. This "double nature" of public relations could only be erased through the process of exercising true public relations practice and constantly explaining public relations' true philosophy to the various Russian publics.

As a result of the efforts of several groups, like journalism educators and editors, public relations was not recognised as a field for some time. It took several years of active practice and many discussions about the true nature of public relations before positive perceptions of public relations began to replace negative ones. Although the problems of understanding and accepting the nature of public relations seem to be irrelevant for modern Russian public relations, some concerns about defining public relations are still in place.

Therefore journalism and business scholars, who were pioneers of teaching and studying public relations, started to define and discuss the conceptual frameworks and worldviews of public relations (Tsetsura 2003). Faculty members who became interested in public relations promoted public relations courses in their departments. The syllabi created for classes were based heavily on Western public relations sources and materials from other areas, depending on what sources were available to faculty members at the time. Because of the lack of contemporary materials in public relations, quite scattered understanding of the field has created advocates and opponents among Russian scholars. Some of them, usually those who had access to the newest research in public relations, argued for US approaches to public relations; others argued for a unique Russian perspective on public relations, which turned out to be a blend of psychological, sociological, and political studies with no public relations theories presented. Most of the works, however, were of an exploratory and descriptive nature.

Most of the Russian research, unfortunately, stays at the descriptive level even today (for instance, research by Alyoshina 1997; Guth 2000; Clarke 2000; McElreath et al. 2001), and a call for problematising public relations through analytical research becomes stronger each year (Tsetsura 2003; Pashentsev 2002).

Among alternative explanations for the development of public relations in Russia, there is a research project by Tsetsura (1999, 2000a) and Tsetsura and Kruckeberg (in press), which proposes that women have played a significant role in the growth of Russian public relations in its earliest stage of development. According to this view, women's role in this process is not only a tribute to feminism, but is a necessary element of Russian PR history.

Although equal rights for men and women have been recognised in Russia, it is truly hard for females to present themselves as leaders in this new professional occupation. Nevertheless, Russian women, as well as their American counterparts, occupy a variety of leading positions, and they work in a wide range of areas in public relations. For example, most of the Russian public relations practitioners currently in the non-profit organisations are women (Tsetsura 1999). A female practitioner, Veronika Moiseeva, is an executive director of the Moscow agency, *Imageland PR Worldwide*. She was also one the first presidents of the Russian Association of Consulting Companies in Public Relations (AKOC). Many women are executive directors and presidents of leading PR agencies and consulting PR firms located in Moscow and St Petersburg, among which are E. Egorova, executive director of the centre of political consulting *Nikkolo M*, E. Sorokina, director of the agency *Obratnaya Svyaz* ('Feedback'), and Y. Rusova, leader of a political consulting firm, *Upravlenie politicheskoj informatsiej* ('Management of political information') (Pashentsev 2002).

2.2. Development of public relations practice

As in most countries, public relations in Russia started with media relations. Female journalists saw public relations as a fresh way to realise their career ambitions. In Russia, where journalism as a field is dominated by males, women were mostly left to cover relatively unimportant news or entertainment-style stories, such as fashion, concerts and movies. That is why public relations, which was regarded as a work in the second-tier of newsworthiness, provided the best opportunity for careers for Russian women at the early stage of the development.

However, in the mid 1980s public relations began to grow and to develop so quickly that it soon became a highly popular and very desirable career, mostly because of the rising opportunities in political and/or governmental consulting. In addition, journalists and sociological scientists began to appreciate the power of public relations in influencing different publics and forming images. Russian male professionals thus started to turn to public relations and soon began to replace females in the highest positions. "The best journalists are leaving journalism for richer pastures in public relations (including serving as political spokespersons)", pointed out Johnson (1995: 181), describing Russian journalism at the time. Nevertheless, many women already had valuable experience in Russian public relations, so they were able to keep their high-level professional positions.

Female public relations practitioners were drawn early to a new professional career and thereby got a credit for their part in the field's development. For instance, the first public relations agency in Voronezh (in the Black-Earth region of Russia), a city with a population of more than one million people, was founded by a female journalist (Tsetsura 1999).

Today, Russian female practitioners work in every area of public relations, such as public affairs, media and customer relations, financial relations, and, surely, in political consulting. Women chair four of the sixteen Moscow public relations agencies that specialise in political consulting (National News Service Agency: Internet archives, 2000). Many other women work for public relations and advertising agencies, as well as in public relations departments of commercial companies in the entertainment and fashion industries; Russian women practice public relations for non-profit and government organisations, banks, as well as corporate organisations. They also conduct research in public relations and teach public relations at Russian universities (Tsetsura and Kruckeberg 2004).

However, as the field develops, female practitioners tend to be substituted by male professionals on the leading positions. They have a harder time getting a raise or promotion. Most of the younger talented professionals work as technicians for political consulting agencies with a shady reputation where they are asked to do a job which is quite controversial from an ethical point of view. They often write blackmailing reports about other candidates and supervise tabloids that are sponsored and published by a single candidate only during the election times (Semenova, as cited in Pashentsev 2002).

The practitioner side of public relations concentrates its efforts on specialised areas, such as corporate and governmental public relations, and, in many cases, ignores other areas of public relations. For instance, Novikov (1999) indicates that political consulting and corporate public relations are two main areas of current Russian practice. Pashentsev (2002) claims that 60 to 70 per cent of all accounts of Russian public relations agencies fall under the category of political public relations. The majority of research published is focused in these two areas. Nevertheless, the public relations field has now defended its right for professional autonomy and has become a vital part of Russian life. In 1996, US$ 100 million were spent on public relations services in the Russian market (Novikov 1999). Primarily in Moscow, agencies and whole alliances of agencies are forming and engaging in campaigns that are designed to attract attention and generate interest in their activities among future professionals, potential clients, and a society at large. Some agencies even conduct seminars and workshops on public relations, which are not connected to a higher education programs at all. Sometimes they invite foreign colleagues to speak to Russian practitioners and create other types of linkages and relationships (Eremin and Borisov 2000). All these efforts of practitioners bring some distraction to the higher public relations education and minimise efforts of educators and researchers to present, analyse, and problematise public relations as a serious field of study.

2.3. Development of education and research traditions in public relations

As public relations became more popular in Russia in the 1990s, the need for education rose. In April 2000, fifty-six Russian higher education institutions offered majors in public relations (Konovalova 2000), in September 2001 there were more than sixty public relations programs (PR News 2001), and by 2002, more than sixty-seven public relations programs were identified (Tsetsura 2002). In 1999, the higher education requirements for public relations majors were defined, and the Federal Russian Committee of Higher Education certified public relations as an official major at Russian universities. This governmental organ not only certifies the guidelines that universities and colleges should follow but also evaluates the institutions for compliance of federal certification standards (Department of Higher Education of Russian Federation, 2000).

Only few universities in Russia, however, actually meet these certification standards (Varustin 2000). Moscow and St Petersburg universities have a large number of standardised programs because of their active development of relations with universities in Europe and Northern America. Thanks to the number of federal grants and the volume of financial aid from independent foundations, many universities – such as Moscow State University, the Moscow State Institute of International Relations, the Moscow Humanitarian Institute, the Moscow State Academy of Management, St Petersburg State University and St Petersburg Electro-Technical University – can afford to invite Western scholars to lecture and conduct workshops on public relations (Alyoshina 1997; Clarke 2000; Guth 2000; McElreath et al. 2001; Newsom, Turk and Kruckeberg 2000).

After about ten years of active implementation of public relations courses into programs in Russia, the significant impact of journalism, political studies, psychology, business, and sociology became obvious. Of course, today there are quite a few sociology and psychology departments who offer public relations majors and minors to their students. For instance, Moscow State University has three departments where public relations is taught from different perspectives: journalism, psychology, and sociology (Pashentsev 2002). In addition, many universities open public relations programs without having any solid background in teaching either of the listed disciplines. Public relations education, it seems, becomes an attractive "bread and butter" for schools and programs that have been experiencing problems bringing in students for paid higher education. Nevertheless, journalism and business areas continue to be main bases for public relations education in the leading public relations programs in the country, including Moscow State University, St Petersburg State University, Voronezh State University, Moscow State Institute of International Relations, and Financial Academy for the Government of Russian Federation (Pashentsev 2002; Tsetsura 2003). Orientation on journalism or business depends on the department at which public relations is taught at a particular university as well as on the expertise of the faculty members teaching specific courses. Thus, public relations programs at Moscow, St Petersburg, Voronezh, and Rostov State Universities are journalism-oriented and programs at Moscow State Academy of Management and St Petersburg Electro-Technical University are business-oriented.

The distribution of public relations programs along these two approaches is fairly even, although the distribution of public relations programs themselves is uneven across different regions in Russia (Tsetsura 2003). For instance, Moscow and St Petersburg have a number of programs, as a result of active development of public relations practices in the Russian capital and the unofficial "Northern capital", as St Petersburg is sometimes called. The development of public relations here is influenced by the incredible market opportunities, the political struggle for administrative positions in the federal government, as well as active relationship-building among universities in Moscow and St Petersburg with universities from Western Europe and the US.

At the same time, universities in other Russian regions, such as Central Europe, Ural, and Siberia, have fewer and less comprehensive programs in public relations (Pashentsev 2002). Some programs from outside of Moscow, however, stand out: for example, Voronezh State and Rostov State Universities are among the few that offer strong programs in public relations outside of the Moscow and St Petersburg (Pashentsev 2002; Tsetsura 2003). Nevertheless, in Voronezh, a city in the Central Black-Earth region with a population of over a million, only two universities offer public relations as a major, whereas in Moscow and St Petersburg there are more than forty programs in public relations. Differences in public relations education are not the only characteristics of different Russian regions, or meta-regions, as Tsetsura (2003) calls them. She claims that geopolitical factors, such as political, economical, and cultural backgrounds and the development of different regions in Russia, directly influence the development of the field. Public relations education, research, and practices as well as specific tactics are different in different meta-regions.

For example, in media relations, Western techniques of developing and distributing press releases are quite successful when used to appeal to Moscow and St Petersburg journalists and editors, while interpersonal techniques and personal friendship as well as personal visits are more helpful in getting publicity in the media published outside of this region, such as in the European part of Russia or the Urals (for more information about this research project, see Tsetsura 2003).

2.4. How language shapes the development of public relations

Modern public relations theory in Russia uses many English words for its concepts, thereby preventing precise translations into Russian to avoid more confusion. This practice began when public relations started to evolve as an independent area of study. Literal, word-for-word translation did not reflect the essence of the concepts. Because of a lack of historic context in Russia, the Russian language often did not have good equivalents for some words, such as "publicity" and "press release". Thus, traditional scholars began to accept loan translations.

Public relations has established in Russia and its concepts and terms have become a part of the Russian lexicon as public relations and marketing had become parts of the Russian social/economic infrastructure.

Of course, the active development of public relations practice has led to an ongoing interest to public relations by scholars.

3.   Typification of current public relations

3.1. Status of public relations in business, administration and society

The development of public relations in Russia significantly differs from the development of the field in Europe and the US. This difference is created not only by field's young age, but also by the lack of Russian theoretical works in public relations. Perhaps, the main characteristic of public relations development in Russia is the absence of a communication tradition. While in many countries communication is a key to understanding the field of public relations, in Russia, communication tradition does not exist. Instead, public relations theory is heavily drawn from a number of different fields, including but not limited to sociology, psychology, business and journalism, whose impact on Russian public relations needs to be addressed.

Another feature of public relations is a wide interpretation of public relations by Russian educators and practitioners. A question of what to call public relations is still a very essential question for many researchers as well as professionals in the field. Often, a whole theory would be developed around this question. As a result, descriptive research that presents public relations from different perspectives appears and tends to be defended over and over. Instead of concentrating on the analysis and problematic of modern state of public relations, researchers argue about grounds and borders between public relations and other activities alike. It is very possible to find Russian books and research projects that would essentially describe public relations only as publicity, political advertising, marketing, corporate advertising, propaganda, or strictly manipulative techniques (Borisov 1998; Egorova-Gantman and Pleshakov 1999; Pashentsev 2002; Yunatskevich and Kulganov 1999).

3.2. Public relations textbooks and best selling practical books

Today business scholars, as a rule, concentrate on management and marketing functions of public relations (business-type public relations), whereas journalism scholars focus on its communication function (journalism-type public relations). Moreover, scholars in psychology, sociology, and political studies bring their own perspectives into the field of public relations. Some books on public relations in Russia are written by political scientists, such as Pocheptsov (1998, 2001). Nevertheless, the quality of most of the books is low, even though a large number of books in public relations have been published in the last five years. Western textbooks, translated into Russian, often are the main source for public relations knowledge for faculty and students of Russian universities. Among other translations, widely used for teaching public relations, are Seitel's *Modern Public Relations*, Buari's *Public relations or trust strategies*, Black's *Public relations: What is it?* and, most recently translated, Newsom, Turk, and Kruckeberg's *This is PR: The realities of public relations*. The latter title is probably the most exciting piece, including a solid overview of public relations theories and practice in the US and presenting challenges and problems of modern public relations in the twenty-first century.

Among the most popular books on public relations are ones that offer practical advice on how to organise political campaigns and use public relations techniques in election campaigns (Maksimov 1999; Pheophanov 2001; Sitnikov and Bakhvalova 2001). Further, political public relations is often analysed in conjunction with political advertising and manipulation, which is a clear evidence that Russian scholars do not make a clear distinction among the three phenomena (Egorova-Gantman and Pleshakov 1999; Pocheptsov 2001). Other Russian textbooks include business-type public relations introductory books by Alyoshina (1997) and Sinyaeva (2000) and journalism-type public relations books (which are written from sociological, political scientific, and journalistic perspectives) by Lebedeva (1999), Pashentsev (2002), Pocheptsov (1998, 2001), Tulchinsky (1994). In Russia, it is easy to find a textbook, self-published by an author or published by a single school or department for teaching their specific public relations courses; in fact, some of the books listed here are published this way. Western textbooks, listed earlier, however, stay as the most popular textbooks among most of the professors at major universities who teach public relations courses (Tulupov, personal communication).

4. Conclusions: state of the art and future of public relations in Russia

4.1. Trends

The professional side of public relations in Russia is characterised by greater emphasis on specific directions of public relations practice. Polit-

ical public relations (relations with national, regional and local governments and electoral relations), media relations, and corporate relations
are the most popular areas in public relations practice. Several Russian
scholars have tried to study public relations in Russia but most of these
efforts concentrate on a functional description of practices rather than on
theorising about them (see, for example, Alyoshina 1997; Maksimov
1999; Sinyaeva 2000; Tulchinsky 1994).

Governmental and political public relations is a specialty in Russian
public relations practice. Public relations scholarship is also concentrated
in this area. Today, the majority of public relations textbooks and case
studies published by Russian scholars almost exclusively cover political
public relations. For example, Pocheptsov (1998) spent much time analysing the nature of political public relations and modern practices in the
field. Pashentsev (2002) presents political public relations in a separate
chapter entitled "Public relations in Russia".

One of the most interesting and provocative discussions in modern public relations theory in Russia concentrates around two views on public relations, "white PR" versus "black PR". These terms were introduced in the
early 1990s and soon became popular among professionals and, later,
scholars. Ethics is the main reason behind dividing public relations practices in to "black" and "white". "Black PR" is associated with manipulative, dishonest, techniques that are used mostly in the area of political
public relations, particularly in election campaigns. "White PR", in contrast, presents a Western, ethical view on public relations, which is drawn
from Grunig's *Excellence Project* (Maksimov 1999). In almost any discussion of public relations practices, public relations scholars, practitioners,
political consultants, and journalists refer to the field in terms of "black"
and "white". But some scholars reject these stark terms. Instead of cat-
egorizing public relations as "black" or "white", they argue that "black"
public relations is not public relations at all, but rather propagandistic efforts (Tsetsura 2000). They point out that "black vs. white PR" discussions
exist mainly because the profession has been slow to adopt ethical standards. Novinskij (2000) argued that in Russia, there is no philosophy and
ethics of public relations per se. Some scholars from the United States
contended that "black" public relations cannot exist because "any misuse
or abuse of public relations is a question, not of "bad" public relations of
which only an individual practitioner can be held responsible, but rather
such misuse or abuse becomes a question of unethical professional
practice which is of collective concern and which must be [the] collective
responsibility of all practitioners" (Kruckeberg 1992: 34).

From a Western perspective, public relations professional ethics is not well understood in Russia. Even though Russian professionals have joined associations such as the International Public Relations Association (IPRA), International Association of Business Communicators (IABC) and the Public Relations Society of America (PRSA), which exhort them to follow codes of ethics, these professionals often consider such codes as idealistic and not practical in the Russian environment (Tulupov, personal communication). The main problem, however, lies in the fact that these Russian professionals themselves argue for ethical public relations in their publications and interviews and accept that they do not act ethically when they break public relations codes of ethics (Pashentsev 2002). The argument that Russian public relations ethics is not the same as Western ethics cannot be accepted in this case: if Russian public relations practitioners do not deny that, for example, publishing press releases for money is wrong, then how can this practice be ethical in Russian public relations?

The problem of paying journalists and editors for publishing publicity materials is a big concern among public relations practitioners today. While the issue originally appeared in Moscow and St Petersburg, now it becomes more and more common in many other regions in Russia. It is often referred to by the slang word *zakazukha*, which means a material in favour of an organisation written by a journalist and published on editorial pages, but was paid for by that organisation. These are called "advertorials" in English. A recent study conducted by Promaco Public Relations, a Moscow-based public relations firm, showed that thirteen out of twenty-one Russian national newspapers and magazines were ready to publish a fake press release (without even checking the facts), charged between US$ 200 and US$ 2,000 for the service (Sutherland 2001). In Russian law this illegal activity is listed as hidden advertising. Unfortunately, the law against hidden advertising which periodically appears in the Russian media is not enforced. Journalists who get paid or public relations professionals who pay for materials to be published are not legally challenged for their wrongdoings. As a result, *zakazukha* is a common Russian practice which creates a strong negative perception of the field (Tsetsura 2000).

The attitudes of some Russian public relations professionals toward this important issue is an area of concern. Russian practitioners, specifically the ones who practice political public relations, readily admit that they do not always practice ethical public relations as presented in the code of ethics of the Russian Public Relations Association. They present what in their view is a plausible excuse for ignoring ethical considerations in their professional practice by citing differences in the mentality of Russian society, which makes it difficult for them to practice specific public relations practices (Tsetsura 2003). Many of them simply say that it is impossible to practice ethical public relations because nobody would pay for it (Maksimov 1999). These excuses seem not to be plausible. First of all, the majority of the practitioners agree that ethics – discussed earlier – needs to be taken into consideration while practicing public relations. Second, Russian scholars constantly argue for ethics of public relations as a unifying element in international public relations (Alyoshina 1997; Egorova 2000; Konovalova 2000; Lebedeva 1999; Pashentsev 2002; Tsetsura 2000a, 2001, 2003). This suggests that the ethics of public relations in Russia requires more attention and further discussion and research.

Russian public relations professional organisations as well as practitioners face the same problem as their many counterparts in other countries: accepted codes of ethics are not enforceable and thus are not practiced (Tsetsura 2001). Although codes of ethics exist worldwide, many point out numerous problems with their reinforcement. One of the goals of public relations practitioners and educators is to find better ways of reinforcing such codes and positioning benefits of following them. This objective can be quite challenging, especially for modern Russian practitioners; however, it is important to continue promoting ethical practices for educational and professional communities in the name of a better future of Russian public relations.

References

Alyoshina, I. (1997). *Public relations dlja menedgerov i marketerov* [Public relations for managers and marketeers]. Moscow: Gnom Press.

Black, Sam (1993). *The Essentials of Public Relations.* London: Kogan Page.

Borisov, B. L. (1998). *Reklama i public relations: Alkhimiya vlasti* [Advertising and public relations: Alchemy of power]. Moscow.

Clarke, T. M. (2000). An inside look at Russian public relations. *Public Relations Quarterly* 45–1, 18–22.

Department of Higher Education of Russian Federation (2000). Novyj gosudarstvennyj obrazovatel'nyj standart po spetsial'nosti "Svjazi s obschestvennostiju" (350400) [New governmental standard in the major "Public Relations". Official document]. www.pr-news.spb.ru/

Egorova, A. (2000). International public relations: Order out of Chaos. A Delphi study focusing on Russia. Master's thesis, University of Lousiana.

Egorova-Gantman, E. and K. Pleshakov (1999). *Politicheskaya reklama* [Political advertising]. Moscow: Nikkolo M.

Eremin, B. and A. Borisov (2000). PR epohi uporjadochennoj demokratii. Electronic version of *Sovetnik* magazine. www.sovetnik.ru/archive/2000/4/article.asp?id=100

Golubkov, E. (1994). *Marketing: Slovar'*. Moscow: Ekonomika: Delo Ltd.

Guth, D. W. (2000). The emergence of public relations in the Russian Federation. *Public Relations Review* 26–2, 191–207.

Johnson, O. V. (1995). East-central and Southeastern Europe, Russia, and the newly independent states. In J. Merrill (ed.), *Global journalism: Survey of international communication*, 177–185. White Plains, NY: Longman.

Konovalova E. (2000), April A za PR otvetish' pered … sovest'ju. Electronic version of *Sovetnik* magazine. www.sovetnik.ru/archive/2000/4/article.asp?id=2

Kostukhina, D. (ed.) (1974). *Marketing: Collected essays*. Moscow: Progress.

Kruckeberg, Dean (1992). Ethical decision-making in public relations. *International Public Relations Review*, 15–4, 32–37.

Lebedeva, T. Y. (1999). *Public relations. Korporativnaya i politicheskaya rezhissura* [Public relations: corporate and political directing]. Moscow: MGU.

Maksimov, A. A. (1999). *"Chistye" i "gryaznye" teknologii vyborov: Rossijskij opy* ["Clean" and "dirty" techniques of political election campaigns: A Russian experience]. Moscow: Delo.

McElreath, M., N. Chen, L. Azariva and V. Shadrova (2001). The development of public relations in China, Russia, and the United States. In R. L. Heath (ed.), *Handbook of Public Relations*, 665–673. Thousand Oaks, CA: Sage Publications.

National News Service Agency of Russia (2000). www.nns.ru/

Newsom, Doug, Judy Vanslike Turk and Dean Kruckeberg (2000). *This is PR: The realities of public relations* (7th edn.) Belmont, Calif.: Wadsworth/Thompson Learning.

Novikov, A. (1999). *Khronologija rossijskih public relations*. Electronic version of *Sovetnik* magazine. www.sovetnik.ru/archive/1999/7/article.asp?id=4

Novinskij, B. (2000). PR: nauka ili remeslo? *RUPR*. www.rupr.ru/news/173192.html?section=articles

Ozhegov, S. (1984). *Slovar' Russkogo yazyka* [Dictionary of the Russian language]. Moscow: Russkij Yazyk.

Pashentsev, E. N. (2002). *Public relations: ot biznesa do politiki* [Public relations: From business to politics], (3rd edn.) Moscow: Finpress.

Pheophanov, O. (2001). *Reklama: Novye texnologii v Rossii* [Advertising: New technologies in Russia]. St Petersburg: Piter.

Pocheptsov, G. (1998). *Public relations, ili kak uspeshno upravljat' obschestvennym mneniem*. Moscow: Tsentr.

Pocheptsov, G. (2001). *Public relations dlya professionalov* [Public Relations for Professionals]. (2nd edn.) Moscow: Refl-book and Vakler.

PR News (2001). www.prnews.ru/news

Sinyaeva, I. M. (2000). *Public relations v kommercheckoj deyatelnosti* [Public Relations in Commerce]. Moscow: Unity.

Sitnikov, A. and N. S. Bakhvalova (2001). *Politicheskoe konsultirovanie: Kurs lektsij* [Political consulting: Lectures]. Moscow: Image-Kontakt.

Sutherland, A. (2001). PR thrives in harder times. *Frontline, IPRA* 23: 5.

Tsetsura, Katerina (1999). Women and the development of public relations in Russia. Paper presented at the Sixty Seventh Annual Convention of Central States Communication Association, St Louis, MO.

Tsetsura, Katarina (2000a). Conceptual frameworks in the field of public relations: A comparative study of Russian and United States perspectives. Master's thesis, Fort Hays State University.

Tsetsura, Katerina (2000b). Understanding the "evil" nature of public relations as perceived by some Russian publics. Paper presented at the International Interdisciplinary PRSA Educators Academy conference, Miami.

Tsetsura, Katerina (2001). Can ethics in public relations finally become international? Dialogic communication as basis for a new universal code of ethics in public relations. Paper presented at the 4th PRSA Educators Academy international interdisciplinary conference, Miami.

Tsetsura, Katerina (2002). Development of public relations theory and practice in Russia: A geopolitical perspective. Paper presented at the 5th PRSA Educators Academy international interdisciplinary conference, Miami.

Tsetsura, Katerina (2003). The development of public relations in Russia: A geopolitical approach. In K. Sriramesh and Dejan Verčič (eds.), *The global public relations handbook. Theory, research, and practice*, 301–319. Hillsdale, NJ: Lawrence Erlbaum Associates.

Tsetsura, Katerina and Dean Kruckeberg (2004). Theoretical development of public relations in Russia. In D. J. Tilson (ed.), Toward the common good: Perspectives in international public relations, 176–192. London: Allyn & Bacon/Longman.

Tulchinsky, G. L. (1994). *Public relations: Reputatsija, vlijanie, cvjazi s pressoj i obschestvennostiju, sponsorstvo*. St. Petersburg.

Utkin, E. and V. Zaitsev (1993). Public relations, ili dobroe imja firmy. *Torgovlja* 4–6: 36–39.

Varustin, L. E. (2000). Sistema obrazovanija public relations pered novym vyborom. *PR News* (On-line) www.pr-news.spb.ru/

Yunatskevich, P. I. and V. A. Kulganov (1999). *Psikhologiya obmana: Uchebnoe posobie dlya chestnogo cheloveka* [Psychology of cheating: A textbook for an honest person]. St. Petersburg.

Chapter 21

Serbia and Montenegro
(The Federal Republic of Yugoslavia)

Milenko D. Djurić

1. National profile

1.1. Overview of national characteristics

The Federal Republic of Yugoslavia is a democratic state with 37 nationalities living on its territory. Yugoslavia consists of the republics of Montenegro and Serbia. On the basis of the Proceeding Points for Restructuring of the Relations between Serbia and Montenegro, the Federal Assembly of the Federal Republic of Yugoslavia made the decision on 4 February 2003 to proclaim the Constitutional Charter of the State Union of Serbia and Montenegro. In this document, it is regulated that the name of the State Union is *Serbia and Montenegro*. Serbia and Montenegro are constituted on equality basis of two member states, the state of Serbia and the state of Montenegro. Serbia includes two autonomous provinces: Vojvodina and Kosovo–Metohija (presently under international administration in line with UNSC 1244). Belgrade is the capital, and is also the administrative, cultural, economic, scientific and logistic centre. Today, Belgrade has more than two million inhabitants and is a major crossroads of the north and the south, the east and the west. The official language is Serbian and the national currency is the dinar[1].

Yugoslavia covers 102,173 sq. km, and, according to the 1991 census, it had 10.4 million inhabitants, by which it ranks fourteenth in Europe. It is estimated that at present – based on projected increase in the population – the country has more than 10.6 million inhabitants. It is situated in the central part of the Balkan Peninsula. Although this is an excellent development advantage, it has led some writers to the conclusion that "the Serbs made a house in the middle of the road", meaning that along with welcome

---

1. The information in this section was taken from the website of the Federal Ministry of Foreign Affairs of Yugoslavia www.mfa.gov.yu.

guests, the unwanted ones dropped by quite often as well. The Republic of Serbia extends to 88,361 sq. km, while Montenegro takes up 13,812 sq. km. The 1991 census reported 9,779,000 inhabitants for Serbia, 615,000 for Montenegro. The average population density per square kilometre is 110 in Serbia and 46 in Montenegro, while on the federal level it is 101.

The Yugoslav economy has faced many difficulties and barriers during the long period of the European Union (EU) sanctions and NATO intervention in 1999. Despite of all problems and destruction, the country is recovering rapidly. All efforts are focused on the economic reconstruction and rebuilding of the infrastructure and the country. The largest part of capacities destroyed during NATO air strikes have been renewed and many enterprises are looking forward to re-establishing business connections with foreign companies. The orientation towards a market economy favours privatisation and creates conditions for a new investment cycle with foreign partners. The government, the financial organisations and institutions, the enterprises and the whole society are going through a fast transition process. Business and market procedures and standards are acquired and the general economic climate is improving each day. A new set of laws, agreed with the European Union, has been introduced, making this country an integral part of contemporary Europe.

In the wake of the democratic changes that took place towards the end of 2000, major changes occurred in Yugoslavia's foreign policy. The chief objective of the new foreign policy has been to create a favourable external, international environment for fundamental internal transformations and reforms, without which any improvement of the general situation in the country can hardly be expected.[2] In other words, it was necessary to find a way out of previous international isolation. Yugoslavia became a member of almost all international organisations (such as the UN and OSCE), international financial organisations, etc. The new authorities restored diplomatic relations with the United States, Great Britain, Germany, France and neighbouring Albania. Relations have been established for the first time with two former Yugoslav republics – Slovenia and Bosnia-Herzegovina – while relations with Croatia have been upgraded to ambassadorial level.

Among the specific aims of Yugoslavia's new foreign policy, two should be singled out in particular. The first one is to get the country closer to European integration, the second, long-term, aim being membership of the

---

2. From the Speech of Federal Minister of Foreign Affairs Mr. Goran Svilanović, University of Fribourg, Switzerland, 21 Jan. 2002.

EU. A second foreign-policy priority is the normalisation and improvement of relations with neighbouring countries. The relations between Yugoslavia and the EU acquired a new dimension after October 2000 and became a strategic priority of the foreign policy. Yugoslavia defined a clear objective of concluding, by 2003 at the latest, the Agreement on Stabilisation and Association with the EU. The admission of Yugoslavia as a full-fledged member by the year 2010 has been set as a long-term objective. In the comprehensive process of Yugoslavia's return to international political and economic integration the European Union represents a key partner and provides the most significant support to political and economic reforms. With the new name Serbia and Montenegro, Yugoslavia has been received as the 45th member state in the Council of Europe on 3 April 2003.

1.2. Facts and figures about public relations in Serbia and Montenegro

The field of public relations is lacking empirically based data. There is no relevant official statistical data referring to the public relations industry. However, the results of the research undertaken in 1988 by Marketing Research Institute (MRI), in 1995 by Profile Public Relations and in 2001 by the Federal Agency for Media and Public Relations Research (FAMPRR) illustrate positive trends in the public relations field in the last decade.

If we compare the results of the first research on the state-of-the-art of public relations from 1988 and 1995 with results of the latest 2001 survey, we see that there is an evident development of public relations practice with recognised status of the independent sector. Significant achievements have been registered in the development of the education sector, in-house public relations departments and the consulting services sector.

The total number of practitioners has been increasing over the past years, though at a slower pace than expected due to the complex political situation and the slowdown of the economy. At the same time, there is an increasing number of companies and institutions, both in the profit and the non-profit sectors, with established in-house public relations departments. While at the end of the 1980s fewer than twenty surveyed companies reported that they had established internal public relations sectors or departments, at the beginning of the new millennium there is an increasing number of companies with internal public relations departments, as reported by 110 companies in the 2001 survey. Top managers in these companies confirmed that public relations is gaining the status of a highly ranked management function in their internal organisational hierarchy. Maintaining mutual understanding and a good relationship with the public is one of the strategic goals of all surveyed organisations.

The results of the survey of the Federal Agency for Media and Public Relations Research (December 2001) indicate that there were around 300 practitioners in the emerging public relations "industry". The majority have been working on a full-time basis in in-house departments. It is estimated that less than 10 per cent have been providing a broad range of public relations services in consulting firms, and public relations institutions focused on education and research in the field. However, in 2003 a significant increase of number of employees is registered in the sector of public relations consultancy practice. On the basis of data collected by the Public Relations Society of Yugoslavia (PRSYU) in April 2003, it is estimated that there is now more than 200 practitioners working in 21 registered public relations agencies. Total number of employees in in-house departments and public relations agencies is estimated to more than 500 practitioners.

The movement towards a market economy, with reforms in financial and tax systems and privatisation process under way, emphasises the importance of public relations specialists. They gain an increasingly important role in the fields of corporate strategic communication, corporate image building, crisis management, public affairs and the promotion of new opportunities to foreign investors.

Since public relations gained the status of academic discipline at university level in 1996, the number of scientific studies on public relations in Serbia and Montenegro is low. The first MA thesis in the field was completed in 1989, and the author elaborated the state-of-the-art of public relations as a profession in Yugoslav companies and institutions (Djurić 1989). Later on, in two doctoral dissertations, the role of public relations was researched in sectors of the army (Bojović 1998) and police (Kešetović 1999). There are also undergraduate papers dealing with the role of public relations in the banking sector and the service industry.

2.   History and developments of public relations

2.1. Development of public relations in practice

Public relations pioneers have been showing their interest in developing public relations practice and education in Yugoslavia since the early 1960s. However, in a centralised planned economy without strong competition in the local market, and with relatively little influence of the public on social trends, a more significant need for public relations practitioners appeared only in the mid 1980s. By now, with the transition to a market-oriented economy and the process of democratisation, public relations is becoming a recognised profession and academic discipline.

In the 1980s, public relations pioneers in Yugoslavia started various initiatives and activities in order to contribute to the affirmation of the profession and the development of education programs. These activities paved the way for the development of the Yugoslav market of public relations services.

The changes during the process of democratisation of Yugoslav society show the increasingly important influence of the entire public in shaping the country's future. Experiences from different crises situations warns that without effective communication it is not possible to provide conditions for a dialogue among various interest groups with conflicting goals. Under these circumstances there is an ever-increasing need for public relations experts competent enough to accept the professional challenges in daily public relations practice. They are expected to provide high professional standards and ethical norms in order to serve to the interest of their organisations and the general public.

The results of research indicate that there is a clear shift of general opinion regarding the definition and image of public relations during the last ten years, from ad hoc improvisation by talented individuals focused on publicity, to day-by-day practice by trained practitioners, based on strategy, with professional responsibilities.

With the democratisation of Yugoslav society comes a strong stimulus for the development of public relations practices. After a long period of embargo pressures and isolation from the international community due to the war and political crises, it seems that the time is right for a new beginning. There is a great need for experts and programs to re-establish links with foreign investors and international institutions and improve the image of the country. The public relations community has an important contribution to make in rebuilding understanding, trust and co-operation with the international community.

2.2. Development of education and research traditions

The development of the education system has been of a great importance for affirmation of the public relations profession in Yugoslavia.

The first initiatives started with seminars and courses at the end of the 1980s. The first certified education program and curriculum for public relations practitioners were promoted in the pioneer project of the School of Public Relations. It started in Belgrade on 14 June 1991, in cooperation of the Yugoslav public relations practitioners and the Yugoslav Institute of Journalism (JIN), together with IPRA and professor Anne van der Meiden, of the University of Utrecht, the Netherlands. This program has been the cornerstone for the further development of public relations education in Yugoslavia.

With the first postgraduate course of public relations specialisation, established in 1996 at the Faculty of Economics, University of Belgrade, managed by professor Dragutin Vračar (of the Faculty of Economics), public relations reached the status of academic discipline. The curriculum was developed in co-operation with professor James E. Grunig (of the University of Maryland, USA) and professor Glen Broom (of the San Diego State University, USA). Since then, public relations has been a core subject, or an optional subject in some other state and private universities.

In 2000, public relations was included as an independent subject in the curriculum of the four-year graduate program in the marketing course at the Faculty of Economics in Belgrade. Also, some other institutions in the system of high education have established a PR curriculum. Due to delays in the development of public relations education programs at universities in Yugoslavia, only 4,6 per cent of the participants in the 2001 survey confirmed that they acquired their basic professional education at institutions of high education.

A great number of short-term public relations seminars, training programs and courses have been organised by specialists and advertising or public relations agencies. In the 2001 survey, 52 per cent of the participants acquired their basic education in public relations courses and seminars, while 43,4 per cent were self-taught. In co-operation with the National Democratic Institute, the Ministry for International Economic Relations of Serbia and the Agency for the Development of Federal Administration, a training program for public relations practitioners in governmental institutions was organised in 2002.

Public Relations has been a challenging field for researchers. In the period from April to August 1988, the first research study in the field of public relations was completed in Yugoslavia. The research project was initiated in Belgrade as a part of an MA thesis in public relations (Djurić 1989), in cooperation with the Marketing Research Institute (MRI) and the Serbian Advertising Association (UEPS). The 500 leading companies and organisations in Serbia, Croatia, Slovenia, Bosnia and Herzegovina, Macedonia and Montenegro were surveyed. In-depth interviews with more than 100 top managers and industry leaders were conducted in the second round of the research. The results illustrated the state-of-the art in the public relations sector at that time and were used as basic guidelines for the actions of pioneers towards the affirmation and development of the profession and education programs in former Yugoslavia.

Two more research projects were completed in 1995 by agency Profile Public Relations, and in 2001 by the Federal Agency for Media and Public Relations Research. These research studies were completed with the intention to provide up-to-date comparative data regarding the state-of-the-art of public relations in Yugoslavia and to identify specific needs and opportunities in the public relations market.

2.3. How language shapes the development of public relations

There is difficulty in trying to define precisely what public relations really is and how to make a strict distinction between it and marketing and advertising. The results of previous research indicate that different terms for the profession are in use in companies and organisations. According to the recommendations of the PRSA Committee on Terminology from the report of 1987, the internationally accepted term "public relations" and the abbreviation "PR" are most commonly used in Yugoslav practice. Also, the translation of "public relations" into Serbian, *odnosi s javnošću* ('relations with the public'), is often used to name the profession.

3. Typification of current public relations

3.1. Status of public relations in business, administration and society

The importance of public relations is growing in the business sector, as well as in the administration sector. Also, public relations has gained socially recognised status of the profession with the important role in establishing conditions for two-way communication and dialog among different interest groups.

Regarding the types of organisation and their main field of work, public relations is gaining more and more importance in the service sector, private companies, the public administration sector, non governmental organisations and in governmental institutions. In the 1960s and 1970s, affirmation of the practice started in the service sector, mainly in hotels and transportation sector. Then, rising number of practitioners have been registered in production companies, the trade sector and banks. During the 1990s the demand for public relations practitioners was at its highest in the service and private sectors, and at the beginning of the new millennium, in the public service and government administration sectors. It is expected that from 2002 more and more companies and governmental institutions will need well-educated and trained public relations practitioners.

The development of the consulting services sector in Yugoslavia started at the beginning of the 1990s. The 2001 survey confirmed that there were twelve registered public relations agencies, and even more advertising and marketing agencies, all offering public relations services. In 2002, there were fourteen public relations agencies at the Yugoslav market registered in Hollis Europe Directory, while in the beginning of 2003 the number raised to twenty one. British based Shandwick was the first international public relations network that started consulting practices in the Yugoslav market in 1998, with Profile Public Relations as its affiliate member. Later, some other foreign agencies and networks entered the market in cooperation with local partners, such as Pristop (Slovenia), McCann-Erickson (Great Britain), Mmd Central and Eastern Europe (Hungary) and Hauska & Partner (Austria).

3.2. Major roles of public relations and typical tasks

The basic goals of practitioners have changed with the development of public relations profession and the Yugoslav market of public relations services. In the beginning, practitioners played the role of communication technicians and communication facilitators. The results of the first research project, conducted in 1988, showed that the basic goals of practitioners in the 500 polled companies were: to increase sales by providing support to advertising campaigns, to place nice stories about companies and their products in the media and thus provide positive press coverage, to create motivation and a team atmosphere among employees and mainly to take care of media relations. Most often, public relations activities were practiced ad hoc on special occasions, or post festum as a company's answer to specific problems or issues, without a consistent long-term strategy. In the polled companies, the most typical activities were: presentations at fairs and exhibitions (92 per cent); support to corporate advertising (91 per cent); house magazines and publications (78 per cent); company and product presentation (77 per cent); protocol and welcome services (68 per cent); special events (66 per cent) and press conferences (52 per cent). Later on, practitioners started to gain the more important role of communication strategist, often at top-management or board level. They have been engaged in continuous practice on a daily basis in order to improve corporate image and to maintain effective communication with media and publics, mainly with consumers. The results of the latest research, conducted in 2001, confirmed that nowadays public relations practitioners face many new challenges in the emerging fields of specialisation in public relations practice: public opinion research, media relations, community relations, crisis public relations, environmental "green" PR, investor relations, financial public relations, issues management, public affairs and lobbying. As the changes in Yugoslav society take effect, a wide range of public relations services will be needed, both at home and abroad.

3.3. The position of public relations in organisations

The profession has reached a more and more important position in all types of companies, organisations and institutions. There is a rising number of organisations in the profit and the non-profit sectors with public relations positioned at the top-level management function in internal organisational structure. Heads of internal public relations departments are often members of management boards. In many other organisations public relations practice is organised within independent public relations departments where average number of practitioners fluctuate from three to five and more. Also in great number of companies and institutions a single person may act as a public relations manager, within departments of marketing and advertising.

From the beginning of 2002, some signs indicated a recovery of the public relations industry in Yugoslavia. There is a growing demand for public relations practitioners. Employment is especially growing in the consultancy sector and non-governmental organisations (NGOs), as well as in governmental organisations and public administration, both on federal and local levels. International companies are also offering new jobs to local practitioners. The real value of effective public relations is anticipated in the whole society especially during the processes of conflicts resolution, economic transition and privatisation.

But in some companies there are still misconceptions about the tasks, goals and relationships between public relations, marketing and advertising. However, there is a growing number of companies which accept concepts of integrated communication, while public relations, marketing and advertising are partners rather than than rivals.

3.4. Current state of education and character of mayor textbooks

The first School of Public Relations in former Yugoslavia, launched in cooperation with IPRA, gave a strong stimulus to further development of public relations education programs. There is growing interest among students and practitioners to study public relations at university level and to innovate their knowledge by attending seminars and training courses.

There are three levels of public relations education programs regarding content of study and total number of working hours. Programs are organised in forms of: (a) two-three days seminars to one week in-house training programs; (b) one semester regular independent subject; (c) two semesters postgraduate specialisation courses.

Postgraduate specialisation courses in public relations are offered at the Faculty of Economics and at the Faculty of Organisational Sciences in Belgrade. From 2000, public relations is included in marketing course at the Faculty of Economics as an independent one semester regular subject. Public relations, as a regular or optional subject, is also becoming the field of study in the journalism, communication, marketing or management programs at some other institutions in the system of high education, namely, the Brothers Karić University, Megatrend, Institute for International Management and English School of Business. Nowadays, besides the more general profile of graduate and postgraduate studies, there is considerable interest in and need for specialised courses and training in different fields of public relations practice. Several private public relations schools, experts and agencies offer short-term seminars, in-house training programs and public relations courses in Belgrade: PRA, Bovan Communications, PRagma, Profile Public Relations, MARK-PLAN and Public Relations Consulting Group.

As a result of the initiative of members of the PRSYU and cooperation with universities, public relations now has academic status. There is a strong initiative to promote high professional and ethical standards in public relations education. PRSYU members will continue to encourage international cooperation in the field of public relations education.

The body of knowledge and literature on public relations have been growing with professional experience of Yugoslav practitioners. Since 1991, nine books on public relations have been written by Yugoslav specialists, together with four translated books: Jefkins (1991), van der Meiden (1993), Wragg (1996) and Black (1997). In three Yugoslav textbooks different aspects of the basics of public relations were elaborated: the role of public relations as a strategic tool of management (Djurić 1992), market communication strategies (Vračar 1996) and business communication, behaviour and image (Filipović, Kostić and Prohaska 2001). In several other books Yugoslav authors have been researching different fields of specialisation in public relations practice: in churches (Šordjan 1993), in the sector of private entrepreneurs' initiative (Džamić 1995), in military organisation (Bojović 1999), in police (Kešetović 2000), speech modelling in public relations (Marković 2000) and public opinion modelling (Jevtović 2003).

3.5. The local scene of public relations in Serbia and Montenegro

The Public Relations Society of Yugoslavia (PRSYU) was founded on 27 January 1993 at the Inaugural Assembly in the Chamber of Commerce in Belgrade as professional association of Yugoslav PR practitioners. All those involved with research, practice and education in the public relations field are welcome to the association. The main goals of PRSYU are: developing and promoting both PR profession and education; establishing contacts and cooperation among Yugoslav public relations practitioners and with international public relations organisations; and introducing and promoting professional and ethical standards in Yugoslav public relations practice.

With the member status of CERP since 1993, the PRSYU has been giving a valuable contribution to the professionalisation and internationalisation of the public relations practice. In 2003 there were around forty individual members in the PRSYU, representing in-house public relations departments, agencies and governmental, educational and research institutions. PRSYU members are also members of other professional public relations organisations, including CERP, EUPRERA, IPRA, IPR, PRSA, IABC and GAPRCM.

In 2001, the PRSYU has joined forces with the leaders of twenty-three national and international associations to establish GAPRCM, a global alliance committed to elevating the standards of the public relations profession and its practitioners around the world. PRSYU members will continue to make an important contribution to the professionalisation of public relations practice and to encourage international co-operation in the field of education and practice.

However, because of the upheavals caused by the Yugoslav crisis in recent years, there are many barriers to the fast revival of public relations business. Most domestic companies have tied up all their funds in reconstruction programs, while many foreign companies are reluctant to invest in public relations campaigns until the political and economic situations have settled down. Conflicting interests among the countries involved in the war, sanctions and different forms of political pressure without conditions for constructive dialogue, have created an unfavourable climate for the local public relations market. There was a sharp decrease in the PR budgets of home and international companies in 1999. This trend led to a temporary fall in total turnover, income and the number of employees in the consultancy sector. Others have moved their offices and exported some of their employees to foreign partner agencies in neighboring countries, providing services from a distance. Since the start of the peace process the situation has significantly improved.

Despite the current limitations and barriers, the local market offers many new opportunities to home-grown and foreign companies and new challenges for foreign investors. At the beginning of 2003, public relations practitioners in twenty one agencies hope that the time is right to meet new challenges and the needs of potential client companies in the emerging public relations market.

3.6. Growing fields and hot issues

The interest of many companies, governmental organisations and institutions is to provide adequate public relations strategies and professional support of practitioners to build closer connections and re-integrate into the European community. There is a great need of funds for financial support to promote new challenges for foreign investors in the local market and to create conditions for local companies to come back to the international market. Urgent actions are needed to improve the image of the country, together with home made products and services, and to get broader international support to the process of economy recovery and privatisation. These are great professional challenges to all public relations agencies and practitioners in Serbia and Montenegro.

At the same time, the profession should soon find the right answers to the growing public criticism, regarding the declining level of responsibility in the manipulative practice of some practitioners and agencies, spin doctors and journalists. Both practitioners and journalists are in danger of losing their credibility because a great number of them isneglect their professional duties, ethical standards and the public's interest. It seems that some public relations "professionals" are at the crossroads and face a dilemma: either to act as a professional communicator for standardised fees, or to act as a professional manipulator and use information and power unethically to reach "higher" goals for huge profits. There are many examples of unqualified practitioners and "spin doctors" who have created misunderstandings, deliberately misrepresented facts, and even openly manipulated the media.

For this reason, professional and ethical standards should be promoted and accepted in daily public relations practice as an effective control mechanism. Now, more than ever, it is necessary to aim all our efforts at rebuilding understanding, trust and cooperation.

4. Conclusions about the state of the art and the future of public relations in Serbia and Montenegro

The unstable environment

With the international support to undergoing a process of privatisation and economic reforms there is a trend of rising optimism regarding prospects for development of a public relations industry in Serbia and Montenegro. With the status of member state in the Council of Europe, Serbia and Montenegro are looking forward to participating in integration initiatives in the European Union and contributing to a stabilisation process in the region. However, in parallel with the optimistic view of the prospects of public relations, some barriers that might hinder the progress of the industry should be considered. These are: the unfavourable economic situation and business climate in Serbia and Montenegro, restricted public relations budgets in many local companies, difficulties in re-establishing cooperation with the international community and the still complex political situation in the region. A specific problem that should be considered is the relatively long period of the slowdown of the economy in Serbia and Montenegro and various political pressures.

The potential and expected economic recovery of the public relations market in Serbia and Montenegro are factors stimulating many home-grown public relations agencies to overcome all barriers and to seek affiliation with international networks, as well as for networks to secure their presence in the market. The results of a recent survey have confirmed that practitioners in Serbia and Montenegro are ready and willing to meet the needs and challenges in the emerging public relations market.

Partnership in communication practice

There are more and more examples of successful cooperation between public relations practitioners and other specialists in diverse fields of market communication in the realisation of global communication. Where there was rivalry before in the competition for limited budgets and dominant role in management structure, now we see ever more that this rivalry is replaced by teamwork and partnership in communication practice within many organisations surveyed.

More important role of public relations practitioners

In an increasing number of companies, practitioners assume a leading role in strategic planning and communication management. They have been employed in almost all types of organisations, in a range from companies and non-profit organisations to government institutions and representative offices of international organisations. They are becoming appropriate people for developing communication strategies and creating corporate identity, corporate culture and corporate image for their companies. They are often in charge of media strategy and managing global (integrated) communication programs. The visible results of their work and campaigns confirm the advantages and the value of a strategic approach to organising an open two-way communication between various organisations and their public.

PR specialisation versus global PR knowledge

With the development of public relations practice in Serbia and Montenegro a greater need for specialisation has emerged. Instead of the need for "global PR specialists" – as was the case at the beginning of the affirmation of the profession – nowadays there is a greater need for specialists in different fields of public relations practice. Increasing significance is attached to public relations specialists in corporate communication management, media monitoring, crisis management, employee relations, issues management, governmental affairs, public affairs and lobbying.

Image improvement campaigns

The unsatisfactory image of many companies, their products and the whole of the State Union of Serbia and Montenegro, at the moment, calls for public relations experts competent to plan and implement strategies and campaigns for image improvement. There is a growing need for effective international representation and strategic communication with opinion leaders and international institutions. The entire venture of image improvement requires public relations specialists, funds for financial support to public relations campaigns, programs for foreign investors and a stage-by-stage approach. Cooperation with international public relations experts, institutions and agencies will be of great importance in the near future.

Professionalisation

In 2002, the contract of cooperation was signed between the Public Relations Society of Yugoslavia (PRSYU) and the International Public Relations Association (IPRA). It should create new opportunities for exchange of know-how and promotion of professional standards and the best international public relations practice.

In an effort to improve the quality of the practice, practitioners in Serbia and Montenegro have supported the adoption of the Code of Athens with other international Codes of Ethics for public relations and the high professional standards defined by professional public relations organisations.

Members of PRSYU and those practitioners who want to secure a socially recognised status for the profession commit themselves to respecting and supporting standards so defined. They are looking forward to establishing cooperation with all regional and international public relations associations and institutions and giving their contribution to the development of the profession. And they are all very optimistic about the future.

References

Black, Sam (1997). *Odnosi s javnošću* [Public Relations]. (Transl. of *The Essentials of Public Relations*, 1993). Beograd: Clio.

Bojović, Mišo (1998). Promena predstave o Vojsci Jugoslavije u javnosti [Change of the Yugoslav Army's Image in the Public]. Ph.D. dissertation, Faculty of Political Sciences, University of Belgrade.

Bojović, Mišo (1999). *Vojska pred očima javnosti* [Army in the Eyes of the Public]. Beograd: Novinsko-informativni centar "Vojska".

Djurić, Milenko (1989). Public Relations: forma komuniciranja preduzeća sa okruženjem [Public Relations: Form of Corporate Communication with Surroundings]. MA thesis, Faculty of Economics, University of Belgrade.

Djurić, Milenko (1992). *Public Relations: ključ uspešnog nastupa na tržištu* [Public Relations: The Key to a Successful Appearance on the Market]. Beograd: Institut za tržišna istraûivanja.

Džamić, Lazar (1995). *Public Relations: fore i fazoni – priručnik za praktične preduzetnike* [Public Relations: Tricks of the Trade. A Guide for Practical Entrepreneurs]. Beograd: UFA Media & SmartCommunications.

Filipović, Vinka, Milica Kostić and Slobodan Prohaska (2001). *Odnosi s javnošću: poslovna komunikacija, poslovni imidž, profesionalno ponašanje* [Public Relations: Business Communication, Business Image, Professional Behaviour]. Beograd: Fakultet organizacionih nauka – Institut za menadžment.

Jefkins, Frank (1991). *Odnosi s javnošću za vaš biznis* [Public Relations for Your Business]. (Transl. of Public Relations for Your Business, 1987). Beograd: Privredni pregled.

Jevtović, Zoran (2003). *Javno mnenje i politika* [Public Relations for your business]. Beograd: Akademýa lepih umetnosti – Centar za Savremenu Žurnalistiku.

Kešetović, Želimir (1999). Odnosi uprave i javnosti sa posebnim osvrtom na odnose policije sa javnošću [Relations between Administration and the Public Featuring Relations between Police and the Public]. Ph.D. dissertation, Faculty of Political Sciences, University of Belgrade.

Kešetović, Želimir (2000). *Odnosi policije sa javnošću* [Police Relations with the Public]. Beograd: Viša škola unutrašnjih poslova.

Marković, Marina (2000). *Poslovna komunikacija: oblikovanje govora u odnosima sa javnošću* [Business Communication: Speech Modelling in Public Relations]. Beograd: Clio.

Meiden, Anne van der (1993). *Public Relations: uvod u odnose s javnošću* [Public Relations: Introduction to Relations with the Public]. (Transl. of Public relations: een kennismaking, 1990). Novi Sad: Prometej.

Šordjan, Zdravko (1993). *Veština odnosa s javnošću* [Public Relations Skill]. Beograd: Teološki institut za obrazovanje, informacije i statistiku.

Vračar, Dragutin (1999). *Strategije tržišnog komuniciranja* [Market Communication Strategies]. Beograd: Ekonomski fakultet. (First publ. Beograd: Privredne vesti Europublic d. o. o., 1996).

Wragg, David (1996). *Odnosi sa medijima* (Media Relations). (Transl. of Targeting Media Relations, 1993). Beograd: Clio.

Chapter 22

Slovakia

Ivan Žáry

1. National profile

1.1. Overview of national characteristics

The modern Slovak Republic was born in 1993, after the velvet divorce
from the Czech Republic in former Czechoslovakia. According the last
census, taken on 26 May 2001, Slovakia has 5,379,455 inhabitants living in
2,883 municipalities. Of these, 51.4 per cent are female; 2,665,837 (49.6 per
cent) are economically active.

An interesting feature of the Slovak Republic is its ethnic diversity.
According the last census these cultural groups are represented: Slovaks
(85.8 per cent), Hungarians (9.7 per cent), Rumanians (1.7 per cent),
Czechs (0.8 per cent), Ruthenians (0.4 per cent) and Ukrainians (0.2 per
cent). The cultural diversity is reflected in Slovakia's linguistic diversity:
languages spoken are Slovak, Czech, German, Polish, Ukranian, Ser-
bian-Croatian, Ruthenian, Hungarian and two dialects of Romani. All
this makes for quite a communication challenge for national and local
authorities – a continuing course in tolerant behaviour and communications. Slovakians must be very successful students and at the same time
teachers of this complex school of tolerance.

Another important feature from the cultural, philosophical and also
communication point of view is the religious diversity and the large number
of church-goers. Comparison with 1991, the proportion of people with any
religious affiliation increased from 72.8 per cent to 84.1 per cent. The share
of people reporting their relations to the Roman-Catholic church increased
from 60.4 per cent in 1991 to 68.9 per cent; for the Evangelic Church of
Augsburg Affiliation, the figures are 6.2 and 6.9 per cent; the Greek-Ortho-
dox church, 3.4 and to 4.1 per cent; the Reformed Christian church, 1.6 and
to 2 per cent. Thus, for Slovakia religion is quite important and religious
consequences or connotations are usually very important in any public
communication. This feature has relevant impact also on public relations.

Administratively, there are eight regions in Slovakia, but there are plans to increase this number to create more homogenous regional entities (see www.statistics.sk/webdata/english/census2001/tab/tab.htm). The Slovak Republic is a candidate member of both NATO and the European Union and will be a full member of both organisations by 2004. This entails new legislation, rules and customs and this, too, is a public relations challenge for Slovakia.

1.2. Facts and figures about public relations in Slovakia

Public relations in Slovakia is in its infancy. Born just after the Velvet Revolution in 1989, it is growing up amid the ruins of the old communist propaganda machine. So it is very early days and data on public relations are difficult to come by. Nevertheless, some observations can be made. There are eleven public relations agencies, all members of the only professional organisation (*Asociácia public relations Slovenskej republiky –* APRSR, Association of Public Relations of the Slovak Republic; see www.aprsr.sk) and several other agencies and individuals operating one-person organisations are observers (2002 figures). In addition, there are up to ten independent agencies. Public relations services are also offered by advertising agencies and such companies as consultancies and advisory firms, which, apart from public relations, also offer services such as media relations, lobbying, training, education – in short, any imaginable aspect of communication. Figures are not available.

The Slovak economic weekly *Trend* recently published (10 April 2002) rankings of sixteen Slovak public relations agencies. Their combined turnover in the year 2001 was € 4.1 million. This figure was confirmed by another magazine specialised in marketing communication, *Stratégie*, which published a similar ranking in 2002, this time of eighteen Slovak public relations agencies; it reported a combined turnover of € 3.9 million. So the public relations market in the Slovak Republic is worth about € 4 million. Unlike numerous major countries, the Slovakian public relations market continues to grow without interruption – even after 11 September 2001.

There are several dozens of registered public relations professionals – members of the PR Club of APRSR, which is an organisation of individuals active in the field. In addition, there are several hundreds of people who are not officially registered in any society or association, working either as independent consultants or as professionals in different communications/public relations positions at both state and private companies.

There are also several dozens of advertising agencies which have – or claim to have – public relations departments or offering "full service", including "below the line" communication or public relations.

Public relations practitioners are a varied group. People coming to public relations are journalists, spokespersons, and students of different fields (but not yet communications or public relations graduates, as there is no specialised education system yet). This is reflected in the level of service on offer: most agencies deal with public relations on a very general level, without any specialization. But this is now changing, as is shown by the way these agencies promote themselves. As to the quality of the agencies, two – Čányiová P&P and ProPublicum – have been awarded official certificates (ISO 9001: 2000), in recognition that their management complies with the ISO standards.

2. History and developments of public relations

2.1. Roots of public relations

We do not have any specific information about public relations in the Nazi Slovak State (1938–1944), but we need to look in archive documents and newspapers from those days. This could be a very interesting study because of the sensitivity of this not so nice part of the Slovak history.

It is difficult to speak of public relations as such in the period that followed – socialism in the former Czechoslovakia (1948–1968) and the federation of Czechs and Slovaks (1968–1989). Public relations was mentioned only in connection with foreign trade activities when dealing with the "class enemy" in order to get some benefits or contracts. Therefore public relations was tolerated and used in former *podniky zahranicneho obchodu* ('foreign trade corporations') – usually in centralised organisations in Prague responsible for dealing with foreign subjects on behalf of the state and other state companies. This mainly involved trade shows, exhibitions, promotions, and similar events.

In normal everyday life in organisations (companies, the government, the army, the communist party) usually the "one-way asymmetric-communication model" was applied. There was no real freedom of speech, organisations of people into democratic associations were not allowed, there was no real freedom of competition – public relations had no chance. The only officially allowed and sacrificed interest were the interests of "working class" (workers, cooperative farmers and working intelligentsia), presented and represented by the communist party. There was a strict and petrified system of party democracy, events, and communications systems: mass meetings, mass events, work place meetings, communist cells bulletin boards, more meetings, tightened discussions with usually pre-planned outcome, etc. The whole mass-media system was ruled and organised by the communist party, without any free flow of information that public relations needs. Foreign media were not allowed to influence Slovak people, people were not allowed to travel freely and show their real opinions. So public relations under communism in Slovakia meant political relations, not public relations. The only form of communication in official life was propaganda, though some marketing communications tools were used in commercial life. The planned, under invested, economy and the poor undeveloped socialist market did not need complex research into the needs of customers.

2.2. The development of public relations in practice

Public relations started to develop in Slovakia after the Velvet Revolution in 1989, which removed the manipulative communist regime. As the democratic changes became visible in the mass media and government, open information and elements of modern public relations started to emerge in the highest state institutions. TV and radio meant a historically significant step, which were still state-owned at the time. Just later the wave of openness and recognition of inevitability of truthful and regular informing of different publics started to emerge for instance in economics, culture, etc. The first two-way communication channels between the Slovak government and general public were established. The press and information department of the Slovak Government Office, under the leadership of Ján Čomaj, Juraj Vereš and Ivan Žáry, worked out strategic information starting points for Leopold Podstupka, the progressive advisor to the Slovak Prime Minister before the Velvet Revolution in the new political and informational reality. This press and information department started the personal and technical development of the government communications structures. For example, materials that had been secret until then were offered to journalists for study, and the first press conferences were held. These press conferences became quite common, and comprehensive communiqués, reporting on the sessions of the government and its presidium, were published. A new daily newspaper was founded *Národná obroda* – its purpose was to liaise government and the general public. Access to information in the Slovak National Council (the Slovak parliament) was facilitated. However, personal, organisational and technical re-engineering of the communications department of the Slovak parliament was not so quick and far-reaching as in the Slovak Government Office.

A further step to systematic work in the field of public relations in the realm of state authorities was the creation of the Slovak Press and Information Service. This institution, with the technical equipment of the former Federal Office for the Press and Information in Prague (which had been one of the Communist tools to control the media), and in close collaboration with the Press and Information Department of the Slovak Government Office, started to prepare daily reports on mass media for members of the Slovak government, parliament and other important state authorities. The aim of the founding fathers of the Slovak Press and Information Service was to build up a modern state information centre which – comparable with the Austrian *Bundespressedienst* ('federal press agency') – would manage the flow of information from the government to domestic and foreign journalists, provide feedback to the government and assist in creating an image of Slovakia abroad. The director of the Press and Information Service was Ladislav Schwarcz, the director of the Press and Information Department of the Slovak Government Office, Ivan Žáry. After leaving their positions in 1992, these two established the first Slovak professional and independent public relations agency, ProPublicum.

Between 1989 and 1993, when the independent Slovak Republic was created, the advertising and communications agencies operating in Slovakia were mainly Czech. The development of public relations in Bohemia (the Czech Republic), and especially in Prague, was ahead of developments in Slovakia. This was partly due to the worldly character of Prague, which, after the revolution, almost immediately became an important centre of European politics, economics, culture, tourism and marketing and strategic communications. Another reason was the fact that before November 1989, public relations were used only in foreign trade organisations, and these usually had their head offices in Prague, the capital of Czechoslovakia. However, officially this "bourgeois method of communication" was used only in the external communications of the communist state, when there was a need to enforce the regime's interests. At that time, Czechoslovakia, with 15 million inhabitants, was a relatively interesting market for transnational corporations and big investors who started establishing their offices in Prague. For instance, Hill & Knowlton opened their Prague office as early as 1991.

The first public relations agencies in Slovakia emerged in 1992–1993. In November 1992 Pro Publicum started its activities (see www.pppr.sk), which from the beginning had a co-operation agreement with Hill & Knowlton. Its first client was *Bratislavská opčná burza* ('Bratislava Option Exchange'), which quickly got the reputation of a modern, flexible and prospective financial institution. In 1993, when the independent Slovak Republic was born, several more public relations agencies were established; among these are Media In (1993), Interel (1996), Omnipublic (1996), Public Plus (1996), Promedia Partner (1997) and Verte (1997). Naturally, from the outset there were also big advertising agencies with their own public relations departments.

Public relations was institutionalised in 1993, when Štefan Jaška, Emil Pícha and Ivan Žáry established the founding committee of the Asociáci a public relations Slovenskej republiky (APRSR, Association of Public Relations of the Slovak Republic; see www.aprsr.sk). In 1995 the first general assembly of APRSR was held, which approved its first statute (by that time Štefan Jaška had left the committee and was replaced by Branislav Zahradník). Ivan Žáry was elected APRSR's first president, the vice-presidents were Nora Paríková and Emil Pícha and Branislav Zahradník, and Dagmar Kéryová and Milan Kisztner were elected presidium members. The general secretary was Silvia Bat'alíková (Kačeríková). The APRSR was established as a non-profit, voluntary organisation, associating professionals from the field of public relations, working in the Slovak Republic. The mission of the association is to contribute to the development of public relations for mutual benefit of individuals, organisations and the whole society. Amongst the goals of APRSR are:

– To enable its members to exchange ideas and practical experience. The APRSR organises meetings of its members with media, clients, discussing different aspects of communications and public relations.
– To improve professional qualifications. Several seminars were organised.
– To gather industry information. Members of the APRSR send important data from the agencies' operations to the headquarters and surveys are offered to industry magazines. The APRSR shares the data with ICCO.
– To inspire scientific research in public relations. This is still a thing of the future, and will only come about when more experts will be prepared to do research in public relations.
– To organise meetings, conferences and events, aimed at the improvement of professional knowledge and skills.
– To deepen professional contacts. In recent years several foreign public relations experts visited Slovakia and met APRSR representatives.

- To organise special social events for the benefit of its members.
- To unify members on the basis of their professional interest, and defend this interest whenever it is needed and appropriate.
- To establish contacts with similar foreign and international associations, partner organisations and other entities in Slovakia. The APRSR joined ICCO. There are quite good contacts with the APRA, the Czech public relations association.
- To keep watch that the code of conduct is respected. The APRSR has an arbitration committee to deal with ethical problems. Until now, however, this body was never consulted.

From the beginning, APRSR has been an organisation of individuals working in the field of public relations, with between 60 and 80 members. Its second general assembly in 1997 approved the Ethical Code of the APRSR and an important change of the statutes, namely, the creation of the Club of PR agencies, which was launched in 1998. After the 1998 general assembly, Ivan Žáry remained president, and Branislav Zahradník, Nora Gubková-Paríková, Dagmar Kéryová, Milan Kisztner, Pavol Lím, Tibor Repta, Michaela Benedigová and Vít Koziak were elected vice-president.

The year 1998 saw a breakthrough for the APRSR, when it changed from an association of individuals to one of agencies. On the APRSR's own initiative, representatives of agencies decided to establish their own club within the APRSR. Founding members were Interel, Media In, Milton (after this folded, its place was taken by AMI Communications Slovakia), Omnipublic, Promedia Partner, ProPublicum, Public Plus and Verte. The main reason for this step was the formulation of common interests and their enforcing, the more transparent public relations market in Slovakia, and the wish for setting professional standards for the profession. All this triggered internal changes in the APRSR, and led to the "Club of the PR agencies" ending up as the main player, with individual members of the association coming in second place. These changes enabled APRSR to participate more actively internationally.

Yet another change came in 1999, when the APRSR was transformed into an association of public relations agencies with the club for individual members. Until then the Association was the body organising individuals only, after the change public relations agencies started to play a significant role. Michaela Benedigová, director of Interel, was elected president and Tibor Repta became coordinator of the individual members. The steering body of the APRSR is the Executive Board, which is composed of statutory representatives of the member agencies. In 2000, APRSR participated in activities of the International Communication Consultancies Organisation (ICCO) and in discussions on global directions of public relations. It has been a full member of ICCO since 2001.

2.3. The development of education and research traditions

There are no provisions for education in communications studies or public relations. The first systematic course in communication and public relations was offered in 2001 by the *Vysoká škola manažmentu*, (College of Management, which is a branch of the American City University, Bellevue), the first Slovak private university. This course is based on the latest knowledge from theory and practice on public relations in the US, the UK and Slovakia. The course is taught in English by this author, and combines classic classroom teaching with up-to-date distance learning, using the latest American literature and multimedia tools, including the Internet and the study on-line centre (see www.vsm.sk). Until now, about 200 students have attended the course.

The first public relations courses for the non-governmental sector (NGOs, not-for-profit organisations) were organised by the Bratislava based Centre for Independent Journalism in early 1990s. "Marketing public relations" is part of the study plans at the Department of Marketing Communication at the Faculty of Arts of the Comenius University in Bratislava. These marketing communications studies were the first in former Czechoslovakia. This author under auspices of the Academy of Education, the Academy of Advertising and the Advertising Academy taught several shorter public relations courses. Some Slovak institutions and state authorities got foreign assistance in the field of management, communications, etc., including special courses and materials featuring public relations. The EU PHARE program, the British Know-How Fund and other bodies financed those programs.

2.4. How language shaped the development of public relations

In Slovakia we use the term "public relations", taken directly from English. However, in practice we also use *strategická komunikácia* ('strategic communication'), *vzťahy s verejnosťou* ('relations with the public') or *vzťahy k verejnosti* ('relations to the public'), *marketingová komunikácia* ('marketing communication') or *podlinkové activity* ('below-the-line activities' such as promotions, events, sponsoring, public relations). The last two terms are used mainly in connection with marketing disciplines, where PR is understood as part of one of the "Four Ps" (Promotion). Sometimes the older term *práca s verejnost'ou* is used ('work with the public', based on the German *Öffentlichkeitsarbeit*), which is perceived as a bit manipulative and pushing public relations more into the direction of spin doctoring and propaganda. This term has certain connotations, associating it with the former communist regime, when "public" was the object of massive propaganda and manipulations.

3. Typification of current public relations

3.1. Status of public relations in business, administration and society

After 1989, when the communist regime was overtaken, further organisations and institutions started to develop, such as business entities, corporations, government and the so-called third sector (non profit / non government). Gradually, these organisations are beginning to realise that there is a crucial need for systematic communications with all important target groups, both internal and external. More and more spokespersons and press secretaries were appointed, and PR departments were established. Among the movers of this development were many foreign entrepreneurs who decided developing their activities in Slovakia. They brought common communications standards used in the more developed world, patterns, practices, demands, experience. However, quantitatively and also qualitatively, this process still runs behind most developed countries, despite the many achievements of the Slovak public relations industry (recall the ISO awards mentioned earlier assigned to two Slovak agencies).

3.2. Dominant roles of public relations and typical tasks

The dominant roles of public relations and the typical tasks of public relations practices are mainly managerial in nature, often complemented with some technical aspects. These are the most visible features of communications tasks of organisations in Slovakia: practical media relations, issuing news releases, organising news conferences, press events, special events, web design, employee communications, producing annual reports, goods and services promotions, etc.

Reflective and educational characteristics are recognised more and more with the progress of understanding of the importance of the strategic, long-term communication needs of different organisations. The development of a professional press and other media also plays an important role here. Magazines such as *Stratégie na Slovensku*, *Marketing magazín* and the economic weekly *Trend* regularly follow what goes on in public relations and communications. They print articles, news, reviews and charts, covering the latest developments in the industry, and discussions on hot issues. In addition *Otázky žurnalistiky* ('Problems of Journalism'), a specialist magazine for the theory, research and practice of mass media, which is already in its forty-fifth year, regularly publishes articles dealing with different aspects of public relations (see www.phil.uniba.sk/~kzur/oz.htm).

3.3. Position of public relations in organisations

Organisations usually do not have autonomous public relations departments. In most cases, public relations is delegated to the marketing department or to the secretary's office, close to management. In other cases it is part of the tasks of an external-relations department. On the other side, internal communications are often the responsibility of human resources units. Understandably, the non-profit sector usually does not have special positions for public relations and communications. There are often ties between certain NGOs and sponsors, who also provide some public relations advice, and there may be links between NGOs and public relations or advertising agencies that support specific programs. Many special courses have been organised by foundations (especially from the US), aimed at strengthening public relations awareness among non-government organisations. Public administration is differentiated as to its level (central, regional, local) and also as to its ties with state or self-government. Government organisations usually have official information units and press secretaries. Self-government tries hard to communicate efficiently without these amenities, having neither enough money, nor experience, nor trained people. However, progress is quick. The situation is improving thanks also to new legislation, giving every citizen the right to get any unclassified information concerning activities of the public administration paid from taxpayers' money (the Free Access to Information Act).

3.4. Current state of education and character of major practical and textbooks

It was mentioned earlier that education in public relations and communication is still in its infancy. The textbooks used the courses organised by the Management School are American (Seitel 2001, for example). The only original Slovak textbook is Žáry (1995). The latest version of this book is available (in Slovak) at www.pppr.sk/english/vbookO.html. Some of the books used are translations into Czech or original Czech texts (for example, Němec 1999).

There are very few books on public relations in the shops. They are usually general publications on public relations – translations without any deeper specialization (with the exception of Němec's Czech book on crisis communication).

3.5. The local scene of public relations in Slovakia

Slovakia has become target market of several global and European public relations networks. There are present network agencies Burson-Marstteller, Edelman, GCI, Hill & Knowlton, Porter Novelli, Interel Marien, etc. Original, native agencies are present, as well.

3.6. Growing fields and hot issues

Hot issues in everyday practice typically revolve around ethical matters. For example, there are some non-transparent relations between some media moguls and public relations agencies, which fly in the face of the relations for media and PR agencies. An old issue is the still current practice of offering free 'advertising' space. For instance, if a company pays for a double spread in the newspaper, the paper will print an interview with the company's boss. Naturally, that interview is not clearly marked as an advertisement. Other ethical issues include the covert payments to journalists to motivate them write "positively" about certain organisations and their products. These things cannot be proved, and those involved deny everything. Newspapers and magazines were very interested in a press release published in 2002 by ProPublicum, based on the results of an IPRA worldwide media transparency survey. A discussion on these issues is now taking place between media owners, journalists and their organisations (see the IPRA worldwide media transparency survey, published on 14 June 2002).

4. Conclusions: state of the art and future of public relations in Slovakia

If we define the beginning of 1990s as the introduction of the public relations profession in Slovakia, then we could describe the beginning of the new millennium as the growth stage. The next stage is maturation. Slovakia will soon be on its way to reach the next level of development of this interesting and challenging communication profession. This is demonstrated by the results of the public relations market, which grows significantly each year, and the increasing awareness of organisations, companies and individuals of the inevitability of permanent efficient communications.

The future of public relations in Slovakia is promising. They are related to further progress of reforms, development of the economy, culture, and political culture, entering further foreign investors, etc. This development is very positive; Slovakia has become a full NATO and EU member (only the agreement of several member states parliaments is to confirm this reality), and thus a free flow of information and communication, including well-established communication patters are shaping the Slovakian public relations environment directly. This development is also challenging the Slovak public relations market. Increasing international competition brings unique opportunities for all public relations players.

References

Němec, Petr (1999). Public relations. *Zásady komunikace s veřejností* [Public Relations: Principles of Communication with the Public]. Prague: Management Press.
Seitel, Fraser P. (2001). *The Practice of Public Relations* (8th edn.). Upper Saddle River, NJ: Prentice-Hall. [With supplements for teachers and exam-building software.]
Žáry, Ivan (1995). *Public Relations: Cesta k úspechu* [Public relations: the Road to Success]. Bratislava. HEVI [The latest version of this book is available free of charge at www.pppr.sk/english/vbookO.html; in Slovak only.]

Chapter 23

Slovenia

Dejan Verčič

1. National profile

1.1. Overview of national characteristics

Slovenia is a small country in Central Europe bordering Austria, Croatia, Hungary and Italy. It became an independent country in 1991. (From 1918 to 1991 Slovenia was a part of Yugoslavia.) It has a population of 2 million people, living on 20.296 sq. km of land, making a GDP of US$ 20 billion. Nearly 90 per cent of the population are ethnic Slovenians, speaking the Slovenian language, and the majority of population is Roman Catholic. In 1999, Slovenia's per capita GDP surpassed that of Portugal and Greece and it entered the new millennium with a per capita GDP that is more than twice that of any of the Central and Eastern European countries (Republic of Slovenia, Ministry of Economic Affairs 2000: 11). Slovenia is one of the ten countries to join the European Union as a full member in 2004.

Although there were public relations-like activities before 1989, the public relations and communication management profession in Slovenia started with the establishment of the first public relations agency, PR Center Ljubljana (now Pristop Communications) in 1989 and the foundation of the Public Relations Society of Slovenia in 1990. But the real growth started only in 1991, when Slovenia became an open, independent, democratic free-market society.

Politics
Slovenia is a constitutional democracy with a division of powers between the executive, legislative and judiciary branches. Its parliament is formed of two chambers. The National Assembly is the highest legislative body and is composed of ninety deputies who are directly elected by citizens through a secret ballot following a proportional voting system. (Proportional electoral systems produce coalition governments. The current one, in 2003, is a coalition of LDS – Liberal Democracy of Slovenia, ZLSD

– United List of Social Democrats of Slovenia, SLS – Slovene People's Party, and DeSUS – Democratic Party of Pensioners of Slovenia). The second chamber of the parliament is the National Council, which is composed according to the principle of corporative representation (through special interest and professional organisations, representing employers, employees, farmers, craftsmen, free-lance professions, universities and colleges, educational system, research activities, social security, health care, culture and sports and local interests) and is unique to the political systems of Western democracies, being closest to the former Irish senate and the former senate of the Free State of Bavaria (Lukšič 2001: 75–76).

Economy
Slovenia is a small open market economy. The total GDP is US$ 20 billion, which is US$ 10,000 per capita. GDP per capita in PPS is 15,000. (PPS is purchasing power standard, which is an artificial currency in which Eurostat expresses GDPs to enable correct comparison of goods and services produced by different countries.) Exports of goods amount to 57 per cent and imports of goods and services to 58 per cent of GDP. The EU-15 countries account for nearly 70 per cent of total Slovenia's external trade. The larger part of GDP comes from services (58 per cent), less from industries (38 per cent) and very little from agriculture (4 per cent). Social partnership exists on all levels from companies to the national level with Economic and Social Council (ESC), a tripartite body representing employees, employers and the government, at the top. The unionisation rate is around 42 per cent (similar to Austria, Italy, United Kingdom, Portugal and Luxemburg). Unemployment, by the standards of the ILO (International Labor Organisation), is around 7 per cent. Slovenia spends 7.8 per cent of its GDP on health and 5.7 per cent on education (The Economist 2002: 202–203; Republic of Slovenia, Ministry of Economic Affairs 2000).

Media
Slovenia is a media-rich society. In 2001, 97.6 per cent of households owned a color TV set (around 60 per cent of them were connected to cable television), 98.6 per cent owned at least one radio and 48.4 per cent owned a computer. The average daily media outreach among the Slovenian population aged 12–65 years was 81 per cent for TV, 68 per cent for radio, 44 per cent for daily newspapers, 32 per cent for outdoor media, and 27 per cent for newspapers and magazines. Of the 600,000 internet users in Slovenia (defined as those who have ever used the internet), 16 per cent can be classified as daily users. Slovenia has five national television channels. *TV Slovenija 1*

and *TV Slovenija 2* belong to the public broadcast system *RTV Slovenija.* *POP TV*, *Kanal A* and *TV 3* are private TV channels. There are eighty radio programs – six national, forty-two regional and thirty-two local. As to the printed press, 914 newspapers and magazines are published regularly, five of which are national dailies (Moûina and Resman 2001: 104–108). Four big media companies control 90 per cent of the daily newspaper market, while *RTV Slovenija* and a private conglomerate, controlling (though not legally owning) both *POP TV* and *Kanal A*, dominate practically the whole of the TV audience (and advertising revenue) market. Concentration in media ownership is counter-balanced by a strong Journalist Society advocating independence and the public service character of journalist profession.

1.2. Facts and figures about public relations in Slovenia

The public relations and communication management profession institutionalised itself in Slovenia only in 1990, when ten practitioners formed the Public Relations Society of Slovenia (PRSS). The current membership is approaching 300. A study conducted by Verčič and van Ruler in 2002 found an average of two people practice public relations activities in medium and large Slovenian companies – 7,040 in total (for-profit sector) or 0.05 per cent of the population. They estimated that current spending on managed communication activities in commercial sector is around 57 billion Slovenian tolars (€ 263 million) or 1.5 per cent of GDP. But only 6 per cent of these companies have a public relations or another communication-specialised department, 37 per cent of them do not have a single specialised communication professional and 60 per cent of the total communication budgets is spent on marketing communication (Verčič and Ruler 2002). A further 60–70 people work in public relations in government, parliament and in the office of the president of Slovenia, around 100 in public relations agencies and an unknown number in the public sector in general (hospitals, utilities, etc.) and in civil-society organisations.

2. History and development of public relations

2.1. Roots of public relations

The roots of managed communication activities in Slovenia are related primarily to the struggle of a small nation to defend its linguistic identity and then to attain a political identity as well. The *Freising Records*, probably dating back to before 1000 AD and written as a travelling bishop's manual, are the oldest known records of persuasive speech in Slovenian. The greatest communicator was the founder of Slovenian Protestantism and the author of the first three Slovenian Alphabet Primers in 1550, 1555 and 1556, Primož Trubar, who was the first Slovenian author to write on the importance of communication. (He was so successful in propagating the Protestant ideas that he was first persecuted and then banished from Slovenia to Germany.) The tradition of Slovenian industrial and trade press goes back to 1843, when the *Kranjska kmetijska družba* ('Agricultural Society of Kranj') published the first issue of *Kmetijske in rokodelske novice* ('Agricultural and Handcrafts News').

During the March Revolution of 1848 by the Central European nations that were part of the Austro-Hungarian monarchy, Slovenians declared a political program, entitled *Zedinjena Slovenija* ('United Slovenia'), which demanded for all Slovenians to be joined into one administrative unit (then still under Habsburg rule) and for Slovenian language to be granted the same status as German. The program became the most important political program for the next hundred years and *Zedinjena Slovenija* became the most important Slovenian political slogan of all times. Between 1868 and 1871 mass political meetings took place under the slogan of United Slovenia. The largest one took place in 1871 and attracted some 30,000 participants. It demanded equality of the Slovenian language and a Slovenian university. It was because those demands were not recognised that in October 1918 the Slovenians joined the Croats and some Serbs in leaving the Habsburg monarchy under whose rule they had been since the fourteenth century, to form a new state. In December of that year this new state joined with the Kingdom of Serbia into the Kingdom of Serbs, Croats and Slovenes, which was renamed the Kingdom of Yugoslavia in 1929. (Similarly, the decision to leave Yugoslavia in 1991 was triggered by Serbian nationalism encroaching Slovenian cultural and educational autonomy.)

From 1945 to 1991 Slovenia was part of the Socialist Federal Republic of Yugoslavia. Public relations-like features of socialist propaganda are still unstudied, but managed communication activities played an important role within that framework. In late the 1960s and early 1970s, socialist, the so-called "self-management", *contacts with the public* (more on that term is explained later on when we discuss language use) emerged. They were not perceived as a management function, but were under trade union jurisdiction. Information and propaganda departments were re-branded "Departments for contacts with the public". At the same time the first interest in public relations developed among social scientists. France Vreg, founder of communication-science studies at the University of Ljubljana, met Scott Cutlip in the 1960s and started translating the second edition of his textbook *Effective Public Relations* (Cutlip and Center 1960) into Slovenian. Pavle Zrimšek, a lecturer at the same department of communication science (established in 1966 at the Faculty of Social Sciences, University Ljubljana) translated a German text on public relations by Hundhausen, *Public Relations: Theorie und Systematik* ['Public Relations: Theory and Practice'] (1969). Neither of these two books was ever published in Slovenian. At the University of Ljubljana, preparations for the establishment of public relations as a separate academic subject have been going on since the late 1960s. The development was stopped by the mid-1970s, by a political directive, and did not continue for another 20 years, either in business or in academia.

Managed communication also played a major role in the social movements of the 1980s and 1990s that changed the political, economic, social and international status of Slovenia. Self-organisation of people, lateral communication and independence of the media were instrumental in these processes (Gruban, Verčič and Zavrl 1994; Verčič 2002).

2.2. Development of public relations practice

Public relations and communication management matured in Slovenia only in 1990s. In the first decade of its existence it went through four phases to become comparable to the current state of the profession in Europe at large (see Table 1).

Table 1. Four phases of public relations development in Slovenia (based on Verčič 2002)

Phase 1: Emergence (1989–1992)	First public relations agencies and departments Establishment of professional association (PRSS) First booklet on public relations
Phase 2: Recognition (1993–1994)	Initiation of annual Bled international research symposia Public relations becomes an academic subject First research on practice in Slovenia
Phase 3: Institutionalisation (1995–1999)	PRSS adopts a Code of Ethics Initiation of annual conferences of professionals First book on public relations
Phase 4: Normalisation (2000–)	Codification of job descriptions, salary levels, etc. Formalisation of professional education Graduate academic education

The drivers of public relations practice development were banks and other financial institutions and telecommunications, primarily operators of mobile telephone networks. The government and the public sector in general, as well as civil society organisations, are lagging behind.

2.3. Development of education and research traditions

The first attempts to introduce public relations as an academic subject at the University of Ljubljana in early 1970s failed and the topic became politically incorrect and unacceptable in the context of socialism (in contrast to advertising and marketing, which were not politically stigmatised and have been taught in academia since the mid 1970s). Education in public relations in Slovenia first developed outside the officially recognised institutions in business training centres (Verčič 1993).

Both academic education and research in public relations and communication management in Slovenia are connected to Larissa A. Grunig and James E. Grunig of the University of Maryland. They first visited Slovenia in 1992 and gave a speech to members of the Public Relations Society of Slovenia. They returned in 1993 to give the first lecture in public relations at the Faculty of Social Sciences, University of Ljubljana, where the field became an academic subject taught at undergraduate level in 1994 and at graduate level in 1998. After several years of intensive preparation, public relations and communication management is to become one of four areas of study within the Department of Communication, with journalism, marketing communications and media studies, both at undergraduate and graduate levels.

Between 1992 and 1994, the "excellence study" (Grunig, Grunig and Dozier 2002) was replicated in Slovenia, comparing Slovenia with the US, Britain and Canada (Verčič, Grunig and Grunig 1996; Grunig, Grunig and Verčič 1998). In 1994, Pristop Communications organised the first international public relations research symposium, which became an annual event. Two books (Moss, MacManus and Verčič 1997; Moss, Verčič and Warnaby 2000), two special issues of the *Journal of Communication Management* (Vol. 3, No. 3, 1999 and Vol. 5, No. 1, 2000) and several books of proceedings materialised the results. Work on an European approach to public relations and communication management (Verčič, Ruler, Bütschi and Flodin 2001) has culminated in *The Bled Manifesto on Public Relations* (Ruler and Verčič 2002).

2.4. How language shapes the development of public relations

The first translation of the English term "public relations" before 1990 was *stiki z javnostjo* (literally, 'contacts with the public'), which, in line with other Slavonic languages, treated the term "public" as an undivisible "general public". Gruban, Maksimovič, Verčič and Zavrl (1990) proposed a new translation, *odnosi z javnostmi* (literally, "relations with publics"), which was adopted by the Public Relations Society of Slovenia as the official term (i.e. *Slovensko društvo za odnose z javnostmi*). Towards the end of the 1990s, the definition of public relations in Slovenia broadened into "total communication" (Åberg 1990) between an organisation and all its publics (Theaker 2001) and synchronised with the European approaches (Ruler and Verčič 2002; Verčič, Ruler, Bütschi and Flodin 2001) that go beyond relational to include discursive and reflective approaches: *celovito komuniciranje* ('holistic communication') and *komunikacijsko upravljanje* ('communication management'). Currently, the three terms (*odnosi z javnostmi, celovito komuniciranje* and *komunikacijsko upravljanje*) co-exist in both practice and in academia – their relations and their future have not yet been decided.

3. Typification of current public relations

3.1. Status of public relations in business, administration and society

In the new millennium, public relations and communication management in Slovenia witnesses a bifurcation in practice between operational (technical) communication staff and managerial work at the strategic level. However, this can be seen only in business, while government, public administration and NGOs are lagging behind in positioning communication at the top level.

Certain elements of strategic work remain undifferentiated at the top corporate level, in the hands of CEOs and their closest collaborators. On the other hand, what van Ruler and Verčič (2002: 14) labelled "reflective characteristics" are divided between general management and top external consultants, while "educational characteristics" are more limited to management; attention to and concern for communicative competence of all members of an organisation is the exception rather than a rule.

3.2. Position of public relations in business

The business sector is by far the largest user of public relations and communication management services in Slovenia, both in terms of number of professionals it employs and in the amount of financial and other resources spent. In the early 1990s there was first a wave of privatisation of previously "socially owned" companies, followed by restructuring and consolidation. The advent of the new millennium brings the opening of the economy as Slovenia enters the EU and adjusts itself to global markets. Cross-border mergers and acquisitions further helped public relations professionals being admitted to boardrooms. Developments, however, are uneven and there are few companies with excellent public relations, many with mediocre or none. Recent research (Verčič and Ruler 2002) found that at least a quarter of the companies have no specialised department handling any kind of communication (external or internal). Marketing departments (regularly doubling as sales departments) are still often domiciles for all communication activities. Recently a reverse trend set in, with public relations directors taking over responsibilities for all communication, including marketing communication activities, and in some cases even strategic marketing.

3.3. Position of public relations in administration

At the centre of the government communication structure is the Public Relations and Media Office with fifteen professionals, all members of the civil service, and a director who is also the spokesperson for the government. Nominally, the director is a civil servant, but he has been replaced each time a new government has taken office. This office is divided into three departments – one for managing domestic, one for international communication, and the third for managing the communication program for Slovenia's accession to the European Union.

Every ministry employs at least one communication professional. The Ministry of the Interior has the largest department, with five communication officers at the ministry, plus eight communication officers at police headquarters – which is part of the Ministry of the Interior – and communication officers posted at police stations around the country. The Office of the Prime Minister has three communication officers. Communication has not gained a proper place in government and in public administration in general. It is still treated as a technical function responsible for information and broadcasting.

3.4. Public relations of NGOs

The specialisation of managed communication function is least developed in non-governmental organisations. This deficiency was recognised by NGO students and activists, and in 2002, when a series of lectures was organised on management of NGOs (and transmitted via student community radio, placed on that radio station's website as audio files and published as a reader; Jelovac 2002), several public relations topics were given a prominent position: policy analysis, relationships between NGOs and public services, the state, the church, political parties and businesses, change of management, public relations, lobbying, negotiations, fundraising, etc. International NGOs operating in Slovenia (Red Cross, UNICEF, etc.) are better in using public relations.

3.5. Public relations agencies

Public relations agencies in Slovenia are domestically owned by their founders as limited liability companies. They are all affiliated with international networks and/or multinationals, but without any equity relationship. The largest one employs over a 100 consultants and technicians. Agencies have an association, which is the Slovenian chapter of the International Communications Consultancy Organisation (ICCO). There are eight members: Imelda, Informa Echo, NT&RC, Prestige, Pristop, SPEM, Studio 3S and Studio Kernel. None can be classified as an exclusively public relations consultancy; at the same time, the major advertising agencies also offer public relations services and there is a process of convergence between advertising/marketing agencies and public relations consultancies. Pristop Communications, with a turnover of € 15 million, is the largest public relations consultancy and at the same time the largest advertising and marketing services group.

3.6. Major textbooks in public relations

Public relations and communication management literature in Slovenian is scarce. There is a booklet, written in 1990 (Gruban, Maksimovič, Verčič and Zavrl 1990), a book from 1997 (Gruban, Verčič and Zavrl 1997) and a reader from 1998 (Gruban, Verčič and Zavrl 1998). These largely draw on standard US textbooks. In 2000, Ašanin-Gole and Verčič published a collection of professional cases from Slovenian practice. In 2002, with a book on media relations (Verčič, Zavrl and Rijavec 2002), the Public Relations Society of Slovenia, in cooperation with the major business-publishing house GV Založba, started a book series that is to publish one original book and one translation per year. Although all these publications are used in formal educational institutions as well, they are primarily targeted at professional readers.

4. Conclusions: state of the art and future of public relations in Slovenia

Public relations and communication management in Slovenia is determined by the historical strive of a small nation to preserve its cultural identity. Language has been and will continue to be an important factor in the development of applied communication practice, favouring native practitioners. Aided by the small size of the country – with a miniature market of only two million people – the Slovenian public relations industry is 100 per cent domestically owned – and is to stay predominantly so, even after the country enters the EU in 2004.

Major changes in the next few years will be in the public sector. It lags behind the private sector in understanding the offerings of professional communication, not only for promotion, but primarily as a means of citizen consultation and participation. Communication as a policy instrument is at the moment still unknown in Slovenia.

Privatisation and deregulation, together with Slovenia entering the EU, will give an additional impetus to a striving profession which is growing rapidly, both in human and in financial terms, and which was unaffected by the recessionary tendencies of the early 2000s felt in the US and in the EU.

References

Åberg, Leif Eric Gustav (1990). Theoretical model and praxis of total communications. *International public relations review* 13–2: 13–16.

Ašanin Gole, Pedja and Dejan Verčič (eds.) (2000). *Teorija in praksa slovenskih odnosov z javnostmi* [*Slovenian public relations theory and practice*]. Ljubljana: Slovensko društvo za odnose z javnostmi/Public Relations Society of Slovenia.

Ašanin Gole, Pedja and Dejan Verčič (eds.) (2000). *Teorija in praksa slovenskih odnosov z javnostmi* [*Slovenian public relations theory and practice*]. Ljubljana: Slovensko društvo za odnose z javnostmi/Public Relations Society of Slovenia.

Cutlip, Scott. M. and Allen H. Center (1960). *Effective Public Relations: Pathways to Public Favor* (2nd edn). Englewood Cliffs, NJ: Prentice Hall.

Economist (2002). *Pocket World Figures, 2002 edition.* London: The Economist.

Gruban, Brane, Dejan Verčič and Franci Zavrl (1994). *Odnosi z javnostmi v Sloveniji: raziskovalno poročilo 1994* [*Public Relations in Slovenia: Research Report 1994*]. Ljubljana: Pristop.

Gruban, Brane, Dejan Verčič and Franci Zavrl (1997). *Pristop k odnosom z javnostmi* [*An Approach to Public Relations*]. Ljubljana: Pristop.

Gruban, Brane, Dejan Verčič and Franci Zavrl (eds.) (1998). *Preskok v odnose z javnostmi: Zbornik o slovenski praksi v odnosih z javnostmi* [*A Step into Public Relations: A Reader on Slovenian Practice in Public Relations*]. Ljubljana: Pristop.

Gruban, Brane, Meta Maksimovič, Dejan Verčič and Franci Zavrl (1990). *ABC PR: odnosi z javnostmi na prvi pogled* [*ABC PR: Public Relations at First Sight*]. Ljubljana: Tiskovno središče Ljubljana.

Grunig, Larissa A., James E. Grunig, and David M. Dozier (eds.) (1992). *Excellent Public Relations and Effective Organizations: A Study of Communication Management in Three Countries.* Mahwah, NJ: Lawrence Erlbaum Associates.

Grunig, Larissa A., James E. Grunig and Dejan Verčič (1998). Are the IABC's excellence principles generic? Comparing Slovenia and the United States, the United Kingdom, and Canada. *Journal of Communication Management* 2–4: 335–356.

Hundhausen, Carl (1969). *Public Relations: Theorie und Systematik* [Public Relations: Theory and Practice]. Berlin and New York: Walter de Gruyter.

Jelovac, Dejan (2002). *Jadranje po nemirnih vodah menedûmenta nevladnih organizacij* [Sailing Through the Rough Waters of NGO Management]. Ljubljana: Radio Študent, Študentska organizacija Univerze v Ljubljani and Visoka šola za management v Kopru.

Lukšič, Igor (2001). *The Political System of the Republic of Slovenia: A Primer.* Transl. Erica Johnson Debeljak. Ljubljana: Znanstveno in publicistično središče.

Moss, Daniel, Toby MacManus and Dejan Verčič (eds.) (1997). *Public Relations Research: An International Perspective.* London: International Thomson Business Press.

Moss, Daniel, Dejan Verčič and Gary Warnaby (eds.) (2000). *Perspectives on Public Relations Research.* London/New York: Routledge.

Možina, Simona Pavlič and Aleksandra Resman (2001). *Facts about Slovenia* (3rd edn). Ljubljana: Government of the Republic of Slovenia, Public Relations and Media Office.

Republic of Slovenia, Ministry of Economic Affairs (2000). *Benchmarking Slovenia: An Evaluation of Slovenia's Competitiveness, Strengths and Weaknesses.* Ljubljana: Republic of Slovenia, Ministry of Economic Affairs.

Ruler, Betteke van and Dejan Verčič (2002). *The Bled Manifesto on Public Relations.* Ljubljana: Pristop Communications.

Theaker, Alison (2001). *Public Relations Handbook.* London/ New York: Routledge.

Verčič, Dejan (1993). Privatisation fuels PR growth. In: R. Sarginson (ed.), *Hollis Europe: The Directory of European Public Relations & PR Networks*, 389–390. London: Hollis Directories Ltd.

Verčič, Dejan (2002). Public relations research and education in Slovenia. In: Stefanie Averbeck and Stefan Wehmeier (eds.), *Kommunikationswissenschaft und public relations in Osteuropa: Arbeitsberichte*, 157–173. Leizig: Leipziger Universitätsverlag.

Verčič, Dejan, Larissa A. Grunig and James E. Grunig (1996). Global and specific principles of public relations: evidence from Slovenia. In: Hugh M. Culbertson and Ni Chen (eds.), *International Public Relations: A Comparative Analysis*, 31–65. Mahwah, NJ: Lawrence Erlbaum Associates.

Verčič, Dejan, Betteke van Ruler, Gerhard Bütschi and Bertil Flodin (2001). On the definition of public relations: a European view. *Public Relations Review* 27–4: 373–387.

Verčič, Dejan and Betteke van Ruler (2002). Public relations and communication management in the Netherlands and Slovenia: a comparative analysis. Paper presented to the Public Relations Division, 52nd Annual Conference of the International Communication Association: Reconciliation through Communication. 15–19 July 2002, Seoul, Korea.

Verčič, Dejan, Franci Zavrl and Petja Rijavec (2002). *Odnosi z mediji* [*Media Relations*]. Ljubljana: GV Založba.

Intermezzo

Civil society and public relations

József Katus

1. Preliminary remarks

When dealing with questions of public relations strategies, politicians, chief executive officers and communication managers are usually preoccupied with the mass media. The impact of mass media on public opinion should, of course, not be underestimated. However, it would be a mistake not to take into account the role of the civil society in its formation. In view of this, we discuss here some dimensions and characteristics of civil society, with special attention to their implications for public relations.

2. Dimensions

Generally speaking, civil society is a social space different from the market or the government. As a phenomenon it is not new – but what is relatively new is its rapidly growing significance and the attention paid to it by politicians and researchers. This has been stimulated by at least five more or less interrelated factors, namely the *perestroika* of the welfare state, the collapse of the dictatorial communist system in Central and Eastern Europe, globalisation, the diffusion of modern information and communication technology (ICT) and the so-called growing gap between citizens and politicians.

As far as the alterations to the welfare state are concerned, it became increasingly clear that it could not realise its pretensions. Consequently, drastic cuts in public spending were considered necessary, whereas functions performed by the state (welfare, health care, culture, etc.) were more and more shifted to the citizens and their voluntary associations. Earlier, when the welfare state was being built, the government increasingly interfered in such fields, taking over tasks that traditionally had been performed by such organisations. Now, however, neo-liberal policy-makers pointed out that citizens' associations should provide such services because they could do it more cheaply and more effectively than the state. At the outset, these organisations were called "non-profit sector", "third sector", "social midfield", or simply as "non-government organisations" (NGOs). In time, "civil society" has found its way into the language, replacing most of these terms.

The collapse of the communist system in Europe greatly stimulated interest in civil society. Before the Communists seized power in 1948 in Central and Eastern Europe, civil society existed there too. However, the new rulers did their utmost to suppress it, eliminating voluntary associations or putting them under party control. Trade unions, women's associations, youth organisations, etc. thus lost their autonomy and became instruments of domination. Nowadays it is recognised that this kind of "social engineering" has badly damaged the societies in Central and Eastern Europe because it undermined their innovativeness as well as their potential to create social capital. It became also clear that a more or less healthy nation is characterised by the presence of, and balance between, three sectors – namely, the state, the market and the civil society. Consequently, the revival of the latter is considered as essential to the sustainable development of the young democracies in Europe's post-communist area.

Globalisation, in turn, is usually seen as a matter of economics, but this is a very limited view that neglects its social, cultural and political dimensions. The German sociologist Beck has a more general approach. He sees globalisation as "the *processes* through which sovereign national states are criss-crossed and undermined by trans-national actors with varying prospects of power, orientations, identities and networks" (Beck 2000; emphasis in the original). To such actors belong, for instance, multinationals, the United Nations, the European Union and the World Bank, but also such non-governmental organisations as Amnesty International and Greenpeace. Globalisation goes with the rise of voluntary associations even on supra-national levels, and with whom governments have to reckon (cf. Eckert 1996). At the same time it boosts the rise of new as well as the vivacity of existing NGOs, which consider globalisation a menace; from their perspective it destroys local cultures and economies, and brings poverty to the majority of mankind. This means clashing opinions, sometimes even violent conflicts between anti-globalisation activists gathering from several countries and what they consider the forces of globalisation. The Internet makes international mobilisation and action organisation relatively easy.

This brings us to the role of ICT. We mentioned earlier that the increasing significance of civil society is also due to its diffusion. This can be explained partly by the fact that the so-called new media have fostered the growth of civil society and the effectiveness of its cognitive praxis. The introduction of the fax, the personal computer and the Internet have facilitated the running of NGOs, enabling them to improve internal communication. In addition, ICT has greatly enhanced their mobilisation potential. It took some time for governments, multinationals and others to realise the implications of this development. Some memorable events certainly made them aware of the need to monitor cyberspace, such as the clash in 1995 between the multinational giant Royal Dutch/Shell and Greenpeace over the Brent Spar oil rig, anti-globalisation actions such as the 'Battle of Seattle', and or the successful international campaign to outlaw landmines (*The Economist* 1999).

The interest in civil society displayed by politicians – mentioned earlier – particularly in Western countries, is not inspired exclusively by neo-liberal policies, but also by the unease with what they call the growing gap between politics and citizens. This gap is expressed by decreasing party membership and declining participation in general and local elections. Seeing this, politicians complain that while citizens turn away from political parties, they tend to support so-called one-issue organisations committed to the protection of the right of minorities, to the fight against poverty, to the preservation of their own cultural heritage, to mention just a few. Those politicians are in fact signalling that politics change, while traditional political parties are losing ground in favour of civil organisations. A similar tendency is perceptible in post-communist countries. Due to the low level of political culture, manifesting itself in corruption and disgusting quarrels, especially young people turn away from political parties in favour of civil organisations (Katus 1999).

3. Characteristics

Turning to civil society once more, we may say that it consists of countless and diverse voluntary associations, including their institutions. Its multiplicity and plurality indicate that it is not dominated by a central power, the ideology of certain political party or an infallible leader (Gellner 1994). (It should be noted, by the way, that voluntary organisations are not necessarily associations of volunteers. A foundation or an association can have, for example, a board and membership consisting of volunteers, while it can have employees, among whom public relation officers. The adjective *voluntary* refers to the fact that such associations come into being because in view of common goals people join voluntarily.) Furthermore, voluntary associations are simultaneously bastions and schools of democracy. They are bastions of democracy because people who join voluntarily defend their collective autonomy against centralistic tendencies. They are schools of democracy because people joining voluntarily learn together how to define common problems, how to find solutions for these and how to work effectively in order to arrive at the envisaged aim. In other words, they learn to cooperate in the formulation and implementation of policies in accordance with democratic habits. Civil society consists not "only" of schools of democracy where people learn how to be autonomous citizens – when people gather voluntarily, they freely discuss politics but also vital questions of an individual or collective nature, exchanging information and evaluating what they see and hear. In this way they are continually shaping their own model of reality, influencing each others' ideas about what is "good" and what is "wrong". In fact, civil society is the arena where values and norms are precipitating, where social information and knowledge are created and diffused.

This cognitive practise (cf. Eyerman and Jamison 1991) encompasses processes of the creation and diffusion of social information and knowledge, as well as processes of problem definition, persuasion and action mobilisation. These often take the form of public debates involving individual citizens, NGOs, mass media, business corporations, political parties and governments. In fact, important issues are usually raised by civil organisations. Or, as Beck (1994) says, "the themes of the future, which are now on everyone's lips, have not originated from the farsightedness of the rulers or from the struggle in parliament – and certainly not from the cathedrals of power in business, science and the state". Raising issues of importance takes place on local, national or international levels. On a local level such issues could be traffic safety, repelling pollution caused by a specific actor, crime prevention, and so on. With issues in mind concerning whole collectives – or even the global community – it is not difficult to realise that our ideas concerning for instance environment protection, the emancipation of women, gay and ethnic minorities, human rights, euthanasia have changed, or are changing, because civil organisations are challenging us to reflect on these, offering at the same time information and knowledge, encouraging responsible solutions of the problems under discussion. It is no exaggeration to say that in a multicultural world, the importance of civil society's cognitive practise is growing – not least because modernisation and social diversity increasingly diminish the role of traditional sources of values and norms.

4. Public relations

The relationship between public relations and civil society is twofold. First, it is obvious that the organisation's own public relations should be tuned to the cognitive practice of civil society. This holds with regard to profit as well as to non-profit organisations. Civil society's cognitive practice includes an ongoing evaluation of the organisation's performance, whose outcomes co-determine its image. In this context, the organisation's credibility plays an important role, and must be confirmed again and again. Civil society's cognitive praxis is a complex process that reflects the formation of opinions, and includes diverse organisations varying from formally established consumer associations to vivid "one-issue" actions groups. The latter consist of citizens who acquire information and knowledge concerning the issue under discussion, and who prove to be able to communicate these effectively. Their effectiveness is sometime quite impressive. To mention just one example, in contrast with other countries, in the Netherlands, since the beginning of the 1970s, no more censuses have been taken although the law prescribed it. This remarkable fact is the achievement of a small "one-issue" action group that succeeded in convincing the people that censuses are dangerous to the privacy of the citizens (cf. Katus 1992).

The other aspect of the relationship between public relations and civil society is that effective public relations is essential to the successful functioning of civil organisations as well. NGOs in Europe's older democracies are, generally speaking, aware of the strategic significance of communication, and those who can afford it employ communication experts. In post-communist countries, the relatively young NGOs usually lack the competencies and financial means necessary for professional public relations. Experience shows, however, that they are increasingly aware of the importance of effective communication with regard to the fulfilment of their mission. Lack of means is compensated by creativity. In other words, they learn by doing how to communicate.

References

Beck, Ulrich (1994). The reinvention of politics: towards a theory of reflexive modernisation. In: Ulrich Beck, Anthony Giddens and Scott Lash (eds.), *Reflexive Modernisation. Politics, Tradition and Aesthetics In the Modern Social Order*, 1–55. Cambrigde: Polity Press.
Beck, Ulrich (2000). *What is Globalisation?* Cambridge: Polity Press.

Eckert, Roland (1996). Private Organisationen an der Hebeln der Macht? Die Entstehung einer globalen "civil society" [Private organizations at the levers of power? The emergence of a global "civil society"]. *Internationale Politik* 51–5: 53–60.

Eyerman, Ron and Andrew Jamison (1991). *Social Movements: A Cognitive Approach.* University Park, Penn.: Penn State University Press.

Gellner, Ernest (1994). *Conditions of Liberty. Civil Society and Its Rivals.* London: Hamish Hamilton.

Katus, József (1992). Why the Netherlands Stopped Taking A Census, paper presented to the 87th Annual Meeting of the American Sociological Association, 20–24 August, Pittsburgh, Pennsylvania, USA.

Katus, József (1999). Experiments in civic education: youth citizenship and NGOs in post-communist countries. In: Sibylle Hübner-Funk and Manuela du Bois-Reymond (eds.), *Intercultural Reconstruction: Trends and Challenges* (European Yearbook on Youth Policy and Research 2). Berlin and New York: Walter de Gruyter.

The Economist (1999). *The non-governmental order.* 11 December.

Chapter 24

Spain

Mª de los Ángeles Moreno Fernández[1]

1. National profile

1.1. Overview of national characteristics

Spain is situated in the south-west of Europe, occupying the larger part of the Iberian peninsula together with two archipelagos and two cities in the North of Africa. It has about 40.5 million inhabitants. Historically, the Spanish population has an Iberic background to which different ethnic groups were added. The main ethnic minority were gypsies since the fifteenth century. But Spain has become a receptor country of emigrants in the twentieth and twenty-first centuries. First, it received prosperous tourists and nowadays African and Latin American workers as well. No official religion is recognised and religious and ideological freedom is guaranteed by the Constitution of 1978, although most Spanish citizens declare themselves to be catholic (Enciclopedia Libre Universal en Español 2002).

After Franco's military dictatorship, a parliamentary democracy was established in Spain. The state is divided into seventeen autonomous regions and two cities with varying levels of autonomy. The main political parties are PP (conservative party), who are currently in power, and the PSOE (social-democrat party). In addition, some nationalist parties play an important role in Spanish political area.

The rate of growth of Spanish economy was 2 per cent in 2002, lower than expected due to the negative economic results in the last part of the year. Unemployment is high, and increased in 2002 there was a trade def-

---

1. The ethnographical research was carried out under the direction of the author. The members of the research team were Laura Juez Royuela, Sara Luna Orobón and José Ángel Mangas. Rocio Prieto Armenteros contributed to the sections on education in public relations. For our ethnographic research we used in-depth interviews with an indicative sample of the best enterprises in the MERCO ranking, which lists public and private best known companies. For agencies we used an indicative sample obtained from the ADECEC, ADC DIRCOM, Agenda de la Comunicación, agencies and rankings published in professional magazines.

icit. Public deficit goals have been achieved by an inflation of 4.7 per cent, but the economy did not really grow (Intermoney 2003).

Consumption is quite diverse among different media. The media which reach a greater part of population is the television (89.9 per cent). Although quite further from it, the radio obtains a 54.7 per cent of population and magazines a 51.4. However, journals reach only 37.4 per cent and the Internet, 22.5 per cent. Television, in spite of being the most consumed media, has not reached the digital age yet. Inadequate public policies have prevented the sustained development of new audio-visual technological media such as satellite, cable and or terrestrial digital television (Bustamante 2000, 2002; Moragas and Prado 2001; Giordano and Zeller 1999; Badillo and Moreno 2001a, 2001b; Moreno 2002).

In Spain, we still did not meet the conditions necessary for public relations, as J. L. Arceo (1988: 24–25, 1999: 58) states until democracy was settled. The task of public relations arrived in the 1960s when the economy began to emerge from the years of dictatorship. The franquist technocrat governments in the 1960s allowed the development of the economy by opening the borders, especially to North American enterprises. With democracy, the Spanish economy grew rapidly in the 1980s – it was almost a virgin market. This made enterprises and institutions consider the importance of communication, though until the end of the 1980s they just focused on advertising. Then, at the beginning of the 1990s, the advertising sector was just one of the sectors to suffer from the worldwide recession. In Spain advertising developed until 1992, partly due to the international events that took place (the Olympic games, the World Exhibition and the fifth centenary of the discovery of America). According to the main analysts (Benavides 1994; Rodríguez 1994), the causes of the advertising crisis were the end of the TV monopoly, the deadlock of advertising creatives in the cultural values of the 1980s, and the over-confident belief in advertising. This last factor made enterprises realise that they had lost control in the management of communication in favour of advertisers. Meanwhile, theories on global, corporate and integral – or integrated – communication arrived in Spain and became widespread in the 1990s. We have witnessed to the spreading of new concepts related to organisational communication as "Corporate" (Rodríguez 1994; Villafañe 1993), *Comunicación Corporativa* (Costa 1995; Alonso 1993; Benavides 2001; Capriotti 1994 and 1999), *Comunicación por objetivos* (Mazo 1994) *Comunicación Global* (Reinares and Calvo 1999) *Comunicación Integral* (Urzáiz 1996) or *Integrada* (Capriotti 1992). The theoretical initiative and the failure of advertising revitalised another communication systems (public relations, direct marketing and promotion), causing a second revolution in public relations in Spain in the last decade (Alternativas de marketing 1995). Moreover, since 1996 the recovering economy has created favourable circumstances for the sector. Anyway, as we will see in the results of our research, it is a limited expansion in qualitative terms, because it is related mainly to marketing communications and mass media relations.

1.2. Facts and figures about public relations in Spain

We have to take into account the professionals of public relations (people and organisms). Nowadays this professional field is not only named with the classic public relations concept, but also with new concepts related to corporate image and communication. As Antonio Noguero (1999: 472) has pointed out, this new terminology was already generalised in the 1980s and we agree with him (Noguero 1991–1992) and José Luis Arceo (1995) that the tasks of corporative communication and image have historically belonged to the area of public relations.

Extensive studies show that in a sample of 283 profit-companies and 178 public and private non-profit institutions active in different sectors, about 75 per cent of the enterprises and 79 per cent of institutions have a communication department (ADC Dircom 2000a: 69, 2000b: 55). On average, communication departments are about six years old; in institutions they are slightly older with eight years (ADC Dircom 2000a: 72, 2000b: 56), but in some top-ranking enterprises, these departments had been established twenty or forty-five years ago (36.4 per cent) – as top-ranking enterprises operate both nationally and internationally, their communication departments tend to be older. Most of the top-ranking enterprises are joint-stock companies, although some are public companies. There are no enterprises or institutions in Spain that invest more than € 120.000 in communication, which means that we are still in an emerging situation (ADC Dircom 2000a: 53). Noguero (1999) notes that in the 1980s, advertising departments tended to have larger budgets than public relations departments.

An average of five people, of whom 3.4 per cent are specialists, work in communication departments. The average age of specialists is 35.3 years in enterprises and 36 in institutions. Enterprises employ more men than women, while in institutions women outnumber men. Most departments have a manager with a degree in journalism (53 per cent in enterprises and 80.8 per cent in institutions). People with a degree in advertising and public relations are more common in enterprises than institutions, although they are outnumbered by people with a degree in economics (ADC Dircom 2000a: 79, 2000b: 60). Managers of communication departments have a degree and 9.8 per cent are postgraduates. Most of them have a degree in journalism (29.4 per cent in enterprises and 66.1 per cent in institutions), though advertising and public relations graduates have increased by 22.6 per cent in institutions (ADC Dircom 2000b: 32). In contrast, enterprises with an excellent reputation offer excellent prospects for public relations. The most common degree among employees of these companies is public relations (27.3 per cent), followed by graduates in journalism (18.2 per cent) and any branch of information sciences (18.2 per cent) in general, specialised technicians (18.2 per cent) and a low percentage (9 per cent) of lawyers and economists. Enterprises have no unified criteria for personal selection, prefer instead experience in advertising companies and mass media.

As for the public relations agencies researched, they have been working for an average of fourteen years, 53 per cent are joint-stock companies and 47 per cent limited liability companies; 73 per cent are independent, 27 per cent are dependent on international agencies; 56 per cent work nationally, 33 per cent internationally and only 11 per cent operate locally. Among specialists in these agencies, 43 per cent have a degree in information sciences, although 75 per cent of agencies declare to have graduates in journalism – this fact explains the relevance of the concept "communication" in denominations – 50 per cent also have graduates in public relations, 25 per cent in economy, 18.8 per cent in marketing, 12.5 per cent in sociology or history and 6.3 per cent in law. Most agencies value previous experience and 25 per cent of these agencies like to train workers themselves. Most agencies were formed in the 1970s and 1980s (Noguero 1999: 478).

2.   History and development of public relations

2.1. Roots of public relations

The main public relations history theorists state that public relations was introduced in Spain in the second half of the twentieth century, and arrived from the US with its enterprises, ideas and the nature of its organisations (J. L. Arceo 1999: 85). Moreover, public relations was imported based on the policies, principles and techniques defined by Bernays in 1923 (Barquero 2001: 223). But until the 1960s, public relations was virtually unknown in Spanish companies, rarely used by those that worked with North American agencies. The only agency with Spanish capital was *SAE de Relaciones Públicas* (Idoeta 1996: 25) but demand grew for public relations services (Noguero 1999: 478) in enterprises and institutions and in 1961 the first professional association was founded (ATRP), which represented Spanish professionals in the *Second International Congress of IPRA*. In 1965 the ARP and the *CENERP* were established. The *Centro Español de Relaciones Públicas* was created by the merger of *Agrupación de Técnicos en Relaciones Pública*s of Barcelona and *Centro Español de Relaciones Públicas* in Madrid. In 1971 it split into *CENERP* of Madrid and *CENERP* of Barcelona (Noguero 1994: 73; Barquero 2001: 245). The ARP, later renamed AERP (*Asociación Española de Relaciones Públicas*), recently integrated into the *Colegio de Profesionales de las Relaciones Públicas y Publicitarios de Cataluña*.

The first magazine dealing with public relations was edited by Fernando Lozano in 1962. The first books – practical and theoretical – were published in the 1960s, too (Barquero 2001: 252). But at that time Spanish enterprises used mainly advertising literature, confusing public relations with the hotel and restaurant business (Idoeta 1996: 25). This changed when, in 1970, the government regulated the field. From then on new enterprises and professionals offered public relations services, differentiating these from advertising. The interest of professionals of communication sciences was roused and in 1973 the *Agrupación Sindical de Técnicos in PR* (Noguero 1994: 77) was born.

The real expansion of the sector took place at the end of the 1970s with the new socio-economic situation of democracy (Idoeta 1996: 25). Multinationals needed to be publicised and media liberation created opportunities to do just that. In the course of the 1980s, the sector expanded in private and public enterprises, focusing on education and sponsorship programs. Advertisers continued having the most successful profession in communication.They criticised public relations efficiency and felt strongly about the separation of the two disciplines (Noguero 1999: 475).

In the 1980s, the Spanish public relations associations established relationships abroad, establishing a collaboration between the FIARP (*Federación Latinoamericana de Asociaciones de Relaciones Públicas*) and the *Consejo Superior de RP de España* (Noguero 1994: 84; 1999: 475).

Public relations education took off in the 1960s, although Richard Jenner had already started some activities in Madrid earlier (Noguero 1994: 69). The *Instituto de Técnicas para la Comunicación Social* in Barcelona organised the first course in 1964. The first Congress of students took place in the same city in 1966 and in 1967 public relations was incorporated in the university program of the *Escuela Oficial de Periodismo* (Barquero 2001: 252–253). In 1968, courses were organised in Escuela Superior de RP of Barcelona University (Noguero 1994: 69–71). In the 1970s, bigger specialisation and professionalisation were favoured, fostered by some theorists (Urzáiz 1971: 121). There were fourteen schools – the two main schools were the Universities of Madrid and Barcelona. In 1971 the first promotion of *Escuela Superior de Barcelona* went out. At the time, other universities and professional colleges were interested in the subject and the *I Congreso Internacional de la Enseñanza y Práctica de las RP* was held. Nevertheless, the main step forward was the inclusion in 1974 of the degree in advertising and public relations in the program of Information Sciences Universities (Noguero 1994: 78). In the 1980s, the degrees of *Universidad Complutense de Madrid* and *Escuela Superior de Barcelona* were consolidated and new Universities of Information Sciences were born, generating a growth in the profession. All these activities resulted in more prestige for the profession, and better career opportunities (J. L. Arceo 1998–1999: 19).

2.2. How language shapes the development of public relations

Yet, the definitive launch of public relations – sometimes called the "second PR revolution" (Alternativas de marketing 1995) – meant a problematic situation for the term. The tasks of press offices and event organisation were extended, while at the same time the introduction of public relations and other systems of communication into advertising agencies, after the crisis, transformed them into plain communications service agencies. At universities, the degree is called "advertising and public relations", but new subjects and different postgraduate studies claim the term "communication" (and other variants, such as, in Spanish, *Comunicación Empresarial, Comunicación Corporativa, Comunicación Integral o Integrada, Comunicación por Objetivos, Comunicación Institucional, Gestión de la Comunicación* and, more recently, *Gestión del Conocimiento*). These terms are also used in academic literature, professional magazines, professional departments and agencies. The main professional associations (DIRCOM and ADECEC) have deleted any reference to public relations from their acronyms. More than half of the enterprises call their managers in communication: "communication manager" (or Dircom), "external" or "institutional relations manager" (also used by press offices), followed by "head of public relations" and "head of corporative communication". Institutions tend to call them "communication service manager" and "press manager" (ADC Dircom 2000a: 32, 2000b: 28). As to departments, the best known enterprises in the survey call them "communication department" (45.5 per cent), "external relations management" (28.3 per cent) or "public relations and protocol department" (9 per cent). Most of them have changed their denomination in the last few years to avoid the suggestion that they dealt with just mass media relations. The agencies in the survey keep the term "public relations" in their name, but also the broader term "communication": 43.8 per cent are called "communication and public relations agencies" or "consulting", 37.5 per cent "communication consulting" and only 6.3, "public relations consulting".

Most best known enterprises (72 per cent) and agencies (75 per cent) have changed their name because they think the new one defines their activities better, but some agencies avoid the term "public relations" because of negative connotations (25 per cent) or because they consider it obsolete (6.5 per cent). As Sara Magallón (1998–1999: 124) pointed out, in every-day use the term "public relations" in Spain means "disappointing", because it is related to doubtful professional activities". Nevertheless, communication managers of enterprises do not adopt the term "communication" unanimously and they do not have a clear understanding of what public relations really is, neither are they clear about its position in relation to communication. Most of them consider it part of communication, 9 per cent consider it equal and 9 per cent identify it exclusively with mass media relations. Forty per cent of the agencies consider public relations as a set of communicational actions, 40 per cent consider it as related exclusively to mass media relations and 25 per cent see it as part of communication.

From our point of view, the change of terminology shows different facts often linked with lack of knowledge about public relations. First, it means a new understanding of *communication by objectives* (Mazo 1994) – that sometimes is ruled by a concept of communication entirely focused on marketing (A. Arceo 1995). Second, it shows the weakening of the public relations concept, caused by professional intrusion and confusion. And finally, it displays the strong predominance of journalists, advertisers and marketing people in this field. It could be said they prefer to avoid the classical public relation concept and use different concepts in order to feel they work in their natural environment.

3.   Typification of current public relations

3.1. Status of public relations in business, administration and society

The importance of communication – even in internal communication (Informpress 1998: 38) – has increased in enterprises in the last years, especially in New Economy enterprises (García 2000: 57). In a sample of 161 organisations, 65 per cent of enterprises and 64.6 per cent of institutions have a communication manager. In institutions, this post was introduced three years earlier, on average (ADC Dircom 2000a: 29–33, 2000b: 27–29). Of communication managers, 91 per cent think they are well considered. Most enterprises see communication as strategic (Villafañe 2001: 108, 2002: 154; Reyes 1999; ADC Dircom 2000a: 54, 2000b: 44) and are mainly interested in getting a good image, even small- and medium-sized companies (Reyes 2001). In enterprises, 72 per cent of communication managers think that communication is fundamentally important. Nevertheless, most of them cannot tell how important communication is in society – only 36.4 per cent think that it is becoming vital. Anyway, 18 per cent feel that there is a long way to go since communication is still unknown in society. Agencies are more pessimistic about this: 56,3 per cent think that there is a total ignorance of communication in society and those who think that communication profession is known think that it has a negative image (18.8 per cent), in contrast with the 12.5 per cent who think it has a positive image.

3.2. Major roles and typical tasks in public relations

In our ethnographical approach, most communication departments prefer the second and fourth models of public relations – as defined by Grunig and Hunt (1984), or Grunig (1992) – at the expense of the first and third models. The success of the second model is based on the preference of the capacity of relations with the media in the profile of communication managers, both in enterprises and institutions (ADC Dircom 2000a, 2000b; Reyes 1999).

Agencies also consider the fourth and second models, in this order, more appropriate. They reject the first model, but 55 per cent support the third. Most communication managers (81.2 per cent) in enterprises defend a symmetrical model; only 18.3 per cent think it unnecessary for organisations to improve the relations with the public. Nevertheless, only

54 per cent of the organisations seem willing to accept the equilibrium, in spite of the criteria of public relations professionals. Of the agencies, 75 per cent choose a symmetrical model; 18.8 per cent support other models, depending on the circumstances. They are clearer on evaluating the position of enterprises: they think that they can accept the equilibrium in a smaller percentage (43.8 per cent), as it depends on the enterprises and on the change proposed. Thus, the preferences of the professionals do not match those of their clients.; and they are unable to do the research necessary to put the two-way models into practice. A. Arceo (1996: 114–115) and M. T. García Nieto (1995) also emphasised the predominance of the second model, in agencies and in the sector of financial institutions, respectively.

As for European public relations roles, 54 per cent of communication departments profess playing all the roles: 27.7 per cent play all but the reflective one and 27.7 per cent play all but the educational role. Therefore, the managerial and the technical roles are mainly used in Spanish enterprises. The educational role is important for training top executives in mass media relations. However, in our opinion, on seeing tasks and investigating results, the reflective role is still very limited: 45.5 per cent admitted that they do not use technical investigation; only 27.3 per cent said they use some previous or evaluative investigation (a lot of companies requested preferred not to answer).

Agencies play all the roles: they all use technical and managerial roles. The educational role is played by 87.5 per cent, oriented specially to mass media relations. Finally, the least adopted is the reflective role, although agencies use it more often than enterprises (62.5 per cent). Most agencies say they do research, especially using qualitative techniques such as focus groups, in-depth interviews and press clippings (used by all of them and showing again the preponderance of mass media relations).

Eighty-five per cent of the tasks of agencies deal with external communication, 15 per cent with internal communication. Only 31.3 per cent of agencies offer internal communication services. But internal communication is much more important in enterprises: 45.5 per cent of them use it.

While in enterprises the communication departments are active mainly in the area of marketing communication, institutions and agencies are more oriented to public relations. In enterprises, after marketing communication, the main activities are corporate communication, mass media relations, internal communication and organising meetings. Institutions

Tasks contratadas outside

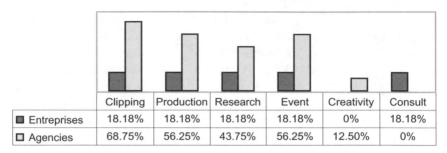

	Clipping	Production	Research	Event	Creativity	Consult
■ Entreprises	18.18%	18.18%	18.18%	18.18%	0%	18.18%
□ Agencies	68.75%	56.25%	43.75%	56.25%	12.50%	0%

Figure 1. Typical tasks of public relations practitioners in enterprises and agencies

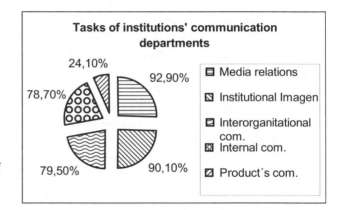

Figure 2. Typical tasks of public relations practitioners in institutions

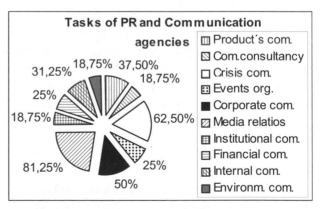

Figure 3.[1] Typical tasks of public relations practitioners in agencies

---

1. Percentages represent the number of enterprises from the sample which use each task; enterprises can use several tasks, therefore the percentages do not add up to 100. Data on institutions data are from ADC (2000b: 72–77).

are based mainly on mass-media relations and corporate communications, followed by inter-organisational communication and internal communication. For example, García Nieto (1996: 98) noted that in public
administration, the relationship with the press is the main activity of
public relations departments. The study of ADC Dircom (2000b) confirms that 80.8 per cent of public organisms declare that they have at
least a graduate in journalism. Agencies are also more oriented to public
relations communication, especially to mass-media relations. Even in the
1980s, the main activities were publishing, mass-media relations and
events (Noguero 1999). It is remarkable that only a few agencies provide
an integrated communication solution. Crisis communication is one of
the more demanded services, followed by corporative communication.
It seems that enterprises hire agencies for specific services for certain
publics, such as institutions and the financial sector. One of the services
whose demand is growing at present is environmental communication.

According to these data, and contrasting practice with the opinion of
the interviewed, the enterprises tend to use the managerial, technical and
educational roles; the institutions the managerial, technical and reflecting roles; and the agencies, the managerial and technical roles, applied
especially to specific situations, though in the consulting communication
sector and in specific programs – such as crisis management and corporative communication – they can offer the reflective role through the use of
knowledge and investigation.

Most enterprises occasionally contract external services (Reyes 1999;
ADC Dircom 2000a: 63), such as consulting, research, clipping, production and event organisation. Agencies use the same external services as
enterprises, apart from consulting communication. In conclusion, we can
say that external services are demanded either in the previous phases (research and consulting) or in the final ones (output and evaluation).

3.3. Position of public relations in organisations

Most enterprises have a communication manager (ADC 2000a: 83;
Reyes 1999) depending on the first or second managerial level. In most
enterprises the communication department is under the general manager
and they usually maintain relations on the same level as the marketing
manager (25.3 per cent) with the human resources manager (24.1 per
cent) and with the general manager (10.8 per cent). In institutions, the
communication department answers to the president, followed by the

general director or assistant director and the general secretary, and maintain relations on the same level as human resources, general secretary and press office chief (ADC 2000b: 62). In most enterprises (63.6 per cent) the communication area consists of a central organ with several offices according to geography or services. In best known enterprises, most communication managers (45.5 per cent) think they must be on the same level as marketing, 27.3 per cent think they must be subordinated to marketing and 27.3 per cent think marketing must be subordinated to communication. As we have seen earlier, according to the tasks performed, communication departments in many of the enterprises are active in marketing communication and public relations communication, whereas agencies are more focused on public relations.

The surveyed enterprises were unwilling to explain their work processes and decision-making models. Most of the time (45.5 per cent) the communication manager is responsible for hiring everything related to communications, although 25 per cent of enterprises declined to answer. Agencies are hired as follows: 50 per cent by the communication manager, 62.5 per cent by the managing director, and 56.5 per cent by the marketing manager. Most of the time (50 per cent) tasks are assigned inside the agency based on preferences of customers.

3.4. Current state of education and research traditions

Nowadays, degrees in public relations are awarded by universities (there are also schools which offer courses in public relations and communication). Twenty-four universities (fourteen public, ten private) offer advertising and public relations degree schemes. The Communication Sciences Faculties offer three degrees: journalism, audiovisual communication and advertising, and public relations. Even in this last one, public relations subjects are subordinated to advertising. The Ministry of Education imposes only two public relations specific subjects and, although most universities have added more optional subjects, there is still an imbalance in comparison with advertising subjects.

The curricula in public and private universities are almost the same. The difference is the duration of the course: this depends on the faculty, and there are more subjects related to public relations in five-year programs. There is also many postgraduate studies, offered by different institutions; these tend to be called "communication studies" rather than public relations.

3.5. Typification of best selling practical books

Public relations professors in Spanish universities use foreign and local handbooks. Foreign books follow mainly the theories of American authors such as Grunig and Hunt (1984); Grunig (1992); Dozier, Grunig and Grunig (1995); Cutlip, Center and Broom (2001); Broom and Dozier (1990); Pavlik (1999) and Wilcox, Autt, Agee and Cameron (2001). As to local books, especially those written by professors from Barcelona and Madrid are popular.

American and Spanish reference books are very different. While the first are based on organisational and mass communication theories and present an exhaustive methodology for the profession, Spanish books focus mainly on conceptual delimitations, epistemology (recently incorporated in academe), history, ethics and new theories of integrated communication and work processes. Moreover, in Spanish books, theory and practice are separated; the main practice books have techniques or case studies published by associations or in collaboration with associations and academics (see ADECEC 1997; Idoeta 1996; A. Arceo 2000). The main journals with wide public relations coverage are *Revista Universitaria de Publicidad y Relaciones Públicas*, published by Universidad Complutense de Madrid and *Questions Publicitarias*, published by the University of Sevilla. The DIRCOM yearbooks and the publications of the *Observatorio del Corporate* and Inforpress are also commonly used.

3.6. Local scene of public relations in Spain

Associationism in public relations emerged, as we have seen, at the same time as the profession, with the traditional rivalry between Madrid and Barcelona. The most important event is the creation of the first professional college in the country, the *Colegio de Profesionales de las Relaciones Públicas y Publicitarios de Cataluña*. The delegation of the *Confederación Europea de Relaciones Públicas* is also based in Barcelona. In Madrid the *Consejo Superior de Comunición y Relaciones Públicas de España*, the *Asociación de Doctores y Licenciados en Publicidad y Relaciones Públicas*, the delegation of the *Confederación Iberoamericana de Relaciones Públicas*, the CERP, the International Public Relations Association and the International Association of Business Communication work at national level. Today, two professional associations have become important: ADC DIRCOM (*Asociación de directores de comunicación*, founded in 1992) and ADECEC (*Asociación de Empresas Consultoras en Relaciones Públicas y Comunicación*); the latter was founded in 1991 and currently represents twenty-nine of the main agencies. Universities have tried closer collaboration several times, but there is still a lot to organise before any other more successful collaboration materialises.

The profession is only officially regulated at Cataluña; as a result, many unqualified people are now active, preventing professionals from getting a better social reputation.

4. Conclusions: state of the art and future of public relations in Spain

Based on interviews with communication managers, agencies managers and theorists, we see three main changes in the last years: (a) enterprises are more conscious of the importance of communication, (b) agencies and departments are more specialised, and (c) the term "public relations" is widely abandoned.

In the late 1990s, the increase of awareness encouraged a revaluation of public relations (Moreno 2000: 50–51), which was of great importance to corporate communications, then only just rebranded (Reyes 1999; López 2001: 89). Enterprises and institutions began to understand the importance of corporate communications (Villafañe 1999; López, 2002: 91). At the level of corporate communications, two related issues can be discerned: reputation and the management of social responsibility. Reputation, as the synthesis of a company's global behaviour (Fombrum 2002; Villafañe 2000), has produced a new kind of appraisal of companies, namely, the *Monitor Español de Reputación Corporativa*, directed by Justo Villafañe. This indicator measures the reputation of companies and has opened a new venue for discussing methods of research as the valuation of intangibles (Moreno 2002: 98–110). As to social responsibility, this has increased in the form of sponsorship in the early 1990s (Piñuel 1994: 30) and will be rising, not only for image improvement or for gains (García 2001: 304–317), but also to get social cohesion among shared values (Montraveta, Sánchez and Valls 2000; Pimentel 2001: 289–303: López 2002: 95–97).

Specialisation can be seen in audience segmentation, channel diversification and the global dimension of communication; in the success and projection of crisis communication and ecological communications (ADC Dircom 2000a; Inforpress 1998; Inforpress-APIE 2000; Cornadó 2000) and the programs with certain special publics, such as internal, institutional and financial sectors. Another dimension of specialisation is caused by the incorporation of the knowledge-based economy and new technologies. Most enterprises or agencies have adapted to the possibilities of the internet and intranets (Lareau 2000). Knowledge management is raising (Villafañe 2001), but is not still a global project for companies as specified programs mainly directed to internal human resources (López 2002: 87)

Public relations are progressively renamed "communication" as a strategic function which surpass mass media relations (Cruz 2001: 51) and integrates communication tasks along the concepts of corporate (Benavides, García and Rodríguez 1999; Reyes 1999; Villafañe 2001). However, this positive development is at the same time a source of controversy, summarized in the following three points.

1. The dispersion of communication functions (Reyes 1999; ADC Dircom 2000a, 2000b), and the confusion about the objectives of public relations cause tensions among marketing, advertising and communication departments.
2. The predominance of mass media relations and marketing communications. The most valued publics for enterprises are customers and the press (ADC Dircom 2000a).
   Therefore, most communication managers are journalists and this can be one of the reasons for (a) the replacement of the public relations concept and (b) the stagnation in the public-information model which pays too much attention to mass media in spite of other channels and publics.
3. Professional intrusion and lack of public relations education. Intrusion (J. L. Arceo 1988: 21; 1998–1999: 18–25; 1999: 31) or the "encroachment process" (Noguero 2000: 59) is an obstacle for integral development of public relations. Interdisciplinarity may be positive (Magaña 1995: 162), provided the professionals of other fields do not avoid theoretical-practical work and the experience in investigation developed by public relations.

Advertising and public relations degrees today offer better education for practitioners and researchers than a degree in journalism. Anyway, according to market demand, it would be better to teach more specific subjects on public relations, mainly on social and organisational research (Aguadero 1993: 193) and on knowledge management.

In summary, agencies encouraged by enterprises and institutional demands are today the pioneers in new trends in communication. Nevertheless, it is necessary to improve evaluative research in order to develop the sought after two-way models and the four roles of public relations.

References

ADC DIRCOM (2000a). *El estado de la comunicación en España I Empresas* [The State of Communication in Spain. Vol. I: Enterprises]. Madrid: ADC Dircom.

ADC DIRCOM (2000b). *El estado de la comunicación en España II. Organismos públicos e instituciones* [The State of Communication in Spain. Vol. II Public Organisms and Institutions]. Madrid: ADC Dircom.

Aguadero Fernández, Francisco (1993). *Comunicación social integrada: un reto para la organización* [Integrated Social Communication: A Challenge for the Organisation]. Madrid: El Ateneo.

Alonso, Rodrigo L. (1993). *Imagen de marca* [Brand image]. Madrid: Acento Gráfico.

Alternativas de marketing (1995). Segunda Revolución de las Relaciones Públicas [Second Revolution of Public Relations], Vol. 3: 1.

Arceo Vacas, Alfredo (1995). Las relaciones públicas y el marketing: crítica a los planteamientos de Kotler [Public Relations and Marketing: a critique of Kotler's approach]. *Questions Publicitarias* 4: 121–133.

Arceo Vacas, Alfredo (1996). El cambio en las relaciones públicas [The change in public relations]. *Revista Universitaria de Publicidad y Relaciones Públicas* 3: 105–118.

Arceo Vacas, Alfredo (2000). *Aplicación de las Relaciones Públicas* [Application of Public Relations]. Madrid: ICIE.

Arceo Vacas, José Luis (1988). *Fundamentos para la teoría y técnica de las relaciones públicas* [Foundations for the Theory and Practice of Public Relations]. Barcelona: Promociones y Publicaciones Universitarias.

Arceo Vacas, José Luis (1995). Las relaciones públicas en la comunicación empresarial e institucional: una introducción [Public relations in management and institutional communication: an introduction]. *Questions Publicitarias* 4: 27–38.

Arceo Vacas, José Luis (1998–1999). Formación y práctica profesional de las publicidad y las relaciones públicas en España [Formation and professional practice of advertising and public relations in Spain]. *Revista Universitaria de Publicidad y Relaciones Públicas* 5–6: 17–32.

Arceo Vacas, José Luis (1999). *Tratado de publicidad y relaciones públicas* [Treatise of advertising and public relations]. Madrid: ICIE.

Badillo, Ángel y Moreno, Ángeles (2001a). La liberalización del audiovisual local: apunte sobre el caso de Castilla y León [The liberalization of the audiovisual local: a note on the case of Castilla and León]. In: Congreso Ibérico de Comunicación, [Iberic Congress of Communication] Málaga: Universidad de Málaga, May 2001 (unpublished proceedings).

Badillo, Ángel y Moreno, Ángeles (2001b). La política de comunicación del Partido Popular: el (extraño) caso de la televisión local [The communication policy of the Popular Party: the strange case of the local television in the *V Congress of Politic Communication and Administration*]. In *V Congreso de Comunicación Política y Administración* [V Congress of Politic Communication and Administration], La Laguna: Universidad de la Laguna/AECPA, Sept. 2001.

Barquero Cabrero, José Daniel (2001). *Comunicación y Relaciones Públicas. De los orígenes históricos al nuevo enfoque de planificación estratégica* [Communication and Public Relations.From the historic origins to the new approach of the strategic planification]. Madrid: McGraw Hill.

Benavides Delgado, Juan (ed.) (1994). *La crisis de la publicidad* [The crisis of advertising]. Madrid: Edipo.

Benavides Delgado, Juan (2001). *Dirección de comunicación empresarial e institucional* [Direction of management and institutional communication]. Barcelona: Gestió.

Benavides Delgado, Juan, Juvenal García and Aurora Rodríguez (1999). La publicidad y el corporate en 1998 [Advertising and corporate in 1998]. In: Justo Villafañe (dir.), *El estado de la publicidad y el corporate en España* [The state of advertising and corporate in Spain], pp. 19–150. Departamento de Comunicación Audiovisual y Publicidad 1, Universidad Complutense de Madrid.

Broom, Glen M. and David M. Dozier (1990). *Using Research in Public Relations, Applications to Program Management*. Englewood Cliffs, NJ: Prentice Hall.

Bustamante, Enrique (2000). Spain's interventionist and authoritarian communication policy: *Telefónica* as political battering ram of the Spanish right. *Media, Culture and Society* 22: 433–445.

Bustamante, Enrique (coord.) 2002 *Comunicación y cultura en la era digital. Industrias, mercados y diversidad en España* [Communication and culture in the digital era. Industries, markets and diversity in Spain]. Barcelona: Gedisa.

Capriotti, Paul (1992). *La imagen de empresa* [The enterprise image]. Barcelona: El Ateneo.

Capriotti, Paul (1994). *Consideraciones sobre la estructura y formación de la imagen corporativa* [Considerations on the structure and formation of the corporative image]. Barcelona: Servicio de Publicaciones Universidad Autónoma de Barcelona.

Capriotti, Paul (1999). *Planificación estratégica de la imagen corporativa* [Strategic planification of the corporative image]. Barcelona: Ariel.

Cornadó, Antonio (2000). La comunicación ante las situaciones de conflicto [Communication in conflict situations]. In ADC Dircom: *Anuario de comunicación 2000*, 136–137. Madrid: ADC Dircom.

Costa, Joan (1995). *Comunicación Corporativa y revolución de los servicios* [Corporative Communication and services revolution] Madrid: Ediciones Ciencias Sociales.

Cruz, Juan (2001). Tendencias en las consultorías de comunicación [Tendencies in the communication consultancies]. *Mk Marketing + Ventas* 155

Cutlip, Scott M., Allen H. Center and Glen M. Broom (2001). *Relaciones públicas eficaces* Barcelona, Gestión. [Transl. of Effective Public Relations (8th edn.), New Jersey: Prentice Hall, 1999].

Dozier, David M, Larissa Grunig and James E. Grunig (1995). *Manager's Guide to Excellence in Public Relations and Communication Management,* Mahwah, NJ: Lawrence Erlbaum Associates.

Enciclopedia Libre Universal en Español (2002). www.enciclopedial.us.es.

Fombrum, Charles (2002). Reputación corporative: su medición y gestión [Corporate reputation: measurement and management]. In ADC Dircom. *Anuario de la Comunicación 2002*, 156–158. Madrid: ADC Dircom.

García, A. (2000). Comunicación y Burbuja financiera [Communication and Financial Bubble]. *Mk Marketing + Ventas* 153:

García Nieto and María Teresa (1995). Los departamentos de comunicación en el sector financiero en España [The communication departments in the financial sector in Spain]. *Questions Publicitarias* 4: 74–88.

García Nieto and María Teresa (1996). Las relaciones públicas en el sector público [Public relations in the public sector]. *Revista Universitaria de Publicidad y Relaciones Públicas* 3: 91–103.

García Perdiguero, Tomás (2001). La evaluación de la responsabilidad social de las empresas [Assessment of the social responsibility of enterprises]. In: Justo Villafañe (dir.), 304–317.

Grunig, James E. (ed.) (1992). *Excellence in Public Relations*. Hillsdale: Lawrence Erlbaum Associates.

Grunig, James E. and Todd Hunt (1984). *Managing Public Relations*. Fort Worth: Harcourt Brace & Jovanovich.

Idoeta, Nerea (ed.) (1996). *El libro práctico de las relaciones públicas: el porqué y cómo de una profesión apasionante* [The practical book of public relations: the how and why of a fascinating profession]. Barcelona: ADECEC.

Inforpress (1998). *IV Informe sobre la Comunicación Empresarial* [IV Report on Management Communication]. Madrid: Inforpress.

Inforpress-APIE (2000). *Las empresas españolas frente a la comunicación on-line* [Spanish enterprises and on-line communication]. Madrid: Inforpress.

Intermoney 2003 PIB en España 4° Trimestre de 2003 [NGP in Spain fourth quarter of 2003]. www.caixatarragona.es.

Lareau, Carlos (2000). El año virtual [The virtual year]. *Anuncios* 80: 56.

López Triana, Isabel (2001). *Observatorio permanente del corporate* [Permanent Observatory of the corporate]. In: Justo Villafañe (dir.), 85–95.

López Triana, Isabel (2002). Observatorio permanente del corporate [Permanent Observatory of the corporate]. In: Justo Villafañe (dir), *El estado de la publicidad y el corporate en España y Latinoamérica* [The Situation of Advertising and Corporate in Spain and Latin America], 85–97. Madrid: Pirámide.

Magallón, Sara (1998–1999). Las relaciones públicas en el ámbito de las ciencias sociales y su papel en las organizaciones [Public relations in the field of social sciences and their role in organisations]. *Revista Universitaria de Publicidad y Relaciones Públicas* 5–6: 139–146.

Magaña, Manuel (1995). Reflexiones en torno a la consolidación de la práctica profesional de la comunicación en España [Considerations about the consolidation of the professional practice of communication in Spain]. *Revista Universitaria de Publicidad y Relaciones Públicas* 2: 161–170.

Mazo del Castillo, Juan Manuel (1994). *Estructura de la comunicación por objetivos* [*Structure of communication by objectives*]. Barcelona: Ariel.

Montraveta, Isabel, Eva Sánchez and Ricard Valss (2000). La responsabilidad social de la empresa [The social responsability of enterprises]. In Projecció Mecenatge Social: *La responsabilidad social de las empresas, Directorio 2000 del Patrocinio y Mecenazgo*. Barcelona: Projecció Mecenatge Social.

Moragas, Miquel de and Emilio Prado (2000). *La televisió pública a l'era digital* [Public television in the digital era]. Barcelona: Portic. Centre d'Investigació de la Comunicació.

Moreno Amador, Eduardo (2002). Panel Delphi: el futuro del corporate en España [Delphi panel: the future of corporate in Spain]. In: Justo Villafañe (dir), *El estado de la publicidad y el corporate en España y Latinoamérica* [The Situation of Advertising and Corporate in Spain and Latin America], 98–110. Madrid: Pirámide.

Moreno, Juanjo. (2000). Nada que envidiar [Nothing to envy]. *Anuncios* 80: 50–51.

Moreno Fernández, María de los Ángeles (2002). *La autopublicidad de televisión española: un sistema de comunicación corporativa, comercial y política. Aproximación económico-política y cultural* [*Self-advertising of Spanish television: a system of corporate, commercial and political communication. An economic-political and cultural approach*]. Doctoral dissertation, University of Salamanca.

Noguero i Grau, Antoni (1991–1992). La comunicación corporativa, un nuevo concepto para usos contemporáneos: introducción al desarrollo conceptual del logotipo y el símbolo [Corporate communication: a new concept for contemporary uses: introduction to the conceptual development of the logo and the symbol]. Revista *Universitaria de Publicidad y Relaciones Públicas* 2: 101–108.

Noguero i Grau, Antoni (1994). La historia de las relaciones públicas en España: 1954–1990 [The history of the Public Relations in Spain 1954–1990]. *Revista Universitaria de Publicidad y Relaciones Públicas,* 1: 67–90.

Noguero i Grau, Antoni (1999). Características principales de la actividad tipificada como industria de las relaciones públicas en España: sujetos promotores y sujetos ejecutores [Main characteristics of the activity defined as industry of the public relations in Spain: developing and executing subjects]. In: J. L. Arceo Vacas (ed.), *Tratado de publicidad y relaciones públicas*, 467–508. Madrid: ICIE.

Noguero i Grau, Antoni (2000). Cross-cultural relations: relaciones públicas interculturales: entendimiento a través del análisis de las diferencias y similitudes culturales [Cross-cultural relations: understanding through the analysis of the cultural differences and similarities]. *Revista Universitaria de Publicidad y Relaciones Públicas* 7: 57–65.

Pavlik, John V. (1999). *La investigación en Relaciones Públicas* [Research in Public Relations]. Barcelona: Gestión 2000.

Pimentel, Aurora (2001). Marketing social corporativo, un enfoque estratégico [Corporative social marketing, a strategic approach]. In Justo Villafañe (dir.), *El estado de la publicidad y el corporate en España y Latinoamérica* [The Situation of Advertising and Corporate in Spain and Latin America], 289–303. Madrid: Pirámide.

Piñuel, José Luis (1994). El volumen de la comunicación en España [The volume of communication in Spain]. *Questiones Publicitarias* 4: 18–37.

Reinares Lara, Pedro and Calvo Fernández, Sergio (1999). *Gestión de la comunicación comercial* [The Management of Commercial Communication]. Madrid: McGraw Hill.

Reyes, Maribel (1999). El corporate en 1998 [The corporation in 1998]. In: Justo Villafañe (dir.), pp. 151–185

Reyes, Maribel (2001). La gestión de la comunicación en las pymes españolas [The management of communication in Spanish small and medium sized companies]. In: Justo Villafañe (dir.), *El estado de la publicidad y el corporate en España y Latinoamérica* [The Situation of Advertising and Corporate in Spain and Latin America], 121–134. Madrid: Pirámide.

Rodríguez Centeno, Juan Carlos (1994). Panorama general de la crisis publicitaria [General view of the advertising crisis]. *Cuestiones Publicitarias* 3: 105–113.

Urzáiz, Jaime de (1971). *Teoría y técnicas de las Relaciones Públicas* [*Theory and Techniques of Public Relations*]. Madrid: San Martín.

Urzáiz, Jaime de (1996). *De las relaciones públicas a la comunicación social integral: nueva estrategia para las empresas e instituciones* [From Public Relations To Integral And Social Communication: A New Strategy For Enterprises And Institutions]. Madrid: San Martín.

Villafañe, Justo (1993). *Imagen positiva: gestión estratégica de la imagen de las empresas* [Positive Image: Strategic Management of the Image in Enterprises]. Madrid: Pirámide.

Villafañe, Justo (ed.) (1999). *El estado de la publicidad y el corporate en España* [The state of advertising and corporate in Spain]. Departamento de Comunicación Audiovisual y Publicidad 1, Universidad Complutense de Madrid.

Villafañe, Justo (2000). La gestión de la reputación corporativa [The management of corporative reputations] en ADC Dircom: *Anuario de comunicación 2000*, 133–134. Madrid: ADC Dircom.

Villafañe, Justo (dir.) (2001). *El estado de la publicidad y el corporate en España y Latinoamérica* [The Situation of Advertising and Corporate in Spain and Latin America]. Madrid: Pirámide.

Villafañe, Justo (dir.) (2002). *El estado de la publicidad y el corporate en España y Latinoamérica* [The Situation of Advertising and Corporate in Spain and Latin America]. Madrid: Pirámide.

Villafañe, Justo, Norberto Mínguez Arraz and Maribel Reyes (2001). La gestión de la comunicación en España: grandes corporaciones, instituciones, pymes [The management of communication in Spain: big corporations, institutions, small and medium sized enterprises]. In Justo Villafañe (dir.), *El estado de la publicidad y el corporate en España y Latinoamérica* [The Situation of Advertising and Corporate in Spain and Latin America], 96–134. Madrid: Pirámide.

Wilcox, Dennis L., Philips Autt, Warren Agee and Glen Cameron (2001). *Relaciones Públicas. Estrategias y Tácticas* [Public Relations. Strategies and Tactics]. Madrid: Addison Wesley.

Chapter 25

Sweden

Bertil Flodin

1. National profile

1.1. Overview of national characteristics

Sweden is a large country – in Europe only Russia, the Ukraine, France and Spain are bigger. This wide-flung country has a small population of about 9 million. Some 85 per cent of its inhabitants live in the southern half of Sweden, in three major urban centres in particular: the capital city of Stockholm (1.7 million, including suburbs), Göteborg on the west coast (800,000) and Malmö in the south (500,000). For a long time, Sweden was ethnically homogenous; today some 20 per cent of the population is of foreign extraction[1].

Sweden is a parliamentary democracy. The monarchy is purely constitutional. In all essentials, the duties of the monarch as head of state are of a representative, ceremonial nature. In the mid nineteenth century, Sweden was one of the poorest countries in Europe with 70 per cent of the population working on the land. Little more than a century later, it was one of the richest and most industrialised countries in the world, and today only 2 per cent work in the agricultural sector. For many years, Sweden's highly developed welfare system gave the country a prominent position in the international debate. The country's economic crisis in the early 1990s, however, led to government cuts, but on the whole the welfare state has survived intact.

In 1991, Sweden applied to join the European Union and an agreement on membership was reached in 1994. The first law on freedom of the press was passed as long ago as 1776. The current law is intended to make it easier for the media to perform their time-honoured task of scrutinising officialdom. All official documents are available to the general public – with just a few, clearly specified, exceptions. Censorship is

---

1. The information about Sweden in this section is taken from the Swedish Institute 2002.

prohibited and anyone communicating information to the media enjoys immunity. Swedes are among the most avid newspaper readers in the world.

1.2. Facts and figures about public relations in Sweden

There has been an exceptional increase among Swedish public relations practitioners in the 1990s. In October 2002, there were more than 4,200 members in the Swedish Public Relations Association (SPRA), which makes it the second largest in Europe. The total number of public relations practitioners is actually higher, but there are no reliable figures. Anyone could call them selves a public relations practitioner and start a consulting firm, since neither certification nor any particular training is required. The figures and information stated below thus only apply to members of the SPRA.

Women increasingly dominate the public relations industry. A survey carried out by the SPRA in 2001 showed that almost 75 per cent of its members, and two out of four heads of public relations, were women (SPRA 2001). Slightly more than 40 per cent of SPRA members are employed by companies in the private sector, 25 per cent work in the public sector, another 25 per cent work for consulting firms and almost 10 per cent work in organisations. The majority of the public relations officers (70 per cent) work in Stockholm and its surroundings. The largest group of the members (29 per cent) are senior executives, about 20 per cent are consultants and almost 30 per cent are technicians. Hierarchically, the majority are positioned directly under the CEO or a senior vice-president. Only 7 per cent work for the marketing manager and 3 per cent for the manager of human resources. About half of them (53 per cent) are permanent members of the dominant coalition.

All members of the association – whether consultants or employees in the private or public sector – believe that business will increase even more in the next few years. In addition, 80 per cent believe that there has been a greater demand for their services in the last two years. The members estimated that their combined public relations budget was between 5.5 and 6 billion Swedish crowns (€ 0.6–0.65 billion).

According to the public relations practitioners, the most important issues in the next five years are strategic planning, a distinctive image, environmental monitoring, internal information, electronic production, business development and media relations (SPRA 2001).

2.   History and developments of public relations

2.1. Development of public relations practice

Unfortunately, there is no detailed research about how public relations has developed in Sweden. In the period after the Second World War there were signs, though, that showed that some professionals in Sweden considered themselves practitioners of an activity that could be defined as public relations. In 1945, the first publication about public relations was edited. The author of *Om Samhällskontakt* (About Community Contacts) introduced the business as follows: "Public relations include all those measures that a firm could possibly take in order to be considered a model firm by the public" (Arbman 1945). Not long afterwards, in 1950, the SPRA was founded. The initial name of the association *Sveriges Pressombudsmän* ('Sweden's press agents'), shows that the business at this time mainly was dedicated towards media relations.

Right from the start there were public relations officers in the private sector as well as in the public sector. The development in the private sector was slow until the beginning of the 1980s, when it suddenly accelerated. Growth in the public sector, on the other hand, was already striking at the end of the 1960s. The reason for this was a substantial reform in municipal structure, which decreased the number of municipalities by 90 per cent, which led to a drastic cut-down in the number of local politicians. Parliament was concerned about this situation and decided to stimulate an increase in municipal public relations.

Whereas the 1980s could be described as a period of stable growth for the industry of public relations, the 1990s were characterised by an explosive growth. The number of members of the SPRA is one indicator: in 1980 there were 676 members, in 1990 this number had gone up to 1,377 members and today (late 2002) there are more than 4,200 members. Another indicator is the number of consultancies that are members of the Association of Public Relations Consultancies in Sweden (PRECIS): four of the consultancies started before 1985, eight of them between 1986 and 1990 and 17 consultancies started in the 1990s.

A number of facts contributed to this development. First, Sweden integrated more and more in the global economy and Sweden's membership of the EU in 1994 manifested its close connection to Europe. Second, there was a dramatic change in the Swedish media landscape in the 1990s. Earlier, the Swedish people were reduced to non-commercial governmental radio and television broadcasting only, but in the 1990s the

Swedes got access to radio stations and TV-channels from all over the world via cable and satellite.

The introduction of new information technology has been exceptionally prompt in Sweden. Simplifying somewhat, the 1990s could be described as the decade when the Internet and the mobile phone became everybody's property. In 2000, 76 per cent of the Swedish population had a computer at home and 80 per cent had access to the Internet (Statistiska Centralbyrån 2001). The highly increased flow of information led to an increased competition for attention among companies, authorities and organisations. This transformed the working conditions and routines of journalists as well as for public relations officers.

Finally, the 1990s implied a new public demand for transparency, openness and participation. This was indicated, for example, by a dramatic increase in memberships in various NGOs and by the fact that confrontations between activists and authorities and companies became a relatively common phenomenon (Granström 2002).

2.2. Development of education and research traditions

The first academic courses in "information technique" started in the early 1970s. The courses lasted one term and were strictly professionally oriented. Courses in mass media and mass communication were developed at the same time. In the 1970s and 1980s, the number of courses increased and at the same time, the subject was considerably diversified and turned into what is today called "Media and Communication Science". This academic discipline has extensive research directed by about sixteen professors.

Education in public relations developed in the discipline of Media and Communication Science. British and American textbooks got in use in the 1980s and it became possible at some universities to write an essay about public relations and obtain a master's degree. The subject was not called "public relations", though, but, among other terms, "planned communication", "organisational communication", "internal communication", and "social communication".

Extensive education and research is taking place today in the field of Media and Communication Science at sixteen different universities and university colleges. Most of it takes place in the faculties of social science and the faculties of humanities. Content wise, the focus is more on the media and less on interpersonal communication (Högskoleverket 2001).

But unfortunately, education in Media and Communication Science has not been able to create a satisfactory training program in public relations. An extensive governmental evaluation of education at all universities and university colleges sums up the conditions in this way: "It is a serious problem that there is no adequate education in strategic information, that is, how information and communication lead the organisation towards its goal" (Högskoleverket 2001).

Research on public relations is very modest in Sweden. The first dissertation was published in 1976, the next one not until 1983. In the 1990s there were only two, and even today (2003) it is unusual to find a doctoral thesis focused on public relations. But there are signs of a change for the better in the next few years. There is considerable interest in public relations among students and in 2003 there are about twenty postgraduates who would like to write their dissertation on the subject (Larsson 2002). There is also a growing demand for professionals with an education in public relations. But there are some obstacles to overcome: the lack of professors specialised in public relations, and the lack of funds for research activities and education for doctoral candidates. A considerably more active participation in international research is also necessary (DIK-förbundet 2002).

2.3. How language shapes the development of public relations

So far, it has not been possible to establish a serious image of public relations. The public often uses the abbreviation "PR", which for many people has negative connotations. This notion of public relations is also found in the daily press, which is somewhat of a paradox since journalists have been using information from public relations practitioners for decades in their daily professional life. At the universities and university colleges the concept of public relations is rarely used. A number of other terms are used instead, such as "organisational communication", "planned communication", "strategic communication" and "integrated communication". It is hardly possible to achieve a research grant on public relations in Sweden today.

The members of SPRA all work in the field of public relations, though many of them do not use the term "public relations professional" to describe themselves. For instance, the first one hundred members in the SPRA roll use as many as twenty-six different titles to name their professions. Only public relations consultants actively use the notion "public relations" (www.precis.se).

3.   Typification of current public relations

3.1. Status of public relations in business, administration and society

Public relations departments are well established in the Swedish private and public sectors. The departments mainly exist in medium-sized and larger companies and also in central and regional public authorities. It is also common to find a well-developed public relations department in NGOs that act on a national basis.

There is a strong belief in the future among public relations practitioners. More than 80 per cent believe that the business will increase and half of them estimate that their own departments will expand within the next few years (SPRA 2001). Practitioners also believe that their services are highly requested. About 80 per cent in the private and the public sector – including consultants – believe that their services have become "more" or "considerably more" sought after in the last two years (SPRA 2001). Their opinion was corroborated by an extensive survey among 800 Swedish top managers. The managers were asked to estimate the value of the public relations officers in the following tasks in the organisation (source: SPRA 2000a):

	Agreed fully/partly:
Consolidate and strengthen the brand	83%
Give constructive criticism and advice in strategic matters	55%
Increase the communicative competence and create added value	53%
Participate in the development of the organisation	57%
Participate in change processes	61%
Support the managers in their communication	89%
Use public relations as a competitive device	66%
Develop public relations strategies	88%
Capacity for crisis management	77%

The general view of how companies, organisations and authorities should conduct their public relations activities is apparent in their communication policies. There is almost complete agreement on which keywords are most important: openness, accessibility, swiftness, honesty, transparency and credibility. This common view could be seen as a strong indicator of the maturity of the industry. So far, however, there are hardly any studies that can confirm that these aims are actually put into practise.

3.2. Major roles of public relations and typical tasks

The Swedish public relations industry of today is highly differentiated and complex. It ranges all the way from the assistant who disseminates information up to a member of the senior management of a large, multinational company. There is also a strong specialisation in the various subject fields, for example, investor relations, crisis communication and media relations.

The members of the SPRA could roughly be divided into three categories; management 29 per cent, technicians 40 per cent and consultants 21 per cent (SPRA 2001).

Over the last decade, the gap between public relation officers and top management has decreased. Today, about two thirds of them are either part of the management group or have direct access to it. It is significant that only a few public relations practitioners are positioned directly below the marketing manager or the head of human resources.

From the description above, it is thus clear that both the management role and the operational role are common for Swedish public relations officers. The result corresponds very well with the Delphi study initiated by the European Public Relations Research and Education Association (Ruler, Verčič, Flodin and Bütschi (2001). The researchers found that besides these two roles, there are also reflective role and educational roles. The reflective role is defined as "to talk about the organisation in society, in order to become responsible. This function has to do with organisational values and norms, and can be seen as a developing function of public relations, as part of the discussion on socially responsible behaviour of organisations". This sounds interesting, but has never been investigated in the Swedish context. An indirect indicator that it is in practice, however, is that two-thirds of the public relations officers believe that environmental monitoring will gain significance and that strategic planning will become the most important field in the future (SPRA 2001).

As to the educational role, there are no current figures to show whether it has been implemented among public relations officers, but it is obvious that one of the most important tasks for public relations officers is to improve the communicative competence within their own organisation.

3.3. Position of public relations in organisations

The overall impression is that the similarities are greater than the differences when it comes to public relations practising in the private and the public sector. There are however some differences that could be partly assigned to the profession's frame of reference, and partly to how the daily work is executed and by what means. One difference is that the private sector generally has more financial resources; another, that the public sector has regulations that require far more openness and which give Swedish citizens and non-citizens (visitors, tourists, immigrant without a Swedish passport, etc.) alike the right to require any information they want, with few limitations. We could add to this that the public sector is expected to make an effort in creating opportunities for a dialogue with all the members of society who would like to have contact, whereas the private sector is not as constrained as this. Naturally, daily professional life reflects the nature of the business. Investor relations are obviously an important part of public relations in the private sector, whereas the public sector is expected to service citizens and adjust the information to the conditions of the receivers. The professional technique is however the same: for example to write a press release or use the intranet.

Unfortunately, there are no basic studies, which could confirm all these impressions. The absence of empirical data is particularly noticeable in regards to the range and alignment of public relations in the non-profit sector.

3.4. Current state of education and character of major textbooks

Education within Media and Communication Science at Swedish universities and university colleges is extensive. Quite a few courses are oriented either towards public relations, planned communication or organisational communication. Only a few universities and university colleges specialise in education in these fields and are able to live up to the excellence in public relations education and research.

Education is principally consensus orientated. It is rare to find course literature with a critical note. Most of the course literature is in English and Swedish, though Swedish titles are few and far between. The most common course book, *Tillämpad kommunikationsvetenskap* (Larsson 2001) is an elementary textbook written by an author with many years of practical and theoretical experience. The literature in English covers a wide field. Naturally, the publications of the researchers in the Excellence project (Grunig 2002) are on the list, but there is also literature on rhetoric and persuasion along with literature on organisation communication and other special fields. A big problem is that we in Sweden do not have possibilities to read public relations literature published in other European countries, such as Germany, Austria and the Netherlands.

3.5. The local scene of public relations in Sweden

The professional practitioners have succeeded in establishing three strong organisations in Sweden. The academic union organisation has a subsection for public relations practitioners, which has almost 3,000 members. The SPRA has more than 4,200 members today, which makes it the second largest in Europe in absolute figures. There is also an association for consultants in public relations (see www.precis.se). Its membership is some thirty consultancy firms as members with about 900 employees, with a combined turnover of about 1 billion Swedish crowns (€ 0.1 billion). There is a striking contribution of foreign ownership, mainly American, among the firms.

3.6. Growing fields and hot issues

The Swedish public and private sectors have been quick to use different kinds of information technology. This has had a profound effect on the businesses that in the last ten years have been working on solving the problem of *how* the information technology is to be used. Today, new channels such as the Internet and intranet are well established and the issues are more about why and when we should use the information technology.

Another hot issue is that Swedish companies increasingly seem to reflect on their role in society, and they seek legitimacy in different ways. An indicator of this development is that companies become more and more detailed in their environmental accounts and also like to describe themselves as "corporate citizens". A side-effect of this development is that ethical issues are more and more emphasised (Flodin 1999). Business associations pursue ethical issues: the consultancy association, Precis, has recently adopted new regulations; other associations in the business arrange seminars and appoint mentors for newcomers within the profession.

An issue that could become hot in the future is how companies can account for their intellectual capital and "intangible assets" (Nordic Industrial Fund 2001). The SPRA has been active in this issue, which of course is a new variant of the classical industry issue: how can we demonstrate the added value of our efforts? (SPRA 2000b).

4. Conclusions: state of the art and future of public relations in Sweden

The last ten years have been successful for the Swedish public relations industry. Whether the first decade of the twenty-first century will be as expansive and dynamic as the last one depends largely on the extent to which public relations practitioners, researchers and educators will succeed in accepting the following challenges:

– To make the public relations industry regarded as serious and a contributor to a positive development in society. Public consciousness considers public relations only as something negative, manipulative or entertaining. Extensive, patient and pedagogical work is required if the public is to get a more nuanced and realistic image of our business.
– To increase research with a critical dimension. Not only instrumental, industry-led research is needed, but research that is capable of analysing public relations from a critical point of view, research that is more focused on public relations as a phenomenon in society rather than as a profession that deals with internal and external communication in organisations.
– To achieve an education that, in volume and quality, corresponds to the demands of the students and the industry. Swedish education needs more teachers with a doctor's degree in line with public relations. Networks are needed that pursue these issues internally in university and university colleges. Teachers and researchers have to apply for support and resources from companies, organisations and research councils.
– To expand international presence. Sweden is not particularly well represented at international conferences on public relations. This is in spite of the fact that the government repeatedly has emphasised the importance of Swedish public relations officers, researchers, teachers and students actively participating in international events.

References

Arbman, Stig (1945). *Om Samhällskontakt* [About Community Contacts]. Stockholm: Industriförbundet.
DIK-förbundet (2002). *Informatörer – ett yrke för framtiden...om utbildningarna hänger med, DIK-förbundet* [Public Relations Practitioners – A Profession For the Future...If Education Keeps Up]. Stockholm: DIK-förbundet.
Flodin, Bertil (1999). *Professionell kommunikation* [Professional Communication]. Stockholm: Styrelsen för psykologiskt försvar.

Granström, Kjell (ed.) (2002). *Göteborgskravallerna* [The Göteborg Riots]. Stockholm: Styrelsen för psykologiskt försvar.

Grunig, James E. (ed.) (2002). *Excellent Public Relations and Effective Organisations.* Mahwah, NJ: Lawrence Erlbaum.

Högskoleverket (2001). *Utvärdering av medie – och kommunikationsvetenskapliga utbildningar vid svenska universitet och högskolor* [Evaluation of Education in Media- and Communication Science at Swedish Universities and University Colleges]. Högskoleverkets rapportserie 2001:25R. Stockholm: Högskoleverket.

Larsson, Larsåke (2001). *Tillämpad kommunikationsvetenskap* [Applied Communication Science]. Lund: Studentlitteratur.

Larsson, Larsåke (ed.) (2002). *PR på svenska* [PR in Swedish]. Lund: Studentlitteratur.

Nordic Industrial Fund (2001). *Intellectual Capital. Managing and Reporting.* Nordika project. Oslo: Nordic Industrial Fund.

Ruler, Betteke van, Dejan Verčič, Bertil Flodin and Gerhard Bütschi (2001). Public relations in Europe: a kaleidoscopic picture. *Journal of Communication Management* 6-2: 166 –175.

Ruler, Betteke van, Dejan Verčič, Bertil Flodin and Gerhard Bütschi (2002). *Report on the Delphi Research Project 2002.* European Public Relations Research and Education Association. Ljubliana: Pristop Communications.

Statistiska Centralbyrån (2001). *IT i hem och företag* [IT At Home and In Companies]. Stockholm: Statistiska Centralbyrån.

SPRA, Sveriges Informationsförening (2000a). *Attitydundersökning om informatörer i företag och offentlig sektor* [Survey about public relations practitioners in privat and public sector]. Stockholm: SIFO.

SPRA, Sveriges Informationsförening (2000b). *Return on Communications.* Stockholm: Sveriges Informationsförening.

SPRA, Sveriges Informationsförening (2001). *INFO 2001.* Stockholm: Sveriges Informationsförening.

Swedish Institute (2002). *General Facts about Sweden.* Stockholm: Swedish Institute.

Chapter 26

Switzerland

Ulrike Röttger

1. National profile

1.1. Overview of national characteristics

Switzerland is characterised by its federal structure, its small size and its different languages. Administratively, Switzerland is divided into twenty-six states (*Kantone*), each of which has its own constitution, government and courts and generally enjoys considerable autonomy. A further characteristic of Switzerland is its high number of small communities and villages, the average number of inhabitants per community being the fourth smallest in Europe: more than half of the 3,000 communities have less than 1,000 inhabitants and only 4 per cent of all communities have more than 10,000 inhabitants. The biggest Swiss cities are Zürich (336,000 inhabitants), Geneva (172,800) and Basle (168,700). Switzerland has 7,258,500 inhabitants, and stretches over 41,293 sq. km. (The information in this section has been taken from www.admin.ch and schweiz-in-sicht.ch.)

There are four official national languages in Switzerland and four linguistic regions that are clearly separated from each another. Only a few cities, situated directly on a linguistic border, are bilingual – for example, Freiburg–Fribourg and Biel–Bienne (German–French). The German-speaking part is the biggest, with 64 per cent of the population. The distribution of the other groups is 19 per cent French, 8 per cent Italian and 0.6 per cent Rhaeto-Romance. The remaining 9 per cent of the population speak other languages. The four linguistic regions have their own newspapers, magazines, radio and television programmes as well as news agencies – the Swiss media map is drawn with borders based on language and culture.

The economic importance of the linguistic regions differs considerably; the important centres of the Swiss economy are mostly in the German-speaking part: 73 per cent of the national income is generated in this part, compared to only 4 per cent in Ticino (the Italian-speaking part), and 23 per cent for the French-speaking part (source: www.statistik.admin.ch, 1998 figures).

A first glance shows that the public relations branch has been developing in parallel with the economic importance of the various linguistic regions. Thus, most of the public relations jobs and the largest number of professionals are to be found in the German-speaking part, whereas in the Italian-speaking part there are but few. Obviously, this is mainly the result of the respective economic structures, not necessarily of cultural differences. The German-speaking part dominates the professional field itself, but also research, scholarship and training in public relations. This also has consequences for this chapter: while we attempt to provide a comprehensive overview of public relations of the whole country, we cannot help a bias towards the German part.

1.2. Facts and figures about public relations in Switzerland

Public relations in Switzerland is in many aspects lacking in empirically data. Current and at the same time comprehensive information does not exist. This is the case regarding both quantity (there is no reliable data available for the number of full-time working public relations experts) and quality (for example, we know little or nothing about the self-awareness of Swiss public relations experts and the way they see their professional role). Well-informed sources estimate that the number of full-time practitioners in Switzerland is between 4,000 and 5,000; by comparison, the same number for Germany is between 10,000 and 16,000 (Fröhlich, Szyszka and Fuhrberg 1998: 5, 7). Keep in mind that these numbers are impressions – they have no empirical basis. Even the Swiss Official Statistics can provide no information about the quantitative side of public relations, as they do not specifically cover the field.

The paucity of data reflects not only the youth of research in public relations in Switzerland, but also the structure and development of this young and dynamic field (see in this context Saxer 1991; Kunczik 1993: 9). As in many other European countries, public relations has gained in importance in the 1980s and the 1990s, and is caught up in an ongoing process of differentiation and diversification of tasks and services (see Szyszka 1995: 317). At the same time it lacks a clear, externally identifiable, outline and structure. In Switzerland, too, public relations is a "general term for a decidedly diverse range of professions and fields of activity" (Szyszka 1995: 318). There are no binding guidelines for training in public relations and no requirements for starting to work in the field; in principle anybody can take it up without any previous special training. But in contrast with most other European countries, Switzerland does have state-approved professional examinations in public relations (the Federal certificate for public relations assistants and the advanced Federal examination for public relations consultants).

Turning now to scientific studies, their number is rather low, as mentioned earlier. Most studies are case studies or undergraduate papers dealing with individual aspects of public relations (e.g. cultural sponsoring by banks, public relations for museums, internal communication in telecommunication companies; see among others Baer 2001; Birrer 2000; Bütschi 1984; Kisseloff 2001; Nievergelt 2001; Schärer 2000). In addition, there are some studies written from an economic point of view and examining the public relations aspect of marketing or corporate communications (see Lindner 1999; Dick 1997).

There are also undergraduate papers that deal with the development of the public relations branch and with communicators in PR (Klar n.d.; Müller 1991; Rhomberg 1991). The results of these three studies give only a partial insight into the current situation of professional public relations in Switzerland: they are outdated, deal only with the German-speaking part and rely solely on interviews with members of the *Schweizerische Public Relations Gesellschaft* (SPRG, 'Swiss Public Relations Association'). It must however be assumed that members of the SPRG belong to a highly professionalised segment of public relations in Switzerland and are not representative for all Swiss practitioners. The most recent of the three studies (Klar n.d.) dates from 1996. In this hitherto unpublished study, members of the SPRG with a consulting or managing function were interviewed. Based on 275 questionnaires (a response of 49,1 %), the study gives information about the academic side of the professional field, about its importance and the ways of securing quality and performing evaluations in daily practice. It appears that about 60 per cent of the interviewed persons have a university degree. Of lesser significance is the diploma for public relations consultants of the *Schweizer Public Relations Institut* (SPRI, 'Swiss Institute for Public Relations'), which about a third of them hold. The background of people taking up public relations is varied: 86 per cent of the interviewees said that they had previously been in another profession – most frequently in journalism, advertising or marketing. As far as teaching and training standards are concerned, a clear majority of the interviewees were in favour of keeping access to the profession open. The majority (77 per cent) is however of the opinion that demand for public relations professionals with a university degree will rise, and 79 per cent believe that a generally approved title for the profession of public relations is necessary.

The deficits mentioned earlier were the starting point for a broad research project financed by the Swiss National Fund, entitled "Public Relations in the Swiss Information Society". (This study is part of a broader study which also comprises the research projects "Cyberpreneurship in Switzerland: Development and Management of Corporate Communications", by U. Geissler and M. Will; see also Geissler and Will 2001; and "Public Relations in government and administration: persuasion, information or dialogue?" by C. Rothmayr and S. Hardmeier of the University of Zürich.) The aim of this project, directed by Otfried Jarren and Ulrike Röttger, is to establish comprehensive knowledge about the structure of the professional field of public relation and the aspects and opinions of professionals in Switzerland, on the one hand, and, on the other hand, to analyse public relations theoretically and empirically as a means of communication used by organisations. It seeks answers to these questions: What are the structural conditions of public relations in organisations? And which factors can be identified supporting or hindering these conditions? Furthermore, the consequences of different types of relationship between organisations and their environments will be analysed, answering the question, Are there really different public relations models depending on the type of organisation?

The attempt to conduct a public relations survey embracing the whole country makes great demands on the project. The task of defining public relations and its exponents in Switzerland and, thus, opening up the profession to a scientific approach, is hindered by the diversity of the professional fields, the lack of standardised titles in the profession, unclear boundaries towards other professions and the lack of a systematic inclusion of the professionals into directories or official statistics. Keeping this in mind, one will regard the definition of the total of the group, not as a requirement for the study, but rather as one of its first results.

In order to solve the problems mentioned earlier, about accessing the professionals, the first step was a thorough evaluation of the relevant literature. Then additional interviews were held with experts who – based on their professional function or position in a professional organisation – enjoy a privileged and broad access to information about the profession of public relations in Switzerland. In addition, a questionnaire was distributed to the leading public relations managers of the biggest companies, administrative bodies on a Federal and Cantonal level, all national non-profit organisations and all public relations agencies in Switzerland, who were asked to complete it. Thanks to this approach it will be possible to establish systematic data for different types of organisation with practitioners, and about the different forms of public relations. This method avoids the distortions, which would have been inevitable had only members of the professional associations been interviewed. To counterbalance the disadvantages of the chosen approach – interviewing leading experts obviously provides no information about practitioners who are not in managing positions – additional data relating to central aspects of the professional field in general was requested from those leading experts.

Examples of these additional data are the number of public relations employees, their age, gender and training. Thanks to these data it was possible to make reliable statements about public relations in Switzerland at meso- and micro-level. Based on this initial preparatory work, 3,037 companies, administrative bodies, non-profit organisations and agencies were identified in 2001 and included in the study. The evaluation of the questionnaires was finished 2002, and the results will be published in late summer 2003 (Röttger, Hoffmann and Jarren 2003).

2. History and developments of public relations

The historical development of the profession in Switzerland has not yet been scientifically researched. We know nothing or very little about the origins and early forms of public relations in Switzerland, though we may assume that it ran parallel with neighbouring countries and the rest of Europe.

2.1. The development of public relations practice

In general, Switzerland has witnessed a general and constant gain in importance of public relations, both quantitatively and qualitatively. As in many other European countries, overall development trends can be described with the catchphrases "increased professionalisation", "feminisation" and the trend to the integration of different forms of communication. This trend (see also section 3.7) has been facilitated by rapid technical progress, which not only leads to a strengthening of cross media and a closer coupling of internal and external communication management, but also increases time pressure on agencies and public relations experts: concepts and project realisation are requested in ever shorter periods and have to be finished sooner and sooner.

2.3. The development of education and research traditions

Apart from some early studies from a strongly economic perspective (Heini 1960; Greber 1952; Helbling 1964; Tondeur and Lerf 1968), Swiss public relations research and training has mostly emphasised the communicational aspect. Leading in this field is the IPMZ – Institute for Mass Communications and Media Research of the University of Zürich, the biggest institute of its kind in Switzerland. Due to its borderline character, quite a number of different scientific disciplines deal with public relations in Switzerland – as in many other European countries – namely, economics, politics, sociology and communication research. The perspectives accordingly vary between placing more emphasis either on a more economic or a more communicational understanding of public relations.

The development of public relations education in Switzerland can be described by the words "expansion" and "differentiation". Over the past few years the number of training possibilities at universities and technical colleges has increased remarkably (see also section 3.4). With the increase in training possibilities, the quality of these courses has become more and more differentiated: apart from seminars at various communication institutes on a regular basis – one of them being the IPMZ – there are currently several options of study: Economic Communication, Corporate Communications and Professional Journalism, and Corporate Communication, which are offered by technical colleges (see section 3.4).

2.4. How language shapes the development of public relations

As mentioned earlier, the language boundaries in Switzerland also form media boundaries. The use of these media in the linguistic regions differs quite considerably. It still needs to be systematically researched whether the different language cultures in Switzerland have any influence on public relations in practice and on the self-awareness of professionals in companies, administrations and non-profit-organisations – and if there is any influence, how that works.

Within the framework of the research project "Public Relations in the Information Society Switzerland", there is a similar study about influences on public relations, based on culture and language. The systematic analysis of specific cultural characteristics of practical public relations is a bit difficult, since comparable aspects and indicators for companies, administrations, non-profit organisations and agencies hardly exist. The development of a specific self-awareness in public relations and of different standards is based on several factors, which interact on different levels. This renders it difficult to identify relevant factors of influence in this complex structure and to make statements about their causal relationships.

As a first step in the above-mentioned project, institutions working in the area of training and research are made the focus of the analysis. Some of the questions of interest are: What kind of text-books (and from which countries) is being used in the institutions of the German-speaking French-speaking and Italian-speaking part of Switzerland? Which theoretical perspectives dominate scholarship and research in the different regions? Which authors are prominently read? Which terms exist to describe the public relations profession (does one speak of public relations, corporate communications or organisational communication)?

3. Typification of current public relations

3.1. Status of public relations in business, administration and society

As a professional field public relations has gained tremendously in importance over the past decades. At the same time the role of public relations in opening up society has been clearly enhanced. This gain in importance, which is connected with a professionalisation of public relations, concerns all parts of society. In politics it plays an important role in the context of the numerous referendum campaigns (see e.g. Baer 2001). Central and currently discussed questions in the area of governmental public relations are the following:

– Which means of communication may and should be used by the Federal Council (*Bundesrat*) and its administration in a referendum campaign?
– Which principles must be adhered to by the Federal Council and by administrative bodies during a referendum campaign?

Based on the idea that the process of forming a political opinion should be free of any governmental interference, the Federal Council formally adopted a passive role in referendum campaigns and with regard to its own information and communication efforts (no active public relations by the members of the Federal Council). Recently there has been a change in this attitude: information and offers of orientation by the administration are now held to be a central requirement for the democratic process of forming a political opinion. Evaluating the flood of information would otherwise overtax the voters.

3.2. Major roles of public relations and typical tasks

Unlike in the US, there has hitherto been no empirical study about PR role-models in Switzerland. Whether the roles of public relations manager and technician discussed in American studies are relevant for Switzerland and, if so, to what extent and how the professionals are divided between these two role models, remains unclear (see e.g. Broom and Smith 1979; Toth and Grunig 1993; Dozier and Broom 1995).

There is a wide range of possible job titles in Swiss public relations, as also in Germany. This is because of the open access to this professional field and due to the lack of a clearly defined (but required) training standard. Common titles are, for example, PR consultant (*PR-Berater*), spokesman (*Pressesprecher*), PR assistant (*PR-Assistent*), PR journalist (*PR-Redaktor*) and Head of Corporate Communications or PR manager (*PR-Manager*) (see SPRG n.d.: 15). According to the experts interviewed for the research project "PR in Switzerland", these job titles are chosen, not based on differences in culture or language, but rather based on the type and the size of the organisation in which they are to be used. The experts claim a kind of tendency for the following pattern: the larger an organisation, the more usually American terms are used (such as Head of Corporate Communications).

The SPRI distinguishes the following job titles in public relations:
– PR executive (*PR-Leiter*)
– PR consultant (*PR-Berater*)
– Spokesman or woman (*Pressesprecher*)
– PR assistant (*PR-Assistent*)
– PR journalist (*PR-Redaktor*)
– PR secretary (*PR-Sekretär*)

According to a survey carried out by the SPRG in 2001, a public relations assistant with a federal certificate (see section 3.4) and two years of work experience earns about SFr 69,000 (€ 45,600) per year. The salary of a PR consultant (with responsibility for employers and budgeting) is much higher with an average of SFr 111,000 (€ 73,350) a year (see www.sprg.ch).

3.3. Position of public relations in organisations

The question whether public relations shows different forms depending of the type of organisation and field of activity is an important one for the ongoing project "Public Relations in the Swiss Information Society". As the data have not been evaluated yet, there is currently no reliable information on the characteristics for public relations in administrative bodies, companies and private non-profit-organisations (NPOs).

In general, the majority of experts interviewed in the course of this project (see above) find no differences in the public relations in different types of organisation. They claim that the professional self-awareness of practitioners in administration, companies and NPOs hardly differs – if at all. A minority finds differences between the public relations in the various types according to the available financial means, the goals set and the forms of message.

The degree of professionalism is described very different: especially administrative bodies seem to lack the understanding for a necessary and permanently required public relations. In most cases they have unrealistic ideas about the possible results of public relations and the costs. From the point of view of the agencies, administrations demand customers since they lack common professional requirements. In contrast, companies have by now realised that they lose if they do not communicate actively.

More differences can be established by evaluating how society looks upon the types of organisation: companies are entitled to make use of as much communication as they see fit, provided that professional standards are taken into account. Administrative bodies enjoy less freedom in their public relations work, for example as regards the funds available. Another question is whether administrations are allowed to use public relations in referendum campaigns – and if they are, to what extent. The interviewed experts perceive a wide range of internal positions for public relations in organisations, but claim that the kind of structural inclusion remains almost the same in each of these types of organisation.

3.4. Current state of education and character of major textbooks

Next to the few offers from some universities, the SPRI is the most important public relations training institution in Switzerland. The training situation in Switzerland differs greatly from that in neighbouring Germany: due to the small size of the country and the different linguistic regions, there are not many competing private institutions offering training courses.

Access to the profession is open and not standardised, but, contrary to other European countries, Switzerland does offer a Federally approved certificate (the federal certificate for public relations assistant and an advanced examination for public relations consultants).

The SPRI was founded in 1969 by the SPRG, the most important professional association in Switzerland. The goals of this association are to increase professional standards; to improve the image of public relations in the eyes of society and to support attempts to establish a kind of public relations based on responsibility (see www.spri.ch). The SPRI offers a variety of additional training courses with many different topics, the most important being the course for public relations assistants and public relations consultants. Participants of both courses can take a final test and obtain a federal diploma. The courses are basically oriented along the role-models of technician or manager. Primary focus of the courses for assistants are the following subjects: concept techniques; public relations instruments, internal and external communication, writing, proof-reading, presentation and communicative behaviour in general. This course is basically aimed at secretarial staff members in public relations, advertising and marketing; it takes about twelve months (parallel to one's main profession), and entry requirements are practical professional experience in the field and/or a relevant degree.

The course for consultants, on the other hand, concentrates on the managing aspect and is aimed at people with several years of work and managing experience in public relations. Most relevant for this course are, on the one hand, the political, legal, social, economic and communicational basic aspects of public relations, and on the other hand, the fundamental and concrete conditions for public relations management and corporate communications. According to the SPRI the would-be public relations consultant will learn in this twenty-month course
– to help establish strategies for their companies;
– to develop and issue public relations strategies and measures;
– to run a public relations department or agency;

– to plan an efficient use of human and financial resources;
– to be competent in the method of environment monitoring and issues
  management.

The SPRI lists in its database about 1,000 graduates from either the course
for assistant or for consultant. Of 195 public relations agency managers interviewed for the study "Public Relations in the Swiss Information Society", 15 per cent have taken the assistant course and 22 per cent, the consultant course; on staff level in the agencies the figures are lower – 14.5 per
cent have taken an assistant course, and 10.5 per cent, a consultant course.

Since 1989, the SPRI – together with the Swiss Italian University in
Lugano (Università della Svizzera Italiana) – has been offering a postgraduate study for a Master of Public Relations (MPR). This study costs about
SFr 35,000 (€ 23,100), entails 1,200 hours of teaching and is open to experienced PR managers. The content of the course is based on US research.

Amongst the universities there are yet no independent studies of public
relations, but a more or less abundant offer of different seminars and
courses specialising in PR. The IPMZ plays a leading role. In Zürich, public
relations courses and seminars are an established part of Media Studies; at
the same time it is approached from a communicational point of view. A
more economic approach is taken by the MCM at the St Gallen Institute
for Media and Communication Management; see www.mcm.unisg.ch).
And over the past years a number of technical colleges have developed new
studies in public relations. The Technical College Lucerne offers studies in
economic communication; the Technical College Solothurn, a post-gradu-
ate course in corporate communication management and the Technical
College Winterthur, in journalism and corporate communication:

As to textbooks, there are few local ones, and which books are used in
courses in the various linguistic regions has yet to be established. The
main difference for the theoretical background is whether public relations
is approached more from a communicational or an economic point of
view. In general in Switzerland the communicational aspect is favoured.
The textbooks used come either from Germany or the United States.

3.5. Best selling practical books in public relations

There are no specific Swiss practice books – apart from very few exceptions (Köcher and Birchmeier 1995; Stöhlker 2001). In most cases the
books used in Switzerland are German or American publications, which

offer tips of best-practice. Characteristics of these "how to" publications are a strong tendency to standardisation (if not towards an ideological point of view: "PR is dialogue and sharing of interests"), little reflection and a total lack of reference to scientific knowledge and models. The role of a go-between between theory and practice is not in the centre of most of the practical books.

3.6. The local scene of public relations in Switzerland

The late 1940s and early 1950s, most European countries, including Switzerland, saw the establishment of professional public relations associations. In 1953 the *Schweizerische Public Relations-Gesellschaft* (SPRG, 'Swiss Public Relations Association') was founded, which keeps its own professional register (BR SPRG). This register lists about 200 names. Since a change in by-laws in 1992 the SPRG is an association with seven regional subsections and a total of 1,300 members. The definition of public relations is given by the SPRG as follows: "PR is the management of communicational processes for organisations and their related groups. PR stands for active communication, dialogue and is part of management" (SPRG n.d.:3–5).

The leading Swiss public relations agencies are organised in the *Bund der Public Relations Agenturen der Schweiz* (BPRA, 'Association of the Swiss Public Relations Agencies'). The BPRA represents the interests of the agencies, it offers suggestions for salaries and fees and encourages quality improvement measures. To become a member of the BPRA, an agency must have been in business for five years, have more than five employees and must offer the full range of PR work ("full range" meaning here consulting, conceptional work and execution). In April 2001 twenty-one agencies were members of the BPRA, generating a combined turnover of SFr 84,8 million (€ 56 million), which represents about 80 per cent of the total turnover for all of Switzerland. Table 1 sets out the turnover figures for services offered by agencies.

A characteristic feature of Switzerland is the small number of large agencies; a nearly non-existing middle level and a large number of small agencies. The dominant role of the German-speaking part of Switzerland can be seen here, too. According to the study "Public Relations in the Information Society Switzerland", the average Swiss agency has 7.8 employees, of which 4.6 are actually working in public relations (the others are to be found in administration, technical support and graphical design).

Compared with the advertising branch, international connections of Swiss agencies are rather less developed and only very few of the global agencies are present in Switzerland. Ten out of the twenty-five leading Swiss agencies claim to be independent and are working only on a national or regional level (see Löffler 2000) and the majority of the remaining fifteen agencies are engaged in rather loose networks.

Table 1. Turnover according to type of service (*source*: www.bpra.ch)

Type of service	1999 (%)	2000 (%)
Total PR-consulting/corporate communication	48.2	42.3
Political-PR/lobbying/public affairs	11.5	17.0
Products-PR/marketing communication	16.6	20.8
Financial PR/investors relations	15.3	11.9
Others	8.5	7.9
Total	100.0	100.0

3.7. Hot issues in public relations in Switzerland

It is difficult to present a complete list of hot issues for Swiss public relations. Based on the technical, social and economic developments in Switzerland, it is possible though to point at crisis management (see the fate of Swissair), issues management and further development in the area of integrated corporate communications as relevant discussions points. In addition, corporate sustainability is an important professional topic. In Switzerland, as in Germany, the area of corporate publishing is growing. Finally, another dominant trend, which is again by no means restricted to Switzerland, is the stressing of the importance of a trademark and the idea of branding, which seems to have become the essence of successful public relations itself.

4. Conclusions: state of the art and future of public relations in Switzerland

Two important developments are: growing professionalism and an increase in the number of female professionals in public relations. The trend to professionalisation is evidenced in particular by the considerable interest in training offers at university level, but also in the interest in subsidiary courses (such courses are offered by the SPRI, for example). In the long run this will lead to a bigger influence of universities on public relations in general. Another aspect of the ongoing trend towards professionalisation in public relations is its differentiation into separate subsections, such as public affairs, investor relations, issues management, and so on. This is especially noticeable in large organisations.

As yet the impact is unclear of the growing number of female professionals on public relations as a profession, for its professionalisation and its status. Initial results of the study "Public Relations in the Swiss Information Society" seem to indicate that the well-known differences from other countries exist in Switzerland as well. For example, the difference in salaries for male and female professionals as well as the difference in their respective professional role models.

The further development in integrated corporate communication is unclear: in practice, only large companies establish such departments. But even here it is clear that integration tends to be implemented more in a formal than in a material sense. Many social, formal and material barriers will have to be overcome before a real integrated communication management can take shape. In its real sense, integrated communication now only exists for a small minority of companies. In Switzerland we find a large number of small and middle-sized companies, which makes the development of integrated communications difficult: they do not enjoy the financial and personal resources necessary to establish integrated communication.

Technical improvements will play another important role in the further development of public relations – see digitalisation and convergence of media. There will be an increase in the speed of communication and of public relations work, and individual and mass communication will grow closer, the merging into one of telephone, television and personal computer will have drastic consequences for the practical side of public relations – the result will be stronger cross-media relations; addressing of shareholder requirements and a closer coupling of internal and external communication management.

Today's rapidity of communication and the gigantic gain in accessible sources of information and in possibilities for companies to pass on information will make the subject of knowledge management a central topic for public relations. The steadily increasing complex reality of public relations cannot be met with knowledge based on best-practice books and a simple listing of formerly successful consulting experiences. In future, a more scientific approach to consultancy will be necessary.

To gain knowledge is one thing – to manage it another: individual training and broadening one's competence as a classic answer to new demands will no longer suffice in future. In order to generate and manage knowledge, new forms of professional networking will gain in importance.

In conclusion, this overview of public relations in Switzerland must point at one dominant characteristic: the trend to internationalisation. Though Switzerland plays a somewhat special role in Europe, it is obvious that its public relations developments are similar at least to those in other German-speaking European countries and that there is therefore no specific and autonomous phenomenom of "Swiss public relations".

References

Baer, Ariane (2001). Parteipolitische Öffentlichkeitsarbeit: Themen- und Ereignismanagement [Party-political public relations: theme and event management]. Master thesis, University of Zürich.

Birrer, Susanne (2000). Public Relations von Nonprofit-Organisationen [Public relations of non-profit organisations]. Master thesis, University of Zürich.

Broom, Glen A. and George D. Smith (1979). Testing the Practitioner's Impact on Clients. *Public Relations Review*, 5–3: 47–59.

Bütschi, Gerhard (1984). Die Erarbeitung eines PR-Konzeptes für den Schweizerischen Zofingerverband [The development of a PR concept for the Swiss Zofingerverband]. Master thesis, University of Bern.

Dick, Marco (1997). Management von Produkt-PR. Ein situativer Ansatz [Management of product PR: a situational Beginning]. (Ph.D. dissertation, University of St. Gallen). Bamberg (n.p.).

Dozier, David M. and Glen M. Broom (1995). Evolution of the Manager Role in Public Relations Practice. *Journal of Public Relations Research*, 7–1: 3–26.

Fröhlich, Romy, Peter Szyszka and Reinhold Fuhrberg (1998). Qualifikationsprofil Öffentlichkeitsarbeit [A profile of public relations]. Bonn. (see also www.pr-guide.de/onlineb/p980903.htm).

Geissler, Ulrike and Markus Will (2001). Gründer-PR während der Internet-Euphorie: Warum die Selbstdarsteller rational handelten. [Public relations for start-ups in times of internet-euphoria] (www.pr-guide.de).

Greber, Emil (1952). Public Relations. Die Politik der Unternehmung zur Pflege der öffentlichen Meinung [Public relations. The policy of the enterprise for the care of the public opinion]. (Ph.D. dissertation, University of Bern). Zürich: Walther.

Heini, Bruno (1960). Public Relations. Die Vertrauenswerbung der Privatunternehmung. Mit besonderer Berücksichtigung der amerikanischen Auffassungen und Methoden [Public relations. Confidence advertisement of private enterprises]. Ph.D. dissertation, University of Freiburg.

Helbling, Alphons (1964). *Public Relations Handbuch* [Public relations handbook]. St Gallen: Zollikofer.

Kisseloff, Irina (2001). Public Relations von Kunstmuseen. Eine Untersuchung der Öffentlichkeitsarbeit als Organisationsfunktion in acht Kunstmuseen der Deutschschweiz [Pub-
lic relations of art museums]. Master thesis, University of Zürich.

Klar, Joachim (n. d.). Professionalisierung im Berufsfeld Public Relations. Eine empirische
Studie zur Professionalisierungssituation in der Schweizer PR-Branche [Public relations
professionalism]. Unpublished manuscript. Zürich.

Köcher, Anton and Eliane Birchmeier (1995). *Public Relations? Public Relations! Konzepte,
Instrumente und Beispiele für erfolgreiche Unternehmenskommunikation* [Concepts, Instruments and examples of successful communication] (2nd edn.). Zürich: Verlag Industri-
elle Organisation

Kunczik, Michael (1993). *Public Relations. Konzepte und Theorien* [Public Relations: Concepts and Theories]. Köln: Böhlau.

Lindner, Holger (1999). Das Management der Investor Relations im Börseneinführungs-
prozess: Schweiz, Deutschland und USA im Vergleich [The management of investor relations during the listing process]. Ph.D. dissertation, University of St Gallen.

Löffler, Jaromir (2000). Wird der Schweizer PR-Markt globaler? [Is the Swiss PR market
globalising?] *Marketing & Kommunikation* 1: 52–53.

Müller, Edith (1991). Das Berufsfeld Public Relations. Eine empirische Untersuchung zur
beruflichen Realität der PR-Schaffenden in der Deutschschweiz. Pubblic Relations
work [Empirical study of the vocational reality]. Master thesis, University of Zürich.

Nievergelt, Suzanne (2001). Public Relations von Nonprofit-Organisationen [Public relations of non-profit organisations]. Master thesis, University of Zürich.

Rhomberg, Karin (1991). Berater für Public Relations: wer sie sind, wie sie es werden. [PR-
consultants: who they are, how they it become] Master thesis, University of Zürich.

Röttger, Ulrike, Hoffmann, Jochen and Otfried Jarren (2003). Public Relations in der
Schweiz – Eine empirische Studie zum Berufsfeld Öffentlichkeitsarbeit [Public relations
in Switzerland. A empirical study of the PR professional field]. Konstanz: uvk Verlags-
gesellschaft.

Saxer, Ulrich (1991). Public Relations als Innovation. Innovationstheorie als public-rela-
tions-wissenschaftlicher (sic!) Ansatz [Public relation as innovation]. *Media Perspektiven*
5: 273–290.

Schärer, Felipe J. (2000). Die Öffentlichkeitsarbeit der NGOs. Das Beispiel der schweizerischen Entwicklungsorganisationen [Public Relations of non governmental organizations].
Thesis University of Bern.

SPRG (n. d.). Public Relations. Selbstverständnis einer Branche und eines Berufsstandes
[Self understanding of the profession]. Zürich.

Stöhlker, Klaus J. (2001). Wer richtig kommuniziert, wird reich: PR als Schlüssel zum Er-
folg [Who communicates correctly, becomes rich: PR as a key to success]. Wien: Über-
reuter Wirtschaft

Szyzka, Peter (1995). Öffentlichkeitsarbeit und Kompetenz: Probleme und Perspektiven
künftiger Bildungsarbeit [Public Relations and qualifications]. In: Peter Szyszka (ed.),
PR-Ausbildung in Deutschland. Entwicklung, Bestandsaufnahme und Perspektiven [PR
education in Germany. Development, fact-finding and perspectives], 317–342. Opladen.
Westdeutscher Verlag

Tondeur, Edmond and Rolf Lerf (1968). Public Relations ohne Schlagworte. Eine Arbeit-
sanleitung für Unternehmer [Public relations without]. Zürich: Verlag Organisator.

Toth, Elizabeth L. and Larissa A. Grunig (1993). The Missing Story of Women in Public
Relations. *Journal of Public Relations Research*, 5–3: 153–175.

Chapter 27

Turkey

Zafer Özden and Mine Saran

1. National profile

1.1. Overview of national characteristics

Turkey is located on two continents – Europe and Asia – and is divided in seven regions. It covers 814,578 sq. km, of which 790,200 sq. km are in Asia and 24,378 sq. km in Europe. Turkey has 65 million inhabitants, 70 per cent urban, the rest rural. Turkey is one of the faster urbanising countries in the world. There are about 3 million Turkish people outside Turkey, mainly in Germany.

Turkey borders Greece and Bulgaria on the European continent, and Georgia, Armenia, Iran, Iraq, and Syria in Asia. It is an integral part of European history, culture, and economy, with its 500 years of history on the continent, and 2,000 years of history cradling the four great civilisations – Greek, Roman, Byzantine, and Ottoman. Turkey has two of the seven wonders of the ancient world (the temple of Artemis and the mausoleum at Halicarnassus), Noah's Ark on Ağrı Dağı (Mount Ararat), Virgin Mary's last home, the oldest American school outside the United States (Robert College in Istanbul), the first church (St Peter's Church) and early churches built by the Christians escaping from Roman persecution. Turks brought coffee to Europe and tulips to the Dutch.

Constitutionally, Turkey is a republic and a democratic, secular state. The Republic of Turkey is defined as a "unitary state", respecting the cultural mosaic and heritage of Anatolia. The vast majority of the country is Muslim (98 per cent) with Christian and Jewish minorities (2 per cent). The constitution protects the social, economic, political, and legal systems against any influence from religious rules. The Turkish language, the sixth most widely spoken language in the world, with its history dating back 5,500 years, is the official language, spoken by 90 per cent of the population. Apart from Turkish, about 70 languages are spoken in different parts of the country.[1]

Modern Turkey's economy is developing rapidly and was identified as one of the most promising emerging economies before the 2001 crisis. It still has considerable potential for growth and could become one of the big global players. Turkey's future, both economically and culturally, will be shaped substantially by its relationship with the European Union. After the EU declared Turkey as a candidate for full membership, the country accepted the concomitant obligations, and, despite claims to the contrary, implemented most of the required legal and administrative arrangements to harmonise with the European Union.

The Turkish Radio and Television Corporation (TRT) has been broadcasting since the early 1970s, and private channels have been active since 1990. Turkish television channels show great variety, with music, news, and documentary channels. The Turkish printed press is diversified with their weekend supplements and added news sections, covering all sorts of different interests. The range of specialised media provides public relations people with an opportunity to place their messages designed for target groups. In the media-ownership structure,[2] the media groups owning these channels and newspapers are among the economic giants of the country, functioning in different sectors. Thus, economically, they are significant partners.

The economic structure of Turkey is determined by the big cities: İstanbul, İzmir, and Ankara. İstanbul (10 million inhabitants) is the biggest city – it is also the centre for trade, finance, industry, tourism, and culture. Ankara (4 million inhabitants) is the capital city, and İzmir (3.4 million inhabitants) is the third biggest city and an important port in Turkey.

1.2. Facts and figures about public relations in Turkey

Turkey, bridging western and eastern cultures, presents an interesting field of study and practice, as its development reflects the changes in society and culture. Attitudes towards public relations reflect the change from traditional eastern ways of trading to western business practices. The public relations profession has developed in tandem with both the economical

---

1. Information about Turkey can be obtained from following websites: www.mfa.gov.tr/grupc/default.htm and www.columbia.edu/~sss31/Turkiye/business.html.
2. See www.cgd.org.tr/yayinlar/media_ownership_structure_in_turkey.doc.

conditions and the cultural changes. It has expanded mainly in big cities where the major international companies operate. There are also some cultural aspects that affect the nature of public relations. For example, the level of economic development and change in the culture determines the perception of the profession. Public relations has had a negative image until recently, because it was seen as a profession of "young ladies wearing stockings under mini skirts".

Academics working in public relations have difficulty finding data and research on the profession, especially in English, and it is not easy to track contemporary research because it is not widely published. It is therefore not possible to give exact figures on the number of public relations agencies and practitioners, or to provide information about titles and positions of the public relations practitioners in organisations. Besides, *Halkla İlişkiler* (which literally means "relations to the general public") is a loosely used term for a wide range of activities; a model working for a nightclub could be introduced as a PR specialist or a PR manager in a news program of a national news channel. To compound the problem of qauntification, the profession is not regulated: there are no legal or professional requirements for establishing oneself as a public relations practitioner – any person with social skills, usually a relative of the company owner, is a serious candidate. At the same time, public relations departments are the first units to be closed when a company meets an economical crisis.

The only tangible source is a survey (Strateji|MORI 1999) conducted among 46 leading firms. This study, carried out in 1999, is the first research to provide a picture of the profession in Turkey. According to the survey, most of the companies view public relations as a one-way communication activity, including activities such as informing customers, organising media relations, reaching the audience with newsletters and news, and publicity. They also consider public relations as a tool for PR activities such as setting up and maintaining good relations with audience and customers. The leading firms in their sectors are serviced by public relations consultancies (26.1 per cent), advertising consultancies (50 per cent), and research consultancies (32.6 per cent). However, public relations is in fourth place as an outside consultancy service with 50 per cent, after advertising (89.1 per cent), research (58.7 per cent) and event planning (56.5 per cent). In this context, another survey,[3] among companies demanding public relations consultancy services, revealed their expectations from public relations activities to be the following:

---

3. See www.kho.edu.tr/yayinlar/bilimdergisi/bilimder/doc/2000-1/bilder-5.doc.

- advantage with low-budget activities
- reaching business objectives with lower expenses
- new and creative public relations projects
- crisis management
- solutions that will help companies increase their prestige and publicity
- supporting marketing communications
- new communications solutions for the identified business problems
- more, and effective, media coverage

On the other hand, it is not possible to give an exact number of professionals in Turkey because there is no research on it. The number of the members of local public relations associations will be provided while looking at the local public relations scene later on. Meanwhile, a survey (Okay and Okay 2001) which was conducted in 2001 among *Halkla İlişkiler Derneği* (HİD, 'Public Relations Association') members yielded interesting results concerning the educational background of the professionals in İstanbul: 66.7 per cent of the members had an undergraduate degree, 26 per cent master's degree, and 5 per cent doctorate degree. Forty per cent of the members are the graduates of Communication Faculties. A notable majority of the members (40 per cent) worked as PR specialists in private organisations, while 20 per cent worked in PR agencies. The remaining 40 per cent of the members were employed in public institutions as PR specialist (1.7 per cent), in advertising (5 per cent), marketing (5 per cent), human resources management (1.7 per cent), academic (8.3 per cent), and other areas (18.3 per cent).

Turkish public relations professionals also cooperate with the international public relations associations so as to increase their market, to improve the standards of the profession, and to represent Turkey internationally. The International Public Relations Association (IPRA) has 64 members in Turkey, including 23 student members. Public Relations Consultancies Inc. (PRCI/ICCO) has been represented in Turkey since 1998 under the title PRCI/ICCO Turkey with seven founding members. PRCI/ICCO Turkey has been organising a number of education seminars and professional activities.

The integration and success of Turkish public relations professionals and companies internationally has helped professional development. A notable sign of the importance given to the public relations profession is the worldwide success of Turkish professionals: Betül Mardin was the first Turkish president of IPRA in 1995, and another leading name in the profession, Ceyda Aydede, who hosted first Council Meeting of 2000 in

Istanbul as a board member, was elected president in 2003. Their professional achievements show not only the success of Turkish public relations
professionals but also the current situation of public relations in Turkey:
the number of successful female practitioners is rising and, encourag-
ingly, they are increasingly running their own companies.

2. History and development of public relations

2.1. Roots of public relations

Contrary to its development in the U.S. and Europe, the public relations
profession emerged under the leading role of the government in the beginning of the 1960s, and made its way in the private sector. Asna (1998:
12) noted that "the concept of PR emerged in Turkey in 1961 when State
Planning Organisation was founded to coordinate the planned economical and social development of the country. The SPO and the Population
Planning Directorate were the earliest organisations having public relations units in Turkey. They were followed in 1969 by Koç Holding Company, a private conglomerate then consisting of 59 companies". The first
Turkish public relations association (HİD) was founded to introduce and
develop the profession in 1972. The first president of the association was
Alaaddin Asna, who also wrote the first book on PR in Turkish in 1969
after his training in U.S. Additionally, Asna founded the first consultancy
company in 1974, and is still one of the prominent figures in the field.

Three projects should be mentioned in the historical development of
PR in state institutions.
1. The MEHTAP Project: *Merkezi Hukumet Teskilati Projesi* ('Central
   Government Organisation Project'). Created in 1962 by the Ministry
   Board. The purpose of this project is to research the distribution of
   the central government functions and to find out if that distribution
   is compatible with the smooth process of state affairs. This project
   emphasised the importance of communication of the central administration with the public. Some years after the MEHTAP project,
   some of the ministries integrated public relations in their policies.
2. *Idari Reform Danisma Kurulu* ('Administration Reform Consultant
   Board'). This board, comprised of ten people, was formed by the Ministry Board in 1971. The board's report mentioned that the units that
   have public relations and public information functions are under different names; so there needed to be a central body to coordinate them.
   The report also stated that the goal of public relations and public infor-

mation services is not only to inform the public about the activities carried out, but also to get the feedback of the public. The report added that these units should work closely with the administration, and people who are trained in the public relations field should be employed. In 1984, the name was changed to Public Relations and Public Information in the ministries that offer public relations services.

3. *Idari Danisma Merkezi* ('Administration Consulting Center'). It was formed by a decision of the Ministry Board in 1966 and closed in 1972. Several ministry representatives and 15 people had been brought to this position by Mayor of Ankara to form this centre. The function of this centre was to answer the questions of the public about state organisations and to facilitate inquiries of the public. Even though it was short-lived, this was considered to be a good public relations tactic. However, a survey carried out in Ankara among 250 people showed that 27.6 per cent of respondents knew about the centre.

The first public relations practitioners were people with experience in journalism and these first public relations professionals were mainly interested in media relations. But today they have different managerial functions and titles paralleling the change in organisations, based on the economical changes. The history of public relations in Turkey, then, shadows capitalist evolution.

2.2. The development of public relations practice

Because of the weak market competition, companies in the private sector did not really need public relations until the 1980s. By then, public relations was widely recognised and developed as a profession and an academic field in universities. In this decade, Turkey implemented some economic reforms for liberalising the economy to integrate it into the international economy, which resulted in the growth of the Turkish economy. As a direct result of economical development and change, modern management principles gained importance in Turkey, thus changing the appearance of the public relations function in organisations. As Melvin L. Sharpe observed in the early 1990s,

> The growth of public relations continues to increase, I was told, because of the competitive need for Turkish corporations to keep pace with European and United States corporate communications advancements. The drive that is improving the profession in Turkey, therefore, is the desire to successfully compete in European and world markets and

the result is improvement of external communications designed to give both government and private sectors of the economy a better face. But public relations professionals are up-front and honest in clearly calling for internal change." (Sharpe 1992: 105)

The competitive need for the Turkish economy and the drive for public relations is even stronger today. Nowadays Turkey's economy is much more integrated with Europe and United States, which increases the need for public relations for Turkish companies operating globally. As a result of the transformation in the economic system and culture, public relations became one of the most popular subjects with university students, which advanced the development of the profession. Graduates with an educational background and professional integrity still struggle to change the image of the profession, and try to assume new roles required by the developments in management areas.

2.3. How language shapes the development of public relations

The common name of the profession in Turkish is *Halkla İlişkiler*. As it is generally believed that public relations as a business and social practice has cultural roots, the words used to describe it have peculiar implications that determine the nature of the profession. *İlişki* is nearly an equivalent of 'relation' but *halk* presents some problems in Turkish as it does not match the meaning of 'public'. *Halk* means 'a mass of people', not a particular target group. Thus, *Halkla İlişkiler* may be viewed as the activities of communication with people in general, but not with a particular group of people, or *kamu* (as is a better equivalent for 'public'). In the discussions about the name of the profession, some academics proposed *Kamusal İlişkiler* (*-sal* is a suffix equivalent with '-ic') as a better alternative. Meanwhile, some companies use the term "public relations" – or its abbreviated form, "PR" – when they want to look posh. Nowadays, some new terms – "communication management", "integrated communication" – have been used as a result of the latest theoretical developments, presented by academics and professionals working in the field. But "public relations" is still the best known and most widely used term.

3. Typification of current public relations

3.1. Status of public relations in business, administration, and society

After 1980, public relations gained importance as a field of study and a profession, due to the changes in the economic system and in society, hand in hand with its development as an academic discipline in universities. Today, public relations is practiced by an increasing number of public relations practitioners with degrees in public relations, economics, or journalism. Apart from university courses, public relations practitioners and would-be professionals can take public relations courses organised by private companies. Public relations departments, firms, and practitioners are a part of the Turkish business world today. We can safely say that public relations has been playing an important role in the development of open and democratic society in Turkey.

Public relations also has a role in government, non-profit organisations, and politics. Almost all public institutions, non-profit organisations, and political parties have public relations departments or public relations workers, as a sign of the need for communication with target groups in a respectful manner, and the need for a positive image. There are numerous departments and titles in public institutions; examples include "Protocol, Press and Public Relations Directorate", "Press and Public Relations Consultant", "Press, Broadcasting and Public Relations Directorate", "Education and Publicity Directorate", "Public Relations and Publicity Directorate", "Publishing and Publicity Directorate", "Advertising and Public Relations Directorate". However, there are some problems in the activities of these public relations departments,[4] which can be identified as follows:

– Public institutions do not consider public relations as a tool of communication for solving people's problems. It is considered a position placed in an organisational chart only because of state planning activities. As a result of this attitude, people's demands and needs are not taken into consideration sufficiently.
– There are organisational problems concerning the structure and position of public relations departments. Therefore, public relations departments and public relations people in public institutions still have to convince top managers about their role and position in the organisational hierarchy. "Public" in public institutions is still understood as a unit organising protocol activities and press relations, and public relations people do not have the possibility of realising the research, planning, execution, and evaluation phases of public relations activities.
– Public relations practitioners in public relations departments lack expertise.

---

4. See www.byegm.gov.tr/yayinlarimiz/kitaplar/turkey2000/ingilizce/developments_in_the
   _economic_sectors/advertising/advertisintg2.htm.

– There are budget problems. In public institutions, most of the budget is spent on public services, and PR departments do not get what they need – the budget is generally hardly enough to pay for salaries and minimum services.
– The principles of public relations have not yet been fully understood in public institutions.

These kinds of problems cause insufficient and ineffective PR activities, and also create a negative effect on the perception of public relations in public institutions. What is needed is a change of understanding and PR professionals with an educational background. Comparing PR activities in the public and private sectors, we can say that PR in the private sector is overshadowed PR in the public sector.

3.2. Major roles of public relations and typical tasks

Empirical studies on public relations models in Turkey do not exist. Evaluating the public relations activities in Turkey according to Grunig's four models, it can be said that organisations are still producing activities for publicity and information. However, it has been observed that some organisations with an established understanding of public relations use the two-way asymmetrical and the two-way symmetrical model only rarely (Okay and Okay 2001: 30–31).

As in the public sector, there is a wide variety of organisational positions and job titles in Turkish public relations, depending on the size of the company and its business area. Other reasons for this variety are the problems in the definition of the profession, and the top executives' view of the PR profession. This is reflected in the multitude of job titles used; to give just a few examples, "PR Manager", "PR Specialist", "Press and PR Consultant", "Press and PR Director", and "Person Responsible for PR". The position of and number of PR practitioners vary according to the size and culture of the company. Most often public relations activities of small-sized and local companies are planned by a public relations specialist or manager working alone. Most of the companies and public institutions have internal public relations departments or units with a public relations manager or specialist, two widely known titles for public relations practitioners.

Public relations firms serve several areas. According to IPRA Referral Service Information (Internationals Public Relations Association

2002–2003: 292–293), which lists the practice areas identified by the members in various countries, Turkish public relations agencies provide services ranging from advertising and marketing to such activities as communication management, consumer relations, corporate communications, crisis management, environmental communications, integrated business communications, international medial relations, and financial communications.

3.3. Current state of education and character of major textbooks

As public relations was viewed as a mass-communication discipline in Turkey, the first public relations courses were given in 1966 in the School of Journalism, part of the Political Sciences Faculty at Ankara University. Public relations education was then moved to public relations departments in communications faculties, and in 1987 it was included in professorial teaching commitments, opening the way for academics. Public relations is now housed in the public relations departments in a growing number of communications faculties (about 27 in 2003) all over Turkey and Cyprus. Courses last four years, including some subsidiary courses in the Radio-Television-Cinema and Journalism departments; they award a "PR Specialist" degree to bachelors graduates. Postgraduate studies are also available, with master and doctorate degrees. Education is provided by faculty staff, and some experienced professionals from both the private and the public sectors are invited for guest lectures. The curricula of the public relations departments differ depending on the status of the university. In state universities, teaching tends to be theory oriented; this due to budget problems and because of the nature of state universities. Private universities, on the other hand, focus more on practical lessons designed for the market. An important contribution of public relations departments in state universities is the increase of educators who can teach both in state and in private universities. Turkish public relations education can be seen as being in a developing stage educationally, abandoning the traditional emphasis on media relations, publicity, promotion, and advertising, and offering courses on new issues such as crisis management, strategic planning, international public relations, and integrated marketing communications.

Some Business and Administration Schools also have public relations courses for their students because public relations is viewed as an important management function, directly tied to meeting organisational objectives, and the businessmen of the future will need an understanding of public relations. Except for the education in public relations departments, there are private public relations courses, organised by private education institutions and companies, and public institutions. In addition, some official institutions (army and police forces, for example) have been teaching public relations to their students.

The relatively short history of public relations in Turkey explains why little is known about social and business aspects of the profession. Another reason for this lack of information is that public relations books in Turkey tend to be Anglo-Saxon oriented. The majority of the books in the field were written by academics, based on English-language originals. However, we cannot say that the American way of public relations is prevalent in Turkey in practice. The public relations profession is practiced in a way heavily affected by the cultural climate of the country; most of the clients are found by personal relations; public relations is still done by the people without formal training; public relations is seen as a prestigious department by company owners, who do not use it in a functional way. In fact, a focus-group survey recently conducted among PR students of two faculties of communication at İstanbul University and Ege University, showed results supporting this condition in Turkey. As Görpe and Saran (2003) note, "during the discussions, there was a tendency to criticise the educational curriculum as well saying that what they do does not match with what they see at school. Internship is seen very important for them, however although it had been thought that it would reinforce what they have learned at school, that is not the case in most experience the students have shared". Therefore, public relations students are also aware of the differences in practice and educational field caused by the business culture in Turkey.

There is a growing number of books on public relations in Turkish today, but most are introductory books written by academics, based on public relations literature in English. Books on public relations have bloomed in recent years, probably under the influence of university education. The increase in the number of public relations departments, and the number of master and doctorate studies has led to the increase in the number of books and articles on public relations. The rise in the sales of business books helped academics to publish their studies. Some books written by social scientists and communication experts can be found in Turkish, but most of the studies on specific areas in public relations are articles in academic journals and professional magazines.

3.4.The local scene of public relations in Turkey

Public relations gained importance in the big cities which have vivid economies. Public relations departments and consultancy firms emerged in open-market conditions, and today, public relations consultancies provide services in cities such as İstanbul, İzmir, Ankara, Bursa and Gaziantep. Almost all large companies have their own public relations departments.[5] A characteristic of local public relations companies is the large amount of small agencies which also serve as advertising agencies. There is no clear distinction between these two types of company, and they generally call themselves "PR and advertising agency".

There are also local associations. These were founded in order to introduce and develop the profession nationwide and in local scale, depending on the location of the associations. HİD (www.hid.org) was founded by the leading public relations professionals in Istanbul 1972, and became a member of CERP (Confederation Européenne des Relations Publiques) in 2002. HİD played an important role in the introduction of public relations in the private sector and the development of the profession. HİD has more than 200 members. *İzmir Halkla İlişkiler Derneği* (HİD, 'İzmir Public Relations Association') was founded in 1985 with the same kind of objectives, and played an important role in the introduction of public relations in İzmir and the Aegean region. HİD has 78 members. *Ankara Halkla İlişkiler Derneği* (AİD, 'Ankara Public Relations Association') (www.ahid.org.tr) was founded in1990 by 25 PR professionals, again with the same kind of objectives; AHİD (81 members) has received PR awards since 1997 to develop the profession in central Anatolia and Turkey. *Bursa Halkla İlişkiler Derneği* (BHİD, 'Bursa Public Relations Association', 39 members) (www.bhid.org) was founded in 1992 to develop the profession in Bursa and neighborhood. *Halkla İlişkiler Danışmanlar Derneği* (HİDD, 'Public Relations Consultancies Association') (www.hdd.org) was founded in 1992, and has 35 members. All these associations pursue similar goals – to establish stricter criteria for the PR profession and improve training.

There are some international agencies in Turkey, such as *Global Tantm: Fleishman Hillard*, which is owned by Ceyda Aydede, President of IPRA. Global Tantm: Fleishman Hillard became an affiliate of Fleishman-Hillard, the leading international public relations agency and made its first steps towards internationalisation in 1992.[6] Founded in 1992,

---

5. See www.globaltanitim.com/eng/about/history.html.
6. See www.prciturkey.com/capitol.html.

Capitol Halkla İlişkiler, representative of Burson Marsteller and Ogilvy PR in İstanbul, has as clients Unilever (Corporate Affairs), Microsoft, Bosch/Siemens/Profilo/Gaggenau White Goods, Danone SA (Corporate, Water, and Dairy Groups), Tekstilbank, AstraZeneca (Corporate Affairs), Peregrine Systems ve Eti Pazarlama.[7] Here is a list of the international agencies in Turkey in 2001:

- ECCO : Plan PR
- Burson Marsteller : Capitol PR
- Ogilvy PR Worldwide : Capitol ECCO : plan PR
- Edelman : Effect PR
- Euro RSCG : Euro RSCG Istanbul
- GCI Group : GCI Istanbul
- Hill&Knowlton : Man PR
International PR Network :
- Leo Burnett : Leo PR
- Porter Novelli International : Unsal PNI
- Weber Shandwick Worldwide : Strateji
- Ketchum : Rekta
- International PR network : A&B
- MMD Central : Mmd PR
- MS&L/Worldcom : Global Tanitim (Hollis Europe Guide 2002[8])

3.5. Growing fields and hot issues

It is not easy to identify any particular hot issues in the public relations profession in Turkey, but one thing that can be mentioned is that current events and research show that there are reliability and image problems in the profession. This leads to debates concerning the ethics of media relations. Public relations professionals state all the time that it is not ethical to bribe or give presents for news placement in the media, and they honestly think that these pay-for-placement practices (or "advertorials") must be eliminated. An IPRA report (www.ipra.com) published in 2002 showed that such a policy is rarely or not generally followed in northern European countries including Turkey. The IPRA national coordinator, Omer Kayalioglu, says, "even though from time to time the media has hesitations regarding the responsibilities it faces, the ration of the news

---

7. See www.hollis-pr.com.
8. See www.hid.org.tr/prg/haberler/haberayrinti.php?Sira_No=2.

published, is not different from markets in central Europe. It is possible to come across news created because of 'non-existent media transparency' only in some magazines. However, this scenario does not prevent the discussion of certain facts about the media". (Kayalioglu 2002: 15). Paralleling these debates, the emergence of a well-informed and sensitive public towards corporate actions with the steps taken to more open and democratic society caused the companies behave much more socially responsible. The goldmine crisis in Bergama (Pergamon) is a case to remember; the villagers of Bergama have been preventing the operations of Normandia Company (formerly Eurogold Company) because it is planning to use cyanide in the gold mine. Such kind of events also made crises management a hot topic among professionals and academics.

As a result of economic and social changes as well as managerial changes, public relations professionals are unwilling to execute just their traditional roles (preparing in-house newsletters and external publications, employee training, protocol activities, organising public relations events, press conferences, etc.). They demand to take part in the strategic decisions, being a part of management team. This leads to another topic – the position and title in organisations. Public relations people still try to convince the managers of their strategic roles in organisations.

The acceptance of the profession is still low; everybody can be a public relations practitioner without any educational background or formal training. Brad H. Hainsworth states four basic requirements that constitute a profession; (1) a well-defined body of scholarly knowledge; (2) completion of a generally standardised and prescribed course of graduate study; (3) examination and certification by a state; and (4) oversight by a state agency which has disciplinary powers over the practitioner's behaviour (Hainsworth 1994: 311). Public relations literature written by academics and professionals provides a well-defined body of scholarly knowledge. Public relations departments in universities all over Turkey have been providing graduate courses and most of their graduates now work in the field, but public relations people cannot have the support of the state for the last two requirements. However, the topic has been debated in Turkey – not only for the graduates of public relations departments, but also for the graduates of Radio-Television-Cinema departments and Journalism departments in Communication Faculties.

Public relations education presents another issue in this context. A debate has been going on about the quality of public relations education in public relations departments, and also in private courses, concerning the curriculum and educators, though the quality of education is expected to improve with the growing number of well-trained teachers. The number of the graduates from PR departments presents another problem, which can be solved only partly after the acceptance of PR as profession with legal arrangements.

4. Conclusion: state of the art and future of public relations in Turkey

In Turkey today, public relations is a widely known field of study and profession, fully accepted economically, culturally, and academically – even though it has some image problems caused by socio-cultural and economic factors. But these problems appear to be resolved by the developments in modern Turkish culture, and public relations is accepted as a useful tool in the advancement of civil society. Despite the economic crisis that Turkey has suffered, the public relations profession is developing, going hand in hand with the integration in the European economy and, in a wider perspective, the global economical changes. Turkey has strong economic ties with Europe and the U.S. in a way that affects the business practices and organisational structures, including public relations. But in spite of all these developments, unfortunately the market for public relations in Turkey has not been developed adequately.

On the other hand, public relations professionals are optimistic and are ready to assume strategic roles. Helped by technical improvements, Turkish public relations agencies and professionals are striving for better services. Most of the public relations agencies and public relations professionals use the internet as an effective communication tool. Turkish public relations people are well aware that we are living in the information age and their profession is essentially about information, and the internet is a new communication tool for them to assemble and distribute information to internal and external publics. Internet public relations is also a hot topic among academics, and some academics began to study and lecture on the subject.

A survey[9] conducted by HİD among public relations agencies gives some clues about the future trends in the profession. According to the results of the survey, expectations are that public relations agencies will change in the following ways:

– public relations will gain importance in marketing communications;

---

9. See www.hid.org.tr/prg/haberler/haberayrinti.php?Sira_No=2.

- companies will demand strategic communications consultancy; that is, they demand planning a program in a competitive environment to identify target markets, preparing appropriate media messages and media planning, timing and budgeting based on facts in the market;
- companies will be served in certain periods of time for special projects;
- results and measurements will gain importance for companies;
- companies in crisis will need the help of PR people;
- PR will gain importance in technology, finance, health, and consumer goods;
- Economic crisis will lead clients to execute creative communications programs with low budgets.

The results of the survey offer a positive future for the profession; public relations agencies think that the expectations of companies they serve will change in 2002 (90 per cent), and hope that the share of public relations in the total communications expenses of the companies will increase (85 per cent).

Meanwhile, there is a strong trend towards a female majority in the public relations profession locally and nationally; the managerial roles of women in organisations and the number of women professionals owning a public relations company are growing; the majority of academics and students in public relations departments are women. It is expected that the increase in the number of female professionals and academics continues in the next few years.

The rapid growth of international business and the revolution in communications have helped the practice of public relations in Turkey. At present, Turkish public relations professionals are familiar with the issues prevalent in the international arena. As a result, public relations in Turkey is still a developing and a promising profession, and is dependent on cultural and economical change. Public relations people with a degree and wide cultural and managerial knowledge growing in number, and these professionals want to assume new roles imposed on them by the changes in the business world.

References

Asna, Alaaddin (1998). Public Relations in Turkey. *International Public Relations Review*, December, 11–12.
Gorpe, Serra (2002). The history and development of public relations in Turkey: a quick glimpse. Lecture, Elon University, 23 May 2002.

Gorpe, Serra and Mine Saran (2003). Student evaluations of public relations and advertising internships. Lecture, Arizona State University, 26 February 2003.

Hainsworth, Brad H. (1994). Professionalism in public relations. *Public Relations Review*, 20-4: 311.

Kayalioglu, Omer (2002). The nature of media in Turkey. *Frontline: The Global Public Relations Quarterly*, 24–3.

Okay, Ayla and Aydemir Okay (2001). *Halkla İlişkiler: Kavram, Strateji ve Uygulamaları* [Public Relations: Concepts, Strategies and Practices]. Istanbul: Der Yayınları.

Sharpe, Melvin L. (1992). The impact of social and cultural conditioning on global public relations. *Public Relations Review* 18-2: 103–107.

Strateji|MORI, Research and Planning Co. (1999). Marketing services sector/Market analysis. Report – 1999.

International Public Relations Association (2003). Membership directory and service guide, 2002–2003.

Intermezzo

Consensus-oriented public relations (COPR): A concept for planning and evaluation of public relations

Roland Burkart

1. Two preliminary remarks

Originally, the COPR model was developed as a tool for evaluating public relations (PR). However, during the evaluation process it turned out to be usable for planning PR, too. Our original case study was concerned with a public dispute about a waste disposal site in Austria (see Burkart 1993, 1994, 2003). Basically, the model relies on two prerequisites and their consequences for PR.

(1) In our present communication society, more and more often the interests of enterprises call for public legitimacy. Anyone who wants to be considered a member of a winning team needs to make the public understand his actions (Münch 1991). Especially in crisis situations this seems to be very important. In such cases companies are forced to present good arguments for communicating their interests and ideas.

(2) From a fundamental point of view, human communication generally can be seen as a process of mutual understanding. Therefore, people working in public relations should remember the following: if they take their jobs seriously, they should look into the requirements and prerequisites of understanding and orientate themselves on these principles.

For many years, James Grunig has argued that primarily in situations with a high chance of conflict, public relations must try to establish mutual understanding between organizations. He adds that for the planning and evaluation of such processes, general theories of communication are more suitable than special theories of persuasion (Grunig and Hunt 1984: 22). The concept presented here matches this position: it makes use of a rather general communication theory for deducting ideas for the analysis of real public relations communication.

2. Communicative principles of mutual understanding

The theory and terms of communication used for the COPR model are the ones established by Habermas (1981) in his theory of Communicative Action. According to this theory, communication always takes place as a multi-dimensional process and each participant in this process needs to accept the validity of certain quasi-universal demands in order to achieve understanding. This implies that the partners in the communication process must trust that they fulfill the following criteria: (a) intelligibility (being able to use the proper grammatical rules); (b) truth (talking about something whose existence the partner accepts); (c) trustworthiness (being honest and not misleading the partner); and (d) legitimacy (acting in accordance with mutually accepted values and norms). As long as neither of the partners have doubts about the fulfillment of these claims, the communication process will function uninterruptedly.

However, these ideal circumstances are rare – we could even say they never occur in reality. Basic rules of communication are often violated and therefore there is a certain "repair mechanism" – the discourse. "Discourse" means that all persons involved must have the opportunity to doubt the truth of assertions, the trustworthiness of expressions and the legitimacy of interests. Only when plausible answers are given, the flow of communication will continue.

Basically, Habermas distinguishes three types of discourse (see Figure 1). In an *explicative discourse* we question the intelligibility of a statement, typically by asking "How do you mean this?", or, "How shall I understand this?" Answers to such questions are called "interpretations". In a *theoretical discourse* we question the claim of truth, typically by asking "Is it really as you said?, or, "Why is that so?" Answers to such questions are called "assertions" and "explanations". Finally, in a *practical discourse* we question the normative legitimacy of a speech act by doubting its normative context, typically by asking "Why have you done this?", or, "Why didn't you act differently?" Answers to such questions are called "justifications" (Habermas 1984: 110). A fourth aspect, namely, the claim of trustworthiness (typical questions are "Will this person deceive me?" and "Is he/she mistaken about himself/herself?"), is an exception, as it cannot be subject to discourse because the communicator can prove his truthfulness only by subsequent actions (Habermas 1981: 69).

Discourses must be free of external and internal constraints. However, this is what Habermas calls "contrafactual" because the "ideal speech situation" that would be required for this does not exist in reality. We only act as if it would be real in order to be able to communicate (Habermas 1984: 180).

Claim	Consent	Type of discourse	Question leading the discourse	Answer
Intelligibility	Mutual intelligibility of a statement	Explicative	How do you mean this? How shall I understand this?	Interpretation
Truth	Shared knowledge about the content	Theoretical	Is it really as you said? Why is that so?	Assertion/ explanation
Trustworthiness	Trustworthiness in each other	–	Will this person deceive me? Is he/she mistaken about himself/herself?	–
Legitimicy	Mutual acceptance of norms	Practical	Why have you done this? Why didn't you act differently?	Justification

Figure 1.   Claims and types of discourses according to Habermas's Theory of Communicative Action

The process of "understanding" is not an end in itself. Normally we pursue the intention of putting our interests into reality (see Burkart 2002: 26). Thus understanding becomes the mean for the coordination of actions, as the participants involved in this process aim at synchronising their goals on the basis of common definitions of a situation (Habermas 1981: 143, 385.) This leads to the conclusion that commonly accepted definitions of a situation need undisturbed processes of understanding as a prerequisite for deciding about what should be done in a given case.

3. Public relations as a process of understanding

The COPR model focuses on the above prerequisites. Public relations managers who reflect on the basic principles of communication will always orientate their activities in accordance with possible criticism maintained by the public. However, the COPR model is not a naive attempt to transfer Habermas's conditions of understanding directly onto the reality of public relations. In view of the theory's contrafactual implications, this would be inadequate. It was rather our goal to gain from Habermas's concept of understanding new ideas for the analysis of real public relations communication. The main impact for the model came from his differentiation of communicative claims, so that this process of questioning can now be analysed more systematically.

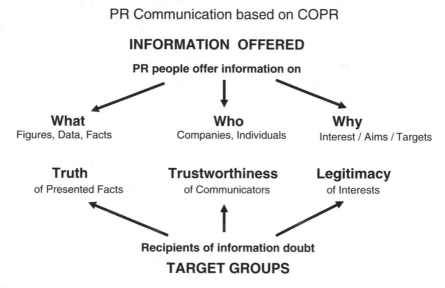

Figure 2. PR communication based on consensus-oriented public relations (Burkart 2003)

Especially in situations when conflicts are to be expected PR managers have to take into account that critical recipients might question their messages. Members of the (involved) target groups will offer their doubts about the truth of presented PR information, especially when confronted with numbers, other data and facts. They will question the trustworthiness of the company and its communicators as well as the legitimacy of the company's interests. This is illustrated in Figure 2. An example may illustrate the above considerations. If a community plans to build a waste disposal site, then this will most likely cause disturbance among the local residents. A citizens' initiative may even be formed that aims at bringing down the project. Normally the local media will support the protests so that a conflict situation can be expected. On the basis of the COPR model, the public relations managers of the company planning the landfill should consider that (a) any assertion they make will be examined concerning its truth – for example, whether figures about the quantity of waste to be deposited are correct, whether air, plants, wildlife, ground-water etc. are really not endangered; (b) the persons, companies and organizations involved will be confronted with distrust – representatives of companies might be taken as biased, for instance, or experts/consultants as incompetent or even corrupt; (c) their intention for building the landfill will be doubted in principle, either because one questions the basic strategy for waste disposal (e.g. by preferring waste avoidance as an alternative for landfills), or because the choice of the site for the landfill is seen as unjustified (because the region has just started developing tourism, for instance).

Only if it is possible to eliminate such doubts, or even better, if doubts are prevented from the very beginning, the flow of communication will not be disturbed. Ways of achieving this goal are presented in Figure 3.

4. Steps and questions for planning and evaluation COPR

In the COPR process four steps with corresponding objectives can be distinguished. These must be adapted to the actual conflict situation, in order to use COPR as a planning tool. This also makes it possible to evaluate the success of public relations activities, not only in a summative sense (at the end of a PR campaign) but also in a formative way (step by step). Figure 3 shows in detail the questions that need to be asked in the case of such an evaluation. ("P" stands for planning and "E" for evaluation the steps of COPR).

In the case of the planned landfill in Austria, the concept of COPR was useful for analysing and explaining the consequences of the public relations activities that the company launched in the conflict that arose from their project. A representative survey showed that the acceptance of building the landfill correlated convincingly with the degree of understanding. Respondents who tended to accept the project were not only better informed but were also less likely to question the trustworthiness of the planners and the legitimacy of the choice of the site for the landfill.

Consensus-oriented public relations (COPR) Questions for planning and evaluation			
	Dimensions of understanding		
COPR-Steps	WHAT Figures, data, facts	WHO Companies, individuals	WHY Interest/aims/targets
INFORMATION			
P	Have the relevant facts been presented?	Have the main company figures been mentioned?	Have the project goals been justified?
E	Did members of relevant publics receive/perceive the information?	Did members of relevant publics receive/perceive the company figures mentioned?	Did members of relevant publics receive/perceive the goals justified?
DISCUSSION			
P	Has a discussion on the relevant facts been organised?	–	Has the legitimacy of the project goals been discussed?
E	Was the truth of the PR statements questioned?	Was the trustworthiness of the communicator/company questioned?	Were any of the justifications presented put into doubt?
DISCOURSE			
P	Were fact-based arguments presented as proof of truth?	–	Were value-based arguments presented as proof of legitimacy?
E	Were these fact-based arguments questioned by members of relevant publics?	Was the trustworthiness of the communicator/company questioned?	Were these value-based arguments questioned by members of relevant publics?
DEFINITION OF THE SITUATION			
	To what extent has consent been achieved concerning facts and fact-based judgments?	To what extent has consent been achieved concerning the trustworthiness of the communicator/company?	To what extent has consent been achieved concerning project goals and value-based judgments?
	Has the result been communicated adequately?		

Figure 3. COPR planning and evaluation (Burkart 2003)

Nevertheless, the COPR model is all but a recipe for generating acceptance. People cannot be persuaded to agree to a project by pressing a "PR button", because acceptance can only emerge among the persons involved if the process of understanding has worked successfully. The prerequisite for this is that the need for dialogue and discourse on the side of the public is taken seriously by the companies and communication managers concerned, especially when the former feel restricted or even threatened by company interests and plans. If companies and PR managers realize the importance of this issue they should really be motivated to make an effort towards mutual understanding.

References

Burkart, Roland (1993*). Public Relations als Konfliktmanagement. Ein Konzept für verständigungsorientierte Öffentlichkeitsarbeit* [Public Relations as Conflict Management. A Concept of Consensus-Oriented Public Relations]. (Studienreihe Konfliktforschung 7)/ Vienna: Braumüller.

Burkart, Roland (1994). Consensus oriented public relations as a solution to the landfill conflict. *Waste Management & Research* 12: 223–232.

Burkart, Roland (2002). *Kommunikationswissenschaft. Grundlagen und Problemfelder. Umrisse einer interdisziplinären Sozialwissenschaft* [Communication science. Essentials and problems. Outline of an interdisciplinary social science]. (4th edn.). Vienna: Böhlau.

Burkart, Roland (2003). Verständigungsorientierte Öffentlichkeitsarbeit. Ein Konzept für Public Relations unter den Bedingungen moderner Konfliktgesellschaften [Consensus-oriented public relations. A concept of public relations under the conditions of modern conflict societies]. In: Günter Bentele, Romy Fröhlich and Peter Szyszka (eds.), *Handbuch Public Relations* [Handbook Public Relations]. Wiesbaden: Westdeutscher Verlag.

Grunig, James E. and Todd Hunt (1984). *Managing Public Relations*. New York: Holt, Rinehart & Winston.

Habermas, Jürgen (1981). *Theorie des kommunikativen Handelns. Bd.1: Handlungsrationalität und gesellschaftliche Rationalisierung* [Theory of Communicative Acts. Vol. 1: Rational Conduct and social rationalisation]. Frankfurt am Main: Suhrkamp.

Habermas, Jürgen (1984). *Vorstudien und Ergänzungen zur Theorie des kommunikativen Handels* [Initial Studies and Amendments to the Theory of Communicative Conduct]. Frankfurt am Main: Suhrkamp.

Münch, Richard (1991). *Dialektik der Kommunikationsgesellschaft* [The Dialectics of the Communication Society]. Frankfurt am Main: Suhrkamp.

Chapter 28

United Kingdom

Eric Koper[1]

1. National profile

1.1. Overview of national characteristics

The United Kingdom (UK) is well known around the world and many people have opinions about the country and its inhabitants without ever having been there. This may be partly because of popular culture supported by print and broadcast media, for example the Sun and the BBC, respectively, but also because of historical experience, which often is war related. The UK could be considered as a brand with national symbols, such as its flag, Queen and Anthem, cultural stereotypes related to a class society, music (Beatles, Rolling Stones), film, drama (Shakespeare), humour (Monty Python, Mr Bean) and eccentric behaviour, and political, economic and industrial power. A study by the British Council,[2] consisting of two surveys undertaken in 1999 and 2000, shows that the UK is the best known country after the US. The UK's main strengths are seen to lie in its economy and institutions, and its main weaknesses in human qualities and social relations, which were singled out in a range of negative personal characteristics such as racism, xenophobia, coldness and arrogance as constituting the biggest drag on the UK's reputation. Tradition emerges as both a major asset and a principal liability.

---

1. Valuable comments on draft versions were made by Jacquie L'Etang, Julia Jahansoozi, Stephanie Ferguson and Paul Elmer. Andy Purcell's study on public relations development in Northern Ireland helped to create insights into developments in other parts of the UK. The chapter was informed by numerous consultations of which the ones with Jon White should be singled out.
2. The British Council carried out a programme of research to find out what "the successor generation, that is, men and women, aged between 24 and 35, well educated, with above-average incomes, and likely to rise to positions of influence in their society" in twenty-eight countries think about the United Kingdom. The interesting results are available online at www.britishcouncil.org/work/survey/index.htm.

The multiple perceptions that exist about the UK relate to the multiple images that are portrayed by business, administration and society at large, and the underlying cultural values of both the sender and receiver. The picture of public relations in the UK should be regarded as one of the many that could be painted and is limited to the author's perception, and the general lack of empirical evidence supporting the arguments and observations made. The picture presented in this chapter is often critical of the current situation, following Kevin Moloney's (1999) argument that the value of public relations in the UK needs to be revisited in theory and practice.

The United Kingdom of Great Britain and Northern Ireland currently consists of England, Wales, Scotland and Northern Ireland. In addition it has a number of dependent areas such as Anguilla, the Falkland Islands, and Gibraltar. The almost 60 million people can be divided amongst the following ethnic groups: English 81.5 per cent, Scottish 9.6 per cent, Irish 2.4 per cent, Welsh 1.9 per cent, Ulster 1.8 per cent, West Indian, Indian, Pakistani, and other 2.8 per cent. The reality is more complex than this, and when considering factors such as migration and marriage it is obvious that these figures can only serve illustrative purposes. The fact that the UK is more than England alone also influences the scale and understanding of public relations practice at local, regional, national and global levels.

English, thanks to a complex set of factors, including British imperialism, is spoken on every continent. More than forty-five countries, such as the UK, Antigua, United States, New Zealand, and South Africa, consider English as their official or first language. India and Guyana are among twenty other countries where English is the educated first language. In many countries it is regarded as the language of success, and it is establishing itself as the international language of business, science, politics, and culture, resulting from major achievements in those areas by the UK and the United States. The UK has numerous worldwide renowned businesses such as Lloyds and BP, scientists such as Isaac Newton (1642–1727) and Michael Faraday (1791–1867), politicians such as Winston Churchill, Margaret Thatcher and Tony Blair, and cultural heroes such as the Beatles, Shakespeare and "James Bond". The UK not only exports culture, but is also influenced by many other cultures, such as African, Afro-Caribbean, American and Asian cultures, resulting in cultural melting-pots that major cities such as London, Manchester and Leeds are. Concern remains with the level of assimilation as mentioned earlier in relation to the British Council study, and as witnessed in occasional violent outbreaks of racial tension, and the persistence of social-economic clusters.

Although English is the predominant language in the UK, there are several other languages, such as Welsh (about 26 per cent of the population of Wales) and Scottish Gaelic (about 60,000 in Scotland). Again, the real situation is more complex and subjective; with many differences in the way people express themselves in English based on social, economic and geographic factors such as heritage, education and place(s) where you live. The point here is that in the UK context, English is often a question of accent, as for example with English-sounding Scottish aristocrats, rather than derived from societal boundaries.

It is impossible to characterise the UK in a few sentences. Detailed facts about the UK can be found in numerous sources such as the, encyclopaedias, tourist guides and the CIA fact book,[3] which, for example, states that "the UK, a leading trading power and financial centre, is one of the quartet of a trillion dollar economies of Western Europe. Over the past two decades the government has greatly reduced public ownership and contained the growth of social welfare programs. Services, particularly banking, insurance and business services, account by far for the largest proportion of GDP while industry continues to decline in importance." This combination of economic factors and its emphasis on services may partly explain the growth and development of public relations practice in private and public sectors in the UK, for which estimates are given in the following section.

1.2. Facts and figures of public relations in the UK

The following figures are often quoted, but their empirical origin has not been established. According to Anne Gregory,[4] the volume of expense on public relations in the UK is estimated to be £1.2 billion per year, with more than 30,000 persons employed in the sector. London is the predominant centre for consultancy practice, with Manchester and Leeds emerging in importance. Public relations people work in private and public sectors, with increasing importance of the latter, where employment and budgets – for example in the National Health Service and Local Government – related to public relations activities have considerably increased in the last two decades. There seem to be two major types of public relations jobs: in-house and consultants. In general one can

3. CIA World Factbook, available at www.cia.gov/cia/publications/factbook/geos/uk.html
4. In her inaugural lecture at Leeds Metropolitan University on 26 March 2003.

state that in-house practitioners serve the interests of the organisations they work for and their activities range from tactics-based entry-level jobs such as public relations or press-officer to senior-level strategic functions such as director of communication or head of public relations. Consultants usually work for different clients and can be kept on a retainer fee to deal with emerging issues, or work on a project such as the organisation of a product launch. Although most of the consultant's work is mainly tactical in nature, there is an increasing trend to develop strategic capacity, which command higher fees and requires more advanced knowledge and skills related to in-depth organisational analysis.

Although only established about thirteen years ago as an academic discipline, there are seventeen universities in the UK that offer public relations programs at under- and postgraduate levels, of which more than half are approved by the Institute of Public Relations (IPR). Despite an increasing number of scholars who carry out valuable research, investment in research is very low – we will return to this later in this chapter. The IPR (see www.ipr.org.uk), with approximately 8,000 individual members, is one of the largest public relations professional bodies in the world. The Public Relations Consultants Association (PRCA, www.prca.org.uk) is the trade association for public relations consultancies in the UK and was set up in 1969. It represents about 70 per cent of the country's public relations consultancies, has over 120 members, who employ about 6,500 people based at over 160 offices throughout the UK. These consultancies are of all sizes, working for clients in all business sectors. Major consultancies, such as Weber Shandwick, have their headquarters in the UK. Other professional bodies that have a presence in the UK include the International Public Relations Association (IPRA), the International Association of Business Communicators (IABC), the European Confederation of Public Relations (CERP) and the European Public Relations Education and Research Association (EUPRERA). The main public relations related trade magazines are *PR Week*, *IPR's Profile*, and recently established students' magazine *Behind the Spin*.

In summary it can be concluded that there is a significant presence of public relations activity in the UK, but that there is a lack of empirical data to support this. Of concern is the emphasis on London, which can partly be explained by its importance as a business and financial centre, which attracted major consultancies. Public relations activities in Northern Ireland, Scotland and Wales are under-researched, but seem to develop, especially in the public sector.

2. History and developments of public relations

2.1. Roots of public relations

In true public relations terms one could argue that public relations, depending on how it is defined, is rooted in mankind itself and may include elements of persuasion and propaganda. People engage in relationships with others from birth. These relationships enhance with the advancement of communication (verbal and non-verbal) and communication technology – take for example the influence of the internet on facilitating synchronous and asynchronous communication. Other roots can be found in philosophy and religion, progressing to psychology and sociology dealing with existence and networks. These general propositions can be applied to any context including the UK. More telling is the empirical study by L'Etang (1998) about the creation of public relations in twentieth-century Britain related to state propaganda and bureaucratic intelligence. This study was based on sixty qualitative interviews and archival research on public relations history in Britain.[5] This section will summarise some of the findings and provides some further insight into more recent developments.

The term "creation" used by L'Etang implies that the public relations occupation can be perceived as a construct. The building blocks can be found within the British political, social, economic and cultural scene in the early 1900s until the 1950s during a turbulent period of European history. Emphasis is on the role of local government in Britain, which contributed to public relations ideology and key concepts of professionalisation. These articulated a strong public service ethos, laying the foundation of the Institute of Public Relations, which was established in 1948. The emphasis is on public services rather than on business, being at the roots of public relations in the UK. However, growth of public relations practice in the last thirty years, especially consultancies, can best be explained in analogy with the US, by developments in the business and financial sectors, especially privatisation, and since the 1980s in communication technology, especially the internet in the 1990s. Miller and Dinan (2000: 5–35) argue that public relations has become big business in the UK, seeping into the very fabric of policy and decision making, can be largely attributed to the changes in the regulation of the market ushered by successive Conservative administrations in the 1980s and 1990s, rather than to a gen-

---

5. L'Etang wrote her doctoral thesis on this subject and is soon to publish a book about the history of public relations in Britain (excluding Northern Ireland).

eralised increase in "promotional culture". They conclude that "a key role of the public relations industry in late twentieth century Britain and a condition for its spectacular growth was to make profits from, and facilitate, the market redistribution of wealth from the poor to the rich" (p. 24).

An interesting video project by Andy Purcell of the University of Ulster gives some insight into the historical evolution of public relations in Northern Ireland from 1961 to 1982. In summary, it became clear that the turbulent political situation and armed conflicts negatively influenced the development of public relations in Northern Ireland. The establishment of Ulster Television in 1959 had a positive impact on the establishment of public relations, being an attraction to key influencers in business and government. Similar to other areas in the UK, the beginning of public relations in Northern Ireland originated in government with a team of journalists and civil servants making up the Northern Ireland Information Service in 1961. In-house public relations activities in the 1960s focused on sponsorship and events on the one hand and community relations and internal communications on the other. In 1965 the first public relations consultancy was a fact with the registration of Public Relations Advice (PRA), which had close ties with the Advertising Agency. Other major factors in the development of public relations in Northern Ireland were the establishment of the Monday Club and the Northern Ireland branch of the Institute of Public Relations in 1965. The Monday Club was a mixture of a weekly news conference and a social event. After 1975 new consultancies were launched, learning their profession in an environment where few wanted publicity or promotion, which required a new type of public relations professionals who were strategically aware.

In conclusion, it is clear that public relations in the UK has its roots in government in the early 1900s, with a delay in Northern Ireland, and in the last decades has significantly grown under influence of business, economic and technological developments.

2.2. How language shapes the development of public relations

The term "public relations" is part of the business, organisational and societal vocabulary in the UK, with emphasis on media relations and publicity. "Public" can mean "in public" or a specific interest group and when added to relations could mean relations with specific publics or relations in public in contrast to in private. Public relations is often negatively labelled as "spin-doctoring" when associated with politics, or as

"PR" when associated with public deceit or basic promotional activities such as canvassing for nightclubs. Despite the negative labelling, resulting from simple or unethical practice, the importance of public relations in function and investment is growing in most sectors mainly as communication and management functions. Although other terms have been introduced, such as "investor relations", "crisis management", "public affairs", "corporate communication" and "communication management", these only explain a particular element of public relations practice and as such fail to explain the understanding of public relations as a function that deals with organisational relationships in public, with the public, for the public. There is indeed an increase in vacancies at higher levels that relate to communication rather than public relations, but this can be regarded as a challenge for public relations to further explain its value to business and society. It can be argued that using other names for the same function works against the building of a good reputation for public relations practice, because it introduces an element of deceit, which is easily detected by the "public" and thus provokes negative labelling, as mentioned before. Jon White (2003) recently stated that public relations still revolves around relationships, be they corporate or political, and thus putting a different "label" on a function does not change the function or its perceived value.

It can be concluded that the term "public relations" still explains the complexity of the practice better than any of the more recently coined terms, but that more explicit efforts should be made to enhance its status by being more transparent and enhancing its value to business and society.

3. Typification of current public relations

3.1. Status of public relations in business, administration and society

Business concerns relate to the cost and value of public relations activities and the capacity and ability of public relations practitioners to deliver. Many consultancies are unfortunately suspected of demanding high fees and raising expectations that cannot be met as expressed in "overpromising and underdelivery." The economic decline in recent years has prompted business to revisit the value of public relations consultants and their investments in public relations. This can be regarded as a positive influence on the further professionalisation of the practice as it requires practitioners to be more reflective and enhance their services. L'Etang

(1999) relates professionalisation to a domain of expertise; the establishment of a monopoly; "social closure", only recognised practitioners are allowed to practice; social status; independent client relations; code of ethics; testing competence; regulating standards; and maintaining discipline. This influence will also mitigate the so called "lip-service" to the strategic elements of the public relations function such as planning, monitoring and evaluation, as practitioners are required to develop more advanced strategic thinking and management skills or else to purchase those skills, for example by recruiting university graduates. (IPR's Gerald Chan (2002) states, "A degree in PR is not necessary, though the industry is beginning to realise the value of PR graduates.") This will not only improve the levels of operation and delivery, but also the status of the practice in business and society.

The public sector in the UK, as mentioned earlier, is increasingly investing in strategic public relations and communication activities based on their needs for improved people's consultation and participation in local services. The need to improve community relations partly derives from citizens' dissatisfaction with public services such as road-gritting in winter, while local government taxation is increasing. At the national level, the ironic public-relations-derived sound bite launched by the Conservative Party in the last elections – "Labour is all spin and no substance" – reflects the negative public perception of public relations when associated with policy and politics, but also the underlying need for improved relationships between government, political parties and their publics. The latter creates an opportunity for strategic public relations practitioners to engage publics with government decision-making. It is interesting to note that the arguments by the Prime Minister, Tony Blair, relating to the UK's participation in a possible war with Iraq, are perceived by many people in the UK as propaganda, and thus regarded with scepticism even though they may be convinced that the regime in Iraq needs changing. So far the emphasis is mainly on the consultation processes, but it is obvious that there is a need for improved participation in local, regional, national and international policy development if the relationship between government and people is to strengthen.

3.2. Major roles of public relations and typical tasks

It is almost impossible to agree on a definition for public relations, and thus even more difficult to define its dominant roles and typical tasks.

Van Ruler et al. (2000) identified four characteristics of public relations, namely, managerial, technical, reflective, and educational. Although this progresses Grunig and Hunt's[6] dominant systems theory (1984), which identified press-agentry, public information, asymmetrical, and symmetrical two-way communication, it could be argued that these descriptive categories obscure the social-psychological dimensions of the different management functions that need support. More specifically, they hardly explain, except for the reflective element, why the public relations functions exist in a particular context, how decisions are made, and how issues such as power, gender, persuasion and culture influence the public relations position in the organisation and its practice. Indeed, it often limits the understanding of the roles by confining them to distinct occupational levels, inputs, activities, outputs and outcomes.

The Institute of Public Relations (IPR), founded in February 1948 with over 7,500 members representative of public relations practitioners at all levels of their careers and in all sectors – for example, consultancy, freelance, in-house, and government – claims to be "the voice of the profession",[7] and describes their vocational and special interest groups as independent practitioners; in-house directors; consultancies, small, medium and large; as well as those who work in specialised areas as diverse as local and central government; charity; health and medical; technology, etc. This could be summarised as consultancy and in-house functions at all levels in the private and public sectors that help an organisation manage its reputation through communication with its publics. The focus of the IPR is mainly limited to reputation derived from and supported by communication activities. This limited view may partly explain why appoximately 25 per cent of the "guestimated" population of 30,000 persons active in the UK's public relations practice is a member of the IPR (the figure of 30,000 is frequently quoted but not supported by any empirical evidence. The difficulty lies in identifying occupational boundaries).

Replacing the term "reputation" with "relationships" and removing "through communication" will widen the tasks and scope of the practice. But more importantly, it changes the balance of power between the organisation and its publics, enhancing symmetry and occupational positioning, including social-psychological dimensions such as social influence, attitude and behavioural change.

---

6. Grunig and Hunt identified these categories in the early 1980s in the US, and the resulting paradigms continue to influence public relations thinking.
7. Point 14 at www.ipr.org.uk/direct/about.asp?v1=strategy [accessed 20 Nov. 2002].

3.3. Position of public relations in organisations

Given the limitations of studies by trade magazines such as *PR Week*'s 2002 salary survey for practitioners in the UK (based on 764 responses, without clear methodological explanation and limited data analysis) one can derive some indication of public relations related jobs in the UK and their perceived value and subsequent status expressed in terms of salary related to age indicators from Table 1 (although studies by *PRWeek* cannot be regarded as representative for the UK practice, it is one of the few that provides insight into the position of public relations practitioners). It can be assumed that income and subsequent status at the most senior levels in public relations is below those at senior management and dominant coalition levels in organisations, and more comparable to the middle-management positions. This may partly explain the desire of public relations practitioners to become more strategic, that is, to climb the ladder, as it is especially at middle-management level where the economic environment is most volatile, and job status varies and is insecure.

The survey also revealed that the vast majority of respondents were Caucasian, confirming some concerns about the need for wider access as supported by the IPR. More importantly, it highlights the absence of multi-cultural perspectives on the management of relationships, which might negatively affect the pursuit of global interests.

The UK Press and Public Relations Handbook 2003 produced by *PR Week* lists the following industry sectors from which public relations income is derived: charity and voluntary sector, consumer durables, Fast Moving Consumer Goods (FMCG) food and drink, FMCG non-food and drink, leisure and travel, professional services, financial services and products, retail, telecommunications, healthcare, media, and dot coms. It also recognises the following sectors in order of income importance: lobbying and public affairs, corporate public relations, business-to business public relations and crisis management. This list could easily be expanded and is indicative of the inter- and multi-disciplinary nature of the occupation, where the specialism is not in a particular sector or product, but in the value added to those by public relations activities.

Public relations is often regarded by lay-persons as a sub-function of marketing and is related to advertising, with a tactical focus on consumer relationships, promotion and "free" advertising. In this context it mainly serves to promote the sales of goods and services, and in marketing terms operates "below the line". There is also overlap with human resource management, especially relating to the communication of activities between an

Table 1. Public relations jobs from senior to junior level with average salary (£) and age
in years

Consultancy	In-house	
	Private sector	Public sector
Chairman/MD	Head of communications	Head of communications
£61,500 | 47 yrs	£51,300 | 45 yrs	£38,000 | 42 yrs
Board director	PR director	PR director
£51,000 | 42 yrs	£65,100 | 43 yrs	£46,400 | 40 yrs
Account director	PR manager	PR manager
£37,200 | 36 yrs	£34,200 | 36 yrs	£28,800 | 38 yrs
Account manager	PR officer	PR officer
£26,600 | 30 yrs	£21,600 | 28 yrs	£21,500 | 35 yrs
Account executive		
£20,000 | 26 yrs		
Freelance		
£43,600 | 44 yrs		

Source: adapted from *PR Week*'s salary survey (Alastair Ray, March, 2002)

organisation and its employees. Public relations claims the communication function as its area of expertise and thus has inroads into human resource, marketing and financial planning, as for example witnessed by the responsibility for in-house newsletters, intranets and the annual report. There is a tendency to engage in too many activities, all requiring basic levels of expertise, which may adversely affect the development of a strong function and identity of the public relations occupation. As mentioned earlier, more emphasis on relationship management, supported by communication activities, could help to clarify the position of public relations within an organisation's operations.

Despite an increasing desire to operate strategically, and being regarded as part of an organisation's dominant coalition and responsible for the strategic management of organisational relationships, most practitioners are employed for communication-related tactical work. The dichotomy between tactics and strategy is expected to accelerate with the possibility that in future the term "public relations" will refer to tactics, and "communication" to strategy. The latter will strive for more recognition and positions at senior management levels, requiring additional skills and knowledge sets. It can be argued that there is no need for this dichotomy to develop in the UK, especially as the value should be seen in relationship management, where communication is used at the technical level. There is an important role for the professional bodies such as the IPR and the PRCA to ensure that the range of functions and levels of public relations practitioners are further developed and explained – not so much in a prescriptive format, but rather in a descriptive manner.

3.4. Current state of education and character of major textbooks

Public relations is taught at various levels, from short professional training courses to full-time postgraduate degrees. In the context of university education, it is preferable to distinguish education from training with education, focusing on knowledge and training on skills. Simplified, training mainly focuses on how to do things while education emphasises its relevance, in other words, why these activities need to be done.

Public relations training in the UK started in the 1930s with formal courses, approximately ten years after public relations was recognised as such. Training courses tend to emphasise practical skills such as writing, presentation and media relations skills, and are offered by numerous courses organised by public and private sector organisations. A quick search on the internet for "PR training in the UK" demonstrates the proliferation of these courses.

Degree courses at universities started in the late 1980s, first at the postgraduate level such as at Stirling in 1988, followed quickly by undergraduate level courses at Bournemouth, Leeds Metropolitan and Central Lancashire. This development was accelerated by the drive for professionalisation of the occupation fuelled by professional bodies such as the IPR. The higher education environment in the UK for the past decade shows increasing numbers of students, shrinking units of resources and increasing emphasis on the quality of learning and teaching (Grantham 1999). Most degree courses (seventeen, and increasing) are approved by the IPR, which rigorously checked for compliance with the Public Relations Education Trust (PRET) matrix. As Alan Rawel (2002: 73) explains:

The IPR has been particularly active in seeking, through its approval process, to influence the content and delivery of PR degrees. It has done this for two reasons. First, there is the need to ensure some measure of consistency between PR students graduating from different universities, if only on account of employer perception. Secondly, and inextricably related, is the continuing scepticism within the UK about the value of PR Bachelors degrees.

L'Etang (2002) adds that most of the seventy-six criteria were geared towards practice rather than the requirements of academia, and as such provoked tensions between academia and practice where the lack of theoretical underpinning could be regarded as a threat to academic freedom. Fortunately, since 2000 IPR approval has become less prescribed, allowing for the necessary academic freedom and career diversity, although its continuing professional development programme (CPD), which is still largely geared towards practice, seems to influence IPR's approval of public relations curricula. An up-to-date list of approved courses can be found at the IPR's website at www.ipr.co.uk.

Even though the number of public relations graduates at under- and postgraduate levels have steadily increased, approximating 2,000 persons estimated over a twelve-year period, this only has had a limited impact on the practice, especially on how public relations activities are carried out, as middle- and senior management levels are mostly occupied by non-(public relations) degree holders. It is anticipated that the influence of graduates will grow and positively impact the practice, but it requires a greater understanding by practitioners about the competences those graduates developed and more importantly need to acquire. There is a mismatch in expectations where employers expect the graduates to be fully trained in the tactical skills, while they are educated to a higher level. Public relations education can be compared to obtaining a driving licence, that is, learners obtain a licence to operate, but have not developed the experience of a driver nor know what car they will drive and how to drive that particular car. Here lies the challenge for the employer to help the employees to develop to their potential.

Public relations practitioners seem to have limited time and funds to invest in continuous professional development (CPD), which is of great concern as the rapid changes in communication technology and public relations functions require regular updating. The "quick fix" approach with emphasis on skills rather than knowledge development seems dominant with about five days of learning per year, spending between £500 and £1,000 (Koper 2000). This is still optimistic compared to Grunig's critical statement about the investments in CPD in the USA during an interview in 2000, where he stated that:

> I'm always amazed at how many people simply practise public relations without ever doing anything to learn how to do it. Many of them just learn on the job, trial and error, they are told what to do and they do it, so it often becomes just mindless kind of attempts to get publicity in the media, without thinking about, you know, managing a public relations programme. So I would say that the majority of practitioners don't spend any time at all in learning (J. Grunig, in Koper 2000).

This obviously depends on how Grunig defines learning, which seems more formal-training related. The Public Relations Education Trust (PRET) Matrix was developed in the UK in the 1990s with and endorsed by the Public Relations Consultants Association (PRCA) and the IPR. It was designed as a basis for self assessment of training needs and career development; appraisal of employees' skills and their development needs; and evaluation of training and education course suitability. It provides a checklist of knowledge, business skills, and public relations skills in relation to five stages of knowledge, skills or experience. The IPR launched its successor on 28 April 2000 and describes it thus: "Developing Excellence, the first continuous professional development (CPD) scheme for PR practitioners will play an important role in raising industry standards. [...] It provides a formal and structured framework for enhancing professional skills and knowledge and recording professional learning in a methodical way." (IPR 2000).

Although mention is made regarding the knowledge elements in the PRET matrix and subsequent CPD programme, it is described in relation to knowing "how to" rather than "why to" and fail to reflect on underpinning theoretical domains such as philosophy, sociology and psychology. There is also a sense of immediacy – that is, they focus on skills and to a certain extent on the knowledge required by today's practice. In contrast, educators need to predict the future needs of the practice as students will graduate several years later. Education also needs to be more reflective and critical analytical, drawing from supporting theories to help learners construct meaning and develop more advanced thinking skills. A tension seems to exist between education and practice where the practice prescribes what competencies a public relations practitioner should have without indicating what role education has to play. This is further complicated and exemplified by the survey on public relations education in Europe, by the European Confederation of Public Relations (CERP, CERP 1991: 1) in its statement "To the question where Public Relations can be situated within the study programme of that University or Institute of Higher Education or which reputation that type of education enjoys in that country, they can usually not answer."

Involvement of professional bodies can be very helpful if they recognise the different perspectives of educators and researchers, allowing them to operate independently to advance the theory and practice. Striving for synergy between research, education and practice benefits from what public relations so often refers to as mutual respect and understanding. The demise of the Public Relations Education Forum (PREF), which brought the UK academics together on a regular basis, is only partly halted by the meetings between academic representatives of IPR approved courses which are organised by the IPR. The absence of non-approved courses should be addressed, but more worryingly is the dependency on one professional body, which might result in narrowing the development and transfer of the necessary body of knowledge.

3.5. Typification of best selling practical books

Most public relations writing is accessible in English, which in theory would benefit public relations practice in the UK. However, American literature is dominant, especially at more advanced level textbooks, but also in modelling the practice. Fortunately, there is a steady increase in research, education and practice material written in the UK and contextualised for the UK. There is also an increase in the use of UK-developed literature in supporting disciplines such as management, marketing, communication, psychology and sociology. Introductory texts by authors such as Sam Black, Philip Kitchen and Alison Theaker or more advanced texts such as by Magda Piezcka and Jacquie L'Etang benefit the understanding of public relations in the UK and its position in a wider context. However, there are too few academic writers in the UK who, like Kevin Moloney, Jon White, Aeron Davis, David Miller and Will Dinan, produce work at the more advanced levels, with the added limitation that much content at the introductory level is related to American developments in public relations. As mentioned earlier, there is a dire need for the practice to invest in fundamental public relations research. A chapter like this would greatly benefit from more fundamental empirical input, helping the practice to develop its unique UK identity.

3.6. The local scene of public relations in the UK

Wilcox, Ault and Agee (1997: 80) state that "any attempt to define a single PR type of personality is pointless, because the field is so diverse that it needs people of differing personalities". This also holds for the local scene of public relations in the UK. The variety of roles and functions in the different sectors as described earlier, together with the support of professional bodies and training and education providers, create a rich diversity which is difficult to capture in a short chapter. An attempt to describe "the local scene" would not do justice to the variety of "scenes". The introduction has already made it clear that the UK is a complex of nations, cultures and habits, and it is logical to conclude that there is no single model of the UK public relations practice.

Although the IPR is one of the biggest professional bodies related to public relations in the world, its 7,500 members are not representative of all practitioners, nor of the way in which they practice. It is interesting to note that the IPR refrains from describing the typical practice or practitioner.

3.7. Growing fields and hot issues

There are numerous current issues related to the economic situation in the UK and subsequent influence on public relations practice, especially related to employment, fee-income and salaries. Public relations activities mainly support organisational goals, but in themselves have little direct influence on the development and management of the core products and services. Strengthening its position at strategic management level might create opportunities for more stability as an organisational function. Public relations will continue to suffer from negative coverage by the media and general public as long as it fails to operate in a transparent and ethical manner. Ethics remains high on the agenda. However, it is questionable if new codes of ethics based on deontological principles will help improve a practice that operates based on utilitarian and situational principles. The value of public relations will ultimately be demonstrated by the quality of the people that work in it. Investment in those people in both developmental and financial terms will further help the public relations occupation to professionalise, and ultimately, as with the medical profession, create legitimacy for its activities. The debate on gender needs to be continued as more women enter the practice, many of them with public relations degrees and with more women studying public relations than men. Although there is some evidence of "shattering" glass ceilings, as for example several presidencies of the IPR, this needs to be further researched. Investments are called for, not only in public relations practitioners, but also in developing organisational understanding of the need to be transparent in practitioners' dealings with their publics if they want to gain trust, which is the foundation of relationships. The recent attention to corporate communication and social responsibility is an opportunity to enhance the reputation of public relations practice.

4. Conclusion: state of the art and future of public relations in the UK

The complexities of the UK as a country and society are reflected in the lack of clear boundaries for the public relations practice. Public relations in the UK has come of age and is gradually becoming more professional. The need for professional communicators at all levels has been established and is expected to expand, that is, the function is growing in recognition. The problem remains who will be able to claim this function, and if there is sufficient expertise within public relations to take up this challenge. Other positive developments relate to the diminishing glass ceiling with more women gaining senior functions, be it that the occupation as a whole seems to have a ceiling of operating at middle-management levels. More investment is needed in education and research to support the ambitions of the practice and to serve the interests of the publics. The lack of empirical data on the practice should be addressed to gauge its value to business and society. Professional bodies such as the IPR and PRCA have an important role to play in the further development of the practice. It is not clear if public relations will further develop a dichotomy related to tactical and strategic functions, and if this transpires into different occupations such as public relations manager versus communication manager or if public relations manages to recapture these occupations.

References

CERP (1991). *Public Relations Education in Europe: Survey of Full Time Study Programmes.* CERP Education.

Chan, Gerald (2002). education.independent.co.uk/careers_advice/az_careers/story.jsp? story=117478 [accessed 2 Feb. 2003].

L'Etang, Jacquie (1998). State propaganda and bureaucratic intelligence: the creation of public relations in 20th century Britain. *Public Relations Review* 24–4: 413–441.

L'Etang, Jacquie (1999). Public relations education in Britain: an historical review in the context of professionalisation. *Public Relations Review* 25–3: 261–289.

L'Etang, Jacquie (2002). Public relations education in Britain: a review at the outset of the millennium and thoughts for a different research agenda. *Journal of Communication Management* 7–1: 43–53.

Grantham, David (1999). IOLISplus – extending the Electronic Learning Environment. *Journal of Information, Law and Technology* 1. (elj.warwick.ac.uk/jilt/99-1/grantham.html).

Grunig, James E. and Todd Hunt (1984). *Managing Public Relations.* New York: Holt, Rinehart & Winston.

IPR (2000). *Profile* 4. (Publication of the Institute of Public Relations).

Koper, Eric. (2000). *Public Relations related to Electronic Learning Environments.* MSc thesis, University of Stirling.

Miller, David and Will Dinan (2000). The rise of the PR industry in Britain, 1979–98. *European Journal of Communication* 15–1: 5–35.

Moloney, K. (1999). Public relations: does the industry need regulating? *Corporate Communications* 4–1: 24–29.

Rawel, Alan (2002). How far do professional associations influence the direction of public relations education? *Journal of Communication Management* 7–1: 71–78.

Ruler, Betteke van, Dejan Verčič, Gerhard Bütschi and Bertil Flodin (2000). *The European Body of Knowledge on Public Relations. Communication management: The Report of the Delphi Research Project* 2000, Ghent/Ljubljana: European Association for Public Relations Education and Research.

White, Jon (2003), lecture at the Universtity of Central Lancashire, 18 Feb. 2003.

Wilcox, Dennis L., Philip H. Ault and Warren K. Agee (1997). *Public Relations: Strategies and Tactics.* New York: Longman.

Chapter 29

New perspectives of public relations in Europe

Günter Bentele

1. Future perspectives for the practical public relations field

This book gives the first systematic overview of public relations in Europe, one that is not only based on subjective beliefs and judgements, but also entails some data. This can be seen as important progress. Moreover, it is written by the most acknowledged experts of their respective countries. At the same time we must confess that we should have much more empirical data to be able to really value what public relations in European countries is all about. All chapters reveal that the science of public relations is not so developed that we empirically know what is going on and why it is as it is. This is not only the case in countries with a recently developed public relations practice, but also in countries in which public relations has existed longer. In most countries statistically representative studies on the whole occupational field have not been in existence for very long.

Nevertheless, if we look at the detailed pictures of so many countries, we first of all may conclude that public relations is a flourishing field, not only in western European countries, but also in the eastern part of Europe. Secondly, we have to admit that it is a field in its infancy, compared with other social science disciplines – even in those countries in which public relations has existed as a profession for a long time. It is hardly recognised as a function at higher levels and it still lacks respect. If we look at the information in the chapters concerning that state of the art in education and research, we have to conclude that these fields are even more in their infancy. There are a lot of educational programs. However, most of these are at bachelor's and "how to" levels. There are hardly any programs at master's level and only some countries have university education at Ph.D. level. When it comes to research, there are hardly any research programs, except for Germany, and to a lesser extent Austria, the Netherlands and the United Kingdom. There is obviously much knowledge reproduction, but not so much knowledge production. That is one of the reasons why there is a lack

of original, culturally embedded textbooks. Many of the educational programs – especially those in countries in which public relations has been developed recently – consequently, have access only to mainstream American textbooks, translated or in English.

It is evident that this will change. The demand for public relations and
communication management can be seen as a trend. The increasing use
of media, growing number of media channels, increasing competition between the channels and the technological developments of digital media
turns our societies into information and communication societies. The
economic and political systems of single countries; economic, political
and cultural globalisation, developments in the information sector; cultural and societal shifts in so many European countries as well as the media systems of European countries and the transformation of media systems into international businesses are major influencing factors of the
development of public relations. The most challenging factor of all, however, will be the so-called *mediatisation* of society. Media and the "media
logic" are becoming the most influential and formative factors for all societal systems. Politics, for example, is increasingly becoming theatre, and
rules of drama start to rule daily political lives to a great extent. Drama
on television replaces former political expertise; in all parts of public life
it is nowadays sometimes even more important to know how to perform
than to know what to perform. All these factors are the basis for the mediatisation of society. Combined with a decline in public confidence in
politics, companies and institutions, a structural growth of the demand of
public relations in its broadest sense can be foreseen. Organisations of any
kind have to communicate, whether they want or not, and the more professional they do it, the more advantages they have. In a mediatised world it
becomes more difficult to differentiate between the original and the fake.
Credibility will be the one key factor of professional communication in this
respect. This necessitates the rise of a public relations profession of a new
type; one that is oriented to high professional standards with, firstly, respect to what to do; secondly, how to do it effectively and efficiently, and
thirdly, how to do it ethically. Our education systems are the basis of this.
Education in turn needs to be fed by academia that should provide theories, methodology and methods, and metatheoretical research.

The value of public relations, the value of the communication function
of organisations (cf. Grunig *et al.* 2002: 90) becomes one of the most important topics in a communication management perspective, either for
the professional field or for public relations research.

Generally public relations is based on trust; its aim is to build trust, keep trust or get it back. Without any doubt we can state that this has become an important societal communication mechanism (cf. Bentele 1994). In a time in which reputation, sustainable development and corporate citizenship are the most important concepts for enterprises, organisations, governments and institutions as well, credibility, trustworthiness and responsibility are the central aims and at the same time the quality measurements of professional public relations.

2. Future perspectives for public relations research in Europe

It is not possible here to give a systematic overview of only the main research activities and theories in all European countries. For some countries such more recent overviews exist (cf. Bentele 1999; Verčič *et al.* 2002). In some of the contributions to this volume one can get an impression not only of research perspectives in European countries, but also about the variety of different theoretical approaches which have been developed in Europe during the last ten years (cf. the articles of Holmström, Merten, Burkart, and others).

If one tries to compare PR research and theory development in Europe and in the USA, one can observe many common interests and structures in theory building and numerous European adoptions of theories and approaches from the US. The writings of James E. Grunig and Larissa A. Grunig and their Excellence Study (cf. Grunig 1992; Grunig *et al.* 2002) in particular, as well as certain American textbooks and many other books and articles, are well known and used in Europe. Some models and theories are quite popular in the academic field. Not so the other way round. Because of the language barrier not many American scholars are able to read or understand languages other than English or American.

Besides common interests and structures, one also can observe some different elements. The most obvious differences in research might be the following:

The leading understanding of public relations within the European scientific community could be somewhat different from some US understanding in several key elements: naming, meaning and relevance of the concepts "relationships" and "communication" or empirical roles of public relations. A Delphi study, conducted by Betteke van Ruler and Dejan Verčič, revealed some differences in comparison with the US situation in this respect (Ruler and Verčič 2002). Such results, highlighting some differences (e.g. a "reflective role of public relations"), have to be discussed deeply and seriously (cf. Grunig and Grunig 2002 and other contributions in Verčič and van Ruler *et al.* 2002) and should be investigated further. Possible differences may have causes in the different traditions of the practical field or academic research itself or in different social structures and in differences of the political or the economic systems of European countries and the US.

In Europe it seems to be more common and more convincing to think of public relations not only as an organisational activity, but also as a social phenomenon, that is, as a phenomenon which has societal functions and impacts on the society and its subsystems like the political system, the economic system, the cultural system or the media system. Ronneberger and Rühl (1992) developed a public relations theory based on systems theory by presupposing – as did Niklas Luhmann – a system-environment paradigm and developing an "equivalence-functionalist" approach. In addition to meta-theoretical reflections, the core of this approach is the differentiation of three levels of analysis: a *macro-, meso-,* and *micro-level* of public relations. At the macro-level, the relationship between public relations and society as a whole is being examined; the authors termed this the *function of public relations.* The meso-level represents interrelations between public relations and other functional systems of society (politics, economics, science, law, leisure, family, etc.); Ronneberger and Rühl chose the term "public relations payments" (and payments in exchange) to designate these relations. The micro-level consists of intra- and inter-organisational relationships; the authors spoke of "public relations tasks" within this context. The social function of public relations was seen by them as providing "autonomously developed decision-making standards for the establishment and supply of effective topics or issues" (p. 252). According to the authors, the intention of public relations is to "strengthen public interests (…) and social trust of the [general] public through follow-up communication and interaction – at the least to manage the drifting apart of particular interests and to avoid the emergence of distrust" (Ronneberger and Rühl 1992: 252).

The question of what impact or which function all organisational activities of all public relations departments of all organisations and all public relations firms in a society have on society seems to be a typical European question rather than an American one. If this is correct, one reason for this could be that for many communication scholars this (theoretical) challenge is interpreted rather as a "sociological" question, not as a challenge for communication science. As one possible answer to this question

Bentele (1998, 2000) differentiates within *a functional model* individual, organisational and societal *functions* of public relations. Organisational and societal functions are differentiated again in *primary* and *secondary* functions. *Monitoring* (observation), *information, communication* and *persuasion* are seen as primary functions, whereas the building of awareness, building of (public) trust, harmonisation, adaptation, integration, early warning (system), image functions, economic functions and the co-building of the public sphere are seen as secondary functions.

Although in the US there are critical perspectives and approaches (cf. Herman and Chomsky 1988; Toth and Heath 1992), the critical tradition in Europe seems to be more traditional and perhaps more developed. One of the critical approaches goes back to the "Frankfurt School" and especially the German sociologist Jürgen Habermas (1990), who had developed quite early a historically grounded theory of the "public sphere" including a critical discussion of public relations and advertising. Habermas (1981) developed a general "Theory of Communicative Action" which is not only seen as a very successful theory, but has also been taken as the basic theory for an Austrian approach of "consensus-oriented public relations", developed in the beginning of the nineties (Burkart 1992, see also his chapter in this book). According to Burkart, consensus-oriented public relations requires communication about the objective, the subjective, and the social world and leads to *understanding* and, consequently, to *agreement*. With four phases (information, discussion, discourse, and situation definition), Burkart suggested a practical model to reach conflict resolution through dialog and conflict analysis. This normative approach has some similarities with the "two-way symmetrical model" of James Grunig (cf. Grunig *et al.* 2002: 306) and had to face similar critical arguments (see Bentele and Liebert, 1995).

European scholars often seem to respect and prefer interdisciplinary approaches: public relations research in European countries is often not only a matter of communication science exclusively, but also a matter of sociology or political science. And if communication scholars deal with public relations, they often try to connect their theories or to embed them in more general social theories, attempting to oversee not only their own discipline, but also the literature published in neighbouring disciplines. This is true for general public relations theories as well as for special theories like campaign theories (cf. Röttger 1997) or even public relations practice.

In European countries some more recent theoretical approaches and theoretical traditions exist that are not very well known in the United

States. Examples include new system-theoretical approaches like the Autopietic System Theory of Niklas Luhmann (for an explanation see Holmström's chapter or constructivist approaches like "radical constructivism"). Whereas a journalism perspective on the same theoretical basis has been developed by Scholl and Weischenberg (1998), Merten (1992, also in this volume) proposed a constructivist perspective for a public relations theory. Public relations is defined here as the "construction of desirable realities". Constructivist and modern system theoretical models go much further than traditional cybernetic models (cf. Cutlip *et al.* 1994: 206), simple system theoretical models (cf. Hazleton 1992) or communication process models (cf. Cutlip *et al.* 1994: 230) which can be helpful to describe organisational and communicative structures but at the same time are not complex enough to describe the complex processes which are taking place in PR.

In Europe some mid-range theories exist, which are quite unknown in the US, partly for the reason that these approaches are not at all available in the English language. Bentele (1994), for example, developed a theory of public trust based on a "reconstructive" approach of mass media communication and public relations (1997). In this approach a model of the societal information and communication process was developed consisting of (social and natural) reality, PR-communicators and media communicators, media reality and the audience, on the one hand, and different rule-governed processes constituting relationships between these elements, on the other.

Another prominent theory and research tradition in Germany is the so-called "determination thesis", a prominent mid-range theory (see Burkart 2002; Schweda and Opherden 1995; Szyska 1997). Similar to Sigal (1973) and Turk (1986) in the United States, Nissen and Menningen (1977) and, subsequently, Barbara Baerns in Germany, examined to what extent and in what form public relations sources were picked up by journalists and used in reporting. The relationship between journalism and public relations in Germany was discussed considering the power each of them has. Baerns (1979, 1991) posited the thesis that *Öffentlichkeitsarbeit* is an important determinative factor for daily media reporting. She concluded that the content of media reporting (news agencies, print or broadcast media) constantly showed large numbers of reports (generally more than 60 per cent) based on public relations. According to Baerns (1991), public relations determines the *topics/themes* as well as the *timing* of media reporting (p. 98). A number of follow-up studies appeared in connection with Baerns' papers. Grossenbacher (1989) gathered similar results in his input–output analysis of press conferences, in which he emphasized the *transformational achievements* of the media concerning the public relations input. Barth and Donsbach (1992) expanded the determination hypothesis by introducing two additional intervening variables: news value and crisis situation. A study conducted by Rossmann (1993) discovered the strong influence of press releases by Greenpeace on media reports; input-output analyses of the Frankfurt Trade Fair (Mathes, Salazar-Volkmann and Tscheulin 1995) revealed that, depending on the type of fair, between 53 and 78 per cent of media coverage was directly *induced* by public relations (p. 167). Another result of this study was the fact that – measured by the elements of information taken up by journalists – PR activities were also surprisingly successful in terms of *evaluation* of importance, success and effectiveness of the fair. Additional studies differentiated the determination thesis. Saffarnia (1993), for example, found that, at an Austrian daily newspaper, the percentage of articles based on public relations sources was 34 per cent smaller than in other research. His study thus put the concept of "powerful public relations" into perspective. An input-output analysis on local politics (Schweda and Opherden 1995) showed similar results.

The above-mentioned studies on the determination thesis indicate that, until today, only the effects of public relations on journalism have been examined. These effects on topic selection and on the timing of making these topics available to the public, however, represent only *one* direction. It seems that a complex *theoretical model* is necessary to examine *reciprocal directions of influence*. One question that needs to be investigated *empirically* is to what *extent*, in which *situations*, in what *form*, and in which *fields of reporting* (municipal, political, business, sports, culture, and science) *mutual influences* can be found. It is reasonable to believe, as journalists do, that the effects of public relations differ depending on the department as well as on the medium. Bentele, Liebert, and Seeling (1997) developed a new model, the *intereffication approach*.[1] With this model, the authors distinguished *induction activities* (communicative stimuli that create responses) from *adaptation activities* (adjustment behavior) on both sides: public relations as well as journalism. Furthermore, they differentiated between a socio-psychological, a factual, and a time dimension. Ben-

---

1. The term was derived from the Latin word *efficare* ('to render possible'), meaning that, in modern communication societies, journalism and public relations render each other possible.

tele, Liebert, and Reinemann (1998), Rinck (1998) and Donsbach and Wenzel (2002) found some empirical evidence for this model.

3. Concluding remarks

The present volume shows the state of the art, important historical aspects and structures of the occupational fields of public relations in European countries. It seems evident that there are not only common or similar elements and features but also much diversity in Europe. The same can be seen if a comparison is carried out between the United States and Europe or another continent (Asia, Africa) in a global context (cf. Sriramesh and Verčič 2003).

In my understanding this book should rather be taken as a starting point to compare different traditions, structures and problems of public relations practice and public relations research in various European countries. At the same time it can be seen as a contribution to an as yet underdeveloped sub-discipline of public relations research: international *comparative studies* in public relations or communication management. Some of the theoretical perspectives, models and approaches can show that European perspectives differ from US perspectives, models and approaches. But the differences have to be described as well as the common features. They have to be understood if we want to understand why they exist. This at least is the common goal of science in general: to look at common features as well as differences, describe them systematically and try to explain them. And that certainly must be the common goal of public relations scholars.

References

Baerns, Barbara (1979). Öffentlichkeitsarbeit als Determinante journalistischer Informationsleistungen. Thesen zur realistischeren Beschreibung von Medieninhalten [Public Relations as determining factor for journalistic information]. *Publizistik*, 24 (3), 301–316.

Baerns, Barbara (1991). *Öffentlichkeitsarbeit oder Journalismus: Zum Einfluss im Mediensystem* [Public relations or journalism: On the impact on the media system]. Köln: Wissenschaft und Politik. [1st edn. 1985].

Barth, Henrike & Wolfgang Donsbach (1992). Aktivität und Passivität von Journalisten gegenüber Public Relations [Activity and passivity of journalists toward public relations]. *Publizistik*, 37(2), 151–165.

Bentele, Günter (1994). Öffentliches Vertrauen: Normative und soziale Grundlage für Public Relations [Public trust: The normative and social foundation for public relations]. In Wolfgang Armbrecht & Ulf Zabel (Eds.), Normative *Aspekte der Public Relations: Grundlagen und Perspektiven. Eine Einführung* [Normative aspects of public relations: Foundations and perspectives. An introduction], 131–158. Opladen: Westdeutscher Verlag.

Bentele, Günter (1997). Public relations and reality: A contribution to a theory of public relations. In Dany Moss, Toby MacManus, & Dejan Verčič (Eds.), *Public relations research: An international perspective*, 89–109. London: International Thomson Business Press.

Bentele, Günter (1999). Public Relations Research and Public Relations Science in Germany, in: H.-B. Brosius & Ch. Holtz-Bacha (eds.). German Communication Yearbook; 181–210. Cresshill, NJ: Hampton Press.

Bentele, Günter (2000). Über die Rolle von PR in gesellschaftlichen Dialogen. [Concerning the Role of Public Relations in Social Dialogues] In: Schell, Thomas von/Rüdiger Seltz (Hrsg.)(2000), *Inszenierungen zur Gentechnik – Konflikte, Kommunikation und Kommerz.* [Putting on Stage Genetic Engineering – Conflicts, Communication and Commerce], 154–168. Opladen: Westdeutscher Verlag.

Bentele, Günter (Ed.) (1998). *Berufsfeld Public Relations.* [Public Relations: The Professional Field.] PR-Fernstudium, Studienband 1, Berlin: PR-Kolleg.

Bentele, Günter and Michel Haller (Eds.) (1997). *Aktuelle Entstehung von Öffentlichkeit: Akteure, Strukturen, Veränderungen* [Current formation of the public sphere: Actors, structures, and changes]. Konstanz: UVK.

Bentele, Günter and Tobias Liebert (Eds.) (1995). *Verständigungsorientierte Öffentlichkeitsarbeit: Darstellung und Diskussion des Ansatzes von Roland Burkart* [Consensus-oriented public relations: Delineation and discussion of an approach by Roland Burkart]. Leipzig: Leipziger Skripten für Public Relations und Kommunikationsmanagement (Vol. 1).

Bentele, Günter, Tobias Liebert and Carsten Reinemann (1998). Informationsfluss und Resonanz kommunaler Öffentlichkeitsarbeit [Information flow and resonance of municipal public relations] (Part 1: Leipzig and part 2: Halle). Unpublished manuscript, Leipzig, Germany.

Bentele, Günter, Tobias Liebert and Stefan Seeling (1997). Von der Determination zur Intereffikation: Ein integriertes Modell zum Verhältnis von Public Relations und Journalismus [From determination to intereffication: An integrated model of the relationship between public relations and journalism]. In G. Bentele & M. Haller (Eds.), *Aktuelle Entstehung von Öffentlichkeit: Akteure, Strukturen, Veränderungen* [Current formation of public communication: Actors, structures, and changes], 225–250. Konstanz: UVK.

Botan, Carl H./Vincent Hazleton, Jr. (Eds.) (1989). *Public Relations Theory.* Hillsdale, N.J.: Erlbaum.

Burkart, Roland (1992). *Public Relations als Konfliktmanagement: Ein Konzept für verständigungsorientierte Öffentlichkeitsarbeit. Untersucht am Beispiel der Planung von Sonderabfalldeponien in Niederösterreich* [Public relations as conflict management: A concept for consensus-oriented public relations. The example of planning hazardous waste depots in Lower Austria]. Wien: Braumüller.

Burkart, Roland (2002). Kommunikationswissenschaft: *Grundlagen und Problemfelder* [Communication science: Foundations and problem areas]. Wien/Köln/Weimar: Böhlau.

Cutlip Scott M., Allan H. Center and Glen M. Broom (1994). *Effective Public Relations.* Englewood Cliffs, NJ: Prentice Hall.

Donsbach, Wolfgang (Ed.) (1997). *Public Relations in Theorie und Praxis: Grundlagen und Arbeitsweise der Öffentlichkeitsarbeit in verschiedenen Funktionen* [Public relations in theory and practice: Foundations and methods of public relations in different functions]. München: Fischer.

Donsbach, Wolfgang and Arnd Wenzel (2002). Aktivität und Passivität von Journalisten gegenüber parlamentarischer Pressearbeit. [Activity and Passivity of Journalists towards press relations activities in parliaments). *Publizistik.* 47 (4), 373–387.

Fröhlich, Romy (1992). Qualitativer Einfluss von Pressearbeit auf die Berichterstattung: Die "geheime Verführung" der Presse? [The qualitative impact of media relations on reporting: The "secret seduction" of the press?]. *Publizistik,* 37(1), 37–49.

Grossenbacher, René (1989). *Die Medienmacher: Eine empirische Untersuchung zur Beziehung zwischen Public Relations und Medien in der Schweiz* [Making the media: An empirical study of the relationship between public relations and the media in Switzerland] (2nd edn.). Solothurn: Vogt-Schild.

Grunig, James E. (1992). The development of public relations research in the United States and its status in communication science. In: Horst Avenarius & W. Armbrecht (eds.), *Ist Public Relations eine Wissenschaft?* [Is public relations a science?], 103–132. Opladen: Westdeutscher Verlag.

Grunig, James E. and Todd Hunt (1984). *Managing public relations.* New York: Holt, Rinehart and Winston.

Grunig, James E. (Ed.) (1992). *Excellence in Public Relations and Communication Management.* Hillsdale: Erlbaum.

Grunig, Larissa A. and James E. Grunig (2002). The Bled Manifesto on Public Relations: One North American Perspective. In: Verčič, Dejan, Betteke van Ruler, Inger Jensen, Danny Moss and Jon White (eds.), *The Status of Public Relations Knowledge in Europe and Around the World,* 25–34. Proceedings of BledCom 2002 in Conjunction with 2002 Euprera Annual Congress.

Grunig, Larissa A., James E. Grunig and David M. Dozier (2002). *Excellent Public Relations and Effective Organisations. A Study of Communication Management in Three Countries.* Mahwah, N.J/London: Erlbaum.

Habermas, Jürgen (1981). *Theorie des kommunikativen Handelns* [A theory of communicative action] (2 Volumes). Frankfurt a.M.: Surhkamp.

Habermas, Jürgen (1990). *Strukturwandel der Öffentlichkeit* [Structural Transformation of the public sphere]. Frankfurt a.M.: Suhrkamp (Original work published in 1962).

Hazleton, Vincent (1992). Towards a Systems Theory of Public Relations. In: Avenarius, Horst/ Wolfgang Armbrecht (eds.)(1992): *Ist Public Relations eine Wissenschaft? Eine Einführung* [Is Public Relations a Science? An Introduction.], 33–45. Opladen: Westdeutscher Verlag.

Hensel, Matthias (1990). *Die Informationsgesellschaft. Neuere Ansätze zur Analyse eines Schlagwortes.* München: Reinhard Fischer.

Herman, Edward S. and Noam Chomsky (1988). *Manufacturing Consent. The Political Economy of the Mass Media.* New York: Random House.

Kunczik, Michael (1993). *Public Relations: Konzepte und Theorien* [Public relations: Concepts and Theories]. Köln: Böhlau.

Löffelholz, Martin (1997). Dimensionen struktureller Kopplung von Öffentlichkeitsarbeit und Journalismus [Dimensions of stuctural links between public relations and journalism]. In G. Bentele & M. Haller (Eds.), *Aktuelle Entstehung von Öffentlichkeit: Akteure, Strukturen, Veränderungen* [Current formation of the public sphere: Actors, structures and changes], 187–224. Konstanz: UVK.

Luhmann, Niklas (1987). Soziale Systeme. Grundriß einer allgemeinen Theorie. [Social Systems. An Outline of A General Theory]. Frankfurt a.M.: Suhrkamp.

Luhmann, Niklas (2000). Die Gesellschaft der Gesellschaft. [The Society of the Society]. Frankfurt a.M.: Suhrkamp.

Mathes, Rainer, Christian Salazar-Volkmann and Jochen Tscheulin (1995). Medien-Monitoring: Ein Baustein der Public Relations-Erfolgskontrolle. Untersuchungen am Beispiel Messe und Medien [Media monitoring: A building block of public relations evaluation. The example of trade fairs and the media]. In B. Baerns (Ed.), PR-*Erfolgskontrolle* [PR evaluation], 147–172. Frankfurt a.M.: IMK.

Merten, Klaus (1992). Begriff und Funktion von Public Relations [The term and function of public relations]. *PR-Magazin*, 11, 35–46.

Neidhardt, Friedhelm (1994). Öffentlichkeit, öffentliche Meinung, soziale Bewegungen [Public sphere, public opinion, social movements] In: F. Neidhardt (Ed.), *Öffentlichkeit, öffentliche Meinungen, soziale Bewegungen.* [Public sphere, public opinion, social movements] Sonderheft 34 (1994) der Kölner Zeitschrift für Soziologie und Sozialpsychologie (pp. 7–41). Opladen: Westdeutscher Verlag.

Nissen, Peter and Walter Menningen (1977). Der Einfluß der Gatekeeper auf die Themenstruktur der Öffentlichkeit [The influence of gatekeepers on the topic structure of the public]. *Publizistik*, 22(2), 159–180.

Rinck, Annette (1998). Interdependenzen zwischen PR und Journalismus: Eine empirische Untersuchung der Medienwirkung am Beispiel einer dialogorientierten PR-Strategie von BMW [Interdependencies between PR and journalism: An empirical study of the media effects of a dialog-oriented PR strategy of BMW]. Unpublished dissertation, Universität Leipzig, Germany.

Ronneberger, Franz, and Manfred Rühl (1992). *Theorie der Public Relations. Ein Entwurf* [Theory of Public Relations. An Outline]. Opladen: Westdeutscher Verlag.

Rossmann, Torsten (1993). Öffentlichkeitsarbeit und ihr Einfluss auf die Medien: Das Beispiel Greenpeace [Public relations and its impact on the media: The example of Greenpeace]. *Media Perspektiven* 93–2, 85–94.

Röttger, Ulrike (Ed.) (1997). *PR-Kampagnen: Über die Inszenierung von Öffentlichkeit* [PR campaigns: On the creation of the public sphere]. Opladen: Westdeutscher Verlag.

Ruler, Betteke van and Dejan Verčič (2002). The Bled Manifesto on Public Relations. In: Verčič, Dejan/Betteke van Ruler/Inger Jensen/Danny Moss/Jon White (eds.)(2002), *The Status of Public Relations Knowledge in Europe and Around the World.* Proceedings of BledCom 2002 in Conjunction with 2002 Euprera Annual Congress. Proceedings, pp. 10–17.

Saffarnia, Pierre A. (1993). Determiniert Öffentlichkeitsarbeit tatsächlich den Journalismus? Empirische Belege und theoretische Überlegungen gegen die PR-Determinierungsannahme [Does public relations in fact determine journalism? Empirical findings and theoretical reflections refuting the determination hypothesis]. *Publizistik*, 38–3, 412–125.

Schenk, Michael (1992), "Informationsgesellschaft im internationalen Kontext." In: Reimann, Horst (Hrsg.)(1992), *Transkulturelle Kommunikation und Weltgesellschaft. Zur Theorie und Pragmatik globaler Interaktion,* 249–262. Opladen: Westdeutscher Verlag.

Scholl, Armin and Siegfried Weischenberg (1998). *Journalismus in der Gesellschaft. Theorie, Methodologie und Empirie* [Journalism in society. Theory, methodology and empiricism]. Opladen: Westdeutscher Verlag.

Schweda, Claudia and Rainer Opherden, Rainer (1995). *Journalismus und Public Relations: Grenzbeziehungen im System lokaler politischer Kommunikation* [Journalism and public relations: Boundary relationships within the system of local political communication]. Wiesbaden: Deutscher Universitäts-Verlag.

Sigal, Leon V. (1973). *Reporters and officials: The organisation and politics of news-making.* Lexington, MA: D.C. Heath and Co.

Sriramesh, Krisnamurthy and Dejan Verčič (Eds.) (2003). *The Global Public Relations Handbook: Theory, Research and Practice.* Mahwah, N.J.: Erlbaum.

Toth, Elisabeth L. and Robert L. Heath (Eds.) (1992). *Rhetorical and Critical Approaches to Public Relations.* Hillsdale, N.J.: Erlbaum.

Szyszka, Peter (1997). Bedarf oder Bedrohung? Zur Frage der Beziehungen des Journalismus zur Öffentlichkeit. [Need or Thread? Remarks on the Relationships between Journalism and the Public Sphere] In: Günter Bentele & Michael Haller (Eds.), *Aktuelle Entstehung von Öffentlichkeit: Akteure, Strukturen, Veränderungen* [Current Genesis of public communication: Participants, structures, and changes], 209–224. Konstanz: UVK.

Turk, Judy VanSlyke (1986). Information subsidies and media content: A study of public relations influence on the news. *Journalism Monographs*, 100, 1–29.

Verčič, Dejan, Betteke van Ruler, Inger Jensen, Danny Moss, Jon White (Eds.) (2002). *The Status of Public Relations Knowledge in Europe and Around the World.* Proceedings of BledCom 2002 in Conjunction with 2002 Euprera Annual Congress. Proceedings, 25–34.

Zerfass, Ansgar (1996). *Unternehmensführung und Öffentlichkeitsarbeit: Grundlegung einer Theorie der Unternehmenskommunikation und Public Relations* [Corporate management and public relations: Outline of a theory of corporate communication and public relations]. Opladen: Westdeutscher Verlag.

Authors

Günter Bentele
Günter Bentele, Ph.D., is full professor of Public Relations at the Institute for Communication and Media Studies, University of Leipzig, Germany. Email: bentele@rz.uni-leipzig.de

Carmel Bonello
Carmel Bonello, M.Sc. (Stirling), M.I.P.R. (UK), is Director of the Public Relations Unit at BPC, Malta's leading marketing communications agency, EBOK's National Coordinator for Malta and Lecturer of Public Relations at the University of Malta. Email: carmelbonello@hotmail.com

Nenad Brkić
Nenad Brkić, Ph.D., is assistant professor of Marketing, Faculty of Economics, University of Sarajevo, Bosnia and Herzegovina.
Email: nenad.brkic@efsa.unsa.ba

Roland Burkart
Roland Burkart, Ph.D., is associate professor at the Institute for Communication Science at the University of Vienna, Austria.
Email: roland.burkart@univie.ac.at

Valérie Carayol
Valérie Carayol is *Maître de Conférences* at the Institut des Sciences de l'Information et de la communication (ISIC), an institute at the University of Bordeaux, France. Email: carayol@u-bordeaux3.fr

Francis Xavier Carty
Francis Xavier Carty, MA, FPRII, is retired Course Leader for the MA degree in Public Relations at Dublin Institute of Technology. He is currently preparing a thesis for his Ph.D. degree in Public Relations.
Email: fxcarty@indigo.ie

Milenko D. Djurić
Milenko D. Djurić, M.A., is the owner of Profile, a public relations agency in Belgrade, Serbia and Montenegro. Email: profile@eunet.yu

Tony Muzi Falconi
Toni Muzi Falconi is president of *Methodos*, a public relations agency; he is also president of FERPI.
Email: tonimuzi@tin.it

Bertil Flodin
Bertil Flodin is a consultant at Con Brio Communications, Stockholm, Sweden. Email: Bertil.Flodin@conbrio.se

Baldwin Van Gorp
Baldwin Van Gorp is a doctoral candidate and a research assistant at the communications department of the University of Antwerp, Belgium.

James E. Grunig
James E. Grunig, Ph.D., is full professor of Public Relations in the Department of Communication at the University of Maryland College Park.
Email: jg68@umail.umd.edu

Larissa L. Grunig
Larissa A. Grunig, Ph.D., is full professor in the Department of Communication, University of Maryland. Email: lg32@umail.umd.edu

Boris Hajoš
Boris Hajos, M.Sc., is project manager of Premisa, the Communications Management Association of Croatia, and Secretary General of the Croatian PR Association. Email: boris.hajos@premisa.hr

Suzanne Holmström
Susanne Holmström. M.A., is a lecturer and a Ph.D. student at the Department of Social Sciences, Roskilde University, Denmark.
Email: sh@susanne-holmstrom.dk

Pål Horsle
Is senior advisor at Stadskonsult, a Directorate for Communication and Public Management, former Director of Advisory Section at the Norwegian Government Central Information Service.
Email: pal.horsle@statskonsult.dep.no or pal_horsle@consultant.com

Melika Husić
Melika Husić is teaching assistant in Marketing, Faculty of Economics, University of Sarajevo, Bosnia and Herzegovina.
Email: melika.husic@efsa.unsa.ba

Ivonne Junghänel
Ivonne Junghänel was assistant at the University of Leipzig and is now PR consultant at the Headquarter of the German Association of the Automotive Industry (VDA) in Franfurt/Main. Email: junghaenel@vda.de

Joszef Katus
Dr. Joszef Katus, Ph.D., is associate professor of government communication at the University Leiden, the Netherlands.

Renata Kodilja
Renata Kodilja, Ph.D., is professor of Public Relations at the University of Udine-Gorizia, Italy. Email: kodilja@uniud.it

Eric Koper
Eric Koper, M.Sc., principal lecturer, leader of the Division of Applied Communication at the Lancashire Business School of the University of Central Lancashire, United Kingdom. Email: ekoper@uclan.ac.uk

Ryszard Ławniczak
Ryszard Ławniczak, Ph.D., is full professor at the Poznań University of Economics, Poznań, Poland, chair holder of the Clair of Economic Journalism and Public Relations, and advisor to the President of the Republic of Poland. Email: kpr@novci1.ae.poznan.pl

Jaakko Lehtonen
Jaakko Lehtonen, Ph.D., is professor at the Department of Communication at the University of Jyväskylä, Finland.
Email: jaakko.lehtonen@jyu.fi;
see also http://viesti.jyu.fi/eng/department/lehtonen.html

António Marques Mendez
António Marques Mendes, M.A., is assistant professor at the School of Media Arts and Communication of the Polytechnic Institute of Lisbon and Managing Director of GlobalCom®, Communication Consultancy,

based in Lisbon, Portugal. Email: amendes@escs.ipl.pt or
globlcom@esoterica.pt. amendes@escs.ipl.pt

Klaus Merten
Klaus Merten, Ph.D., is full professor of communication science at the
University of Münster.

Angeles Moreno Fernandez
Mᵃ de los Ángeles Moreno Fernández, Ph.D., is a researcher in Public
Relations at the Rey Juan Carlos University of Madrid, Spain.
Email: a.moreno@cct.urjc.es

Karl Nessmann
Karl Nessman, Ph.D., is assistant professor in public relations at the Institute for Media and Communication Science of the University of Klagenfurt, Austria, and Leader of the stream on public relations.
Email: karl.nessmann@uni-klu.ac.at

Zafer Özden
Zafer Özden, Ph.D., is associate professor of Public Relations in the Fac-
ulty of Communications at Ege University in İzmir, Turkey.
Email: zaf@iletisim.ege.edu.tr

Luc Pauwels
Luc Pauwels, Ph.D., is a former communication manager, and currently
associate professor of communication science at the University of Antwerp, Belgium. Email: Luc.Pauwels@ufsia.ac.be

Juliana Raupp
Juliana Raupp, Ph.D., is scientific assistant at the Institute of Media and
Communication Studies at the Free University of Berlin, Germany.
Email: raupp@zedat.fu-berlin.de

Ulrike Röttger
Ulrike Röttger, Ph.D., is full professor of Public Relations at the Institute
for Communication Science at the Westfälischen Wilhelms-Universität
Münster, Germany. Email: ulrike.roettger@uni-muenster.de

Betteke van Ruler
Betteke van Ruler, Ph.D. is full professor of Communication and Organisation at the Department of Communication Science at the University
of Amsterdam, the Netherlands. Email: bvanruler@fmg.uva.nl

Mine Saran
Mine Saran, Ph.D., is an assistant professor of Public Relations in the Faculty of Communications at Ege University in İzmir, Turkey. Email: saran@iletisim.ege.edu.tr

José Viegas Soares
José Viegas Soares, Ph.D., is full professor of Semiology and Semiotics at the School of Media Arts and Communication of the Polytechnic Institute of Lisbon, Portugal. Email: jsoares@escs.ipl.it

György Szondi
György Szondi is senior lecturer in Public Relations at the School of Business Strategy, Leeds Metropolitan University, United Kingdom. He taught Public Relations at Concordia University in Estonia and at the College of Business and Management Studies in Hungary. His professional experience includes working for Hill and Knowlton in Hungary and London.

Kaja Tampere
Kaja Tampere, M.A., lecturer at Tartu University, Estonia, and doctoral student at Tartu University, Estonia and Jyväskylä University, Finland. Email: kajata@jrnl.ut.ee

Ana Tkalac
Ana Tkalac, Ph.D., works at the Faculty of Economics, University of Zagreb, Croatia. Email: atkalac@efzg.hr

Katerina Tsetsura
Katerina Tsetsura, M.A., is a doctoral candidate in the department of communication at Purdue University, USA. She holds an MA from the Voronezh State University in Russia. Email: tsetsura@purdue.edu

Dejan Verčič
Dejan Verčič is partner in Pristop d.o.o. and assistant professor of Public Relations and Communication Management at the University of Ljubljana, Slovenia. Email: Dejan.Vercic@Pristop.si

Prodromos Yannas
Prodromos Yannas, Ph.D., is full professor of International and European Relations and chairperson of the Department of Public Relations and Communication at the Technological Educational Institution (TEI) of Western Macedonia, Greece. Email: yannas@kozani.teikoz.gr

Ivan Žáry
Ivan Žáry is head of the Marketing and Communications Department of the College of Management of the City University, Bellevue, USA in Bratislava, Slovakia. He is also director general of ProPublicum, Hill & Knowlton International Associates Group, Bratislava, Slovakia.
Email: zary@internet.sk, see also http://www.pppr.sk/english/izarye.html

Minka Zlateva
Minka Zlateva, Ph.D., is associate professor; she holds the UNESCO Chair "Communication and Public Relations" at the Faculty of Journalism and Mass Communication of the Sofia University "St. Kliment Ohridski" and she is a member of the managing board of the Bulgarian Public Relations Society. Email: zlateva@asico.net